FLASHBACK HISTORY

PLAINS INDIANS

Susie Brooks

PowerKiDS press.

New York

Published in 2010 by The Rosen Publishing Group, Inc.
29 East 21st Street, New York, NY 10010

First Edition

Original series design: Dave West
Illustrator: Ian Thompson
Layout for this edition: Alix Wood
Editor for this edition: Katie Powell

Library of Congress Cataloging-in-Publication Data

Brooks, Susie.
  Plains Indians / Susie Brooks.
     p. cm. — (Flashback history)
  Includes index.
  ISBN 978-1-4358-5519-9 (library binding) —
  ISBN 978-1-4358-5520-5 (pbk.) —
  ISBN 978-1-4358-5521-2 (6-pack)
1. Indians of North America—Great Plains—Juvenile
literature. 2. Indians of North America—Great Plains—
History—Juvenile literature. I. Title. II. Series.

E78.G73B695 2010
978.004'97—dc22

2009002159

Picture Credits: Front cover: Werber Forman Archive:
Department of Library Services, American Museum of Natural
History, American Museum of Natural Hsitory,
plus Barbara Feezor-Stewart, p23(r) (P. Hollembeak); Archives des
Jesuites St Jerome, Quebec, Canada/Father Nicholas Point's Collection
p41(t); The Trustees of The British Museum, p13, p15(tl), p20(b), p22, p23(l), p24/25, p25, p27(t)
p33(t); Buffalo Bill Historical Center, Cody, WY, p18 (Painting: *The Storyteller* by Charles M. Russell (1864-1926)
gift of William E. Weiss), p30/31, p43(b); Bruce Coleman, p12(l & r), p41(b); Stuart Connor, p33(b); The Denver
Art Museum, p15(tr), p15(b), p26, p38/39; Deutsches Ledermuseum/Schuhmuseum, Frankfurt, endpapers; Richard
W. Edwards Jr., p19 (Weyer International, Toledo, Ohio); Emilia Civici Musei, Italy, p32; Barbara Feezor-Stewart,
p42(l); Glenbow Archives, Calgary, Canada, p8(r); Gloria Goggles, p12/13 (Fremont Photography); Hastings
Museum & Art Gallery, p39 (b) (Peter J. Greenhalf); Indian City, USA, p17(r); Joslyn Art Museum, Omaha,
Nebraska, USA, p24 (Painting: *Pehriska-Ruhpa (Two Ravens), Hidatsa Man,* p27(b)) (Painting: *Chan-Cha-Uia-
Tuen, Teton Sioux Woman (Woman of the Crow)* and p30 (Painting: *Mato-Tope (Four Bears), Mandan Chief,* by
Karl Bodmer (1809-1893)), p36/37 (Painting: *Encampment on Green River* by Alfred Jacob Miller (1810-1874));
Museum of the American Indian/Heye Foundation, p20(t); The Museum of Fine Arts, Houston/The Hogg Brothers
Collection, gift of Miss Ima Hogg, p40 (Painting: *The Emigrants* c.1904 by Frederic Remington (1861-1909);
Pipestone National Monument, Minnesota, p21(l) (Ephraim Taylor); Provincial Museum of Alberta,
Canada/Ethnology Collection, p28/29(t); Smithsonian Institution, p8(b), p14;Staaliche Museen Preubischer
Kulturbesitz/Museem Fur Volkerkunde, Berlin, p16; Taylor Archive, p17(l), p21(r), p28/29(b), p32/33, p34, p34/3.
p36, p42(r), p43(t); Illustrtaions reproduced in Catlin's *O-kee-pa,* published by Trubner & Co of London, 1867,
p28, p29; University of Nebraska Press, p31 from *A Pictographic History of Oglala Sioux* by Amos Bad Heart Bu
Werner Foreman Archive, p8(l), p38

Manufactured in China

CONTENTS

Words that appear in **BOLD** can be found in the glossary on page 44.

WHO WERE THE PLAINS INDIANS?

Long before white people came to North America, the land was ruled by native tribes. Early white settlers called them "Indians," though they are mostly known as Native Americans today. There were many Indian tribes, all across America. This book is about those who lived on the **Great Plains**.

PLAINS TRANSPORT ▼

The **travois** was like a cart without wheels, made of two long poles. Goods were strapped on and pulled by dogs or horses.

LIFE ON THE PLAINS ▲

The Great Plains are grasslands with hills, valleys, and streams but very few trees. Summers are hot, and winters very cold. The Plains Indians had to learn to find shelter and food. Luckily, there were lots of wild animals to hunt for meat and skins.

DISTINCTIVE LOOKS

Wolf Robe (left) was a chief of the Cheyenne tribe. The Plains Indians were generally tall and slim, with small hands and feet bronzed skin, and brown eyes. They had straight black hair, usually worn in braids.

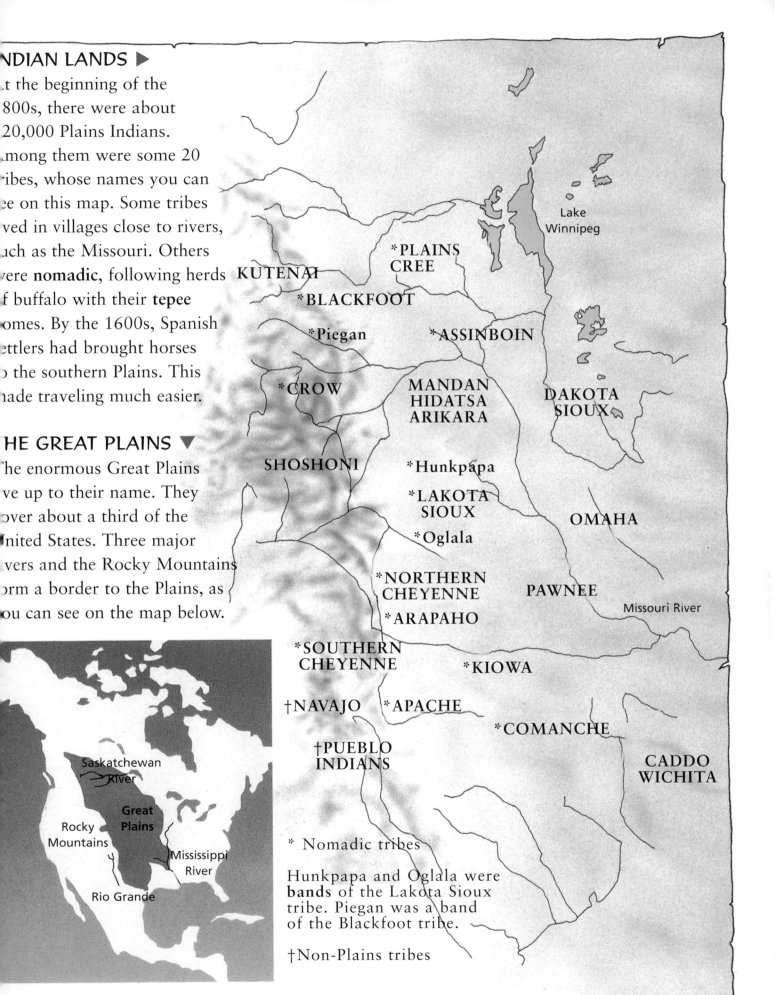

INDIAN LANDS ▶

At the beginning of the 1800s, there were about 20,000 Plains Indians. Among them were some 20 tribes, whose names you can see on this map. Some tribes lived in villages close to rivers, such as the Missouri. Others were **nomadic**, following herds of buffalo with their **tepee** homes. By the 1600s, Spanish settlers had brought horses to the southern Plains. This made traveling much easier.

THE GREAT PLAINS ▼

The enormous Great Plains live up to their name. They cover about a third of the United States. Three major rivers and the Rocky Mountains form a border to the Plains, as you can see on the map below.

KUTENAI

*PLAINS CREE

*BLACKFOOT

*Piegan

*ASSINBOIN

*CROW

MANDAN HIDATSA ARIKARA

DAKOTA SIOUX

Lake Winnipeg

SHOSHONI

*Hunkpapa

*LAKOTA SIOUX

*Oglala

OMAHA

*NORTHERN CHEYENNE

PAWNEE

*ARAPAHO

Missouri River

*SOUTHERN CHEYENNE

*KIOWA

†NAVAJO

*APACHE

*COMANCHE

†PUEBLO INDIANS

CADDO WICHITA

Saskatchewan River

Great Plains

Rocky Mountains

Mississippi River

Rio Grande

* Nomadic tribes

Hunkpapa and Oglala were **bands** of the Lakota Sioux tribe. Piegan was a band of the Blackfoot tribe.

†Non-Plains tribes

TIMELINE

	PRE-1600	1600-1650	1650-1700	1700-1750	1750-1800
EVENTS IN PLAINS REGIONS	Around 18,000 BCE, early ancestors of the Native Americans cross the **Bering Land Bridge** from Asia into North America.	Shoshone tribes have been living in the north and central Plains for thousands of years. Ancestors of Mountain Crow Indians move to the Plains. **Stone-headed club**	Dogs are still the main means of transportation on the Plains. Southern tribes trade with Spanish settlers for horses.	The Shoshone are forced off the Plains into the Rocky Mountains, by tribes such as the Blackfoot, who have guns.	Increasing white settlements drive tribes from the east, southeast, and southwest onto the Great Plains. Guns and warfare become more common.
EVENTS IN AMERICA	1000 CE The Viking Leif Ericson discovers present-day Canada. 1492 Christopher Columbus arrives in the Caribbean and claims the New World for Spain.	1607 British settlers arrive in Virginia. 1620 The British ship *Mayflower* arrives at Plymouth Rock, Massachusetts.	1680 Pueblo Indians fight the Spanish in the Great Pueblo Revolt.	Navajo Indians learn to weave by copying the Pueblo Indians. **Navajo blanket**	1776 The Declaration of Independence is signed, freeing America from the British Empire. 1789 George Washington becomes the first U.S. President.
EVENTS IN BRITAIN	**Guy Fawkes**	1605 Guy Fawkes tries to blow up the Houses of Parliament. 1616 William Shakespeare dies. 1649 King Charles I is executed.	1660 Charles II becomes King of England. 1666 The Great Fire of London destroys the city.	1727 The scientist Sir Isaac Newton dies.	1765 Scotsman James Watt invents the steam engine. By the end of the century, the Industrial Revolution has begun and factories have become common place.
EVENTS AROUND THE WORLD	2650 BCE The Great Pyramid is built at Giza, Egypt. 570 CE The Islamic prophet Mohammed is born. **Great Pyramid**			1730 Peter II of Russia dies of **smallpox**.	1773 An English explorer, Captain James Cook, crosses the Antarctic Circle.

1800-1850	1850-1900	1900-1950	1950-1990	1990-2009
Plains Indian culture reaches its peak. There are thought to be 60 million buffalo on the Plains. White explorers and artists begin to visit.	White settlers fight with some Plains tribes. At the Battle of Little Big Horn in 1876, the Cheyenne and Sioux win. By 1890, most Plains Indians are forced to live in reservations.	White **hide** hunters make the buffalo almost extinct. The native way of life suffers. 1924 Native Americans gain U.S. citizenship and the right to vote.	Reservations become more independent as oil, coal, and gas are found on their land. Native American life becomes stronger again.	Many Native Americans are now well educated and go to college. Most groups maintain their rights and traditions.

Pipe tomahawk

1800-1850	1850-1900	1900-1950	1950-1990	1990-2009
1823 *The Last of the Mohicans*, a book about American Indians by James Fenimore Cooper, is published. 1841 Canada is granted self-government.	1852 *Uncle Tom's Cabin*, by Harriet Beecher Stowe, highlights the cruelty of slavery. 1861–1865 The American Civil War takes place between the northern U.S. states and the Confederate states of the South.	1904–1914 The Panama Canal is built. 1929 The Wall Street Crash starts a worldwide financial crisis – the Great Depression.	1963 President John F. Kennedy is assassinated. 1969 Neil Armstrong is the first man on the moon.	2001 Terrorists strike New York and Washington, D.C. 2009 Barack Obama is elected 44th U.S. President.

1800-1850	1850-1900	1900-1950	1950-1990	1990-2009
1815 French Emperor Napoleon I is defeated at the Battle of Waterloo. 1837 Queen Victoria begins her 64-year reign.	1854 The Crimean War breaks out between Russia and Europe. It includes the disastrous Charge of the Light Brigade.	1914 World War I begins in Europe. 1929 The engineer John Logie Baird invents color TV.	1953 Queen Elizabeth II is crowned. 1962 The Beatles have their first hit, *Love Me Do*.	1997 Princess Diana is killed in a car crash in France. 2007 Gordon Brown succeeds Tony Blair as Prime Minister of the U.K.

Atomic bomb

1800-1850	1850-1900	1900-1950	1950-1990	1990-2009
1835 The English naturalist, Charles Darwin, studies wildlife on the Galapagos Islands. As a result, he publishes *The Origin of Species* in 1859.	Over 55 million people leave Europe to settle in America.	1939 World War II begins. 1945 World War II ends when the first atomic bombs are dropped on Hiroshima and Nagasaki, Japan.	1952 A fish called a coelacanth, thought to have been extinct for 50 million years, is caught near Madagascar.	2003 Tribal warfare breaks out in Darfur, Western Sudan.

VARIED CULTURE

Most of the tribes in this book came originally from northern and eastern America, settling on the Great Plains from around 1730. They spoke about six languages between them, with several different **dialects**, too. Each tribe had its own name and customs, though they all shared a similar way of life. This began to change when white people arrived on the Plains. White settlers hunted buffalo in huge numbers and drove the Indians from their lands. By 1890, the native culture was almost destroyed.

HORSE POWER

The Spaniards took horses to North America in 1541, but they didn't trade them with the Indians until the 1600s. Southern tribes such as the Comanche were the first to benefit. They then traded the animals farther north.

WHAT FOOD DID THEY EAT?

The Plains Indians had to hunt, gather, or grow all of their food. Some tribes farmed crops, such as corn or maize, beans, and pumpkins. But most relied on wild animals and wild fruits and vegetables. The prairie

turnip, for example, grew naturally on the Plains in the summer. The Indians could dry it and save it for the winter months.

TYPICAL FOODS ▶

Gloria Goggles, of the Arapaho tribe in Wyoming, prepared these Plains foods. The dried turnips will last for several years if they don't get damp. Some of the meat has been dried, too. The rest is mixed with herbs and made into a type of sausage.

BUFFALO ▼

Buffalo are the largest mammals in North America. They roamed the Plains in millions, providing the Indians with plenty of meat. Before the tribes had horses, they captured buffalo in pens or drove them over cliffs to kill them. They hunted pronghorn antelope in a similar way.

Dried prairie turnips

Corn

Pronghorn antelope

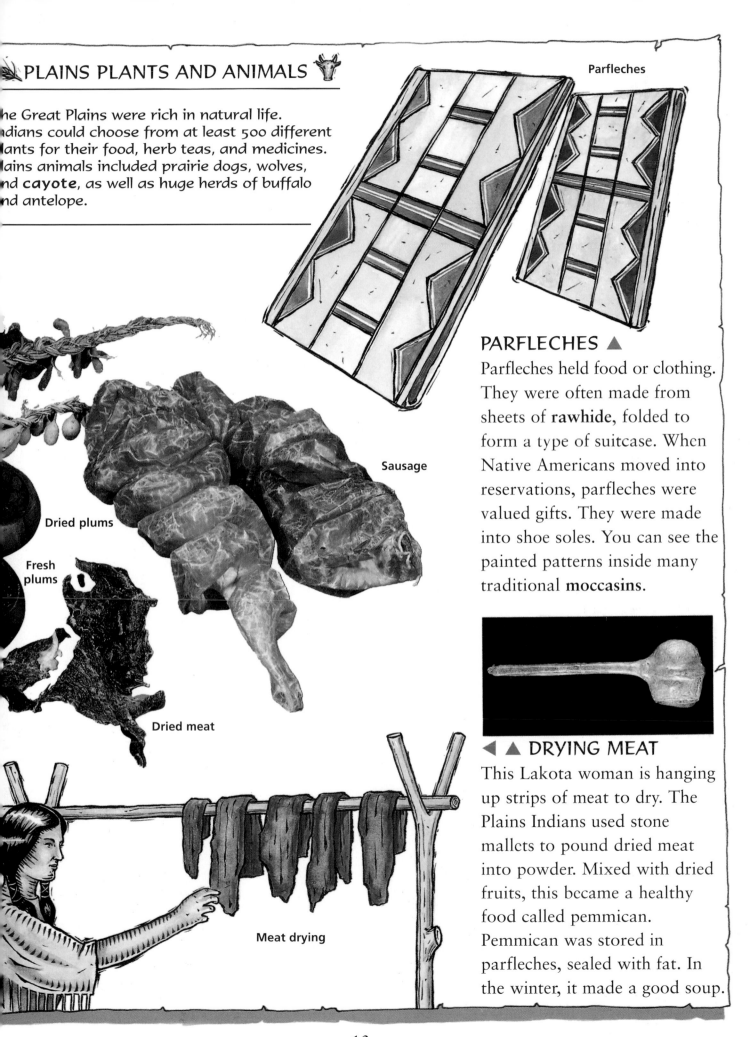

PLAINS PLANTS AND ANIMALS

The Great Plains were rich in natural life. Indians could choose from at least 500 different plants for their food, herb teas, and medicines. Plains animals included prairie dogs, wolves, and **cayote**, as well as huge herds of buffalo and antelope.

Parfleches

Sausage

Dried plums

Fresh plums

Dried meat

Meat drying

PARFLECHES ▲

Parfleches held food or clothing. They were often made from sheets of **rawhide**, folded to form a type of suitcase. When Native Americans moved into reservations, parfleches were valued gifts. They were made into shoe soles. You can see the painted patterns inside many traditional **moccasins**.

◄ ▲ DRYING MEAT

This Lakota woman is hanging up strips of meat to dry. The Plains Indians used stone mallets to pound dried meat into powder. Mixed with dried fruits, this became a healthy food called pemmican. Pemmican was stored in parfleches, sealed with fat. In the winter, it made a good soup.

WHAT WAS FAMILY LIFE LIKE?

Family was very important to the Plains Indians. Before a man could marry, he had to prove he was a good enough hunter to provide for a wife and children. Some Indian men had several wives, often choosing sisters so they didn't fight! Mothers were always with their babies, but everyone helped to look after older children.

DADDY'S BOYS ▶

Fathers took their turn at babysitting. They enjoyed playing games and teaching youngsters new skills. This Cheyenne father is posing with his sons, who look a little startled by the camera. They are all wearing traditional clothes, made by the women of the family.

 ## GUARDIAN SPIRITS

The Plains Indians believed in guardian spirits, who gave them protection through life. Boys were usually sent out to find their spirit, spending four days and nights on a hilltop alone. Some boys had dreams, or visions, of animal spirits such as buffalo, bears, wolves, and eagles. These were thought to pass on their strength and skills. Many Plains Indians wore a lucky charm representing their spirit guide.

COMFORTABLE CRADLE ▶

Newborn babies slept in cradles like this one, usually made by their grandparents. A soft animal skin bag was stretched over two wooden boards, strapped together with rawhide. This could be carried safely on a horse's back during travel.

BALL GAMES ▶

Playing sports was great training for boys, who would grow up to be hunters. It kept them fit and taught them skills and speed. Indians all over America loved playing shinny, a game a bit like hockey. They used a wooden stick to hit a ball made of **buckskin**-covered clay. The ball above is decorated with colorful beadwork.

◀ DOLLS

Dolls were usually sewn from soft buckskin. They had painted or beaded faces and their hair was real human hair. A Lakota girl owned the two shown here. Their clothing is typical of her tribe.

Hoop and pole game

FAMILY GAMES ▶

Many adult Plains Indians loved playing the hoop and pole game. You can read more about it on page 22. Horse racing was popular, too. All Indians learned to ride at an early age.

DID THEY LIVE IN HOUSES?

Nomadic tribes, who lived on the move, made tepee homes out of buffalo hide. These were easy to carry, put up, and take down. Supported by wooden poles, they withstood strong winds in the winter and were cool during summertime. More settled tribes, such as the Mandan and Omaha, built larger earth lodges but still used tepees on hunting trips.

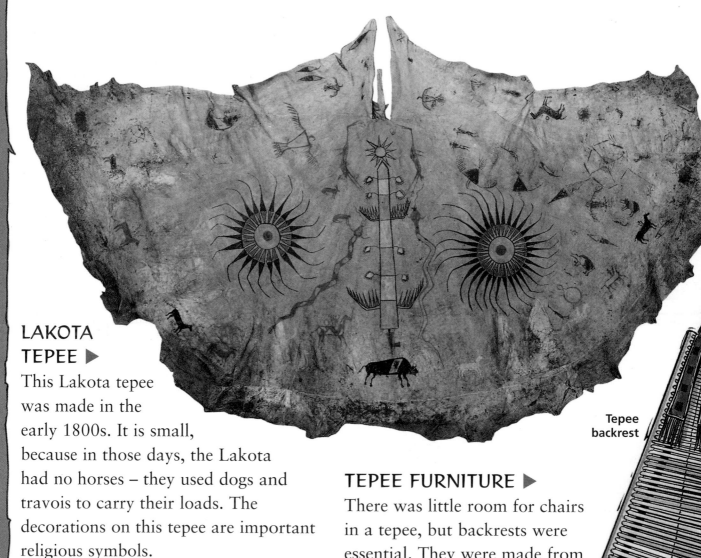

LAKOTA TEPEE ▶

This Lakota tepee was made in the early 1800s. It is small, because in those days, the Lakota had no horses – they used dogs and travois to carry their loads. The decorations on this tepee are important religious symbols.

Paintings of tepees

Tepee backrest

TEPEE FURNITURE ▶

There was little room for chairs in a tepee, but backrests were essential. They were made from thin willow rods, laid across wooden poles.

or the Plains Indians, swimming in the
ver was as good as having a bath. Indian
amps also had a "sweat lodge," which was
ke a sauna. Sweating got rid of dirt and
as thought to cleanse people spiritually.
airbrushes were made from porcupine tails,
nd toothbrushes from frayed twigs. The
ains Indians apparently had very white
eeth. Their sugar-free diet probably helped.

Inside a tepee—the space
at the back was usually
kept for important
people and
sacred objects.

TEPEE HOME ▶

he round door of a tepee
ways faced east, toward the
sing sun. Inside, the lower
alls were lined with skins to
eep out drafts. In the middle
f the floor was a small fire
or cooking and warmth.
eople slept on simple willow
ats or buffalo robes.

ETTLED LODGES ▲ ▶

ome-shaped earth lodges like
e ones above made sturdy,
ettled homes. For special
eremonies, they could fit
bout 40 people inside. Grass
dges (right) were similar, but
ere used only by the Caddo
nd Wichita tribes.

DID BOYS AND GIRLS GO TO SCHOOL?

Children didn't go to school. They learned from their families and tribes. Copying adults taught them skills such as hunting, and needlework. They learned about religion in ceremonies, and about history through storytelling and picture-writing.

STORYTELLING ▲

Storytelling, as shown in the painting above, was a very important part of Indian life. It helped people to understand their tribe's history, culture, and religion. Listening to stories and legends also brightened up the long, dark winter nights.

PICTURE-WRITING ▼

The Plains Indians used picture-writing instead of letters and words. Warriors' names were shown by **glyphs** above their heads. These men are named Whirlwind Bear and Medicine Crow.

1851-52

THE WAYS OF ANIMALS ▼

Stuffed animals, like the otter and black-footed ferret below, were used to teach children about wildlife. Boys in particular needed to understand animal behavior and characteristics if they were to be good at hunting. The Crow and Blackfoot Indians used stuffed animals as sacred symbols, too.

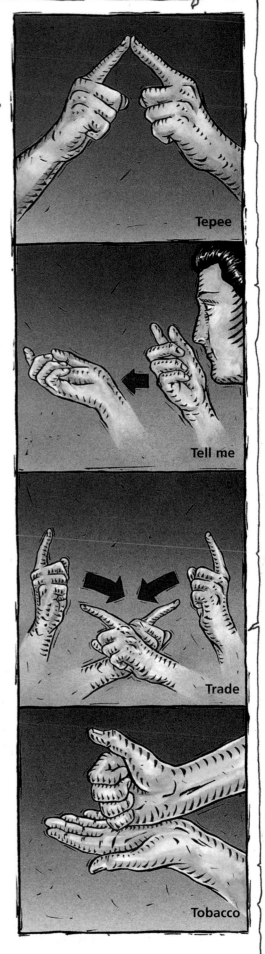

Tepee

Tell me

Trade

Tobacco

BROWN HAT'S HISTORY

Below, you can see a pictograph, made by a Lakota artist named Brown Hat. It starts on the left with an Indian trading blankets and other goods. In the middle are various battle images, showing warriors being wounded by arrows. In 1869–70, a woman was killed by a falling tree.

SIGN LANGUAGE

The Plains Indians spoke many different languages and dialects. Even tribes that lived fairly close together found it difficult to know what their neighbors were saying. They could, however, communicate using sign language. You can see in these pictures how each hand sign conveyed an idea, rather than a spelt word. Tepee, for example, is a simple tent shape made with two fingers. Sign language is said to be five times faster than speaking. It was very useful for making **treaties** and for trading—both with other tribes and with white people who visited the Plains.

1869-70

19

WHAT WORK DID PLAINS INDIANS DO?

Work for the Plains Indians revolved around hunting. The men went out to kill buffalo, deer, and antelope for their meat, skins, and horns. Women skinned and cut up the animals, dried the meat, and treated the hides. They also cooked and sewed. Children worked, too, looking after their younger brothers and sisters and the horses.

MAKING MOCCASINS ▶

Women made moccasins to fit each person's feet. They cut the soles out of thin rawhide and the tops from soft, tanned skin. The shoes were sewn together using **sinews** for thread, and decorated with beads and **quills**. Patterns were typical of the wearer's tribe.

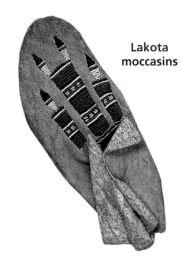

Lakota moccasins

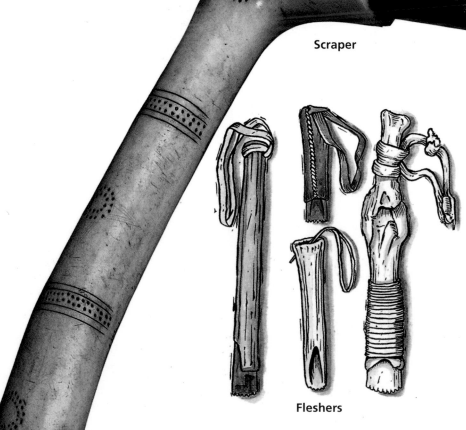

Scraper

Fleshers

◀ TREASURED TOOLS

Tools like these on the left helpe women to prepare animal skins. To take off the animal hair, they used a scraper, often made of ell horn with a metal blade. A woman marked the handle for each new hide she prepared, and often this was passed on down through the family. A chisel-shaped flesher removed the animal's fat from its skin. Early fleshers were made from bone, but later they had iron blades.

MAKING PIPES ▼

Smoking pipes was a regular Plains Indian pastime, and different pipes were made for different occasions. Women only smoked everyday pipes, while elaborate ones were used in special ceremonies. This pipe was made by a Sioux or Pawnee Indian before 1850. It is carved from **catlinite** stone. Native artists at the Pipestone Quarry in Minnesota still make pipes today.

TANNING HIDES ▼

Tanning made animal skins soft and supple. After removing the hair and flesh, women scraped the skin to an even thickness. Then they washed it, stretched it, and rubbed it with a softening paste of animal liver and brain.

TRAPPING EAGLES

Of all the birds swooping across the Plains, the Indians worshipped the eagle. They used the feathers of this mighty creature to decorate headdresses and costumes for their tribal leaders. Young golden eagle feathers (white with dark tips) were particularly attractive and valuable. Just 15 feathers could be traded for a horse.

As the birds grew older their feathers became mottled, but they were still precious. Families went on eagle-trapping trips to catch them. They dug a pit, covered it with leaves and put fresh meat on top. A hunter hid inside the pit to kill the bird as it dived down and plunged inside.

WHAT DID THEY DO IN THEIR SPARE TIME?

The Plains Indians always made time for games, storytelling, and dancing. The men loved sports and were members of **warrior societies**. They dressed up and danced at special ceremonies, sometimes pretending to be animals. Women played games, and also held needlework clubs.

HOOP AND POLE GAME ▲

This painting from 1834 shows winter with the Hidatsa tribe. The men are playing the hoop and pole game, one of the most popular Plains Indian sports.

Players had to try to hit a rolling hoop using darts or spears. It was all about skill and chance. The Pawnee tribe sometimes played the game as a magical performance for calling buffalo.

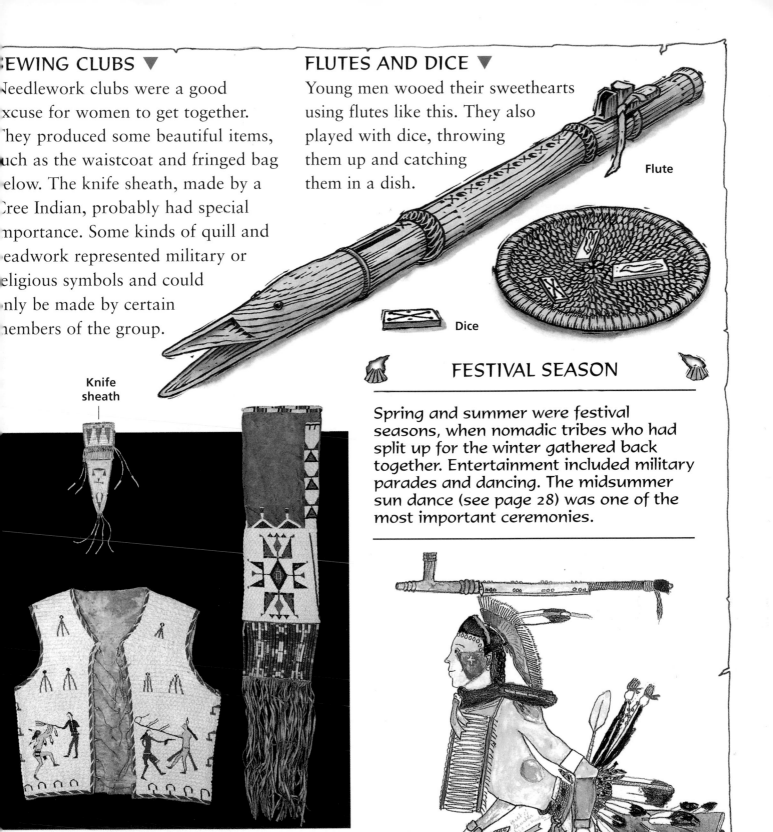

SEWING CLUBS ▼

Needlework clubs were a good excuse for women to get together. They produced some beautiful items, such as the waistcoat and fringed bag below. The knife sheath, made by a Cree Indian, probably had special importance. Some kinds of quill and beadwork represented military or religious symbols and could only be made by certain members of the group.

Knife sheath

FLUTES AND DICE ▼

Young men wooed their sweethearts using flutes like this. They also played with dice, throwing them up and catching them in a dish.

Flute

Dice

FESTIVAL SEASON

Spring and summer were festival seasons, when nomadic tribes who had split up for the winter gathered back together. Entertainment included military parades and dancing. The midsummer sun dance (see page 28) was one of the most important ceremonies.

THE GRASS DANCE ▶

Many Plains Indians did the Grass dance, though it had a different meaning for each tribe. For the Hidatsa, it represented the life of a warrior. Warriors carried grass in their belts for lighting fires when they were out at war.

Hidatsa Grass dance

WHAT DID PLAINS INDIAN MEN WEAR?

Each Plains Indian tribe had its own traditional dress. Most clothes were made from tanned skins, particularly deer and antelope. Women made the clothes, decorating them on special occasions with paintings, quills, and fringing. Men usually wore moccasins, long leggings, a **loincloth**, and a belt, with a shirt or buffalo robe on top.

PEHRISKA-RUHPA ▼

Pehriska-Ruhpa was an important Hidatsa Indian. Below, he is wearing a quilled shirt, fringed with hair and **ermine**. A painted buffalo robe is draped over his shoulders and he carries a ceremonial pipe.

EAGLE HEADDRESS ▶

Only a very distinguished warrior could wear a headdress like this one. It is made of 30 precious tail feathers from young golden eagles. The feathers related to acts of bravery by the warrior and his men. Styles like this were typical of central Plains Indians, such as the Lakota and Crow.

24

IMPORTANT MEN ▶

In some tribes, a grizzly bear necklace was a sign of great bravery and high position. A man's importance depended on his generosity, treatment of others, and leadership skills, as well as his courage in battle.

Grizzly bear claw necklace

MOCCASINS ▼

The Crow moccasins below were made in the 1850s. They had soft buckskin tops, rawhide soles, and laces at the front.

Moccasins wore out quickly, so Plains Indian men took several pairs when they went out to war. This meant a lot of work for the shoe-making women back home.

BUFFALO ROBES ▼

The Crow Indians made the finest robes and traded them with other tribes. Buffalo robes were decorated to show the achievements of the owner, such as capturing guns, taking scalps, and giving away horses or blankets. The warrior's robe below indicates a captured bow, guns, a horn full of gunpowder, and a shot bag for carrying lead shot.

Hidatsa warrior

WHAT DID WOMEN AND CHILDREN WEAR?

Women and girls traditionally wore deerskin dresses. They draped a deerskin tail around the neck, or made a beaded collar to look like a tail instead. Boys ran around in leggings, loincloths, and occasionally, plain shirts. Buffalo robes kept them warm. No one on the Plains had underwear, so in very cold weather, they wore two layers of clothing. Elaborate costumes were kept for special occasions.

Boot moccasins

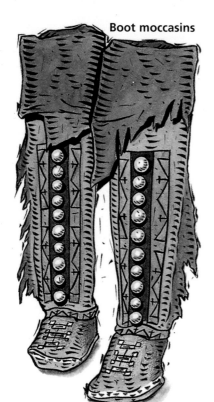

◀ LEGGINGS AND MOCCASINS

In the southern Plains tribes, such as the Comanche, women wore bootlike moccasins. These ones are made of dyed buckskin, with silver buttons down the front. Women farther north wore a type of leg-warmer, stretching from ankle to knee and held up by garters.

CLOTH DRESSES ▶

By 1870, Europeans were trading plenty of cloth on the Plains. This Cheyenne girl's dress is made of wool from England. The cowrie shell decorations were traded, too. They became very popular in the 1880s.

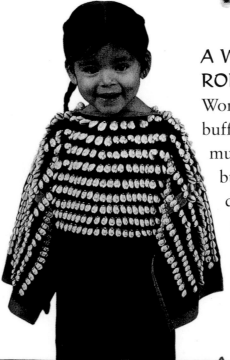

A WOMAN'S ROBE ▶

Women wore buffalo robes much like men's, but they were decorated differently. Female robes usually had geometric designs. The pattern on the robe above is called a "box and border." It symbolizes different parts of a buffalo.

A GALA DRESS ▶

A gala dress like this was worn on special occasions. It is made from two whole deerskins, laced together at the sides. The cape at the top has Lakota patterns in beadwork and colored cloth. Heavy fringes add a final decorative touch.

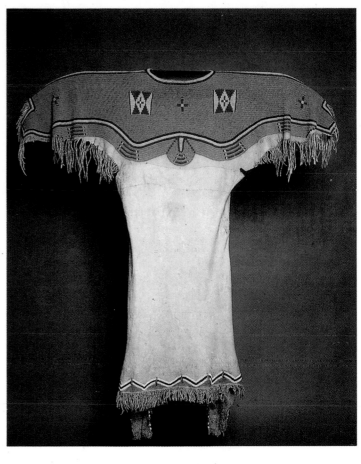

Buffalo robe

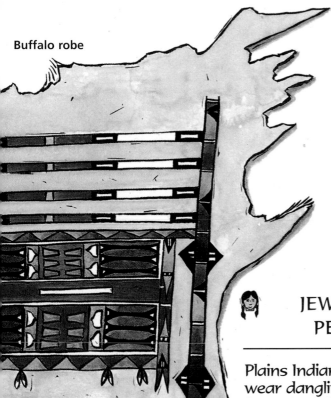

JEWELS AND PERFUME

Plains Indian women liked to wear dangling earrings made from traded seashells or metal. They were decorated with beads or quills. Beads were also worn in the hair, and a painted red parting showed that a woman could still have children. Sometimes, ladies scented their clothes with a herb called sweetgrass.

A SIOUX WOMAN'S ROBE ▶

Chan-Cha-Nia-Tenin belonged to the Sioux tribe. Here she is wearing a summer robe made from smooth, tanned hide. The "box and border" design stands out in bright colors.

WHAT WAS THE PLAINS INDIANS' RELIGION?

Religion guided the Plains Indians through life. They believed in an upper world, ruled by powerful Thunderbird spirits, as well as a deeper underworld. Underwater spirits controlled the animals and plants. Spirits were thought to give people good or bad health and to lead them into an afterlife.

A MEDICINE BUNDLE ▶

Medicine bundles were important holy items, thought to have great healing and protective powers. They were owned by chosen keepers and opened in special ceremonies, sometimes to cure the sick. Inside was a medicine pipe and other objects, such as skins, feathers, and bones. These all had a spiritual meaning.

Blackfoot medicine bundl[e]

BUFFALO DANCE ▼

This Mandan man is performing a Buffalo dance. He is drawing on the spirit of the animal, to make sure the next hunt goes well.

SUN DANCE ▶

This photo shows the start of a four-day sun dance, an important ritual across the Plains. During the ceremony, dancers pushed skewers through the skin on their chest. The skewers were tied by leather thongs to a central pole. Dancers gazed at the sun and were thought to draw power from the earth through the pole.

POWERFUL SPIRITS

ome tribes believed in an
ll-powerful Great Spirit, called
Wakan Tanka by the Lakota.
verything and everyone had
 spirit that was connected to
his great creator. If a Plains
ndian was in trouble, he or
he would call on the spirits
or help. A tribe's spiritual
eader, or medicine man, had
pecial powers to communicate
ith the spirit world.

◀ O-KEE-PA CEREMONY

The Buffalo dance was an
important part of a Mandan
ceremony called O-kee-pa.
Another aspect of this festival
was self-torture, which
was thought to release
supernatural powers. George
Caitlin, a famous explorer,
was the first white man to
witness the O-kee-pa. When
he described what he had
seen, few people believed him.

MEDICINE PIPE ▼

Medicine pipes were used to summon healing spirits
in ceremonies across the Plains. This one is
decorated with eagle feathers, ermine,
horsehair, and an eagle head.
Each tribe had its own
traditions around
the medicine
pipe.

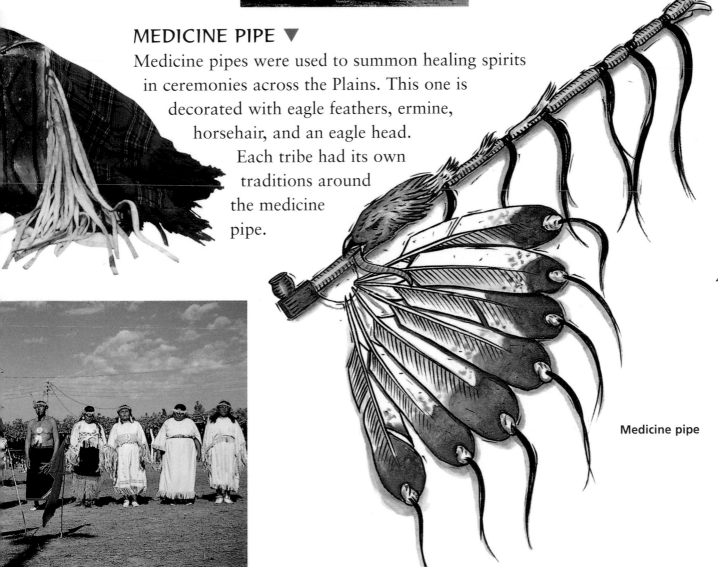

Medicine pipe

HOW DID THEY GOVERN THEMSELVES?

There was no official government among the Plains Indians. Instead, important decisions were made by a **tribal council**. Each tribe was made up of different bands, and the bands all chose a leader to represent them on the council. Women were not usually voted into the council, but everyone respected their wishes and views.

RED CLOUD'S SHIRT ▼

Red Cloud was a leader of the Oglala Lakota. In the 1870s, he visited Washington, D.C. for meetings with the U.S. government. He wore this shirt, beaded and fringed with human hair. The blue and yellow represent sky and earth powers.

◄ MATO-TOPÉ

Mato-Topé was a famous Mandan chief, also known as Four Bears. You can tell his importance by his magnificent headdress, made of golden eagle feathers and buffalo horns. The curved knife on top is a record of a fight with a Cheyenne chief, and the feather and scalp on his spear show other victories. When the skin for his shirt was tanned, a border of fur was left at the bottom for decoration.

LAKOTA CHIEFS ▲

An Indian historian named Amos Bad Heart Bull drew the picture above. It shows a young Lakota war chief, Crazy Horse of the Oglalas, following the famous spiritual leader, Sitting Bull. The Lakota tribal council was made up of important elders who had lived long and successful lives. Other tribes elected leaders in different ways.

The Sioux nation

THE SIOUX NATION ▶

This diagram shows the various Sioux tribes of about 1850. At the time, there were a total of about 25,000 Sioux Indians. The Teton, meaning "those who dwell on the prairies," called themselves Lakota. They were split into seven main groups.

SIOUX

WAHPETON MDEWAKANTON YANKTONAI YANKTON
WAHPEKUTE SISSE TON

TETON

BRULE
BROILED MEAT PEOPLE
BIG LEGGED HORSES
BOIL THEIR DISHES
BAD ARMS
BORN IN MIDDLE
COWEATERS

BLACKFEET
THE CUTS
BLACKFOOTED ONES
BAD LOOKERS
CAMP NEXT TO
CROW FEATHER

OGLALAS
TRUE OGALA
RED WATER
OLD SKIN NECKLACE
NIGHTCLOUD
RED LODGE
SHORT HAIR

TWO KETTLE
NO DIVISIONS

MINICONJOU
RIVER THAT FLIES
EAT NO DOG
SHELL EARRING
LEJA GA DAT CAH

SANS ARC
SANS ARC
RED WATER
HAM EATERS

HUNKPAPA

DEVILS MEDICINE MAN
HALF BREECH CLOUT
FRESH MEAT NECKLACE
SLEEPY KETTLE
SORE BACKS
THOSE THAT CARRY BAD BOWS

WERE THE PLAINS INDIANS ARTISTS?

Art was a big part of Plains Indian life. They developed their style of work over hundreds of years. Paintings were mainly done on useful items such as clothes, tepees, and sacred objects. Stone and wood were carved into beautiful pipes and symbols of historic events. Men did most of the painting and carving, and women excelled at needlework.

SIOUX SHIRT ▶

The painted war scenes on this Sioux shirt show the owner's bravery. The warriors appear to be riding sidesaddle, but they were probably drawn in this way to show their spirits were one with their horses. The man on the red horse is wearing a soldier's coat and top hat. Clothes like this were given to important Indians at white **trading posts**.

PAINTING TOOLS ▼

To paint a skin, the Indians used a stick to scratch an outline. Then they added color using "bone pens." These were like felt-tip pens, that soaked up the paint through holes in the bone.

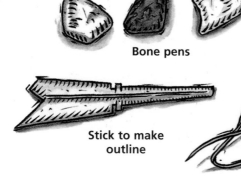

Bone pens

Stick to make outline

Paint pouch

BULL BEAR'S ROBE ▶

This huge buffalo robe may have belonged to the Oglala chief, Bull Bear. The holes around the edge show where it was stretched for tanning. Two of the painted warriors are holding large red scalps – you can see the hair hanging down. To the right of them is a Pawnee warrior with a shield. The green figure on the left is probably a Pawnee woman being captured by the Sioux.

◀ CARVING STONE

Carving was a skilled job. Traditional pipe makers used a hard stick and sand to drill into chunks of stone. It took about an hour to make a hole just an inch or so deep. The decorative pipe below was probably a gift to white soldiers who visited the Plains.

MONTANA WARRIOR ▶

This petroglyph was made in Montana, probably in the late 1700s. By this time, many Plains Indians had horses and guns, and war between tribes was common. This warrior is holding a broken spear and his horse has no tail. Men tied up their horses' tails for battle.

PETROGLYPHS

Petroglyphs are pictures carved in rocks or caves. The Indians created them using tools made of a very hard stone called flint. Petroglyphs can be found throughout the Great Plains—some date back to the 1600s or earlier. They often show animals, plants or human figures and can tell us a great deal about Plains life long ago.

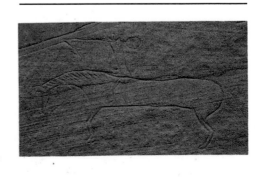

HOW DID THEY RECORD THEIR HISTORY?

The Plains Indians passed on much of their history by word of mouth. Some tribes also used a type of calendar, with important events painted on a huge animal hide. This was called a Winter Count, because most Indians counted the years by winters. Some tribes may have started these calendars long before they moved to the Plains.

LITTLE BLUFF'S PAINTED TEPEE ▶

The tepee on the right was given by the Cheyenne to the Kiowa Indians. It commemorates a peace treaty between the two tribes. The black stripes indicate successful war parties, led by the Kiowa chief, Little Bluff. The pictures record other events of the tribe, including Indians fighting soldiers with guns.

◀ LONE DOG'S WINTER COUNT

Left is a winter count made by Shunka Ishnala (Lone Dog) of the Sioux. It starts in the middle with the winter of 1800, then continues in a spiral path. The black disk near the end shows an eclipse of the sun in 1869. After this comes a symbol with 30 black lines, representing 30 Sioux who were killed by Crow Indians.

Pictograph histories varied between tribes and changed quite a lot over time. The pictures on the left were probably done by the Blackfoot tribe. You can see a gun being captured (a), a warrior with a shield (b), and a chief in a horned headdress being speared (c). What can you see in the Sioux pictures on the right? One is a battle scene, with hoof prints to show how the enemy was surrounded and killed.

GROUP DRAWING

Picture-writing was a man's job, and often he would ask his friends to help. This made big jobs like decorating tepees much quicker and more fun.

HISTORY KEEPERS ▼

In some tribes, such as the Cheyenne, certain men were picked as keepers of the tribe's history. They had to promise to tell the tribal history only to other keepers, who had to agree that it was correct. Records of events passed from generation to generation in this way.

Picture-writing ancient symbols

WHAT DID THE PLAINS INDIANS TRADE?

Through trade, the Plains Indians bought what they couldn't provide for themselves. Nomadic hunters traded meat and skins for crops grown by villager tribes. European goods, such as kettles and guns, were also bought. Food, weapons, and other items changed hands across America and beyond.

RENDEZVOUS ▼

A rendezvous was a great trading center, where tribes gathered at certain times of year. The painting below shows a rendezvous on the Green River, Wyoming in the 1830s.

TRADE GOODS ▶

This Hidatsa shirt was traded in the mid-1800s. In the 1860s, the Blackfoot would offer up to ten buffalo robes for a gun like the one below.

Flintlock gun

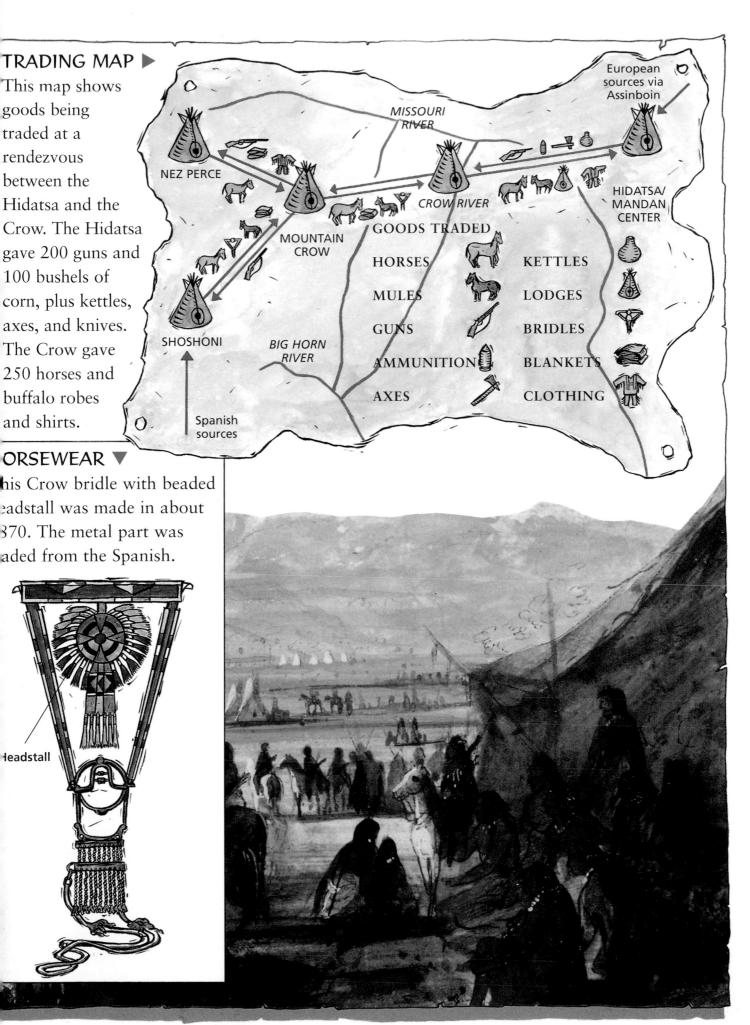

TRADING MAP ▶

This map shows goods being traded at a rendezvous between the Hidatsa and the Crow. The Hidatsa gave 200 guns and 100 bushels of corn, plus kettles, axes, and knives. The Crow gave 250 horses and buffalo robes and shirts.

HORSEWEAR ▼

This Crow bridle with beaded headstall was made in about 1870. The metal part was traded from the Spanish.

Headstall

MAP LABELS

NEZ PERCE

MISSOURI RIVER

European sources via Assinboin

MOUNTAIN CROW

CROW RIVER

HIDATSA/ MANDAN CENTER

SHOSHONI

BIG HORN RIVER

Spanish sources

GOODS TRADED

HORSES
MULES
GUNS
AMMUNITION
AXES

KETTLES
LODGES
BRIDLES
BLANKETS
CLOTHING

WHAT WAS PLAINS INDIAN WARFARE LIKE?

Competition for land and buffalo sometimes led to battles. In the early days, wars were rare, but the introduction of guns in 1740 gave some tribes more power. For example, the Blackfoot and Cree forced the Shoshone and Kutenai off their land and the Apache lost to the Pawnee. Most wars were about taking horses and counting **coup**, rather than destroying tribes.

SHIELDS ▶

This large rawhide shield was used in the days before horses. It had a soft buckskin cover and lucky charms attached. Most shields were painted with designs to protect the warrior. Later shields, used on horseback, were smaller.

Whistle

WHISTLES ▶

War leaders communicated using long whistles made of bone from the wings of eagles. Often, these were engraved with lightning symbols, which were thought to have protective powers.

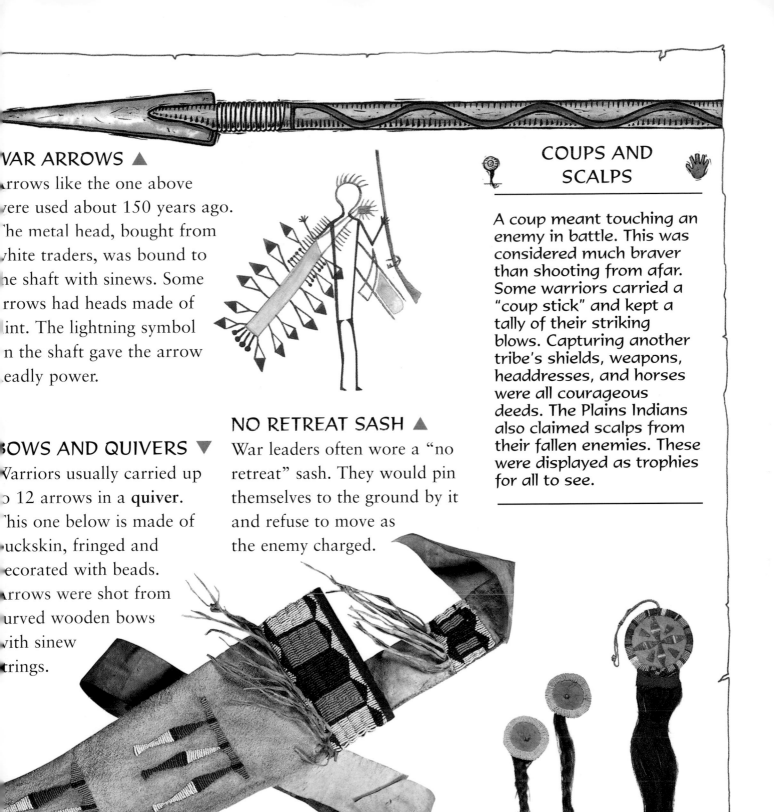

WAR ARROWS ▲

Arrows like the one above were used about 150 years ago. The metal head, bought from white traders, was bound to the shaft with sinews. Some arrows had heads made of flint. The lightning symbol on the shaft gave the arrow deadly power.

BOWS AND QUIVERS ▼

Warriors usually carried up to 12 arrows in a **quiver**. This one below is made of buckskin, fringed and decorated with beads. Arrows were shot from curved wooden bows with sinew strings.

NO RETREAT SASH ▲

War leaders often wore a "no retreat" sash. They would pin themselves to the ground by it and refuse to move as the enemy charged.

COUPS AND SCALPS

A coup meant touching an enemy in battle. This was considered much braver than shooting from afar. Some warriors carried a "coup stick" and kept a tally of their striking blows. Capturing another tribe's shields, weapons, headdresses, and horses were all courageous deeds. The Plains Indians also claimed scalps from their fallen enemies. These were displayed as trophies for all to see.

SCALPS ▶

Chief Crazy Crow of the Blackfoot took these two small scalps from Crow and Kutenai enemies. The larger scalp, embroidered with porcupine quills, is probably Mandan.

HOW DID THE PLAINS INDIANS CHANGE?

Contact with white people brought the Plains Indians many things that improved their lives. These included blankets, knives, scissors, combs, needles, beads, and most importantly, horses and guns. Relations between white people and Indians were peaceful at first, but battles soon began as white people threatened to take control of the natives' land.

WHITE SETTLERS ▲

In the 1840s, white people began pouring across the Plains to settle in the western United States. Their wagons often came under attack from Indians, who worried that their land was being invaded. The white travelers also brought diseases, such as **cholera** and smallpox, which affected the Natives badly. By 1859, at least 30,000 Plains Indians had died.

◀ FUR TRADERS

A Blackfoot artist made this sketch in about 1840. It shows white men trading bottles, flasks, buckets, and kettles in return for furs. At the bottom of the picture, the Indian's shirt fringe is shaking. This is to show the terrible effects that whiskey had on the tribesmen, who had never drunk alcohol before. Tea and coffee were also introduced by white traders.

Beaver tail knife

Trade knife

GUNS ▶

arly guns were hard to ad onto horseback. ribes used bows nd arrows until ifles came in e 1870s.

◀ PIPE TOMAHAWK

The pipe tomahawk doubled as a pipe and a weapon. It was invented by whites, but became very popular among Indians.

CUSTER'S LAST STAND ▼

From the 1860s, the U.S. government began to move Native Americans into reservations. Chief Sitting Bull and his followers tried to resist. On June 25, 1876, they defeated General Custer's army at the Battle of Little Bighorn. General Custer died alongside 200 of his men.

Pipe tomahawk

Winchester rifle

ONCE I WAS A WARRIOR

he reservations system ave white people more ights to the land. They lowly took over the Plains, uilding farms, killing the uffalo, and destroying the ative way of life. The Battle f Wounded Knee in 1890 narked the end of the Plains ndians' freedom. Sitting ull's song describes ow things ad changed:

iki'cize	a warrior
waon'kon	I have been
wana	now
hena'la elo	it is all over
iyo'tiye kiya	a hard time
waon	I have

WHAT ARE THE PLAINS INDIANS DOING TODAY?

While the arrival of white settlers forced Indians to change their lifestyle, the Plains Indians clung to their identity. In 1924, they were given U.S. citizenship and the right to vote. Now Native Americans are rebuilding their culture and have a say in how their reservations are run. They are represented in the U.S. government and get financial support for their industries, schools, and tourist activities.

TOURISM ▶

Tourism is important to today's Plains Indians. They still carve beautiful ornaments and pipes to sell. Some reservations are open to the public, too.

◀ SCHOOLS

In the 1880s and 1890s, many children were sent off the Plains to white schools. Today, schools on reservations teach traditional values as well as math, history, and other subjects. Many pupils go on to college, like this Dakota girl.

TRANSPORTATION ▼

Modern life has brought cars and trucks to Indian reservations, many of which are huge. The Navajo Nation measures over 25,870 square miles (67,000 square kilometres). As you can see from the sign below, the Oglala Lakota even have their own airport.

PINE RIDGE–OGLALA SIOUX AIRPORT
PINE RIDGE, SOUTH DAKOTA
DEDICATED TO THE MEMORY OF ALL VETERANS OF ALL WARS
NW–SE LANDING STRIP PAVED 60'X 5,200' LIGHTED
E – W LANDING STRIP PAVED 50'X 3,000'
PAVEMENT DESIGNED FOR 23,000–LbS. SINGLE GEAR AIRCRAFT

VEHICLES PROHIBITED ON RUNWAYS
VIOLATORS TRESPASSING BEYOND AUTO PARKING LOT FENCE
MAY BE FINED $360.00 OR 6–MONTHS IN JAIL, Or Joe E. Bluehorse Representative   G. Wayne Tapio Pine Ridge Village Representative

DO NOT DRIVE ON RUNWAYS

POPULATIONS

European diseases had a drastic effect on Plains Indian numbers. For example, smallpox killed so many Mandan people that their population dropped from 1,600 in 1837 to just 150 in 1850. But tribal numbers are rising again. The 2007 **census** recorded about 3 million Native Americans living throughout the U.S.

TRADITION MEETS TECHNOLOGY

Plains Indians are now able to combine their traditional skills with modern technology. The Lakota have developed new beadwork designs using computer graphics. The patterns on the shoes, cap, and ball below are examples of this type of work.

THE CROW FAIR ▲

The Crow woman and horse above are dressed up for the famous Crow Fair. This takes place every August along the Little Bighorn River in Montana. Tribes and tourists come from all over the country to see one of the world's largest collections of tepees. There are also dances and horse races for the children, and a horseback parade.

43

GLOSSARY

BANDS Smaller groups within a tribe, who lived and traveled together.

BERING LAND BRIDGE A stretch of land that joined present-day Alaska and eastern Siberia many thousands of years ago. Later, the sea rose over this land and it became the Bering Strait.

BUCKSKIN A type of leather made of softened deerskin.

CATLINITE A soft, red stone named after the American explorer and painter George Catlin.

CAYOTE A type of wild dog, smaller than a wolf.

CENSUS An official population count.

CHOLERA A highly infectious disease, caused by contaminated food or water.

COUP Touching an enemy in battle, often with a "coup stick." Counting coup was a measure of bravery among warriors.

DIALECT A regional variety of a language.

ERMINE White winter fur of the stoat.

GLYPH A symbol or character that conveys a particular meaning.

GREAT PLAINS A huge, grassy area in central North America.

HIDE A raw, untanned animal skin.

LOINCLOTH A strip of soft, tanned skin (or later cloth) that men wore between their legs. It was folded over a belt at the front and back.

MOCCASIN Traditional Plains Indian shoe, usually made of deerskin or other soft leather.

NOMADIC Describing people who move their homes from place to place, usually following animals to hunt.

PICTOGRAPH A series of pictures painted on a hide or wood, usually as a record of events or spiritual experiences.

QUILL A spine from a porcupine, or sometimes the stiff part of a feather. Native Americans dyed quills and used them for decorative work.

QUIVER A container for arrows, usually carried by a strap over the shoulder.

RAWHIDE Dehaired and cleaned hide that becomes hard and stiff when dry.

SINEW Tough, stringy fiber that attaches muscles to bones.

SMALLPOX A highly infectious disease that included fever and a blistery rash.

TANNING The process of cleaning and softening rawhide to make it into leather.

TEPEE A tent made of buffalo hide, supported on wooden poles. From about 1870, the hide was replaced with canvas.

TRADING POST A place where Indians met with white people to trade.

TRAVOIS Two long poles, attached at each side of a horse or dog, with a platform for carrying luggage.

TREATY A formal agreement, such as a peace agreement between tribes.

TRIBAL COUNCIL A group of elected men who made decisions for the tribe.

WARRIOR SOCIETY Groups of men who had their own traditions, and who were responsible for the safety of the tribe.

INDEX

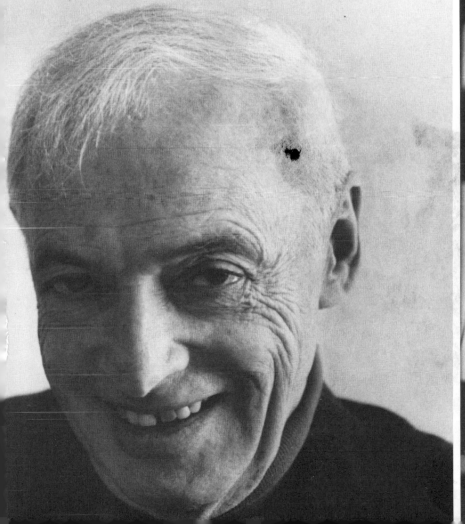

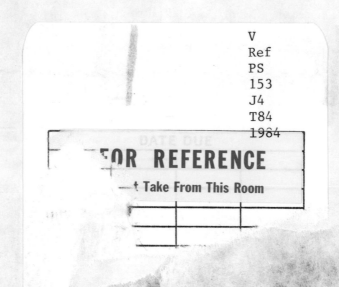

Twentieth-Century American-Jewish Fiction Writers

Dictionary of Literary Biography

1: *The American Renaissance in New England*, edited by Joel Myerson (1978)
2: *American Novelists Since World War II*, edited by Jeffrey Helterman and Richard Layman (1978)
3: *Antebellum Writers in New York and the South*, edited by Joel Myerson (1979)
4: *American Writers in Paris, 1920-1939*, edited by Karen Lane Rood (1980)
5: *American Poets Since World War II*, 2 volumes, edited by Donald J. Greiner (1980)
6: *American Novelists Since World War II*, Second Series, edited by James E. Kibler, Jr. (1980)
7: *Twentieth-Century American Dramatists*, 2 volumes, edited by John MacNicholas (1981)
8: *Twentieth-Century American Science-Fiction Writers*, 2 volumes, edited by David Cowart and Thomas L. Wymer (1981)
9: *American Novelists, 1910-1945*, 3 volumes, edited by James J. Martine (1981)
10: *Modern British Dramatists, 1900-1945*, 2 volumes, edited by Stanley Weintraub (1982)
11: *American Humorists, 1800-1950*, 2 volumes, edited by Stanley Trachtenberg (1982)
12: *American Realists and Naturalists*, edited by Donald Pizer and Earl N. Harbert (1982)
13: *British Dramatists Since World War II*, 2 volumes, edited by Stanley Weintraub (1982)
14: *British Novelists Since 1960*, 2 volumes, edited by Jay L. Halio (1983)
15: *British Novelists, 1930-1959*, 2 volumes, edited by Bernard Oldsey (1983)
16: *The Beats: Literary Bohemians in Postwar America*, 2 volumes, edited by Ann Charters (1983)
17: *Twentieth-Century American Historians*, edited by Clyde N. Wilson (1983)
18: *Victorian Novelists After 1885*, edited by Ira B. Nadel and William E. Fredeman (1983)
19: *British Poets, 1880-1914*, edited by Donald E. Stanford (1983)
20: *British Poets, 1914-1945*, edited by Donald E. Stanford (1983)
21: *Victorian Novelists Before 1885*, edited by Ira B. Nadel and William E. Fredeman (1983)
22: *American Writers for Children, 1900-1960*, edited by John Cech (1983)
23: *American Newspaper Journalists, 1873-1900*, edited by Perry J. Ashley (1983)
24: *American Colonial Writers, 1606-1734*, edited by Emory Elliott (1984)
25: *American Newspaper Journalists, 1901-1925*, edited by Perry J. Ashley (1984)
26: *American Screenwriters*, edited by Robert E. Morsberger, Stephen O. Lesser, and Randall Clark (1984)
27: *Poets of Great Britain and Ireland, 1945-1960*, edited by Vincent B. Sherry, Jr. (1984)
28: *Twentieth-Century American-Jewish Fiction Writers*, edited by Daniel Walden (1984)

Documentary Series:

1: *Sherwood Anderson, Willa Cather, John Dos Passos, Theodore Dreiser, F. Scott Fitzgerald, Ernest Hemingway, Sinclair Lewis*, edited by Margaret A. Van Antwerp (1982)
2: *James Gould Cozzens, James T. Farrell, William Faulkner, John O'Hara, John Steinbeck, Thomas Wolfe, Richard Wright*, edited by Margaret A. Van Antwerp (1982)
3: *Saul Bellow, Jack Kerouac, Norman Mailer, Vladimir Nabokov, John Updike, Kurt Vonnegut*, edited by Mary Bruccoli (1983)
4: *Tennessee Williams*, edited by Margaret A. Van Antwerp and Sally Johns.

Yearbook:

1980, edited by Karen L. Rood, Jean W. Ross, and Richard Ziegfeld (1981)
1981, edited by Karen L. Rood, Jean W. Ross, and Richard Ziegfeld (1982)
1982, edited by Richard Ziegfeld; associate editors: Jean W. Ross and Lynne C. Zeigler (1983)
1983, edited by Mary Bruccoli and Jean W. Ross; associate editor: Richard Ziegfeld (1984)

Dictionary of Literary Biography • Volume Twenty-eight

Twentieth-Century American-Jewish Fiction Writers

Edited by
Daniel Walden
Pennsylvania State University

A Bruccoli Clark Book
Gale Research Company • Book Tower • Detroit, Michigan 48226
1984

Advisory Board for
DICTIONARY OF LITERARY BIOGRAPHY

Louis S. Auchincloss
John Baker
D. Philip Baker
A. Walton Litz, Jr.
Peter S. Prescott
Lola L. Szladits
William Targ

Matthew J. Bruccoli and Richard Layman, *Editorial Directors*
C. E. Frazer Clark, Jr., *Managing Editor*

Manufactured by Edwards Brothers, Inc.
Ann Arbor, Michigan
Printed in the United States of America

Library of Congress Cataloging in Publication Data
Main entry under title:

Twentieth-century American-Jewish fiction writers.

(Dictionary of literary biography; v. 28)
"A Bruccoli Clark book."
Includes index.
1. Novelists, American—20th century—Biography.
2. American fiction—Jewish authors—Bio-bibliography.
3. American fiction—20th century—Bio-bibliography. I.
Walden, Daniel, 1922-   . II. Title: 20th-century American-
Jewish fiction writers. III. Series.
PS153.J4T84   1984   813'.5'0935203924   [B]   84-4014
ISBN 0-8103-1706-0

For Beatrice Schulman Walden, my L'am, whose love and spirit sustained me;
and for our children Moss and Ruth (and little David),
the fruits of our vine, our past and our future.
Mazeltov. Shalom.

Contents

Contents

Plan of the Series

The advisory board, the editors, and the publisher of the *Dictionary of Literary Biography* are joined in endorsing Mark Twain's declaration. The literature of a nation provides an inexhaustible resource of permanent worth. It is our expectation that this endeavor will make literature and its creators better understood and more accessible to students and the literate public, while satisfying the standards of teachers and scholars.

To meet these requirements, *literary biography* has been construed in terms of the author's achievement. The most important thing about a writer is his writing. Accordingly, the entries in *DLB* are career biographies, tracing the development of the author's canon and the evolution of his reputation.

The publication plan for *DLB* resulted from two years of preparation. The project was proposed to Bruccoli Clark by Frederick G. Ruffner, president of the Gale Research Company, in November 1975. After specimen entries were prepared and typeset, an advisory board was formed to refine the entry format and develop the series rationale. In meetings held during 1976, the publisher, series editors, and advisory board approved the scheme for a comprehensive biographical dictionary of persons who contributed to North American literature. Editorial work on the first volume began in January 1977, and it was published in 1978.

In order to make *DLB* more than a reference tool and to compile volumes that individually have claim to status as literary history, it was decided to organize volumes by topic or period or genre. Each of these freestanding volumes provides a biographical-bibliographical guide and overview for a particular area of literature. We are convinced that this organization—as opposed to a single alphabet method—constitutes a valuable innovation in the presentation of reference material. The volume plan necessarily requires many decisions for the placement and treatment of authors who might properly be included in two or three volumes. In some instances a major figure will be included in separate volumes, but with different entries emphasizing the aspect of his career appropriate to each volume. Ernest Hemingway, for example, is represented in *American Writers in Paris, 1920-1939* by an entry focusing on his expatriate apprenticeship; he is also in *American Novelists, 1910-1945* with an entry surveying his entire career. Each volume includes a cumulative index of subject authors. The final *DLB* volume will be a comprehensive index to the entire series.

With volume ten in 1982 it was decided to enlarge the scope of *DLB* beyond the literature of the United States. By the end of 1983 twelve volumes treating British literature had been published, and volumes for Commonwealth and Modern European literature were in progress. The series has been further augmented by the *DLB Yearbooks* (since 1981) which update published entries and add new entries to keep the *DLB* current with contemporary activity. There have also been occasional *DLB Documentary Series* volumes which provide biographical and critical background source materials for figures whose work is judged to have particular interest for students. One of these companion volumes is entirely devoted to Tennessee Williams.

The purpose of *DLB* is not only to provide reliable information in a convenient format but also to place the figures in the larger perspective of literary history and to offer appraisals of their accomplishments by qualified scholars.

We define literature as the *intellectual commerce of a nation*: not merely as belles lettres, but as that ample and complex process by which ideas are generated, shaped, and transmitted. *DLB* entries are not limited to "creative writers" but extend to other figures who in this time and in this way influenced the mind of a people. Thus the series encompasses historians, journalists, publishers, and screenwriters. By this means readers of *DLB* may be aided to perceive literature not as cult scripture in the keeping of cultural high priests, but as at the center of a nation's life.

DLB includes the major writers appropriate to each volume and those standing in the ranks immediately behind them. Scholarly and critical counsel has been sought in deciding which minor figures to include and how full their entries should be.

Wherever possible, useful references will be made to figures who do not warrant separate entries.

Each *DLB* volume has a volume editor responsible for planning the volume, selecting the figures for inclusion, and assigning the entries. Volume editors are also responsible for preparing, where appropriate, appendices surveying the major periodicals and literary and intellectual movements for their volumes, as well as lists of further readings. Work on the series as a whole is coordinated at the Bruccoli Clark editorial center in Columbia, South Carolina, where the editorial staff is responsible for the accuracy of the published volumes.

One feature that distinguishes *DLB* is the illustration policy—its concern with the iconography of literature. Just as an author is influenced by his surroundings, so is the reader's understanding of the author enhanced by a knowledge of his environment. Therefore *DLB* volumes include not only drawings, paintings, and photographs of authors, often depicting them at various stages in their careers, but also illustrations of their families and places where they lived. Title pages are regularly reproduced in facsimile along with dust jackets for modern authors. The dust jackets are a special fea-

ture of *DLB* because they often document better than anything else the way in which an author's work was launched in its own time. Specimens of the writers' manuscripts are included when feasible.

A supplement to *DLB*—tentatively titled *A Guide, Chronology, and Glossary for American Literature*—will outline the history of literature in North America and trace the influences that shaped it. This volume will provide a framework for the study of American literature by means of chronological tables, literary affiliation charts, glossarial entries, and concise surveys of the major movements. It has been planned to stand on its own as a vade mecum, providing a ready-reference guide to the study of American literature as well as a companion to the *DLB* volumes for American literature.

Samuel Johnson rightly decreed that "The chief glory of every people arises from its authors." The purpose of the *Dictionary of Literary Biography* is to compile literary history in the surest way available to us—by accurate and comprehensive treatment of the lives and work of those who contributed to it.

The *DLB* Advisory Board

Foreword

For the Jews from the cities, towns, and *shtetls* of the Old World arriving in the United States at a time of national reform, of primary importance were the problems of adjustment to the new culture and reconciliation of their old-country culture with that of the New World. Scrambling for a dollar, all family members working, they endured so that their children might become Americans. "Who has ever seen such optimism?," asked Harry Golden. For the American-Jewish writer, under the pressures of the Americanizing process, new problems were added. With disdain for his parents' ways, dress, and accent, he often opted for the New at the expense of the Old. Traditions, values, religion—all were subordinated to the need to emulate the Americans or the Jews who were no longer greenhorns. As the works of those writers from Abraham Cahan on in the first generation, and from Samuel Ornitz through Henry Roth to Saul Bellow in the next, show, Jews who bridged the two cultures in a host country wrote of the ongoing bridging experience. Their literary talents explored the sociological dimensions of a minority. As Jewish self-consciousness benefited from the national and international processes, so the American-Jewish writer wrote of himself, his people, anti-Semitism, the war, middlebrow America, and the attempt to understand himself and the society he inhabited.

For the more than two million Eastern European Jews who came to the United States between 1880 and 1920, the transatlantic crossing from the Old World to the New was, in the words of one commentator, "a kind of hell that cleanses a man of his sins before coming to the Land of Columbus." From poverty, pogroms, and degradation, from hundreds of years of powerlessness, despair, and deferential adjustment, from a world of ghettoes in which they knew who they were and what their values were, the Eastern European Jews came to a land where opportunity, success, and the American Dream ruled. No longer was the study of the Torah a sign of achievement; as Abraham Cahan's David Levinsky was told, it was the American Dream that one had to achieve in the New World. True, there was a good chance of some upward mobility. But, sprinkled in with the possibilities of success—for one's children if not for oneself—were the bitterness of disillusion, the unsureness of identity, the world of values in process. To David Levinsky's "peculiar state of mind that the experience [of seeing the Statue of Liberty] created in me," were contrasted Michael Gold's condemnatory words, that this "is a land where the lice make fortunes, and the good men starve," and Genya's disappointment, in Henry Roth's *Call It Sleep,* on seeing her husband for the first time in months: "Ach! Then here in the new land is the same old poverty." In the conflict of cultures that was the life of the new immigrants, it was the New World with its new values that triumphed.

American-Jewish writers have had to fashion their products out of the life they knew, and they worked usually in an uncaring or hostile framework. For too long, as in the case of black literature, stereotypes persisted, drawn mainly by the host culture but aided and abetted by the minority. Overcoming these images was one aspect of the writers' problem. Learning the language and the symbols was another. Most important, the writers had to deal with a Jewish image brought into existence by Gentiles and Jews both and then create what had never existed before—an American-Jewish literature.

By the 1920s, America's Jews, now American Jews, with one foot in the old country and one in the new, were struggling with problems no longer tied to the ghetto. As Jews, their adherence to traditional values and ethics was honored. As American Jews, shown in Samuel Ornitz's anonymously published novel *Haunch, Paunch and Jowl* (1923), the compulsion to succeed and to wield power, no matter how correctly, surfaced for the first time. Though it was an isolated case, surrounded by pathos and humor, Meyer Hirsch's rise as chronicled by Ornitz went beyond David Levinsky's acceptable entrepreneurship in its earthiness—so much in the Yiddish tradition—and grotesqueness. As the drama of the generations was played out, Jews as Jews and as American Jews rebelled against their parents, struggled for their own identities, succeeded and failed, cried and laughed, as did others.

In the 1930s, in the grip of the Great Depression, Jews moved into prominence in literature. Nathanael West, Daniel Fuchs, Michael Gold, Henry Roth, and Meyer Levin were some of those in whose novels social and economic, generational and religious problems appeared. Writing about intellectuals and workers, hoboes and farmers, they concentrated on the attempts of people to identify with the poor and the oppressed. Some glorified the new energy of the Soviet Union or the Communist party at home as alternatives to what appeared a sick society. Michael Gold's *Jews Without Money* (1930), a novel from an ideologue, surprisingly kept to its last pages a plea for Communist brotherhood. Most Jewish writers, characteristically, reflected the external pressures of a depression-ridden society in which Jews struggled to be Americanized and survive. Many also joined in the decade's widely supported protests, spearheaded by President Roosevelt's New Deal for some and the Communists' program for others. Exchanging religious attachments for secularism, they sought new answers, perhaps new messiahs, in the social order. As Michael Gold wrote, "We had not Santa Claus, but we had a Messiah." No wonder he promised his mother, ideologically, "I must remain faithful to the poor because I cannot be faithless to you."

It was unusual that Henry Roth's *Call It Sleep* (1934) shifted focus in so many ways. Unlike any other novel of the era, this superb psychological work narrated from the viewpoint of a child summed up the truths and the traumas of the immigrants' experience. Confronted by a father who was maddened by ghosts of the past and by present poverty and despair, little David Schearl balances his existence precariously between the traditional values of his mother and the *cheder* (religious school) and those of the outside world. The most Freudian of the interwar novels, involved with oedipal conflict, God, and phallic imagery, it is, said Leslie Fiedler, "the best single book by a Jew about Jewishness written by an American, certainly through the thirties and perhaps ever." Whether *Call It Sleep* is a proletarian novel, which I doubt, is unimportant. What comes across is the inner psychic pain of the second generation and its social and familial revolts.

Jews in the United States have responded in many ways to the pressures of the New World. Some from the beginning and into the present desired to be and were quickly or eventually assimilated. Some attempted to find a middle way by which they could become Americans and still retain their sense of being Jews. Some were so alienated or estranged as to drop out and pass into the great other—the Gentile world. Still others were doubly alienated, no longer at home either in the Jewish or non-Jewish context. And some didn't care one way or the other. Meyer Levin, accepting biculturalism, wrote, "Godless though I profess myself, I have responded with more than warmth to the mystical elements of Chasidism. As a writer, I have considered that I

accept the material as folklore. But in my soul I know that I take more than this from these legends." Ben Hecht vacillated from self-hating and nearly anti-Semitic prose to some essays and stories in the 1940s calling on Jews to defend Jewish rights. For Saul Bellow, who has had no struggle in identifying himself as Jewish, there has been unconcern for the definition of what that means.

Though some critics have termed these authors collectors of pathological characters, anti-Semitic, or simply nonwriters because their concerns are not in accord with a set of predefined goals, it is clear to me that they are writers first, who are Jews. I realize that some will ask that a writer be held to a specific commitment (individually defined), to a specific religious framework in which the writing goes on, but searching for truth takes many forms. One form it will take only perilously is that of the didactic story or essay; however, the search must take the form that the characters and their situations determine. If Jews in America are religious or not, or are rooted in the values of the past or not, so be it. If they are engaged in a generational conflict, so be it. And if they are Americans who are Jews, trying to find their way in a world that has meanings and structure somewhat different from that of the past, or that seems to lack meaning, or that needs new interpretations of the past, so be it. The writer's province is insight and honesty, not religious or political activism, and the degree to which he succeeds as a writer, as an American-Jewish writer, is the most important criterion.

From World War I through World War II, American literature was dominated by concepts such as alienation and the wasteland. In spite of the fact that estrangement produced some masterpieces, its time passed. When the older generation moved on, there seemed to be few replacements. At this point, in Bellow's opinion, the writer had to exercise his own intelligence, to think, and not merely of his own narrow interests and needs. For Bellow, who had no fight about being a Jew—"I simply must deal with the facts of my life, a basic set of primitive facts," he said in 1964—the Jewish people's experience was a universal metaphor. Inasmuch as the modern writer specializes in what have been called grotesque facts and cannot compete with the news itself, as both Bellow and Philip Roth pointed out, he must go beyond reality. He must turn away from current events, for what seems lacking, concluded Bellow, is a firm sense of a common world, a coherent community, a genuine purpose in life. Man has to strive for a life of significant pattern.

With the same goals in mind, Bernard Malamud has quested for moral salvation and self-realization. Whether he is writing about Morris Bober and his assistant, or Fidelman, or a Levin who would like to be a "Free-man" in a world that is not easy for Jews, the theme of meaningful suffering is present. Bober, for example, knows painfully that he has been a failure in the eyes of the world. But, as becomes clear in the end, he is a good man in the biblical sense of the word. One of the Hasidic rabbis said that he would rather be devout than clever, but rather than both devout and clever, he should like to be good. Becoming the essential Jew, therefore, is what is sought. And that goal is at least distantly related to what Bellow refers to as consummation of a heart's need.

That there are similarities in the works of some American-Jewish writers can be demonstrated. The differences are more striking. Philip Roth, for instance, has written most often about extreme behavior in ordinary situations. From the beginning, he has been concerned with men and women whose moorings have been cut, who have been swept away from their native shores and out to sea, sometimes on a tide of their own righteousness or resentment. Take "The Conversion of the Jews," a story of a Jewish boy who could no longer stomach his rabbi's evasions and thus responds as a child who can no longer act like "a little rabbi." Take Alexander Portnoy, a productive member of society on the job, whose problems, rightly or wrongly understood, lead him to live beyond his psychological and moral means. In short, we learn from Roth, the fantastic situation must be accepted as reality at the same time as the reality of the fantastic and horrible. Or, to go back to an earlier explanation, the world of fiction, wrote Roth, "frees us of circumscriptions that society places upon feeling . . . and allows both writer and the reader to respond to experience in ways not always available in day-to-day conduct."

In the second half of the twentieth century the American-Jewish writers came of age. They were American writers, of course, but they were also American-Jewish writers because they were born Jewish, and, regardless of the intensity of their religious or cultural commitment, they have written about some essential aspect of the Jewish experience in America. Unlike the Lost Generation writers—Gentiles who seldom wrote about urban or ethnic conditions—the Jewish community was defined enough to support their work. In the early 1940s, American-Jewish writers responded as no other group to the country's urgent cultural need. The biblical past, the rise of Hitler, the Holocaust, the new State of Israel, and the need of Americans to again believe in humanity helped. As Saul Bellow put it, affirming his belief in the humanity of the patriarch Abraham, he knew his debt—it had to do with the presence and continuation of life.

In the 1970s and since, a most extraordinary development has been the emergence of a group of writers who write out of a sense of ongoing Jewish identification. Cynthia Ozick, Norma Rosen, and Hugh Nissenson, for example, have written of the centrality of the Jewish experience. In Nissenson's *A Pile of Stones* (1965), *Notes From the Frontier* (1968), *In the Reign of Peace* (1972), and *My Own Ground* (1976), there has been an attempt to examine the relationship of Jews to their religion in view of a God who is often absent or less than ideal. In Ozick's *Trust* (1966), *The Pagan Rabbi and Other Stories* (1971), *Bloodshed and Three Novellas* (1976), and *Levitation* (1982), there is an effort to develop a genuinely Jewish art in English along with what Ozick calls the "Judaization" of English.

As Ruth Wisse put it in a *Commentary* article in 1976, "Having no longer to defend themselves from real or imagined charges of parochialism, the new Jewish writers of the 70s are free to explore the 'trivial' and particularistic aspects of Judaism, and even, turning the tables, to speculate on the restrictive limits of English as a literary language." In other words, with an interest in trying to find out what it is like to think and write like Jews, they are using Jewish history and legend, they are not drawing caricatures, and they may be creating or completing what has been called one of the most distinctive cycles of literary expression in our time.

Twentieth-Century American-Jewish Fiction Writers contains essays on fifty-one authors whose novels and short stories deal with or come out of their American-Jewish experience. The writers may deal with that experience overtly or covertly, positively or negatively, confronting alienation, identity, acculturation, or assimilation. In this sense, writers such as Cahan, Bellow, and Ozick clearly fit in. On the other hand, some writers—West, Trilling, and Mailer, for example—are included because, although their fiction is not as overtly drawn from the Jewish experience, they are products of the Jewish cultural environment. In sum, it is the importance of the American-Jewish experience in shaping a writer's fictional world that has been crucial in my determination to include that author.

—Daniel Walden

Acknowledgments

This book was produced by BC Research. Karen L. Rood is senior editor for the *Dictionary of Literary Biography* series. Margaret A. Van Antwerp was the in-house editor.

The production manager is Lynne C. Zeigler. Art supervisor is Claudia Ericson. The production staff included Mary Betts, Rowena Betts, Patricia Coate, Lynn Felder, Kathleen M. Flanagan, Joyce Fowler, Laura Ingram, Patricia C. Sharpe, Joycelyn R. Smith, and Meredith Walker. Jean W. Ross is permissions editor. Joseph Caldwell, photography editor, did the photographic copy work for the volume.

Walter W. Ross did the library research with the assistance of the staff at the Thomas Cooper Library of the University of South Carolina: Lynn Barron, Sue Collins, Michael Freeman, Gary Geer, Alexander M. Gilchrist, Jens Holley, David Lincove, Marcia Martin, Jean Rhyne, Karen Rissling, Paula Swope, and Ellen Tillett. Valuable help was given also by the South Caroliniana Library at the University of South Carolina, and by staff members of the Richland County Public Library in Columbia, South Carolina: Information Services staff Sarah Linder, Sarah Shaw, Helen Young, Dot Wilson, Jennifer Walker, Maryann Fowler, and Tine Culler; and Periodicals staff Janice Yelton and Cathy Barber.

Twentieth-Century American-Jewish Fiction Writers

Dictionary of Literary Biography

Nathan Asch
(10 July 1902-23 December 1964)

Eva B. Mills
Winthrop College

See also the Asch entry in *DLB 4, American Writers in Paris, 1920-1939.*

BOOKS: *The Office* (New York: Harcourt, Brace, 1925; London: Holden, 1926);
Love in Chartres (New York: A. & C. Boni, 1927; London: Holden, 1927);
Pay Day (New York: Brewer & Warren, 1930);
The Valley (New York: Macmillan, 1935);
The Road: In Search of America (New York: Norton, 1937).

OTHER: "In the Country," in *The American Caravan*, edited by Van Wyck Brooks and others (New York: Macaulay, 1927), pp. 515-525;
"In the City," in *The Second American Caravan*, edited by Alfred Kreymborg, Lewis Mumford, and Paul Rosenfeld (New York: Macaulay, 1928), pp. 631-641;
"Heart's Desire," in *American Stuff*, edited by Henry G. Alsberg (New York: Viking, 1937), pp. 82-95;
"In Search of America," in *The 30's: A Time to Remember*, edited by Don Congdon (New York: Simon & Schuster, 1962), pp. 284-306.

PERIODICAL PUBLICATIONS: "The Voice of the Office," *transatlantic review*, 1 (June 1924): 414-420;
"Marc Kranz," *transatlantic review*, 2 (August 1924): 144-153;
"Gertrude Donovan," *transatlantic review*, 2 (December 1924): 608-622;
"Dying in Carcassonne," *Forum*, 84 (November 1930): 305-310;

Nathan Asch, circa 1937

"Tod Eines Helden," *Neue Rundschau*, 42 (January 1931): 95-107;
"Im Stillen Thal," *Neue Rundschau*, 42 (November 1931): 668-682;
"Moses," *New Yorker*, 8 (2 April 1932): 23;
"The Program Continues," *New Republic*, 74 (20 March 1933): 189;

3

"Cross Country Bus," *New Republic*, 78 (25 April 1934): 301-314;

"Mr. Bromley's Tonsils," *New Yorker*, 10 (28 April 1934): 19-20;

"Truth, Beauty, and Efficiency," *New Yorker*, 11 (2 November 1935): 71-72;

"Route 61," *New Republic*, 85 (15 January 1936): 380;

"Marked Tree Arkansas," *New Republic*, 87 (10 June 1936): 119-121;

"Deep South," *New Yorker*, 13 (10 April 1937): 5;

"WPA Adult Education," *American Federalist*, 45 (April 1938): 386-390;

"On War Policy," *New Republic*, 99 (June 1939): 147-148;

"Five to Seven," *New Yorker*, 16 (18 May 1940): 42;

"The Works," *New Yorker*, 16 (27 July 1940): 24-26;

"A Home for Emma," *Yale Review*, 31 (December 1941): 350-374;

"Late-afternoon Sun," *New Yorker*, 18 (8 August 1942): 44-45;

"Mary," *Contact*, 1 (8 August 1942): 18-44;

"The Lake: A Story," *Virginia Quarterly Review*, 22 (Summer 1946): 386-393;

"Young Man on His Way," *New Yorker*, 22 (22 June 1946): 26-28;

"Inland Western Sea," *New Yorker*, 26 (29 April 1950): 29-35—

"Only So Big—A Puzzler," *Commentary*, 14 (November 1952): 489-491;

"Game," *Commentary*, 15 (March 1953): 280-284;

"The Nineteen Twenties: An Interior," *Paris Review*, 6 (Summer 1954): 82-92;

"Women in Munich," *Contact* (July/August, 1964);

"My Father and I," *Commentary*, 39 (January 1965): 55-65.

Not until after World War II did scholars and critics begin to pay much attention to American-Jewish writers as a group. Many of these—Norman Mailer, Philip Roth, and others—have received public acclaim. While not all sharing the same tradition—one need only contrast the tradition informing the work of Saul Bellow and that informing the work of Isaac Bashevis Singer—most of these writers draw on some identifiable tradition. Certainly Nathan Asch is an American-Jewish writer, but he felt he had no tradition. Asch questioned his being an American and being a Jew and often wondered whether he was a writer. In 1936 he wrote his mother: "What does it mean to be a European Jew? To feel you are a Jew and yet you are not anything that Jews are known to be? To have no conscious Jewish culture..., to have never been in a Synagogue, to have known no Yiddish; but to go to a European school, and speak a European language and have European friends, and symbolically not to wear a kaftan, but to wear the European clothes, and yet to be a Jew?"

Yet, like many Jewish writers, throughout his life and in his writing he searched for a spiritual identity and in the process examined his own past and tried to come to terms with the present.

Asch, the first child of the well-known Yiddish novelist Sholem Asch and Mathilda Spira Asch, was born in Warsaw, Poland. At age ten, after having spent a few months with his maternal grandfather in Lodz, he joined the family in Paris, where the Asches had migrated. There he met émigré artists, including Chagall, Kissling, and Pascin, who later, when Asch returned to Paris during the 1920s, spoke with longing of their visits to the Asch family's beautiful home in Chatillon, a suburb of Paris. Within three years of settling in Paris, shortly after the outbreak of World War I, the Asches were again on the move—to America. There they settled on Staten Island in a neighborhood where there were no Jews. Nevertheless, young Asch did have extensive contact with Jewish writers living on the West Side of New York whom he met through his father, already one of the most prominent Yiddish writers of that time. Asch attended the public schools in New York City; he also studied at Syracuse University and at Columbia, but he never graduated from college.

In light of his father's strong identity with the Jewish and Yiddish language and culture, one might well ask why Nathan Asch was obsessed with his own rootlessness. Leaving aside psychological interpretations, one can readily see that Asch's frequent moves and his exposure to various nations and languages would raise questions in the mind of a sensitive child and young man. On the one hand, Asch seems almost emblematic of the wandering Jew; on the other, he is a precursor of a whole generation of writers, Jew and non-Jew alike, searching for their roots.

At age twenty-one, Asch returned to Paris, where his career as a serious writer began in 1924 with the publication of three stories in the *transatlantic review*. "Gertrude Donovan," "Marc Kranz," and "The Voice of the Office" later appeared as episodes in his first novel, *The Office*, published in 1925.

Asch soon became a member of the expatriate colony in Paris. He counted among his friends Josephine Herbst, John Herrmann, Kaye Boyle, Evan Shipman, Ford Madox Ford, Ernest

Hemingway, Malcolm Cowley, Eugene Jolas, and Pierre Loving, who in a 1925 article for the *Paris Tribune* called Asch one of the most interesting and promising young writers. Even after returning to the United States in 1926, Asch kept in touch with Robert McAlmon, Morley Callaghan, and Paul Shinkman, who spoke of him as "that well-known Quarterite . . . now in New York." Asch and his wife, the American Lysel Ingwersen whom he met and married in France, lived among former expatriates in Connecticut and in the same boardinghouse with Hart Crane in Paterson, New Jersey. In 1929, their only child, David, was born in New Milford, Connecticut. Though always pressed for money, Asch seemed relatively satisfied. He was writing, and his work was being published.

His novel *The Office* had already appeared. The novel, a series of sketches narrating the effects of bankruptcy on the employees of a firm, was praised by many reviewers for its experimentation with structure, language, and point of view. The effect of the book upon the reader, according to one critic, "is like the experience of the art-viewer who observes a gallery of pictures." Walter Yust, in *Literary Review*, found fault in the book—"too ostentatiously restrained when it is restrained and too callously violent when it's violent"—and Joseph Wood Krutch was cautious with praise in a review for *New York Herald Tribune Books*. For Krutch, the novel's virtues and failings were typical of "much contemporary fiction"; Asch had mistaken "surface novelty for profundity" and imagined "that an ingenious scheme is sufficient to make a great work."

Asch had started his second novel, *Love in Chartres* (1927), in Paris but revised the manuscript after his return to New York. In this work, a fictionalized account of Asch's love affair with Lysel Ingwersen, the young American writer decides that he must forego marriage in favor of his career, breaks off the relationship in Chartres, and goes to Paris to write. Though the novel did not sell well, reviewers were mostly laudatory. At least one, however, complained that Asch's style was forced and unreal and reproached the novelist for not probing the psychological depths of his characters. Asch and Ingwersen were divorced three years after the novel was published.

Asch was beginning to make a name for himself, not only in America but also on the Continent. His third work, *Pay Day*, (1930), was published simultaneously in the United States and in Germany; a year later it appeared in Hebrew translation in Warsaw. Although featuring a Jewish protagonist, Harry Grossman, the narrative centers on the contrast between the young Grossman's hedonistic pursuit of pleasures and the night's sobering event—the Sacco-Vanzetti execution. The *Nation*'s reviewer found it "an excellent study of the type," but one which according to the critic for *New York Herald Tribune Books* does not slight the "messy details" so often missing in the "dissections of mental and moral fibre of the younger generation."

Although Asch sometimes felt rejected by the New York publishing establishment, he was pleased by the popularity of his works in Germany, where translations of *The Office*, *Pay Day*, and several of his short stories sold well until Hitler outlawed all Jewish writing. Possibly as a result of his divorce, his lack of success in America, and his concern about the events in Germany, Asch became more conscious of his rootlessness. Unsure of himself, Asch felt he was neither a Jew nor an American. In January 1931, shortly after he returned from a trip to France to see his parents, he wrote Malcolm Cowley: "I am not American, and probably if I never went back to Europe and lost all contact with it, and remained in America I still would never be an American. Which probably explains why they read me in Germany and Russia more than they do here. But the curious thing is that I love this place and feel no sympathy with Eastern Europe. . . . I feel clean in America and not in Germany. . . . So you see I have no place anywhere, . . . I love America, and am not an American, not liked by Americans."

In spite of these doubts about himself, Asch had two more novels published during the 1930s: *The Valley* (1935) and *The Road: In Search of America* (1937), composed of tales and sketches in the manner of *The Office*. The sketches in *The Valley* concern the problems faced by rural men whose land has become barren. Most reviewers suggested that, as in his earlier works, Asch was looking at what one critic called the "outer aspects" of life. H. W. B. in the *Saturday Review of Literature* cast Asch as a "sympathetic outsider taking notes." Horace Gregory found *The Valley* "a reassertion of those qualities which have made his [Asch's] prose distinctive"— a judgment shared by many others.

The Road: In Search of America depicts people, places, and events from all over the American continent. According to some reviewers, though Asch showed sympathy and understanding, his writing at times bordered on sentimentality; others chose to emphasize the influence of Dos Passos, Sherwood Anderson, and Ernest Hemingway they perceived in Asch's latest book. Asch had gathered the material for this, his last work, while on a bus trip across the United States. Some of the sketches were first

7 Nov
1949

THE MYSTERIOUS LOLA

Probably, the coincidence wouldn't have struck Audrey so,
if earlier that day she hadn't decided finally to get rid of
the sofa.   But the whole unpleasant business had been
furthest from her mind, when after the movies she and Ed and
the Grants had thought they'd find out what this new place
where they played jazz was like: - and who would be considering
an old-fashioned, black horsehair sofa, misgotten during an
enthusiastic moment at an auction, while trying to find a
table in a crowded, dimly-lighted room, where a combination
of piano, clarinet and drums was playing Dixieland style?
What Audrey had been thinking was, "There's a table.   That
man with the patch on his eye, I hope I won't have to sit
next to him, he's staring at me."   But she did have to
sit next to him, and as he rose to make room for her, she
thought, "Oh, my God, he's drunk!"

The man was drunk, but he was controlling himself. After
she sat down, he sat down, too, in the chair beside her. She
felt the two chairs touching, then she felt his elbow pressing
against her arm, and she heard him whisper, she knew it was to
her:

"I've got a buyer for the sofa, Lola."
Audrey exclaimed, "What?"
Ed asked, "What's the matter?"

Revised typescript page from the second draft of a short story by Asch (Dacus Library, Archives & Special Collections, Winthrop College) published in the *New Republic*, along with reviews Asch regularly wrote for that journal between 1931 and 1939. Asch's trip ended in Hollywood, where he found work as a scriptwriter for Paramount Pictures. Later he moved to Washington, D.C., to accept a position with the education program of the Works Progress Administration.

Letters to his family, particularly his mother, and friends reveal his intense feelings of loneliness and rootlessness. He was determined to find a home. In 1936 he applied for a Guggenheim Fellowship to visit Poland and his relatives scattered throughout Europe. He particularly longed to see his maternal grandfather with whom he had lived for several months before leaving Poland and who, he knew, could give him much of the information he needed about his extended family. The proposal he submitted to the foundation poignantly describes his feelings: "The problem to be examined is one of rootlessness. Most writers, like most people, have within them the memory of a home — physical: they spent their childhood in one house, went to one school, grew up, played, fought in one neighborhood — a spiritual home: they relax in one language, one region, one country. They are motivated by its tabus, are moved by love for it, are loyal to it. As is in a tree, from old roots to new leaves, their past flows in an unbroken line into their present, sustains and explains it. There seems to be, there seems always to have been, a quality to being native. It is a quality the writer of this statement does not possess." Asch did not receive the fellowship, despite recommendations from Stephan Zweig and Malcolm Cowley.

During World War II, Asch enlisted in the U.S. Army Air Force, while his second wife, Carol Tasker Miles of Philadelphia, whom he had married in 1939, joined the WACS. He served by doing journalistic work in London for the air force and later as a member of the occupation forces in Paris after the liberation of that city. After the war, he and his wife bought a house in Mill Valley, California — a home she still occupies. While Asch continued to write, Carol Asch worked at a variety of jobs, providing the family's main support. During the McCarthy era she was temporarily suspended from her job with the Civil Service Commission as a result of an investigation by the House Un-American Activities Committee that probed her husband's supposed left-wing activities during the 1930s and her father-in-law's connections with Soviet Russia.

Encouraged by his wife, Asch wrote feverishly, occasionally having pieces accepted for publication by such magazines as the *New Yorker* or *Commentary*. One of these, "Only So Big — A Puzzler," was a humorous piece documenting the depiction of Jews in literature as "little." It contained quotations from some fifty authors, Jews and Gentiles, Americans and Europeans, and included a citation from Asch's own writings. During the late 1940s he spent most of his time and energy writing his most ambitious novel, "Paris Is Home," completed in 1947. Malcolm Cowley was enthusiastic about the book and wrote Asch that it contained some of the best writing Asch had ever done and that "it shouldn't be merely accepted by the publisher but accepted with enthusiasm . . . and reviewed on page one or at least page three of the Times and Herald Tribune." But, Cowley added, Asch needed to make revisions, assuring him that it was worth the time and effort it would take. Publishers shared both Cowley's enthusiasm and his reservations. Harold Strauss's evaluation of the book — contained in a letter to Maxim Lieber, Asch's literary agent — is representative: "Everyone [who has read the manuscript] is enthusiastic about the descriptions of postwar Paris. Everyone is captivated by Asch's evocation of the strange postwar mood among the occupation personnel. But *only* because it is fiction can *Paris Is Home* be called a novel. The structure is almost nil. . . . There is no true ending to the book; it merely stops when Kranz decides to go home. Few or none of the moral issues are resolved. Mr. Asch is no novice. I think the crux of the matter hinges on his development of the clash of moral values. Kranz never moves one way or the other in the book as it stands. . . . I admit that this is not a matter of minor editorial revision but requires that a new series of climactic episodes be built into the book."

In letters to Cowley, Asch spoke of revising material, but it seems that he was not revising "Paris Is Home." None of the extant manuscripts of the novel show revisions, as do some of Asch's other manuscripts. The book was submitted to dozens of publishing houses but was never accepted. Only one short section, a twenty-page excerpt entitled "The Nineteen-Twenties: An Interior," appeared a few years later in the *Paris Review* with a laudatory introduction by Cowley. As late as 1955, Knopf was inquiring about the possibility of publishing the novel.

During the early 1950s, Asch planned that "Paris Is Home" would be part of a series of novels, tentatively titled "Marginal Man" — "the story of forty years in the life of a Jew from Eastern Europe in the West" that "would take seven to eight years to write." Of this projected series, Asch completed only "London is a Lonely Town," a work that also went the rounds of publishers for several years but was never accepted. The major obstacle to publication—so clearly identified by Harold Strauss, Malcolm Cowley, and others—was Asch's difficulty in synthesizing his material and distancing himself from it. Undoubtedly Asch wrote well and was most effective in depicting places, time, mood, feeling, emotion, and sensation. His letters, as well as the character sketches of people he had known—his father, maternal grandfather, other members of his family—and of public figures such as Hart Crane attest to his artistry. Most of his writing (*Love in Chartres* is the exception) is episodic. It lacks the continuity and the unity that were missing from his own life. In his later years, Asch recognized this characteristic of his art. When telling Cowley about the sketches he was writing, tentatively titled "Gallant Ladies and Illustrious Men," he saw they did not fit together. He hoped to publish them some day as a miscellany, but he did not want them published while he and some of his subjects were still living. The only exception he made was for a long piece, eighty-two typewritten pages, he had written about his father. This piece, the last one by Asch ever published, appeared as "My Father and I" in the January 1965 issue of *Commentary*—a month after Asch died.

Although none of the novels Asch wrote after the war was ever published, Asch continued to write and enjoyed writing. Two short novels, "The Shrewd and the Mad" and "The Livelong Day," and a longer one, "Celia," also made the rounds of publishers without success.

Toward the end of his life, Nathan Asch no longer seemed preoccupied with finding his roots. He could relax with his wife at home in Mill Valley, among furniture he had crafted himself, teaching occasional writing classes to eager adult students in his home and writing for himself. He had grown his own roots. He died of lung cancer at age sixty-two.

References:

Kay Boyle and Robert McAlmon, *Being Geniuses Together, 1920-1930* (Garden City: Doubleday, 1968);

Morley Callaghan, *That Summer in Paris* (New York: Coward-McCann, 1963);

Malcolm Cowley, *And I Worked at the Writer's Trade* (New York: Viking, 1978);

Cowley, *A Second Flowering* (New York: Viking, 1973);

Samuel Putnam, *Paris Was Our Mistress* (New York: Viking, 1947).

Papers:
Copies of published and unpublished manuscripts as well as letters and other memorabilia are in the Archive Collection at Winthrop College, Rock Hill, South Carolina. Asch's letters to Malcolm Cowley and other materials are with the Cowley papers at the Newberry Library, Chicago.

Saul Bellow
(10 June 1915-   )

Keith M. Opdahl
DePauw University

See also the Bellow entries in *DLB 2, American Novelists Since World War II, DLB Yearbook: 1982,* and *DLB: Documentary Series 3*.

BOOKS: *Dangling Man* (New York: Vanguard, 1944; London: Lehmann, 1946);
The Victim (New York: Vanguard, 1947; London: Lehmann, 1948);
The Adventures of Augie March (New York: Viking, 1953; London: Weidenfeld & Nicolson, 1954);

Seize the Day (New York: Viking, 1956; London: Weidenfeld & Nicolson, 1957);
Henderson the Rain King (New York: Viking, 1959; London: Weidenfeld & Nicolson, 1959);
Recent American Fiction (Washington, D.C.: Library of Congress, 1963);
Herzog (New York: Viking, 1964; London: Weidenfeld & Nicolson, 1965);
The Last Analysis (New York: Viking, 1965; London: Weidenfeld & Nicolson, 1966);
Mosby's Memoirs and Other Stories (New York: Viking,

1968; London: Weidenfeld & Nicolson, 1969);

Mr. Sammler's Planet (New York: Viking, 1970; London: Weidenfeld & Nicolson, 1970);

The Portable Saul Bellow (New York: Viking, 1974);

Humboldt's Gift (New York: Viking, 1975; London: Secker & Warburg, 1975);

To Jerusalem and Back; A Personal Account (New York: Viking, 1976; London: Secker & Warburg, 1976);

Nobel Lecture (New York: Targ Editions, 1976);

The Dean's December (New York: Harper & Row, 1982; London: Secker & Warburg, 1982).

PLAYS: *The Last Analysis*, New York, Belasco Theatre, 1 October 1964;

Under the Weather (A Wen, Orange Soufflé, Out From Under), London, 7 June 1966; Festival of Two Worlds, Spoleto, Italy, 14 July 1966; New York, Cort Theatre, 27 October 1966.

OTHER: Isaac Bashevis Singer, "Gimpel the Fool," translated by Bellow, *Partisan Review*, 20 (May-June 1953): 300-313;

"Distractions of a Fiction Writer," in *The Living Novel*, edited by Granville Hicks (New York: Macmillan,1957), pp. 1-20;

Great Jewish Short Stories, edited with an introduction by Bellow (New York: Dell, 1963);

"Literature," in *The Great Ideas Today*, edited by Mortimer Adler and Robert M. Hutchins (Chicago: *Encyclopaedia Britannica*, 1963), pp. 135-179;

"Zetland: By A Character Witness," in *Modern Occasions*, edited by Philip Rahv (Port Washington, N.Y.: Kennikat, 1974), pp. 9-30.

SELECTED PERIODICAL PUBLICATIONS:
Fiction:

"Two Morning Monologues," *Partisan Review*, 8 (May-June 1941): 230-236;

"A Sermon by Dr. Pep," *Partisan Review*, 16 (May-June 1949): 455-462;

"The Trip to Galena," *Partisan Review*, 17 (November-December 1950): 769-794;

"Address by Gooley MacDowell to the Hasbeens Club of Chicago," *Hudson Review*, 4 (Summer 1951): 222-227;

A Wen, Esquire, 63 (January 1965): 72-74ff.;

Orange Soufflé, Esquire, 64 (October 1965): 130-136;

"Silver Dish," *New Yorker*, 54 (25 September 1978): 40-62;

"Him with His Foot in His Mouth," *Atlantic*, 250

Saul Bellow, 1950s

(November 1982): 115-144.

Nonfiction:

"The Jewish Writer and the English Literary Tradition," *Commentary*, 8 (October 1949): 366-367;

"Dreiser and the Triumph of Art," *Commentary*, 11 (May 1951): 502-503;

"Man Underground," *Commentary*, 13 (June 1952): 608-610;

"Laughter in the Ghetto," *Saturday Review of Literature*, 36 (30 May 1953): 15;

"How I Wrote Augie March's Story," *New York Times Book Review*, 31 January 1954, pp. 3, 17;

"Deep Readers of the World, Beware!," *New York Times Book Review*, 15 February 1959, pp. 1, 34;

"Where Do We Go From Here: The Future of Fiction," *Michigan Quarterly Review*, 1 (Winter 1962): 27-33.

A sober evaluation of his work leaves no doubt that Saul Bellow is one of the important writers in American literature. As one of two living American Nobel Prize-winners in literature, he inherits the mantle of Hemingway and Faulkner, even though he himself has not become a culture hero. Nor has he, like Borges or Márquez, become a cult figure; when in 1979 the *New York Times Book Review* asked twenty leading intellectuals which books since 1945 would count among the hundred important books in Western civilization, Bellow was not mentioned. He *is* mentioned elsewhere, however, and with the highest praise possible. Who are "the great inventors of narrative detail and masters of narrative voice and perspective" according to Philip Roth? "James, Conrad, Dostoevski and Bellow."

Bellow has in fact always enjoyed the kind of reputation that is won by solid and accomplished work. He is a private person, and in his public appearances he is sometimes distant or moody, without those manufactured public outlines (sportsman, Southern gentleman) that give easy popular identification. But he is also our preeminent public spokesman, the writer who catches and articulates the sometimes hidden feelings of our era. Bellow puts flesh on those abstract and cliché-ridden bones, showing what alienation actually is on a winter afternoon, say, or precisely how our culture crushes a mediocre man. Does America mean opportunity? Bellow's fiction takes a larky young man about the country, exploring exactly what opportunities await him. Is life a mixture of the sublime and the vulgar? Bellow in his last novel before winning the Nobel Prize shows just what that mix can look like.

Bellow was born in Lachine, Quebec, just two years after his parents, Abraham and Liza Gordon Bellows, had emigrated from St. Petersburg, Russia. His father was a daring and not always successful businessman who in Russia had imported Egyptian onions (Bellow describes him as a "sharpie circa 1905"), and in the New World attempted several often unconventional businesses. A family portrait in 1922 shows the father to be a stocky, erect man with the touchy look one would expect from Bellow's fictionalized accounts of him. Bellow's mother in the same picture is handsome, with large gentle eyes and a broad forehead. Bellow himself—the seven-year-old Solomon Bellows—is alert and knowing, the baby among two sisters and a brother, staring down the camera with something of his father's insouciance.

The Bellows lived in a slum on St. Dominique Street "between a market and a hospital," Bellow has said. "I was generally preoccupied with what went on in it and watched from the stairs and windows." His father, who blamed himself for the family's poverty, worried that Solly would see too much; and the boy did see violence and sexuality, saying

later that the raw reality of Dominique Street made all else in his life seem strange and foreign. "Little since then has worked upon me with such force," Bellow has written, as he has returned to the scene in *Dangling Man* and *Herzog*. He lived amid the color and spirituality of an earlier era, for Lachine was "a medieval ghetto . . . ; my childhood was in ancient times which was true of all orthodox Jews." By the age of four he knew the book of Genesis in Hebrew. "You never got to distinguish between that and the outer world."

Lachine was also a verbal environment, teaching young Bellow Hebrew, Yiddish, French, and English. He spent a year in the Royal Hospital (in the TB ward, he says, though he didn't have TB) with nothing to do but read. But by the time his family had moved to Humboldt Park in Chicago, when he was nine, he was healthy enough for sports as well as his many intellectual projects. Humboldt Park was a neighborhood of immigrants, filled with the cultural and intellectual activity of sidewalk orators, branch libraries, and mission houses that would provide a debating club a meeting room. By the time he attended Tuley High School, Bellow had such pals as Isaac Rosenfeld, Sydney J. Harris, who would become the newspaper columnist, Oscar Tarkov, and David Peltz, his good friend to this day, who remembers that "Solly Bellows was the most precocious of the lot—a good runner on the track team, a fair swimmer, middling tennis player, but a remarkable writer even then. . . ." The boys were leftist in politics, and at one time crazy about surrealism.

But at home all was not well, for the father—by all accounts an impetuous, pretentious man—continued to have financial problems, and a fatal accident involving his uninsured coal truck made the family labor for years to pay off the debt. Bellow's mother died when he was fifteen, and when he was seventeen he and Sydney Harris ran away to New York for a few weeks to peddle (unsuccessfully) their first novels.

If Chicago had been a shock to the young Canadian, he had persevered. He attended the University of Chicago, where he felt the dense cultural atmosphere to be suffocating, and transferred to Northwestern, where he founded a socialists' club and graduated in 1937 with honors in sociology and anthropology. He reportedly wished to study literature, but was advised that anti-Semitism would thwart his career, and so he accepted a scholarship to study anthropology at the University of Wisconsin, where his professor told him he wrote anthropology like a good novelist. In Chicago on New

Year's Eve, 1937, Bellow married Anita Goshkin, a social worker, and abandoned his graduate work. "In my innocence," he has said, "I had decided to become a writer."

It was a bold decision at that time, and such boldness has characterized Bellow's work ever since. His greatest strength as a novelist is his style, which is fluid and rich, picking up the rhythms and energy of Yiddish and the plain speech (and sharply observed detail) of the Middle West. His style is precise and lucid and gives off an air of absolute integrity—an integrity that has at times gotten Bellow into trouble, for as a writer he is as stiff-necked as his father looks. Again and again over his career, Bellow has followed his imagination wherever it may lead. In an era of experimentalism he has been a realist, claiming that "the development of realism in the nineteenth century is still the major event of modern literature." During the 1940s, in a time of deep social concern, Bellow dramatized a sense of the transcendent. When alienation was popular, Bellow celebrated accommodation. He reacted to the popularity of the Jewish novel by turning to a WASP protagonist (in *Henderson the Rain King*), and he met America's new youth culture head-on with the creation of a seventy-year-old protagonist (in *Mr. Sammler's Planet*). And yet in most of these ventures he was successful, largely because of his fertile imagination and clarity of mind.

Bellow's largest difficulty as a writer lies in plot. He has confessed this difficulty, and many critics believe his novels to be formless. If Bellow's characters are colorful and his situations telling, he characteristically gives too much, too many ideas for us to know the central one and too many characters, too many memorable details, for us to discern a simple story. No doubt Bellow is not as formless as he seems, since his point is often the subtle insight of the realist, so easily lost among his comic characters and rich descriptions, and he himself is the most diligent of craftsmen, working through draft after draft. But the fact remains that his art is one of clearing and solidifying an abundance of materials, and when he has finished with the process the reader too has a way to go.

And indeed, one of Bellow's central themes is precisely this density of life. So too is the malice or nastiness of his protagonist and those around him. Another theme is the experience of transcendence and the fact that the issues that confront us are ultimately metaphysical or religious, an element that provides one of the keys to Bellow's style, as the sense of a special meaning or significance just out of

reach adds another dimension to his precisely detailed physical world. A society that can invent the inner life but give it no nourishment, a universe that requires the self to twist himself to survive within its force, a protagonist seeking most of all to cure himself of some unknown malady—all of these are typical Bellow themes.

And so too is the theme of his Jewishness, but in a special and rather independent way. Although Bellow's mother wished him to become a Talmudic scholar like many others in her family, Bellow himself has insisted that he is not that exotic creature, the Jew who writes in English, but an American writer—a Western writer who happens to be Jewish. "I did not go to the public library to read the Talmud," Bellow says of his Chicago days, "but the novels and poems of Sherwood Anderson, Theodore Dreiser, Edgar Lee Masters, and Vachel Lindsay." Bellow nevertheless is singled out by Alan Guttmann in *The Jewish Writer in America* (1971) as portraying the full range of American Jewish experience, and Bellow's comedy, intellectualism, moral preoccupation and alienation, his concern with the family and with rough Eastern European immigrants, his obsession with the past and with the dangers of an alien world, his emphasis on purity, his sense, as Alfred Kazin says, "of the unreality of this world as opposed to God's"—all of these elements bespeak his deep Jewish concern.

And indeed, the fact that he is Jewish added a special tension to his decision to be a writer, for he would enter a world dominated not only by WASPS but by WASPS from New England. He worked for the Work Projects Administration doing biographical sketches of midwestern writers and then taught at the Pestalozzi-Froebel Teacher's College. He went to Mexico in 1940, writing the never-published novel "Acatla," and lived, he says, a bohemian life. But these years were not all gaiety: "I sat at a bridge table in a back bedroom of the apartment while all rational, serious, dutiful people were at their jobs or trying to find jobs, writing something." After lunch with his mother-in-law, in whose apartment he lived, he would walk the city streets. "If I had been a dog I would have howled," he has written. He managed in 1941 to place a short story about a young man waiting for the draft in the *Partisan Review*; the next year another, about the Trotsky assassinations, appeared. And in 1943 *Partisan Review* published part of his new novel in progress.

Perhaps the most memorable quality of this first novel, published in 1944 as *Dangling Man*, is the tone of voice: modeled after that of Rilke's *Journal of*

My Other Self, the voice is frank and honest, compensating for its self-pity by the depth and precision of its observation. Taking on Ernest Hemingway, the most famous writer just then, the protagonist Joseph jibs at the hard-boiled: "If you have difficulties, grapple with them silently, goes one of their commandments. To hell with that! I intend to talk about mine, and if I had as many mouths as Siva has arms and kept them going all the time, I still could not do myself justice."

Like Bellow himself, Joseph has been kept dangling by his draft board, bound in the red tape surrounding his Canadian birth. His ostensibly formless journal is actually shaped by his increasing lack of self-control, as he records the failure of his attempts to write or prepare himself spiritually for the army, and then his disappointment with his friends and his wife, his in-laws and his mistress. Wanting to forge a self that would be "a member of the Army, but not a *part* of it," he must watch himself become overwhelmed by a hundred trivial details, as his self-control leaves him and the nasty bad temper he has remarked in others comes to dominate. When he strikes his landlord and realizes that his sense of the strangeness and impermanence of the world has grown, he, like Dostoevski's Underground Man, throws in the towel, crying "Long live regimentation."

One critic thought Joseph was a "stinker," but other reviewers gave the book a remarkably affirmative judgment. Even the names of the reviewers tell us a great deal, for Edmund Wilson, Peter DeVries, Diana Trilling, and Delmore Schwartz all felt this first novel worthy of their attention. Edmund Wilson called it "one of the most honest pieces of testimony on the psychology of a whole generation," and George Mayberry proclaimed the creation of a complex character like Joseph "an event that is rare and wonderful in modern American writing." Subsequent critics have found the book narrow and Bellow's attitude toward Joseph uncertain. To some, Joseph at the end rejoins society and thus is not ironic; to others, he is totally defeated, surrendering his individuality, a reading the echo from Dostoevski's "Notes from Underground" would support. Bellow's novel is a lively and even memorable work, with many striking figures, even if the author himself has confessed that he cannot bear to reread it.

Bellow's own dangling was ended by the army for medical reasons, and in 1943 he began to work for Mortimer Adler's "Great Books" project for the *Encyclopaedia Britannica,* reading he says some 60 of the 443 works indexed. He joined the merchant marine, which stationed him in New York, and then worked for the Maritime Commission onshore. After the war, Bellow decided to stay in New York, tasting, he has said, the intellectual life of the Village and enjoying the pleasures of fatherhood with the birth of his son Gregory. He reviewed books, edited, wrote reports for the founder of Penguin books, and in a clash that served him well, spent two days as movie reviewer for *Time*, until Whitaker Chambers reportedly picked a quarrel and fired him on the spot—an event he would include in his next novel, *The Victim* (1947).

Joseph in *Dangling Man* had complained that upon awaking he went "in the body from nakedness to clothing and in the mind from relative purity to pollution" when he read the newspaper and admitted the world. To Joseph the world is a war that can kill him, but it is also the physical universe itself. In *The Victim* this impurity pursues the protagonist Asa Leventhal as Kirby Allbee comes one hot summer night to accuse the solitary and anxious Leventhal of causing his ruin. Leventhal had quarreled with Allbee's boss, prompting Allbee's loss of his job, he claims, and thus his drinking and the loss of his wife. Following Dostoevski's *The Eternal Husband*, Bellow explores the intense and ambivalent relation between the two men, as Allbee presses deeper and deeper into Leventhal's life, taking money, a bed in his apartment, liberties with his mail, and finally a whore in Leventhal's own bed—an impurity that is still not the final one, since Allbee slips into the apartment late at night to attempt suicide in Leventhal's kitchen.

Was Asa Leventhal responsible? A parallel plot suggests he was not, for he mistakenly assumes the blame in a death for which he had no responsibility at all. Both Leventhal and Allbee are victims of an oppressively dense world—one of the finest creations in the novel, as Bellow catches the summer heat of New York—and of their inability to discern a clear order in it. Each argues for a version of reality that the other cannot accept. Allbee cannot bear the notion of an impersonal universe in which he might be harmed for no reason at all. He must find an agent—a Jew. To Leventhal, on the other hand, such a "human" universe is ominous, frightening, a world in which he could be ruined overnight. Allbee appears inexplicably, emerging from a crowd in a park as an embodiment of the city streets which Leventhal, like his immigrant forebears, considers full of impurity and danger: "He really did not know what went on about him," Leventhal thinks, "what strange things, savage things."

The Victim is a remarkable advance over *Dangling Man*, for though it is dense and claustrophobic it is also rich and full of an absolutely honest life. It raised some eyebrows, coming as it did only two years after the death camps had been opened, for to critics such as Theodore Ross in the *Chicago Jewish Forum* Allbee and Leventhal are too much alike. Was this the time to show that the psychology of Jew and bigot can be similar? Bellow had insisted on paying the Jew the same tribute he would pay all human beings, neither more nor less, and in Allbee he captured the unconscious subtleties of Jewish self-hatred, making him a messenger from not just a destructive world but Leventhal's own psyche. Leventhal's alienation is that of modern man, moreover, for by showing Jew and Gentile to be alike Bellow shows that at this time we are all Jews.

Although *The Victim* was not praised as much as it deserves (critics now judge it to be one of Bellow's best works), it was sufficiently recognized to win Bellow a Guggenheim Fellowship for 1948, freeing him from teaching at the University of Minnesota, where he had been in 1946 and 1947. In France on his fellowship he began a third novel in the same serious vein as his first two, but found he needed a relief. He took to writing a "memoir" of Chicago—which in France had become exotic to him, he says—and by 1949 had turned to it almost exclusively. "Augie was my favorite fantasy," he has said of the Chicago book. "Every time I was depressed while writing the grim one I'd treat myself to a fantasy holiday." He wrote *The Adventures of Augie March* (1953) while on the move, in trains and in cafés in Paris and Rome, in Minneapolis where he returned to teach in 1949, in a cold-water flat in New York where he lectured at New York University, at Princeton where he was a Creative Writing Fellow, and even in the editorial offices at Viking Press. At some point he felt such revulsion with the "grim" work he had begun that he slid some 100,000 words down an incinerator.

Thus *The Adventures of Augie March* begins as the opposite of Bellow's serious concerns, best defined perhaps in terms of Asa Leventhal's fear of the streets. Bellow had known a lad like Augie: "He came of just such a family as I described. I hadn't seen him in 25 years, so the novel was a speculative biography." And what was particularly speculative was Bellow's definition of the young man as an enthusiast who is swept up by the people he loves, sometimes in a sexual swoon and at others as an admiring disciple. Can a young man in a harsh world of force survive without weapons other than

affection and tolerance and a lack of calculation? The answer lies in the adults who surround Augie and are as large and threatening as they would appear to a child. They exist with a Balzacian vigor and importance that testifies to human worth as they act upon their environment, but they also overwhelm the passive young Augie, who becomes another Bellow hero oppressed by the world.

At first he manages to survive, and Bellow's point is clear. Augie's childhood is dominated by the wonderful Grandma Lausch, whose world is every bit as dramatic and cynical as the czar's court, and whom Bellow describes as the equal of the great politicians of the world. And so too is the crippled Einhorn, even if his kingdom is a West Side neighborhood and his courtier (and male nurse) the young Augie. Augie serves the North Shore matron Mrs. Renling (until he is taken as her gigolo and she wishes to adopt him) and acts as an aide-de-camp to his ambitious brother Simon, who marries into a wealthy family. In each case, Augie observes not only that "it wasn't so necessary to lie," as he says in the first chapter, rejecting Machiavellian cynicism, but also that these egotists finally do themselves in. Grandma Lausch's children treat her with the same impersonality she had tried to teach Augie. Simon is tormented by his position, and Einhorn outsmarts himself. Only Augie, larky, impetuous, sensual, accepting—the very opposite really of Bellow's usual protagonist and thus a true fantasy for Bellow—only Augie it seems is escaping a harsh and destructive world.

And yet Augie doesn't escape either. Bellow's insistence that these Chicago-neighborhood characters are of the same caliber as mythic and historic greats can work both ways. His references and allusions enrich and elevate the story, but they also darken it, reminding us of the terror at the heart of our myths and legends. Or to put it another way, Augie's style is Whitmanian in the way it picks up everything, relishing its energetic catalogues; but at the same time and in much the same way as Whitman, it contains a belying strain, a shrillness. Augie March is the Jew accepting all of America, Norman Podhoretz has said, and accepted in return, except for his "quality of willed and empty affirmation."

For the truth is that Augie is hit again and again, and we can measure the novel's progress by noting Augie's responses. In the first chapter Augie is beaten up by neighborhood punks (including Augie's good friend) for being a Jew: "But I never had any special grief from it," Augie says, "or brooded, being by and large too larky and boisterous to take it to heart. . . ." By the middle of the novel, when Augie is beaten up in a labor strike, he flees full of rage and terror. He goes to Mexico with his lover Thea, another Machiavellian who plans to hunt iguanas with a trained eagle, and suffers a concussion that makes him spend depressing weeks on the mend. When he cheats on Thea, she tells him he is not a man of love at all, but isolate or indifferent, a fact that Einhorn had earlier described as Augie's "opposition." "Me, love's servant?," Augie wails. "I wasn't at all!"

Bellow's fantasy has simply turned into his old nightmare, and the book becomes the memoir of a rather scarred and saddened middle-aged man who defines himself as one singing in the middle of a desolate and frozen farm field. Like the novel after which it was modeled, *Adventures of Huckleberry Finn*, *The Adventures of Augie March* is unable to sustain its original serenity.

Reviewers in 1953 took Bellow's intention for the deed, however, praising the novel for its energy and acceptance and stylistic fireworks. Even though it won a National Book Award in 1954, Bellow himself today has reservations, commenting that "I got stuck in a Sherwood Anderson ingenue vein: here are all these people and isn't life wonderful! By the last third of the book I wasn't feeling that way any more." The novel had emancipated Bellow from grim labor, at any rate, but what seems notable today is not so much the sweep and energy of the work, particularly in the large numbers of characters, as the warm tone of its voice and the precision of its details. Augie promises to tell the truth, to close in on his experience, which makes the book not so much a picaresque novel skating on the surface of life as a deeper, closer investigation of what a life over a period of years actually is. Bellow had grown up on the naturalistic work of Dreiser, Dos Passos, and Farrell, and he retains their sense of a cruel world of force, but he transforms it here into something less mechanical, less deterministic or external, focusing more on the perception and history and feeling of the inner protagonist—who finds a triumph finally in consciousness if not in love.

Bellow taught at Bard College in 1953-1954 and at the University of Minnesota the next year. He won a second Guggenheim Fellowship which permitted him to spend 1955 in Nevada and California, and then, having terminated his troubled marriage, he was free to marry Alexandra Tschacbasov and settle down—after almost two decades of moving about—in Dutchess County, New York, near Tivoli. It was during these same five years that he wrote the short works that would make up his next book, *Seize the Day* (1956): "Looking for Mr. Green" (1951), "A Father to Be" (1955), "The Gonzaga Manuscripts" (1956), the title novella, and a one-act play, *The Wrecker* (1954). The novella "Seize the Day" reflects the important fact that Bellow's novels are usually written over a period of years and thus do not belong to the year or even the decade in which they see publication. A friend of Bellow's reports seeing *The Victim* in two different versions by 1945, which means its composition may well have overlapped that of *Dangling Man*. When an interviewer grouped "Seize the Day" with Bellow's work in the 1940s, Bellow didn't argue with him, saying only that he had written it over a period of years. The fact remains, however, that the novella reflects a pattern of variety in Bellow's work, as each novel seems to contrast in tone with its predecessor. *The Adventures of Augie March* sprawls and attacks the world with energy; it made Bellow well known in the world of letters. "Seize the Day" is tight and sets an elegiac tone; it may well be the work that insures Bellow's position in the world of important writers.

The story recounts a day in the life of a failing middle-aged American, Tommy Wilhelm, who has made a series of poor decisions that land him jobless in his early forties at the Hotel Ansonia, where his father lives in retirement. Tommy wants his father's help—and is denied. He wants his substitute father's help too, and this father, the sometime psychologist Tamkin, is the character Bellow now finds most interesting in the tale, for "like most phony phonies, he is always somewhere near the truth. . . . But Tamkin's truths aren't really true." As he treats patients over the phone and spouts existential clichés, Tamkin promises to cure all of Tommy's troubles. He will make him strong, teaching him to "seize the day"—the very vagueness of which is Bellow's point—and he will make him financially comfortable, too, using his money to speculate on the grain market. Bellow begins the novella with Tommy emerging from his room, assuming a bold front. He gives over the first three sections to Tommy's past and his breakfast with his father, and the second three to his relations with Tamkin. In the last, climactic section, Tommy's disgusted father disowns him and Dr. Tamkin, having lost Tommy's last remaining savings, disappears.

Tommy's defeat makes many readers uncomfortable, and several reviewers termed "Seize the Day" an interim work, filling the time after *The Adventures of Augie March*. Since 1956 the novella's reputation has grown steadily, however, until, as

Alfred Kazin puts it, "none of his works is so widely and genuinely admired as this short novel." The reason lies in the calm and solidity of Bellow's art. The tone is almost Olympian in its treatment of Tommy's sloppy sentimentality, and Tommy himself is a significant creation. He is at once the ultimate antihero (Herbert Gold called "Seize the Day" "one of the central stories of our day") and yet a worthwhile man, and likable, with "a large, shaky, patient dignity." He is cheerful and without malice. He cares for his loved ones. More important, he is intelligently aware, undergoing his experience with depth and sensitivity.

But the finest accomplishment of the story, and certainly one of the remarkable conclusions in American literature, is the novella's climactic scene. Tommy at one moment is on the New York streets, desperately looking for Tamkin and feeling the pressure of the crowd, "the inexhaustible current of millions of every race and kind pouring out, pressing round, of every age, of every genius, possessors of every secret," and at the next inside a funeral parlor, where it is suddenly "dark and cool," and where "men in formal clothes and black homburgs strode softly back and forth on the cork floor, up and down the center aisle."

In a few moments he stands before the corpse, a man he had never known, and begins to cry. He sobs at first for the man, "another human creature," he thinks, but soon he cries for himself and for all his troubles. "Soon he was past words, past reason, coherence," Bellow writes. "The source of all tears had suddenly sprung open within him, black, deep. . . ." The other guests envy the dead man, to have such mourning, but Tommy does not stop. His grief becomes a definitive and strangely triumphant moment, as the flowers and lights and music fuse within him, pouring "into him where he had hidden himself in the center of a crowd by the great and happy oblivion of tears. He heard it and sank deeper than sorrow, through torn sobs and cries toward the consummation of his heart's ultimate need."

In the first version of this concluding paragraph, as originally published in the *Partisan Review*, Bellow included "and by the way that can be found only through the midst of sorrow," implying what the prose rhythms suggest, which is that the humiliating moment is some kind of victory. Critics disagree about Bellow's final meaning, puzzled, as Brendan Gill puts it, by the sense that Tommy is "sobbing his heart out over his plight and yet feeling rather better than usual," but almost all readers sense the authority of the scene. As Alfred Kazin says of the whole novella, "It has a quite remarkable intensity of effect without ever seeming to force one."

More specifically, the circumstance of Tommy finding his way to a stranger's funeral crystallizes Tommy's situation and needs. For he needs a father and has been denied, seeking help from people "dead" to him. He has sought all day to hide his failure, to put up a front, and here he is publicly reduced to truthfulness. Bellow himself has said that he wanted to dramatize the way New Yorkers fulfill intimate emotional needs through strangers, and so Tommy turns from his psychologist (the professional stranger) to an alien corpse—where he finally finds fulfillment. The scene gathers together other themes as well, for Tommy all day has been sinking in his tears and here drowns; he had rejected his Jewish heritage, anglicizing his name, and here grieves before the Star of David; Tommy has been a masochist too, seeking pain in a classic case of Reichian pathology, as Eusebio Rodríquez has shown, and here he finally lets go, dissolving his destructive rigidity to permit a healthy venting of emotion. Since Tommy has had mystical promptings that his suffering somehow has a transcendent purpose, Bellow's point is also that Tommy sinks to a truer, more spiritual level of being accessible only when he is stripped of worldly pretensions.

Henderson the Rain King (1959) did not receive effusive praise when it was published, but it did not diminish Bellow's reputation either. Bellow wrote it in 1957 in Tivoli, New York, the period during which his second son, Adam, was born, and in 1958 at the University of Minnesota (an anchor for Bellow in these years and the place where he was friends with John Berryman), and then the next year in Europe, having won a two-year Ford Foundation grant.

This book about a WASP millionaire's trip to a dreamlike Africa illustrates the fertility and variety in Bellow's imagination and his desire, as he said later, to develop "a fiction that can accommodate the full tumult, the zaniness and crazed quality of modern experience." Henderson is a gigantic man in body and emotion, six foot four inches tall with "an enormous head, rugged, with hair like Persian lambs' fur. Suspicious eyes, usually narrowed. Blustering way. A great nose. . . ." He is an heir to a fortune, a hard drinker, a bully, a fighter, a man fleeing death. When the comedy of Henderson's brawling is done, his character remains formed in malice. He is nasty to his wives, torments the neighbors, breaks glass on tourist beaches. His rages finally scare the family cook to death, making him seek a salvation in Africa where, he says, "the world which I thought so mighty an oppressor has removed its wrath from me." Henderson (whose initials and taste in guns are the same as Hemingway's) is the militant, insecure American who attempts to prove his manhood by killing. He is also the intelligent and sensitive man who suffers from his knowledge of human limitation. Confessing that he is most like the character Henderson, "the absurd seeker of high qualities," Bellow comments that "what Henderson is really seeking is a remedy to the anxiety over death. What he can't endure is this continuing anxiety . . . which he is foolhardy enough to resist."

In Africa Henderson encounters a harsh desert environment with a fierce white light—in essence, the inhuman physical universe. Although the novel has many realistic touches, it is essentially a fantasy, a trip deep within the Africa of Henderson's mind. For in this wasteland, reminiscent of the sheer raw power of the naturalistic world, Henderson discovers first a tribe which reacts to its environment with a soft, worshiping attitude, loving its cows and its dimpled and smiling old queen, and then (after he has harmed the gentle Arnewi irremediably by blowing up their water supply) a fierce and willful and manipulative tribe that beats its gods and threatens to kill its king. Part of Bellow's point is Henderson's desire to serve a community even though it involves often bizarre and dangerous conditions, as in the case of the marvelously relaxed Wariri King Dahfu, who studies Emerson, William James, and Wilhelm Reich and who will be unceremoniously strangled if he fails to satisfy any one of his forty wives. To make the anxious Henderson equally serene, Dahfu takes him into a lion's den, where he teaches him to emulate the lion. Dahfu's tribe believes that he is not completely king until he captures the soul of his dead father . . . in a live lion. Although educated in the Western empirical tradition, which would scoff at such a view, Dahfu accepts these conditions, and is killed in the attempt.

When Henderson then feels himself cured or freed from the world's wrath, he stumbles in explaining the cause, for he claims it was not the lion's cruel indifference that freed him but the love of the Arnewi—a statement that grows more out of Bellow's desire than the novel's events. The truth seems to be that Bellow's imagination drives (as in *The Victim* and "Seize the Day") to a final scene of violence or death which once experienced leaves the protagonist relieved and joyful. Bellow's burden as the maker of plots is to justify not just the death but the joy. And when he fails to do so, as in *Henderson*

the Rain King, critics complain about a murky ending.

Henderson the Rain King is an amusing novel and a good introduction to Bellow's work. Henderson is a truly comic character, and Dahfu's theories are good intellectual fun. Bellow is bolder than he had been in his previous work (it is from *Henderson* that he dates his maturity as a writer), for he here openly makes a connection between the force of the universe, particularized in the sun, say, or in an octopus's eye, and a human or spiritual principle. But Bellow once again sought variety, turning in the hectic next five years to a realistic work. He spent much of 1959 in Europe and the next year at his country home in Dutchess County. With Keith Botsford and Aaron Asher he edited the periodical the *Noble Savage*, which published writers such as Ralph Ellison, Thomas Pynchon, Josephine Herbst, and John Hawkes. He taught at the University of Puerto Rico and then settled down to his third marriage, with Susan Glassman, whom he wed in December 1961. Much sought after as a leading novelist, he taught a course in 1962 on "The Modern Novel and its Heroes" at the University of Chicago. The next year, with a new child on the way (Daniel, born in 1963) and a desire to return to his roots, Bellow left New York for Chicago, where he accepted a permanent position at the University of Chicago on the Committee on Social Thought.

In Chicago Bellow sought a greater freedom to work, a desire which bore fruit the next year with the publication of *Herzog* and the production of *The Last Analysis*. The play was a lighthearted episodic farce Bellow hoped would survive because of its entertaining qualities. The novel was more serious, embodying the theory he had announced in 1961 that a novelist must be permitted to deal with ideas. The play flopped, and the novel was a best-seller for six months. "I received two or three thousand letters from people pouring out their souls to me, saying 'This is my life, this is what it's been like for me,'" Bellow said after the publication of *Herzog*. "And then I understood that for some reason these themes were visited upon me, that I didn't always pick them, they picked me." Since the novel covered events similar to those of Bellow's life, portraying an intellectual professor devastated by the betrayal of wife and friends, some of the interest in the novel was that of a roman à clef. But most of the people who bought it were not in on the gossip; the novel articulated their own anger, their own frustration—precisely that frame of mind that characterized the late 1960s as tempers flared (and letters flew) over the issues of free speech, racial injustice, and war. Writing as early as 1960, Bellow anticipated the mood of the coming decade.

The story consists of Moses Herzog's memories as he putters alone about his country home—technically the place at which the action takes place, since everything that follows is a memory in Herzog's mind. Herzog remembers himself in New York, where he had stayed a few days after teaching a course, and then in Chicago, where he had lurked outside his estranged wife's apartment before suffering a minor auto accident, and a brief incarceration, from which the police freed him to go back to his country home in western Massachusetts.

If the geography is simple, however, the story is not. Since Herzog writes letters to all kinds of people and remembers all kinds of earlier events, the novel seems disorganized. Critics divide largely into those who forgive this disorganization (since it reflects Herzog's mind) and those who do not. And once again the protagonist at the end feels somewhat better, but the reader is not certain why. And yet the truth is that the book, which Bellow rewrote at least thirteen times, is indeed well formed. Moses Herzog had decided early in the story to shift from an emotional, "personal" life, such as the one in which his wife Madeleine abused him, to a more rational, civil, moderate one—he will shift, as he says in a letter to Eisenhower, from Tolstoy to Hegel. And much of the novel flows from this decision: he leaves Martha's Vineyard in part two because to him it represents the emotional or personal life since he had come there seeking comfort from a friend. He reviews his intimate family and friends in part three because they too sought salvation in the personal. He carps about Ramona (who gives him gourmet dinners and what she thinks is gourmet sex) because she would cure him by means of the "personal life." Resolved to do something, he awaits his lawyer in a courtroom that portrays the horrors of the personal or sexual life and shows how the impersonal machinery of the court may give true justice.

In part six he flies to Chicago, contemplating murder of his ex-wife and her lover in order to protect his daughter Junie, reportedly locked crying in an auto outside Madeleine's apartment, but he decides once more (as the novel catches the realistic zigzags of a man trying on a new mode) that he is being extreme and indulging in personal "drama."

Thus each of the novel's sections (there are nine in all) dramatizes Bellow's theme. After he is caught the next day with the gun in his pocket, Herzog finds himself standing before a police

Dust jacket for Bellow's second National Book Award-winner

sergeant, next to Madeleine, who in pure hatred seeks to have him imprisoned. "Her voice went up sharply, and as she spoke, Herzog saw the sergeant take a new look at her, as if he were beginning to make out her haughty peculiarities at last. . . . 'One of those was for me, wasn't it!' she says of the bullets. 'You think so? I wonder where you get such ideas? And who was the other one for?' He was quite cool as he said this, his tone was level. He was doing all he could to bring out the hidden Madeleine, the Madeleine he knew."

When the sergeant lets him go, Herzog receives a symbolic justice. The friends and relatives and even doctors who had witnessed his divorce had all failed him, but the civil authority had not. And having gotten justice he feels better. One of the problems with the novel, however, is that he feels an ecstatic joy that goes far beyond fair treatment. The truth seems to be that this novel too must be viewed as not so much a thematic statement as an experience. Herzog in Chicago undergoes a purgation, first in the pondered murder and then in being jailed. Madeleine's lover Gersbach, whom Herzog had stalked with a gun in his pocket, becomes the parallel to Allbee, Dahfu, Tommy's dead stranger—and so too, in the cell that means ruin and death, does Herzog himself.

Herzog is notable for the controversy it caused. Bellow's second National Book Award-winner, it was praised and highly criticized. Alfred Kazin called it Bellow's "most brilliant" novel while Brendan Gill termed it "faultless." Other critics worried that Herzog pondered only himself, making the novel solipsistic. The key question is whether or not Herzog succeeds in making a character of himself as he looks back. Does Herzog get out of his own mind? His ability to see himself from the outside and with precise detail suggests that he might. Bellow's theme at any rate is something very much like solipsism, as Herzog is imprisoned in the "private" life.

But however one evaluates the structure of the book, *Herzog* is perhaps most notable for the style, which represents Bellow at his very best. Herzog's double remove permits Bellow to dote on detail, to slow the action when necessary to make the scenes live. And since Herzog does a great deal of observing, the novel finds its center in its descriptions. The prose is charged, rich, full of the specifics and precisely defined impressions that create the feel of mid-1960s American life. Herzog's pain seems to intensify his perception, but in many ways the novel is almost a culmination of the realistic movement, defining just that moment before the ripeness turned. Because Herzog is deflected from his course not by any insight or charged drama but by the sight of kindly Gersbach giving little Junie a bath, *Herzog* is a defense of the realistic mode, holding that the significant levels of life are often the common, whether in the home or outside in society—a view Herzog himself embraces (rejecting the fashionable existentialism) and then in his life dramatizes.

But once again Bellow was not content to work in a single key. *Herzog* joins *The Victim* and the novella "Seize the Day" to define Bellow's realistic work (a mode which more than one critic feels to be Bellow's best), but Bellow in 1964 also wrote a wilder, more fantastic piece in the play *The Last Analysis*, which he saw performed in fall 1964 and which climaxed a long interest in the theater. One of his early essays had been about the season's Broadway plays, and in 1952 he had seen *The Victim* as adapted for the stage by Leonard Lesley. He had collaborated on a dramatization of "Seize the Day" and had included a one-act play, *The Wrecker*,

among the pieces in the collection *Seize the Day*. Bellow also seems to have been motivated financially, for his novels had not made him a great deal of money, and his coming book—about a professor who writes letters to famous intellectuals—did not promise to be a best-seller. Zero Mostel would play the lead in "Humanitis," as *The Last Analysis* was originally entitled, and the play, Bellow thought, would be easy to write. He saw the theater as a form of freedom, since the footlights required a more direct, less subtle approach. He would supply the skeleton, as it were, and string some vaudevillelike bits together on it—a play with energy and emotion and sprawl not too unlike some of the work in the Yiddish theater.

By 1964, though, Bellow complained that he was writing himself into his grave. Mostel backed out, to be replaced by Sam Levene, and Bellow found playwriting more demanding than he had imagined. He persevered, however, presenting a comedian who has slipped in his career because of his seriousness and who now, in his New York warehouse studio, seeks to combine laughter and home-style psychoanalysis. The protagonist, Bummidge, seeks a cure for "humanitis," and his technique, he says, is to act out "the main events of my life, dragging repressed material into the open by sheer force of drama." In the first act he struggles to get enough money to go on closed-circuit television before a gathering of psychoanalysts and talks about his performance with his associates and relatives—his agent Winkleman, his mistress Pamela, his sexy but platonic secretary Imogen, his sister, his wife, his son—many of whom resent the money he is squandering. He rehearses his method, and then in the second and final act gives his lecture-demonstration, taking himself through the birth trauma, conflicts with his father, sexual adolescence, marriage, and then death, the experience of the last triggering an ecstatic state in which he disposes of all those who had obstructed him and determines to proceed with an institute to advance his new therapy.

So goes the published version of the play, which Bellow tells us is a substantial rewrite of the original, much tightened and simplified—abandoning the vaudevillian looseness for form and stressing the mental comedy of Bummy's method. The Broadway version flopped after twenty-eight performances, receiving poor reviews even though journalists such as John Simon tried gallantly to save it, arguing that it was the most substantial piece of comic drama produced that season. And such, at least in Bellow's rewrite, it seems to be. Bellow plays with ideas, providing a protagonist who seeks to discover what is wrong with himself by exploring the past. Bellow finds a way to visualize the internal. He combines a comedy of ideas—having fun not only with Freud but also with the intellectual's search for health—and a physical stage comedy, reminiscent of vaudeville.

Bellow's second effort in the theater did no better. For the production *Under the Weather*, Bellow combined three one-act plays, two of which have been published: *A Wen*, a delightful comedy about a scientist who has found the experience of winning the Nobel Prize less intense than the glimpse of a birthmark on a woman's thigh (a glimpse he seeks to duplicate, in middle age, with the same surprised lady) and a somewhat darker comedy, *Orange Soufflé*, about a Polish whore who wants to move in with her elderly and wealthy WASP customer. *Under the Weather* was produced in London, Spoleto, and New York, but failed to catch on.

In the novel *Herzog* Bellow attempted something like the comedy of serious thought, while in the play *The Last Analysis* he presented a clown reaching for serious ideas. Both works define a mode that would dominate Bellow's fiction for the next eighteen years, and that is the reliving of the past. *The Adventures of Augie March*, of course, was a memoir, and Henderson attempts to reach the dead parents for whom he yearns. In *The Last Analysis* and *Herzog*, however, Bellow discovered a new center, as the protagonist relives his memories. The result was not only the creation of a special richness and color, always contrasting past and present, but a special style, one with the leisure to look and replay and sort and arrange and explore the past. "I think of myself as horribly deprived of people whom I loved and who are dead," Bellow confessed recently. "These memories serve to resurrect feelings which, at the time, I didn't want to have. . . . Now I realize how much emotion was invested in them, and I bring them back."

This mode is expressed in the best story in Bellow's next published work, *Mosby's Memoirs and Other Stories* (1968), a more or less "made" book designed to keep Bellow's name before the public and perhaps to capitalize on the great success of *Herzog*. Bellow continued to teach in Chicago in the years following *Herzog*, although he took time out in 1967 to cover the Six-Day War for *Newsday* and in 1968 to receive the Croix de Chevalier des Arts et Lettres from France. He had begun the novel that was to become *Humboldt's Gift*, but upon hearing an anecdote about an old man witnessing a pickpocket at work, shifted to the manuscript that would be-

come *Mr. Sammler's Planet*. He had also found time to write two short stories, "Mosby's Memoirs" (1968) and "The Old System" (1967), to which he added "Leaving the Yellow House" (1957) and several tales already published in *Seize the Day*.

The best story of the group is "The Old System," in which the well-known scientist Samuel Braun, transparently Bellow himself, indulges in what became a characteristic Bellow posture in the late 1960s and 1970s: the middle-aged man remembering his Jewish relatives, losing himself in a colorful and exotic past. The characters are mysterious to Braun, who loves them. He ponders their reality, their evolution, the strangeness of their being. They are in one sense crude and grasping immigrants from Eastern Europe who would embarrass a third-generation Jew. But they are also vital and proud and fierce. They seem to Braun to be more intensely alive, or at least more passionate, than his modern colleagues. And indeed they are, for the remarkable story begins when Braun's fierce and fat cousin Tina, having reneged on a business deal with her brother Isaac, misses out on the fortune Isaac proceeds to make. The disappointment makes her claim Isaac cheated her, and she refuses to see him even though Isaac, as an old-fashioned believer in family, is scandalized. He spends years trying to see her, but it is only on her deathbed that she sends Isaac a message: he may visit if he pays her $20,000. To Braun remembering all this, the issue is why he is so moved now, why the event seems so precious to him. As he looks at the stars which make the episode and all else seem insignificant, he still glories in the magnificence of Tina's will and of her capriciousness—as she refuses the money when it is offered—and of her sassing the fate that gave her a fat body and the death that will soon come. He glories too in the integrity of Isaac and the old system to which he clung.

And thus it seems ironic that Bellow's next novel be marred by a lack of caring. *Mr. Sammler's Planet* (1970) was well but somewhat absentmindedly received, as though the reviewers praised Bellow by rote; a few years later it was attacked by radical young critics for political reasons, in part because Bellow had declared his independence from the liberal establishment in 1965 by attending the White House dinner that Robert Lowell, protesting Vietnam, had boycotted.

A stubborn and difficult writer, Bellow had written about an elderly man in a decade obsessed with American youth. In this novel, as in *Herzog*, Bellow seemed to test both his readers and his own powers. Artur Sammler is an old Polish Jew who, having lived in London in the 1930s, where he knew many of the Bloomsbury group, and having survived Nazi atrocities, has the civilized tastes of the intellectual English and the wisdom of the survivor. Around him he finds a host of modern young nieces, nephews, and acquaintances who reject all limits on their desire. They know no sexual bounds, no moral imperatives, no common civility. Sammler alone in New York quietly pursues something like duty. When his crazed daughter Shula steals a manuscript to help her father with his study of H. G. Wells, he doggedly seeks to return the manuscript. When his friend and benefactor Elya Gruner lies mortally ill in a hospital, Sammler alone among even the man's children pays homage to the dying.

The plot, which Bellow seems to have formed with a Wellsian casualness, consists largely of the young interfering with these two tasks and is typified in the running story of Sammler's relations with the black pickpocket, whose crimes he has witnessed on a bus and who follows Sammler to his apartment foyer to threaten the old man by exposing himself. Sammler mentions the incident to his opportunistic friend Feffer, only to discover later (in too much of a coincidence) the black struggling with Feffer because he had taken pictures of the crime. And when Sammler asks his ex-son-in-law to intervene, the younger man hits to kill. In contrast to such madness, Sammler at the end praises his friend Elya Gruner, who (though sometimes an abortionist for the mob) had known how to be kind. And to do his duty. Moderation, limits, rationality—all we have, Sammler suggests, is simple human decency. Gruner had met "the terms of his contract," Sammler concludes, "The terms which, in his inmost heart, each man knows. As I know mine. As all know. For that is the truth of it—that we all know, God, that we know, that we know, we know, we know."

Mr. Sammler's Planet is vintage Bellow, full of the precise detail and lively ideas and honest feeling that provide Bellow his strengths. If it is true, as several critics have charged, that Mr. Sammler is too right and the city too wrong, it may well be that this is the best novel the reader could hope for, written as it was so close in time to the controversial period it takes as its subject. And certainly the character of Sammler, who has survived the Holocaust, waking from a pile of corpses to kill fascists in his escape, is an excellent point of view from which to examine and judge American culture. Bellow captures better than anyone the feel of American society in the late 1960s, with its blend of social rebellion, sexuality, racial unrest, and personal aggrandizement.

Those who criticize the book have a point, too, however, although it is not a political one. Sammler's rational conservatism is totally responsible, whether we agree with it or not, for it is the result of a calm choice. "Without limits you have monstrosity, always," he says. "Within limits? Well, within limits monsters also appear. But not inevitably." What does mar the novel, finally, is Sammler's basic feeling of revulsion toward the world, both in its social form, which is cheap and distracting—Gruner's daughter worries about her sex life as her father dies—and in terms of all matter. Like Yeats sailing to Byzantium, Mr. Sammler has no use for the natural physical world, or what he calls "creatureliness.... Its low tricks, its doggish hind-sniffing charm." Sammler yearns to be "a soul released from Nature, from impressions, and from everyday life."

Herzog had balanced precariously between a sense of the world's beauty and its ugliness. In *Mr. Sammler's Planet* the balance is tipped, and the result is not only a book that turns sour but also one that tolerates a certain contrivance of plot, as though corny or mechanical events were a true parallel to a corny or mechanical world. Sammler on the move, fending off the crazed youth, is unconvincing. Sammler alone with his thoughts and memories, in what is now Bellow's most typical mode, is mellow and believable.

Mr. Sammler's Planet won a National Book Award in 1971. While continuing to teach at the University of Chicago (where he had become chairman of the Committee on Social Thought) and coping with the public and bitter dissolution of his third marriage, Bellow worked on two novels, segments of which were published in 1974. One of these was *Humboldt's Gift*, which in 1975 became his seventh novel and which nominally won him the 1976 Nobel Prize.

Many reviewers praised the book, and *Newsweek* did a cover story on America's leading writer, but other critics were disappointed. "The book is not very real," Alfred Kazin confessed, although large pieces of it were. Part of the trouble seemed to be the combination of the realistic and the manic: Bellow attempted to work grotesque gangsters into a finely detailed world, and it did not work. And then the plot creaked, even though Bellow had been true to his vision once again, for if the world of affairs is contrived and vulgar, what kind of plot must a realist provide? Bellow had defined his basic intention in this novel in 1963, discussing "Literature" for *Encyclopaedia Britannica:* few modern novelists, he noted, dramatize a spiritual experience. If they feel they are important, writers "ought

Drawing of Bellow by David Schorr

him to the altar. But during all these events, Citrine moves inward in memory and meditation, seeking the images that Rudolf Steiner had promised would give spiritual salvation.

What is interesting thematically in *Humboldt's Gift* is the equation within Citrine's inner life of his meditation of spirit and his memories of his friend. Both of these exist in saving opposition to the world, although Humboldt's actual gift combines the sublime and the vulgar, for it consists first of a movie scenario on which they had collaborated and which proceeds to earn Citrine a small fortune, and then of a scribbled sentence at the end of a farewell letter: "We are not natural beings but supernatural beings."

The chief critical issue in the novel, aside from Bellow's struggle to mesh his transcendental philosophy with commercial America, is how Bellow in the same book can write both brilliantly and ineptly. Bellow moves from passages such as

> She threw a very good pass—a hard, accurate spiral. Her voice trailed as she ran barelegged and made the catch on her breast. The ball in flight wagged like a duck's tail. It flew under the maples over the clothesline.

to passages such as this:

> I met Kathleen at a cafe and showed her the clippings. There was more in the same vein. I said, "Thraxter has a terrible weakness for making major statements. I think I might just ask for the three guns to be applied to the back of my head and the triggers pulled rather than sit through those seminars."
> "Don't be too hard on him. The man is saving his life," she said.
> "Also it's a fascinating thing, really. Where does he make the ransom pitch?"
> "Here. . . ."

Bellow at his worst sounds like an amateur playwright providing background information as he moves his characters on- and offstage. Thus the later parts of the novel fall off, becoming talky and cranky, as though (as reportedly is the case) Bellow took to talking his novel to a stenographer, like the later Henry James, or as though his troubled personal life had taken its toll. The truly fine early parts of the book were written not too long after *Herzog*, while the later parts, developing some of the disenchantment with the real world Bellow expressed in *Mr. Sammler's Planet*, came since 1969.

Critics have not really done justice to the fact

to show us the actualities of a religious life." *Humboldt's Gift* is a fascinating book because it does precisely that.

The story is told from the point of view of Charles Citrine, a well-known dramatist who reminisces about his friendship with Humboldt, a poet who combines qualities of John Berryman, with whom Bellow had been close friends at Minnesota, and Delmore Schwartz, whom Bellow had known in New York. It was in fact shortly after Schwartz died in 1966 that Bellow began the novel, much of which consists of Citrine trying to hang on to his memories of Humboldt and do a little anthroposophical meditation while being harassed by gangsters, lawyers, bimbos, and creeps—some funny and some not. All of them are typified by Cantabile, to whom Citrine owes money and who has Citrine's car smashed in by baseball bats and later forces the playwright to watch him defecate. An ex-wife is suing Citrine, and a mistress—the sensual Renata, an uninhibited woman who makes one think of a witty and tough Ramona—is attempting to lead that good writing seems to exist in a delicate balance or tension that the reader can sometimes see come and go. One thinks of Mark Twain, and then, perhaps, the Bellow of *Humboldt's Gift*, for this novel contains writing as good as any that Bellow has done and also the very worst that he has done. Perhaps Bellow said what he had to say in *Herzog* and now marks time. Certainly *Mr. Sammler's Planet* is very much like a brilliant piece of journalism, providing a highly intelligent man pondering our civil disruption.

And yet Bellow has always surprised his readers, and the wise Bellovians would expect to be surprised again. Bellow's 1976 book is the journalistic *To Jerusalem and Back; A Personal Account*, published after Bellow had accompanied his new wife, Alexandra, professor of mathematics at Northwestern University, to Israel. There he had adopted a fascinating premise: what could a practitioner of the humanities add to the politics and propaganda and terror of the Israeli-Arab conflict? Could he penetrate the confusion to find some kind of order? Bellow had contemplated a book on Chicago and had served as a journalist during the Six-Day War. Could he now make some kind of

contribution to solving Israel's troubles? The book describes Bellow's travels, his interviews with Israeli and American leaders, and his dinner conversations with the powerful and the humble, and then—and not least important—his reading and research into the problem.

Bellow's writing is lucid and detailed, and not without humor, as an Hasidim, for example, is offended by Bellow's eating habits and offers to send him money each month if he will return to orthodoxy. But at the end the rational and well-meaning Bellow is forced to conclude that the situation is even more dangerous than he had supposed, for he finds that nations (and their leaders) do not act consistently with even their own self-interest. If only they recognized their goals and sought them ruthlessly, Bellow suggests, the struggle would have some order. But both Arab and Jew act irrationally, creating a dangerous and unpredictable mix. That bystanders such as Jean-Paul Sartre or the United States will make use of the conflict for their own purposes—again inconsistently and irrationally defined—only makes the issue worse.

Bellow's most recent novel examines another situation out of control and represents again the

Bellow, 1980s (photo by Layle Silbert)

Dust jacket for Bellow's most recent novel. The author's contrast of life in a Communist society with life in the United States drew mixed reviews.

humanist's look at an important human issue. In *The Dean's December* (1982), Bellow contrasts communism and capitalism or, more accurately, the human failure of both systems. In this novel, Albert Corde, a dean of students at a Chicago college, has accompanied his sensible astronomer wife, Minna, to Bucharest, where her mother lies ill in a hospital. There petty communist officials make it difficult for Minna to visit the dying woman, a communist official now fallen from favor, and finally permit her only one visit—she must choose the time. Corde's wife must suffer the ordeal of her mother dying alone, without her daughter at the bedside.

As Minna hurries about the city seeking help, Corde passes the time in a chilly apartment remembering the problems he left back in Chicago. He had published a set of articles on the black underclass of the city and had insisted upon the prosecution of two blacks in the murder of a white student. His articles had upset liberals, who mistook his bleak honesty for racism, and so too had his insistence that the murderers be prosecuted. Corde could lose his job as dean, since it was injudicious of him to confront a problem as intractable as the Chicago ghetto,

and certainly the acquittal of the black defendants in the murder case would mean that his insistence upon prosecution had been an error. While Minna struggles with a communist bureaucracy, Corde struggles with an American one. But because Corde is isolated in the Rumanian apartment, the chief drama in this novel is in meditation: Corde *thinks* about his problems, as the story passes back and forth between the present and the past, between action and analysis, between suspense and a reflection that Henry James might have found delightful.

But of course, the issues are not a delight. Bellow places his protagonist six thousand miles from Chicago to obtain distance from America's mammoth and emotional social problems. Corde's articles (recently published in *Harper's*, he says) are in fact leftovers from Bellow's abandoned book about Chicago and include a fine description of dialysis at the Cook County Hospital as well as several interviews, one with the public defender in a troubling case. A middle-class housewife had been abducted and raped and had sought refuge in private homes only to be turned back into the arms of her captor, who then murdered her. The public defender blandly tells Corde that the white woman had acquiesced; she had been sitting alone in the abductor's car. She had been dazed, Bellow suggests, and her black murderer had been dazed too: people suffer and commit atrocities like sleepwalkers. But the point of Corde's meditation is justice: the blacks must be held responsible for their crimes, Corde believes, and so too must the whites who are callous about human suffering. Corde is especially scornful toward the "media intellectuals," or those journalists and academics who have studied the lower class and have come up with nothing but jargon.

Corde's position as a journalist and an academic is thus very much to the point. Modern problems are so large that citizens must rely upon information supplied to them. But those charged with the responsibility of supplying such information have failed: "The language of discourse had shut out experience all together." Corde wrote his articles, we understand, "to recover the world that is buried under the debris of false description or non-experience."

And does Bellow himself "recover the world"? Because the specialists have failed in terms of language and perspective, Bellow provides a rationale for the participation of the humanist in public issues. But in doing so he makes an ambitious claim for his own novel. Does he succeed? Several reviewers found *The Dean's December* to be a considerable achievement. Bellow compares not just capitalism and communism, or a world in which "people have to be human without freedom" and one in which "they succeed in not being human with it," but the intersection in each society of the State and the person. Bellow in Rumania permits us to look at the State through the eyes of personal need, as in Minna's story, and then in Chicago to glimpse the individual—the suffering black—through the eyes of the State or the public officials who administer it. In both Rumania and America, the society parcels out pain to the individual. Ironically, in this intersecting set of contrasts and similarities, the communist state works in terms of the individual, singling out Minna's mother, while the capitalistic society works in terms of the larger group, creating a community (a commune) of deprivation and despair.

And yet the novel is flawed too, by what increasingly seems to be Bellow's carelessness. Bellow's style can flash to life at any moment, but it can also go dead. The plot concerning Minna's mother seems true and right; the murder trial in Chicago is contrived and wooden, full of desperate characters who are not so much shown as discussed. Bellow's description of Bucharest is so fine that John Updike proclaimed Bellow "one of the rare writers who when we read them feel to be taking mimesis a layer or two deeper than it has gone before." But Bellow's dialogue is formal, "talky," full of information that should be shown. Bellow forgets to ground his dialogue in a human relationship that will anchor it and make it part of the story and instead attempts to reveal events by having people talk about them.

Thus the reviewers had mixed feelings about *The Dean's December*, treating Bellow with respect but acknowledging the book's deep flaws. Those who praised the novel did so on the grounds of Bellow's style and the immediacy of his descriptions. Those who criticized it (for reasons other than political ones) tended to refer to what has come to typify Bellow's later work, the juxtaposition in the same book of two different tones, two kinds of experience, or two levels of imagination. Bellow presents in his last three novels both a quiet, realistic level of experience, usually surrounding his protagonist's personal life, and then a manic one, full of energy and color and involving the external world or an eccentric who represents that world. What seems to have happened is that history has thrown Bellow a curve: as the public realm has become progressively more complex and uncontrollable, Bellow has had greater trouble uniting his two modes. The manic tone that Bellow once used as comic relief is now a form of verisimilitude, true to the public life, and the result in the novel is a series of jolts as we move from one tone to the other, from what Bellow controls to what he simply describes. And yet Bellow himself feels this disunity, for he carefully positions his protagonist to cope with it, giving him the leisure to think and a vantage point far enough away from the chaos—in terms of his years, say, or his sojourn in far-off Rumania—to gain perspective on it.

But whatever his difficulties, Bellow continues to write fascinating fiction, struggling to close the gap between private and public experience. He himself has continued to live in Chicago, writing and teaching, and seems to have achieved his own orderly life, with the end of a public lawsuit by his third wife. Will his work last? Even as fads come and go, even as Ph.D.'s study Bellow's difficulty with plot and others study Bellow's great success in style, even as the world whirls about him, Bellow's novels give evidence of lasting. Perhaps the most accurate testimony to Bellow's strength is given by his friend Richard Stern, when he asks, "How many American writers have published first-rate imaginative books over a thirty year period? Perhaps three, Henry James, Faulkner and now Bellow."

Interviews:

Gordon Lloyd Harper, "Saul Bellow: An Interview," in *Writers at Work: The "Paris Review" Interviews*, Third Series (New York: Viking, 1967), pp. 175-196;

Joseph Epstein, "A Talk with Saul Bellow," *New York Times Book Review*, 5 December 1976, pp. 3, 92-93.

Bibliographies:

B. A. Sokoloff and Mark Posner, *Saul Bellow: A Comprehensive Bibliography* (Folcroft, Penn.: Folcroft Library Editions, 1972);

Marianne Nault, *Saul Bellow: His Works and His Critics* (New York: Garland Publishing, 1977);

Robert G. Noreen, *Saul Bellow: A Reference Guide* (Boston: G. K. Hall, 1978).

References:

John J. Clayton, *Saul Bellow: In Defense of Man* (Bloomington: Indiana University Press, 1968);

Sarah Blacher Cohen, *Saul Bellow's Enigmatic Laughter* (Urbana: University of Illinois Press, 1974);

Robert Detweiler, *Saul Bellow: A Critical Essay* (Grand Rapids, Mich.: Eerdmans, 1967);

Robert R. Dutton, *Saul Bellow* (New York: Twayne, 1971);

Daniel Fuchs, *Saul Bellow: Vision and Revision* (Durham, N.C.: Duke University, 1984);

David D. Galloway, *The Absurd Hero in American Fiction: Updike, Styron, Bellow, Salinger* (Austin: University of Texas Press, 1966; revised edition, 1970);

Chirantan Kulshrestha, *Saul Bellow: The Problem of Affirmation* (New Delhi: Arnold-Heinemann, 1978);

Irving Malin, *Saul Bellow's Fiction* (Carbondale: Southern Illinois University Press, 1969);

Malin, ed., *Saul Bellow and the Critics* (New York: New York University Press, 1967);

Keith Opdahl, *The Novels of Saul Bellow: An Introduction* (University Park: Pennsylvania State University Press, 1967);

G. I. Porter, *Whence the Power?* (Columbia: University of Missouri Press, 1974);

Earl Rovit, *Saul Bellow* (Minneapolis: University of Minnesota Press, 1967);

Brigitte Scheer-Schaetzler, *Saul Bellow* (New York: Ungar, 1972);

Tony Tanner, *Saul Bellow* (Edinburgh & London: Oliver & Boyd, 1965; New York: Barnes & Noble, 1965).

Papers:

Bellow's manuscripts are at Regenstein Library of the University of Chicago. This is an extensive collection, including manuscripts from most of the novels, many different working drafts, letters, and memorabilia. Several manuscripts of *Seize the Day* are at the Humanities Research Center, University of Texas, Austin.

E. M. Broner
(8 July 1930-   )

Cathy N. Davidson
Michigan State University

SELECTED BOOKS: *Summer is a Foreign Land* (Detroit: Wayne State University Press, 1966); *Journal/Nocturnal and Seven Stories* (New York: Harcourt, Brace, 1968); *Her Mothers* (New York: Holt, Rinehart & Winston, 1975); *A Weave of Women* (New York: Holt, Rinehart & Winston, 1978).

PLAYS: *Summer is a Foreign Land*, Detroit, Studio Theater, Wayne State University, 1967; *Colonel Higginson*, Detroit, Studio Theater, Wayne State University, 1968; *The Body Parts of Margaret Fuller*, Detroit, Hillberry Theatre, 1976; New York, Playwrights Horizons, 1976; Princeton, N.J., McCarter Theatre, 1977.

OTHER: *The Lost Tradition: Mothers and Daughters in Literature*, edited by Broner and C. N. Davidson (New York: Ungar, 1980).

PERIODICAL PUBLICATIONS: "A Woman's Passover Haggadah," by Broner and Naomi Nimrod, *Ms.*, 5 (April 1977): 53-56; "Broner on Broner: The Writing of Humor, or A Funny Thing Happened to Me on the Way to a Tragedy," *Regionalism and the Female Imagination*, 3 (Winter 1977-78).

E. M. Broner (photo by Layle Silbert)

In her fiction, Esther Masserman Broner simultaneously experiments with narrative form and emphasizes the continuity of myth, folklore, and tradition. As her most recent novel, *A Weave of Women*, especially demonstrates, Broner succeeds in finding new forms for fiction, forms that incorporate both dramatic presentation and poetic language and, at the same time, encompass a radical feminist reordering of social and fictional hierarchies. Her most important contribution to contemporary literature is the way in which she employs an inheritance of Yiddish and Hebrew themes and tones in an experimental fictional mode that celebrates the female hero.

Broner was born in Detroit at the beginning of the Depression into a gifted family. It is not difficult to see in her work the influence of each of her parents. Now retired, her father, Paul Masserman, was a journalist and a noted Jewish historian, while her mother, Beatrice Weckstein Masserman, had acted in the Yiddish theater in Poland. At seventeen Broner went to New York, where, she says, her first job was at Coney Island painting messages on the backs of turtles: "It taught me to be concise." After her marriage to artist Robert Broner, she lived on the West Coast, in the South, and then returned to live in New York. The Broners were part of the literary and artistic scene of Greenwich Village in the 1950s. But they returned to Detroit to raise their four children. Broner earned her B.A. and M.F.A. from Wayne State University. Her Ph.D. is from the Union Graduate School in New York. A recent recipient of a National Endowment for the Arts fellowship, Broner now divides her time between Detroit, where she is writer-in-residence at Wayne State University, and Manhattan, where she does much of her writing.

Broner's fiction explores the relationship between the past and the present. The past, in her novels, can be both an inheritance and a curse. In much of her work characters struggle with history to wrest from it a place for themselves. In *A Weave of Women*, for example, a group of women from various nations meets in Israel to re-create and re-form Jewish patriarchal history. This is an important concern of Broner's personal life as well. She has coauthored a woman's Haggadah, recently performed a ceremony for "Excommunicating the Excommunicators" (in order to honor women of various religions who have been excommunicated for their political beliefs) at the 1980 meeting of the College Art Association, and annually holds a woman's seder in New York for feminist artists, writers, editors, politicians, and other friends. She frequently speaks at conferences on the role of women within a patriarchal religious tradition.

Broner's first book, *Summer is a Foreign Land* (1966), is a verse drama which foreshadows the themes in her later fiction. Broner notes that the drama was influenced by Hasidic literature as well as by the resonances of the Yiddish theater and the daily conversations that she overheard as a child in Detroit: "The political arguments in the backroom of my grandfather's little grocery store, the daily reading aloud of the Yiddish papers, the conversation at the vegetable stands with the tradesmen, the family club meetings were used in the play." According to Broner's preface, the drama was written "in honor of the pioneers who came to Ellis Island and those of their American descendants who chose to make themselves uncomfortable in a comfortable world." It centers on the death of the Baba, the Russian-Jewish matriarch who possesses magical gifts inherited from her ancestor, Mechirch, the "righteous one, a master of the souls of men." From Mechirch, Baba inherited three wishes, two of which she used to help her family escape from Russia to America. As she lies dying, her grandchildren surround her, hoping for the gift of the third wish.

Broner's second book, *Journal/Nocturnal and Seven Stories* (1968), also celebrates those who choose to remain uncomfortable, who choose to retain an ethnic, sexual, or political commitment

that violates the prevailing mood of their time and place. The title novella is printed in two separate columns on the page, each column recording one half of the double life that the main character, named only the Wife, is forced to lead. An early feminist work, the novella *Journal/Nocturnal* is set during the Vietnam War and is the story of a woman married to a liberal professor who actively opposes the war. By night the Wife shares the bed of the Guest who is a proponent of the war. Passive and confused, the Wife criticizes and defends the war, depending upon which man she is with at the time. Her situation, stricken and divided, represents America torn by the war, and, at the same time, the conflict in Vietnam represents the situation of women, divided and conquered. The book reflects Broner's continuing commitments to both the peace movement and the women's movement. It is also noteworthy that one of the stories included in the volume, "The New Nobility," received an O. Henry Award for short fiction in 1968.

In Broner's first novel, *Her Mothers* (1975), the protagonist, Beatrix Palmer, is a writer and, also like Broner, a graduate of an all-Jewish public high school in Detroit during World War II. The novel derives partly from Broner's research for a nonfiction book about mothers and daughters, a book no doubt inspired by the fact that she is a mother of two daughters. But *Her Mothers* is not essentially autobiographical. It is more a biography of a nation divided by the so-called generation gap of the 1960s and early 1970s. The novel's form is that of the quest romance, but Broner inverts archetypal quest patterns. Beatrix is a mature woman searching for her missing adolescent daughter, Lena. As she searches, she also remembers her own years as an adolescent daughter and continues, too, her research on a book called "Unafraid Women." Toward the novel's end, the daughter and mother reunite. Beatrix and Lena meet in Florida where they go swimming together in the ocean. Their mutual frustration leads to a violent physical struggle, alternately a watery battle and a passionate, symbolic embrace. This reunion results in further division but that division leads to still another attempt at a truce, if not a reconciliation. The ending itself is the final answer to the riddle/refrain repeated throughout the novel: "Mother, I'm pregnant with a baby girl." "Why is she singing?" "Because she's unafraid."

Like Broner's other works, *Her Mothers* is a technically ingenious book. The frequently repeated refrain takes on different meanings in its different contexts and allows the promise of the ending. There is also an effective dislocation of chronological time and a reordering of events according to a deliberate pattern of associations and juxtapositions. Continually the search for Lena is interrupted by Beatrix's searches into her own past for herself, for lessons from her Jewish upbringing, history, and religion. Simultaneously developed is a parallel search for heroic women from the past and the ambivalence of discovering matriarchs who denounced women—Sara, Rivkah, Lea, Rachel—or the ambiguous matriarchy of American mothers Margaret Fuller, Emily Dickinson, Louisa May Alcott, and late nineteenth-century black feminist writer Charlotte Forten.

Like *Her Mothers*, Broner's most recent novel, *A Weave of Women* (1978), was written mostly while Broner was a resident at the MacDowell Writer's Colony in New Hampshire and at Ossabaw in Georgia. The novel was greatly influenced by the year Broner lived in Israel, teaching women's studies and creative writing at the University of Haifa, learning Hebrew, and giving readings and lectures throughout the country at institutions such as Hebrew University, Bar-ilan, and Ben Gurion University. In *A Weave of Women*, women from Israel, England, Germany, and America meet and live together in a small stone house in the Old City in Jerusalem. Twelve women and three "wayward girls" come together to help each other and, in the process, envision a woman's utopian society. They rewrite myths, traditions, and religious ceremonies.

They endure the hostilities of men and women who resent their radical reformation of sacred rituals. The fifteen characters finally find themselves challenging social precept and biblical law, again a reflection of the author's particular interest as a social activist.

A Weave of Women is a technically innovative work, written in prose but also, by turns, poetic, lyrical, and dramatic. Each of the characters has a story to tell and only gradually do the fifteen tales interweave into a saga of oppression and joy, revenge and celebration. The book continues the themes set forth in the earlier novels, this time extending the female quest into the spiritual as well as the political and psychic realms. The women of the house create ceremonies to celebrate stages in a woman's life including the advent of menstruation, love, marriage, birth, motherhood, menopause, and death. There are abandonments, betrayals, disappointments, and deaths, but the novel ultimately ends triumphant, affirming the strength of a female tradition that the different characters discover and create during the course of the novel itself.

Broner's fiction has gained increasing critical attention and is at the forefront of a contemporary burgeoning of fiction by Jewish feminists. As a reviewer for *Ms.*, a frequent speaker at women's conferences, a playwright, and a novelist, Broner has added an important counterbalance to the prevailing masculine tradition in contemporary American-Jewish writing.

Abraham Cahan
(7 July 1860-31 August 1951)

Jules Chametzky
University of Massachusetts

See also the Cahan entries in *DLB 9, American Novelists, 1910-1945*, and *DLB 25, American Newspaper Journalists, 1901-1925*.

SELECTED BOOKS: *Social Remedies* (New York: New York Labor News Co., 1889);
Yekl: A Tale of the New York Ghetto (New York: Appleton, 1896);
The Imported Bridegroom and Other Stories of the New York Ghetto (New York & Boston: Houghton Mifflin, 1898);

The White Terror and the Red: A Novel of Revolutionary Russia (New York: Barnes, 1905; London: Hodder & Stoughton, 1905);
Rafael Naarizokh: An Erzaylung Vegin a Stolyer Vos Iz Gekommen Zum Saykhl ["Rafael Naarizokh: A Story of a Carpenter Who Came to His Senses"] (New York: Forward Press, 1907);
Historia fun di Fareingte Shtaaten ["History of the United States"], 2 volumes (New York: Forward Publishing Company, 1910, 1912);
Neshoma Yesoroh ["The Transcendent Spirit"];

Fanny's Khasonim ["Fanny's Suitors"] (New York: Forward Association, 1913?);

The Rise of David Levinsky (New York & London: Harper, 1917);

Bleter fun Mein Leben, 5 volumes (New York: Forward Association, 1926-1931); volumes 1 and 2 republished as *The Education of Abraham Cahan*, translated by Leon Stein, Abraham P. Conan, and Lynn Davison (Philadelphia: Jewish Publishing Society of America, 1969);

Palestina ["Palestine"] (New York: Forward Publishing Association, 1934);

Rashel: A Biografia ["Raschell: A Biography"] (New York: Forward Publishing Association, 1938);

Yekl and The Imported Bridegroom and Other Stories of Yiddish New York (New York: Dover, 1970).

Abraham Cahan was a founder of the great Yiddish newspaper the *Jewish Daily Forward* in 1897 and its senior editor from 1903 until his death in 1951. In this role he played a crucial part in the acculturation of the Eastern European Jewish immigrant through the paper's persistent use of an Americanized Yiddish and with the popularizing and instructive features he introduced into its pages (such as the "Bintel Brief"—letters to the editor). He also produced a considerable body of fiction, mostly written in English from the 1890s until 1917. These stories and novels deal largely with the themes of accommodation and acculturation of the immigrant. As an imaginative writer and journalist Cahan was unique, mediating among several languages and cultures: Yiddish-Jewish, American-English, Russian. At the very beginning of the development of a significant American-Jewish literature, Cahan was a pioneer explorer of the duality of Jewishness and Americanism—a subject that has occupied every consciously American-Jewish writer in the twentieth century. His masterwork, *The Rise of David Levinsky* (1917), richly articulates an experience that is a central cultural reality not only to Jews in a country that has been called "a nation of immigrants."

Cahan was born in Podberezy, a small village near Vilna, a historic center of Jewish learning that Napoleon once called "the Jerusalem of Lithuania." His grandfather had been a rabbi, his father a *melamed* (teacher of young children) and small businessman. Cahan was educated in various Hebrew schools, studied briefly in a yeshiva, and mastered Russian in order to attend in 1877 the newly founded Vilna Teachers' Institute—a government-sponsored school for Jewish teachers in which Yiddish was prohibited. By the time he was

Abraham Cahan, circa 1925 (Jewish Daily Forward)

graduated and certified in 1881, he had broken with traditional Judaism and been converted to socialism. He had joined an underground anti-Czarist group that read the revolutionary literature of the day, so that he was in danger when a wave of repression followed the assassination of Czar Alexander II in 1881. When the police searched Cahan's room in the provincial town in which he held his first teaching position, he knew it was time to flee. Almost by chance he joined a group of immigrants bound for America, crossed the Russian border illegally with false papers, and eventually landed in the United States on 6 June 1882. At the time he considered himself primarily a Russian revolutionary with very shadowy ideas at best about America. As he wrote in his autobiography, not until he saw a cat on the dock did he believe the United States existed in the same world as Russia, Austria, and England.

Initially, Cahan was immersed almost entirely in the world of the Russian-Jewish East Side intelligentsia. He quickly became a leading figure, renowned as a radical agitator who, two months after his arrival, gave the first socialist speech to be delivered in the U.S. in Yiddish; as a labor organizer who in 1884 helped organize the first Jewish tailors' union; and as a radical editor who in 1886 coedited the first Yiddish-language socialist weekly (*Neie Tzeit*). He was protean in his gifts and activities: he was also for many years a teacher of English in Young Men's Hebrew Association evening schools that became part of the public school system and a journalist who wrote in three languages. These occupations pushed him into broader currents of New York and American life—a life whose color, pace, and variety, and in which "a shister [shoemaker] became a mister and a mister a shister" always fascinated him. Within a year of arrival, his first piece in English appeared, a letter denouncing the Romanovs in Russia, published on the front page of the *New York World*. He was also contributing to Russian newspapers and journals in St. Petersburg and continued his prolific Yiddish radical journalism well into the 1890s.

In 1897, shortly after a factional dispute forced him to resign from the newly founded *Daily Forward*, he was employed by Lincoln Steffens in the city room of the *New York Commercial Advertiser*, a connection that lasted four years. During that time Cahan expanded his knowledge of American life, working as a police reporter, writing human-interest stories about Jewish life on the East Side and recording immigrant dramas at the point of entry, doing interviews with figures as varied as William McKinley, Prince Kropotkin, and Buffalo Bill. His first novel in English, *Yekl: A Tale of the New York Ghetto* (1896), and numerous stories had been published by then, so he cut quite a figure with the young intellectuals and aspiring writers Steffens brought to work for him. Among these was Hutchins Hapgood who, like Steffens, loved the Jewish East Side and, led and instructed by Cahan, produced in 1902 his beautiful study of the inner life of that district, *The Spirit of the Ghetto*. In turn, Cahan brought over to his Yiddish journalism and increasingly moderate socialism the pragmatic and liberal tendencies of the *Commercial Advertiser* experience.

When Cahan left the *Commercial Advertiser* he thought he would continue his efforts at a literary career in English. In 1903 the Kishinev massacre of Jews was an event that focused for Cahan and other Jewish intellectuals committed to universalist enlightenment ideals their deep, irrevocable involvement with a specifically Jewish fate and identity. Cahan was the undisputed leader of Jewish jour-

nalism, with a solid reputation and connections in the American literary community. When he was asked to return to the editorship of the *Daily Forward*, he could not refuse. With the stipulation that he would have absolute command of the enterprise, he returned to the world of Yiddish journalism for the rest of his long life.

Throughout Cahan's early career, one can discern the outlines of his unique abilities and the special position he occupied. First of all, his was a complex sensibility, that of an intellectual and writer nurtured by Russian and American cultures as well as by a distinctly Jewish life. These elements were always to remain part of him, complicating the effort at cultural synthesis he often attempted, trying to reconcile the contradictory elements of an experience that was to some extent paradigmatic for his immigrant generation. He was an interpreter of American life to his Jewish readers, while American journals solicited his views on Russian revolutionary matters and on the effects of the Dreyfus affair among Jews. His literary masters were mostly Russian (Tolstoy and Chekhov, chiefly), which was the language of his intellectual development, but he read Henry James and all of William Dean Howells, and English was the language of his serious literary aspirations. His chief gift as a journalist and imaginative writer was his ability to gauge his different audiences and to be a lucid interpreter for them of unknown areas of life and thought.

Cahan began to write fiction cautiously—in Yiddish, for the *Arbeiter Zeitung*, a radical paper he edited for the Socialist Labor party. His first story was "Mottke Arbel un zayn shiddokh" (1892). It tells of a low-bred immigrant whose modest success in America enables him to contract a marriage arrangement by mail with the daughter of his former employer in Russia; at the end he is frustrated when his prospective bride leaves the boat on the arm of another immigrant to whom she became engaged on the voyage. The story was well received by Cahan's readers, encouraging him in his budding literary aspirations. Its translated version, called "A Providential Match," was published in *Short Stories* in 1895 and was read by William Dean Howells, who remembered Cahan from an earlier meeting when Howells was engaged in research for *A Traveler from Altruria* (1894). On the strength of this story Howells encouraged Cahan to do a longer work in English on New York's growing East European Jewish community. The result was *Yekl: A Tale of the New York Ghetto*.

First, however, Cahan wrote another story in

Yiddish called "Die Zwei Shiddokhim" ("The Two Matches")—a slight tale involving a misunderstanding about romantic proprieties which leads to two unsuccessful marriages—and an ambitious didactic novel that was serialized for many issues in the *Arbeiter Zeitung*. The novel, never translated into English, was called *Rafael Naarizokh* and subtitled in its earliest book version *A Story of a Carpenter Who Came to His Senses* (1907). By 1917 the novel had gone through six editions, the final one considerably enlarged over the first. It tells of a simple immigrant's growing class-consciousness in America and his conversion to socialism—the ultimate "Song of Songs" that he has been looking for all his life. Largely a vehicle for transmitting socialist ideas, the story avoids dry didacticism (usually) through its twenty-one chapters with sharp use of details from the street, shop, and café and overall wit and humor.

Rafael, its central character, is innocent but good-natured, with considerable charm—traits that alleviate the weight of theory and polemic that freight the book. He also employs a homey vernacular to communicate his ideas, mostly to his crusty wife, who also enlivens the proceedings by her earthiness. For years Cahan had been writing a column called "The Proletarian Maggid [Preacher]" in which he drew socialist morals from traditional Torah stories, and another entitled "The Hester Street Reporter," which recorded ordinary events of everyday East Side life. Both efforts proved valuable training for the developing realist writer, providing the foundation for *Rafael Naarizokh* and the fiction in English that followed.

Yekl, sponsored and supported by Howells, was to make Cahan part of the New York literary scene. Howells had retitled the novel (Cahan at first had called it "Yankel the Yankee") and helped get it published. He then reviewed the book in glowing terms for the *New York World*, hailing Cahan, along with Stephen Crane, as "a new star of realism." Although the novel did not sell well, it tapped an important spring of creativity in Cahan. *Yekl: A Tale of the New York Ghetto* is a short novel, significant for Cahan personally and also a significant moment in America's cultural and literary life. It is perhaps the first novel written in the period of the so-called second immigration by an immigrant wholly about the immigrant experience—about the gains and losses involved in adaptation to the new land. Its persistent vitality is attested to by the success in the 1970s of the film *Hester Street*, based on the novel.

The novel's central character, Jake Podgorny ("Yekl" in the old country), discards almost all his Old World values in a mere three years and is seemingly self-satisfied with a crude smattering of new ones. Apparently single as the story opens, Jake flirts with the women in his shop, enjoys dance halls, and prides himself on picking up the slang of sports, unaware of the incongruities of his fractured English. The drama of the story involves his response to the European wife, Gitl, for whom he sends when he guiltily recalls his duty. Her Old World ways alienate him, and despite her efforts to change he divorces her in order to marry a more Americanized young woman with whom he had become involved earlier. Slight though it seems as a story, and callow though the hero is, serious themes are explored in the novel. Jake has experimented with an unfamiliar emotion called love and, at the end, feels stirring in himself, however faintly articulated, guilt and uncertainty about his condition. Part of Cahan's achievement in *Yekl* is to identify the clash between a dense and exciting new reality and the pull of a dreamlike past. He also sees that the clash is poignant, because those involved are unable in an unfamiliar language and culture to articulate or control the feelings of fragmentation, incompleteness, that accompany it. It is the quintessential immigrant or ethnic theme, explored by Cahan in the areas of sex and language that became staples of imaginative treatments by later generations of writers.

In the spate of stories that followed *Yekl*, Cahan moved from exploration of the interesting social surface of this experience to, ultimately, more penetrating psychological investigation of its inner meanings. Thus in the collection *The Imported Bridegroom and Other Stories of the New York Ghetto* (1898), "A Providential Match," "A Sweat-Shop Romance," "A Ghetto Wedding," "Circumstances," and the title story all deal with the social dimensions of Jewish-American immigrant ghetto life, emphasizing the impact of America upon the immigrant, much as in *Yekl*.

In "A Sweat-Shop Romance" Cahan introduces some of the realities of the sweatshop—the crowding, the scramble for work—but not too starkly; there is an attempt to make the characters rounded people, capable of human emotions, rather than protest-poster figures—voiceless victims merely. The dialogue is realistic, though the tale, written before *Yekl*, ends in a romantic glow (in his autobiography Cahan wonders "how on earth did it pop into my head?"). The others were written after *Yekl* and show more sophistication—even the slight O. Henry-like tale "A Ghetto Wedding" (in which the impoverished couple are disappointed by the small amount of gifts they receive after investing all they own in a splashy wedding) ends in a magical moment when they are suddenly surprised on the dismal streets by a feeling of bliss in their union. "Circumstances" is the brilliant tale of a Russian-Jewish intellectual couple whose marriage and aspirations disintegrate under the brutal economic impact of their New York ghetto existence. It combines a critique of the shallowness of American culture with an understanding that anti-Semitism made life in Russia also impossible for them. "The Imported Bridegroom" is the longest story in the collection and in its sophistication and complexity the climax of Cahan's development as a writer up to 1898. A retired wealthy widower named Asriel Stroon, unhappy with American prospects, brings from his home village in Russia a bridegroom steeped in traditional religious learning for his modern and Americanized daughter. The daughter agrees to marry the pious talmudist only if he agrees to study (secretly) for medical school. The tables are turned on the father when the learned prodigy abandons religion for skeptical and secular ideas. The imported bridegroom disappoints Asriel's daughter as well by going beyond her bourgeois aspirations for him (she is an "alrightnik," a term Cahan coined), becoming a pure intellectual passionately concerned with impractical political and philosophical ideas.

The six stories Cahan published in leading periodicals between 1899 and 1901 broke new ground for him, probing more deeply into the psychological consequences of the clash of cultures embodied in the immigrant experience. In their order of publication, these stories are "The Apostate of Chego-Chegg," "Rabbi Eleizer's Christmas," "The Daughter of Avrom Leib," "A Marriage by Proxy: A Story of the City," "Dumitru and Sigrid," and "Tzinchadzi of the Catskills."

"The Apostate of Chego-Chegg" is about a young Jewish woman who becomes a Christian in Poland in order to marry the Polish youth she loves. In America she decides to leave him because she misses intensely the sense of community provided by the old faith but then, responsive to his loneliness and need of her, chooses not to abandon him. The story is almost allegorical, transplanting an Old World *shtetl* and its values to a Long Island pastoral setting in order to probe questions of attitude, belief, and behavior appropriate to the New World. Cahan works out a complex attitude toward past and present, suffused with an understanding of the shifts and bewilderments the immigrant's condition engenders. "Rabbi Eleizer's Christmas" and "The

Daughter of Avrom Leib" are stories written from deep within knowledge of Jewish life, which is presented without apology to an American audience. The title characters are, in a sense, displaced people, but in their acceptance of the realities of their condition and the richness of their Jewish experience, there is no room for the reader to feel superiority—a clear shift from *Yekl*. Rabbi Eliezer is a book peddler on the East Side whose Old Testament appearance encourages two Gentile social workers to look upon him as a kind of exotic art object. On his part, however, his articulate comprehension of the concrete realities of his own situation (Cahan allows him fluent English) undercuts any effort to see him so condescendingly. In "The Daughter of Avrom Leib" an alienated but successful immigrant businessman (a forerunner of David Levinsky) woos a cantor's daughter out of a sentimental yearning for an image of wholeness he glimpses in Jewish ritual and religion. Because she is aware of his self-centeredness and inability to see her truly as an Other, her final acceptance of him is ironic and uncertain, lending the story a decidedly modern flavor.

The other stories are about non-Jewish immigrants but explore further the themes of displacement, fragmentation, and loneliness. "A Marriage by Proxy" and "Dumitru and Sigrid" are primarily anecdotes, drawn from Cahan's experience as a reporter. The first is about an Italian couple whose marriage is arranged by mail through the intercession of his handsome young brother; the union suffers from that unpromising beginning, but after advice from a fortune-teller, it works. The second is slightly more complex, about a couple—he Rumanian, she Swedish—who meet in the detention shed at Ellis Island, communicate movingly with the aid of dictionaries, fall in love, and are separated. When they meet again years later they cannot recapture in their harsh new immigrant English the depth of feeling of the earlier time. There is a serious theme at work here, despite Cahan's anecdotal style.

"Tzinchadzi of the Catskills" is more ambitiously conceived and executed. Tzinchadzi is a Georgian immigrant, a master horseman who originally came to America to perform at the Chicago World's Fair. The narrator meets him at a Catskill resort where the bearded horseman appears in order to sell Circassian wares to the bored guests. The narrator meets him again years later on the Staten Island ferry—Tzinchadzi has shaved his beard, taken the name Jones, and become a successful American businessman. His last words, in this the last short story Cahan wrote—"I have plenty of money; but if you want to think of a happy man, think of Tzinchadzi of the Catskills, not of Jones of New York"—anticipate Cahan's major achievement, *The Rise of David Levinsky*.

After "Tzinchadzi of the Catskills" Cahan briefly attempted a free-lance existence. He planned a novel called "The Chasm" that he never completed and for which no manuscript has been found and wrote upon the editor's request a Yiddish novella for the *Forward* entitled *Neshoma Yeseroh* (a term for the transcendent spirit that supposedly descends on Jewish households on the Sabbath). In *Neshoma Yesorah* Cahan deplored to everyone's satisfaction the loss of idealism in the Jewish socialist community. The novella, along with another written a few years later, *Fanny's Khasonim* ("Fanny's Suitors"), has never been translated into English.

Cahan's eerily prophetic novel *The White Terror and the Red: A Novel of Revolutionary Russia* was published in 1905, shortly before the first Russian Revolution and its cruel aftermath in anti-Jewish riots. The novel was his longest book to date (forty-two chapters) and grappled with reconciling a Jewish consciousness to the demands of a revolutionary spirit. It focused on the events leading up to and following upon the assassination of Czar Alexander in 1881—a fateful year for Cahan that set in motion Cahan's ultimate transformation from Russian revolutionary to Jewish intellectual and leader.

The novel recounts the involvement of a fictitious Russian prince, Pavel Boulakoff, with a Jewish revolutionary named Clara Yavner: their participation in the underground movement between 1874 and 1881 culminates in their arrest and imprisonment. It is a highly tendentious and didactic novel, despite Cahan's theoretical expression of opposition to and usual avoidance of such writing. Into its long and sometimes implausible narrative Cahan puts all he knows about clandestine politics and terrorism, the workings of Russian autocracy, and especially Jewish life and thought in the Pale. The material often appears in essayistic chunks, but by and large the novel is informative and worth reading. The most interesting sections deal with the efforts of Jewish intellectuals to come to grips with the anti-Semitism unleashed by the regime after the assassination. Factions of the revolutionary movement encouraged the pogroms, thinking they would be the first step in a general uprising of the peasantry. For Jewish comrades this misbegotten notion produced an existential crisis in which all their ideas had to be reevaluated in the crucible of experience. Of those who were not thoroughly dis-

illusioned or turned to private concerns exclusively, most became "particularist," turning to one or another form of Jewish nationalist consciousness. Cahan still retains nostalgia for the incandescent idealism of many of the revolutionaries—a feeling that was to cause him to welcome the 1917 revolution and not turn against it until its murderous attitude toward social democracy became abundantly clear—but he is clear-eyed about the disfigurement of those ideals by anti-Semitism. For all its faults and longeurs, *The White Terror and the Red* is a serious effort to inform his American audience about a world rooted in a historical reality they knew little of, one to which no intelligent person dared be blind. Cahan was for this public a uniquely knowledgeable interpreter of that experience.

In the eight years following, Cahan enjoyed his unusual status and influence in the Jewish world, highlighted by a triumphant ceremony for him in Carnegie Hall on the occasion of his fiftieth birthday. The *Daily Forward* was a powerful force in the community; his voice was attended to in labor circles as well as in the columns of advice he gave out to the ever-growing immigrant reading public; he printed the work of Peretz and Sholem Aleichem and translations of other writers; he was in many respects a fulfilled man. When *McClure's* magazine, a leading muckraking journal, wanted to do a piece on the success of Jewish immigrants in the business world, Cahan was obviously the person to turn to. In 1913 he accepted the commission to write two articles on the subject, but he subtly transformed the task: instead of a couple of factual articles, he composed a two-part quasifictional account of a successful businessman and called it "The Autobiography of an American Jew." It was so successful the editor asked for two more installments. These four pieces became the basis for *The Rise of David Levinsky*, published four years later.

The audacity of the book is for Cahan, the old proletarian *maggid* whose life had been spent, as he said, largely in study and writing, to tell his version of the saga of the East European Jews in New York through the first-person narration of a wealthy garment manufacturer looking back on his life and success with a mixture of self-satisfaction and regret. Into the novel Cahan put all his accumulated knowledge about writing as well as about the Jewish immigrant experience.

At the age of fifty-two and in possession of two million dollars, David Levinsky looks back upon his life. He starts with his past in a Russian *shtetl*, where his mother is killed by brutish Gentiles, and his arrival in America in the 1880s with four cents in his pocket. Ten of the novel's fourteen sections deal with the American experience: Levinsky's early dreams of college, his involvement in the clothing industry, his rise from peddler to rich man, his disappointing loves. There are vivid scenes of New York's teeming streets, the insides of shops and factories, of kitchens and apartments where generational and family conflicts are being fought out in unprecedented ways. Cahan also describes Catskill resorts, real estate speculations, and presents, above all, detailed and expert accounts of the East European Jewish takeover of the ready-made clothing industry from the German Jews. If that were all, the book would be a treasure trove of sociological and historical value; but there is more—chiefly the portrayal of the effects these changes have upon the character and soul of David Levinsky. Levinsky is in some respects a reflective intellectual, and behind him—the successful capitalist—is Cahan the reflective socialist. The ironies and subtleties are manifold. For all his supposed candor, there is something guarded in Levinsky—failures of love and a distancing of feeling emerge as the chief thread in his narrative, perhaps as a consequence of Levinsky's language that is, ultimately, lifelessly correct and formal, perhaps as part of the supreme egoism of a chilling Dreiseresque titan of industry.

At the end Levinsky questions whether his rise (the title consciously echoes Howells's *Silas Lapham*) has made him happy. He answers, predictably enough, no—he would rather have made it in a more soul-satisfying profession than business. There is much that is self-serving in Levinsky the millionaire's yearning for a more spiritually fulfilling destiny than mere material success. Yet there is a real sense in which he expresses a heartfelt and very American sense of unease at the unsatisfactoriness of his life. He notes in the conclusion that "his past and present do not comport well"—searching still for an elusive wholeness in what should be a secure American identity. One is left with a haunting sense of unfinished business in this question of who and what Americans are, as individuals and as a people—a conclusion not unlike that of *The Great Gatsby*, in which Nick Carraway observes "so we beat on, boats against the current, borne back ceaselessly into the past." That journey and the hoped-for integration of incongruous elements is a pilgrimage often made in fictional images of the American experience, and in his masterful recognition of these issues in *The Rise of David Levinsky* Abraham Cahan has written, in the guise of an "immigrant novel," an American classic.

After *The Rise of David Levinsky* Cahan was never again to attempt that journey fictionally. It was as if he had exhausted the theme or at least could go no further than this treatment of the lacerating effects of dislocation and fragmentation. Cahan turned almost entirely to the public arena. There was the World War, in which Cahan initially supported Germany against czarist autocracy but later was fully supportive of the U.S. government. The *Daily Forward* was the center of news for Jews anxious about their kin in the eastern war zones. After the war Cahan made several journeys abroad for Jewish causes. In the 1920s and 1930s he introduced the work of Sholem Asch and of Isadore Joshua Singer and Isaac Bashevis Singer to his readers. He wrote several books in Yiddish—on his two visits to Palestine recording the modulation of early anti-Zionist views and his sympathy with the socialist idealists there; on a Yiddish actress; on politics; his valuable five-volume memoir (only two volumes of which have appeared in English translation). Politically he was a power, actively anti-Stalinist, anti-fascist, and finally pro-New Deal; active and feisty always, he personally covered the Lindbergh kidnapping trial at the age of seventy-five. Increasingly imperious with old age, sharp and acerbic almost to the end, Cahan gave up the day-to-day running of the *Daily Forward* after suffering a stroke in 1946. He wrote his last book review in 1948. He died in 1951, a few years after his wife, Anna Bronstein Cahan, to whom he had been married for sixty years. They had no children.

Only recently is Cahan being seen as the first and foremost figure of the long and distinguished line of American-Jewish writers in this century. The themes he established, the methods he explored were unerringly central. He was the first to try to hold in an enriching equilibrium a European sensibility, a Jewish life, and the native American ground. If a Yiddish sensibility is indeed a factor, however transformed, in the work of more recent Jewish writers, the chief bearer and transmitter of this legacy is undoubtedly that fierce old ancestor of them all, Ab. Cahan.

Bibliographies:
Ephim Jeshurin, *Abraham Cahan Bibliography* (New York: United Vilner Relief Committee, 1941);
Sanford E. Marovitz and Lewis Fried, "Abraham Cahan (1860-1951): An Annotated Bibliography," *American Literary Realism, 1870-1910*, 3 (Summer 1970): 197-243.

References:
Jules Chametzky, *From the Ghetto: The Fiction of Ab-*

raham Cahan (Amherst: University of Massachusetts Press, 1977);

Alan Guttmann, *The Jewish Writer in America: Assimilation and the Crisis of Identity* (New York: Oxford, 1971);

Irving Howe, *World of Our Fathers: The Journey of the*

East European Jews to America and the Life They Found and Made (New York: Harcourt Brace Jovanovich, 1976);

Ronald Sanders, *The Downtown Jews: Portraits of an Immigrant Generation* (New York: Harper & Row, 1969).

Arthur A. Cohen
(25 June 1928-   )

Diane Cole

SELECTED BOOKS: *Martin Buber* (London: Bowes & Bowes, 1957; New York: Hillary House, 1957);

The Natural and the Supernatural Jew (New York: Pantheon, 1962; revised edition, New York: Behrman House, 1979);

The Carpenter Years (New York: New American Library, 1967; London: Hart-Davis, 1967);

The Myth of the Judeo-Christian Tradition (New York: Harper & Row, 1970);

A People Apart: Hasidim in America, photographs by Philip Garvin (New York: Dutton, 1970);

In the Days of Simon Stern (New York: Random House, 1973; London: Secker & Warburg, 1974);

If Not Now, When? Toward a Reconstitution of the Jewish People; Conversations Between Mordecai M. Kaplan and Arthur A. Cohen, by Cohen and Kaplan (New York: Schocken, 1973);

Osip Emilievich Mandelstam: An Essay in Antiphon (Ann Arbor, Mich.: Ardis, 1974);

Sonia Delaunay (New York: Abrams, 1975);

A Hero in His Time (New York: Random House, 1976; London: Secker & Warburg, 1976);

Acts of Theft (New York: Harcourt Brace Jovanovich, 1980; London: Secker & Warburg, 1980);

The Tremendum: A Theological Interpretation of the Holocaust (New York: Crossroad, 1981).

OTHER: *A Handbook of Christian Theology*, edited by Cohen and Marvin Halverson (New York: Meridian, 1958);

The Anatomy of Faith: Essays by Milton Steinberg, edited with an introduction by Cohen (New York: Harcourt, Brace, 1960);

Humanistic Education and Western Civilization: Essays

for Robert M. Hutchins, edited with an introduction by Cohen (New York: Holt, Rinehart & Winston, 1964);

Arguments and Doctrines: A Reader of Jewish Thinking in the Aftermath of the Holocaust, edited by Cohen (New York: Harper & Row, 1970);

The New Art of Color: The Writings of Robert and Sonia Delaunay, edited with an introduction by Cohen (New York: Viking, 1978);

The Jews: Essays from Martin Buber's Journal "Der Jude," 1916-1928, edited with an introduction by Cohen (University: University of Alabama Press, 1980).

SELECTED PERIODICAL PUBLICATIONS: "Why I Choose To Be a Jew," *Harper's* (April 1959); republished in *The Judaic Tradition*, edited by Nahum N. Glatzer (Boston: Beacon Press, 1969), pp. 744-755;

"Ferreting the Word," *Congress Bi-Weekly* (21 June 1974): 16-17;

"Our Narrative Condition," *Present Tense*, 8 (Summer 1980): 58-60.

As author or editor of nearly twenty books, Arthur A. Cohen has produced work whose erudition, invention, and passion have established him as one of American Judaism's foremost men of letters. Although probably best known for his 1973 novel, *In the Days of Simon Stern*, Cohen has distinguished himself as theologian, novelist, art historian, and literary critic.

Arthur A. Cohen was born in New York City on 25 June 1928. He received his bachelor's degree from the University of Chicago in 1946 and a master's degree in 1949. While at Chicago, Cohen, the son of Isidore Meyer and Bess Junger Cohen,

Arthur A. Cohen, 1976 (photo by Pepe Diniz)

affluent, nonobservant Jewish parents, underwent a religious crisis when confronted, as he put it, with "the recognition that Western culture is a Christian culture, that Western values are rooted in the Greek and Christian tradition." Having never before considered the question of faith, Cohen weighed the possibility of converting to Christianity, but "retraced the path backwards through Christianity to Judaism" under the guidance of rabbi and philosopher Milton Steinberg. This experience, described in Cohen's essay "Why I Choose To Be a Jew," lies at the heart of much of Cohen's work. His concern with what he has called, in the title of one book, *The Myth of the Judeo-Christian Tradition* and his attempt to discover a workable theology for Judaism are two of his most insistent themes.

In 1950, Cohen left Chicago to study medieval Jewish philosophy at the Jewish Theological Seminary in New York. After two years, however, he left to pursue a career in publishing.

In 1951, while still at J.T.S., Cohen had founded the Noonday Press with the poet Cecil Hemley. When Cohen left Noonday in 1954, he founded another publishing house, Meridian

Books. He remained its president until 1960. He moved to Holt, Rinehart & Winston in 1962, where he served first as the director of its religion department, and then, from 1964 until 1968, as editor in chief and vice-president of the General Books Division. Since 1974 he has owned and run Ex Libris, a Manhattan bookstore specializing in the original documents of twentieth-century art. He is married to the artist Elaine Firstenberg Lustig and has one daughter, Tamar Judith Cohen.

During his years in publishing, Cohen managed to pursue a life in Jewish scholarship. His first book, *Martin Buber*, was published in 1957 as part of the British series Studies in Modern European Literature and Thought. In this concise yet comprehensive introduction to the Jewish thinker, Cohen traces Buber's search for "the Holy within the concrete."

Cohen's own beliefs and theological biases are more evident in his next full-length book, *The Natural and the Supernatural Jew,* published first in 1962 (a revised edition appeared in 1979). A critical survey of Jewish thought from the late fifteenth century to the present, it is perhaps his best known work of theology. Here Cohen distinguishes between what he calls the natural Jew, who is shaped by history and environment, and the supernatural Jew, whose messianic faith transcends history.

Concerned "less with Jewish history as such . . . than with a specific phenomenon: the Jewish mind as it has thought and continues to think about its supernatural vocation," Cohen nevertheless presents his argument in the context of history—the history of Jewish theology. Cohen augments his earlier study of Buber with discussions of Moses Mendelssohn and other figures of the German Enlightenment and of such figures of the German Jewish Renaissance as Hermann Cohen, Leo Baeck, and Franz Rosenzweig, the last of whom Cohen counts as a major influence on his own work.

Cohen sees all these thinkers as having existed in a continuum. With the advent of American Judaism in this century, however, Cohen asserts that "The continuity is broken. There is no chain of succession which binds the traditions of European Jewry to the traditions of American Judaism; no neat lines of transfer and influence. . . . Whether the Jewish genius for religion will display the tensility, urgency, and creativity to make American Judaism something more than a boring legacy of conservation remains to be seen."

Sadness and anger can be sensed in the book's last third, which describes the predicament of American Judaism today and pleads for a new approach to Jewish theology. Cohen, who is essentially Orthodox in his beliefs, takes particular exception to the views of Mordecai Kaplan and the Reconstructionist movement. "The future of Judaism as a civilization," Cohen writes, "rests only upon a renewal of Israel's relation with God and consequent restimulation of the vocation of Jacob, which was to wrestle with God until He be found and to release Him only after having won from him the promise of salvation."

In parts of this book, as in others, Cohen himself seems to be wrestling with faith or history. As he seeks to discover a language to describe his beliefs, Cohen often rises to an impassioned eloquence. On occasion, the language can become clotted, and to the lay reader some points may be lost in philosophical terminology. This last fault is minor, however. Cohen's books are never dry, even in their most complex arguments. His voice is clear and vital because his ideas are both reasoned and deeply felt. However much one wishes to argue with Cohen—and many of his essays invite controversy—the reader always feels himself to be in the presence of a brilliant thinker who stubbornly insists on being

heard and who will wait, with the same stubborn patience, for his questions to be answered.

These qualities are nowhere more evident than in *The Tremendum: A Theological Interpretation of the Holocaust* (1981). Conceding that his critics were correct in that previously "I had ignored Auschwitz," Cohen grapples with the recognition of radical evil. He asserts that the enormity of the Holocaust demands the creation of a new theological language which will force a rethinking and will therefore allow discussion of what happened in the death camps. In that new language, the concept of God—the Jewish God as well as the Christian God—must be redefined since the Holocaust must be seen as an event in human, not simply Jewish, history.

This final argument amplifies Cohen's concluding plea for the founding of a "Judeo-Christian humanism" in his 1970 collection of essays, *The Myth of the Judeo-Christian Tradition*. Jews and Christians, Cohen asserts in this volume, do not share a common religious or doctrinal tradition; rather they have lived in theological enmity. What separates the two religions is their basic views of the messiah: the Jews, in rejecting Jesus as the messiah, continue to await redemption.

Redemption: this theme comes to mind immediately in thinking of Cohen's fiction. While the reader of Cohen the novelist need not be aware of Cohen the theologian, the author's philosophical and theological pursuits do spill over to enrich his four novels. In fact, it is the very wealth of his ideas that gives his novels their distinctive cast.

Though less successful than his later books, Cohen's first novel, *The Carpenter Years* (1967), is a skillful rendering of Jewish life in Christian America. The protagonist Morris Edelman transforms himself from a doubting New York Jew into Edgar Morris, the Christian director of a small-town YMCA, where his abandoned son Danny tracks him down to confront him with the past. According to Cohen, this story "set forth some of the premises of Jewish anti-Christianity"—the main one being that "The Jewish myth of the Gentile was as banal and foolish as most anti-Semitism."

But the book also concerns the spiritual quest, in America's secular society, of the father and his estranged son. Edgar's conversion to Christianity seems less a renunciation of the Jewish religion than an abandonment of the American-Jewish dream of success. To Edgar, Judaism does not mean faith, but an immigrant's drive to raise his family out of poverty. He fails in business and therefore feels himself to be a failed Jew. Uncomfortable among

Jews, Edgar feels further alienated as a Jew among Christians. When Edgar flees his singularly unappealing, guilt-inducing wife at last, he finds in his new identity as a Christian more comfort than faith as he learns to be simply ordinary. "It's the carpenter years of Jesus that interest me, the unknown years, where all of us live and die most of our lives," a minister tells Edgar. The demand is not to become famous, or successful, but "to become exemplary while remaining unimportant."

Like his father, Edgar's son Danny feels boxed in by his mother and her Jewish God who "only care about death." He seeks solace in psychology—a new God. His final, brief encounter with his father in some way redeems him—it frees him from the past. He is lucky. Edgar chooses not to be a Jew, but it does not free him from himself.

Though the novel commands interest and respect, there are flaws. It lacks the imaginative freedom and inventiveness that characterize Cohen's other novels, particularly *In the Days of Simon Stern*. A sense of constraint pervades the book—it is shorter by half than his subsequent novels. The tone is severe, and the characters do not seem to know how to laugh, especially at themselves. While Cohen is probably right to identify the American Jew's attitude toward his religion with his feelings about his family, Edgar's Jewish wife suffers her fate so coldly that it's no wonder that any man would wish to leave her.

Nevertheless, *The Carpenter Years* does succeed in giving dramatic life to its characters' spiritual conflicts. Cohen is at his liveliest here when the dialogue turns to philosophical debate. The characters, like their author, care fiercely about ideas, and the reader unwilling to follow a discussion and perhaps learn something new ought to stay away from the work of Arthur A. Cohen.

Cohen has said that in his novels he seeks to give the reader "a tale plus something else." He sees fiction as a "smuggling device" which will allow him to follow the advice of philosopher Franz Rosenzweig "to smuggle Jewish ideas into general culture." Cohen's modestly accomplished first novel began that task; in his second, he revealed himself a master—both at smuggling and at creating novels.

In the Days of Simon Stern displays Cohen's gifts both as a storyteller and as a thinker. He has justly described the book as a "ragbag" of Jewish history, literature, and ideas, with digressions that range from a parable about the last Jew on earth to discussions of the meaning of the Jewish holiday Purim and the nature of the Holocaust. A few of these could be cut without loss. And yet for the most

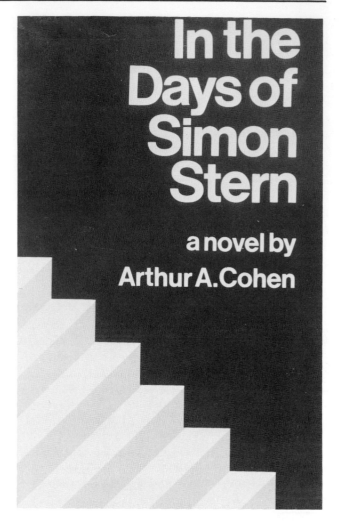

Dust jacket for the 1973 novel that Cohen termed a "ragbag" of Jewish history, literature, and ideas

part, the book's tales within tales and essays within essays fit together. The novel's unifying principle is its energy—the energy of imagination.

The blind scribe Nathan of Gaza chronicles the life and times of Simon Stern, messiah. The son of immigrant parents, Simon grows up in poverty on New York's Lower East Side. Simon is wealthy in money-making schemes, however, and soon makes a fortune in real estate. His rise from floor-sweeper to millionaire would please anyone who holds the American dream dear.

Tragedy soon strikes, however. In keeping with a secret family prophecy, Simon's parents die in a fire for which he is inadvertently responsible. Although the law clears him of blame, Simon accepts his burden of guilt. How will he redeem himself? The family prophecy also holds that Simon is the messiah—the one who will redeem others.

At the start of World War II, Simon hears Chaim Weizmann tell an audience at Madison Square Garden something that few Americans wish to believe, that fewer still wish to be responsible for knowing. Weizmann reports that millions of Jews are being murdered by Hitler. With growing anger, Simon decides that it is time "to begin the work of redemption." He creates a Society for the Rescue and Resurrection of the Jews. With his millions, he will redeem a "symbolic remnant of survivors" by bringing them to America and installing them in a compound on the Lower East Side. Simon envisions that compound—outwardly modest, but whose interior is built to resemble the Second Temple—as "a small Bene Brak as in the days after the destruction of the ancient Temple." A flowering of Jewish cultural and intellectual achievement will take place there. The Jews will not only survive; their spirits will be healed also, and as a people, they will endure. But the survivors of Auschwitz will also "testify to the world that it is a monstrous place. . . . We shall hold up to the world the mirror of its desecration."

Simon's post-Holocaust plan ends in yet another holocaust, as it must. It must because history declares it so; the first and second temples were destroyed, and so is this attempted third one. History, in Cohen's view, repeats itself endlessly. Its cycles and patterns, he has written, present us with "a series of partial avowals and partial refusals of redemption." When Simon's compound goes up in flames, the reader understands that another cycle has ended; yet another is about to begin.

The reader also perceives that if Simon Stern is not the true messiah, neither is he the false one—not another Sabbatai Zevi. For blind Nathan of Gaza (whose name also belonged to Sabbatai Zevi's best-known follower and "prophet"), Simon is the literal savior who brought him from Auschwitz to America. For others, Simon is a messianic bearer who keeps hope alive, who reminds us of the existence of God and the possibility of redemption.

"In the end, to save his skin, Sabbatai Zevi converted to Islam, confusing his followers," Cynthia Ozick pointed out in her review of Cohen's novel. "In the end, Cohen's messiah flees the closed ghetto built out of his sacred passion for saving Jews. . . . The strangeness and the exhilaration and the power of this novel lie just in this ancient and perplexing question: whether the holy sparks that the messiah draws down from heaven are meant to fall into the uncleanness of 'the large world,' which is always the present world of all our lives; or whether the messiah must continue to tarry. In the Days of Simon Stern answers in the voice of

Scheherazade—she who, like the Jews, is every moment wary of her survival."

"The messiah is a real moment, never a psychological conceit," Nathan writes in his chronicle's last paragraph. "I think of Simon Stern as one correct moment." To believe in Simon Stern—in spite of personal rage and in the face of evil—is to affirm the words of Maimonides: "I believe in the coming of the Messiah, and even if he tarries, I will await his coming every day."

Cohen's next novel, *A Hero in His Time*, appeared in 1976. It tells the story of a minor Soviet-Jewish poet who must choose between the conflicting demands of conscience and those of the repressive Soviet state, even if to follow conscience may be to risk survival. Cohen's short book on the real-life Soviet-Jewish poet Osip Mandelstam had appeared in 1974, and while the fictional poet's artistic achievement is in no way comparable to that of Mandelstam, one figure is reminiscent of the other.

In discussing Mandelstam in *Osip Emilievich*

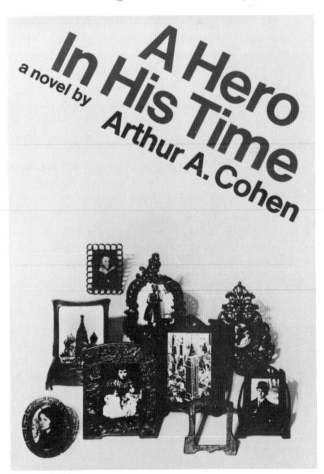

Dust jacket for Cohen's novel about a Russian-Jewish poet who must choose between the demands of his conscience and those of the Soviet state

Mandelstam: An Essay in Antiphon, Cohen had focused on the poet's determination to continue writing poetry—and to remain in the Soviet Union—in spite of official harassment and persecution. In both his literary essay and in his novel, Cohen wishes to discover why it is that some men will give in—either to the pressures of the state or to suicide—while others refuse. Cohen believes that for Mandelstam, the assimilated Jew who often used Christian imagery in his poetry, at least part of the answer resided in his faith.

For the fictional Yuri Isakovsky, who in addition to being a poet is the editor of a small journal of ethnic music, the spiritual dilemma arises when the Soviet government orders him to embark on an official visit to New York. There he is to deliver a poem to a Soviet secret agent. Embedded in the poem is a coded message. But the poem—which Yuri must acknowledge as his own—does not meet the poet's artistic standards. In improving its stanzas, Yuri revises the secret message out of existence.

The book's tone is satiric, and as in all good satire, beneath the humor lies great anger. In the sections set in Moscow, Cohen details the ways in which an oppressive state controls and corrupts its citizenry—through fear, intimidation, and the promise of material rewards for those who shape their morality to fit the official state mold. Cohen's portrait of an official "people's poet"—a man whose career and ego remind one of Yevtushenko—is particularly scathing. What interests Cohen more than those who conform, however, are those who rebel. *A Hero in His Time* dramatizes Yuri's decision to join that last group.

His inward journey occurs during his actual journey to New York. Cohen views the city humorously, through Yuri's eyes, but the contrast between the closed society of the Soviet Union and the open society we know here is not always flattering. "In our country," Yuri observes while in New York, "it's almost a crime for old people and peasants to believe in God, but certainly a crime for an editor of an important Soviet journal. . . . But the amusing thing is that it is also a crime in this country, punishable not by loss of job and income, but by contempt. These people, not unlike ourselves, think such beliefs as all right for children, ladies, and high-strung mental cases, but not for scientists and intellectuals."

The key to Yuri's perseverance lies in his faith—both in God and in art. Pressed to defect in order to gain artistic as well as religious freedom, Yuri refuses. America may be Simon Stern's haven; for Yuri, the only refuge is his art. At novel's end,

Yuri's return to the Soviet Union strikes him as an act of tenacity rather than of heroism, for he cannot write his poetry except in his native Russian. As for Soviet Jewry, Yuri explains to an uncomprehending American, "if all leadership of Jews gets out, two million ordinary, uneducated working-class Jews will be deserted, left to their fate. No one to worry about them." His act is also redemptive: even if he is imprisoned, he will have proved that his soul belongs to himself alone. He will have preserved the freedom of his imagination.

Unlike *In the Days of Simon Stern*, *A Hero in His Time* does not attempt to cram a 4,000-year heritage into a single volume. It does address a wide range of moral, aesthetic, political, and religious dilemmas. Yuri's journal—which is interspersed throughout the narrative—at times reads like short sketches for longer essays which the poet (or Arthur Cohen) will someday compose. The book entertains and instructs. These twin goals may be old-fashioned, but while the book cannot duplicate its predecessor's explosive energy, its execution is controlled and fresh.

Yuri Isakovsky's religion is literature; the hero of Cohen's most recent novel, *Acts of Theft* (1980), worships art. The novel differs from the work that preceded it in that it contains no overt Jewish themes. Like *In the Days of Simon Stern*, *Acts of Theft* does include many philosophical and theological digressions. But Stefan Mauger, the main character in this novel, more closely resembles a sinner than a messiah. An impoverished Austrian aristocrat, sculptor (he is a student of Brancusi), and art collector, Mauger masterminds a heist of pre-Columbian art treasures in Mexico. As the plot unfolds, Mauger and Cohen's other characters—a collection of art critics and aficionados—debate the meanings and manifestations of idolatry, art, and religious faith.

Cohen is himself the owner of a rare book and art gallery in New York City, and his wife is an artist. A man of diverse interests and talents, Cohen has also written and edited books about the twentieth-century artists Robert and Sonia Delaunay. *Acts of Theft* therefore may in some sense be seen as an attempt to combine Cohen's career as an art historian and collector with his deeper theological interests.

Unfortunately, the result is not entirely successful. Mark Shechner, writing in the *New York Times Book Review*, complained that "Mr. Cohen is basically an essayist starting out with a problem and seeking to concretize it in fiction. Since the problem here is theophany, knowledge of the Infinite, Mr.

Cohen plies us with vivid and passionate yearnings that overpower his plot and overwhelm his sentences."

Cohen is currently completing a new novel, "An Admirable Woman," whose main character bears a strong resemblance to—but is not, he says—Hannah Arendt.

Cohen sees himself in the tradition of European rather than American writers, and his estimation is just. Cohen is never afraid to take the risk of exposing his audience to ideas. His sensibility is that of the novelist-philosopher. To be sure, there are moments in his novels when the reader cries for more story and less philosophy, but the characters about whom Cohen chooses to write are no less caught up in the vast life of the mind than is the author himself.

Cohen is reminiscent of the European rather than the American tradition, too, in his refusal to be classified as one kind of writer only. He is both theologian and novelist. Though ideas attract him, he is not satisfied with ideas in the abstract. His imagination also seizes on the dramas that make up people's lives. There would be no point in discuss-

ing faith, after all, if there existed no men and women to believe—or to deny belief. Cohen's purpose as a writer is not to convert readers, but to illuminate the intricate and various pathways of faith and to show the blackness of history. In presenting his vision of the world, Arthur A. Cohen helps clarify our own. His voice arouses his readers to thought, perplexity, the possibility of faith, and finally, the perception of art.

References:
Diane Cole, "Profession: Renaissance Man; Profile of Arthur A. Cohen," *Present Tense*, 9 (Fall 1981): 32-35;

Thomas Lask, "Publishing: From Art Books to a Novel About Art," *New York Times*, 22 February 1980, III: 24;

Cynthia Ozick, "In the Days of Simon Stern," *New York Times Book Review*, 3 June 1973, p. 6;

Peter S. Prescott, "The Last Jew," *Newsweek*, 81 (11 June 1973): 108;

Mark Shechner, "Graven Images and Other Temptations," *New York Times*, 9 March 1980, III: 10.

E. L. Doctorow
(6 January 1931-   )

Mildred Louise Culp

See also the Doctorow entries in *DLB 2, American Novelists Since World War II*, and *DLB Yearbook: 1980*.

BOOKS: *Welcome to Hard Times* (New York: Simon & Schuster, 1960); republished as *Bad Man from Bodie* (London: Deutsch, 1961);
Big As Life (New York: Simon & Schuster, 1966);
The Book of Daniel (New York: Random House, 1971; London: Macmillan, 1971);
Ragtime (New York: Random House, 1975; London: Macmillan, 1976);
Drinks Before Dinner (New York: Random House, 1979);
Loon Lake (New York: Random House, 1980; London: Macmillan, 1980).

PLAY: *Drinks Before Dinner*, New York Shakespeare Festival, Estelle R. Newman Theatre, 22 November 1978.

PERIODICAL PUBLICATIONS: "The Bomb Lives!," *Playboy*, 21 (March 1974): 114-116, 208-216;
"After the Nightmare," *Sports Illustrated*, 44 (28 June 1976): 72-82;
"False Documents," *American Review*, 231, no. 26 (November 1977): 215-232;
"Living in the House of Fiction," *Nation*, 226 (22 April 1978): 459-462;
"Dream Candidate: The Rise of Ronald Reagan," *Nation*, 1 (19-26 July 1980): 65, 82-84.

One of the most celebrated and controversial novelists of the past two decades, E. L. Doctorow has an uncanny ability to reach both the general audience (*The Book of Daniel, Welcome to Hard Times*, and *Ragtime* have been made into movies) and the literary scholar, with works that challenge and expand accepted definitions of the art of the novel. He

E. L. Doctorow (photo by Layle Silbert)

has distinguished himself among American-Jewish writers by the diversity of his work: an allegorical Western, a science-fiction satire, three novels (one with a large component of poetry), and a play. Doctorow is discussed primarily as an innovator in narrative technique. Yet he is also a distinctly Jewish writer, his replication of characters and events throughout his work reflecting his concern for the persistence of moral crises in history and calling into question modern responses to the problems of evil and individual responsibility.

Born in New York City on 6 January 1931 to David Richard and Rose Levine Doctorow, he attended the Bronx High School of Science before enrolling at Kenyon College, where he studied with John Crowe Ransom. He received his A.B. with honors in 1952 and was awarded an L.H.D. in 1976. Senior editor of the New American Library from 1959 to 1964, editor in chief at Dial Press, 1964-1969, Doctorow was writer-in-residence at the University of California at Irvine (1969-1970) and later served on the faculty at Sarah Lawrence College and Yale University. In 1972 Doctorow received a National Book Award nomination for *The Book of Daniel*; in 1976 he won the National Book Critics

Circle Award and an Arts and Letters Award from the American Academy and National Institute of Arts for *Ragtime*. He lives in New Rochelle, New York, with his wife, Helen Setzer.

Doctorow's novels are demanding reading. His heroes, while not always Jewish, are with one possible exception intellectuals trying to make sense of a chaotic world infused with violence and evil. And his plots, simple and absorbing but seldom linear, serve as vehicles to analyze the composing process as a parallel to life itself. *Welcome to Hard Times* (1960), Doctorow's Western, has been described by Victor S. Navasky as "a play against the genre." An allegory, it belongs essentially to a Jewish literary tradition, focusing on the radicality of evil and the inexplicable cruelty of the alien aggressor toward an insulated community. Set in the Dakota Territory, *Welcome to Hard Times* is narrated by Mayor Blue, the first in Doctorow's series of characters who speak about the act of writing. The plot is a unified, seemingly simple one, beginning with the brutal ravaging of a small town by Turner, the "Bad Man from Bodie," and ending with Turner's bloody retribution. Through the tale Doctorow explores the awesome force of rampant evil, the impotence of reason without will, and the morbid predictability of both. Turner is evil incarnate, and the Old West of *Welcome to Hard Times* prefigures the Holocaust. When the town becomes a conflagration in Turner's hands, its inhabitants' passivity is terrifying. Molly Riordan, the town's conscience, urges the mayor to confront Turner and she herself tries to stop Turner with a stiletto—a reminder of the impotence of weapons in the face of intractable evil. Molly's attraction to Turner symbolizes a universal fascination with the demonic. And Blue, the self-styled "promoter" of the town whose compulsive record-keeping—"it was something that had to be done"—represents the inability of the intellectual to control evil, fails to recognize the strength of Turner's power and allows it to become superhuman.

In *Welcome to Hard Times*, despite what David Emblidge has called "a spirited hopefulness," there is little cause for hope, and the radical evil is not confined to a single cowboy. *Welcome to Hard Times* is, as Marilyn Arnold has observed, "a testimony to human stories that keep repeating themselves," an early indication of Doctorow's theme of replication. The death of the Bad Man is not the end of the evil that motivated him. Wirt Williams has remarked that Doctorow, like Conrad, suggests our ability to resist evil psychically. Yet when Blue concludes the narrative, no progress has been made. "Nothing is

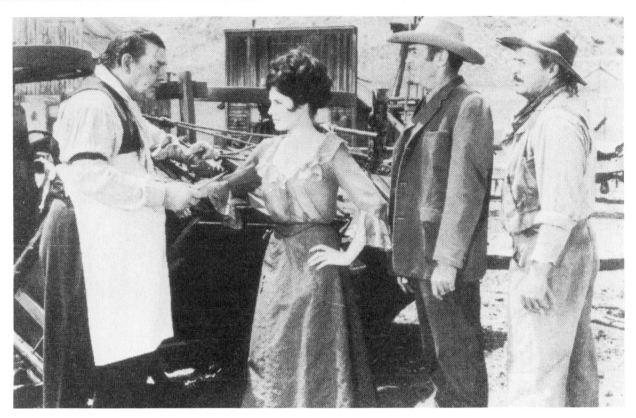

Lon Chaney, Janice Rule, Henry Fonda, and Alan Baxter in the 1967 film version of Doctorow's first novel, Welcome to Hard Times

ever buried," he says, "the earth rolls in its tracks, it never goes anywhere, it never changes."

While *Welcome to Hard Times* explores the nineteenth-century West, *Big As Life* (1966) is set in the New York of the future. Intended as satire, *Big As Life* is Doctorow's most neglected work, partly, perhaps, because the satire itself is uneven and diffused. A pair of giant creatures, "big as life," position themselves over the Pan-American Building and refuse to budge, sending the city into panic and prompting the president to send in the army and blockade Manhattan. Posited against the government's overreaction is the empty response of Wallace Creighton, the satirized intellectual who reacts like the historian he is: like Mayor Blue, he will keep records. But the satire breaks down, apparently, as the creatures become more predictable, less monstrous. Their oblivion to the panic around them, and their show of affection for each other, is mirrored in the private sweetness of a human couple, Red Bloom and Sugarbush. As Creighton comes to realize, the parallel is no accident. The creatures are monstrous products of our world; "we're joined to them, they are in our world, they *are* our world and if we destroy them we destroy ourselves." That ob-

servation, however, makes the satire less pointed. Which response is the appropriate one—the ineffective intellectualizing of Creighton, the simple-mindedness of the military, the oblivion of the lovers? If, as Barbara Estrin has suggested, *Big As Life* is a vision of Armageddon, Doctorow is indicting man's inability to respond at all. Creighton reacts to disaster by the single-minded pursuit of his record-keeping, and Red returns to hearth and home.

While satire may not be Doctorow's forte, *Big As Life* does prefigure his next work, artistically and ideologically iconoclastic, filled with grotesque minor characters, and challenging in its questions about the human condition. Published in 1971, *The Book of Daniel* was Doctorow's most compelling novel up to that time. Narrated by Daniel Isaacson Lewin, a graduate student at Columbia who is trying to piece his life together, *The Book of Daniel* addresses, on one level, events of the McCarthy era, specifically the case of Julius and Ethel Rosenberg, Jews electrocuted in 1953 after their conviction for espionage. Enigmatic like his Old Testament namesake, Daniel is writing in the late 1960s. His quest is agonizing and ends, as Richard Schickel has pointed out, without a shred of certainty "about the meaning of anything." The ambiguity is at once irritating and arresting. But Doctorow's failure to provide answers is evidence of a maturing of his craft. Doctorow himself admitted, in his 1977 essay "False Documents," that he had become "more interested in discovering what may be wrong with us than in expressing pieties."

Much of Doctorow's effect results from the way he approaches the art of composition in the novel. In Daniel's scrambled, episodic narration, the act of writing becomes itself part of the story; Daniel the narrator becomes linked with Mayor Blue of *Welcome to Hard Times* and anticipates the Little Boy of Ragtime and the poet in *Loon Lake*. The experiments with voice and point of view in *The Book of Daniel* suggest Doctorow's impatience with fictional forms, his attempts to reform the novel by reconstructing it. Moreover, as he has hinted in "Living in the House of Fiction," those experiments may be a metaphorical statement on "our need to transform our lives and remake ourselves."

On several levels, *The Book of Daniel* is Doctorow's most overtly Jewish work. It draws upon Jewish history and culture—the biblical Daniel, for instance, figures prominently in the narrative—and like its Old Testament namesake, it is filled with dreams and visions that remain unexplained. Daniel's sprawling ruminations call up the pogroms of czarist Russia, the great wave of Eastern European migration at the turn of the century, the sweatshop existence of first-generation immigrants, and, in Daniel's obsession with the eloctrocution of his parents, the horror of the Holocaust and the world that could permit such horror to occur. Politically, too, the novel is self-consciously Jewish, concerned as it is with class struggle and the oppression of political outcasts. When Paul and Rochelle Isaacson are imprisoned for their Communist sympathies, their incarceration suggests a wider imprisonment, that of America during the McCarthy era. If Doctorow's Daniel discovers anything, it is that for Jews there will be more questions than answers. Juxtaposed to references to the Old Testament God of justice, Daniel's story is painfully ironic. And Daniel himself becomes a prophetic figure, delivering truths that we do not want to hear, castigating us with political complacency in a nuclear age. In *The Book of Daniel*, and in his essay "The Bomb Lives!" (1974), Doctorow explores humanity's responses to the technology it has created.

Ragtime, written while the author was a Guggenheim fellow, took the literary world by storm when it appeared in 1975. An antinostalgic

Dust jacket for Doctorow's fourth novel, which focuses on the experiences of three American families during the period just before World War I

novel of replication set in the decade prior to World War I, *Ragtime* "rags" an array of historical figures, including Houdini, William Howard Taft, J. P. Morgan, John D. Rockefeller, Jung, Freud, Henry Ford, Big Bill Haywood, Scott Joplin, Emma Goldman, Thomas Edison, and Archduke Ferdinand. So carefully does Doctorow weave history with events of the imagination that by the end of the novel the nature of historical truth is called into question.

The main fictional figures are part of a triptych of families through which Doctorow delineates the American experience at the turn of the century. The first is headed by Father, the quintessential American who earns his living by manufacturing flags, bunting, and fireworks and for whom America is most properly WASPish: "no Negroes . . . no immigrants." Mother reinforces the vestiges of Victorian prudery; Mother's Younger Brother defies those standards in some of Doctorow's most graphic sex scenes; and the Little Boy in the sailor blouse records the scene. Cultural counterparts of this family are the Jewish Mameh, Tateh, and Daughter and the black family grouping of

Coalhouse Walker, Jr., Sarah, and her infant.

Through the experiences of these families Doctorow reveals a world in flux, modern culture at its birth—an era of frustration and violent change. Immigrant life on the Lower East Side and Coalhouse Walker's extended rampage both give the lie to Father's pristine vision of America. Younger Brother's sexual experience with Goldman and Evelyn Nesbitt ends in a shower of sperm "like falling ticker tape," a symbolic outpouring of frustration over the satisfactions of post-Victorian morality.

Finally, *Ragtime* is another reminder that for Doctorow writing is performance. Through the Little Boy, for whom the world, like statues in the park, seems constantly to be composing and recomposing itself "in an endless process of dissatisfaction," Doctorow creates a self-reflexive novel, one that questions not only the nature of historical truth but also the authority of the narrative voice. Critical reception of the novel has been generally favorable, though varied. Daniel Zins contends that ethnicity and racial unrest are the key issues for Doctorow; for Cobbett Steinberg the novel is a tribute to the oppressed. And, as Jonathan Raban observes, the book is Jewish, its tenements evoking the fiction of Abraham Cahan, Henry Roth, and Bernard Malamud.

Doctorow's one foray into drama, *Drinks Before Dinner*, is an almost plotless two-act play. The vision of *Drinks Before Dinner* is of a disturbingly post-existentialist world. At a gathering of friends, the main character, Edgar, whips out a pistol and harangues the others at gunpoint. Despairing about life in our time, Edgar articulates the theme that Doctorow pursues in his other works: if our civilization is to continue, we must overhaul it, while doing something about ourselves. For the distraught Edgar, automobiles become symbols for the senseless enslavement of humanity by technology; we create them, he says, then they entrap us in an automotive existence. Edgar laments that cars "suggest the dreariness of biology, the predictability of the plan of mindless excess by which we reproduce ourselves." Suicidal and out of control, Edgar presents an apocalyptic scenario that concludes with a vision of nuclear destruction.

Edgar's despair contrasts with the resigned optimism of Joel, a physician who works with "disgusting and degrading means of dying" and, almost ritualistically, performs the same operation five or six times a day. In the face of this dull existence, Joel endures. What sets him apart from the other characters is his ability to accept life for what it is,

and to keep going. Joel's response to Edgar may well be the most memorable lines in the play: "So it is clear, then, that those who do best in life are those who get on with it. Life is surely merciful to those who get on with it." A play of ideas and words, *Drinks Before Dinner* rests—as Doctorow himself admits in his introduction—on "a sense of heightened language." The barrage of words reflects Doctorow's genius as a writer, but most of his critics and his audience were unprepared for it. Judging by reviews of its 1978 production, *Drinks Before Dinner* is less effective on stage than on paper.

Loon Lake (1980), a story set during the Depression, reflects in some senses both Doctorow's most successful writing and least satisfying techniques. The novel represents the author's belief that the boundaries of fiction must be extended. In *Loon Lake*, however, the problem rests in the extension of narrative voice, an intense interiority so distressingly drawn out that the compelling quality that works so well in, say, *The Book of Daniel*, is obscured. In *Welcome to Hard Times* Doctorow demonstrates the fluidity of life; in *Loon Lake* he experiments with the fluidity of art, creating an impressive structure that suffers from less-than-successful tone and theme.

The story is narrated from several points of view, including those of Warren Penfield, a failed poet, and Joe Korzeniowski of Paterson, New Jersey. Through frequent shifts in narrative voice Doctorow assaults the most enduring fictive convention, the chronologically ordered plot. In part the brilliance of *Loon Lake* lies in Joe's tale of his life, wandering among carnival people, then living and working at the estate Loon Lake, later laboring among factory workers in Steubenville, Ohio. Through Joe's wanderings Doctorow presents a panorama of American life. What Joe comes to realize, partly through F. W. Bennett, the wealthy industrialist who owns Loon Lake and supports Penfield, is that "poverty is not a moral endowment," that the wealthy may be as scarred as the poor by their experiences. A novel of replication, *Loon Lake* suggests an underlying sameness in the lives and experiences of its characters and, by implication, of all men and women in all times. There is a sameness, too, in the need for moral regeneration. As Robert Towers has pointed out, the lake functions symbolically as a vehicle for rebirth. As the loon must dive into its blackness to resurface, be fed and replenished, so humanity must immerse itself into the depths of its being if it is to sustain itself.

The poetry of *Loon Lake* is striking yet integrated beautifully into the prose. Diane Johnson has noted that it reflects Doctorow's key moral preoccupations, from capitalism to sex. But it is more than that. Through its computer imagery and language, the poetry shows how thoroughly technology permeates even the most personal and creative of human endeavors. Technology merges with sexuality and reminiscence: "Come with me / Combust with me" and "Data comprising life F. W. Bennett undergoing review" are daring songs of American life, daringly expressed. In the poetry Doctorow is once again more than simply a quasi-historian or social/political critic. He is also calling into question the art of novel writing.

Like most novelists, Doctorow respects the boundaries of tradition. In *Loon Lake* he has created a romance in the manner of Hawthorne and social realism after Abraham Cahan and Michael Gold. Yet he will be remembered for his experiments with those boundaries: overlapping genres in *Welcome to Hard Times* and *Big As Life*, integrating fiction and history in *Ragtime*, toying with narrative voice in *The Book of Daniel* and *Loon Lake*. His next novel, Doctorow projects, will emphasize language rather than plot. But for him the two are inseparable. His concern for the pluralism of American society is mirrored in the variety of his experiments with fictive conventions; his continual grappling with the problems of the permanence of evil and the responsibilities of modern mankind are themes as time-honored as the novelistic tradition he respects. For Doctorow, writing is an act of recovery and discovery, the process of composition akin to the moral need to create and recreate. In Doctorow's hands, the novel becomes a distinctly American document that looks backward in criticism and forward in nervous anticipation, that indicts our inequities yet celebrates our diversity, that shows a distressing sameness while holding out the promise of change.

References:

Marilyn Arnold, "History as Fate in E. L. Doctorow's Tale of a Western Town," *South Dakota Review*, 18 (Spring 1980): 53-63;

Mildred L. Culp, "Women and Tragic Destiny in Doctorow's *The Book of Daniel*," *Studies in American Jewish Literature*, 2 (1982): 155-166;

David Emblidge, "Marching Backward into the Future: Progress as Illusion in Doctorow's Novels," *Southwest Review*, 62 (Autumn 1977): 397-408;

Barbara L. Estrin, "Surviving McCarthyism: E. L. Doctorow's *The Book of Daniel*," *Massachusetts Review*, 16 (Summer 1975): 577-587;

Diane Johnson, "Waiting for Righty," *New York Review of Books*, November 1980, pp. 18ff.;

Jonathan Raban, "Easy Virtue: On Doctorow's *Ragtime*," *Encounter*, 46 (February 1976): 71-74;

Bernard Rodgers, "A Novelist's Revenge: *Ragtime*," *Chicago Review*, 27 (Winter 1975-1976): 138-144;

Richard Schickel, "Review of *The Book of Daniel*," *Harper's*, 243 (August 1971): 94;

Cobbett Steinberg, "History and the Novel: Doctorow's *Ragtime*," *University of Denver Quarterly*, 10 (Winter 1976): 125-130;

Wirt Williams, "Bad Man from Bodie," *New York Times Book Review*, 25 September 1960, p. 51;

Daniel Zins, "E. L. Doctorow: The Novelist as Historian," *Hollins Critic*, 16 (December 1979): 1-14.

Stanley Elkin
(11 May 1930-   )

Doris G. Bargen

See also the Elkin entries in *DLB 2, American Novelists Since World War II*, and *DLB Yearbook: 1980*.

BOOKS: *Boswell: A Modern Comedy* (New York: Random House, 1964; London: Hamish Hamilton, 1964);

Criers and Kibitzers, Kibitzers and Criers (New York: Random House, 1966; London: Blond, 1967);

A Bad Man (New York: Random House, 1967; London: Blond, 1968);

The Dick Gibson Show (New York: Random House, 1971; London: Weidenfeld & Nicolson, 1971);

Searches and Seizures (New York: Random House, 1973); republished as *Eligible Men* (London: Gollancz, 1974);

The Franchiser (New York: Farrar, Straus & Giroux, 1976);

The Living End (New York: Dutton, 1979; London: Cape, 1980);

Stanley Elkin's Greatest Hits (New York: Dutton, 1980);

George Mills (New York: Dutton, 1982).

PERIODICAL PUBLICATIONS: "A Sound of Distant Thunder," *Epoch*, 8 (Winter 1957): 39-57;

"The Party," *Views*, 4 (1958): 37-51;

Review of *The Fixer* by Bernard Malamud, *Massachusetts Review*, 8 (Spring 1967): 388-392.

Stanley Elkin (photo by Herb Weitman)

Among American-Jewish writers, Stanley Elkin has a very special place. Like other writers of his American-born generation, he deals with a heritage rather than the personal experience of immigration or of the Holocaust. While some young writers continue to sound traditional themes or to chant nostalgic hymns to a diminished sense of peoplehood, others have sought a new mode in black humor, a movement shared with non-Jewish authors. Elkin's career as a writer exemplifies a new style of ethnic concern and a new concern for non-ethnic style.

Only about half of Elkin's heroes are Jewish. They are invariably secular Jews with little commitment either to Judaism or to peoplehood. Indeed, locution (Jewish humor) and the usual vocation of his protagonists (salesmanship) are the only vestiges justifying ethnic categorization. In the course of Elkin's career, Jewishness has become increasingly vestigial.

One might, from the biographical facts, have expected stronger ties. Stanley Elkin was born of American-Jewish parents on 11 May 1930 in New York City; he was reared in Chicago and received both a B.A. (1952) and an M.A. (1953) from the University of Illinois, Urbana. His career as a writer was nurtured by both his parents. In fact, he claims that his mother, Zelda Elkin (née Feldman), "Made up my mind" to become a serious novelist by sending him to Rome and London on "a Mother's grant." There he was able to devote his wholehearted attention—previously divided between his teaching job at Washington University, St.

Louis, and the finishing of his dissertation on William Faulkner for the University of Illinois, Urbana (1961)—to the writing of his first novel, *Boswell: A Modern Comedy* (1964). While his mother is to be credited with making possible this first and major breakthrough, the writer's father, Philip Elkin, inspired many of the themes prevalent in the fiction, from the obsession with professional jargon to the fascination with heroes who are literal or symbolic salesmen. On 1 February 1953 Elkin married Joan Marion Jacobson. Since 1960 he has been teaching English at Washington University; except for various visiting professorships, he has been faithful to St. Louis, where he lives with his wife, an accomplished painter, and their three children.

Elkin started out with markedly Jewish themes. He was inspired by his salesman father's gift for telling stories, especially stories about Jews. "A Sound of Distant Thunder" (1957) and "The Party" (1958) both have conventional sets: a small store in a Jewish neighborhood about to be taken over by blacks and an upwardly mobile Jewish family about to lose its sense of tradition. However, the two stories foreshadow typical Elkinesque interests transcending the urge to preserve an ethnic identity. In both stories the traditional reverence for the past strikes the protagonists as anachronistic while full immersion into mainstream American culture appears to them as a betrayal. Rejecting past and present, they opt for the timeless, for beauty, symbolized by chinaware in one case and by fairy tales in the other.

After his first venture into long fiction with *Boswell: A Modern Comedy*, which featured a non-Jewish protagonist, Elkin's breakthrough as a Jewish writer came with his collection of short stories, *Criers and Kibitzers, Kibitzers and Criers* (1966). In fact, these stories, roughly half of which can be counted as Jewish, were so well received that Elkin, who thinks of himself primarily as a novelist, has been stuck with the label of short-story writer ever since. The collection's title story and "I Look Out for Ed Wolfe" are frequently anthologized. Although perhaps Elkin's funniest in terms of ethnic humor, these stories may at the same time be his most tragic. In the title story, Greenspahn, a former kibitzer, learns not only that his store is beset by petty thieves but also that his own son, whose recent death he mourns, was among the despoilers. The protagonist of "I Look Out for Ed Wolfe"—reared in a Jewish orphanage—is a salesman who sells out literally and metaphorically in an allegorical examination of his orphan existence. Although these early heroes are Jews who suffer, they are not, like the heroes of

Dust jacket for Elkin's fourth novel, often considered his best expression of contemporary Jewishness

Bernard Malamud or Edward Lewis Wallant, Jews *because* they suffer. Self-pity is overcome by Elkin's linguistic resourcefulness.

Elkin's second novel, *A Bad Man* (1967), further transforms the theme of suffering and the claims of humanism based upon suffering. Caught between his still-peddling and quite literally crazy Jewish father and his boringly Americanized son, department-store owner Leo Feldman looks for an existential experience in which to find his fate. He willfully maneuvers himself into prison, where he comes to affirm rather than bemoan his self-construed, metaphorical orphanhood. He plays down his Jewishness and his family ties; he sells himself to others and hopes thereby to find a place in the family of man.

A death in the family inspired Elkin to write a novella about the Jewish funerary ritual of sitting *shiva*. In "The Condominium," originally published in the three-novella collection *Searches and Seizures* (1973), Marshall Preminger inherits his father's apartment. While mourning his father, he reflects about condominium dwellings and their untraditional life-style, but his preconceived academic notions about alienation blind him to the positive aspects of his father's bachelor freedom. Rather than reveling in his orphanhood like Leo Feldman, he succumbs to suicidal despair. Lacking the creative drive, the resourcefulness, indeed, the obsession that distinguishes the typical Elkin protagonist, Marshall fails to emulate his father. Hoping to find a community to shelter him from the loneliness associated with modern freedom, he jumps from the condominium balcony and enters the ultimate home—death.

Elkin's fourth novel, *The Franchiser* (1976), best epitomizes his sense of contemporary Jewishness. Adapting and transforming traditional Jewish themes, Elkin begins with the Depression years that buffeted not only the Jewish minority but all of America as well. Ben Flesh, the first Elkin orphan to be adopted, is taken into a Jewish family of eighteen twins and triplets who suffer from uncommon diseases. Absurdity is added to absurdity. The head of this Jewish family, Julius Finsberg, made a fortune during the Depression, succeeding brilliantly in musical comedy, a genre dominated by Jewish composers and lyricists who seemed uncannily in touch with America's conception of America. Through Ben Flesh's career, sponsored by a Jewish fortune and aiming at the homogenization of America, the assimilatory trend begun in the Depression is developed to a logical extreme. Ironically, the hero becomes one with an America that is stricken by the energy crisis—a painful analogue to the multiple sclerosis that affects both Ben Flesh and Stanley Elkin. As the Finsbergs die of their freakish disorders, the hero returns to an orphan existence, to lonely freedom and independence, Elkin's hallmark of modernity. Identity no longer comes from ethnic roots, unless modern Jewishness is thought of not as a preparation for peoplehood but as a capacity to endure loneliness.

Although Elkin continues to touch upon Jewish themes, he tends to steer clear of the traditional problems faced by Jewish immigrants concerned about assimilation into mainstream America. Despite the desire of many younger Jews to recover a nearly forgotten cultural heritage, didactic nostalgia is a poor substitute for the drama of ethnic culture shock that was the origin of American Jewish literature. If Elkin has deemphasized the narrower aspects of his heritage, he has not been engaged in renunciation but rather in a search for more universal themes.

The protagonists of Elkin's surrealistic triptych of related stories, *The Living End* (1979), do not simply cross state lines, like franchiser Ben Flesh in his cadillac "home"; now the characters migrate between Heaven and Hell on the one hand and the twin cities, Minneapolis-Saint Paul, on the other. The symbolism of the tales ("The Conventional Wisdom," "The Bottom Line," "The State of the Art"), if not the parodic style, is distinctly Christian.

Finally, the picaresque and the surrealistic are united in Elkin's most recent novel, *George Mills* (1982). The non-Jewish protagonist, George Mills, roams about in time and space and breaks through the barriers that had confounded and intrigued an earlier Elkin protagonist, Dick Gibson, a radio-personality protagonist of Elkin's third novel, *The Dick Gibson Show* (1971). Characters whose lives cover a millennium, all males, share the same name (George Mills) and presumably the same fate (all are "God's blue collar worker"). Although linked by their obsession with family lore, the Millses could hardly be more different from each other. It is indeed a long journey from the first George Mills, a crusader whose mission ends in a medieval Polish salt mine, via the nineteenth-century George Mills, who is finally released from an Ottoman harem through the serendipitous intervention of Moses Magaziner (the only significant Jew in the novel) and is sent home (which, turns out, by accident, to be America rather than England), to the contemporary George Mills, whose charitable mission to Mexico shifts the mode of the novel from the comic to the tragic.

George Mills is not only a fabulous concoction of all of Elkin's previous themes; it is a superb achievement all its own. As if to defy those critics who complain about lack of plot, all the George Millses go purposely if not joyfully astray. While each individual George Mills is a humble, vulnerable, struggling individual, together they achieve mythic dimensions. In the manner of a Zen paradox, diversity is found in uniformity over generations of Millses, their individual fates reflected in their collective one, and vice versa. Whether the prison is Leo Feldman's (in *A Bad Man*) or those of George Mills in the Polish salt mine or the Ottoman harem, the existential situation is the same. Ultimately, Elkin is more concerned with the universal than the ethnic. In his own words, he is most concerned with "the writers who are stylists, Jewish or not. Bellow is a stylist, and he is Jewish. William Gass is a stylist, and he is not Jewish. What I go for in my work is language." That style takes priority over themes is perhaps best illustrated by his heroes' love

Dust jacket, with caricature by David Levine, for Elkin's novel in which all the characters share the same name

of making speeches which sparkle more with the passion of poetic rhetoric than with the logic of the businessman's agenda. Professional success is never a vital consideration; bewitching the audience with language for the sake of language is.

References:

Doris G. Bargen, *The Fiction of Stanley Elkin* (Bern & Frankfurt: Lang, 1980);

Bargen, "The Orphan Adopted: Stanley Elkin's *The Franchiser*," *Studies in American Jewish Literature*, 2 (1982): 132-143;

Kurt Dittmar, "Stanley Elkin, 'I Look Out for Ed Wolfe,'" *Die amerikanische Short Story der Gegenwart*, edited by Peter Freese (Berlin: Erich Schmidt Verlag, 1976), pp. 252-261;

Allen Guttmann, *The Jewish Writer in America: Assimilation and the Crisis of Identity* (New York: Oxford University Press, 1971), pp. 79-86;

John Leonard, "Stanley Elkin, Nice Guy," *New York Times Book Review*, 15 October 1967, p. 40.

Irvin Faust
(11 June 1924-   )

Julia B. Boken
State University of New York At Oneonta

See also the Faust entries in *DLB 2, American Novelists Since World War II*, and *DLB Yearbook: 1980*.

BOOKS: *Entering Angel's World: A Student-Centered Casebook* (New York: Bureau of Publications, Teachers College, Columbia University, 1963);
Roar Lion Roar and Other Stories (New York: Random House, 1965; London: Gollancz, 1965);
The Steagle (New York: Random House, 1966);
The File on Stanley Patton Buchta (New York: Random House, 1970);
Willy Remembers (New York: Arbor House, 1971);
Foreign Devils (New York: Arbor House, 1973);
A Star in the Family (Garden City: Doubleday, 1975);
Newsreel (New York & London: Harcourt Brace Jovanovich/Bruccoli Clark, 1980).

SELECTED PERIODICAL PUBLICATIONS: "The Dalai Lama of Harlem," *Sewanee Review*, 72 (Spring 1964): 223-243;
"Operation Buena Vista," *Paris Review*, 35 (Fall 1965): 87-105;
"The Double Snapper," *Esquire*, 64 (December 1965): 180-182, 304-308;
"Simon Girty Go Ape," *Transatlantic Review*, 21 (1966): 66-75;
"Gary Dis-Donc," *Northwest Review*, 9 (Summer 1967): 6-18;
"Melanie and the Purple People Eaters," *Atlantic Monthly*, 248 (December 1981): 70-77.

OTHER: Paul Cain, *Fast One*, afterword by Faust (Carbondale: University of Southern Illinois Press, 1978).

Although literary critics have delineated writers such as Bernard Malamud, Saul Bellow, Philip Roth, Norman Mailer, Joseph Heller, Wallace Markfield, Cynthia Ozick, and, certainly, Irvin Faust as American-Jewish writers, Faust considers himself an American writer who was born Jewish, with all of its varying associations. He stated, in an interview in 1977, "I have this Jewish-American base. . . . I don't see myself as a stereotype Jewish-American writer, and yet I suppose that out of that

Irvin Faust at a party honoring publication of his most recent novel, Newsreel *(photo by Layle Silbert)*

wellspring much has developed." Willy, the protagonist in Faust's 1971 novel, *Willy Remembers*, is of German ancestry and is rather anti-Semitic; in fact, he is anti almost everything except his own concept of America and his two sons. Buchta of *The File on Stanley Patton Buchta* (1970) has a middle-European heritage but is not Jewish. All of Faust's other protagonists are Jewish, yet religion or ethnicity does not play a highly significant role in their portraiture. All of his protagonists suffer angst, a reflection of the artist at work, not necessarily an ethnic manifestation.

One of Faust's short stories, "Jake Bluffstein and Adolf Hitler," concerns an anti-Semitic Jew. Although painful for him to write, Faust feels that the story has meaning for a broad spectrum of people and groups: "I felt that it was important to talk about self-hatred. I think it's important to bring it out in the open, even to the extent that it becomes a psychosis, which it did in Jake's case."

Faust believes that every Jew "is living on the edge of the holocaust today." Israel has liberated Jews to a degree because there *is* this country. It validates the world of Jews who want to be remembered for having lived, to leave their footprints in the sand of history. All in all, though, Faust's writing, he is certain, strikes "a resonance with the intelligent reader who may or may not be a student of the Jewish experience." Above all, Faust's work exhibits a deep-rooted love for America and its history that the author knows well and which he uses as an integral part of all of his novels. And unlike the works of some other writers with a pronounced Jewish background, Faust's books do not cause the reader strain to plumb meaning without knowing the Cabala, various rituals or biblical heroes, and allusions. In a sense, Faust's Bible is American history (or the experience as history), and this mindset becomes the wellspring of most of his fictional world.

Faust has published six novels, a collection of short stories (plus several uncollected ones), and a casebook of studies on students and their problems. One of his novels has been adapted into a movie of the same title, *The Steagle* (1971), starring Richard Benjamin. In 1983 a story which appeared in *Atlantic Monthly* (December 1981), "Melanie and the Purple People Eaters," was selected for inclusion in *O. Henry Prize Stories*. His unpublished novels include a 600-page historical novel on early colonial New York (1740-1830) featuring Marinus Willett, another depicting a numbers runner from Harlem in the 1930s, and several pieces of varying lengths on the inner life of horse racing. Faust is experimenting with several different modes, including the mystery genre.

Faust is particularly interested in the novels of Charles Dickens, William Dean Howells, Edith Wharton, and Stephen Crane. Further, he is partial to Chekhov, especially his plays, and believes that this Russian writer predated the modern sensibility. The mood and dialogue (even in translation) of a Chekhov play is appealing to him. Like many of his generation, he has been an admirer of James Joyce and his language, especially of *A Portrait of the Artist as a Young Man*, *Dubliners*, and *Ulysses*. Among modern American writers, John Cheever stands preeminent. "Cheever is probably overall the greatest American talent since World War II," says

Faust. He also enjoyed the early Saul Bellow novels, *Dangling Man* and *Henderson the Rain King*. His favorite reading is in history—all periods and countries, but especially American history.

Irvin Faust was born in Brooklyn and, apart from leaving the greater New York City area for wartime service, continues to call Manhattan home. This area, where he lives with his wife Jean, is the setting in the main of virtually all of his works. He admits to a love/hate for New York City and he calls his experiences there "integrative, disintegrative [following World War II] and then reintegrative." In *A Star in the Family*, he writes, "N. Y. is where it was, is and always will be." He enjoys the ethnic and cultural diversity and, above all, the energy of the City, that energy which has been transmuted into all of his fiction.

Faust's parents, Morris and Pauline Henschel Faust, were Jews. His father was an immigrant; his mother was born in the United States and her father was native-born as well. His maternal grandfather was probably the only Jew who fought with the U.S. Army against the Apaches, actually hunting Geronimo, under General Crook. Faust was reared in a Brooklyn-Queens household, with his father's heroes, the liberals Benjamin Nathan Cardozo, Sol Bloom, and Emanuel Celler and Judge Samuel Leibowitz.

His background of education and training is atypical in the sense that he did not major in English, literature, or writing in college. Irvin Faust attended City College of New York, where most of his training was in physical education, with a minor in biology. This facet of his background together with his passionate interest in sports is evident in his writing.

In 1949 he began a teaching career in Harlem, where he encountered at firsthand a broad ethnic mix, including blacks, Puerto Ricans, and Orientals. Searching for a more dynamic avenue to reach students, he began graduate training in guidance and counseling at Teachers College of Columbia University. He remained there to complete his doctoral studies in guidance and career counseling. His experimental case studies were accepted, despite their unorthodoxy, as the dissertation, which was eventually published by Teachers College under the title *Entering Angel's World* (1963). Faust then became a guidance counselor in a public high school and is now guidance director in a New York school. Like many writers in the past, Chekhov, T. S. Eliot, and Wallace Stevens, he combines two careers successfully.

Only when his doctoral adviser, Raymond

Patouillet, insisted that Faust's written work showed a dramatic turn of phrase did he begin to think of writing fiction. He began a class with the novelist and short-story writer R. V. Cassill. His first piece of fiction, "Into the Green Night," written for this class, was published by the *Carleton Miscellany* in Minnesota. His writing career was thus launched; short stories were accepted and published by *Transatlantic Review, Paris Review*, and other magazines.

Random House's editor, Robert Loomis, liked Faust's stories well enough to publish his first book of them, *Roar Lion Roar and Other Stories*, in 1965. Publishing a book of short stories before the author has had a novel published is relatively rare in the publishing world. In this collection the title piece, "Roar Lion Roar," takes its name from the fight song of Columbia University and is a bittersweet story of an uneducated Puerto Rican boy whose identity with and devotion to the Columbia football team and its performances become his hallmark. He gives his life for the Lions, although the team ironically is unaware of his existence. The ivy league college commanding Morningside Heights is contrasted with the environment of an academically impoverished minority youth, presenting a situa-

tion that continues to plague this university, located literally on the fringes of Harlem.

The stories and characters in *Roar Lion Roar* are as diverse as the City with its polyglot inhabitants. A premonitory one is "Philco Baby," published long before the popularity of the Walkman and the heavy portable radio sets that blare in the American streets of the 1980s, radios which symbolize a kind of machismo or the insulation of the individual or the desire to be noticed. "Madras Rumble," another story in the collection, is worth mentioning not only because it introduces another cultural type (a Far-Eastern Indian) but also because it begins to exemplify Faust's humor, which is a vital, integral part of the tone in all of the novels.

Roar Lion Roar becomes a prelude to Faust's interest in writing about the way an individual lives within his own perceptions. Faust says, "Generally, my character is living by the accoutrements of his source and our culture. These people are often 100% committed and passionate and live, in an existential sense, in quite normal ways, within that internal parameter." The psychologist Carl Rogers, Faust insists, would understand this phenomenon. Their breakdown occurs when their "props" are

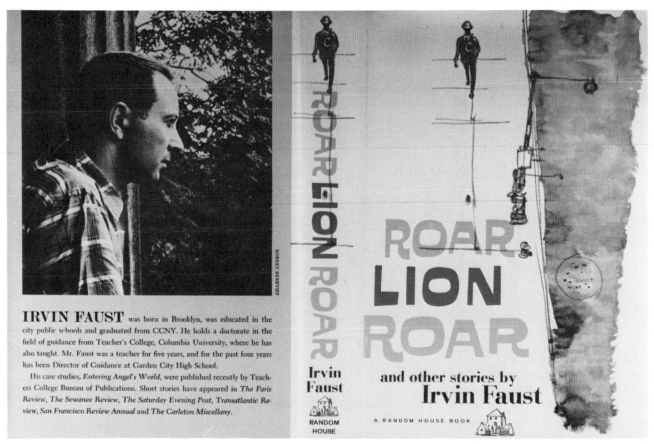

Dust jacket for Faust's first published book of fiction, a collection of ten short stories, eight of which have teenage protagonists

removed. As outsiders might view them, many of the characters in *Roar Lion Roar* hold unorthodox views of America. They can be seen as maladjusted, even psychotic, but their methods of dealing with their lives stem from their cultural bedrock—urban life, poverty, unexamined perceptions, cultural artifacts, especially the radio, music, and the mass media television and the cinema.

Faust compares the writing of a short story and a novel to the difference between a studio and a large one-family house. "The short story requires exactness. It is confined in space, yet it must work within such space. In writing a novel, the artist can rummage from the basement through the living floors and even up to the attic." Space is less constrained and there is more leisure time.

Not only pressed by editors but also wishing to try different modes, Faust began a novel, the idea being precipitated by the Cuban missile crisis during the presidency of John F. Kennedy, an important leader in the novels of Faust. Out of this contemporary and frightening event, *The Steagle* (1966) began emerging. It is the story of a college professor, Harold Aaron Weissburg. The novel covers a twelve-day period during which Weissburg is so cataclysmically disoriented and at the same time liberated by the Cuban missile crisis that he leaves his family, his job, and his comfortable cocoon to return to Chicago where he had been stationed during World War II and then continues his odyssey throughout the Midwest and on to the West Coast in a search of past time, which was more bearable and more glamorous, certainly less lethal. Weissburg's emotion is reflected in the terrain he covers, as the hero, like many archetypal heroes, rises from the nether regions for a return and the *accommodation de crise*, limited though it be in the lecture hall of academe. Faust focuses on an important and highly significant event in the life of his generation—the watershed of World War II, during which he served in the European theater, the Philippines, and in Japan. This historical event becomes a litany but never a threnody in his novels.

The title refers to a wartime professional football team created by the temporary merger of the Pittsburgh Steelers and the Philadelphia Eagles. In *The Steagle*, Faust uses another element which will become one of his hallmarks—the intersecting of reality and fantasy. For seven days, Harold Weissburg's fantasies become his realities. Faust writes, "The challenge was to sustain the intensity, the fever, and to fuse his inner and outer lives so that something coherent would emerge." Many of these fantasies revolve around sex—and a limited fulfillment. Sex for Faust in this novel becomes primarily an appetite, phrased in the disparaging terms of most servicemen, with little or no thought after the act. It is a mode of action, not a prelude to a healthy relationship with women. In Faust's other novels, sex is linked to an aspect of a character's history and value system, consciously and unconsciously. Many such erotic scenes, whether in fantasy or reality, become the focus of hilarity, as in *Foreign Devils* when Benson at first refuses to capitulate to the sexual voracity of the Empress Dowager of China, somewhat reminiscent of Byron's *Don Juan*.

In *The Steagle* another favored theme of Faust is the identity of the Jewish protagonist with Gentiles or the urgency to focus his perceptions through WASP types. These WASP heroes are generally historical figures such as Andrew Jackson, Theodore Roosevelt, Woodrow Wilson, and especially Franklin Delano Roosevelt, and eventually more contemporaneous figures such as Gen. Dwight D. Eisenhower and John F. Kennedy. Emerging also is Faust's respect and love of history, which he has read extensively, researched, and digested. Contemporary society becomes a chord with history in the fiction of Irvin Faust.

Always attempting a further extension into new fictional techniques, Faust wrote his second novel, *The File on Stanley Patton Buchta*, published in 1970. Faust insists that many of the critics misperceived this novel because of their belief that the protagonist was simply "an indolent cop." The novel is decidedly more complex. Buchta is uncommitted, unaware of himself and of his values. Slipping easily and unquestioningly into the role of triple agent provocateur (almost Russian-like), without taking a stand, Buchta is whirled into a hurricane of events. When the rioting subsides, he pays for his driftage when he loses the woman whom he unwittingly loved. Harlem is an integral part of the novel and Buchta lives there for no apparent purpose. Not unintelligent and certainly possessing the strategy for survival, like all Faust's protagonists, Buchta—after the deluge—will continue to lead an unexamined life. Faust intimates ironically that Buchta, unlike his middle-namesake, General Patton, will continue his gelatinous existence in and around Morningside Heights, a metaphor for the policeman's distancing from self and from the people he is hired to protect. The novel is Faust's existential statement in fiction: the USA played games or drifted in not definitively selecting either direction or values, and the country was finally jerked into action by such cataclysms as unrestricted submarine warfare in 1916 and 1917, Pearl Harbor in 1941, and the Tet offensive in 1968. Careful readers of this novel will see the student riots of the 1960s on the launching pad.

Willy Remembers (1971) is for Faust the novel that most nearly coincides with his intentions. He departs structurally by cutting into the present and the past, a technique that mirrors the thoughts of the near-senile protagonist, who is a veteran of the Spanish-American War. Again, a war integrally defines the consciousness of a man during his long life, as war—whether it be termed a conflict or an intervention—also defined and continues to define the United States. Willy is a German-American bigot, limited and fixed in amber, but he worshiped his two sons and he loved his country all of his life. Ironies heavily vein the book—and the death scene of his younger son is a cameo that haunts the memory. Faust's commentaries in the novel on sex with German women (in World War II) might have been sober, even dour; these episodes, on the contrary, turn out to be written in a way that stylizes his novels—hilarity of episode and tone. Although the reader may be unsympathetic to much of Willy's value system, the Spanish-American War hero himself emerges as a likable figure of energy, wit, commitment, and above all, survival. "Willy," says Faust, took *him* over and "in his quasi-senile way commented on the American scene with what I think is more accuracy than clear-headed commentary could have provided."

Another kind of conflict highlights Faust's *Foreign Devils*, published in 1973 and structurally his best book, according to the author. The novel is a book within a book (the double-box mode of the Chinese puzzle). Its idea was generated by Nixon's trip to China (a kind of invasion) and by Faust's deep-rooted interest in history and his extensive research into the Boxer Rebellion, the colonial invasion of China in 1900, and the semimystical resistance of the Chinese. (The Boxers actually believed that they could not be killed by Western bullets.) The novel within the novel is written by a Richard Harding Davis type, a war correspondent whose prose is florid, with Faust echoing the popular style for readers in the early 1900s. Sidney Benson (once Birnbaum), who is writing the novel, is a substitute teacher in real life. His fictional creation (within the fictional creation) is the reporter Norris Blake, who like Lancelot searches for his holy grail, though in the form of stories and scoops, and who like other heroes (Candide and the tilter at windmills) distributes his largesse and rescues the oppressed while he collects materials for the readers back home. His ego is unsinkable. Benson is a participant, of course, an *engagé*, and the correspondent's exploits, given the sweeping Chinese terrain, become as grandiose as the reporter himself, though they are tempered by some historical truths. The conclusion of *Foreign Devils* returns to the grim reality of Benson's roots—to his senile father, who is incapable of delight in historical perspectives. The young American nation, in all innocence, is a vortex symbolized then and now by the taking on of the Oriental ancients with the "help" of other nations who will again in that corner of the world seduce Americans into fighting their brand of war. *Foreign Devils*, about the flexing of muscles of a youthful country, also stretches the fictional technique of Irvin Faust.

A Star in the Family (1975) is Faust's third novel that builds on a radically different structure. Time and space are completely fractured and disjunctive. It is the story of a Jewish-American stand-up comic, Bart Goldwine. His story unravels from a series of interviews of people who passed through his stormy life, with the comic's asides to his biographer who is assembling these anecdotes and remembrances of Goldwine's rise and precipitous fall from popularity and wealth. Goldwine is disturbed at other people's multifaceted views of him but disguises his reactions since the comedian is always a comedian. There is a kind of pointillism in the contouring of Goldwine, who looks back on his life with a masked cynicism of one who is aware of his final failure and who shrouds his self-hatred with wry wit.

Bart Goldwine's life is a composite of impersonations, especially of the main demagogues of World War II—Stalin, Mussolini, and Hitler. There is a chapter on the comedian as he serves with the U.S. Army in Europe and in the army of occupation in Japan. Its disjunctive style makes the reader leap from time present to World War II and back again as Goldwine shuttles between that which was and that which is now with his biographer, the fractured structure mirroring the emotional breakdown of the comic. Goldwine serves in the European theater and is pressed by Major Danforth to leave the English boondocks as a radio operator in the army for London as a comedian. He leaves a very accommodating Englishwoman as well. Jokes are plentiful, and Faust knows his historical stuff as Goldwine is accompanied by commentators drawn from history—Alfred Dreyfus and Benjamin Disraeli, who become his conscience and whose stichomythic remarks readily reveal pithy certitudes. (Goldwine to Dreyfus: "They crucified you." Dreyfus: "An old role for a Jew.") History for Faust becomes also a companion and an ethical code.

Goldwine's rise is meteoric. Hollywood makes him rich, but his relationships suffer. Alcohol becomes indispensable to him, but the Brooklyn-born Jew copes and shuttles between movies and television and makes people all over the world laugh with his impersonations, especially that of his quintessential hero, J. F. K.

The novel's two pages subtitled "Research: Performance, November 22, 1963," are a riotous but ironic mélange of jokes and allusions to everything from cruel humor concerning Mrs. Abraham Lincoln to commercials to Bostonian accents, interspersed with references to the just-slaughtered political hero. It ends with, "Ask not—No-o-o-o-o-o-o-o-o-o-o-o-o-o-o-." The subsequent dialogue between Goldwine and the biographer heightens the irony with the comic's forbidding this material to be used and the consequent quitting/firing of the biographer. The ruin of Kennedy's Camelot causes national mania and blasts personal relationships.

A Star in the Family was almost universally misinterpreted by the critics, who insisted that Goldwine was patterned after Lenny Bruce, a cult figure at that time whose life was being transposed to film. Faust says nothing could be further from the fact. He actually does not admire Lenny Bruce, as he does the Goldwine figure, and the character was his own artistic creation, with echoes or superimpositions of comics such as Morey Amsterdam, Milton Berle, Phil Silvers, among many others. Goldwine, unlike Lenny Bruce, takes no trendy political stance and is actually unashamedly pro-American.

This bittersweet novel of Goldwine's rise and fall, coalescing in the gold and the wine of the Kennedy days when Americans felt charmed and warmed by the White House and, like their president, could laugh easily, pays tribute to the age of the stand-up comic. These funsmiths circled the country, made their yearly appearances at the Borscht Belt in the Catskills, and opened their wit to the world through television in its early days. Faust remembers them well. *A Star in the Family* once again emphasizes Faust's devotion to meaningfully interspersing history with the moment—the blending of fact and fantasy.

Faust's eighth published book is *Newsreel* (1980), a novel employing time in traditional chronology—from 1946 to 1968. Manny ("Speed")

Finestone, the protagonist, reached his finest hour when he served with honor and distinction during World War II and became a captain decorated for his valor. His subsequent years are lived in nostalgia as he yearns to recapture those glorious days.

Faust believes *Newsreel* to be his most "complete" book. It is his statement on middle-aged America's locus today as it resists letting go of the old, treasured time under attack from the blatant new. The U.S. with its problems multiplied in superpowerdom has finally emerged from Eden. Many of the country's facets are presented in the book—movies, television, sports, war history (especially World War II), New York City's history, Columbia University (when General Eisenhower was president of this center of learning), New York State history, commercials, giant shopping malls, magazines, newspapers: a newsreel compilation of them all. Finestone is obsessed with the leader Eisenhower (although a Republican) who becomes a university's and then the country's president, as he had once been fixed on his much-admired F. D. R. *Newsreel* unwinds before the reader and before the characters as Finestone is coping with his search for his moments of glory. The frustration and anger of Finestone reflect in the novel's tone of abrasiveness. In his life he terminates one marriage and begins another, only to have that crumble as well. He writes to the White House proposing his daughter in marriage to David Eisenhower. (What better fantasy than to have his daughter coupled with the family of that ex-commander now-president whom he deeply admires?) Movies are spotlighted in the novel as Faust intersperses cinematic history with events of the plot: Finestone takes his second wife and later his girl friend through New York State to Niagara Falls, with obsessive flashes and recollections of the movie *Niagara*, starring Marilyn Monroe, a darling of the Golden Age. From New York City to the Falls, the history of the state obtrudes insistently with minutiae. (For example, Mark Twain was indeed buried in the Empire State.) Jim Ryun, the sprinter in the Olympic finals, appears on television and controls the erotic pleasures of Finestone and his companion. Faust's use of recalled trivia is incremental until the reader is led to remember the glory that was and the sleaze that is.

Having lost his third woman in the novel (and perhaps his daughter as well), Finestone is purged of his block and resumes his writing. A flip remark, as he glances at the Palisades: "Hey Yonkel, does love *really* conquer all?" and the reply, "Why not?," may in fact refer to the many kinds of love for Finestone—of his writing, his country, his finest

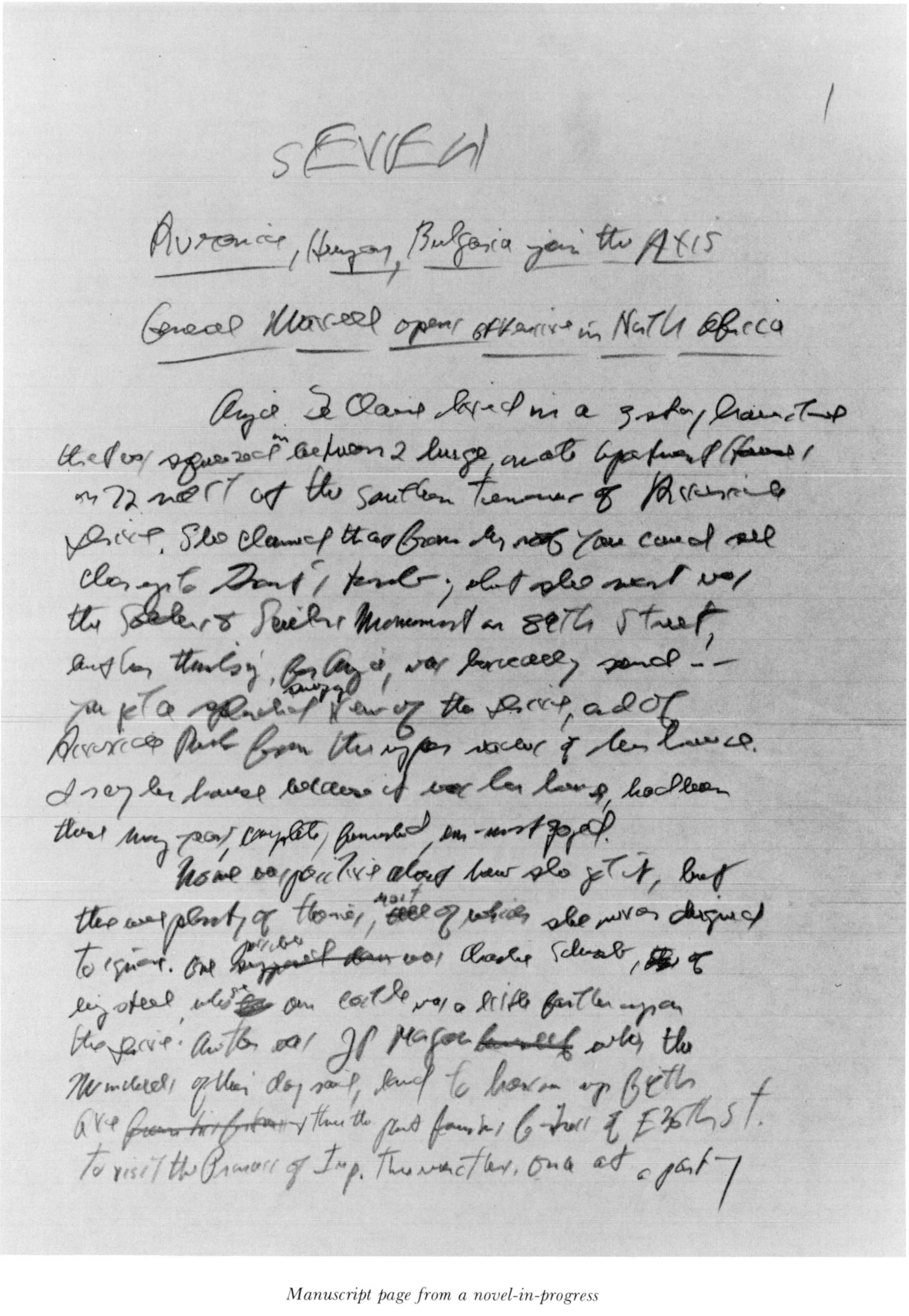

1

SEVEN

Rumania, Hungary, Bulgaria join the AXIS

General Wavell opens offensive in North Africa

Manuscript page from a novel-in-progress

hour serving the U. S., never to be repeated but echoed only in his fiction.

The hallmarks of Faust's writing are many, but predominant are his love of and encyclopedic recall of American (and European) history and his use of historical fact in his art, counterpointed with his love of fantasy, especially the cinema. Although Faust is almost Proustian in his seizing and focusing on the moment of glory and success, his heroes and other characters do not yield passively and nostalgically to their pasts. They (like Finestone) struggle to face the hurly-burly and establish themselves in the present. Above all, his characters are survivors.

Faust agrees with the interpretation that the tone of his novels virtually becomes a character, as Hardy's heath looms like a person. Such tone is set by some of the liveliest dialogue in modern American fiction. Conversation runs, gambols, sings, dives, skyrockets, becomes almost psychedelic in its range in a recapturing of the diversity that is America, which he loves, and Europe as well. Critics praise what must be Faust's total recall in capturing patterns of speech.

Humor also is a significant trademark of Faust. Very often it stems from a literal use of language. It results, too, from language that echoes the "insanity" of daily life. Rhythm piles on rhythm, and Faust's American symphonies strike their chords and discords with a seemingly unending variety of people—from college professors, policemen, war veterans, and comedians to writers, Puerto Rican and black youths, to East Indians, black and white women of many backgrounds and countries, salesmen, con artists, and the man on the street.

Faust's characters do not build empires, but they fight wars, report on them, teach the country's young, record America, dream the American dream that never was. They always cope and all survive.

Faust unifies the electric current of the multimedia present and the historical past, that which roots us but does not petrify us. Faust, somewhat like Dr. Faustus, commands the historical moment to stay and be meaningful, to blend that which was heroic with the present moment to make it not only fulfilling but also touched with dynamic possibilities.

References:

Matthew J. Bruccoli, "Irvin Faust," in *Conversations with Writers II* (Detroit: Bruccoli Clark/Gale Research, 1978), pp. 46-72;

R. V. Cassill, "Willy Remembers," *New York Times Book Review*, 29 August 1971, pp. 5, 26;

Ivan Gold, "Life as News," *New York Times Book Review*, 13 April 1980, pp. 15, 32;

Richard Kostelanetz, "New American Fiction Reconsidered," *Tri-Quarterly*, 8 (Winter 1967): 279-286.

Edna Ferber
(15 August 1885-16 April 1968)

Steven P. Horowitz and Miriam J. Landsman
University of Iowa

See also the Ferber entry in *DLB 9, American Novelists, 1910-1945.*

BOOKS: *Dawn O'Hara: The Girl Who Laughed* (New York: Stokes, 1911; London: Methuen, 1925);

Buttered Side Down (New York: Stokes, 1912; London: Methuen, 1926);

Roast Beef, Medium; The Business Adventures of Emma McChesney (New York: Stokes, 1913; London: Methuen, 1920);

Personality Plus; Some Experiences of Emma McChesney and Her Son, Jock (New York: Stokes, 1914);

Emma McChesney and Co. (New York: Stokes, 1915);

Fanny Herself (New York: Stokes, 1917; London: Methuen, 1923);

Cheerful, By Request (Garden City: Doubleday, Page, 1918; London: Methuen, 1919);

Half Portions (Garden City: Doubleday, Page, 1920);

$1200 a Year, by Ferber and Newman Levy (Garden City: Doubleday, Page, 1920);

The Girls (Garden City & Toronto: Doubleday, Page, 1921; London: Heinemann, 1922);

Gigolo (Garden City: Doubleday, Page, 1922; London: Heinemann, 1923);

"Old Man Minick" and Minick, by Ferber and George S. Kaufman (Garden City: Doubleday, Page, 1924; London: Heinemann, 1924);

So Big (Garden City: Doubleday, Page, 1924; London: Heinemann, 1924);

Show Boat (Garden City: Doubleday, Page, 1926; London: Heinemann, 1926);

Mother Knows Best: A Fiction Book (Garden City: Doubleday, Page, 1927; London: Heinemann, 1927);

The Royal Family, by Ferber and Kaufman (Garden City: Doubleday, Doran, 1928; London: French, 1929);

Cimarron (Garden City: Doubleday, Doran, 1930; London: Heinemann, 1930);

American Beauty (Garden City: Doubleday, Doran, 1931; London: Heinemann, 1931);

Dinner at Eight, by Ferber and Kaufman (Garden City: Doubleday, Doran, 1932; London: Heinemann, 1933);

They Brought Their Women (Garden City: Doubleday, Doran, 1933; London: Heinemann, 1933);

Come and Get It (Garden City: Doubleday, Doran, 1935; London: Heinemann, 1935);

Stage Door, by Ferber and Kaufman (Garden City: Doubleday, Doran, 1936; London: Heinemann, 1937);

Nobody's In Town (Garden City: Doubleday, Doran, 1938; London: Heinemann, 1938);

A Peculiar Treasure (New York: Doubleday, Doran, 1939; London: Heinemann, 1939);

The Land is Bright, by Ferber and Kaufman (Garden City: Doubleday, Doran, 1941);

No Room at the Inn (Garden City: Doubleday, Doran, 1941);

Saratoga Trunk (Garden City: Doubleday, Doran, 1941; London: Heinemann, 1942);

Great Son (Garden City: Doubleday, Doran, 1945; London: Heinemann, 1945);

One Basket: Thirty-One Short Stories (New York: Simon & Schuster, 1947);

Your Town (Cleveland: World, 1948);

Bravo!, by Ferber and Kaufman (New York: Dramatists Play Service, 1949);

Giant (Garden City: Doubleday, 1952; London: Gollancz, 1952);

Ice Palace (Garden City: Doubleday, 1958; London: Gollancz, 1958);

A Kind of Magic (Garden City: Doubleday, 1963; London: Gollancz, 1963).

SELECTED PLAYS: *Our Mrs. McChesney*, by Ferber and George V. Hobart, New York, Lyceum Theatre, 19 October 1915;

Minick, by Ferber and George S. Kaufman, New York, Booth Theatre, 24 September 1924;

The Royal Family, by Ferber and Kaufman, New York, Selwyn Theatre, 28 December 1927;

Dinner at Eight, by Ferber and Kaufman, New York, Music Box Theatre, 22 October 1932;

Stage Door, by Ferber and Kaufman, New York, Music Box Theatre, 22 October 1936;

This Land is Bright, by Ferber and Kaufman, New York, Music Box Theatre, 28 October 1941;

Bravo!, by Ferber and Kaufman, New York, Lyceum Theatre, 11 November 1948.

SELECTED PERIODICAL PUBLICATIONS: "Joy of the Job," *American Magazine*, 85 (March 1918): 34-35;

"No Apologies Needed for American Art," *Bookman*, 52 (November 1920): 219-220.

Edna Ferber was one of the most popular Jewish-American women writers in history. She was a best-selling author as well as a critically successful one and the first Jewish-American woman to win the Pulitzer Prize for the novel. Not only was she widely read in the United States, but her fiction was also translated into several foreign languages and distributed worldwide. In the course of her career, which spanned more than a half-century, Ferber produced more than twenty volumes of fiction and collaborated on eight plays, most of them written with George S. Kaufman. Additionally, many of Ferber's works, including *Giant, Show Boat, Cimarron*, and *Ice Palace*, have been made into successful Hollywood movies. Her writing was highly acclaimed by such notables as Rudyard Kipling and James M. Barrie, and Columbia University awarded her the honorary degree of Doctor of Letters in 1931 in recognition of her literary excellence. Almost all of Ferber's novels were best-sellers, and many of her works were included in high-school and college English curricula.

Ferber was born in Kalamazoo, Michigan, to Jacob Charles and Julia Neumann Ferber. Her father was a first-generation Hungarian-Jewish immigrant. Her mother was a second-generation German Jew from Chicago. As a result of Jacob Ferber's business failures, the family moved often, from Kalamazoo to Chicago, to Ottumwa, Iowa, and Appleton, Wisconsin.

The Ferber family's move to Appleton was precipitated by an anti-Semitic incident. According to Ferber, her parents were victimized in an unsuccessful lawsuit they had filed against an employee accused of theft. Although there were witnesses to

The house in which I was born. Kalamazoo, Michigan. August 15, 1885. Edna Ferber.

American, a writer, and a Jew in that order. Her books were regionally oriented, with each novel describing a different part of the United States. Ferber considered the working class the backbone of America and gave them a prominent position in her fiction. Many of her strongest characters were women who established their identities through their work rather than through their relationships to men. Almost all of Ferber's works contained at least one Jewish character, but this person was usually peripheral to the narrative. She portrayed Jewish Americans as people whose work, hopes, and aspirations were identical to those of their compatriots.

Ferber became popular with the publication of her Emma McChesney stories. In 1911 she sent *American Magazine* a story whose protagonist was Mrs. Emma McChesney, a traveling businesswoman and divorced mother with one son. The editors found the character of Emma McChesney innovative and potentially profitable, and Ferber wrote more than twenty stories based on that character.

the crime, those individuals denied knowledge of the incident in court, refusing to testify against one of their own kind.

Ferber graduated from high school in Appleton and worked as the first female newspaper reporter for the *Appleton Daily Crescent*. The townspeople, as Ferber recalls in her 1939 autobiography, *A Peculiar Treasure*, often reacted unfavorably to her unusual occupation, but she enjoyed newspaper work and eventually landed a higher-paying job for the *Milwaukee Journal*. However, she had a nervous breakdown and returned to live with her family in Appleton. It was at this time that she began her fiction-writing career with the novel *Dawn O'Hara: The Girl Who Laughed* (1911), the story of a newspaperwoman in Milwaukee. Originally she was dissatisfied with the work and threw it in the trash, but her mother salvaged it, and this became her first published novel. Ferber's first publication was a short story, "The Homely Heroine," which appeared in *Everybody's Magazine* in 1910. Her first story collection, *Buttered Side Down*, was published in 1912.

The central concern in Ferber's fiction is the glorification of America. She considered herself an

Ferber in 1904, the first female reporter for the Appleton Daily Crescent

The McChesney stories were written over a period of several years, from 1912 to 1915, and were well known in their time. In fact, when Ferber was covering the Democratic convention as a reporter for the *Chicago Tribune*, Theodore Roosevelt asked her when McChesney was going to remarry. According to Ferber, Roosevelt expressed the typical male viewpoint. Women preferred that Emma remain single.

Ferber firmly believed that women should work. In an essay entitled "Joy of the Job," (1918), she emphasized the importance of work to a human being's individual growth. She expressed pride in working three hundred and fifty days out of the year, a pattern she continued throughout her life. Ferber stated that the value of work was priceless and that once the habit was acquired, it could not be easily forsaken.

The prominent theme of the McChesney stories is work. Emma McChesney appears as a hardworking saleswoman for Featherloom petticoats, who, out of economic necessity, travels from place to place to make a living for herself and her son. McChesney is much harangued because she is a working woman in a nontraditional occupation, a situation with which Ferber herself was well acquainted. The McChesney stories were collected in three volumes—*Roast Beef, Medium* (1913), *Personality Plus* (1914), and *Emma McChesney and Co.* (1915)—and in 1915 Ferber and George V. Hobart collaborated on *Our Mrs. McChesney*, a play based on these stories.

Ferber's next endeavor was a semiautobiographical novel entitled *Fanny Herself* (1917), the story of a Jewish girl growing up in a small midwestern town. In *A Peculiar Treasure*, Ferber acknowledged that much of the book was based on her own experiences: "Certainly my mother, idealized, went to make up Molly Brandeis. Bits and pieces of myself crept into the character of Fanny Brandeis. Appleton undoubtedly was the book's background, and little Rabbi Gerechter and Arthur Howe and Father Fitzmaurice and a dozen others formed the real basis of the book's people."

The novel expresses Ferber's views of the Jewish people, endowed with certain adaptive qualities as a result of the oppression they had suffered over the past thousands of years. In the words of the novel's Irish priest, "You've suffered, you Jews, for centuries and centuries, until you're all artists—quick to see drama because you've lived in it, emotional, over-sensitive, cringing, or swaggering, high-strung, demonstrative, affectionate, generous."

In 1921, Ferber published a novel entitled *The Girls* which she expected to become a best-seller. While the reception of this book did not meet her expectations, that of her next novel, *So Big* (1924) did. It was an enormous success and was awarded a Pulitzer Prize.

So Big concerns an idealistic, hardworking farm woman named Selina Peake DeJong and her son, Dirk. Selina exemplifies the strong, virtuous female who works endlessly and unselfishly to provide for her child. Dirk, on the other hand, represents the type of person who sacrifices principles for materialistic success: he rejects his initial aspiration of becoming an architect in favor of the less demanding but financially profitable vocation of selling bonds.

In *So Big* work again appears as the prominent theme. However, this time it is placed in the context of family relationships. Like Molly Brandeis in *Fanny Herself* and Emma McChesney, Selina Peake DeJong is forced to labor because her husband died at a relatively young age. In this regard she resembles Ferber's mother as well. Julia Ferber had always had a strong hand in running the family business, but she was forced to take full responsibility when Jacob Ferber lost his eyesight.

Although Ferber had written *Our Mrs. McChesney* with George V. Hobart, it was not until her collaboration with George S. Kaufman that she felt satisfied with her playwriting. Ferber, always fascinated by the spoken word, initially aspired to be an actress—a "blighted Bernhardt," she termed herself in *A Peculiar Treasure*. While a senior in high school she won the Wisconsin State Declamatory Contest; it was this honor that led to her writing job for the *Appleton Daily Crescent*.

In 1924 Kaufman approached Ferber with the idea of converting one of her short stories—"Old Man Minick"—into a play. Even though Ferber disagreed with his choice of story (she wanted to use "The Gay Old Dog"), she heartily agreed to work with him on this endeavor. Although the production of *Minick* was not very successful, Ferber and Kaufman continued to work together for many years and created such popular dramas as *The Royal Family*, produced in 1927, *Dinner at Eight* (1932), and *Stage Door* (1936).

It was at the opening night party for *Minick* that Ferber first heard the term *show boat*, from her director Winthrop Ames. Her investigation of this phenomenon led to the creation of the novel *Show Boat* (1926), perhaps Ferber's most famous work. It has been translated into eleven languages and has served as the basis of a musical play, a radio program which ran for over six years, and four separate motion pictures. The musical continues to be performed today, no doubt owing largely to the score written by Jerome Kern and Oscar Hammerstein II, which contains such popular standards as "Ol' Man River" and "Can't Help Lovin' Dat Man."

Ferber called *Show Boat* her "oilwell" because of the tremendous revenues she received from it. The work itself was pure Americana. As the title indicates, it concerns one of the showboats that traveled the Mississippi River in the latter half of the nineteenth century. The most controversial aspect of the novel is the theme of miscegenation between a black woman (who is light enough to be taken for white) and a white man. Again, the themes of hard work as an essential part of a fulfilled life and of women's need to labor as hard (or harder) than men are evident.

Ferber's next great success was *Cimarron* (1930), a novel set in late nineteenth-century Oklahoma. The background of *Cimarron* is the opening up of the Oklahoma territory, the discovery of oil, and the consequent overnight growth of the region. The book's central characters are Yancey Cravat, a small-town newspaper editor, and his wife, Sabra, a woman of genteel upbringing who eventually enters political life as a member of Congress.

Ferber's intention in writing *Cimarron* was vastly different from the public's impression of it. As she put it in *A Peculiar Treasure*, she considered the work to be "a malevolent picture of what is known as American womanhood and American sentimentality. It contains paragraphs and even chapters of satire and, I am afraid, bitterness, but I doubt that more than a dozen people ever knew this. All the critics and the hundreds of thousands of readers took *Cimarron* as a colorful romantic western American novel."

Although the general public admired *Cimarron*, it was hostilely received in Oklahoma. Ferber was flooded with vilifying letters from the state, and several Oklahoma newspapers published editorials against her, including one which attacked her Jewishness by asking, "Why doesn't she stay in the ghetto where she came from?"

One of the more interesting episodes in *Cimarron* contains a Jewish character named Sol Levy, an immigrant who has somehow ended up in the small Oklahoma town and is ostracized and persecuted by the citizenry. In one scene, in which a group of men try to force Levy to drink whiskey, Yancey rushes to Levy's defense: Levy's "face was deathly white. They had shot off his hat. He was bareheaded. His eyes were sunken, stricken. His

head lolled a little on one side. His thick black locks hung dank on his forehead. At that first instant of seeing him as he rushed out of his office, Yancey thought, subconsciously, 'He looks like—like—' But the resemblance eluded him then. It was only later, after the sickening incident had ended, that he realized of whom it was that the Jew had reminded him as he stood there, crucified against the scale." Ferber's use of this scene suggests her resentment of Christians' antagonism toward Jews. Coming from a reformed Jewish family, Ferber herself was not very religious, and she perceived few differences between Jewish and Christian Americans. She believed anti-Semitism to be a philosophy espoused by the unsuccessful in society.

The success of such books as *Cimarron, Show Boat,* and *So Big* established Ferber's reputation as a regional author. She continued working in this vein with her next book, *American Beauty* (1931). This novel incorporates over 200 years of Connecticut farm history, beginning with the English colonization of New England and ending in modern times with immigrant Polish peasants working the land and making it fertile again. As in her other novels, the characters who work the hardest are the most positively drawn, while those who merely exploit natural resources are negatively portrayed.

The book was published in one of the worst years of the Depression, and, understandably, the popular reception was not as enthusiastic as it had been for her previous books. People could not afford to buy the novel, and its theme of hard labor eventually paying off rang false to many in that bleak year. However, Rudyard Kipling sent a personal letter to Ferber's publisher and asked the company to send his congratulations. He then stated, "I don't think her own people realize her value as an historical painter—yet. They will later."

The novel *Come and Get It* (1935) is similar in theme to *American Beauty*. It concerns the despoilment of Wisconsin and Michigan timberlands. Again, the characters who exploited the land for their own capitalistic gain are seen as wicked, while those who loved and cared for the land are positively drawn.

A Peculiar Treasure (1939), Ferber's first autobiography, was written as a response to the growth of Nazism and fascism, in the United States and abroad. The title comes from the Book of Exodus, and indeed, Ferber views America as "the Jew among nations" in the opening pages of the book. America, like the Jewish people, she believed, was resourceful, envied, ethical, and maligned by others.

Ferber states in *A Peculiar Treasure* that the book is "the story of an American Jewish family in the past half a century and as such a story about America which I know and love." She considered herself a fervently patriotic American, yet felt that this in no way interfered with her pride in her Jewish heritage. Instead she viewed her Jewishness as having made her a better American. For Ferber, Judaism was more of a culture which was primarily concerned with moral behavior than a religion.

Although Ferber saw herself as a pioneer in terms of being a woman in a predominantly male profession and consistently included strong female characters in her fiction, she did not place much emphasis on her own sexual identity. Instead, she was concerned mostly with her vocation as a writer. However, she did believe that one could not be a good author and a wife-mother simultaneously and attributed her never marrying to this belief.

Giant (1952) was perhaps Ferber's most notorious regional novel, because of its unflattering presentation of the State of Texas. The work describes the ranch industry and millionaire ranch owners. The story begins with the marriage of Les-

Ferber with James Dean on the set of the 1956 Warner Bros. film Giant *(Sanford Roth-Photo Researchers)*

lie Lynnton, an aristocratic Virginian, to Jordan Benedict, head of the Reata ranch in Texas, and much of the plot concerns Leslie's acculturation to the Texas way of life. In nearly every way, from their eating habits to their style of dress, Leslie finds Texans to be vastly different from the Americans she had known. She is also appalled by the Texan's discrimination against the Mexicans, who live in dire poverty in contrast to the ranchers' extravagant life-style. *Giant* proved to be immensely popular, and the novel was made into a film starring James Dean, Elizabeth Taylor, and Rock Hudson.

Ferber admitted her personal dislike of Texas, insisting that size should not be confused with greatness. She seemed to think that Texans regarded their state as superior to the rest of the United States, and this attitude conflicted with her own ideas about America. Ferber saw America as an amalgamation of different religions and ethnicities, none any better than the others, and resented the chauvinism which she found in Texas.

After the publication of *Giant*, Ferber visited Israel and compared the new nation to the Lone Star State: "Israel was a sort of Jewish Texas—without oil wells." Ferber's analogy referred to her perception of Israeli people as arrogant, ignorant of the world beyond the Israeli borders, and lacking in basic manners. The concept of a nation based on membership in a religion—even her own—conflicted with Ferber's sense of identity as a pluralist and an American.

Ice Palace (1958) was Ferber's last novel. The book concerns Alaska, which she visited often during the novel's five-year-writing period. Although *Ice Palace* is not as cohesive a work as her previous novels, it did bring her acclaim. She was credited with putting Alaska in the public eye and facilitating its transition from a territory to statehood. In fact, the *Anchorage Daily Times* paid her tribute by calling her "a twentieth-century version of Harriet Beecher Stowe."

The novel revolves around one character who wants Alaska to remain a territory so that he can exploit its natural resources and another who dreams of making Alaska a state and bettering the conditions of all the residents. The book follows in Ferber's tradition of regional novels, as again the author asserts her concern for the ecology and her distaste for capitalists who exploit the land.

Ferber's last work was her second autobiography, *A Kind of Magic* (1963). Like *A Peculiar Treasure*, it was written with the intent of glorifying life in America. However, *A Kind of Magic* is less interesting because it provides no new revelations about

Ferber shortly before her death (photo copyright © by Halsman)

the age of eighty-two, five years following publication of *A Kind of Magic*, Edna Ferber died of cancer after a lengthy bout with the disease. Perhaps the *New York Times* evaluated her career best in its front-page obituary on 17 April 1968: "With a love and enthusiasm that gained her world fame, Miss Ferber wrote about the United States for four decades. Her novels became minor classics and earned her a fortune as well as many honors. . . . Her books were not profound, but they were vivid and had a sound sociological basis. She was among the best-read novelists in the nation."

Although she was not commonly thought of as a Jewish writer, Ferber's Jewishness provided her with a unique perspective in viewing America. It provided her with a double vision—one which allowed her to love America openly on the one hand and yet be critical of its faults on the other.

Bibliography:
V. J. Brenni and B. L. Spencer, "Edna Ferber: A Selected Bibliography," *Bulletin of Bibliography*, 22 (1958): 152-156.

Biography:
Julie Goldsmith Gilbert, *Ferber: A Biography* (Garden City: Doubleday, 1978).

Ferber's life. She had much trouble writing the book, as she suffered from tic douloureux which bothered her during the last ten years of her life. At

Papers:
The principal collection of Ferber's papers is at the State Historical Society of Wisconsin.

Leslie Fiedler
(8 March 1917-   )

Stephen J. Whitfield
Brandeis University

SELECTED BOOKS: *An End to Innocence: Essays on Culture and Politics* (Boston: Beacon, 1955);
Love and Death in the American Novel (New York: Criterion, 1960; revised edition, New York: Stein & Day, 1966; London: Cape, 1965);
No! In Thunder: Essays on Myth and Literature (Boston: Beacon, 1960; London: Eyre & Spottiswoode, 1963);

The Second Stone: A Love Story (New York: Stein & Day, 1963; London: Heinemann, 1966);
Waiting for the End (New York: Stein & Day, 1964; London: Cape, 1965);
Back to China (New York: Stein & Day, 1965);
The Last Jew in America (New York: Stein & Day, 1966);
The Return of the Vanishing American (New York:

Leslie Fiedler (photo courtesy of SUNY at Buffalo News Bureau)

Stein & Day, 1968; London: Cape, 1968);

Nude Croquet: The Stories of Leslie Fiedler (New York: Stein & Day, 1969; London: Secker & Warburg, 1970);

Being Busted (New York: Stein & Day, 1969; London: Secker & Warburg, 1970);

Unfinished Business (New York: Stein & Day, 1972);

To the Gentiles (New York: Stein & Day, 1972);

Cross the Border—Close the Gap (New York: Stein & Day, 1972);

The Stranger in Shakespeare (New York: Stein & Day, 1972; London: Croom Helm, 1973);

The Messengers Will Come No More (New York: Stein & Day, 1974);

Freaks: Myths and Images of the Secret Self (New York: Simon & Schuster, 1978; Harmondsworth, U.K.: Penguin, 1981);

The Inadvertent Epic: From Uncle Tom's Cabin to Roots (New York: Simon & Schuster, 1979);

Olaf Stapledon (Oxford & New York: Oxford University Press, 1982);

What Was Literature? (New York: Simon & Schuster, 1982).

The roster of "great critics and historians of American literature in this century," the *New York Times Book Review* once announced, "would have to include Leslie [Aaron] Fiedler, by far the least academic, [and] the most voluble, diverse, uneven, divisive, [and] rambunctious." Although Fiedler himself has wryly noted that the adjective "controversial" has become associated with his name so frequently as to seem part of it, few scholars would dispute that Fiedler's identification of sexual and racial motifs, which owes much in boldness and terminology to psychoanalytic theory, has decisively shaped the interpretation of letters in the United States. His fecund essays and books, especially *Love and Death in the American Novel* (1960), have been distinguished by exceptional freshness of insight, ambitiousness of assertion, and pungency of expression. He has also had three novels, three novellas, and a collection of short stories published, though his fiction has not earned him the same measure of attention—or admiration—as his criticism.

This remorseless explorer of national myths, especially the romance of the West, was born in Newark, New Jersey, the son of a pharmacist, Jacob J. Fiedler, and Lillian Rosenstrauch Fiedler. He was educated in Newark's public schools and then commuted to New York University, which granted him a bachelor's degree in 1938. Fiedler received a master's degree from the University of Wisconsin the following year and his doctorate from the same institution in 1941. During World War II, he studied at the Japanese Language School at the University of Colorado; and until 1945, Lieutenant Fiedler served in the U.S. Naval Reserve as a Japanese interpreter. He did postdoctoral work at Harvard in 1946 and 1947. Fiedler's marriage to Margaret Ann Shipley ended in divorce after thirty-four years in 1973, when he married Sally Andersen. He has six children from his first marriage and two stepchildren from his second.

Unofficial membership in the New York Jewish intelligentsia did not lapse, even though, for two decades (1941-1943, 1947-1964), Fiedler taught English at Montana State University. Such displacement undoubtedly stirred his interest in the consequences of ethnicity and marginality and in the complications of cultural estrangement. Having switched allegiance from the mild Trotskyism of his adolescence to the psychoanalytic and mythic speculations of Freud's *Totem and Taboo*, Fiedler was especially fascinated by the disabling role of guilt in distorting relations between Jews and Gentiles, Indians and palefaces, blacks and whites, and foreigners and Americans overseas. He himself was ceremoniously inducted into the Blackfoot tribe.

No one developed better than Fiedler the knack of finding subconscious fears lurking in shifts of identity. No one could convert a stereotype into an archetype faster than the author of *Love and Death in the American Novel*, which argues for the persistence and pertinence of the dream of a buddy system involving a white male and a dark companion removed from the control (and rivalry) of women. Fiedler claimed that the "failure of the American fictionist to deal with adult heterosexual love and his consequent obsession with death, incest and innocent homosexuality" affected daily life and influenced "the writers in whom the consciousness of our plight is given clarity and form." Startling at first, Fiedler's thesis has become widely accepted, despite vigorous dissenters. Philip Rahv, whose

Partisan Review had published the essay that first propounded this interpretation of American literature, later dismissed it as "a talented young man's *jeu d'esprit*," though Rahv conceded that Fiedler "is nothing if not brilliant." Irving Howe condemned *Love and Death in the American Novel* as "sophisticated crankiness" because of its absence of modulation and qualification and its neglect of those writers who cannot be incorporated into the thesis of the book.

Fiedler continued to insist upon the "duplicity and outrageousness" of American novelists, although his own fiction—while testifying to his fascination with ethnicity—was drawn to "adult heterosexual love" rather than to homoerotic themes. In 1957 he won an award from the National Institute of Arts and Letters for "excellence in creative writing," though his first novel was not published until six years later. *The Second Stone: A Love Story* is a dissection of Americans in Italy, where Fiedler himself lived as a Fulbright fellow and lecturer from 1951 to 1953. Clem Stone, a barely published writer, has been living in Rome in the 1950s. He falls in love with Hilda, the wife of his boyhood friend Mark Stone, though Clem continues to express an abiding love for his own wife. The book includes several comic episodes, such as a First International Conference on Love, as well as a Communist riot that Clem inadvertently provokes on May Day. The author's own brilliant critical powers could not be suppressed when he turned to the composition of his fiction, and the result is a self-conscious design. In *The Second Stone* Clem and Mark are presumably meant to represent the bifurcated identity of Samuel Clemens, whom Fiedler has argued was a subversive artist wearing an entertainer's mask. It was Clemens who developed the myth of American innocents abroad.

Fiedler's first novel was not very well received. Granville Hicks voiced objections that others have applied to the range of Fiedler's fiction: "Not only do the satirical passages come close to a too easy kind of burlesque; there is a great variation of tone in the more serious portions of the novel." Hicks nevertheless acknowledged that the author had "a gift for fiction, though his grip on his craft is uncertain."

A second novel published two years later, *Back to China* (1965), is also devoted to the subject of an extramarital affair. The protagonist is a middle-aged Jew who teaches philosophy at a university in Montana. He is given the improbable name of Baro Finkelstone, which means—as the *New Republic's* Guy Daniels explained—that "this confessional tale lays *bare* the truth about . . . a *fink*." Through a series of flashbacks, it is disclosed that a Japanese urologist and a beatnik Sioux scholarship student, with whose Japanese wife Finkelstone has been committing adultery, have both died. Finkelstone is in fact responsible for the deaths of neither the Japanese father figure nor the Sioux surrogate son; but his guilt is so burdensome that the *New Republic* labeled the book "one of the most confused . . . in modern fiction." *Time* considered *Back to China* "grotesque and often unpleasant, but it is also funny and unexpectedly successful as the study of a converse Candide," who is seeking to repent for "the worst of all possible selves." The novel can also be read as a converse *End to Innocence* (1955), Fiedler's first collection of essays that flayed liberalism for its assumption that it was without sin during the New Deal and thereafter.

The title story of his next work of fiction, *The Last Jew in America* (1966), is perhaps Fiedler's most successful. An aged Jew who had come West to disseminate socialism is dying; and the effort to gather a *minyan* in a campus community of assimilated Jews to pray for him on the Day of Atonement is by turns comic and pathetic. What makes "The Last Jew in America" memorable, however, is not its clever plotting but its resourcefulness in striking the most compelling of themes in American-Jewish fiction: assimilation and its discontents. The other two tales in the collection are much less resonant. In "The Last WASP in the West," a poet from the same imaginary western town finds himself the only Gentile at a crass Jewish wedding in New Jersey, and for a moment he believes that virtually all the students at the university back home are Jews as well. In "The First Spade in the West," the black owner of a cocktail lounge, who believes himself to be the great-grandson of the slave who accompanied the Lewis and Clark expedition, seeks recognition from the white fathers of the city. He ends up compromised, having spent a night with a wealthy white woman who dies while her husband is in a drunken stupor.

The Last Jew in America is enlivened by wickedly satirical thrusts that often cannot be differentiated from vulgarity and tastelessness. Fiedler has a habit of calling a Negro a spade; and Rahv once asserted that Fiedler "is virtually allergic to tact." The author himself has cheerfully pleaded guilty to this charge, thus helping to demonstrate the theory of sociologist John Murray Cuddihy that Jewish intellectuals feel peculiarly afflicted by "the ordeal of civility."

In any event Fiedler did not surrender his cosmopolitanism in teaching in the West; his stay in Montana was interrupted by frequent lectures and visiting professorships at universities throughout the United States and in Europe. In 1964 he moved to the State University of New York at Buffalo. The author of the once notorious "Come Back to the Raft Ag'in, Huck Honey!" became the Samuel Clemens Professor of English. Having written about the drug experience in *Back to China* and in his eccentric analysis of mythic Indians, *The Return of the Vanishing American* (1968), Fiedler became the faculty adviser to a student organization advocating the legalization of marijuana. Fiedler denied having taken illegal drugs himself; but in 1967 he was arrested for having "maintained a premise"—his home—where marijuana was allegedly smoked. The case against Fiedler was based on the testimony of a police agent equipped with a radio-listening device who was a guest in Fiedler's home. This sentence—six months in prison — was reversed by the New York Court of Appeals after the case received international publicity.

In 1969, the same year that his account of his legal tribulations, *Being Busted*, was published, Fiedler gathered his short stories together in *Nude Croquet: The Stories of Leslie Fiedler*. The title story is probably the most widely known and originally appeared in *Esquire*. This fable of middle-aged, defeated Jewish intellectuals and their wives (a couple of them young second wives) is set in a bizarre mansion in New Jersey. Croquet is played, but the rules require disrobing, which reveals the indignity of aging. By the end of the story, the wife of one has-been writer has goaded him so mercilessly that a fatal heart attack results.

Among the other noteworthy contributions to the collection are "The Stain," which treats black self-hatred; "Dirty Ralphy," whose subject is Jewish self-hatred; "Let Nothing You Dismay," whose protagonist is the puzzled child of a Jewish-Gentile marriage; and "The Girl in the Black Raincoat," a fantasy about the seduction of humanities professors. Fiedler was himself an early champion of the mystical writings of Simone Weil, and his vaguely Hasidic parable of self-sacrifice, "The Dancing of Reb Hershl with the Withered Hand," is among the best of his stories. Yet the permanence of Fiedler's fiction cannot be predicted with any confidence, since its subordination to preoccupations better developed in his nonfiction is often a deterrent to aesthetic enjoyment. Fiedler's novels and stories, for all their savvy and fluency, lack the piquancy, vitality, and sheer pyrotechnics that make his criticism so indispensable.

five

he doubted whether he dould finish it, confessing that " there is a wrong kind of fire burning in my head and I don't think I can write." But write he did, ~~kh~~ ~~fmxxkhexfixxkxt~~though predictably enough he ended bp writing-- for the first time in his career-- against rather than for or to his audience. ~~And once he~~ was done, he ~~xxkxxxkxdxixxx seems to have drawn back into himself~~ ~~xxx~~ produci~~ng~~ no long fiction for three years and never again readi~~ng~~ any review of his own work. Yet he ~~knew~~ that Martin Chuzzlewit , despite its reception, was " in a h hundred points immensely the best work" he had published.

~~Andxwikhxkhisxjudmenxtxixxamxur~~

And with this judgment I concur, though I understand too why the critics of his time demuured; since~~xgxxxxkxxxkxixixxxxxximexxgxxxxxxxxxxixxxxxxxxxxximm~~ingly ~~un-Dickension sort~~ ~~lingly un-Dickensian kind~~ ~~sort~~ It is , to begin with, often truly "disgusting" ~~and~~ nowhere "life-enhancing" or beautiful: a work, in short, as ~~g~~ ~~misanthropic~~ and offputting as the Fourth Book of Gulliver's Travels." The Voyage to the Houynyms", however, is redeemed by the elegance of its structure and the precision of its language, while Martin Chuzzlewit~~x~~ is ~~inxxxx~~ artistically a mess~~x~~; betraying everywhere , as ~~an early~~ revi~~c~~wer noted, signs of" fast writing and careless composition." The same charges could, of course, ha~~d~~e been made against all of ~~his earlier~~ novels, but the critics seem not to have taken them seriously enough to ~~here measured them against~~ by esthetic standards, ~~or~~ ~~Besides, they were probably, too~~ busy laughing and crying. But Martin Chuzzlew is too grim for easy t~~x~~ laughter or tears; and it boasts in the text itself of being not a mere entertainment but a serious study of human selfishness. On first reading, indeed, that ~~novel seems to fall~~ between two stools; being neither, like, ~~the earlier~~ Oliver Twist, loved by children and appealing to the dhild in all ~~of us~~, nor, like the ~~later~~ Hard Times, fare for adult tastes only

Finally, however, , ~~ifxxixxixxxxtx~~transitional ~~as it is~~, it demans to be read as ~~the last of Dicken's pop romances rather than~~ the first of his art novels, ~~which is to say~~ the sort of good bad book, ~~naive and mythological,~~ which though a failure by elitist critical standards, somehow refuses to die. ~~And like~~s in the case of all such books, what is best in it is what is ~~unxxxi~~unplanned and inadvertent, dreamed rather than c~~xxixxxxxxxxxxxxx~~ means first of all ~~Mxxxxxxmp~~Sairy Gamp, ~~xhxx~~ who ~~seems to making~~ make ~~her~~ appearnace ~~against the author's will~~ forcing herself into the book ~~only~~ after it is one third over, ~~the~~ refusi~~ng~~ to disappear until the very end, though she can only with violence be forced in~~to~~ the plot or made to s~~eem~~ relevant to the book's main theme.

She is, an immensely complex character, Mrs. Gamp, who ~~begins as~~ a comic grotesque embodying Dicken's contempt for the medical profession and his

Revised typescript page from an essay on Martin Chuzzlewit

In any event, he has turned away from the study and composition of serious fiction in recent years and has devoted himself instead to the iconography of popular culture. In 1974 he produced a science-fiction novel set in twenty-fifth-century Palestine, *The Messengers Will Come No More*. In reviewing it for the *New York Times Book Review*, Robert Alter observed that it might have been entitled "The Last Jew in the Cosmos." The theme of ethnic extinction, Alter added, "has only been impoverished by the temporal and spatial projection and the abstraction it has undergone" since "The Last Jew in America." Fiedler has long been an unusually perceptive student of the relationship between Jews and American popular culture; his columns, often on that topic, originally appeared in the magazine *American Judaism* and have been collected in a book of essays, *To the Gentiles* (1972). His writings have often drawn attention to the relevance of his own ethnic background. It is certainly not idle to speculate that his own dissident stance, his lifelong interest in outsiders, his intellectual pride, and his eagerness to unmask the secret intentions at the heart of American literature are intimately connected to his Jewishness.

Even readers who manage to resist Fiedler's arguments and who cannot accept his methods or conclusions can appreciate his supple and graceful prose, punctuated by original wit. Virtually all of Fiedler's pages betray an intelligence that is radically discontented with received—and especially respectable—opinion. His books are a monument to an engaged—and engaging—mind.

Reference:

Max F. Schulz, *Radical Sophistication: Studies in Contemporary Jewish/American Novelists* (Athens: Ohio University Press, 1969), pp. 154-172.

Bruce Jay Friedman

(26 April 1930-   )

Evelyn Avery
Towson State University

See also the Friedman entry in *DLB 2, American Novelists Since World War II*.

BOOKS: *Stern* (New York: Simon & Schuster, 1962; London: Deutsch, 1963);
Far from the City of Class and Other Stories (New York: Frommer-Pasmantier, 1963);
A Mother's Kisses (New York: Simon & Schuster, 1964; London: Cape, 1965);
Black Angels (New York: Simon & Schuster, 1966; London: Cape, 1967);
Scuba Duba: A Tense Comedy (New York: Simon & Schuster, 1968);
The Dick (New York: Knopf, 1970; London: Cape, 1971);
Steambath (New York: Knopf, 1971);
About Harry Towns (New York: Knopf, 1974; London: Cape, 1975);
The Lonely Guy's Book of Life (New York: McGraw-Hill, 1976).

SELECTED PLAYS: *Scuba Duba: A Tense Comedy*, New York, New Theatre, 10 October 1967;
Steambath, New York, Truck and Warehouse Theatre, 30 June 1970.

OTHER: *Black Humor*, edited by Friedman (New York: Bantam, 1965).

SELECTED PERIODICAL PUBLICATIONS: "The Imposing Proportions of Jean Shrimpton," *Esquire*, 63 (April 1965): 70-75, 148-150;
"Celine," *New York Times Book Review*, 5 February 1967, pp. 1, 52;
"Arrested by Detectives Valesares and Sullivan. Charge: Murder," *Saturday Evening Post*, 240 (22 April 1967): 38-42, 45-47;
"Look Mao, I'm Dancing," *Esquire*, 77 (April 1972): 55, 58;
"Hi, This is Bruce Jay Friedman, Reporting from Hollywood," *Esquire*, 86 (August 1976): 56-58;
"Living Together," *Esquire*, 96 (December 1981): 118-123;
"Detroit Abe," *Esquire*, 99 (March 1983): 234-239.

Bruce Jay Friedman (photo © Jerry Bauer)

Author of four novels, two collections of short stories, a book of satiric essays, and many articles, Bruce Jay Friedman gained recognition in the 1960s as a seriocomic writer. Labeled a black humorist, an ambiguous term he himself coined, Friedman caricatures the lives of neurotic, partially assimilated Jewish-Americans. Unlike Saul Bellow and Bernard Malamud, he avoids the immigrant experience and Yiddish heritage, concentrating instead on a transient, impersonal, highly materialistic America.

Although some of Friedman's short-story characters are Gentiles, his novels center on Jews alienated from Christian America and ignorant of their own roots. Shallow and status-conscious, his Jews are born losers, comic exaggerations of the victim and the bungler. Episodically structured and very colloquial, Friedman's fiction depicts an absurd and fragmented America. In such a world, the individual is weakened; the family is perverted; and the once taboo—adultery, alcoholism, drug abuse, and random violence—becomes common.

To some extent, Friedman, according to Max Schulz, "draws deeply upon his past for his fiction."

Born on 26 April 1930 in the Bronx, he was reared there by his parents, Irving and Molly Liebowitz Friedman, and developed an interest in writing while working on his high-school paper, the *Clinton News*. After graduating from DeWitt Clinton High School in 1947, Friedman majored in journalism at the University of Missouri, where he received his B.A. in 1951. Both his urban background and Midwestern experiences are evident in such works as "Far From the City of Class," "The Subversives," *A Mother's Kisses*, and *The Dick*. A stint as a United States Air Force correspondent and feature writer (1951-1953) provided material for several short stories and for his first novel, *Stern* (1962).

Critically acclaimed for its offbeat humor and sharp insights, *Stern* has been described by Gerald Weales as a "surrealist fantasy which is always either sexual or violent." Others view the novel's bumbling, paranoiac protagonist as a perverse Walter Mitty, nurturing misfortune, inviting rejection and disaster. Grotesque and pathetic, Stern's life is a travesty of the American dream. Despite the outward trappings—a family, suburban home, and secure job—the thirty-four-year-old Stern is miserable, suspicious of his flirtatious wife, uncomfortable with his aloof neighbors, and uneasy as an editor for a label manufacturer. Even his son Donald is a trial and a disappointment, "a lonely boy who sucks on blankets." Worse, Stern's self-contempt makes him prey to the neighborhood anti-Semite who has insulted his family and "peered between [his wife's] legs."

Humiliated by the incident and his impotency, Stern develops an ulcer, the physical symptom of his obsession. Though the illness lands him in a bizarre rest home, ironically he finds companionship and achieves manhood there. Among the crippled and demented, Stern parodies the all-American male by contributing to a sandlot-baseball victory, joining in a tavern fight, and engaging in sordid sex. However, his newly won confidence vanishes when he reenters the real world where he must prove himself again. After "the mildest nervous breakdown," Stern challenges his anti-Semitic nemesis, but the fight is indecisive, a perfect description of his past and future. A closing image of Stern, emotionally detached, posing as a family man, highlights his predicament. Too self-conscious, too conformist, Stern seems incapable of deep, responsible relationships. In many ways, he, dependent on others for his identity, resembles David Riesman's "other directed man" in *The Lonely Crowd* (1958). Stern is not alone. Mouthing clichés and slogans, most of Friedman's characters, Jews and Gentiles, occupy similar Madison Avenue wastelands. His Jews, how-ever, are doubly burdened. As marginal men in a gilded society, they are denied their authentic heritage. Stern, for example, is a victim of a superficial Hebrew-school education, Judaically ignorant parents, and carnival Passover rituals. Though he longs to be one of "the chanting sufferers at the synagogue," he feels "phony, . . . a loner" in the traditional setting. Offered an opportunity, years later, to be accepted in a small-town synagogue, Stern, then an air force officer, bungles it. By pretending to be an unmarried pilot, by sexually exploiting one of the congregant's daughters, he betrays his wife, the congregation, and himself. Predictably, momentary pleasure gives way to guilt and then flight.

Betrayal and guilt are trademarks of Fried-man's fiction in which oppressor and victim are often one, the bizarre is normal, and everything has a price. *Far from the City of Class and Other Stories* (1963), his first collection of short stories, echoes *Stern* and foreshadows later works. Although not explicitly Jewish, the tales include characters, dialogues, and incidents from lower-middle-class ethnic backgrounds. "When You're Excused, You're Excused" does contain a Jewish protagonist and situation. In this extended shaggy-dog tale, Mr. Kessler violates Yom Kippur, the Day of Atonement, by exercising in the gym, eating ham, smoking pot, committing adultery—all of which he rationalizes as necessary for his health. When con-fronted, however, by a companion's ignorance of an obscure Jewish baseball player, Kessler is morally outraged and bites off a piece of his ear.

A hypocrite who betrays his family and his values, Kessler resembles Gordon and Merz, two hustlers in "Foot in the Door." Ultramaterialistic, they negotiate with their families' health and honor for carpeting, promotions, and mistresses but are ultimately trapped by the crass commercialism they represent. Three other tales, "Far from the City of Class," "The Trip," and "The Good Times," are later expanded in *A Mother's Kisses* (1964), Fried-man's second novel.

Published five years before Philip Roth's con-troversial *Portnoy's Complaint*, *A Mother's Kisses* lam-poons the Jewish-American mom. Similar in sub-ject, both novels concern a young Jewish man and his frustrated, overbearing mother. Like Sophie Portnoy, Friedman's character Meg is an energetic, demanding woman chained to an ineffectual hus-band and pathologically attached to her son. Both mothers spy on their children, manipulate their lives, and exploit their guilt; but Meg's actions are

more brazen, Friedman's novel more burlesque. Moreover, Meg is a middle-aged exhibitionist, flaunting her figure, convinced that every male, including her son, desires her. Unlike the sen-timentalized Yiddish mama of stage and fiction, Meg is a source of embarrassment and suffering to her children.

Set in a summer resort, a Brooklyn apartment, and on a Midwestern college campus, the novel traces a brief, transitional period in the life of Joseph, an overprotected adolescent seeking inde-pendence but thwarted by his mother. As a younger copy of Stern, he is also physically and psychologi-cally scarred, tormented by an infected arm and wounded ego. Like Stern, he lacks a positive Jewish identity and responds primarily to anti-Semitic in-sults or threats. Joseph's "kike-man" is a Jew-baiting lifeguard whom he attacks, much to his mother's surprise and consternation.

Deflated by the experience, Joseph, somewhat like his Old Testament namesake, is in an alien land, cut off from his people. But unlike the biblical fig-ure, Friedman's protagonist performs no miracles, possesses no faith, and is denied an authentic com-munity. The novel's few references to American Judaism are negative, portraying it as materialistic, vulgar, and hypocritical. The sole religious scene occurs in an off-campus church basement, tem-porarily the site of Jewish services. In an extended ecumenical parody, a young rabbi solicits funds, a patronizing Christian couple absorbs "Hebrew cul-ture," and Meg exclaims Christ's name in a tribute to brotherhood. In a variety of ways Meg typifies the confused Jewish-American, uncertain of religious law, of the rabbi's role, and of the Jew's relation-ship to Gentiles. Thus she regards "true Jewishness" as flourishing in a church "without a Torah" and prayers. Though she disparages fund-raising, she slips the rabbi a donation. She is suspicious of Jew-loving Christians, even though her closest friends are Gentiles. Alternately critical and accepting, trusting and skeptical, Meg is the quasi-assimilated Jew, touching both worlds but not entirely comfort-able in either.

As a product of his mother's neuroses, Joseph is a comic victim, financially exploited and romanti-cally repudiated. While a waiter at a Jewish resort, he is overworked and underpaid, spurned by a sexy girl and pursued by a sickly one. Rejected by Co-lumbia University, Joseph, thanks to his mother, enrolls in Kansas Land Grant Agricultural College, where a couple of neurotic Jews and a husbandry curriculum threaten his sanity. Unable to adjust to the Gentile world or to accept the Jewish one,

Charles Grodin and Jenny Berlin in The Heartbreak Kid, *based on Friedman's story "A Change of Plans"
and released by 20th Century-Fox in 1972*

Joseph, like Stern, is the perpetual outsider, the typical Friedman protagonist buffeted by fate and fear.

Sometimes, as Friedman illustrates in his second story collection, *Black Angels* (1966), the enemy is not anti-Semitism but "the contemporary mayhem [which] scars even the traditional . . . family." One of the stories, "The Enemy," pits two sisters against an "interloping in-law" whom they blame for their brother's insanity. Replete with paranoia, senility, and rage, the tale burlesques the Jewish family and its trouble-making matriarchs. In "A Change of Plans" family discord begins shortly after the wedding, when Cantrow, an immature groom, decides his wife is repulsive and dumps her for an attractive Gentile girl. Friedman's story, which served as the basis of the 1972 film *The Heartbreak Kid*, highlights marital infidelity and family frailty as well as the appeal of WASP beauty to insecure Jewish men.

Similar concerns appear in Friedman's first drama, *Scuba Duba: A Tense Comedy*, published in 1968. An off-Broadway success for more than a year, the play centers on Harold Wonder whose wife is involved with a refined, accomplished black man. As a so-called liberal, Harold must divest himself of racial stereotypes and confront reality, a crumbling marriage and changing society.

Friedman's novel *The Dick* (1970) reveals the impact of the tumultuous 1960s on the outsider. In a desperate attempt to be assimilated Kenneth LePeters, a lonely and self-conscious Jew, has changed his name from Sussman, become a police department public-relations man, and purchased a house on "Detective Hill." Like Stern and Joseph, he craves companionship and approval but is denied both. Even his hard-won transfer from public relations to detective duty does not alter his role as a New York Jewish misfit. A scar, dividing his face in two, symbolizes LePeters's psychological conflict and miserable condition. Unlike earlier Friedman protagonists, he breaks with the past and affirms his individuality. Influenced by culture of the 1960s, he rejects his unfaithful wife and flees with his teenage daughter to a new freedom. In a rapidly changing society, Friedman suggests, daring and adaptability are necessary for survival. Despite a relatively positive conclusion, *The Dick* is not as effective as *Stern*. Superficially, LePeters appears decisive, but he has not solved his problems, merely run from them.

Moreover, as one reviewer put it, Friedman's third novel is stylistically full of "gimmicks . . . which have degenerated into formula . . . and cheaply won laughs[s] that depend on tag line[s]."

Steambath (1971), Friedman's second play, locates the protagonist, Tandy, in a steamy, overheated afterlife, where he argues with God, a Puerto Rican bath attendant, that he should be restored to life. In a predictable Friedman reversal Tandy concludes that his life has not been admirable and that his case is weak.

Friedman's most recent fiction is stultifying, as claustrophobic as a steambath. Technically a novel, *About Harry Towns* (1974) consists of six sections, almost short stories, which skim the life of Harry Towns, a self-centered, fortyish Jewish screenwriter. Separated from his wife, depressed by his parents' deaths, experiencing the proverbial midlife crisis, he embraces the swinging life—partying, gambling, using drugs—but is left more desolate. Geographically mobile and culturally uprooted, Harry represents the contemporary self-indulgent American, severed from family, community, and tradition.

A pathetic figure, even his Jewishness is an accident of birth recalled during crises. Confronted by his parents' deaths, he relies on the funeral director to choose a rabbi and then mistakes conservative clothes, a reasonable fee, and an effective eulogy for sincerity and spirituality. Shallow and gullible, Harry credits the rabbi with nearly "get-[ting] him back to religion" until the second funeral when he discovers him more an actor than God's servant. Enraged that the rabbi is more concerned with his Hollywood connections than with his father's death, Harry crudely rejects his invitation to meet him in Israel: " 'I don't give a shit about Israel,' said Towns. It wasn't true. He did give a shit about Israel. When the chips were down, he was still some kind of Jew."

Unfortunately, the evidence of Harry's Judaism, or of his sensitivity, or responsibility is absent from the novel. The truth is that Harry does not care about anyone or anything. Had he been won over to religion, the experience would have been trivial; tripping on God would have temporarily replaced snorting cocaine. Harry Towns is not much of a Jew or a man. A disappointment to his son, whom he claims to love, Harry needs external highs because he is empty, a shell of a person incapable of loving or living. Disordered and meaningless, his life reflects nothing of a rich Judaic heritage, only a vulgar American materialism. Less conventional and more self-pitying than Stern or

Joseph, Harry forfeits the reader's sympathy because he is a victim of his own poor choices. Nor is the conclusion persuasive when he vows to reform, to "treat each human being . . . with generosity—until such time as he found reason not to." Once again Friedman's affirmation is unexpected; his point of view is unclear. Does the novel satirize Harry Towns's life, sympathize with it, or combine both attitudes? Can a character be both a cad and a schlemiel? While the questions raised are important, the characters, mere skeletal sketches, are not. The book is lifeless, lacking the humor and spontaneity of earlier works.

Friedman's latest work, *The Lonely Guy's Book of Life* (1976), is a satiric guide which spoofs the single man's condition and semiseriously offers helpful hints. Although praised by Herbert Gold, the irony is strained and the humor is not sustained.

Two recent short stories also reveal the defects of Friedman's most recent writing. "Living Together" (1981) veers between satire and melodrama as middle-aged Pellegrino falls in love with an intense, possessive woman whom he later considers rejecting but does not. Given his girl friend's al-

Dust jacket for Friedman's latest book, a parodic guide to happiness for the single man

coholism, overweight, and total dependency, the happy ending is obviously ironic, the story a heavy-handed romantic satire.

"Detroit Abe" (1983) begins promisingly enough with Abrahamowitz, a forty-eight-year-old frustrated untenured college instructor, confronting his lonely, monotonous existence. Aloof from his colleagues, detached from his students, deserted by women, Abrahamowitz even considers seeking comfort in a synagogue, but he concludes that he is not that desperate yet. In some respects he resembles Seymour Levin in Malamud's *A New Life* (1961), but the similarities are superficial. While Levin becomes more sensitive, sacrificing personal desires for principles, Abrahamowitz becomes more self-centered, forsaking his morals for money. In a vividly described chance meeting with a black pimp, Abrahamowitz is offered a fortune if he replaces the pimp, destined for prison. Initially repelled, he reconsiders and agrees to the venture. Though his rationalizations are comic, an inversion of conventional morality, the humor seems pointless. What

does a pale, middle-aged Jewish college professor turned pimp represent? Perhaps the story offers a clue in its definition of irony, which, according to Abrahamowitz, is "when you can't make out the intentions of the author and when the hero ends up in puzzled defeat." Unfortunately the definition applies to much of Friedman's recent work. Despite vivid description, effective dialogues, some memorable characters, Friedman's recent writing is unfocused. Both the author and his heroes seem uncertain of their roles, and the reader remains puzzled. Having drifted from his early concern with anti-Semitism and self-conscious Jews, Friedman has not yet found another effective subject.

References:
"An Interview [with Bruce Jay Friedman]," *Notre Dame Review*, 1 (1 March 1974): 16-19;
Stanley Kaufmann, "Frightened Writer," *The New Republic*, 155 (8 October 1966): 20-37;
Max F. Schulz, *Bruce Jay Friedman* (New York: Twayne, 1974).

Daniel Fuchs
(25 June 1909-)

Gabriel Miller
Rutgers University

See also the Fuchs entries in *DLB 9, American Novelists, 1910-1945*, and *DLB 26, American Screenwriters*.

BOOKS: *Summer in Williamsburg* (New York: Vanguard, 1934; London: Constable, 1935);
Homage to Blenholt (New York: Vanguard, 1936; London: Constable, 1936);
Low Company (New York: Vanguard, 1937); republished as *Neptune Beach* (London: Constable, 1937);
Stories, by Fuchs and others (New York: Farrar, Straus & Cudahy, 1956); republished as *A Book of Stories* (London: Gollancz, 1957);
Three Novels by Daniel Fuchs—includes *Summer in Williamsburg*, *Homage to Blenholt*, and *Low Company* (New York: Basic Books, 1961); republished as *The Williamsburg Trilogy* (New York: Avon, 1972);

West of the Rockies (New York: Knopf, 1971; London: Secker & Warburg, 1971);
The Apathetic Bookie Joint (New York: Methuen, 1979; London: Secker & Warburg, 1980).

SELECTED SCREENPLAYS: *The Big Shot*, by Fuchs, Bertram Millhauser, and Abem Finkel, Warner Bros., 1942;
The Hard Way, by Fuchs and Peter Viertel, Warner Bros., 1943;
Between Two Worlds, Warner Bros., 1944;
The Gangster, Allied Artists, 1947;
Hollow Triumph, Eagle Lion, 1948;
Criss Cross, Universal, 1949;
Panic in the Streets, adaptation, 20th Century-Fox, 1950;
Storm Warning, by Fuchs and Richard Brooks, Warner Bros., 1951;

Daniel Fuchs

Taxi, by Fuchs and D. M. Marshman, Jr., 20th
    Century-Fox, 1952;
The Human Jungle, by Fuchs and William Sackheim,
    Allied Artists, 1954;
Love Me or Leave Me, by Fuchs and Isobel Lennart,
    M-G-M, 1955;
Interlude, by Fuchs and Franklin Coen, Universal,
    1957;
Jeanne Eagels, by Fuchs, Sonya Levien, and John
    Fante, Columbia, 1957.

OTHER: "Pioneers! O Pioneers!," in *Story in
    America*, edited by Whit Burnett and Martha
    Foley (New York: Vanguard, 1934).

SELECTED PERIODICAL PUBLICATIONS:
    "Where Al Capone Grew Up," *New Republic* (9
    September 1931);
"Dream City or the Drugged Lake," *Cinema Arts*
    (Summer 1937);
"My Sister Who is Famous," *Collier's*, 100 (4 Sep-
    tember 1937);

"Crap Game," *New Yorker* (25 December 1937);
"Last Fall," *Saturday Evening Post*, 210 (5 March
    1938);
"Such a Nice Spring Day," *Collier's*, 102 (23 April
    1938);
"Shun All Care," *Harper's Bazaar* (May 1938);
"Getaway Day," *Collier's*, 102 (10 September 1938);
"Lucky Loser," *Collier's*, 102 (15 October 1938);
"A Matter of Pride," *Collier's*, 102 (22 October
    1938);
"Life Sentence," *Collier's*, 102 (19 November 1938);
"Give Hollywood a Chance," *Esquire* (December
    1938);
"Fortune and Men's Eyes," *Saturday Evening Post*,
    211 (10 December 1938);
"If a Man Answers, Hang Up," *Collier's*, 103 (22
    April 1939);
"Crazy Over Pigeons," *Collier's*, 103 (29 April 1939);
"A Girl Like Cele," *Redbook* (April 1939);
"The Woman in Buffalo," *Esquire* (April 1939);
"Not to the Swift," *Collier's*, 103 (13 May 1939);
"Toilers of the Screen," *Collier's*, 104 (8 July 1939);
"The Hosiery Shop," *Harper's Bazaar* (1 Spetember
    1939);
"The Politician," *New Republic*, 100 (11 October
    1939);
"A Mink Coat Each Morning," *Collier's*, 105 (27
    January 1940);
"Pug in an Opera Hat," *Collier's*, 105 (23 March
    1940);
"Daring Young Man," *Collier's*, 106 (24 August
    1940);
"Racing is a Business," *Collier's*, 106 (5 October
    1940);
"The Fabulous Rubio," *Collier's*, 107 (4 January
    1941);
"Strange Things Happen in Brooklyn," *Collier's*,
    107 (1 February 1941);
"The Long Green," *Cosmopolitan* (February 1951);
"Writing for the Movies," *Commentary* (February
    1962).

Daniel Fuchs is a writer of major importance
in the American-Jewish literary tradition, although
his novels are neither as generally recognized nor as
widely read as befits his achievement. His following,
though small, includes such distinguished novelists
and critics as Irving Howe, Leslie A. Fiedler, Mordecai Richler, John Updike, and Howard Moss. His
most recent work, *The Apathetic Bookie Joint* (1979),
received the kind of review evaluation accorded the
most distinguished writers. Yet despite such accolades, Fuchs's name is not well known, even in

academic circles, nor is his work easily available.

Fuchs was born in New York City to immigrant parents. His father, Jacob Fuchs, came to America from Russia when he was seventeen years old; his mother, Sara Cohen Fuchs, emigrated at age thirteen from Poland. Fuchs grew up in primarily Jewish areas of the city, spending his early childhood on Manhattan's Lower East Side and then, at the age of five, moving with his family to the Williamsburg section of Brooklyn, which was to become the greatest influence on his artistic imagination.

The Williamsburg of Fuchs's youth was ethnically mixed; later there would be a more substantial Jewish migration, but in 1914, the area was true melting-pot New York. Fuchs's own block was Jewish, but the neighborhood was parceled into sections, each with its own ethnic group. The children formed gangs, both for adventure and for protection. In an early piece, "Where Al Capone Grew Up" (1931), Fuchs described the environment: "The district as I knew it in my boyhood was still comparatively free of serious crime. . . . At this stage rough-house was mainly semi-pastime in nature, providing a kind of sporting *gradus honorum* for all red-blooded youths. But boy gangsters grew up into men, the East Side influence was strong, and hooliganism became in one generation a business colorlessly operated by many of the very individuals for whom it had been a boyish sport." At the time of the move to Williamsburg, Fuchs's father set himself up in a new business, selling newspapers to the construction crews at work on the Whitehall Building on Battery Place; when the building was completed, he set up a concession stand where he sold papers, magazines, and candy. This business provided his son one form of escape from Williamsburg, which he would later describe as a "closed-in canyon." Jacob Fuchs brought home many magazines, including *Punch*, *Tatler*, *Life*, and *American Mercury*, and the young Fuchs read them all. Novels, however, were his first love, and his enthusiasm encompassed the works of Dickens and Thackeray, as well as the modern fiction of Lawrence, Maugham, Joyce, and the avant-garde writers in *transition*.

A second passion, and source of influence later, was the movies. Within a short distance of his home were seven movie theaters; the programs were changed regularly, and Fuchs went to the movies at least twice a week. As well as a way of becoming Americanized, the movies provided the young Fuchs, and many like him, a means of escape, more immediate and more powerful even than reading, from the depressing world of Williamsburg. In Fuchs's words, "what these pictures did—with their virility and vigor, their command of life and consistently positive statements—was to act against the fear that possessed and constricted us." This fear, transferred from parents to children, was the last effect of the oppression of the Old World and of the hardships of adjusting to the New. The experience of the movies plays a central role in Fuchs's fiction; it has shaped his style, his attitudes, and his vision.

Fuchs practiced his writing skills while attending City College, from which he graduated in 1930, a philosophy major. His major achievements as a writer are the three novels he wrote in the 1930s during summers off from teaching public school. Read in sequence, his three Williamsburg novels are a testament of a writer's quest, a struggle for a design, a knowing, and, finally, a sad acknowledgment that the only answer to be found was in acceptance of the ironic dimensions, both comic and tragic, of human nature.

Summer in Williamsburg (1934) is an attempt by a young writer to find some meaning in his experience of growing up in Williamsburg. Philip Hayman, Fuchs's persona in the novel, sets out at the suggestion of a neighbor to make "a laboratory out of Williamsburg" and thus to discover clues to the meaning he seeks. The novel is panoramic, employing a cinematic method as it moves from event to event, character to character. Often, parallel scenes comment on one another, enlarging and expanding the significance of each individual scene.

Philip's seriousness contrasts to the less noble quest of his friend Cohen, a romantic schlemiel who tries to instill meaning and beauty into his life by posturing alternately as a misunderstood artist, a political revolutionary, and a rejected lover. The youthful idealism of these boys, who are treated humorously and affectionately by Fuchs, sets off in turn the corrupt figure of Philip's gangster-uncle Papravel, who strong-arms his way to dominance of the bus routes from Brooklyn to the Catskill resort area. Papravel is at the same time a parody and an indictment of the success ethic in America. The novel, however, is dominated by failures: Philip's father, a man of honesty and sensitivity who ends up with nothing but "a cigarette and a window"; and Sussman the butcher, whose suicide opens the novel and presages the subsequent suicides of his wife and children. It is all of this that Philip tries to put together and understand.

Summer in Williamsburg is Fuchs's most ambitious novel, crowded with people and events, an endeavor to present life as he knew it in its entirety. If the book suffers from some of a first novel's excesses and an occasional loss of control, it is nonetheless remarkable for what it does accomplish. Like Fuchs's other Williamsburg novels, this narrative is set in summertime, that time of year when life is most directly exposed, when feelings and anxieties become sharpened as people crowd the streets to escape the oppressive heat of closed-in places. Fuchs's people are poor, sweating, pained Jews who inhabit claustrophobic tenement apartments in a squalid Jewish section of New York City. It is easy to explore life in Williamsburg, where nothing has to be pared away. Here one can see life in the raw and perhaps discover its meanings in stark relief.

The lives depicted and the incidents related in *Summer in Williamsburg* finally add up to very little, as the novel simply reflects in vivid detail the inevitable collapse of youthful romantic dreams under the pressure of an unrelenting harsh reality. Most explicit, however, is its statement of Fuchs's own attitudes about fiction: finding that life lacks direction, catharsis, or completion, he despairs at the novelist's attempts to find, and achieve, a design. In some passages of *Summer in Williamsburg*, more determinedly than in any of his other works, he exhibits the contradictory and incomplete nature of experience: "These were people as God made them and as they were. They sat in the sunshine going through the stale operations of living, they were real, but a novelist did not write a book about them. No novel, no matter how seriously intentioned, was real. The progressive development, the delineated episodes, the artificial climax, the final conclusion, setting the characters at rest and out of the lives of the readers, these were logical devices and they were false. People did not live in dramatic situations." And he laments the shortcomings of the novelist's art: "How marvelously writers were able to perceive, clear-cut and with sureness, the causes and the actions of their characters. In life no man was known, even to himself, but in these novels the authors were able to explain their people logically. What wonder-makers! What liars." *Summer in Williamsburg*, however, presents a poignant and profound record of experience, despite such disclaimers. It is a first novel of extraordinary talent.

The next two novels demonstrate Fuchs's mastery of form. *Homage to Blenholt* (1936) is a comic and vibrant novel, full of the kind of youthful idealism and zest lacking in the first novel. The protagonist, Max Balkan, is again a dreamer, longing to escape Williamsburg. Fantasizing about heroism and grandeur, he concentrates on thinking up get-rich-quick inventions which he hopes will bring him wealth and power. The novel develops around his plans to attend the funeral of Blenholt, commissioner of sewers, whom Max considers "a hero in this flat age," someone who sought heroism by building a machine of gangsters and political hacks. Flanking Max is another hopeless dreamer, Munves, whose greatest joy in life is to seek out errors in the footnotes of prominent etymologists. Another friend, Coblenz, is openly rebellious to life in Williamsburg and lives his life in defiance of its social conventions, scorning work and spending his time betting on the horses. Finally, as in *Summer in Williamsburg*, there is a father figure, another sweet and generous man who is beaten down by the harsh economic realities of the New World. Formerly a Yiddish actor who traveled all over the world playing great classical roles, Mr. Balkan is now reduced to carrying a sandwich board that advertises Madame Clara's Scientific Beauty Treatments. Laughed at by his wife, he asks nothing of life beyond occasional moments of peace and quiet.

Homage to Blenholt is Fuchs's most focused examination of the comic contradiction between dreams and reality, as his protagonist is firmly brought to confront the truth about his chosen hero and about himself. In scenes that anticipate Nathanael West's *The Day of the Locust* (1939) Fuchs exposes Max Balkan to the sudden violence that mobs unleash because of frustration, debased dreams, and empty lives. The novel, by its end, has shifted from broad comedy to tragic overtones of human entrapment, as Max must learn to live without his sustaining fantasies and to accept the cruel realities of Williamsburg. He and Munves both are to marry—women in Fuchs's novels are realists, who understand that they have to cope with the economics of Williamsburg—and in thus shouldering responsibility, they abandon their dreams in favor of running a delicatessen. As Mr. Balkan observes: "Much had gone out of Max, aspiration, hope, life. His son would grow old and . . . die, but actually Max was dead already for now he would live for bread alone. . . . Walking out of the house . . . it seemed to the old man that this death of youth was among the greatest tragedies in experience and that all the tears in America were not enough to bewail it." In *Low Company* (1937), Fuchs abandons the questioning tone of the earlier novels. The wide-eyed dreamers are gone; Fuchs is no longer searching for solutions. *Low Company* is a dramatized world view, a portrait of a world on the verge of collapse, a nightmare landscape where everyone and everything is dreck. It is also Fuchs's most surely plotted work.

The novel's locale is Neptune Beach (Fuchs's version of Brighton Beach), a grim wasteland of vice, corruption, and murder, where escaping misery can be man's only goal. Prostitution is big business and violence the chief occupation of the novel's characters. The protagonist is Moe Karty, a wretched failure obsessed with gambling. He has deserted his family and now lives in the basement of Spitzbergen's soda parlor, plotting his daily betting strategies. Having squandered all of his money, he tries to borrow constantly, most persistently from Shubunka, a small-time operator of houses of prostitution who is having his own problems with organized crime. In one of the novel's central scenes, Shubunka is beaten up on the beach by some of the mob's henchmen. Crying for his dignity and his life, he shouts: "Who am I? A dog? You have no right to do this! It is not the way for one human being to treat another! . . . We must not be like animals to each other! We are human beings altogether in this world." The words of Fuchs's *Luftmenschen*, his humane fathers, have now been put into the mouth of one of his most grotesque characters, who is not pleading for any positive ideal but merely defending small-time prostitution against organized crime. The novel concludes with the beating of Moe Karty by his brother-in-law and some hired thugs to whom he owes money, the murder of Spitzbergen by Karty, and the exile of Shubunka. In *Low Company* Fuchs anticipates West in his depiction of the surreal and grotesque and in the vision of mob anger and loneliness. In contrast to West, Fuchs demonstrates restraint and a dedication to realism that allow the violence and resulting sense of despair to remain convincing.

Although his Williamsburg setting is specifically a Jewish milieu and nearly all the characters in the three novels are Jews, many of them closely tied to their immigrant roots, Judaism as a religion and a force that shaped social and familial attitudes is strangely missing in the world of Fuchs's work. Certainly it does not hang over his characters as it has in the work of an earlier generation of American-Jewish writers, such as Abraham Cahan, Anzia Yezierska, and even Samuel Ornitz. Fuchs's narratives include no references to religious ritual, Old World attitudes, or even to exotic Jewish foods.

Fuchs himself, although the child of first-generation immigrants, received no religious education and was never bar mitzvahed, which might explain the absence of religious ritual from his books. What is surprising, however, is not that religion plays no part in the lives of the young men and women in the novels (the second generation), but that it is seemingly of no interest even to the parents and grandparents, people who, surely, had been steeped in it in the Old World.

There are several reasons for this religious void. Fuchs's characters reflect the fact that America turned out to be a country whose streets were not, after all, paved with gold. His people must spend all their energies struggling to make a living and then resting so that they can work the next day. There is time for little else, even love. There is certainly no time for religion; life in America has beaten any love of God or Jewish heritage out of them. Nevertheless, though there is a strong element of social criticism in the novels, Fuchs was not out to decry the immigrant condition. He was not a radical writer, nor did he write proletarian novels—he was clearly not in the political mainstream of his time. Fuchs merely wrote about the realities of the world within which he lived, and if his novels imply a critique of the American capitalist system, nowhere does he suggest any alternative. He distrusted all isms, and his novels are in no sense political.

Instead, Fuchs's novels expose a spiritual vacuum at the core of existence, finding it so profound as to be impenetrable. Directly concerned with the moral bankruptcy of the modern age, his plots are full of gang wars waged by both adults and children, murder, prostitution, and suicide. Fuchs's fictional universe, like that of many modern writers, operates without benefit of God or inherent spiritual values. At first he seems to question and to protest: God Himself makes an appearance in *Summer in Williamsburg*, but only as a figure of almost comical indifference and clearly an object of the author's scorn. By the time of *Low Company*, Fuchs has learned to accept this barren moral landscape and to live in it.

The central theme of Fuchs's fiction, then, is the estrangement resulting from this spiritual isolation. His vital consciousness of mankind's helplessness before the overwhelming forces of circumstance, of little man's insignificance before a universe gigantic and impersonal, ties him closely to his ancestors, the classic Yiddish writers of the nineteenth century. In fact, Fuchs's first two novels are rooted in certain conventions of that literature.

Whether or not Fuchs himself was aware of these conventions, the Williamsburg of his youth was full of the very kinds of characters who populate Yiddish fiction; he surely knew there people familiar with Jewish culture, who could tell him stories and teach him the traditional themes and types. His early writing represents one of the truest and most fully realized pictures of immigrant Jewish life in America.

Among the nineteenth-century Yiddish writers, a common theme was the concept of *golus* (exile). Historically a people with no homeland, a community continually denied dignity, respect, and a secure place among their fellow human beings, the Jews lived under the difficult irony of being taught that they were the chosen people of God yet experiencing only the pain of rejection and persecution. Despite, or perhaps because of, the attitudes of the outside world, the Jews of eastern Europe were a coherent and unified group, held together by strong religious and spiritual ties and a sense of identity.

Fuchs's concept of estrangement is intimately connected with the historical reality of the *golus*, but his people are not unified by any sense of destiny. When, occasionally, his characters try to get together, they find themselves unable to communicate; invariably they destroy, or at least hurt, one another. Fuchs's Williamsburg novels are a clear explication of the sense that the very conditions of life doom man to failure and that there is nothing anyone can do about it.

The lives of Fuchs's protagonists have thus been destroyed before their quests for meaning, for glory, or for success have begun. Having no one on whom they can depend and no sense of tradition or belonging, theirs is a fatal heritage of deprivation, a harsh life in Europe that has led to one of economic failure in America. None of Fuchs's characters realizes his goal, and none succeeds in finding love: "Love is a hot joke," as one remarks. Fuchs is fond of the metaphor of the butterfly trapped in a subway train; his early protagonists, with their dreams of beauty and romance, are like the butterfly, trapped in an environment that closes them in and offers no escape.

Closely tied in to the image of the trapped dreamer/idealist is Fuchs's use of the Yiddish character-type, the schlemiel. A luckless, usually comical bungler, the schlemiel often gains a measure of nobility in retaining, against all external humiliation and disappointment, a sense of his own uniqueness and of the legitimacy of his own values. As Ruth Wisse states in *The Schlemiel as Modern Hero*, "the schlemiel represents the triumph of identity despite the failure of circumstance." The emphasis in Jewish writing on the schlemiel character is closely related to the stress placed upon the theme of antiheroism. Classical Jewish writers have tended to admire not the great overreachers of tragedy but those able to live and endure in silence: Tevye the dairyman is a famous example. The little man (*Dos Kleine Menschele*), the poor but proud householder trying to maintain some kind of status in the world as he continually grows poorer, appeals to the sensibility of the Jewish writer.

Fuchs's schlemiels partake of this tradition, exhibiting all the familiar characteristics of the type, but in the end no victory, real or psychological, awaits them. They remain victims, are cheated, destroyed, or even killed. Fuchs's two most lovable characters, and two he obviously admires, are the fathers of the protagonists of his first two novels. Both Mr. Hayman and Mr. Balkan demonstrate the peculiarities of the schlemiel-type and the moral resolution that must support it: both have learned to live with dignity, to be honest, loving, compassionate, and good, and to retain their principles and their ideals rather than to trade them for the financial success which is enjoyed by others around them and which tempts their sons to seek other, gaudier heroes. It is Fuchs's love for these little men, coupled with his increasing awareness that such principles can produce only impotence and failure in the modern world, that seems, ultimately, to prompt his disgust and his resignation to the ugly realities of life.

This sense of despair and emphasis on defeat, however, is not the whole story. The early novels are not merely a bitter record of nihilism, for Fuchs's sadness is balanced by his sense of responsibility and his profound compassion for his characters. Despite the fact that he believed there were no solutions, his fiction is a record of a quest for an answer. The defeats of his protagonists, especially his dreamer/schlemiel characters, is painful because the quest is so earnest, so full of hope, and, most important, because Fuchs's great sympathy for his characters gives them a profound sense of dignity. It is the maintenance of this complex and precarious balance which distinguishes Fuchs's novels.

Part of this creative tension derives from Fuchs's use of comedy. His style mixes irony and humor with a catalogue of sordid detail; critic Harold Beaver has noted Fuchs's mastery of the "undercutting rhythms and idioms of American Jewish humor." Comedy consists in the recognition of the disparity between the realities of actual existence and the grand ideals by which people attempt to live; Fuchs's achievement is that he accepts both, discovering human life to be meaningful, and even, at times, noble, while at the same time ludicrous and pathetic. Finally, comedy is an important vehicle for Fuchs because it celebrates endurance, and it is important that most of his characters manage to endure and do so with some measure of dignity.

Low Company was to be Fuchs's last novel for many years, although most reviews the Williamsburg novels received were quite good; the *New York Times* singled out Fuchs as a major talent. (When the books were republished in one volume in 1961, reviews again were excellent.) Depressed, however, by poor sales (the three books sold about two thousand copies), in 1937 Fuchs accepted a thirteen-week screenwriting contract at RKO and went to Hollywood. His dissatisfaction with what he found there is recorded in two of his best short pieces, "Dream City or the Drugged Lake" (1937) and "A Hollywood Diary" (1938). Fuchs returned, however, in 1940, and, with the exception of some time spent in Europe and time spent in World War II military service, where his commanding officer was film director John Ford, he has been in California since then. For many years Fuchs wrote mostly film scripts, although he did have several short stories (the best appeared in the *New Yorker*) and essays published. His best film works are the screenplays for *Hollow Triumph* (1948) and *Criss Cross* (1949) and the adaptation for *Panic in the Streets* (1950). He also adapted *Low Company* for the screen as *The Gangster* (1947), and he won an Academy Award for his original story for the film *Love Me or Leave Me* (1955).

Fuchs's Hollywood novel, *West of the Rockies*, his first in thirty-four years, appeared in 1971. The setting is Palm Springs and the characters are wealthy, but Fuchs's vision has not changed. The people are still "low company," their lives morally bankrupt; they scurry about to avoid facing their inner emptiness and the wasteland around them. The novel deals with the mental disintegration of Adele Hogue, a movie star whose antics have forced the production she is working on to close down. In an effort to placate her, the studio sends Burt Claris, a grifter, minor press agent, and her former lover, who is to entice her to go back to work. The novel concentrates on their pasts and their present encounter. *West of the Rockies* differs sharply from Fuchs's earlier work in style, substituting a poetic, dreamlike quality, more attuned to the ephemeral nature of the Hollywood life-style, for the dogged realism of the Williamsburg novels.

Dust jacket for Fuchs's Hollywood novel about the mental disintegration of movie star Adele Hogue

Fuchs's most important work of fiction since the 1930s appeared in 1979 in *The Apathetic Bookie Joint*, a collection of his best short stories and essays. The single previously unpublished contribution is the novella "Triplicate," which is Fuchs's most openly autobiographical work of fiction, explaining much about his art and his attitudes toward it. Stylistically "Triplicate" seems a cross between *Summer in Williamsburg* and much of Fuchs's Hollywood writing. It possesses that sense of life experienced which characterizes the early novel, and it also has a protagonist who is a writer very concerned about form. At one point the protagonist thinks about his own art: "For Rosengarten, what was of most importance in a piece of writing was a certain exhilaration, a life, a liveliness, a sense of well-being arising from the scene and the people, hard for him to describe or even to understand clearly, and yet the thing that gave him a sinking terror when it was missing, when he knew it wasn't there." Like *Summer in Williamsburg*, "Triplicate"

1-13   the trick: the nishvishendick, sweeping
               "uninterpreted"scene

                            following on after the Prescott
                            uninter reted

1. you lose yourself - immersed, artless, nishvishendick
   all the things that have to be said, that makes it possible - the simulated densit
     the illogicality - what he did - that he does it
    how Louis made it possible, handling the car, just leave it there, I'll pick it
up, the cigarette, the reticence

2. how it came about, what made it so
   her vehemence
   how now since we last saw her
   she determined, engulfed, swept up
                    pushes it all behind her, the hallucinations, the
                    neuroses, the scalp-burning/
   it wasn't enough for her
   so, in passing, through the back door, you work it in, Melanie,
   standing guard, on the watch, getting past her, so they had to come here
                        the flair of her, accepting it,
                        the criminal illicit act
        3. the reproach, the dead of the siesta, the bare boards,
        the wooden plank, the sadness, the shabbiness, the
        desolation, the sun-bathed studio dressing-room suites

4. the diffidence, the ambivalence, the unease
   the Pinter wit; get the feel, the sense of Claris being in there with her (as
     before, in the 2nd scene, in the Harry-FAdele, the Claris-Adele)
   ***the thing that happnes   / the immediacy, the fact that he's in there with her
   he sees her through the mirror, the lubricious itch, the realism, the uneasiness,
  the heimish thing there / the face that doesn't go with her, that she can't relate
      the Pinter wit, awkwardness, abrasion: all this hell bewing, and they there,
                                        to herself
   he on the edges, shifting, the dangers he's running, hidden,
  the way of her
  everything against her/ and the Geraldine Page elation, gloating
                    he fends with her, spars, ginger - dry, tart
here the switch
  she was determined to thwart, resist Harry, hold them off, although it made no sense
  he remembered how her whole body trembled, shook
    the fierce Hayward hatred, loathing,
    lose yourself in this: the rawness, the crudities, how he knowing it all, having
  it all on her, could rap her, make her feel like nothing, no mystery for him
  how these things happen, how it miscarries, the int nse devotion, adoration,
the detestation - I think of you the first thing when I wake up in the morning, the
last thing before I fall asleep at night. (The thing he omitted)

5. the main thing, must maintain through the end the fierce determination, to stand o
6. get the Zhivago - all this, now make a density, things constantly happening - the
way she throws herself away, laying the agent, he anonymous, nothing to her, they
fall in together - the illusion of love, the kisses, the embraces, the fondling,
the acrobat's body, the ways of fornication, this knavish thing people relentlessly
do, out of all reason - the reproach, the flush on her fa e, the absorption they
get when they're being laid, the cheeks young and round,

                                       leaving it outrageously nowher
                                       leaving it the uninterprete scen
to do more; to make the scene as scene;   sustaining it, outrageous again,
the electric thing; the reality - need a   the jump cut
line, something

Page of Fuchs's notes for West of the Rockies *(Muger Memorial Library, Boston University)*

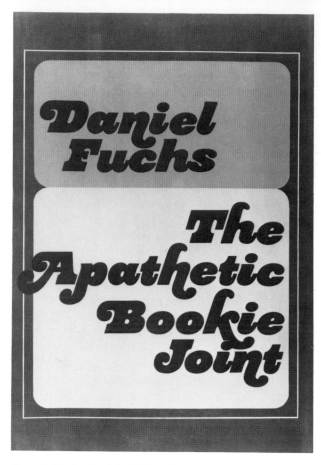

Dust jacket for Fuchs's 1979 collection of short fiction which includes the previously unpublished Hollywood novella "Triplicate"

greater distance. There are no heroes or villains, nor does either good or evil seem to exist. Instead, the reader is introduced to a series of characters who, through their dialogues and monologues, reveal confused and painful private dilemmas and struggles. This novella, which may therefore appear shapeless, is simply a presentation, a slice of life. Its significance in the Fuchs canon derives from the undertone of renewed compassion, as the author for the first time embraces in total acceptance and love the life he recreates, comprehending the contradictions, the tragedies, and even death.

In many ways "Triplicate" resembles James Joyce's "The Dead." Both novellas detail the events of a party, portraying numerous characters who dodge in and out, speak, and try to create impressions. In both, the action seems casual as fleeting moments crystallize. The important link, however, is in the endings, both epiphanies that demonstrate an enlargement and generosity of spirit. Joyce's protagonist achieves spiritual awakening through a recognition of love and his kinship with all of the dead, evoking a larger identification with the life of man, a life which has endurance because of works, artistic and otherwise. Fuchs, too, like Joyce's Gabriel Conroy, now partakes of this larger vision, and like Joyce, he closes his novella with an eloquent, sympathetic meditation on death, which, paradoxically, dwells fondly and gratefully on the small joys of the living: "Sometimes as you move along in a crowd, a woman's face will suddenly flash out at you, a resemblance to someone who died a long time ago, someone you haven't even thought about in years, and it comes to you with a pang—the life going on, everything as usual, and your friend not there. That's the rub, the shiver. The most vivid idea I have of what death is like is when I'm here, in California or New York, and think of London, the theaters, the parks, the greenery, the normal life of the city going on as it always goes on, except that you're not there, without you. . . . The young girls in the late fall afternoons, the smell of snow in the air, the feel of winter coming on, the people getting out of cabs, bringing home packages, going to restaurants, the streetlamps lighting up, the bustle, the life—no more, no more, no more."

Of all the Jewish novelists who came of age before the American-Jewish literary renaissance in the 1950s and 1960s, Fuchs was among the most gifted. His novels display a mastery of various forms and styles. *Summer in Williamsburg*, primarily naturalist in tone, captures uniquely the world of the immigrant Jew in America. *Homage to Blenholt* is more indebted to the novel of manners, and in it

achieves in a grander format what some of Fuchs's best short stories provide in miniature—a vivid representation of life as it is, dramatized not in movement toward or around a central episode but through the aggregate revelations of people coming and going, engaging in bits of conversation and action. The technique is very Chekhovian, and if Fuchs is in the debt of a literary master, it is Chekhov.

"Triplicate" captures the sense of liveliness and exuberance of the Hollywood social whirlwind, exhibiting the egoism of its people and also their eloquence and drive. More compelling, however, is the portrait of the loneliness behind the facade, the deep feeling of isolation suffered among individuals crowded together at a Hollywood party, talking but not communicating and unable to escape the solitude of their own beings.

Fuchs no longer judges his characters; he began to adopt a detached perspective in *Low Company*, and he maintains in "Triplicate" an even

Fuchs displays a gift for exuberant comedy. *Low Company*, Fuchs's masterpiece, has a more surreal flavor and offers one of the most damning and violent visions of America written. The Hollywood writing is more lyrical, almost stream-of-consciousness, as Fuchs moves between past and present, East and West. It is Fuchs's virtuosity as a stylist and his honesty in presenting a grim, compelling, but compassionate view of the world that will assure him a place in the front rank of American-Jewish writers.

References:
Irving Howe, "Daniel Fuchs: Escape from Williamsburg," *Commentary* (6 July 1948): 29-34;
Gabriel Miller, *Daniel Fuchs* (Boston: Twayne, 1979).

Michael Gold
(Irwin Granich)
(12 April 1893-14 May 1967)

Richard Tuerk
East Texas State University

See also the Gold entry in *DLB 9, American Novelists, 1910-1945.*

SELECTED BOOKS: *Life of John Brown* (Girard, Kans.: Haldeman-Julius, 1924);
The Damned Agitator and Other Stories (Chicago: Daily Worker Publishing, 1926);
120 Million (New York: International Publishers, 1929);
Money (New York: French, 1929);
Charlie Chaplin's Parade (New York: Harcourt, Brace, 1930);
Jews Without Money (New York: Liveright, 1930; London: Douglas, 1930);
Battle Hymn, by Gold and Michael Blankfort (New York, Los Angeles & London: French, 1936);
Change the World! (New York: International Publishers, 1937);
The Hollow Men (New York: International Publishers, 1941);
The Mike Gold Reader: From the Writings of Mike Gold (New York: International Publishers, 1954);
Mike Gold: A Literary Anthology, edited by Michael Folsom (New York: International Publishers, 1972).

SELECTED PLAYS: *Hoboken Blues*, New York, New Playwrights Theatre, 2 February 1928;
Fiesta, New York, Provincetown Playhouse, 1929;
Battle Hymn, by Gold and Michael Blankfort, New York, Federal Theater Project, 1936.

OTHER: *Hoboken Blues*, in *The American Caravan*, edited by Van Wyck Brooks and others (New York: Macaulay, 1927).

Michael Gold (a pseudonym for Irwin Granich) is best known for his autobiographical novel, *Jews Without Money* (1930), a sympathetic treatment of tenement life at the beginning of the twentieth century on the Lower East Side of New York City. Hailed as the first important work of American proletarian literature, Gold's book about growing up in poverty continues to stir the imagination of generations long removed from the immigrant neighborhoods of the Lower East Side. Although he wrote many short stories and poems, several plays, and hundreds of essays, his fame rests on this single book.

Gold was born Itzok Granich on 12 April 1893 on Chrystie Street in New York City, the son of poverty-stricken Jewish immigrant parents from Bessarabia. His father was a peddler and suspender maker. His family's poverty was so great that he had to quit school at the age of twelve, when he went to work for the Adams Express Company as a night porter, clerk, and driver. (That he hated the job is indicated in *Jews Without Money* by his having an Adams Express wagon kill Mikey's sister, Esther.)

In 1914, Gold became a radical. In "The Writer in America" (1953), he tells how: he "stumbled into a big demonstration of the unemployed in Union Square. I listened to the speakers [one of

Michael Gold (New York Public Library Picture Collection)

whom was Elizabeth Gurley Flynn]. An army of cops attacked us out of nowhere. I saw a woman worker slugged to the ground. I rushed impulsively to help her and was slugged by a sweaty cop with the eyes of a killer." At that demonstration he bought his first copy of the *Masses* with a dime he "had been saving for emergencies." In "Jack Reed and the Real Thing" (1927), he writes that his reading of the *Masses* "was the beginning of my education." It inspired him to write a poem on unemployment which was published in the *Masses* in August 1914. Entitled "The Three Whose Hatred Killed Them," this was the first of Gold's many poems on social topics in which he imitated the style of one of his heroes, Walt Whitman. Also as a result of reading the *Masses*, he became an active participant in radical movements. Shortly after its formation, he joined the American Communist Party and remained an active member for the rest of his life.

Gold attended New York University for one year, and in spite of his lack of formal education, in the fall of 1914 he was admitted to Harvard as a provisional student. Although he seems to have done well academically, he ran out of money, had a

nervous breakdown, and was forced to quit before the semester was over. Out of this episode eventually grew "Love on a Garbage Dump" (1928), a short story in many ways typical of Gold's work at its best. In the beginning of the story the narrator writes: "Certain enemies have spread the slander that I once attended Harvard college. This is a lie. I worked on the garbage dump in Boston. But that's all." The narrator is in love with two women: one is a fellow worker at the dump; the other he never sees but often hears playing the piano in a house on Beacon Hill. When he finally visits his coworker at her home, before satisfying his desires she asks him for a dollar. On his way home, feeling disgust at having to pay a dollar, he stops to listen to the piano music played by the other woman he loves. When a policeman roughly demands that he move along, he decides that his fellow worker had every right to ask for a dollar. A capitalist system forces her to need the money, and she should not feel ashamed to ask for it from a fellow worker, nor should a fellow worker feel disgust at paying it. The real villain is the unseen woman who has time to play the piano while others labor so that she may enjoy the fruits of a corrupt capitalist system. Thus, a story that begins as a devastatingly realistic yet highly symbolic look at some of the most degrading kinds of labor imaginable becomes an overly sentimental vehicle for Communist doctrine. In fact, in story after story and essay after essay, Gold allows Communist doctrine to interfere with his abilities as a writer, just as in his literary criticism he judges writers not on the basis of their ability to handle words but on the basis of their treatments of the working classes and their calls for an end to the capitalistic system.

Often he tacks Communist doctrine onto stories in melodramatic ways. In "Faster, America, Faster," collected in *120 Million* (1929), he writes of a private train chartered by a Hollywood producer. On the train the producer tries to seduce his new leading lady (a teenager) while his friends drink and his previous leading lady becomes jealous. In the meantime, the fireman kills the engineer and starts to make the train go faster and faster. Finally, the train crashes, killing not only the fireman and the moviemakers but also the porters. At the end of the story a farmer carrying a sickle comes upon the wreck, followed by a laborer carrying a hammer, as a red star rises in the east. Yet rather than showing solidarity among workers, the story really explores what Gold in "On a Section Gang" in *120 Million* calls "the Adamic curse that has been laid on the American labor movement," namely, the tendency of workers to fight among themselves.

From 1914 to 1917 Gold contributed often to the *Masses* and the Socialist paper the *New York Call*. He also began to show an interest in the theater. In 1916, George Cram Cook of the Provincetown Players staged Gold's one-act play entitled *Down the Airshaft*. Later that same season, another one-acter, *Ivan's Homecoming*, was produced. In 1920, the Provincetown Players produced *Money*, another one-acter. As a result of his involvement with the Provincetown Players, Gold met Eugene O'Neill, who praised Gold's work.

To avoid the draft, Gold fled to Mexico in 1918. When he returned, he became a member of the editorial board of the *Liberator*, to which he was elected at the end of 1920. Until 1921, he wrote as Irwin Granich, but then, as he explains in "The Writer in America," he took the name of the father of a friend of his. The father was a Civil War veteran, Corporal Michael Gold, "an upright, fiery old man. . . . I took his name for a pen-name when I needed one, and he never seemed to mind or to reproach me." The immediate impetus for his taking a pen name was the raids Attorney General A. Mitchell Palmer was conducting against so-called foreign radical organizations. The name stuck.

In 1922, Gold was one of three editors of the *Liberator*. The *New Masses* began publishing in 1926. In 1928, when the periodical was almost bankrupt, Gold became its editor and, as one critic put it "revised it in his own image." The periodical became devoted entirely to the ideals and aspirations of the radical workers, and its pages were devoted to articles and creative pieces by workers.

During the 1920s Gold spent time at other pursuits, taking a trip to California in 1923 and 1924 and traveling to Europe and the Soviet Union in 1925. In 1926, he wrote two more plays, *Hoboken Blues* and *Fiesta*. Far more ambitious than his earlier one-acters, *Hoboken Blues* was published in *The American Caravan* in 1927. An experimental drama set in Harlem and Hoboken, *Hoboken Blues* is, according to Gold's stage directions, to have an entirely black cast, with white characters portrayed by blacks in white face.

Subtitled *The Black Rip Van Winkle: A Modern Negro Fantasia on an Old American Theme*, the play focuses on Sam Pickens, who journeys from Harlem to Hoboken seeking work playing his banjo in a circus. When he gets there, he finds that Hoboken is anything but the paradise he expected. In fact, he discovers that blacks, especially unemployed ones, are not welcome. In a series of surrealistic scenes, Sam gets various jobs, including one that requires him to use his head as a target for baseballs, but each

job proves to be degrading and intolerable. Finally, he is beaten by the police and, as a result, wanders for twenty-five years, during which he fantasizes that as a result of a factory workers' revolution he has been elected president of Hoboken. When he returns to Harlem, he discovers that his wife has married Butler, an undertaker-turned-nightclub-owner, and is about to leave Butler because he has mistreated her and is about to force Sam's daughter to marry Rosewater, owner of a rival nightclub that is ruining Butler's business. At the end of the play, after Sam is reunited with his family, he is co-opted by the system: he accepts a job working for Rosewater in his nightclub as a star vaudeville attraction; he will be billed as "Lazarus, risen from de dead, in a banjo solo and talk on hell—Rip Van Winkle in a song and dance and travelogue—Jesus Christ, crowned wid barbed wire, in a snappy American monologue." He still retains his utopian vision, and finally asks, "why can't there be a place for de poor men, black and white, where birds sing sweet, and every house is full of music, and dere's sunflowers round de factory door? Where no one is hungry, where no one is lynched, where dere's no money or bosses, and men are brudders?" With surrealistic settings and actions, this drama still is of interest, not so much because of its plot—which is rather unoriginal—or its dialogue—which is often stilted—as for its staging and ideas. Many of its scenes, especially those set in Harlem's streets, are vibrant with energy.

Gold had trouble finding a producer for the play. After Paul Robeson refused to play the lead, the Provincetown Players decided not to produce it. The financier Otto Kahn liked it, and his New Playwrights Theatre did produce it in 1928. But Gold's all black cast became an all white cast, and the actors were instructed to mingle with the audience during intermission distributing balloons. The play was a failure.

Fiesta is based on Gold's experiences in Mexico. Produced in 1929 at the Provincetown Playhouse, it received mixed but largely negative reviews. He wrote several more plays, most notably *Battle Hymn*, which he based on his 1924 book *Life of John Brown* and on which Michael Blankfort collaborated. This play was produced by the Federal Theater Project in 1936. Gold, however, never achieved his ambition of becoming a prominent playwright.

In 1917, a piece of Gold's autobiographical fiction had been published in the *Masses*. In the 1920s he started working seriously on his autobiographical novel *Jews Without Money*. Later that decade several episodes appeared in the *New Masses* and *Menorah Journal*, and H. L. Mencken, who later became one of Gold's villains, published vignettes from it in the *American Mercury*.

In *Jews Without Money* Gold is at his best. Like "Love on a Garbage Dump," *Jews Without Money* is a vivid portrayal of life among the poor and oppressed. Like "Love on a Garbage Dump," *Jews Without Money* ends with a call for revolution which Mikey, the protagonist and narrator, becomes convinced is "the true Messiah." But in *Jews Without Money*, the relatively brief radical ending does little—if anything—to destroy the poignancy of the material that comes before it. Some critics feel that the whole novel points inevitably toward the radical ending. Others see the ending as a flaw. The main characters in the novel are Herman, Mikey's lead-poisoned painter father, who, as a result of a serious fall which makes him afraid to return to the scaffold, ends up selling rotting bananas on the streets; Katie, Mikey's sympathetic, strong, loving mother, who keeps the family together; Esther, Mikey's only sibling (Gold himself was one of three brothers), who meets an early death; and Mikey. The novel tells of dreams turned to dust as immigrants come to America hoping to find the *goldineh medina* (the golden land) and instead find the land of sweatshops and Tammany Hall. Expecting to make a fortune in the New World, Herman finds himself caught in the "trap" of abject poverty. Katie, who retains her strength throughout the book, keeps the family's morale high even after Herman's accident and Esther's death. When the book ends, Mikey too has been entrapped by poverty, dashing Herman's hopes that even though he himself could not escape, his son would be able to.

A very popular book, *Jews Without Money* was translated into several languages, including Esperanto, and republished as a paperback in 1965, when Avon omitted the last few paragraphs—the radical ending—of the book. Shortly thereafter, Avon issued a complete version.

After *Jews Without Money*, Gold continued to write short stories, essays, and poems. Critics agree

Woodcuts by Howard Simon for Gold's 1930 novel Jews Without Money

that none of his later creative efforts match his one novel. Far too often his works become excuses for preaching sermons on the virtues of communism and the ills of capitalism. For him, Russia was the utopia his parents had sought in the New World. In Russia, he wrote, workers joyfully do their jobs; true genius is recognized and nourished; exploitation never occurs; and men live in brotherhood and harmony. Even the excesses of the Stalin era seem neither to have bothered him nor to have changed his beliefs. He considered those writers and intellectuals who defected from the Communist party to be traitors to the workers' cause. In his study of American literary tradition, *The Hollow Men* (1941), in spite of his own strong Jewish identification, he especially berates those authors who defected from communism after the "Hitler-Stalin Pact" of 1939. In "The Writer in America" he traces the tradition of American literature from Bronson Alcott, Emerson, Thoreau, and Whitman as one devoted to "utopian communism" and the replacement of capitalism "with a system of brotherhood and collective ownership," and he praises Mark Twain as "a subversive conspirator." During the McCarthy era, he remained outspoken in his devotion to the Communist cause.

In the 1930s Gold began to write a regular column for the *Daily Worker* entitled "Change the World." He collected many of these columns into his 1937 book of the same title. His last column was published in the *Worker*, the semiweekly successor to the *Daily Worker*, on 31 July 1966.

During the last years of his life, he lived in California. He contributed articles to the *People's World*, a West Coast radical journal, and to the Yiddish *Freiheit*, a New York-based paper. In February 1967, after suffering a stroke, he entered a Kaiser Foundation Hospital near San Francisco. On 14 May 1967 he died.

Although most of Gold's writings are forgotten—probably justly so—*Jews Without Money* endures. A classic portrayal of tenement life in pre-World War I New York City, it remains a vivid account of a sensitive child's coming of age in a New World that is anything but a land of milk and honey. It captures for all time the usually vibrant, sometimes subdued spirit of the ghetto in which Gold himself lived as a child and young man.

References:

Daniel Aaron, *Writers on the Left: Episodes in American Literary Communism* (New York: Harcourt, Brace & World, 1961), pp. 84-90;

Charles Angoff, *The Tone of the Twenties and Other Essays* (South Brunswick, N.J.: Barnes, 1966), pp. 182-188;

Michael Brewster Folsom, "The Education of Michael Gold," in *Proletarian Writers of the Thirties*, edited by David Madden (Carbondale: Southern Illinois University Press, 1968), pp. 222-251.

Gerald Green
(8 April 1922-   )

Judith Rinde Sheridan

BOOKS: *His Majesty O'Keefe*, by Green and Lawrence Klingman (New York: Scribners, 1950; London: Hale, 1952);

The Sword and the Sun (New York: Scribners, 1953);

The Last Angry Man (New York: Scribners, 1956; London: Pan, 1959);

The Lotus Eaters (New York: Scribners, 1959; London: Longmans, Green, 1960);

The Heartless Light (New York: Scribners, 1961);

The Portofino P.T.A. (New York: Scribners, 1962);

The Legion of Noble Christians; or The Sweeney Survey (New York: Trident, 1965; London: Longmans, Green, 1966);

To Brooklyn with Love (New York: Trident, 1967);

The Artists of Terezin (New York: Hawthorn, 1969);

Faking It; or The Wrong Hungarian (New York: Trident, 1971);

The Stones of Zion: A Novelist's Journal in Israel (New York: Hawthorn, 1971);

Block Buster (Garden City: Doubleday, 1972);

Tourist (Garden City: Doubleday, 1973);

My Son the Jock (New York: Praeger, 1975);

Gerald Green (photo by Layle Silbert)

The Hostage Heart (Chicago: Playboy Press, 1976;
    London: Allen, 1976);
Girl (Garden City: Doubleday, 1977);
An American Prophet (Garden City: Doubleday,
    1977);
Holocaust (New York: Bantam, 1978; London:
    Corgi, 1978);
Cactus Pie: Ten Stories (Boston: Houghton Mifflin,
    1979; Leighton Buzzard, U.K.: Melbourne
    House, 1980);
The Healers (New York: Putnam's, 1979; Leighton
    Buzzard, U.K.: Melbourne House, 1979);
The Chains (New York: Seaview, 1980; Leighton
    Buzzard, U.K.: Melbourne House, 1980);
Murfy's Men (New York: Seaview, 1981).

SCREENPLAY: *The Last Angry Man*, Columbia,
    1959.

TELEPLAY: *Holocaust*, NBC, 1978.

Gerald Green is best known as the author of
the teleplay for the 1978 television mini-series
Holocaust, the novelization of which became a best-

seller. This work led to a renewed awareness in the
United States and Europe of the horrors of Germany's Third Reich. The theme of *Holocaust*,
humankind's capacity for brutality and the individual's potential for courage and nobility, is recurrent in Green's work and was established in his first
critically recognized and perhaps most artistically
satisfying novel, *The Last Angry Man*, which later was
adapted to the movies. A prolific writer, Green has
incorporated issues of social importance in his fiction and nonfiction. Most often he has achieved
popular rather than critical success.

Born in Brooklyn, New York, the son of
Samuel Greenberg, a physician, and Anna Ruth
Matzkin Greenberg, Green studied at Columbia
University, earning an A.B. in 1942 and an M.S. in
journalism in 1947. From 1942 to 1946 he served
with the Armed Forces Network in Germany, in the
United States Army, Ordnance, and achieved the
rank of sergeant. In 1950 he became producer and
writer with the National Broadcasting Company
and contributed to such programs as "Today,"
"Wide Wide World," and "Chet Huntley Report-
ing." He also wrote and produced documentaries.
Green lives in Stamford, Connecticut, is married to
Marie Pomposelli, and has three children.

Two of his most vital novels, *The Last Angry
Man* (1956) and *To Brooklyn with Love* (1967), draw
heavily on biographical material. At the center of
both novels is a brilliant, caring general practitioner
whose uncompromising honesty and short temper
results in a dwindling practice. Dr. Samuel Abelman
in *The Last Angry Man* and Dr. Sol Abrams in *To
Brooklyn with Love* are modeled after Green's father.
Both novels are set in the 1930s in a decaying section
of Brooklyn characterized by a polyglot, multiracial,
impoverished population. While not practicing
Jews, the doctors are influenced by humanism and a
commitment to family and education which reflects
prototypical Jewish concerns.

Like Green's father, Abelman and Abrams are
lovers of Thoreau and escape the grime of urban
life by lovingly tending a backyard garden.
Moreover, both are men who possess rare physical
strength as a result of youthful involvement with
gymnastics. Their affinity for the values of American Transcendentalists link them with characters
created by Green's more famous contemporaries,
Saul Bellow and Bernard Malamud.

Both Samuel Abelman and Sol Abrams fight
continuing battles against those they often refer to
as the "galoots," people who thrive on meanness,
who belong to the "great brotherhood of bullies and
bastards." Their everyday struggles against the de-

structive individuals who populate Brooklyn are put into a larger perspective by the historical background of the novels. In both novels, through radio broadcasts and newspaper accounts, the increasing power of Hitler is documented, and Brooklyn becomes a microcosm which mirrors world events. The petty cruelties experienced daily by Abelman, Abrams, and Abrams's son, Albert, prepare them to accept what was for most people incomprehensible. Sam Abelman's attitude toward the rising specter of Nazism is powerfully set forth in *The Last Angry Man*: "Hitler did not surprise Sam Abelman at all. Everybody was wringing their hands now that the little bastard was proving he wasn't fooling, that he really meant to kill every Jew in the world. Where were all of them when the lights went out? . . . Kicking Jews in the ass was a fine old European custom. Dimly, he seemed to recall something about pigs eating Jews in the streets of a Russian village. There was the final equation, truer and more inevitable than anything Einstein could formulate: A pig may eat a Jew, but a Jew may not eat a pig."

The Last Angry Man is narrated by Woodrow Thrasher, a television producer who decides to use

David Wayne and Paul Muni in The Last Angry Man. *Green wrote the screenplay for this 1959 Columbia film based on his first novel.*

Dr. Abelman as the focus of a live television program, "America, U.S.A." All attempts by Thrasher to portray Abelman as a stereotypically good man with a "heart of gold" who unselfishly and happily serves his community are stymied by Abelman's complexity and the horrors of ghetto life. Through the character of Thrasher, Green attacks the tendency of television to distort truth in favor of increasing the commercial appeal of its programs. Green's concern with the ethics of journalism is a recurrent theme in his work.

Ultimately Thrasher is humanized by his encounter with Abelman and comes to understand his responsibility as a journalist to tell the truth. In the novel's final paragraph, Thrasher formulates a credo for all writers, one to which Green clearly subscribes: "the word need not be destructive, or fraudulent or malign. The usages of the word were multiform, and if the word could be used to debauch and deceive, it could also be used to create and to uplift."

In a later novel, *The Heartless Light* (1961), Green returns to themes of journalistic responsibility when he attacks television, radio, and print journalists who in the course of reporting the story of a kidnapping all but forget the victims, a four-year-old girl and her parents, in their heartless and sensationalistic presentation of events.

The 1959 film version of *The Last Angry Man*, scripted by Gerald Green, was a popular and critical success. Paul Muni was nominated for an Academy Award for his performance as Dr. Abelman. Lester D. Friedman in *Hollywood's Image of the Jew* (1982) cites the film as one of the few produced in the 1950s which presented a "well rounded Jewish character." Friedman characterizes the 1950s as a period in which filmmakers portrayed Jews mainly as caricatures; hence the portrait of Dr. Abelman as a mixture of stubbornness, argumentativeness, dignity, and decency was a significant departure.

In his recently published novel *The Chains* (1980) Green again employs the Brooklyn of his youth for his setting. In this novel the characters of Dr. Abelman and his young nephew Myron Malkin reappear. Now a reporter for the fictional World News Association, Malkin provides the narrative frame in the form of a journal he keeps for a book to be written about the Chain family. Dr. Abelman's actions and words emerge in the form of recollections by the novel's central characters. Abelman continues to embody the highest standard of morality in an essentially amoral world.

The novel records the history of a family which achieves wealth, prominence, and respect-

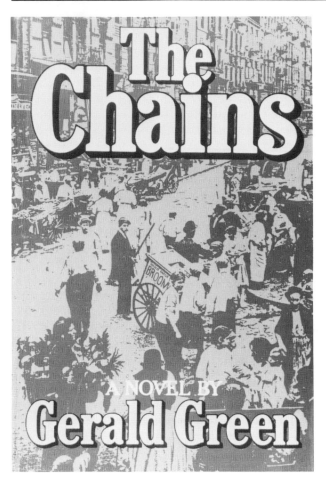

Dust jacket for Green's most recent novel, about a Jewish family's involvement with the underworld in 1930s New York

Increasingly in his work Green has attempted to comprehend and at the same time remind his readers of the reality of the Holocaust. In *The Legion of Noble Christians* (1965), Buck Sweeny, an Irish *luftmensch*, is commissioned by Sherman Wettlaufer, a wealthy Jewish-American entrepreneur, to record and reward the efforts of individual Christians who at personal risk saved Jews from concentration camps and slaughter. In the course of the novel, noble Christian clergy and citizens throughout Europe recount not only their own acts of courage but also the horrific brutality against which they reacted. The novel inculpates Christianity for a history of anti-Semitism and the Vatican for acts of indifference, and through the character of A. C. Stonebreaker, a one-time liberal novelist now a wealthy right-wing polemicist, those who would deny the accuracy of the accounts of Nazi brutality and European compliance are also indicted.

The Artists of Terezin (1969) is a nonfiction memorial to a group of painters who, while incarcerated in Theresienstadt, the "model" concentration camp located in Czechoslovakia, worked in secret to document the atrocities they witnessed. Here Green celebrates the heroic tenacity of the human spirit. The book contains an introduction, a compilation of the works of art, and an analysis of those works. *The Artists of Terezin* was researched and written at the same time as *Holocaust*, which incorporates the existence of these artists and their eventual discovery and torture into its fictionalized account. In *Holocaust* Karl Weiss is an artist who shares the fate of the real-life counterparts.

In *The Artists of Terezin* the painters Otto Ungar, Leo Hass, Biedrich Fritta, and Felix Bloch embody what Green believes to be the true responsibility of the artist. In the introduction Green states: "The battle never ends. You destroy Nazism and something else turns up. Something always does. If it isn't Yagoda or Eichmann, it's the Chicago cops, and I trust no one thinks that George Wallace and the worst of his people will just go away. Do your own thing, as the contemporary cant puts it, but some—people like the artists of Terezin—have a broader commitment. And thank God for them." This sense of the artist—painter or writer—as one with a moral obligation to use his craft to mirror higher truths, to affirm spiritual qualities of character and to record humankind's history of brutality, and the rejection of art for art's sake, fiction about fiction, strongly connects Green with the majority of Jewish writers.

Green's belief that the events of the Holocaust have not been explored fully is also stated in *The*

ability. The origin of the Chain wealth, however, lies in the underworld activities of "Crazy" Jake Chain. Jake began his climb out of poverty as a union strong man and later formed a partnership with his son Martin in a highly successful bootlegging operation. A beautiful distant cousin, Eva Heilig, articulates the social ideals which initially inspired the union movement of the 1930s—ideals which became anachronistic in the face of the violent battles between workers and management and the subsequent involvement of organized crime. *The Chains* may well be viewed as a Jewish version of Mario Puzo's *The Godfather*, because it focuses on the underside of the American dream as lived by immigrant groups in great urban centers. Harshly realistic in style, the book is especially noteworthy for Green's accuracy in recording scenic detail and dialogue. It does suffer, however, from awkward and contrived construction in Green's use of Malkin's journal notes as a narrative frame.

Artists of Terezin. He argues that "It is not as some critics contend, that the death camps have made topical writing impossible. Rather they have given us too much to write about." For this reason *Holocaust*, his most famous work, evolved.

Holocaust focuses on the plight of a German family of assimilated Jews. Dr. and Mrs. Weiss are always compassionate, loving, and dignified, even in the face of savagery. Their gentle natures prevent them from fully accepting Nazi threats until it is too late. They die in Auschwitz as does their oldest son, Karl. Their daughter Anna, deranged after her rape by Nazis, is gassed in a euthanasia center at Hadamar. Their youngest son, Rudi, the work's true hero, becomes a partisan in the Ukraine. He survives and immigrates to Israel. The story of the Weiss family is counterpointed with the story of Eric Dorf and his family. An insecure lawyer, Dorf joins the Nazi party at his wife's insistence and becomes Gestapo chief Reinhard Heydrich's chief assistant who provides euphemistic legal language to justify the "final solution."

Holocaust, as a television mini-series, inspired tremendous controversy. Elie Wiesel in a *New York Times* article, "Trivialization of the Holocaust," attacked the work as "untrue, offensive, cheap," filled with "contrived situations, sentimental episodes, implausible coincidences." Many criticized the television media for juxtaposing the drama with commercials selling deodorant and dog food. But most, including concentration-camp survivors, found *Holocaust* to be an important and long-awaited reminder of facts too easily forgotten. While all recognized that no medium could fully re-create the horror of the Third Reich, Green was applauded for providing a historic framework and conveying a sense of the vast numbers killed as well as humanizing camp victims through the Weiss family. Green also attempted to tell the tale without stereotypes and included heroic Christians as well as Jews who cooperated with their Nazi captors.

A side effect of the showing of *Holocaust* and the success of its novelization, according to *Newsweek*, was revived support for Israel. Green's own commitment to Israel is recorded in *The Stones of Zion: A Novelist's Journal in Israel* (1971), which shows Green, an amateur archaeologist, gaining insight into the ancient history of Israel. He also better understands the present-day struggle and his own feelings as an American whose Jewishness had been tenuous at best.

In a 1977 interview with *Publishers Weekly*, Green describes his novels as "thematic." He explains, "I hate to sound like a sociologist, but I want to write about important issues." His concern with broad social issues and with conveying a moral perspective may well be an outgrowth of his years as a working journalist.

Yet Green's need to tackle themes of great social significance results at times in fiction filled with strained characterizations and overly complex and awkward plots. Book reviewers have praised Green's scope and intent but also have noted that his writing lacks stylistic elegance.

At his best Gerald Green is a fine and entertaining storyteller capable of creating memorable characters. His books champion moral decency and oppose oppression of all kinds. A believer in the individual's ability to survive with spirit intact, Green finally must be viewed as an optimistic writer who seeks affirmations, yet never ignores the overwhelming brutality which has marked the twentieth century.

References:

John F. Baker, "*Publishers Weekly* Interviews Gerald Green," *Publishers Weekly*, 211 (7 March 1977): 10-11;

Lester D. Friedman, *Hollywood's Image of the Jew* (New York: Ungar, 1982);

Elie Wiesel, "Trivialization of the Holocaust," *New York Times*, 16 April 1978, II: 1.

Ben Hecht

(28 February 1894-18 April 1964)

Mark Bernheim
Miami University

See also the Hecht entries in *DLB 7, Twentieth-Century American Dramatists; DLB 9, American Novelists, 1910-1945; DLB 25, American Newspaper Journalists, 1901-1925*; and *DLB 26, American Screenwriters*.

SELECTED BOOKS: *The Wonder Hat*, by Hecht and Kenneth S. Goodman (New York: Shay, 1920);

The Hero of Santa Maria, by Hecht and Goodman (New York: Shay, 1920);

Erik Dorn (New York & London: Putnam's, 1921);

1001 Afternoons in Chicago (Chicago: Covici McGee, 1922; London: Grant Richards, 1923);

Gargoyles (New York: Boni & Liveright, 1922);

Fantazius Mallare: A Mysterious Oath (Chicago: Covici McGee, 1922);

The Florentine Dagger: A Novel for Amateur Detectives (New York: Boni & Liveright, 1923; London: Heinemann, 1924);

Cutie, A Warm Mamma, by Hecht and Maxwell Bodenheim (Chicago: Hechtshaw, 1924);

Humpty Dumpty (New York: Boni & Liveright, 1924);

Broken Necks and Other Stories (Girard, Kans.: Haldeman-Julius, 1924);

Tales of Chicago Streets (Girard, Kans.: Haldeman-Julius, 1924);

The Kingdom of Evil: A Continuation of the Journal of Fantazius Mallare (Chicago: Covici, 1924);

The Wonder Hat and Other One-Act Plays, by Hecht and Goodman (New York & London: Appleton, 1925);

Broken Necks (Chicago: Covici, 1926);

Count Bruga (New York: Boni & Liveright, 1926);

Infatuation, and Other Stories of Love's Misfits (Girard, Kans.: Haldeman-Julius, 1927);

Jazz, and Other Stories of Young Love (Girard, Kans.: Haldeman-Julius, 1927);

The Policewoman's Love-Hungry Daughter and Other Stories of Chicago Life (Girard, Kans.: Haldeman-Julius, 1927);

The Sinister Sex and Other Stories of Marriage (Girard, Kans.: Haldeman-Julius, 1927);

The Unlovely Sin and Other Stories of Desire's Pawns

Ben Hecht (Culver Pictures)

(Girard, Kans.: Haldeman-Julius, 1927);

Christmas Eve (New York: Covici Friede, 1928);

The Front Page, by Hecht and Charles MacArthur (New York: Covici Friede, 1928; London: Richards & Toulmin, 1929);

The Champion from Far Away (New York: Covici Friede, 1931);

A Jew in Love (New York: Covici Friede, 1931; London: Fortune, 1934);

The Great Magoo, by Hecht and Gene Fowler (New York: Covici Friede, 1933);

Actor's Blood (New York: Covici Friede, 1936);

To Quito and Back (New York: Covici Friede, 1937);

A Book of Miracles (New York: Viking, 1939; London: Nicolson & Watson, 1940);

Ladies & Gentlemen, by Hecht and MacArthur (New York, Los Angeles & London: French, 1941);

Fun To Be Free, Patriotic Pageant, by Hecht and MacArthur (New York: Dramatists Play Service, 1941);

1001 Afternoons in New York (New York: Viking, 1941);

Concerning a Woman of Sin (New York: Armed Services Edition, 1943);

Miracle in the Rain (New York: Knopf, 1943);

A Guide for the Bedevilled (New York: Scribners, 1944);

I Hate Actors! (New York: Crown, 1944);

The Collected Stories of Ben Hecht (New York: Crown, 1945);

A Flag Is Born (New York: American League for a Free Palestine, 1946);

The Cat That Jumped Out of the Story (Philadelphia: Winston, 1947);

A Child of the Century (New York: Simon & Schuster, 1954);

Charlie: The Improbable Life and Times of Charles MacArthur (New York: Harper, 1957);

The Sensualists (New York: Messner, 1959; London: Blond, 1960);

A Treasury of Ben Hecht (New York: Crown, 1959);

Perfidy (New York: Messner, 1961);

Gaily, Gaily (Garden City: Doubleday, 1963; London: Elek, 1964);

Letters from Bohemia (Garden City: Doubleday, 1964; London: Hammond, Hammond, 1965);

In the Midst of Death (London: Mayflower, 1964).

SELECTED PLAYS: *The Wonder Hat*, by Hecht and Kenneth S. Goodman, Detroit, Arts and Crafts Theatre, 1916;

The Hero of Santa Maria, by Hecht and Goodman, New York, Comedy Theatre, 12 February 1917;

The Egotist, New York, Thirty-ninth Street Theatre, 25 December 1922;

The Front Page, by Hecht and Charles MacArthur, New York, Times Square Theatre, 14 August 1928;

The Great Magoo, by Hecht and Gene Fowler, New York, Selwyn Theatre, 2 December 1932;

Twentieth Century, by Hecht and MacArthur, New York, Broadhurst Theatre, 29 December 1932;

Jumbo, by Hecht and MacArthur, New York, Hippodrome, 16 November 1935;

To Quito and Back, New York, Guild Theatre, 6 October 1937;

Ladies and Gentlemen, by Hecht and MacArthur, Martin Beck Theatre, 17 October 1939;

Christmas Eve, New York, Henry Miller Theatre, 27 December 1939;

Fun to Be Free, Patriotic Pageant, by Hecht and MacArthur, New York, Madison Square Garden, 1941;

Lily of the Valley, New York, Windsor Theatre, 26 February 1942;

We Will Never Die, New York, Madison Square Garden, 9 March 1943;

Swan Song, by Hecht and MacArthur, New York, Booth Theatre, 15 May 1946;

A Flag Is Born, New York, Alvin Theatre, 5 September 1946;

Hazel Flagg, New York, Mark Hellinger Theatre, 11 February 1953;

Winkelberg, New York, Renata Theatre, 14 January 1958.

SELECTED SCREENPLAYS: *Underworld*, Paramount, 1927;

Scarface, United Artists, 1932;

Design for Living, Paramount, 1933;

Twentieth Century, Columbia, 1934;

Crime Without Passion, by Hecht and Charles MacArthur, Paramount, 1934;

Viva Villa!, M-G-M, 1934;

Once in a Blue Moon, by Hecht and MacArthur, Paramount, 1935;

The Scoundrel, by Hecht and MacArthur, Paramount, 1935;

Barbary Coast, by Hecht and MacArthur, United Artists, 1935;

Nothing Sacred, United Artists, 1938;

Gunga Din, by Hecht and MacArthur, RKO, 1939;

Wuthering Heights, by Hecht and MacArthur, United Artists, 1939;

Angels Over Broadway, Columbia, 1940;

Spellbound, United Artists, 1945;

Notorious, RKO, 1946;

Miracle in the Rain, Warner Bros., 1956;

A Farewell to Arms, 20th Century-Fox, 1957.

Over a career spanning nearly half a century, Ben Hecht wrote highly individual works which earned him a place in both popular culture and American literature. An outspoken, abrasive personality, he was often at the center of self-created controversies in which he was pitted against middle-class values at odds to his own on topics ranging from class relations to international politics, sexual mores to anti-Semitism. By his own words a "child of the century," he was preternaturally aware of playing center-stage roles in many of the great dramatic events of early- and mid-twentieth-century history. In the decades since his death, his literary reputation, which declined steadily under the generalized impression that he sold out to Hollywood, has continued to languish, although for a time in the early 1920s he was thought one of America's most prodigious talents and indeed exerted strong influences upon important later writers such as Nathanael West and Saul Bellow. Today Hecht is best known as a spinner of tales, a rapid-paced journalist of the Chicago school of tough, urban portraiture, although cinema historians continue to explore the question of his notable contributions to film, and his international reputation is selectively high. Modern French cinema, for example, has noted its indebtedness to him (Jean-Luc Godard commented in 1968, "Ben Hecht . . . is forgotten today, but in my opinion he invented eighty percent of what is used in American movies today"), while largely for political reasons, his works remain in disfavor in England and Israel.

Ben Hecht was born on the Lower East Side of New York to Russian immigrant parents and attended the Broome Street grammar school, after which his family removed to Racine, Wisconsin. There he spent an American youth and early adolescence far removed from the tenements he continued to recall as characterizing New York until he returned years later as a famous journalist. The lure of Chicago as Midwestern metropolis drew Hecht as it did many other members of the literary world who abandoned small-town American life in the years preceding World War I. At the age of sixteen in 1910, following a celebrated youth in Racine, where he had performed as magician and acrobat at a circus and as a ten-year-old violinist, Hecht fled the University of Wisconsin to surface in Chicago and fall into a rough-and-tumble assignment gathering photographs of criminals for the *Chicago Journal*. The teenage Hecht received a colorful introduction to the Chicago underworld, as he later recalled it in *A Child of the Century* (1954), a kaleidoscope of "haunted streets, studios, whore houses, police stations, courtrooms, theater stages, jails, saloons, slums, mad houses, fires, murders, riots, banquet halls and bookshops. . . . I ran everywhere in the city like a fly buzzing in the works of a clock . . . and buried myself in a tick-tock of whirling hours that still echo in me."

Hecht came to know and recognize those of merit in the city, which already had a reputation for political corruption on a grand scale. He developed an early distrust for political machinery and those who both greased it and made it go: Hecht con-

tinued for decades to attack political establishments and politics in the United States and abroad, and the only elected leader he ever expressed deep admiration for was Theodore Roosevelt. This strong streak of surface anarchism characterizing Hecht's philosophy apparently resulted from the pervasive, albeit exciting, corruption of public service he witnessed the strong men of Chicago politics exercising over an uncomprehending public. Furthermore, Hecht's scorn for middle-class complacency (strongly akin to H. L. Mencken's favorite target, the "booboisie") may also date from these early lessons in the workings of ward democracy as practiced by the bosses of Chicago. It is said that Mencken—another early Hecht hero—never rejected a story Hecht sent him for publication, starting with one for which he paid forty-five dollars in 1917 for the *Smart Set*. Hecht formed a strong admiration for Mencken's caustic wit when it was put in motion against the cultural philistinism of conservative American tastes, and the connections between Hecht and German radical experimentation in the arts which flourished in the 1920s on both sides of the Atlantic may have been inspired by Mencken's translations of Nietzsche's writings on the need for aesthetic and moral "supermen," as opposed to the uncomprehending masses of modern life.

Hecht had sketches published in Margaret Anderson's trend-setting *Little Review*; "The Sermon in the Depths," based upon his readings in the French symbolists and decadents and employing intricate, ornamental wordplay and descriptive tours de force, appeared there in 1915, when Hecht was twenty-one. Mencken also published in 1917 a play which Hecht wrote with Maxwell Bodenheim, part of a long literary and personal association which was to produce parodies of each other's style as well as serious joint works, and, given the tragic demise of Bodenheim (saved from a pauper's grave in part through Hecht's charity), a demonstration of contrasting success and failure within the American literary dream. At this time, Hecht also worked on a full-length play with Sherwood Anderson, another of his Chicago group, based on the life of Benvenuto Cellini. Despite the obvious attraction of the Renaissance man's extraordinary career for the members of the Chicago Renaissance group, the play was never completed.

Hecht left the *Journal* for the *Chicago Daily News*, where he was to achieve his greatest fame as a newspaperman and one of the master reporters of his time, a go-getter who never failed to get a sensational angle on the news or make it himself. Al-

Hecht in 1919, when he was a reporter for
the Chicago Daily News

inspired by Chicago rather than New York or New England—profoundly influenced German writers: Chicago-style crime, jazz, violence, and heavy industry figure prominently in Brecht and Kafka, for example.

Always an active cross-fertilizer of literary attitudes, early in his Berlin stay Hecht formed a friendship with George Grosz, then a leader in Dadaist "happenings" and other revolutionary artistic events and movements. Later Grosz and Hecht were to work together in America; during Hecht's assignment in Berlin, Grosz helped him to remain close to the center of political and artistic unrest, where Hecht saw proof of the unstable nature and uncertain future of both modern art and modern politics, especially *en masse* city life. Perhaps most significantly, much of what Hecht observed around him figured prominently in his early fiction, notably *Erik Dorn* (1921), a largely autobiographical work which appeared a year after he left Berlin.

Erik Dorn at the time was viewed as an important novel by a new writer, uniting the influences of European modernism with a distinctly original American character type to create a portrait of the alienated urban intellectual at war with a society which cannot fathom his peculiar blend of callousness and sensitivity. The novel also begins Hecht's long dissection of the institution of marriage, in this case coming at a time when sexual and social mores were rapidly changing. Yet nowhere is there much of the pervasive neo-Freudianism of the 1920s: Hecht preferred a mixture of formlessness, Expressionist exaggerations, and stylistic experimentation. The result was his most distinctive novel: roughly divided into geographical segments corresponding to the major steps in Hecht's own career to date, *Erik Dorn* traces the growing frustrations of a brilliant young master reporter who is stifled by both marriage and homeland. From Chicago to New York to Berlin he is driven by estrangement to enact estrangement, compulsively seeking fulfillment with one hand while pushing away all human contact with the other. Hecht provides Dorn's opposite in the steady young lawyer Hazlitt, but both men and both leading female characters, Anna and Rachel, are equally engulfed in the meaninglessness of furiously empty lives. Each lives with yet apart from others, and only Anna, Dorn's deserted spouse, eventually finds a living-death reconciliation with an early admirer. Dorn, acquitted of the murder of his rival through an act of heroism on the part of a German noble, ends more alone than ever, observing and recording the living of life by others around him. The book is both highly polished and crude, an

though he stayed at the *Daily News* until 1923, he was sent to Berlin (without a knowledge of German) as its correspondent from December 1918 until early 1920, an experience which proved enormously productive and stimulating. High living had brought him to an $8,000 debt by his departure, but never one to be held back by material need, Hecht found that his few dollars went far in the inflationary German economy and soon established himself in an existence which resembled his daredevil Chicago days. Living at such a pitch, Hecht discovered that although the time spent in Berlin was not long, it produced cultural influences which persisted and propelled him into the avant-garde. A man always open to new trends, as well as a ready initiator, he ended by absorbing stimuli from the fertile Berlin cultural scene of the immediate postwar years, and by acting as a major force in the countermovement of American culture abroad in the 1920s. The image of America which Hecht helped to spread—a portrait of the United States odd instance of pseudoproletarian fiction written by a sophisticated elitist.

Although the reader never sees any of Dorn's supposedly brilliant writings, giving the novel a curiously unformed quality because its chief figure is unchanged from beginning to end, its thinly veiled portrait of the rebellious writer seeking to transcend human limitations does achieve a combination of heroic and antiheroic characteristics which reappear in many of Hecht's later works: "Hechtian man"—a hard-boiled sentimentalist, a "Don Quixote of disillusionment" who suffers the anguish of alienation in an urban environment to whose stimulation he is bound. Finally, *Erik Dorn* remains an outline of problems felt rather than thought through or expressed. The main character's sufferings, for example, are never given form beyond the expression of disgust over a too-devoted wife who cannot fathom her husband's metaphysical longings. But neither can the reader, since Dorn cannot, or will not, himself. It is assumed that here Hecht was charting the dissolution of his own first marriage to reporter Marie Armstrong, which lasted from 1915 to 1925 and produced his daughter Edwina. In 1925 Hecht married Rose Caylor, with whom he apparently had far more in common: they successfully collaborated literarily, and she is represented in *Erik Dorn* by the mysterious Rachel Laskin, a daughter of immigrants and fellow-sufferer of urban anxieties. (Hecht and Caylor's daughter, Jenny, born in her father's middle age, became a child actress on whose behalf Hecht embroiled himself in several controversies seeking to further her career.)

In Chicago Hecht became a leader of the so-called Chicago Renaissance which flourished until the mid-1920s and included such figures as Sherwood Anderson, Floyd Dell, Kenneth Rexroth, Maxwell Bodenheim, and Carl Sandburg, who had become the film critic for Hecht's newspaper by the time Hecht returned from Germany. Even more deeply in debt, Hecht churned out columns for the *Chicago Daily News* from June 1921 until October 1922 under the title "1001 Afternoons in Chicago." Hecht's narratives were concerned with the unknown and often sordid side of big-city life, and he considered his beat to be the off-beat: in a distillation of Naturalistic principles with Expressionistic love for the grotesque, he haunted back alleys, morgues, flophouses, speakeasies, and divorce courts. The life of the city in its often seemingly unlivable conditions became his precinct, and without social agitation or propagandizing, he turned the light of journalism upon corners otherwise un-illuminated. Throughout, the figure of the reporter, observing all, recording, detached yet very much a part of the scene, is never absent. Hecht was already in the process of forming the public's notion of investigative reporting that he would help bring to the stage several years later in *The Front Page*. Critic Harry Hansen called Hecht "the Pagliacci of the fire escapes," and the epithet stuck.

In the meantime, Hecht entered the first of his many public controversies, this time over the appearance of his "pornographic" novel *Fantazius Mallare*, subtitled *A Mysterious Oath* (1922) and published in a limited edition at a time when conservative elements were decrying changes in public morality. The Watch and Ward Society, the Society for the Suppression of Vice, and other such groups had already censored Anderson, Dell, Dos Passos, and others when Hecht's *Gargoyles* (1922), a novel imitative of Dreiser (who had tried to lure Hecht to Hollywood as early as 1915), drew their wrath for its attack upon middle-class morality. *Fantazius Mallare* was another matter: even by today's standards, the short confessional work with its scatalogical foreword is rather startling in the tradition of French *décadence*, relating the erotic fantasies of a narrator in the style of Huysmans who seeks to annihilate both himself and a gypsy waif by arousal to heights of passion. The work featured endpapers and drawings by Wallace Smith done in the fashion of Aubrey Beardsley, complete with phallic representations in the borders. It quickly brought about a lawsuit which Hecht and Smith, although represented by Clarence Darrow, lost; they were fined $1,000. The scandal at the time cost Hecht his position, in effect propelling him into one of his most productive phases: *1001 Afternoons in Chicago* appeared in 1922, collecting his sketches from the *Chicago Daily News*; *The Florentine Dagger*, a mystery story Hecht dictated in thirty-six hours to win a $2,500 bet, in 1923; and *Cutie, A Warm Mamma*, a satire written with Bodenheim, in 1924. That same year Hecht also produced *Humpty Dumpty*, a novel repeating the themes of *Erik Dorn*, and *Broken Necks and Other Stories*, a collection of stories written for Mencken and others, which included such suggestive titles as "Tales of Chicago Streets" and "The Policewoman's Love-Hungry Daughter."

Although at this time much of Hecht's energy was involved in Florida land-speculation schemes, his reputation as an erotic writer was growing, and in this light he was often taken more seriously than he may have desired. Decades later, looking back at his youthful posturings on the moral fringes of society, Hecht was able to draw distinctions between his rejection of the sort of relations that led to the economic and spiritual bondage he called marriage and the freer unions he envisioned as liberating because partners were aware of their own fallibilities and avoided a serious performance. The erotic impulse in Hecht's works was always strong, though occasionally unpredictable, and more often than not sought to shock and prod the public to reexamine its own duplicities. Sex as the ego's expression formed a great part of the vitality Hecht sought to infuse into life, a liberating force which could separate the "half-dead" (one of his favorite phrases) from the truly alive, those with whom Hecht always sympathized. The tension between the individual and his circumstances remained a constant in Hecht. But the difficulties of being understood by mass audiences for whom he manifested an elitist scorn remained a permanent condition under which he labored, and the fame accompanying his transition into a successful playwright and screenwriter did nothing to clarify the often muddled philosophical bases of his thought.

For a time Hecht wrote and published the *Chicago Literary Times*, which has been described as America's first underground newspaper, and he worked on *Count Bruga*, a ribald lampoon of the career of Bodenheim, which appeared in 1926. By this time he had already removed to New York and begun collaborating with Charles MacArthur, a lifelong friend. Together they wrote *The Front Page*, which opened on Broadway in 1928 and became one of the most successful of all period vehicles. The play has enjoyed numerous revivals and had three screen versions. A *piece à clef*, the play was by far the most successful work of either Hecht or MacArthur and has profoundly influenced the journalistic profession and the public's conception of it. The plot is based on the true story of an escaped prisoner about to be executed unjustly for political motives, by chance discovered hiding in the pressroom of the Chicago Criminal Courts Building by the star reporter assigned, against his will, to cover the event. The gruff bureau chief, the reporter eager to leave on his marriage journey, the wisecracks, the cynical gallows humor—all have become clichés of the popular image of the newsroom. The play also achieved a certain notoriety owing to its occasionally rough language; as Tennessee Williams noted, *The Front Page* "uncorseted the American theatre."

Hecht and MacArthur, the latter at the time about to marry Helen Hayes, succeeded later together with screen adaptations of *Gunga Din* (1939) and *Wuthering Heights* (1939) and original screenplays for *Crime Without Passion* (1934) and *The Scoundrel* (1935). In 1934 they collaborated on the successful screen version of their greatly popular 1932 play *Twentieth Century*. The first film version of *The Front Page* was produced by Howard Hawks in 1931 (Hecht wrote *Scarface* for him the following year).

Herman Mankiewicz and Hecht in a scene from the silent film More Soup, *produced at Paramount as a Christmas gift for Adolph Zuckor*

Hecht had already been involved in Hollywood since the closing days of silent movies, having been invited by Herman Mankiewicz to write scripts for sums of money much larger than he could have hoped to earn from serious fiction. At the height of his movie career in the 1930s, at a salary of $1,000 a day, Hecht was able to clear income in the hundreds of thousands of dollars, although his high style of cross-country living apparently consumed the greater part of it, forcing him to take more assignments, many of which were completed anonymously, with screen credits attributed to others. (He was reputed to have rewritten much of *Gone With the Wind* in three days, without having read the novel.) He also directed several films (*The Scoundrel, Crime Without Passion*) under a special agreement with Paramount. His first effort, *Underworld*, a silent film written in 1927 for Josef von Sternberg (for which he received one of the first Academy awards given for scriptwriting), launched Hecht upon the creation of a cynical yet sentimental criminal characterization which has continued to dominate American gangster films since. In *Scarface*, which Hecht described as the story of Al Capone superimposed on that of the Borgias, Paul Muni, George Raft, and Howard Hawks received first recognition, while the movie created the image of gangsterism in much the same fashion as *The Front Page* did for journalism, again showing Hecht's power as image maker.

Among Hecht and MacArthur's most successful scripts, *Twentieth Century* continued the tradition of mild lampoon of upper-class mores. The story concerns a theatrical couple—a leading lady and a Broadway producer—aboard the Twentieth Century Limited train; although she is bound for Hollywood, he is bent on convincing her to stay in New York, and naturally enough, they fall into each other's arms by zany coincidences and arch contrivings. The film, starring John Barrymore and Carole Lombard, appealed to the Depression audiences for its spoof of the rich and pretentious. In 1938 Hecht wrote *Nothing Sacred*, starring Carole Lombard, directed by William Wellman, and produced by David Selznick. One of Hecht's favorite stories, the plot carries on his predilection for debunking middle-class values and gullibility; Hecht by this point was viewed as a clever Hollywood sophisticate, and the screwball antics of his screenplays became further vehicles for his curious blend of cynicism and sentimentality, which mass audiences found appealing.

In the meantime, however, Hecht had written *A Jew in Love* (1931), which proved to be his last major novel for twenty-five years, one which tended to alienate him further from any world but Hollywood. The book may be Hecht's most curious one, for the aura of Jewish *selbst-hass* (self-hate) has long surrounded it, and even Hecht's radical about-face transformation into Jewish patriot in the early 1940s has never erased fully the negative impression of *A Jew in Love*. Disillusionment and alienation dominate the unsuccessful novel, which presents stereotypes and caricatures of scheming, disreputable assimilationist Jews leading empty parasitic existences, ominously foreshadowing the tide of anti-Semitism already building throughout the Western world. Before a decade had passed, Hecht strongly regretted the book, which far outsold any of his other fiction and is unsympathetic, to say the least, to its unsavory Jewish characters. Ostensibly the story of a roguish publisher, Jo Boshere (born Abe Nussbaum), the story was viewed as perhaps based on Hecht himself, Bodenheim, and publisher Horace Liveright. It is a dark work, telling of tangled, reprehensible personal relations built on deception of the self as well as of others, and represents Hecht at his most cynical, totally lacking compassion and even sentimentality. The book immediately preceded Hecht's greatest successes in Hollywood but marks the nadir of his fiction, although its effects were later counterbalanced, to Hecht's mind, by his metamorphosis into defender of the faith at the end of the decade.

In the years following *A Jew in Love*, Hecht had several collections of short stories and novellas published, many drawn from movie ideas never realized, others from incidents recalled from his crime-reporter days in Chicago: *The Champion from Far Away* appeared in 1931, *Actor's Blood* in 1936, and *A Book of Miracles* in 1939. Most of the stories are macabre or bizarre in their settings, plots, and contrivances. A sense of spiritual collapse appears in many, as extraordinary people find themselves in reduced circumstances and either farce or melancholy results. "The Masquerade" tells of a convicted murderer about to be hanged who asks to be permitted to don women's clothing and makeup on the gallows. *A Book of Miracles* interestingly contains the first indication of Hecht's growing Jewish sensibility: "The Little Candle" concerns a rabbi committing suicide during a pogrom. Hecht also wrote many successful film scripts during this time, combining sophistication with cynicism to charm 1930s audiences. The film *Design for Living* (1933), directed by Ernst Lubitsch, was adapted from Noel Coward's play and satirizes both American philistines and phony expatriates. Early in the next de-

Hecht in the 1940s during rehearsal for a radio show based on his story "Specter of the Rose," about a ballet dancer accused of murder (The Bettmann Archive, Inc.)

cade Hecht did some of his finest screenwriting for Alfred Hitchcock's *Foreign Correspondent* (1940), for which he received no screen credit, *Spellbound* (1945), and *Notorious* (1946).

Before these films, Hecht had already undergone his best-known change of heart and become a rabid propagandist for Jewish self-defense and nationalism. Although for the greatest part of his life he had scrupulously avoided Jewish commitment of any kind, he apparently discovered in the rising tide of anti-Semitism a cause to believe in with all his energies, and he reacted to anti-Jewish sentiments and acts with ferocity.

Hecht's first antifascist sentiments are mildly expressed in his 1937 play, *To Quito and Back*, but it was apparently the threat he felt to both his "people" (as he decided to call them) and his nation that led him to espouse anti-isolationist views as early as 1939. At the time Hecht was loudly pro-British (he was to change this stance following the war) and outspokenly anti-German. The latter opinion he defended on the basis that the Germans he had known and admired in the years immediately following the war had manifested none of the insane egotism of the Nazis; they had a creative, humorous energy, apparently untouched by mass fanaticism during his own stay there. Hecht noted that in 1939 he discovered his own identity as well as patriotism, and he became active in the Fight for Freedom movement which attacked Lindbergh and other isolationists and protectionists, seeking to mount support for the British in the expected showdown with Germany. His wartime novella, *Miracle in the Rain*, published in 1943 and filmed in 1956, was designed to boost home-front morale with its story of a supernaturally heroic soldier.

At the same time, Jewish sentiment came with a rush to Hecht, as he reported in the well-known manifesto "My Tribe is Called Israel": "I had before then only been related to Jews. In that year I became a Jew and looked on the world with Jewish eyes." Hecht sentimentally asserted that he felt the Nazi movement directed at him personally, and even more so, "The compelling thing that had thrown me into the Jewish fight was that I loved Jews." In 1941 Hecht's articles, including "My Tribe is Called Israel," for the experimental New York newspaper *PM* appeared as *1001 Afternoons in New York* (illustrated by Grosz, now in America). Making his transformation complete and public, Hecht loudly denounced Nazi atrocities throughout occupied Europe, accurately forecasting even greater calamities to come and calling for absolute Jewish solidarity. He lauded Sholom Aleichem; he attacked Joseph Kennedy for allegedly trying to muffle Jewish opinion in this country to protect British interests in Palestine; he threw himself with all his energy into trying to organize support in Hollywood for the Committee for a Jewish Army of Stateless Palestinian Jews. Approached because of his stance by representatives of the right-wing terrorist organization the Irgun Zeva'i Le'umi (IZL), he joined actively to support the American League for a Free Palestine and the Hebrew Committee of National Liberation.

Torn between backing the British war effort against Germany and opposing British restrictions of Jewish immigration to Palestine, Hecht wrote *A Guide for the Bedevilled* (1944), a work of pure polemic seeking to analyze the roots of anti-Semitism in the anti-Semite himself and often indulging in vitriolic abuse of the German national character. Hecht claimed that Germans and Nazis deserved each other, that Nazism somehow corresponded to the lowest of human motivations such as he had originally seen in Chicago jails thirty years before—pure animalism, savage and destructive egotism gone wild. *A Guide for the Bedevilled* set itself "to write of Jews with love and of their enemies with hatred," and Hecht proved himself up to the task, going so far as to claim that Mozart and Wagner were not Germans, but converted Jews. In "My Tribe is Called Israel," he noted that "I write of Jews today . . . because that part of me which is Jewish is under violent and ape-like attack. . . . I have tried in my small way to bring into the long-battered soul of the Jew the pride and mental stamina many Jews like myself feel." Years later, in his memoirs, *A Child of the Century* (1954), he looked even further back: "I became a propagandist for Jews. . . . I did all these things partly out of my own needs. But much of what I have done . . . has been done because I loved my family. It was they who were under attack by the German murderers and the sly British. It was they who, long dead, suddenly set up a cry in me for Palestine. Although I never lived 'as a Jew' or even among Jews, my family remained like a homeland in my heart." Hecht thus defined his Judaism largely in terms of others' views of him, but clung to it with a passion equal to his occasional disdain for his Jewishness. Among his most sentimental stories of this period is "God Is Good to a Jew," a highly charged story of Jewish solidarity which appeared in July 1943 in *Collier's*, at a time when Hecht was speaking out largely alone against wartime atrocities.

The war over, Hecht redoubled his efforts and clearly felt the British a fair target. He worked tirelessly to raise funds for the Irgun and obtain illegal arms for the coming struggle. The Irgun named a cargo ship for him, and he organized a star-filled show, proudly titled *A Flag Is Born*, at the Alvin Theatre in New York in 1946. The play calls for violent opposition to British intransigence as justified in terms of compensation for the war crimes against European Jewry, and it launched Hecht on a collision course with the ruling Zionist powers who counseled moderation toward a gradual transition to independence. Over one hundred pages of *A Child of the Century* detail Hecht's tireless efforts on behalf of the Irgun rightists, culminating in his utter disillusionment following the sinking of the *Altalena* in Tel-Aviv harbor during the War of Independence and the fragmentation of the Irgun faction. Hecht withdrew in disgust at what he viewed as outright Jewish treason committed by the Ben-Gurion ruling party in Israel, although he continued to proclaim himself a Revisionist and three years before his death launched a last attack at Zionism in *Perfidy* (1961), in which he raked over the Kastner-Greenwald libel case which split public opinion in Israel along establishment-

opposition lines. The book only increased official Israeli disapproval of Hecht and his works, which were also boycotted in England for the inflammatory nature of his urgings to Irgun terrorists to attack the British and rejoice in their elimination. Old friends like Henry Luce and Edward G. Robinson dropped Hecht entirely, and he was called in the British press "a Nazi at heart." Years later, during the Cyprus crisis of the 1950s, Hecht continued to berate England publicly. As a propagandist he demonstrated the same sense of loud effectiveness and bombast, mixed with a lively journalistic style that could not be ignored and was as likely to offend as it was to attract.

In the last decades of his life, Hecht worked often with Gene Fowler on screenplays, although his contributions were not noted in the credits. In 1952 Hecht, Charles Lederer, and I. A. L. Diamond wrote *Monkey Business*, a 1930s-style Hollywood comedy, and it was about this time that Hecht began his obsessive efforts to launch his daughter's career as a child actress. He also worked on *A Child of the Century* for more than a decade, seeing it appear as he turned sixty and gather much favor-

Hecht's daughter Jenny in her first show, Midsummer, *Hartford, Connecticut, 1952 (photo by Halley Erskine)*

able criticism as a major American autobiography. In the *New York Times Book Review* Saul Bellow noted, "Among the pussycats who write of social issues today, he roars like an old-fashioned lion." The massive work involves the enormous cast of the famous and near-famous—as well as the unknown—Hecht dealt with in his varied careers. Three years later Hecht's only biography, *Charlie*, a study of Charles MacArthur, appeared, although it is equally about Hecht himself and their long closeness. *Gaily, Gaily*, a collection of nine tales of Hecht's wild youth, was published in 1963. Posthumously, *Letters from Bohemia* (1964) collected correspondence Hecht had received from his illustrious friends and collaborators, presenting miniature portraits of Mencken, Anderson, Grosz, Bodenheim, and others. His last years were marked by more controversy over the story that he had ghostwritten Marilyn Monroe's memoirs, by articles in *Playboy* magazine, as well as a year's run as host of a television talk show in which he regularly offended large groups of viewers, especially when he revealed his close ties to underworld figures such as gangster Micky Cohen, who had contributed heavily to the Irgun cause. Shortly before he died, he worked on the film script for the James Bond spoof *Casino Royale*, and he was also increasingly concerned with analyzing correspondences between the underworld of his youth and the more sophisticated criminal elements of mid-century. Hecht died suddenly of a heart attack at age seventy in New York.

In a recent biography, *The Five Lives of Ben Hecht*, Doug Fetherling distinguishes his careers as iconoclast, bohemian, sophisticate, propagandist, and memoirist. He notes that throughout them all, Hecht remained maverick, gadfly, and a juggler of "special effects," the creator of a new cinematic style and a genuinely unique individual who bridged popular and intellectual cultures at several key points which bear his distinctive signature to this day. From his early works for Emma Goldman to those for the Marx Brothers, he was "an anarchist of emotions . . . [and] an optimist about the future of pessimism" who chose for the epigraph to *A Child of the Century* a line from the book of Job: "But there is a spirit in man. . . . Fair weather cometh out of the North."

Biography:

Doug Fetherling, *The Five Lives of Ben Hecht* (Toronto: Lester & Orpen, 1977).

Papers:

The major collection of Hecht's papers is at the Newberry Library, Chicago.

Joseph Heller

(1 May 1923-   )

George J. Searles
Mohawk Valley Community College

See also the Heller entries in *DLB 2, American Novelists Since World War II*, and *DLB Yearbook: 1980*.

BOOKS: *Catch-22* (New York: Simon & Schuster, 1961; London: Cape, 1962);
We Bombed in New Haven (New York: Knopf, 1968; London: Cape, 1969);
Catch-22: A Dramatization (New York: French, 1971);
Clevinger's Trial (New York: French, 1973);
Something Happened (New York: Knopf, 1974; London: Cape, 1974);
Good As Gold (New York: Simon & Schuster, 1979; London: Cape, 1979).

PLAYS: *We Bombed in New Haven*, New Haven, Yale School of Drama, 4 December 1967; New York, Ambassador Theatre, 16 October 1968;
Catch-22, East Hampton, New York, John Drew Theater, 13 July 1971;
Clevinger's Trial, London, 1974.

SCREENPLAYS: *Sex and the Single Girl*, by Heller and David R. Schwartz, Warner Bros., 1964;
Dirty Dingus Magee, by Heller and others, M-G-M, 1970.

OTHER: "Catch 18," in *New World Writing No. 7*

Joseph Heller (photo by Thomas R. Koeniges, courtesy of Newsday)

(New York: New American Library, 1955), pp. 204-214;

"World Full of Great Cities," in *Nelson Algren's Own Book of Lonesome Monsters*, edited by Algren (New York: Lancer, 1964).

PERIODICAL PUBLICATIONS: "I Don't Love You Any More," *Story*, 28 (September/October 1945): 40-45;

"Castle of Snow," *Atlantic Monthly*, 181 (March 1948): 52-55;

"Girl From Greenwich," *Esquire*, 29 (June 1948): 40-41, 142-143;

"A Man Named Flute," *Atlantic Monthly*, 182 (August 1948): 66-70;

"Nothing To Be Done," *Esquire*, 30 (August 1948): 73, 129-130;

"McAdam's Log," *Gentleman's Quarterly*, 29 (December 1959): 112, 166-176, 178;

"Too Timid to Damn, too Stingy to Applaud," *New Republic*, 147 (30 July 1962): 23, 24, 26;

"Catch-22 Revisited," *Holiday*, 41 (April 1967): 44-61;

"How I Found James Bond," *Holiday*, 41 (June 1967): 123-125;

"Love, Dad," *Playboy*, 16 (December 1969): 181-182, 348.

Despite his relatively small output, Joseph Heller is considered a major contemporary author. His reputation rests principally on his first book, the experimental antiwar novel *Catch-22*, one of the most highly regarded American fictions since mid-century. Heller's work is assigned in college literature courses and has generated a substantial body of scholarly criticism. *Catch-22* has been made into a film; Heller appears on television; his novels are offered as book club selections. He is a rarity among writers, having secured both academic acclaim and popular success.

Heller was born to Russian immigrant parents in the Coney Island section of Brooklyn, New York, at that time a heavily Jewish enclave. His father, a bakery-truck driver, died after a botched operation when the boy was only five years old. Heller, his older brother, and their mother were left to fend for themselves in the carnival-midway atmosphere of Coney Island. Several critics have suggested that Heller's characteristic mode of cynical, street-wise humor may have been nurtured by these early experiences and surroundings.

He attended Coney Island's Public School No. 188 and Abraham Lincoln High School. After graduating in 1941, Heller worked briefly in an insurance office and as a blacksmith's helper in the Norfolk Navy Yard, enlisting in the United States Army Air Force in October 1942. Discharged as a first lieutenant in 1945, he married the former Shirley Held of Brooklyn. Heller then attended college under the G.I. Bill, enrolling at the University of Southern California. Soon he transferred to New York University, where he was elected to Phi Beta Kappa and graduated with a B.A. in English in 1948. His first published short stories were beginning to appear in such magazines as *Esquire* and the *Atlantic*. He earned an M.A. from Columbia University in 1949 and spent the academic year 1949-1950 as a Fulbright scholar at Oxford University. After two years as an English instructor at Pennsylvania State University, he began his career as an advertising copywriter for *Time* (1952-1956) and *Look* (1956-1958) before becoming promotion manager at *McCall's* (1958-1961). During this time he continued to write short fiction and began writing occasional scripts for movies and, under the pseudonym Max Orange, for television. But the most significant activity during this period of Heller's career was the slow and painstaking creation of his masterpiece, *Catch-22*. Since the great success of that novel, Heller has been able to pursue his craft full-time, although he has renewed his academic ties, having taught creative writing at Yale University and the City University of New York. A member of the National Institute of Arts and Letters, Heller resides in an apartment building on Manhattan's Upper West Side, summering in fashionable East Hampton on Long Island. Although he is socially acquainted with other writers—notably Mario Puzo and Kurt Vonnegut—many of his closest friendships date from grade school.

It has been said—somewhat too reductively—that his principal theme is death. While the specter (and the actuality) of death is certainly present in Heller's books, there are other preoccupations as well. In a 1975 interview Heller himself cited his concern with "the closeness of the rational to the irrational mind, the location of reality." This latter interest, a central feature of Heller's fiction, finds expression in his seriocomic manipulation of language. Repeatedly, words are used in grimly oxymoronic, paradoxical ways to limn a world in which nothing is what it seems, where zany dislocation and irrational disorder are the norm. The purpose of this verbal stratagem is to challenge received versions of reality. Heller's books depict a corrupt society in which the abuse of authority is endemic. He asserts that language has become a vehicle of debasement and is itself debased in the service of an amoral expediency. Constituting a Swiftian indictment of a whole mode of thought and discourse, his books argue that we can no longer distinguish between truth and falsehood, reality and unreality, right and wrong. Treading a thin line between bemused contempt and outraged indignation, he has been aptly described as a black humorist, a purveyor of comic despair.

In *Catch-22* (1961) and the related plays, Heller's target is the military; in *Something Happened* (1974), the corporate realm; and in *Good As Gold* (1979), the government. Like the social historian C. Wright Mills, he sees these complementary bureaucracies as the seats of power in contemporary America, and he attacks them with vengeful acerbity. In each context, he focuses on an alienated, antiheroic protagonist struggling to identify his own priorities and reconcile them with the larger system by which he is ensnared and controlled. In presenting his characters' misadventures, he alternates between straightforward, realistic narration and grotesque, comic exaggeration, thereby creating an uneasy sense of dislocation that mirrors the protagonists' own confusions. Several critics have said that Heller's questers are autobiographical

projections, and to some extent this appears to be the case. If his characters are not actual personae, they at least share many of the author's beliefs and feelings. Referring to *Catch-22* and *Something Happened*, Heller told a *Paris Review* interviewer that "neither . . . was intended to be autobiographical." But elsewhere he has said, "My point of view is there in both books, and not in the slightest concealed, I hope."

Catch-22 grew out of the author's combat experiences during World War II. A bombardier with the 488th Squadron of the 12th Air Force, Heller flew sixty missions over Italy and France. Like his protagonist John Yossarian, Heller underwent an epiphany during a nearly disastrous mission over Avignon, suddenly recognizing the true magnitude of war and of his own mortality. While Yossarian's subsequent depredations—and the bureaucratic extremes that he encounters—are clearly an exaggeration of Heller's experiences, the novel contains characters, scenes, and observations drawn directly from life.

Among the most acclaimed books of the modern period, *Catch-22* has been translated into more than a dozen languages and has sold more than ten million copies. The 1970 film version, a Paramount Pictures release written by Buck Henry, directed by Mike Nichols, and starring Alan Arkin, contributed greatly to the novel's popularity. During the politically tumultuous 1960s, the term *Catch-22* became a household expression, and Heller was catapulted into the role of campus hero and antiwar activist. Critical response to *Catch-22* has been voluminous and almost entirely laudatory, although the novel received mixed reviews upon initial publication. Appearing in 1961, perhaps it was a few years ahead of its time; its highly experimental treatment of chronology, its absurdist vision, and its madcap energy are striking even now.

Catch-22 is different from other antiwar novels such as Erich Maria Remarque's *All Quiet on the Western Front* (1929) in that it transcends its genre, becoming a critique not just of war and the military establishment but also of the exasperating illogic of life itself. The term *Catch-22*—defined by *Webster's New World Dictionary of the American Language* (2nd College Edition) as "a paradox in law, regulation, or practice that makes one a victim of its provisions no matter what one does"—is a highly existential construct, suggesting that the human predicament is somehow ambiguous, circuitous, and unfathomable. Thus when Yossarian feigns derangement in an attempt to be excused from flying further combat missions, he is told that his attempt itself attests

Heller (right) with director Larry Arrick during the 1971 run of Heller's play Catch-22, *John Drew Theatre, East Hampton, New York*

to his sanity, and his request is therefore denied. As one critic expresses it, "the comic formula 'Catch-22' seems to apply to God's laws as well as to man's; or, rather, men project their own irrationality on God." Hence, the novel ultimately posits an irresolvable conflict between "irrational conformity" (embodied by characters such as Milo Minderbinder, a mess officer turned syndicate head who masterminds a black market and bombs his own men for profit) and "rational revolt" (typified by Yossarian and his roommate Orr, whose successful escape to Sweden inspires the protagonist's later defection). The book proposes that the rational revolt is the only viable avenue to self-validation, even while acknowledging that such rebelliousness is doomed in the face of an all-encompassing absurdity.

Influenced by the work of Celine, Nabokov, Kafka, and other masters of literary innovation, Heller structured *Catch-22* in a highly unconventional fashion; events are disjointed, scrambled in time. Although there is a semblance of plot—framed by Yossarian's visits to the hospital—the novel's chronology is interior and psychological rather than actual. This unusual handling of time

sequence, coupled with Heller's habitual use of comic non sequitur—both in the dialogue and the authorial narration—and the book's generally antinomian coloration, qualifies it as an example of the experimental fiction that has proliferated since mid-century—literature which *Catch-22* has actually helped to promote. The book has not only added a new term to the language but has also exercised a considerable influence on subsequent works. In addition, the novel has generated an outpouring of scholarly exegesis, as critics have scrutinized its surrealism, its black humor, its mock-epic qualities, its labyrinthine structure, and various other controversial features.

Yet the novel is not as radical as it appears. As the critic Frederick Karl has said, *Catch-22* "derives from the tragic undertones of Ecclesiastes with its monody against vanity, egoism, hypocrisy, folly. . . ." Similarly, Daniel Walden has cited Deuteronomy 30:19 ("Therefore choose life") to show that in its affirmative thrust, *Catch-22* embodies the traditional prophetic injunction to live morally. This is consistent with Heller's own observation that the novel's "structure is more radical than the content. The morality is rather orthodox —almost medieval. . . . the seven basic virtues and seven

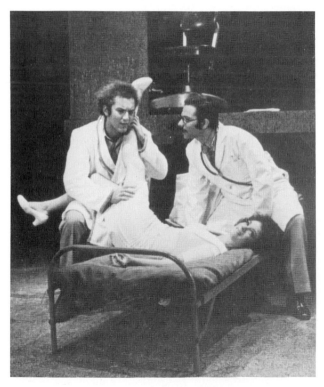

John Pleshette as Yossarian, Marcia Jean Kurtz as Nurse Duckett, and William Reilly as First Doctor, in a scene from the John Drew Repertory Company's production of Catch-22

deadly sins are all in their proper place."

This moral concern also informs Heller's plays. He has written a three-act dramatic version of *Catch-22* and a separate but thematically similar two-act play entitled *We Bombed in New Haven*. (In addition, he has composed a short dramatic piece entitled *Clevinger's Trial*, based on the trial scene in the novel.) Heller's endeavors in this area have generally met with critical favor, but really his plays are only reflections of his first book. While some commentators have applauded the stage version of *Catch-22* as having a separate life of its own, actually their remarks are too generous. Likewise, *We Bombed in New Haven*, though correct and moving in its treatment of war's consequences, would probably not have attracted much notice strictly on its own merits.

We Bombed in New Haven is less directly autobiographical than Heller's other writings, although its essential convictions obviously were formed by the author's military service. Adamantly antiwar, it is more uncompromising than *Catch-22*, in which Heller objects not so much to war itself but to the military superstructure. *We Bombed in New Haven* is unqualifiedly denunciatory. The ending involves Captain Starkey, who is forced to conscript his own son and slate the boy for certain death; Heller's implications are quite clear. "Now, none of this, of course, is really happening. It's a show, a play in a theater, and I'm not really a captain. I'm an actor," Starkey explains. Heller's message emerges unmistakably when Starkey continues, "There has never been a war. There will never be a war. Nobody has been killed here tonight. It's only . . . make-believe . . . it's a story . . . a show. Nobody has ever been killed." Perhaps understandably, critics have tended to respond more to Heller's thesis than to the play as a whole. Persuaded by the content, they have tended to excuse some rather damaging inadequacies of form. The play is a bit too chaotic, a bit too excessive in its burlesque. Surrealistic in the manner of Edward Albee's *The Sandbox* or Tom Stoppard's *After Magritte*, it lacks the control and tightly symbolic cohesion of those more accomplished works. It closed after eighty-six performances at Broadway's Ambassador Theatre.

In *Something Happened*, however, Heller returned to the novel genre and to his earlier powers. But this book is a real departure from *Catch-22*. Perhaps the most immediately obvious difference is the protagonist, Bob Slocum. Heller's only first-person narrator, he is totally unheroic. While Yossarian personifies the ethical impulse, Slocum is a moral cipher, neither worthy nor unworthy. His personality is intended to embody what Heller sees as the deadening torpor of the business world. Here again, many details parallel events in Heller's background. Heller's brief employment as a file clerk for a casualty insurance company after graduation from high school finds its way into the novel, as does Heller's later career at *Time, Look*, and *McCall's*. Although the company for which Slocum works goes unnamed and his duties are unspecified, he occupies the middle-management corporate realm, territory with which Heller is obviously familiar. Indeed, Heller has revealed in conversation that Slocum is employed by *Time*, and that many of Slocum's ideas are the author's own.

The book has the feel of being spoken rather than written, and Slocum's manner of expression—flat, ordinary, unexciting—is an accurate reflection of his personality. Even the seven chapter titles ("I get the willies," "The office in which I work," "My wife is unhappy," "My daughter's unhappy," et al.) are miniature studies in resigned monotone. Whereas Yossarian is concerned not simply with surviving but with preserving his honor in what he perceives to be a dishonest world, to Slocum survival is everything. He is an integral part of the corporate atmosphere that surrounds him. While Yossarian steadfastly resists regimentation and restrictions, Slocum conforms punctiliously to the system that he despises.

The difference between the two protagonists is essentially the difference between innocence and experience. Although no naif, Yossarian maintains a high-minded sense of individual responsibility to self. But Slocum—older, lacking in illusions, and basically corrupted—has long since relinquished such idealistic notions. Jaded and world-weary, Slocum is presented as a sort of modern American Everyman. A principal theme of *Something Happened* is the bankruptcy of the contemporary middle-class American experience, and it finds expression in Slocum's preoccupation with loss. His feeling is that something has gone out of the American reality, that the world as he knows it is no longer hospitable to virtue. In this, *Something Happened* has much in common with the novels of John Updike. Like Updike's fictions, Heller's book is a novel of manners, mercilessly accurate in its rendering of social disorders.

Preoccupied with the dreadful emptiness of a certain sector of modern life, the novel offers none of the stated affirmations that we sometimes get from, say, Saul Bellow or Bernard Malamud, and none of the comic relief that characterizes Kurt Vonnegut's books or *Catch-22*. It does, however, convey an implied affirmation; relevant and ultimately humanistic, the novel functions not only as an indictment but also as a recommendation for something better. And although the book's gloominess and deadpan delivery alienated some reviewers, *Something Happened* is now gaining recognition as a major work. In at least one respect it is actually superior to *Catch-22*. Dependent on boisterous exaggeration, the earlier novel sometimes verges on self-parody. *Something Happened* is more sophisticated. Heller turned here from hyperbole to implication, and by opting for a less strident, less obvious approach, he produced a more mature work. In *Something Happened* Heller significantly expanded his range and again asserted himself as a writer of considerable stature.

Good As Gold, however, is a disappointment. Heller's most recent novel lacks a clear focus. Really it is three books in one: a Jewish family comedy, an academic satire, and a political lampoon. These several strands are too loosely intertwined. The result is a rambling, shapeless, nearly 450-page novel that contains many sections of good material but fails as a whole. Some commentators have suggested that this may have been caused by hasty composition. Whereas Heller took practically twelve years per novel to craft *Catch-22* and *Something Happened*, he wrote *Good As Gold* in less than half that time.

Protagonist Bruce Gold, like Yossarian and Slocum, has much in common with Joseph Heller. Like Heller, Gold is a product of Coney Island; he has attended college on the G.I. Bill and spent a year at Oxford; he holds a master's degree from Columbia; he is an author and a college professor; he has been married for some time to a patient, supportive wife; he is a father; he exercises in a mid-Manhattan gymnasium; and he writes in a studio apartment near Central Park. Significantly, he alone among Heller's protagonists is Jewish. In short, many of the particulars of Gold's life are similar or identical to those of the author's. And Heller has again acknowledged the autobiographical quality of his work, dedicating this book to the "several gallant families and Numerous unwitting friends whose Help, conversations, and experiences play so large a part."

Although Gold aspires to a career in government, he views the Washington scene as an empty charade and shares Heller's belief that "No one governs. Everyone performs. Politics has become a social world." Gold courts political appointment solely for personal gain: financial, sexual, and social. To Gold, the social component is the most compelling. Like Philip Roth's Alexander Portnoy,

he is ambivalent about his Jewishness and yearns for admission to the restricted enclaves of WASP privilege, even as he ridicules the WASP mentality. He endures the madly anti-Semitic ravings of an eccentric, alcoholic Virginia aristocrat whose endorsement will supposedly ensure Gold's acceptance; on the other hand, he is testy in response to veiled prejudice and castigates Henry Kissinger as a disgrace to the Jewish people. In all of this, the narrative alternates between straightforward, realistic depiction and wild overstatement. But Heller is guilty of the imitative fallacy. Like Gold, he cannot seem to decide how serious he is. Consequently, none of the book's several subjects emerges with any degree of credibility.

The family material is basically realistic, as are the academic scenes. But the Washington-based episodes are sheer foolery, as Heller releases a rabidly vitriolic pasquinade on Capitol folderol. His unrelenting scorn for the government is conveyed mainly through his facetious use of language. As in *Catch-22*, officialdom speaks a form of double-talk: Gold is repeatedly given such advice as "We'll want to move ahead with this as speedily as possible, although we'll have to go slowly," and "We'll want to build this up into an important public announcement, although we'll have to be completely secret." Such passages are juxtaposed with actual newspaper clippings and columnists' reports on Kissinger, along with outright authorial denunciations of the former secretary of state and other public figures, including Irving Kristol and Sidney Hook. Elsewhere Heller's victims are assailed pseudonymously, although in every case the person's actual identity is obvious. But the jokes—and the animus—quickly become predictable. Coupled with awkward authorial intrusions, a highly self-conscious use of Yiddish and Yiddish-influenced sentence structure, and several other indiscretions, the book's repetitious dependence on non sequitur and easy one-liners finally relegates *Good As Gold* to secondary status.

The novel has the feel of a warm-up, an unedited first draft. In the concluding scene, Gold—who is under contract to write a book about "the Jewish experience" but has had difficulty defining it for himself—is seen groping at last toward a deeper understanding of his heritage. Like Roth's protagonist at the conclusion of *Portnoy's Complaint*, Gold may be ready to begin his real story only now that *Good As Gold* has ended. To the extent that Gold "is" Heller, such a reading bodes well for contemporary American-Jewish fiction. Until the publication of *Good As Gold* Heller had not been generally thought of as a Jewish writer. But he may now be ready to explore in greater depth the issues of ethnic identity that he merely toys with in *Good As Gold*. Just as Roth had first to indulge his experimental impulses before producing his mature works, Heller in *Good As Gold* may simply be performing a cathartic exercise in preparation for something more substantial. Conceivably, his best writing may be still ahead of him.

References:

Nicholas Canaday, "Joseph Heller: Something Happened to the American Dream," *CEA Critic*, 40, no. 1 (1977): 34-48;

Barbara Gelb, "Catching Joseph Heller," *New York Times Magazine*, 4 March 1979, pp. 14-16, 42, 44, 46, 48, 51, 52, 54, 55;

Frederick Kiley and Walter McDonald, eds., *A "Catch-22" Casebook* (New York: Crowell, 1973);

Susan Strehle Klemtner, " 'A Permanent Game of

Excuses': Determinism in Heller's *Something Happened*," *Modern Fiction Studies*, 24 (Winter 1978-1979): 550-556;

Wayne C. Miller, "Ethnic Identity as Moral Focus: A Reading of Joseph Heller's *Good As Gold*," *MELUS*, 6, no. 3 (1979): 3-17;

James Nagel, ed., *Critical Essays on Catch-22* (Encino, Cal.: Dickenson, 1974);

"Playboy Interview: Joseph Heller," *Playboy*, 22 (June 1975): 59-61, 64-65, 68, 70, 72-74, 76;

George Plimpton, "The Art of Fiction LI: Joseph Heller," *Paris Review*, 60 (Winter 1974): 126-147;

Robert M. Scotto, ed., *A Critical Edition of Joseph Heller's Catch-22* (New York: Dell, 1973);

Alden Whitman, "Something Always Happens On The Way To The Office: An Interview With Joseph Heller," in *Pages: The World of Books, Writers, and Writing*, volume 1, edited by Matthew J. Bruccoli and C. E. Frazer Clark, Jr. (Detroit: Gale, 1976), pp. 74-81.

Laura Z. Hobson

(19 June 1900-   )

R. Barbara Gitenstein
Central Missouri State University

BOOKS: *Outlaws Three*, by Hobson and Thayer Hobson as Peter Field (New York: Morrow, 1933);

Dry Gulch Adams, by Hobson and Thayer Hobson as Peter Field (New York: Morrow, 1934);

A Dog of His Own (New York: Viking, 1941; London: Hamilton, 1941);

The Trespassers (New York: Simon & Schuster, 1943; London: Gollancz, 1944);

Gentleman's Agreement (New York: Simon & Schuster, 1947; London: Cassell, 1948);

The Other Father (New York: Simon & Schuster, 1950; London: Cassell, 1950);

The Celebrity (New York: Simon & Schuster, 1951; London: Cresset, 1953);

First Papers (New York: Random House, 1964; London: Heinemann, 1965);

I'm Going to Have a Baby (New York: Day, 1967; London: Heinemann, 1967);

The Tenth Month (New York: Simon & Schuster, 1971; London: Heinemann, 1972);

Consenting Adult (Garden City: Doubleday, 1975; London: Heinemann, 1975);

Over and Above (Garden City: Doubleday, 1979);

Untold Millions (New York: Harper & Row, 1982);

Laura Z: A Life (New York: Arbor House, 1983).

Laura Z. Hobson, most famous as a spokesman for liberal causes, writes of tolerance for all varieties of human existence. She demands that readers look at unacknowledged prejudices and try to overcome them. She is particularly sensitive to the hypocrisy of the empty-souled liberal's pat phrases of tolerance which cover a fear of anyone who is different.

Hobson was born in 1900 to Adella Kean and Michael Zametkin (editor of a Yiddish newspaper and labor organizer). After her childhood on Long Island, Hobson earned an A.B. at Cornell University and in 1930 married publisher Thayer Hobson, later adopting two sons (Michael and Christopher). Until 1934, she worked as an advertising copy-

Hobson's parents, Adela Kean and Michael Zametkin. In her autobiography Hobson recalls them as "unlike the usual immigrants dwelling in novels, for they were both teachers and writers, my father the first editor of the Jewish Daily Forward, *one of its founders before the celebrated Abraham Cahan took over, . . . and my mother for twelve of her middle years a regular columnist on a lesser Jewish newspaper,* The Day."

human being's responsibility is not only to recognize the rights of others but also to destroy vestiges of inherited prejudices by trying to place himself in the situation of the other. In her attempt to enlighten her readers, Hobson most often writes from the point of view of the majority group. In order to accomplish her goal of instruction in tolerance, she creates spokesmen who rise above their classes by their sensitivity to the predicaments of others.

Hobson's autobiography is her fiction in another mode. According to Sybil Steinberg in *Publishers Weekly*, "Those who have read Hobson's nine novels already know a great deal about [her], although they may be generally unaware that all were based on episodes from the author's own life." Steinberg then proceeds to list these "episodes" and the novels that correspond: a child of socialists (*First Papers*, 1964), an advertising copywriter (*Untold Millions*, 1982), an unwed mother (*The Tenth Month*, 1971), the mother of a gay son (*Consenting Adult*, 1975), a critic of fascism (*The Trespassers*, 1943), and an opponent of anti-Semitism (*Gentleman's Agreement*, 1947). The three novels not listed here further

Laura Z. Hobson about the time The Trespassers *was published (photo by Halsman)*

writer. In 1935, she obtained a divorce. Since the mid-1930s, Hobson has made a reputation in several areas of publishing as well as in the capacity of a creative writer. She has worked as consultant and promotion director for such journals as *Time, Life, Fortune, Sports Illustrated*, and *Saturday Review*; she worked for one year as a reporter for the *New York Evening Post*; she has had short stories published in *Collier's, Ladies' Home Journal, McCall's*, and *Cosmopolitan*; she collaborated with Thayer Hobson on two Westerns written under the joint pseudonym Peter Field (*Outlaws Three*, 1933, and *Dry Gulch Adams*, 1934); and she has written two works of juvenile fiction (*A Dog of His Own*, 1941, and *I'm Going to Have a Baby*, 1967), nine novels for adults, and, most recently, her autobiography, *Laura Z.* (1983).

Hobson's major theme is that individuals of a minority group ought to have the same rights of freedom as individuals of a majority group. Each support Steinberg's statement in that they, too, are based on events of Hobson's life: she was a parent (*The Other Father*, 1950); she was one who suddenly achieved and suffered fame (*The Celebrity,* 1951); she is a Jew who has queried her Jewish identity (*Over and Above*, 1979).

Hobson's most famous novel, *Gentleman's Agreement*, is the best example of her technique and her most important themes. Philip Green, a Protestant-born journalist, moves from the West Coast of the United States to a new job at *Smith's Weekly* on the East Coast, where he is virtually unknown. His first assignment, an analysis of American anti-Semitism, and his decision to assume the identity of a Jew set the stage for the revelation of not merely blatant prejudice, but also hypocritical prejudice from his liberal friends. For instance, Philip's new girl friend, Kathy Lacey Pawling, is worried about what ruse to employ when she must introduce her future fiancé as a Jew to her establishment family and friends; his future in-laws, who own a cottage in Darien, Connecticut, a restricted community, feel they ought not sell the cottage to Philip and Kathy. The network of prejudice even reaches to Detroit, where Philip's sister worries about her husband's job being in jeopardy because of his Jewish relations. Philip learns that in some cases people are not "consciously antisemitic. . . . They despise it; it's an 'awful thing.' But . . . they help it along and then wonder why it grows." When Philip's son becomes the butt of anti-Semitism at school, Philip learns the angry resistance of a father, and his bitterness makes him reject the gentleman's agreement of polite prejudice.

The book was quite successful. Though some critics charged Hobson with overwriting, most critics admired both her skill in telling the tale and the powerful feelings behind that tale. E. R. Embree of the *Chicago Sun Book Weekly* felt "the story was not as good as the sermon"; the reviewer for the *New Yorker* found the book "slick." But William Du Bois (*New York Times*) and Struthers Burt (*Saturday Review of Literature*) described the book as brilliant. The most cogent criticisms of the novel pointed to Hobson's rather unconvincing ending, in which not only is Philip's article based on his experiences as a Jew well-received but also Kathy learns the error of her prejudiced ways. In contrast to pictures of the Nazi concentration camps, Hobson's consequences seem pallid. But her American view of anti-Semitism proved popular, for in 1947, Elia Kazan made a successful film of *Gentleman's Agreement* with Gregory Peck in the starring role.

In Hobson's other novels, the problem which

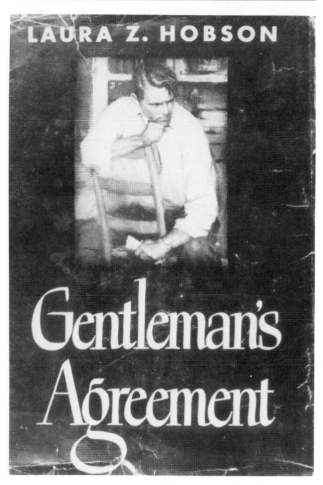

Dust jacket for Hobson's best-known novel, the story of Protestant journalist Philip Green who assumes the identity of a Jew to investigate anti-Semitism in America

evokes from her the sympathetic concern evident in *Gentleman's Agreement* is homosexuality. *Consenting Adult* is the tale of Tessa Lynn's growing understanding of her son Jeff's homosexuality. Years of reading, interviews with medical doctors and psychiatrists, and her own growing acceptance allow Tessa to attain a more generous attitude toward homosexuality. When she hears of his involvement in Gay Rights and when she greets his male lover at her home for the first time, she recognizes the transformation in Jeff as his own acceptance of himself. She is now able to purge her own mind of prejudices which she has come to see as a sort of voyeurism. She can accept the two young men at her door as consenting adults who have chosen to live with one another.

Though *Consenting Adult* did not receive the amount of critical attention that *Gentleman's Agreement* did, the response was as complimentary as that the earlier novel had enjoyed. There was a similar questioning of the success of the ending of this novel, but the praise of Hobson's courage and of the powerful pleas for tolerance was consistent. For example, Martin Duberman's *New York Times* review argued the great value of approaching this topic from the parent's point of view, and though he found the novel flawed, he also described it as "courageous." In *Consenting Adult*, as in *Gentleman's Agreement*, Hobson seems able to address a major social issue and awaken readers to prejudices against one who is different from the majority. There is a distance between the author and her Gentile, male spokesman in *Gentleman's Agreement* that is not apparent in the Jewish-born mother, who has a career as a journalist and espouses liberal causes in *Consenting Adult*. The added warmth in the 1975 novel, however, hinges on the fact that Jeff is Tessa's son, whereas the Jews are only the subjects of Philip's story.

Of Hobson's novels for adults, only two have Jewish characters who figure significantly as Jews in the fiction: *First Papers* and *Over and Above*. In the first of these, the Ivarins are more significant as portraits of liberals at the turn of the century than they are as portraits of Jews. The novel is an accurate representation of the intellectual, agnostic, liberal atmosphere in which Hobson herself grew up. On the other hand, *Over and Above* asks whether denial of Jewishness is satisfactory in contemporary America. Amy Maxe, daughter of the intellectual-agnostic Jewish past, learns from Eph, a Zionist and her daughter's former boyfriend, to reidentify with Jewish peoplehood. In fact, *Gentleman's Agreement*, which has no major characters who are Jewish, is the novel which best articulates Hobson's concern for tolerance of Jews.

In her novels, however, "the Jewish Question" is a liberal cause, different from the more current concern of some American-Jewish authors who see Jewishness as essential to their identities. Hobson does represent a significant element in the American-Jewish writing of the 1930s and 1940s which aligned liberal causes with Jewishness and in fact added a "Jewish accent" to some of the left-wing political issues of the time. In this capacity she belongs with the broad outlines of American-Jewish literary tradition.

"The Z is for Zametkin, my maiden name, and I have clung to it through all my years because it held my identity intact before that Anglo-Saxon married name of Hobson.

"I was born Laura Zametkin in New York City when the new century was five months and nineteen days old...I can truly say that the century was young when I was young, was in its middle years when I was middle-aged and now is in its late years during my own late years...

"In this one nothing will be made up, nothing invented, nothing knowingly shaded to put a better light on some crisis, no special pleading to exonerate me in some misfortune...If it is written here, it will be true..."

—LAURA Z. HOBSON, in *Laura Z*

ISBN: 0-87795-524-7

Laura Z

LAURA Z. HOBSON

ARBOR HOUSE

Laura Z

A LIFE

BY
LAURA Z.
HOBSON

Dust jacket for Hobson's autobiography, published in 1983. In the "Afterword—and Foreword" she announces plans for volume two: "This, then, is not the end of my story, but only a pause in the telling of it, with this brief postscript doubling as a preface for the rest of it still to come."

Erica Jong

(26 March 1942-   )

Emily Toth
Pennsylvania State University

See also the Jong entries in *DLB 2, American Novelists Since World War II*, and *DLB 5, American Poets Since World War II*.

BOOKS: *Fruits & Vegetables* (New York, Chicago & San Francisco: Holt, Rinehart & Winston, 1971; London: Secker & Warburg, 1973);

Half-Lives (New York, Chicago & San Francisco: Holt, Rinehart & Winston, 1973; London: Secker & Warburg, 1974);

Fear of Flying (New York, Chicago & San Francisco: Holt, Rinehart & Winston, 1973; London: Secker & Warburg, 1974);

Here Comes and Other Poems (New York: New American Library, 1975);

Loveroot (New York: Holt, Rinehart & Winston, 1975; London: Secker & Warburg, 1977);

The Poetry of Erica Jong (New York: Holt, Rinehart & Winston, 1976);

How to Save Your Own Life (New York: Holt, Rinehart & Winston, 1977; London: Secker & Warburg, 1977);

Selected Poems, 2 volumes (London: Panther, 1977, 1980);

Four Visions of America, by Jong, Thomas Sanchez, Kay Boyle, and Henry Miller (Santa Barbara: Capra Press, 1977);

At the Edge of the Body (New York: Holt, Rinehart & Winston, 1979);

Fanny: Being the True History of the Adventures of Fanny Hackabout-Jones (New York: New American Library, 1980; London: Granada, 1980);

Witches (New York: Abrams, 1981);

Ordinary Miracles (New York: New American Library, 1983).

OTHER: *Stories by Colette*, foreword by Jong (New York: New American Library, 1975).

SELECTED PERIODICAL PUBLICATIONS: "The Artist as Housewife / The Housewife as Artist," *Ms.*, 1 (December 1972): 64-66, 100, 104-105;

"The Writer as Sexual Guru," *New York*, 7 (20 May 1974): 80-82;

Erica Jong, early 1970s (photo by Peter Trump)

"Remembering Anne Sexton," *New York Times*, 27 October 1974, VII: 63;

"Writing a First Novel," *Twentieth-Century Literature* (October 1974): 262-269;

"Marriage, rational and irrational," *Vogue*, 165 (June 1975): 94-95;

"Writer Who 'Flew' to Sexy Fame Talks About Being a Woman," *Vogue*, 167 (March 1977): 158, 160;

"Creativity vs. Generativity: the Unexamined Lie," *New Republic*, 180 (13 January 1979): 27-30.

Her first novel, *Fear of Flying*, gained worldwide fame for Erica Jong as a writer about women's literary and sexual adventures. But the reputation of *Fear of Flying* has overshadowed Jong's achievements as a poet, social critic, and writer concerned with satire, Jewishness, and women's independence.

Like Isadora Wing in *Fear of Flying*, Erica Mann was born into a family of Jewish painters, musicians, and intellectuals and grew up on the Upper West Side of New York City. Eda Mirsky Mann was a painter; Seymour Mann, a musician and composer, was also an importer of giftware. As an adolescent, their daughter Erica wrote constantly, producing journals, notebooks, and stories she illustrated herself—but her heroes were always white Anglo-Saxon Protestant males, with such names as Mitch Mitchell and Duane Blaine.

As a student at Barnard College, from which she graduated in 1963, Erica Mann edited the college literary magazine and produced poetry programs for the campus radio station—while writing poems in imitation of male writers, among them Yeats, Auden, and Dylan Thomas. Soon after graduation she married a Columbia student, Michael Werthman, but the marriage lasted only a year and a half.

As a Columbia graduate student in English literature (M.A., 1965), Erica Mann wrote a master's thesis on Alexander Pope's "Eloisa to Abelard," suggesting that Pope viewed himself through Eloisa's *persona* and that he (probably unconsciously) equated his disabilities as a hunchback with Eloisa's social limitations as a woman. "Eloisa to Abelard" is also a mock-memoir, purporting to be Eloisa's true confessions—much as *Fear of Flying* was taken to be Erica Jong's.

In 1966 Erica Mann married Allan Jong, a Chinese-American psychiatrist, and went with him to Germany, where he did his military service until 1969. She taught at the University of Maryland Overseas Division, worked briefly as a door-to-door saleswoman for investment opportunities, and continued to write poems, but in Heidelberg she also began confronting her own subject matter. She saw the World War II death camps and later wrote in "The Artist as Housewife/The Housewife as Artist," published in *Ms.*, that "Germany was an overwhelming experience. Suddenly I felt as paranoid as a Jew in hiding during the Nazi period. For the first time I began to confess to my primal terror, to my sense of being a victim. . . . From persecuted Jew to persecuted woman is not a very long step."

She began reading women poets who wrote about women, especially Anne Sexton and Sylvia Plath, and began writing poems from her own experiences as a Jew and as a woman. For instance, "The 8:29 to Frankfurt," first published in the *Beloit*

Poetry Journal (Winter 1968/1969) under the name Erica Mann and reprinted in *Fear of Flying*, describes a German train conductor who "goose steps / down the corridor." Though he resembles a "pink marzipan pig," his voice and uniform signify authority—and the poem's speaker imagines that the journey will end in a death camp. But finally someone nudges her awake, the conductor smiles about the weather, and the sunlight seems "suddenly benign as chicken soup."

By the time Jong published her first poetry collection, *Fruits & Vegetables*, in 1971, she had found her own subject matter and voice, with a highly original, satiric perspective. She endows fruits and vegetables with human characteristics, notably the onion, admirable for "its capacity for self-scrutiny . . . the onion searches its soul & finds only its various skins. . . ."

Fruits & Vegetables includes poems on aging and artificiality in women, on painting, on Germans, and on Sylvia Plath; but the main subjects are love, death, sex, and food, viewed with sudden, oddly comical insights. Moreover, in *Fruits & Vegetables*, Jong uses for humor language that has traditionally been considered off limits for women. There are also somber notes in *Fruits & Vegetables*, and some of them concern Jewishness. "The Heidelberg Landlady," for instance, lost her father in World War I and her husband in World War II but insists, "You can't judge a country / by just twelve years." She and her mother are shown cultivating their plants, hoping for the sun, and "living in a Jewless world without men."

In her second collection, *Half-Lives* (1973), Jong works on inventing a style to represent what she sees as the extremes of her character: despair and wild hilarity. Some poems are deadly: "The Man Who Can Only Paint Death," "The End of the World," "Why I Died." Some of the most deadly lines appear in the long prose poem "From the Country of Regrets," including a lethal fantasy about rich merchants in another country who are hated and finally purged in pogroms called "Regrets."

But other poems in *Half-Lives* expand the limits of permissible language, such as "Seventeen Warnings in Search of a Feminist Poem," which includes such lines as "Beware of the man who denounces his mother; he is a son of a bitch." "Seventeen Warnings" is among the first Jong works praised by some critics for its witty portrayal of feminist anger and condemned by others for its open, down-to-earth qualities. Other poems in

Half-Lives also poke fun at men—"The poet of sulks" who confuses a woman poet's poems and her cooking in "The Bait."

Jong won the Alice Faye di Castagnolia Award of the Poetry Society of America for *Half-Lives*; she had also won *Poetry* magazine's Bess Hokin Prize, *New York Quarterly*'s Madeline Sadin Award, and a grant from the New York State Council on the Arts. Her poetry has been well received by other poets and critics—among them Muriel Rukeyser, Anne Sexton, and Louis Untermeyer—who called her poems "sly but penetrating, witty but passionate, bawdy and beautiful."

Fear of Flying (1973), Jong's first published novel, was a change in genre but not in the common theme Jong sees in all her work: "the quest for self-knowledge." *Fear of Flying*'s Isadora Wing has more in common with Erica Jong than the search for truth, however: she shares Jong's age, her appearance, her education; has had two husbands; and published a successful poetry collection.

As Isadora tells her story, she is both frightened of life and jaded. Marital sex has lost its bite and become more like Velveeta than the rare goat cheese she would like: "luscious, creamy, cloven-hoofed." At a Vienna psychiatrists' convention, Isadora seizes the opportunity to leave Bennett, her Chinese-American psychiatrist husband, and romp aimlessly around Europe with Adrian Goodlove, a British analyst. Isadora describes her feelings and adventures in mostly comic and very earthy prose, notably her fantasy of the guilt-free sexual experience, "when you came together zippers fell away like rose petals. . . ." The experience is brief, anonymous, and perfect—and it was thoroughly shocking to many *Fear of Flying* reviewers.

Fear of Flying is essentially a literary novel, a Bildungsroman with strong parallels to the *Odyssey*, Dante's *Inferno*, and the myths of Daedalus and Icarus. But many critics ignored the book's literary aspects and focused exclusively on the sex in it.

Jong has insisted that the novel is about unfulfillment—and indeed, Adrian Goodlove is often impotent and the other men in the novel usually somehow lacking. Apparently thinking *Fear of Flying* was intended to portray all women, Paul Theroux in the *New Statesman* accuses it of "picturing woman as a hapless organ animated by the simplest ridicule." Other critics also overstressed the sexual references, but some readers saw that Jong was breaking new ground, especially for women writers.

Dust jacket for Jong's first novel, described by John Updike as "a winner. It has class and sass, brightness and bite."

"*Fear of Flying* feels like a winner. It has class and sass, brightness and bite," John Updike wrote in the *New Yorker*. Henry Miller praised it in the *New York Times* as a "female *Tropic of Cancer*," giving women a chance to "find their own voice and give us great sagas of sex, life, joy, and adventure." *Fear of Flying* has paved the way for other women writers to describe women's sexual longings in more earthy language, and recent academic critics, such as Elaine Showalter, Joan Reardon, and Susan Koppelman, have considered the book a milestone for American fiction.

Fear of Flying also describes Isadora's recognition of her Jewishness with her femaleness. Before living in Germany, she knew almost no Yiddish, was fourteen before she ever attended a bar mitzvah, and celebrated neither Christmas nor Chanukah—only "The Winter Solstice." In Heidelberg, miserable during her husband's tour of duty, Isadora realizes that "intensely Jewish" means "intensely paranoid." She discovers censored books, hiding the truth about the extermination of the Jews; she finds a secret Nazi amphitheater in the hills above the city. In Heidelberg, Isadora Wing says, "I began to write as if it were my only hope for survival, for escape."

Isadora's Jewishness also plays a part in Adrian's ambivalent reactions to her. "It's just that Jewish girls are so bloody good in bed," he says—then later calls her "bloody Jewish . . . mediocre at other things, but at suffering you're always superb." Isadora's Jewishness and femaleness intersect in her constant feelings of guilt, and in her challenge: "Show me a woman who doesn't feel guilty and I'll show you a man."

Fear of Flying ultimately sold over six million copies in twenty countries. By the time her third collection of poems, *Loveroot*, appeared in 1975, she and Allan Jong were divorcing.

Loveroot records transitions in Erica Jong's life from 1968 until 1975, when she went to live with Jonathan Fast, a novelist, in California. *Loveroot* begins with a self-portrait in which "I, Erica Jong," having endured "three decades of pain . . . declare myself now for joy." The *Loveroot* poems satirize male poets and critics, make fun of "Penis Envy," and celebrate women writers, especially Sylvia Plath, Anne Sexton, and Colette. The confessional poems in *Loveroot* explain the breakup of her marriage to her "silent muse," with whom she "felt no bondage / in this air we share" ("For My Husband"). She mourns Anne Sexton's suicide and celebrates her own new love as salvation ("Eating Death, for Anne Sexton").

The themes in *Loveroot* anticipate Jong's second novel, *How to Save Your Own Life* (1977), a more serious sequel to *Fear of Flying*. In *How to Save Your Own Life*, Isadora and Bennett's marriage dies; the poet Jeannie Morton (who resembles Anne Sexton) takes her own life. Isadora meets the novelist Kurt Hammer, who resembles Henry Miller and tells her that life is full of excuses not to live: she should seek joy and "watch out for the death-people." Isadora finds the joy with Josh Ace, a warm young writer who shares her sense of humor. With Josh, she relearns how to laugh.

How to Save Your Own Life is also a feminist mock-memoir, describing in comic detail what happens to Isadora Wing after publication of *Candida Confesses*, her best-selling novel about sex and adventure: again, much of the story borrows from Erica Jong's life. The later Isadora has more women friends, who illustrate women's problems and possibilities. One fights with Isadora about Jewish

female guilt; another has an affair with Isadora, a comical meeting of Jewish chutzpah and WASP "coolth." But Isadora learns the most from Jeannie Morton, who before her death teaches Isadora "the courage to be a fool."

At the Edge of the Body (1979), Jong's next volume of poetry, is more reflective than her earlier work. She includes poems about dogs, moving from witty to serious observations; about house-hunting; and about death: "Flesh is merely a lesson. / We learn it / & pass it on" ("The Buddha in the Womb"). The feminist subjects are still present, with new insights into women's anger, which must be turned "where it belongs": to the fathers, husbands, and brothers who oppress ("The Deaths of the Goddesses"). But Jong's own anger at men is muted, she reveals, for the man in her life is her friend as well as her lover ("The Truce Between the Sexes").

Jong has said that as she grows older, she becomes more herself—and writes now from a mature tranquillity. She and Jonathan Fast were married on Christmas Eve 1977, and their daughter, Molly Miranda Jong-Fast, was born in 1978, while Jong was on page 420 of her latest novel, *Fanny: Being the True History of the Adventures of Fanny Hackabout-Jones* (1980).

Jong calls Fanny a "very modern wench in eighteenth century dress," though *Fanny* is in the tradition of Fielding's *Tom Jones* and John Cleland's *Fanny Hill* (to which it is, in part, an answer). Fanny, a red-haired would-be poet, has adventures with highwaymen, pirates, bawdy-houses, and witches and has a feminist analysis for much of what happens—while Jong uses the eighteenth-century novel form to satirize both Fanny's century and her own. *Fanny* purports to be a letter from Fanny to her daughter, Belinda—reflecting Jong's own concern with mothering a daughter and making her an independent woman.

"*Fanny* is the most radical book I have written," Jong says. Fanny has more courage than Isadora Wing, and much less internal conflict. She shows, Jong says, "what women can be at their boldest." Fanny needs to be strong—to escape seduction by Alexander Pope, among others. Of Pope, Fanny's stepsister observes that "just as his Back is deform'd, so his Masculine Appendage must be similarly gothick and strange"—and Fanny discovers the truth while Pope is insisting, "Whate'er is, IS RIGHT." *Fanny* satirizes, but more gently, the masculine pretensions that were also Jong's targets in earlier books. The witches represent a matriarchal religion, an underground survival of feminism giving Fanny a reservoir of strength. The witches

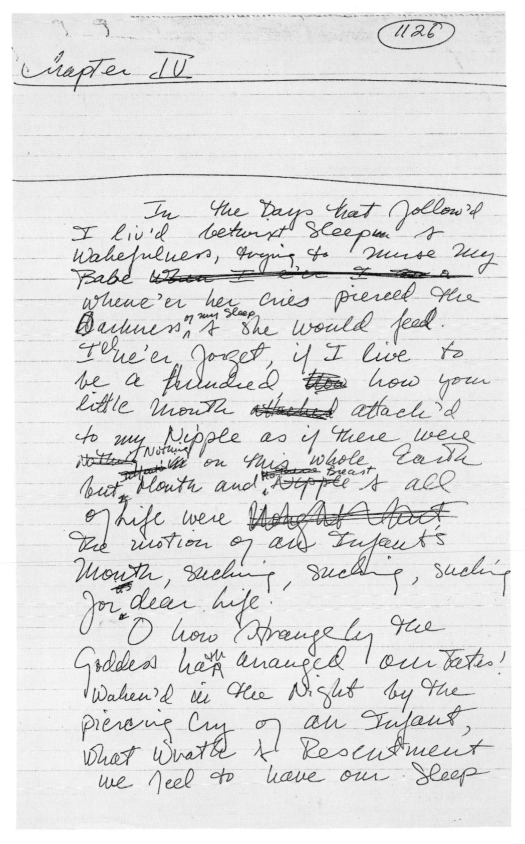

Manuscript page from Jong's most recent novel, Fanny: Being the True History of the Adventures of Fanny Hackabout-Jones *(1980)*

Jong about the time Fanny *was published*
(photo by Elizabeth Gee)

Erica Jong continues to write poetry, has begun another contemporary novel, and will co-produce the film version of *Fanny*. Her 1983 poetry collection, *Ordinary Miracles*, includes meditations on the breakup of her marriage to Jonathan Fast, which ended in 1981. Though her overall subject matter has become less openly autobiographical and confessional, she retains the same satirist's view she described to *Playboy* in 1975: "I see the world as a tremendous circus. . . . My real view of the world is a satirist's view, and more often than not, I find the games we play to gain status very foolish."

Interviews:

"Interview with Erica Jong," *New York Quarterly*, no. 16 (1974): 22ff.;

Elaine Showalter and Carol Smith, "Interview with Erica Jong," *Columbia Forum*, 4 (1975): 12-17;

"*Playboy* Interview: Erica Jong," *Playboy*, 24 (September 1975): 61-64, 66-73, 76, 78, 202-203;

Barbara A. Bannon, "*Publishers Weekly* Interviews Erica Jong," *Publishers Weekly*, 211 (14 February 1977): 8-9, 12;

Ellen Frankfort, "Erica Jong: an Intimate Conversation," *Viva* (September 1977): 44, 46, 80, 85-87.

References:

John L. Kern, "Erica: Being the True History of the Adventures of Isadora Wing, Fanny Hackabout-Jones, and Erica Jong," *Writer's Digest*, 61 (June 1981): 20-25;

Henry Miller, "Erica Jong's *Tropic*," *New York Times*, 20 August 1974, p. 38;

Joan Reardon, "Fear of Flying: Developing the Feminist Novel," *International Journal of Women's Studies*, 1, no. 3 (1978): 306-320;

Paul Theroux, "Hapless Organ," *New Statesman*, 87 (19 April 1974): 554;

John Updike, "Jong Love," *New Yorker*, 49 (17 December 1973): 149-151.

also give Fanny her most important principle: "Courage is the only Magick worth having."

Jong's research for *Fanny* inspired her next book: *Witches* (1981), a brew of prose and poetry about the world of witchcraft. Jong's text, with Joseph A. Smith's illustrations, explores the figure of the witch as historical and mythical, as Halloween hag and exotic seductress. The book also includes recipes for love potions, formulas for spells and incantations, and "a ghoulish gallery of witches' familiars."

Roberta Kalechofsky

(11 May 1931-   )

Ruth Rosenberg
University of New Orleans

SELECTED BOOKS: *George Orwell* (New York: Ungar, 1973);

Justice, My Brother (Montreal: Writers' Cooperative, 1974);

Stephen's Passion (Marblehead, Mass.: Micah Publications, 1975);

La Hoya (Marblehead, Mass.: Micah Publications, 1976);

Orestes in Progress (Marblehead, Mass.: Micah Publications, 1976);

Solomon's Wisdom: A Collection of Short Stories (Marblehead, Mass.: Micah Publications, 1978);

Rejected Essays and Other Matters (Marblehead, Mass.: Micah Publications, 1980).

OTHER: "To Light a Candle," in *New Voices 3*, edited by Charles Glicksberg (New York: Hendricks House, 1958);

"His Day Out," in *Best American Short Stories of 1972*, edited by Martha Foley (Boston: Houghton Mifflin, 1972);

"Cheever," in *Encyclopedia of World Literature in the Twentieth Century*, volume 4 (New York: Ungar, 1975);

"Abraham and Isaac," in *The Enduring Legacy: Biblical Dimensions in Modern Literature*, edited by Douglas C. Brown (New York: Scribners, 1975);

"My Mother's Story," in *The Woman Who Lost Her Names: Selected Writings by American Jewish Women*, edited by Julia Mazow (San Francisco: Harper & Row, 1980);

Echad: An Anthology of Latin American Jewish Writing, edited by Kalechofsky (Marblehead, Mass.: Micah Publications, 1980);

South African Jewish Voices: Echad 2, edited by Kalechofsky (Marblehead, Mass.: Micah Publications, 1982);

Phoenix Rising: Contemporary Jewish Writing, edited with contributions by Kalechofsky (Marblehead, Mass.: Micah Publications, 1982).

SELECTED PERIODICAL PUBLICATIONS: "Epiphany," *Works*, 1 (Spring 1968);

Roberta Kalechofsky

"A Dispute with Gloria Steinem," *Branching Out*, 1 (December 1973);

"Montreal Writers' Cooperative," *Branching Out*, 1 (March/April 1974);

"Realities," *Forum*, 15 (Winter 1974);

"My Mother's Story," *Forum*, 15 (Winter 1974);

"Secular Democracy or Religious Nationalism," *Genesis 2* (March 1975);

"Ben Yehoshua on the Problem of Being an Israeli Writer," *Genesis 2* (December 1975);

"The No-Travels Journal," *Northeast Rising Sun* (May 1976);

"Two Eastern European Views: *Jacob the Liar* by

Jurek Becker, and *This Way for The Gas, Ladies and Gentlemen* by Tadeusz Borowski," *Genesis 2* (September 1976);

"Reflections from A Park Bench," *Forum*, 17 (Winter 1976).

Roberta Kalechofsky is not only an acclaimed novelist, an accomplished lecturer, a prizewinning short-story writer, an essayist, an editor, and a translator, but she is also a publisher and an active spokesperson for the small presses. She was contributing editor to *Margins,* a review of small-press books, and dedicated her first book to the small-press movement. She made the decision to found her own press after she received her one hundred first rejection slip on 11 May 1975, which happened to be her forty-fourth birthday. She justified the decision by pointing to a distinguished list of predecessors who had printed their own works: Mark Twain, Edgar Allan Poe, Stephen Crane, William Blake, Walt Whitman, Gertrude Stein, and Mary Baker Eddy. She at first intended to call her press Hogarth II after Virginia Woolf's publishing house, but decided instead, since she specializes in Jewish fiction, to name it after the Hebrew prophet Micah.

She says that she discovered how Jewish she was by writing. She credits authorship and motherhood as being the two "shaping experiences" which forced her to make conscious her commitment to her heritage. She was deeply moved by the responsibility of being the mother of two Jewish sons. And her religious-allegorical novels show continual concern with the historical destiny of the Jews. Some of her shorter fictions are vibrant retellings of Bible stories; others are meditations on the death camps. Anthologies she has edited introduce African and Latin-American Jewish writers to an American audience. This series of volumes is called Echad after the Hebrew word for *one*.

The drive to found a community out of many distant voices derives from her early background. She was raised by a succession of relatives after her parents were divorced when she was about a year old. She says, "I lived in many households, among all kinds of people: Orthodox Jews, assimilated Jews, rich families, and poor families." Her father, Julius Joseph Kirchik, a lawyer, married Naomi Jacobs in 1930, in Brooklyn. The marriage had been arranged by a matchmaker. Naomi Jacobs, in Kalechofsky's words, "a glamorous, flamboyant person, who was said to resemble Jean Harlow," had been born in Brooklyn on 7 July 1909. Although she had been trained as a Hebrew teacher, she never

taught, because "like a Jamesian character, she had inherited enough money so that work never entered her life." Although she did not value intellectuality, she did treasure Yiddishkeit, often taking her daughter to the Yiddish Theater on the Lower East Side or playing Yiddish records for her. They faithfully listened to the Yiddish hour on the radio. From her mother's home at East 9th Street and Avenue H in Brooklyn, Kalechofsky moved to Brownsville, East New York, where both sets of grandparents lived. The paternal grandparents, with whom she stayed for a time, are poignantly described in the short story "From a Park Bench." About them she said: "It was my grandmother who always told me to study to be something. But it is my grandfather's stories and legends that live on through my own writing and identity. They were very religious people."

The continual adjustments demanded of her in being raised by a succession of relatives gave her an extraordinary resilience and imposed the necessity of inventing her own continuity among such a shifting cast of characters. In a recent letter Kalechofsky notes, "Living in many different households is very difficult when you are young, but it gives you quite a valuable foundation to draw upon later." Thus, out of these bewildering circumstances, she precociously shaped an identity and gathered materials for her later fictions.

At Midwood High School she was strongly influenced by her English teacher, Mrs. Rose Risikoff, who urged her to take her talent for writing seriously and persuaded her to work on *Patterns*, the high-school literary magazine. Kalechofsky majored in English at Brooklyn College and minored in secondary education, going back to Midwood to do her student teaching. She served as the literary editor of *Voices*, her college magazine, and knew when she graduated in 1952 that she would be a writer. She credits Professor Marjorie Coogan with having instilled confidence into her. Coogan helped her to get a part-time instructorship at the University of Connecticut in 1952. There, at Storrs, she became a faculty adviser for the campus magazine. In 1953 she left to marry Robert Kalechofsky, and they both continued their graduate work at New York University. In February 1956 she completed her master's thesis on "The Structure and Symbolism of Hawthorne's Work." Her husband's dissertation was on "Mathematical Models of Piaget's Cognitive Theories."

From 1956 to 1959, and again from 1962 to 1963, she taught at Brooklyn College, also finding time to serve, in 1958, as a junior editor at Funk and

Wagnalls. While her husband was teaching at Stony Brook as one of the founding faculty who helped to establish the mathematics department, their first son, Hal Joshua, was born, on 10 January 1960. His brother, Neal Frederic, was born in Schenectady, on 24 December 1963, while his father was teaching at Union College. Robert Kalechofsky joined the faculty of Salem State College in Marblehead, Massachusetts, in September 1966.

While the children were still small, Roberta Kalechofsky began work on her doctorate. "Getting a degree with two young sons was a terrible strain. I have a dim recollection of having had a tension headache for two years." She had finished her course work before they were born, but studying for the qualifying examinations and writing the dissertation while they were still toddlers was an enormous exertion. She received her Ph.D. in 1970.

Her dissertation, with Professor David H. Greene at NYU, was on "The Political Novels of Joyce Cary." Kalechofsky dealt with *Prisoner of Grace, Except the Lord,* and *Not Honour More.* Her passionate advocacy of Cary is expressed in a long essay, "History as a Multi-Level Experience," which made the rounds of the periodicals from 1970 to 1975. She finally published it herself in *Rejected Essays and Other Matters* (1980), along with the rejection slips that it had accumulated. In it, she says that "in neglecting Cary, the public has deprived itself of one of the wittiest and most insightful writers on the workings of democracy, and on modern consciousness in the range of its expressions." She herself learned, through her minute analyses of Cary's novels, the technique of blending wit and lyricism.

In the summer of 1971 Kalechofsky's short story "His Day Out" was published in the *Western Humanities Review*, and it was then reprinted in Martha Foley's *Best American Short Stories of 1972.* It depicts an anxious mental patient's reluctance to leave his analyst. Lionel Enzino tries every ruse possible to remain in the safety of the Craigmore Institute for the emotionally disturbed. The story builds to its ironic climax with swift thrusts. "Lionel dreaded his day out. He wished he could give it to someone who would appreciate it. He did not." Agonizing in advance over every gesture, rehearsing every move in a cold sweat, he allows Dr. Benson to force him to take a day off. His worst anxieties are realized as a crazed gunman shoots at him in a diner. He thinks, as he cowers, whimpering, against the counter, "Dr. Benson, you're never going to believe this."

In 1973 Ungar published Kalechofsky's monograph *George Orwell*, and the family moved to Edmonton, Canada, for her husband's sabbatical

from Salem State College at the University of Alberta. There she volunteered to help in the founding of Canada's first feminist magazine, *Branching Out.* The founders of *Branching Out* began with an initial fund of sixty dollars, which they chipped in themselves for postage. This experience confirmed Kalechofsky's conviction that one must forge one's own readership. "It's a gamble, but if you believe in what you are doing, then you must do it." The success of this enterprise showed her that a grassroots operation could work. She has since reprinted some of her position papers on feminism, originally published in *Branching Out*, in *Rejected Essays and Other Matters*. Of particular interest is "Where We Differ: Comments on Jewish Feminists," her carefully researched article on the position of the Jewish woman in daily life throughout history.

In 1974 the Montreal Writers' Cooperative published Kalechofsky's novel *Justice, My Brother*. It earned distinguished reviews and, in the words of one critic, "deserves an honored place on everyone's bookshelf, in everyone's memory."

When she was asked why she had chosen Mexico as a setting for this novel and impoverished peasants as protagonists, Kalechofsky explained that these best embodied her theme. She was dealing with the problems of rage and hatred and did not want to employ characters sophisticated enough to psychoanalyze their feelings. Kalechofsky did an enormous amount of research for this novel. The details of daily life in the village of Netzahualcoytl gain authenticity and immediacy from an anthropological study. However, the harsh and brutal incidents are the author's own invention. She says that she was "going through a gothic phase" at that time.

In this brooding, oneiric novel, Julio Donajcro, a Mexican peasant, is "marked for death" by his younger brother, Ricardo, whom he has wronged. Ricardo, with a rifle strapped to his saddle, gallops toward Julio's farm to revenge himself. Julio's assembled sons watch their uncle shoot and miss. In superstitious terror, Julio forces his family to become vagrants. They flee from city to city, always encountering Ricardo, never perceiving that under the influence of Father Ferenza, Ricardo is slowly being transformed from a would-be murderer to a saint. At first the priest employed him as his servant and then gradually instructed him until Ricardo became his assistant and a *rezandero*, one who alleviates the sufferings of the poor. As Ricardo becomes more selfless, Julio lusts only after his lost authority. He loses a leg, then has a stroke, becomes a pauper, and returns to his farm to die. The *rezan-*

dero who is summoned to administer the last rites to this dirty cripple with matted hair sees the terror blazing in his eyes but does not recognize his brother, whom he blesses.

In 1975 the Kalechofskys returned to Marblehead, Massachusetts, where Robert still teaches at Salem College. Roberta finds it ironic that her home is about a mile's distance from the Hawthorne family landmarks and that she can visit Nathaniel Hawthorne's grandfather's grave on her way home from shopping. She suspects that literary fate might be involved in their having settled in Salem, where Hawthorne grew up, since she had spent so many years concentrating on Hawthorne's work.

It was in 1975 that the Kalechofskys decided to found a "two-person publishing house" for which they would do the layout, typesetting, and designing. The books that they produced were so elegantly

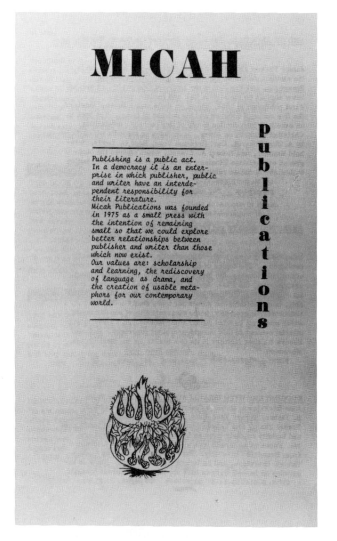

MICAH

Publications

Publishing is a public act. In a democracy it is an enterprise in which publisher, public and writer have an interdependent responsibility for their literature. Micah Publications was founded in 1975 as a small press with the intention of remaining small so that we could explore better relationships between publisher and writer than those which now exist. Our values are: scholarship and learning, the rediscovery of language as drama, and the creation of usable metaphors for our contemporary world.

*Brochure for the press founded by Kalechofsky
and her husband, Robert*

bound and so beautifully illustrated that they were nominated two years in a row by the *Library Journal* as among the best small-press releases of the year. They formulated their goals as the fostering of traditional literary values, those of "scholarship and learning, the rediscovery of language as revelation and drama, and the creation of usable metaphors for our contemporary world."

These precepts are rigorously practiced by Roberta Kalechofsky. Each of her novels derives from exhaustive scholarship. The first step in her composing process is to study the map of the area she is writing about. Her knowledge of the terrain, the flora and fauna, and the climate for *Stephen's Passion* was amassed by studying the diaries of missionaries and the journals of explorers. She finds that the notes of the latter are usually thorough and precisely detailed. It is only after internalizing the topography of a region that she begins to write.

The novel *Stephen's Passion* (1975) was Kalechofsky's first self-publishing venture. It is set in Guyana partially because the 1967 atlas that she was using indicated that the border between Guyana and Brazil was an "Area in Dispute." The phrase clung to her mind with symbolic force. It became in her view "practically a metaphor for the conflict between Christians and Jews" and seemed the perfect location for a religious-allegorical novel. In a 1971 *National Geographic* she had read "Mesa del Nayar's Strange Holy Week," an article about the Easter celebration among the Cora Indians of Mexico. She transposed these Indians' reenactment of the Crucifixion into the unmapped interior of the Guyanese jungles. She invented Indian tribes—the Ackawois, the Wapisanis, the Wai-Wais—whose cultures have partially yielded to the domination of missionary clergymen. Father Aigin, Reverend Newton, and Father Reuchlin each have their own interpretations of Christianity. Each has his own method, related to his particular personality, of imposing his views on the natives, and each is in conflict with the others.

The novel describes the excursion through this jungle by a pair of explorers: a Brooklyn-born Jewish cartographer, Stephan Werner, and an anthropologist of Dutch descent, Peter van de Groot. The Jew endures a broken leg, malaria, and an encounter with alligators, only to be crucified by the native followers of a fanatic missionary when a "spontaneously ignited mob" of Ackawois suddenly transforms their Easter Week Passion play into a reality. Their death hunt becomes "a macabre alchemy of victim, persecutors, and timing." The meditation on maps with which the novel opens symbolizes the courageous but futile attempt to chart the unknown. The barbarous jungle noises — "grinding, sucking, gnawing, slithering" — represent the forces that resist taming.

Reviewer Michael Scott Cain hailed the novel as "well-crafted, adventurous, probing, and deeply affecting." In *Small Press Review* Ellen Ferber wrote: "What Stephen encounters in the jungle, along with heat, bugs, and the oppressive sense of unseen presences can be compared with what happens in *The Heart of Darkness.* . . . It's always surprising that the fulfillment of a gradually revealed pattern is so satisfying, even in its agony." According to Terrie Gregory in the *Madison Review of Books*, "It's an intellectual exercise" to read Kalechofsky. "It's also a fist's thrust to the gut."

Kalechofsky's next book, the novella *La Hoya* (1976), takes as its title the Spanish word for *grave* or *pit*. Set in seventeenth-century Spain, it is dedicated to the victims of inquisitions and to the children who must learn of these episodes. The mood is established through stark woodcuts and excerpts from medieval documents recounting the torture of heretics in lurid detail. Kalechofsky then begins by a meditation on El Greco's painting *The View of Toledo*.

The authorial comment on this 1603 landscape is that everything in it seems to be descending, to have been pulled downward: "It is as if the world were being sucked down some hole behind a bush, probably where the town's cesspool is kept." In Kalechofsky's meditation, from the lowest corner of the picture three children emerge. Tomé, whose uncle is a torturer for the Inquisition, tells Alejo and Rafael that he knows of a secret spot from which they can watch the proceedings. The two older boys stare in fascination and afterward repetitively play out what they have seen as a game. Rafael is so horrified that he screams out. Haunted by the dying man's eyes, he can no longer sleep. After each nightmare, he hears his aunt's voice telling him: "Debes olvidarlo (You must forget it)." But he can never forget. Having so intensely participated in the heretic's torment, he is condemned to reenact it. At the end, Tomé and Alejo tie Rafael to a tree, placing a burning faggot in the kindling beneath his feet. And the harsh tale resolves itself back again into a painting: "Then all locked into landscape with a title: Boy tied to a tree in a ditch." This slim novella poses, by its own elegant patterning, the ultimate challenge to the theory of mimesis. Not even El Greco, who spent a lifetime painting modes of aspiration, asserting on canvas the spiritual pull exerted by heaven, could transcend human suffering.

"There is a gravitational pull exerted by history on the psyche of human beings." Seldom has the relationship between art and life been more severely tested than in the pages of *La Hoya*.

Kalechofsky's next self-published novel, *Orestes in Progress* (1976), has as its only survivor a three-legged mutt, Aleph, who pitifully tries to arouse his master Morris Bloom from the sleep of death. This most ambitious of all her books to date, two sections of which had been previously published in quarterlies, is complex and technically sophisticated. The novel is structured so as to erase as much of the sense of chronological time as possible by constantly connecting the past with the present. Each section is coherent in itself, related to its adjoining sections by leaps in time. John Orestes is both the Greek hero and the "all American boy," born to accomplish everything, except the forging of his own identity. His mother relives the destiny of Clytemnestra, who was killed by her son. The tragic fate of John's family drives him into an obsession with justice, which leads to his death. This kind of destiny, grounded in family tyranny, is contrasted with Rabbi Morris Bloom's tragedy, grounded in an obsession with political tyranny, in particular with the fate of the Jewish people. This contrast is sharpened through allusions to James Joyce's *Ulysses* in that the two protagonists are related as Stephen Daedalus and his spiritual father Leopold Bloom are. The title is, of course, ironic. John Orestes's "progress" is none at all. He has fled from Middletown, Massachusetts, and the tragic deaths of his parents, Chlore and Basil, to find temporary refuge with the Kunz family in New York. There he is forced to witness further domestic tragedy as Georgie Kunz, the witless, stammering youngest son, murders most of his family in a senseless dispute over their maid. Then John seeks out his parents' closest friend, Rabbi Bloom, only to find that he has become an insomniac, walking about the city all night with his dog, mourning the Holocaust. The second irony intended in the title is that in matters of ethics there has been no "progress" since the time of Aeschylus. In matters of rage, revenge, family relations, things are still what they were in the days of the ancient Greeks.

Kalechofsky says she was once asked how she could go on living without believing in progress. She answered that she found this a very strange question. "I feel that life itself is its own justification. The Jewish part of me, as opposed to the part that is impressed with the Greek tragedians' view, believes that God's best gift was life; that God delights in life, in fact, as life delights in life. I don't feel obliged to question it, anymore than my dogs do. They obey the instinct to life unquestioningly."

Orestes in Progress is full of virtuoso passages, brilliant parodies, dazzling conversations, interpolated tales, episodes of bravura. It is endlessly inventive. There is a hallucinatory dialogue with Hammurabi, a historical account of anti-Semitism in nursery rhymes, a shtetl tale of a pogrom, an epistolary account of a duel over a French mistress, a high-comedy tour of a soap factory. Bill Katz in the 15 December 1976 *Library Journal* called it "a find for the serious reader. . . . a carefully plotted tale of the 'post-holocaust generation.' "

Kalechofsky's mastery of the short-story form has been widely acknowledged. One of her stories was published in one of Martha Foley's anthologies of the year's best stories, and a second received honorable mention. A third, "Abraham and Isaac," first published in the Long Island University magazine, *Confrontations*, was republished in Douglas C. Brown's *The Enduring Legacy: Biblical Dimensions in Modern Literature* (1975), which also contains contributions by D. H. Lawrence and William Faulkner. "My Mother's Story" is included in a collection of *Selected Writings by American Jewish Women*, edited by Julia Mazow (1980).

In 1978 Kalechofsky assembled ten of her short stories into a collection called *Solomon's Wisdom*. The stories show her almost uncanny gift for finding the most telling perspective from which to view an event. For example, the sacrifice of Isaac begins from Sarah's point of view. Her helplessness is grounded in her recognition of her husband's character: "Sarah looked at him with the settled irritation of a wife married for half a century to a stubborn man." In the title piece, the story of Solomon's decision over the infant begins with a brutal battle between the contesting mothers, Haggith and Ohalah, two notorious whores. "Epitaph for an Age" is told from the point of view of a good citizen whose wife is dying. His futile efforts to stop the sealed boxcars passing through his village to the death camps are frustrated not by evil but by the democratic process itself. Each of his neighbors is involved in his own utopian project, and he cannot rouse them to concerted action. "Reflections from a Park Bench" works its magic through the angle of narration. The speaker, who is reminiscing about his grandparents, is now the very age that they were when he was a child. He recalls that elderly Orthodox couple who succumbed to their orphaned grandson's yearning and hung up a Christmas stocking for him. Now, dozing in the sun, he muses: "The park is wintry and grey, with something of the atmosphere that must pervade the undramatic apostasy of old people, the very mood perhaps with which my grandmother stood at my door in her flannel bathrobe and listened for my reaction. Something of both their attitude, mechanical, repetitive, whining, sensing that all, all is in the hands of a miracle, comes to me as shocking in its wisdom."

Of *Solomon's Wisdom* Isaac Mozeson wrote in *Judaica Book News* that "Kalechofsky's eye for detail and her psychological perceptions are masterly," and Kirk Polking, in *The Writer's Digest*, concluded that "Ms. Kalechofsky is possibly one of the best writers in the country."

Translating some of the contributions from the Spanish herself, Kalechofsky edited and published *Echad: An Anthology of Latin American Jewish Writing* in 1980. "I learned a great deal about the workings of language by doing the translations," she commented recently; "it was personally instructive going from one tongue to another, weighing their values, seeking equivalents." The volume, supported by a grant from the National Endowment for the Arts, brings together twenty-four writers from twelve Latin American countries. In addition to poetry and fiction, it contains interviews, scholarly articles, and essays.

The second volume in the Echad series was supported by a grant from the Massachusetts Council on the Arts and Humanities. Published in 1982 as *South African Jewish Voices*, it presents work by Nadine Gordimer, Lionel Abrahams, Dan Jacobson, Jillian Becker, Barney Simon, and others and was very favorably reviewed in *American Jewish Archives* (November 1982) by Rabbi Anthony D. Holz, who headed a congregation in Praetoria: "it not only vividly brings home the loveliness of the country, but also the frightening incomprehensibility and grotesqueness in the lives of its people." Finally, he concluded, here is a book which "captures the unique reality" of this land.

The third volume in the Echad series is called *Phoenix Rising* to symbolize "the feat of overcoming collective despair" of the post-Holocaust generation of American-Jewish writers. Published in 1982, it contains two new stories by Roberta Kalechofsky, as well as two of her poems, and works by Menke Katz, Stanley Nelson, Shelley Ehrlich, and others. The next Echad book will be called *Jewish Writing From Down Under* and will feature authors from Australia and New Zealand. This fourth member of the series is part of an ambitious project to complete a multi-volume global anthology of Jewish writers.

Also published by Micah Publications in 1982 was a book of interviews, conducted in Hebrew and

Page from Kalechofsky's notes for the short story "My Poor Prisoner," included in the Micah anthology Phoenix Rising translated into English by Esther Fuchs. In this volume, entitled *Encounters with Israeli Authors*, nine of Israel's leading writers speak about their lives and their art. Each author is introduced with a biography and a portrait. Fuchs, who compiled the volume, is an Israeli now teaching at the University of Texas.

Operating her own small press has allowed Roberta Kalechofsky to take the sorts of risks with promising, but unknown, authors that large commercial publishers who must worry about profits are no longer willing to take. She launched the writing careers of Fred Mandell and Thomas Friedmann and plans to publish several books each year from the manuscripts that are submitted to her. She considers this a vital service; as she writes in "Publishing as She Is Done Now, Writing As It

Ought Always To Be," in *Rejected Essays*: "Literature, as I believe that word is meant, is a way in which civilization keeps its grip on sanity and comes to terms with reality, a way in which it transmits to its children the record of its struggle for survival and leaves them for an inheritance the only thing worth inheriting: vision."

In 1982 Kalechofsky received a fellowship in creative writing from the National Endowment for the Arts for the purpose of completing a book on the era of the Black Death. This book, entitled "Bodmin: 1349," explores the relationship of Christians and Jews against the backdrop of feudal Europe. Kalechofsky does not regard it as fiction or nonfiction but prefers to describe it as "a work of the religious and historical imagination."

Johanna Kaplan
(29 December 1942-   )

Peter Shaw

BOOKS: *Other People's Lives* (New York: Knopf, 1975);
O My America! (New York: Harper & Row, 1980).

SELECTED PERIODICAL PUBLICATION: "Scenes From a 'Special' Classroom," *Commentary*, 51 (May 1971): 69-76.

In her fiction Johanna Kaplan explores the Jewish experience in America, especially as it has been lived in New York City. Her concern is with the fully integrated, Americanized generation that grew up in the 1940s and 1950s. Jewishness and the Jewish tradition remain important for her characters, but neither of these defines them, for their experience is as American as it is Jewish.

Kaplan was born in New York, grew up in the borough of the Bronx, and attended Music and Art High School in Manhattan. She studied at the University of Wisconsin, received a B.A. from New York University in 1964, and earned a master's degree in special education from Teacher's College, Columbia University in 1966. Her father, Max Kaplan, was born and raised on New York's Lower East Side and became a New York City schoolteacher. Her mother, Ruth Duker Kaplan, was born

in Poland and came to the United States as a teenager. From her parents, then, Kaplan had a view of both the old country from which the American Jews had emigrated and the immigrant experience of the New York ghetto. Her mother was an active Labor Zionist, a circumstance that is reflected indirectly in the political and intellectual themes of Kaplan's fiction.

Kaplan's stories, published between 1969 and 1973 and collected in her first book, *Other People's Lives* (1975), deal with secular, middle-class family life in New York City. In them Kaplan is often concerned with the relationship between the generations and with differing attitudes toward the Jewish experience. The members of Kaplan's fictional older generation include both foreigners and native-born Americans, both Jews and non-Jews. All of the characters were alive during World War II and have been touched by it to one degree or another. The children come to terms with this past in their own sometimes comic, sometimes melancholy ways.

In "Sickness," a child's experience of the Jewish past is restricted to the romanticized versions that she finds in her history books on the one hand, and on the other to her mother's recollections of a

Johanna Kaplan (photo by Layle Silbert)

Polish childhood. While home from school for a few weeks on account of illness, Miriam observes the life of her Bronx apartment house. Images of the heroic Jewish past from her books interweave with the concerns of the partly immigrant population of the building. Kaplan's comic talent, which was to flower in her novel, *O My America!*, is evident in the speech and behavior of the heroine's mother, her schoolmates, and their parents. By the end of the story, though, the naively presented past of the young girl's books has played through her sensibility in such a way as to lend a historical and even tragic significance to the mundane, daily existence of the apartment house.

An equally subtle epiphany occurs in "Sour or Suntanned, It Makes No Difference," chosen for inclusion in Irving Howe's 1977 anthology, *Jewish American Stories*. The story takes place at a Zionist summer camp, where Miriam is cast in a play about the Warsaw Ghetto to be performed on Parents Day. At the end of that long, distracting day, as she sits among the other campers on a crude representation of a Warsaw street she becomes a part of Jewish history. The lilt of immigrant and New York speech is reproduced here with a verve and humor

that belie the underlying literary subtlety. Thus Miriam is addressed by her friend Bryna:

> "I could be going horseback riding in Riverdale right now. Where I live, it's practically the country."
> "Where you live is the Bronx," Miriam said. "On your letters you put Bronx, New York, and you even write in a zone number."

Similarly, in "Loss of Memory is Only Temporary," the relationship between an aunt and her niece is presented in the aunt's immigrant speech, but the reader must pay attention to the aunt's point of view or risk being taken in by her earthy, and therefore presumably good-hearted, simplicity.

The collection's title novella, "Other People's Lives," employs the oddly revealing point of view of an unwanted, maladjusted young girl who has been sent to live with an eccentric bohemian family on New York's Upper West Side. The household consists of a middle-aged German immigrant wife, Maria, her American ballet-dancer husband who is in the hospital dying, her seven-year-old son, and the neighbors in their apartment house who constantly wander in and out of the family's life. The young boarder tends to view these "other people's lives" in the light of her lonely need, yet her conception of them proves to be a profound one.

As the character of Maria emerges she grows in stature from a distracted housewife into a figure of nobility. The reader comes to value the peasantlike wisdom which she applies with equal weight to her husband's imminent death and to mundane, practical matters. Her simple sentiments, expressed in slightly faulty English, come to appear more humanly significant than the artistic pretensions, the community spirit, or the political convictions of the friends who surround her.

Although the milieu of "Other People's Lives" is Jewish, Maria is not. Yet her neighbors' jokes about her German past, which must have been steeped in anti-Semitism, have the surprising effect of casting her experience in the context of twentieth-century displacement and exile. As a result this non-Jewish character becomes the vehicle for giving significance to the Jewish experience.

The stories collected in *Other People's Lives* originally appeared in *Commentary* and *Harper's* magazines. The volume was nominated for a National Book Award and for the Ernest Hemingway Foundation Award and won the Jewish Book Award for fiction in 1976. Since 1968 Johanna Kaplan has been employed as a teacher of mentally disturbed children in the psychiatry department of Mount Sinai Hospital in New York. She described her work in "Scenes From a 'Special' Classroom," published in *Commentary* in May 1971, and her art in a 1975 interview with Helen Dudar for the *New York Post*.

Between 1969 and 1980, when her first novel appeared, Kaplan was awarded a New York State-CAPS grant and a fellowship from the National Endowment for the Arts. She was an instructor at the Breadloaf Writer's Conference in Middlebury, Vermont, and she gave readings from her work at colleges and at the 92nd Street YMHA in New York City. She is a reviewer of contemporary fiction for the *New York Times Book Review* and for *Commentary* magazine.

In some ways Kaplan's novel, *O My America!* (1980), represents a departure from her previous fiction. Its central character, the New York Jewish intellectual Ezra Slavin, is at once more intellectual and more flamboyant than her earlier characters. Also, the historical sweep of his life story is broader and the political and intellectual issues that he raises more explicit than any she had dealt with before.

Born in 1910, Slavin was a young radical in the 1930s, a skeptic with regard to World War II, and a critic of conformity in the 1950s. Then, as a result of his championing of youth and opposition to the Vietnam War, he is taken as a media hero in the 1960s. His story amounts to the biography of a representative of his generation. Reviewers noted the resemblances between Slavin's career and that of the social critic Paul Goodman, among others.

O My America! consists of a reconstruction of Slavin's life. He is seen partly through documents—his letters, interviews, news clippings, eulogies, and published essays—and partly through the recollections of his daughter, Merry. She is another of Kaplan's removed, sharply observant narrators—this time possessed of a mature, sophisticated intelligence.

The themes of Kaplan's stories reappear in the novel in more overtly political forms. Thus the critique of Slavin's politics recalls the treatment of Rebecca Relkin in "Other People's Lives." In the *New Leader* critic Pearl K. Bell called Rebecca "a grotesque, exasperatingly poignant avatar of the Jewish-radical heyday in prewar New York." Ezra Slavin represents the same type viewed as a public figure. This time, as a result, the author's insights concern not only matters of style and outlook but also the worldly consequences of a Jewish radical's lifestyle and point of view. Once again these have to do with the family, the relationship between gener-

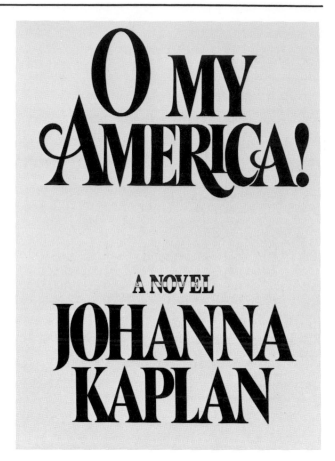

Dust jacket for Kaplan's 1980 novel, winner of the Edward Lewis Wallant Award, the Kenneth B. Smilen/Present Tense Literary Award, and the Jewish Book Award for fiction

ations and the Jewish past—which in this case is inextricably intertwined with the American past and American traditions.

In his quirky originality and lifelong antibourgeois and antiestablishment prejudices, Slavin reaches back to American Emersonianism as much as he does to nineteenth-century Jewish Labor radicalism. Without sacrificing her talent for capturing the crucially intimate details of people's lives, Kaplan found in Slavin a vehicle for a more comprehensive treatment of the twentieth-century condition.

O My America! was nominated for an American Book Award and won the Edward Lewis Wallant Award, the Kenneth B. Smilen /*Present Tense* Literary Award, and the Jewish Book Award for fiction, all in 1981. The novel's portrait of Slavin was widely praised, notably by Pearl K. Bell in a review essay in *Commentary* (April 1981). Some reviewers missed the portrait's critical bite, mistaking authorial empathy with Slavin's vigor and humor for approval of his sexual and other peccadilloes. Kaplan's comic gift also came in for praise: more than one reviewer was taken with Sybil Roizman, a politically aware matron who remarks of some people she knows: "they're not political at *all* . . . they don't even go to concerts!"

Most characteristic of Kaplan are the extended monologues of Ffrenchy Meisel, Slavin's illegitimate, wayward teenage daughter through a nearly forgotten liaison. The monologues richly, comically reproduce the speech of an ill-educated high-school girl: "Like if *I* was gonna be sick anyplace, I would *definitely* pick India, Definitely! Because—because in *India*, if you get sick they are *truly* mellow about it, they really are!" At the same time Ffrenchy's inanities amount to a critique of Slavin's beliefs, for they suggest that his practice of free thought and free love must eventually lead to the dead end of such an imagination as hers.

Johanna Kaplan's work bears comparison with her contemporaries Jerome Charyn, Robert Kotlowitz, Jay Neugeboren, Hugh Nissenson, and Cynthia Ozick. It is her distinction both to have rendered closely the speech and thought patterns of characters drawn from contemporary life and at the same time to have consistently viewed their lives in the context of Jewish tradition. Kaplan's relationship to that tradition is suggested by her remark in acceptance of the Jewish Book Award in 1976 that she could never forget the obligation impressed on her in youth "to benefit and answer to the common good." Her fiction holds to this imperative even when most critical of the Jewish radical tradition from which it derives.

Reference:

Helen Dudar, "Interview with Johanna Kaplan," *New York Post*, 10 May 1975.

Harry Kemelman
(24 November 1908-   )

Sheldon Hershinow
Kapiolani Community College, University of Hawaii

BOOKS: *Friday the Rabbi Slept Late* (New York: Crown, 1964; London: Hutchinson, 1965);

Saturday the Rabbi Went Hungry (New York: Crown, 1966; London: Hutchinson, 1967);

The Nine Mile Walk: The Nicky Welt Stories of Harry Kemelman (New York: Putnam's, 1967; London: Hutchinson, 1969);

Sunday the Rabbi Stayed Home (New York: Putnam's, 1969; London: Hutchinson, 1969);

Weekend with the Rabbi (Garden City: Doubleday, 1969);

Common Sense in Education (New York: Crown, 1970);

Monday the Rabbi Took Off (New York: Putnam's, 1972; London: Hutchinson, 1972);

Tuesday the Rabbi Saw Red (New York: Arthur Fields' Books, 1973; London: Hutchinson, 1974);

Wednesday the Rabbi Got Wet (New York: Morrow, 1976; London: Hutchinson, 1976);

Thursday the Rabbi Walked Out (New York: Morrow, 1978; London: Hutchinson, 1979);

Conversations with Rabbi Small (New York: Morrow, 1981).

Harry Kemelman's best-selling series of mystery novels made its debut in 1964 with *Friday the Rabbi Slept Late*, which won the Edgar Award of the Mystery Writers of America for best first novel. The seven books in the series, each named for a different day of the week, have made Kemelman's protagonist probably the most famous rabbi in all fiction. Set in a small New England community of Jews and Gentiles, these self-contained but sequential narratives have created an original type of mystery-detective story. While Kemelman relies on suspense and armchair detection to carry his plots, his real interest is in other and richer lodes: social commentary, religious philosophy, and human nature.

Born in Boston to Isaac and Dora Prizer Kemelman, Kemelman has continued to live in the Boston area. He attended Boston Latin School (1920-1926), Boston University (A.B., 1930), and Harvard University (M.A., 1931; postgraduate study, 1932-1933). After leaving Harvard, Kemelman taught English in Boston area high schools and, later, in the evening division of Northeastern

Harry Kemelman

mystery writer for his short stories published in *Ellery Queen's Mystery Magazine* (later collected under the title *The Nine Mile Walk*, 1967). The hero of these stories is Nicky Welt, Snowden Professor of English Language and Literature at a New England university, who uses his superior intellect to solve murders for his friend, the county attorney. In his introduction to *The Nine Mile Walk*, Kemelman explains that at first he refrained from writing longer mysteries because he felt that "the classic tale of detection was essentially a short story—the primary interest on the problem, with the character and setting emerging as adjuncts."

Later, Kemelman conceived a desire to write a novel explaining—via a fictional setting—the sociological situation of the Jew in suburbia. His first attempt was titled "The Building of a Temple," an examination of suburban Jews living in a Yankee community. This was, doubtless, in part an autobiographical account of Kemelman's own experience with life in suburban Boston, where he too was one of the few Jews who suddenly found themselves in a position of leadership in organizing a temple after the rapid influx of young Jewish couples to the suburbs after World War II. An editor observed that the book lacked real excitement and suggested, almost as a joke, that Kemelman adapt the content to the detective-story format. Reluctant at first, Kemelman came to see that the idea had possibilities. By creating a rabbi detective he could retain the classical mystery element of an intellectual outsider while bringing in an ethnic and religious component: the rabbi's involvement in solving the crime would naturally be precipitated by his role as interpreter of the Law, and his superior reasoning power could then stem from his training in Talmudic logic. Moreover, the murder would provide only one thread in a far larger fabric; the real subject would be the entire community—with its history, manners, and mores—in which the murder occurred. *Conservative Judaism*'s review of *Friday the Rabbi Slept Late* confirmed Kemelman's success with the mystery format: "It contains within it a more balanced, accurate, truthful description of a contemporary Jewish community and synagogue board than almost any work of 'serious literature.'"

In the course of the series, Rabbi David Small is drawn into various intrigues by virtue of his position as titular head of a small Jewish community in Barnard's Crossing, Massachusetts (modeled on East Bedford, Massachusetts). In *Friday the Rabbi Slept Late* he solves the murder of a young girl whose body is found in the rabbi's parked car in the temple parking lot; in *Saturday the Rabbi Went Hungry*

University. In 1936 he married Anne Kessin, a medical secretary-technician, with whom he has had three children. During the war years Kemelman worked as the chief wage administrator (civilian) for the U.S. Army Transportation Corps in Boston and later became the chief job analyst and wage administrator for the New England Division of the War Assets Administration. From 1949 to 1963 he operated his own business and did free-lance writing before accepting an assistant professorship in English at Franklin Technical Institute. In 1964 he became associate professor of English at Boston State College, where he remained until his retirement in the early 1970s. During his postretirement years Kemelman has continued to write and has traveled extensively with his wife.

Although Kemelman's father, a diamond merchant, had little interest in Judaism and Kemelman grew up without the benefit of formal religious instruction, he gained from his Orthodox grandparents a strong sense of Jewish identity, which surfaced with startling effect in his mystery novels.

In creating the books about Rabbi Small, Kemelman combined two separate interests. He had already established a reputation as a talented

(1966), he demonstrates that Jewish scientist Abe Hirsch's apparent suicide was really a murder and then proceeds to solve the crime; *Sunday the Rabbi Stayed Home* (1969) finds him drawn into the problems of the youth culture; *Monday the Rabbi Took Off* (1972) has the rabbi, on sabbatical in Israel, indirectly involved with Arab terrorism and the killing of an Israeli citizen; *Tuesday the Rabbi Saw Red* (1973) takes place at a small liberal arts college where the rabbi teaches a course in Jewish philosophy and lends his talents to tracking down the murderer of a colleague; *Wednesday the Rabbi Got Wet* (1976) concerns a pharmacy, mixed-up prescriptions, and the murder of an invalid who is a large contributor to the temple. In *Thursday the Rabbi Walked Out* (1978) the rabbi solves the murder of an old-style eccentric who is the town millionaire and self-proclaimed anti-Semite.

As mysteries these are all intriguing and suspenseful whodunits and incorporate the expected measures of guilt, suspicion, and character study, complete with the revelation of the behind-the-scenes reality beneath appearances. But the Rabbi books are much more than this. Kemelman's purposes are best appreciated when his novels are turned upside down and inside out. Kemelman himself has said: "I am not engaged in writing detective stories that make use of an unusual amateur detective, a rabbi. Rather I am engaged in writing stories about a rabbi who happens to get involved in murder mysteries which serve somehow to heighten the differences with the congregation. Basically, the thesis is this: The average American Jew, as represented by the congregation in Barnard's Crossing, not having thought very much about his religion, is confronted by one, the rabbi, who has a profound knowledge of its tenets."

As teacher and philosopher of Judaism, young Rabbi Small views himself in the uneasy position of mediator between the dominant Yankee culture and his Jewish congregation. In the course of solving the various murders by the use of Talmudic logic, the rabbi finds himself having to explicate to his Gentile fellow-townsmen the Jewish view on topics ranging from petitionary prayer to suicide, emphasizing, for the characters as for the reader, the often radical differences between Jewish and Christian doctrines and attitudes. At the same time, he must constantly remind his assimilation-minded congregation of their own distinctive Jewishness. In performing his dual role, the rabbi is revealed to be an isolated man of uncompromising integrity and inventive wisdom. He is set off from the Gentile community, on the one hand, by his Jewish beliefs, and from his own temple membership, on the other, because of his refusal to strive for the accommodation of his religion to the American way of life.

By using the rabbi as an outsider figure, Kemelman's novels offer an unexpected stripe of social commentary on American life, drawing on a relatively foreign perspective. The rabbi acts as a point of cultural convergence between traditional Judaism and modern American middle-class secular and Christian life. His characterization is that of a moral man who through intelligence and insight is able to bridge historical and cultural gaps to deal with modern life and its problems on an ethical basis derived from beyond and outside the vision of the dominant culture. Uncompromising but simultaneously flexible, he must mediate between the worlds of Judaism and Christianity as an ambassador without portfolio. At the same time, he must explain his religion and tradition to the Jews themselves in his role as another kind of mediator: between Old World Orthodox Judaism and his assimilationist suburban community. *Books and Bookmen* praised Kemelman's understanding of human nature and his ability to disclose character, which have the effect of "throw[ing] a searchlight beam on what is *terra incognito* to the non-Jewish reader."

The rabbi's role throughout the novels is one of guardian of the special qualities of Judaism which set it apart from the non-Jewish world. In fact, he constantly perceives that the major threat to Judaism is the tendency of his congregation to want to camouflage or to forget their special designation of the Chosen People. While others, Christians and Jews alike, point to the similarities between the two traditions, it is Rabbi Small's self-elected duty to point out the differences, which are often radical ones. Far from being a conciliatory peacemaker, if anything, he acts to accentuate disparities and contradictions where none were thought to exist before.

This aspect of the rabbi's role emerges most strikingly in his dealings with Christians. In the course of the seven novels, the rabbi frequently has to point out philosophical differences, even in areas which at first appear only remotely connected with religious observance. One minor but pithy example occurs in the first novel when the city fathers, mostly as a gesture of goodwill and support for the rabbi, who is himself under a cloud of suspicion of murder, offer him the honor of blessing the boats in the Boat Race Week opening ceremonies. There at first appears to be nothing the least controversial in this well-intentioned gesture. However, the rabbi is

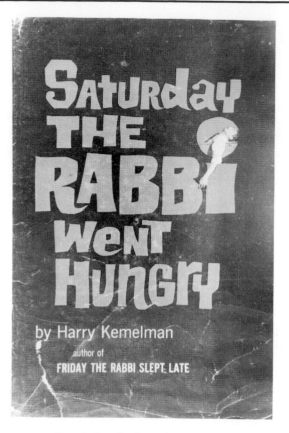

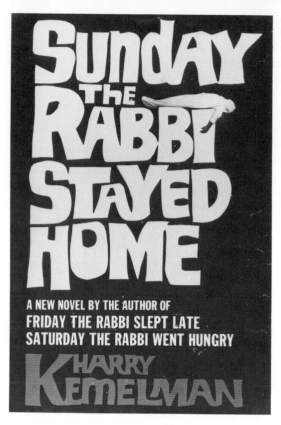

Dust jackets for four of Kemelman's seven mysteries about crimes solved by Rabbi David Small

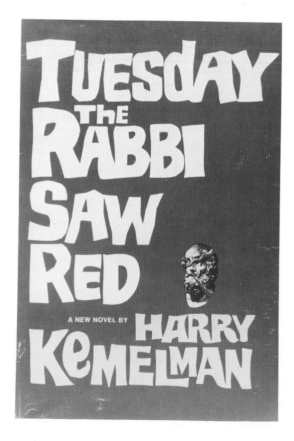

obliged to set the good men straight by explaining the Jewish attitude toward prayer, which is not petitionary but an offering of thanksgiving for blessings one has already received.

Although Rabbi Small customarily spends most of his philosophizing time in the series explaining the differences between Judaism and Christianity to non-Jews, one cannot assume that such distinctions are intended only as enlightenment for Gentiles. As one of the rabbi's Jewish students in his class on Jewish Philosophy at Windemere Christian College asks, "How can we know about Judaism if we don't have anything to compare it to?" By extension, one can infer that the many comparisons between Judaism and Christianity are intended for Jewish readers as well as Gentile ones. This double appeal of the novels is even more apparent when one considers the other side of the rabbi's role as spiritual head of the Jewish community. In dealing with his congregation, Rabbi Small must continually remind well-intentioned but ill-informed leaders of the temple of the traditional spirit of Judaism. So difficult and thankless is this task that throughout the series the rabbi is in danger of losing his job. One of the major interests in each book centers around the politics of the temple and the question of whether the rabbi will be allowed to continue as its adviser, since his wisdom and remonstrances are actually resented by the guilty congregation as a sort of restraint on their easygoing attitudes about religious identity and ritual. One of Kemelman's main achievements is his skillful method of interweaving temple intrigue with the murder investigation. In *Friday the Rabbi Slept Late*, for example, the rabbi's solving of the murder causes the leader of the opposition to agree to the renewal of the rabbi's contract and gives him a powerful ally who supports him throughout the series in other episodes of the ongoing conflict, when the rabbi is faced with new (and younger) temple leaders.

The root of Rabbi Small's conflict with his congregation lies in their differing views of the place of Judaism in modern America and of the role of the rabbi. The assimilation-minded congregation wants, basically, to minimize the differences between Jews and their Gentile neighbors. They wish to have a rabbi who will be a good representative to the Gentile community, someone of imposing demeanor who can make an impressive appearance on a platform, someone who, as Al Becker, leader of the opposition in *Friday the Rabbi Slept Late* puts it, "can carry on the public relations job that the position requires." In short, "an Episcopal Bishop sort

of man." Rabbi Small, however, is a thin, pale, bespectacled young man with "a scholarly stoop" who is absentminded about appointments, careless about his appearance, and uncompromising in his principles.

Throughout the series other conflicts arise because of attempts by segments of the congregation to reform various aspects of the temple's activities to bring them more in line with the predominant Christian (American) practices. In *Saturday the Rabbi Went Hungry* an expansion-minded board of directors tries to play fast and loose with the rabbi's ruling about the burial of a possible suicide in order to receive a large contribution from a rich member—who will donate funds for a new (unnecessary) building only if his own rigidly old-fashioned and ritualistic understanding of the Jewish attitude toward suicide is allowed to prevail. In *Sunday the Rabbi Stayed Home* a new president of the congregation and his friends initiate a program of social action as a demonstrative show of support for the Civil Rights movement—at the expense of other needs of the temple. The rabbi counters by maintaining that unlike Christians, Jews have always been involved with life on this earth and its many injustices. Thus no special show of support is necessary or appropriate. In the same book, a well-meaning director of the religious school attempts to "jazz up" the Passover seder with a mod theatrical performance. In *Tuesday the Rabbi Saw Red* the rabbi tangles with a fashionable and influential family whose daughter wants the rabbi to perform a wedding catered by a nonkosher firm. In *Wednesday the Rabbi Got Wet* the rabbi again comes close to losing his job when he stands against a plan for the temple to purchase a retreat in the country for mystical communion with God. *Thursday the Rabbi Walked Out* finds Small squaring off against feminists who challenge Judaism's traditional attitude toward women.

Throughout all of these conflicts Rabbi Small remains unflappably calm in his insistence that Judaism is not just another sect having minor doctrinal differences from other denominations: "We are a nation of priests, dedicated to God because he chose us." With enviable self-confidence and self-knowledge, he attempts to adapt the spirit of traditional Judaism to modern conditions, resisting the inflexible rituals of the piously orthodox on the one hand and the assimilationist reforms of identity-seeking suburbanites on the other.

Occasionally in the series, Rabbi Small feels disillusioned about his lack of success with his congregation, sensing keenly that he is out of place in modern America. The rabbi's usual measured optimism is more than a few times challenged and subdued. His battles in and outside the temple then make him pause to consider whether all the suffering he is subjected to (first as a Jew and second as a rabbi) is worthwhile. But the rabbi always concludes, as he says to his wife in the first book in the series, that "The congregation needs me. . . . Without me or someone like me, you know what happens to these congregations? As religious institutions, that is as Jewish institutions, they dry up."

At the heart of Rabbi Small's disagreements with his congregation—and central to Kemelman's view of Judaism—is the insistence that the role of the rabbi is not one of leader, spokesman, or moral exemplar but one of judge and teacher; he is a man admired for his knowledge of Jewish law and his ability at *pilpul*, the method of Talmudic disputation that involves hair-splitting distinctions about an interpretation of law. "The Talmud [commentaries on the law]," according to Rabbi Small, "deals with everything. . . . Particular situations differ from age to age, but the general principles remain the same." The philosophical procedures established by Talmudic tradition give him an uncanny ability to see the third side of any question.

It is precisely the rabbi's ability to apply the general principles of the Talmud to present-day situations, using Talmudic logic, that unites the mystery elements of the books with the Jewish subject matter. The rabbi's ability to solve practical, contemporary problems, by extrapolating from Talmudic precedents, wins him the admiration of both civil authorities (police, detectives, district attorneys) and members of his temple. In this way, Kemelman presents a picture of Judaism as a practical religion whose ancient principles and pragmatic outlook are eminently well suited for the modern world because of their secular outlook, intellectual basis, and ethical content. Perhaps, as readers can often guess from the way the rabbi's "comparative religion" lectures progress, Christianity is often at a disadvantage as a rival problem-solving and ethical system. Rabbi Small tells his class at Windemere that Judaism, as a religion built around ethical behavior rather than personal salvation, depends on the satisfaction of facing reality: "It doesn't permit us to dodge problems, but it does help us to solve them, if only by recognizing that they exist. And after all, isn't that what the modern world is beginning to do?"

In presenting this vision to a mass audience by way of detective fiction, Kemelman demonstrates that formula works of popular literature in fact can be effective in communicating serious ideas, allowing in the process considerable literary creativity. As social commentary, Kemelman's books raise questions about the viability of the Jewish community in America. These are questions that will not go away. Rabbi Small endures the perennial ill will of his wayward and headstrong congregation by telling them about the importance of being Jewish—and, therefore, different. Kemelman speculates about the dangers of the melting pot, collective forgetfulness, assimilation, economic affluence, and secularism as they affect the very existence of Jewish identity. Throughout the novels, a central question is pressing: what impact will the "loss of consciousness" among Jews have on the future of the Jewish community and on the larger issue of Jewish survival?

As literary works, the Rabbi books have added a new and needed dimension to the image of Jews in contemporary American literature. Or perhaps it would be more accurate to say that Kemelman puts into popular form many of the concerns of pre-World War II chroniclers of Jewish experience in America, such as Abraham Cahan, Meyer Levin, Daniel Fuchs, Isaac Rosenfeld, and Ludwig Lewisohn. In Kemelman's books the reader observes Jews in ordinary circumstances, living more or less average lives as suburbanites with strongly assimilationist leanings, trying as much as possible to lead normal lives, torn between the American Dream and the Jewish way of life whose differences, Rabbi Small insists, should be more, not less, marked. However, unlike earlier writers who depicted everyday life in an immigrant milieu, Kemelman provides a new prototype for the Jewish protagonist: that of the unalienated outsider whose strength comes from an appreciation of what he has to offer to the world as a Jew. And unlike such schlemiel characters as Bernard Malamud's Morris Bober and Saul Bellow's Herzog, practical failures who nonetheless achieve a sort of moral or ethical victory in defeat, Rabbi Small is a portrait of a model man based on practical, not ethereal, principles. In fact, the rabbi's appeal goes beyond his ethnic character. He is really outside the traditions of defensiveness in nostalgia, pessimism, irony, and "Jewish" humor. He is an optimist, despite the setbacks he suffers; his vision is definitely forward-looking—to the future Judaism has in offering a valid creed to modern man beyond its exotic tribal origins, past glories, or romanticized hardships. As Rabbi Small tells his class at Windemere College, "After thousands of years it appears our way is at last coming into style."

References:

Sheldon Hershinow and Margaret King, "Judaism for the Millions: Harry Kemelman's 'Rabbi Books,' " *MELUS*, 5 (Winter 1978): 83-93;

Margaret King, "The Rabbi's Week," *Antioch Re-view*, 57 (Winter 1979): 113-117;

Daisy Maryles, "Harry Kemelman: Creator of the World's Best Known Rabbi," *Jewish Digest* (December 1975): 45-47.

Bruno Lessing
(Rudolph Block)
(6 December 1870-29 April 1940)

William J. Burling
Pennsylvania State University

BOOKS: *Children of Men* (New York: McClure Phillips, 1903; Edinburgh & London: Blackwood, 1904);

With the Best Intention (New York: Hearst's International Library, 1914; London: Hurst & Blackett, 1915);

Lapidowitz the Schnorrer, "With the Best Intention" (New York: Hearst's International Library, 1915);

Jake—Or Sam (Privately printed, 1919).

Bruno Lessing, the pseudonym for Rudolph Edgar Block, is best remembered as a writer of short stories dealing with life in the ghetto on the East Side of New York during the last years of the nineteenth century and the early years of the twentieth. Lessing's terse style, vaguely reminiscent of Chekhov's, captures the pathos of the hardships and the subtle humor and insight to be found in the day-to-day milieu of the Jewish community.

Little is known of Lessing's early life except that he was born in New York City. While attending the College of the City of New York, he began reporting for the *New York Sun* in 1888. He later became Sunday editor for the *New York Recorder* and also reported for the *New York World*. After graduating from CCNY, Lessing became comic-supplements editor for the Hearst syndicate, a position he held for twenty-eight years.

His first book, *Children of Men*, appeared in 1903. This collection sweeps the range of the Jewish experience in the ghetto, offering a panorama of the plight of the naive, optimistic new arrivals as well as the hardened, sometimes disillusioned, ex-perienced veterans. The twenty-three stories vary in their attention to Jewish problems and in quality, but according to Meyer Waxman, in his 1941 *History of Jewish Literature*, the collection "expresses the best that there was in this Anglo-Jewish fiction during its early stages."

The stories are set against the backdrop of Jewish life but often deal with universal themes. "A Rift in the Cloud," for example, renders the sad plight of a Hungarian Jew ostracized by the tight-knit society of the Houston Street area because of the sordid reputation of his family in the Old World. More of a sketch than a developed story, as are many of Lessing's shorter pieces, the events of a particular evening when Polatschek suddenly picks up a violin and plays wonderfully, gaining the admiration of his compatriots (which he then rejects), reveal Lessing's sensitivity for the commonplace and his tendency to moralize about faults shared by all people. Another tale, "End of the Task," portrays the final days of a girl working in a sweatshop. She becomes enthralled with a painting depicting a rural scene which reminds her of her girlhood in Russia, so her boyfriend, in an act of desperation and affection, steals the painting without her knowledge and presents it to her. After her death, the young man returns the painting, is convicted of theft, and imprisoned. The emphasis upon the pathos and irony of the human condition is generally characteristic of Lessing's fiction during his early period.

Demonstrations of faith in the face of extreme adversity or unexpected success also receive frequent attention from Lessing. "The Unconverted,"

September 1911 comic by Rudolph Dirks. Dirks began the Katzenjammer Kids *in 1897 when Lessing, comic-supplements editor for the Hearst Syndicate, suggested that he model a feature on Wilhelm Busch's cartoon series,* Max und Moritz.

for example, examines the strength and peace of mind which arise from faithful adherence to Orthodox Jewish tradition, a point made by the portrayal of a Protestant missionary who decides against attempting to convert any Jews. Success demands faith, also, as Lessing demonstrates in "The Americanisation of Shadrach Cohen." Here, an Orthodox Jew asserts his faith and business savvy to such a degree that his sons, who are eager to become "Americanized" and who have abandoned many of the Orthodox ways, return to tradition and gain the lasting respect of their father, the irony being, of course, that the elder Cohen definitely is not Americanized. Lessing also pictures the result of lost faith, as in "Without Fear of God." A Jew leaves the synagogue after losing his wife and children to hunger, disease, and the sweltering conditions of the tenements, lives as an outcast, and finally goes insane. As the reviewer for the *New York Times* noted: "it is pathos that Mr. Lessing handles best," and Harry Thurston Peck stated in *Bookman*: "Many have written of this life before, but no one . . . with so genuine a sympathy."

In the years following *Children of Men* Lessing continued to work for the Hearst chain as a comics editor, creating or discovering such favorites as "Happy Hooligan" and "The Katzenjammer Kids." He also began to publish the first of some eighty stories that appeared between 1906 and 1919 in *McClure's, Muncey's, Ladies' Home Journal, Hearst's Magazine, Collier's, Everybody's,* and *Cosmopolitan,* with more than sixty appearing in the last. In an unsuccessful private venture Lessing published *Jake–Or Sam* (1919), an extended version of one of his short stories.

Lessing's political interests are revealed by a notable incident in 1909. Judge Gaynor, seeking support for his candidacy for mayor of New York, solicited the aid of William Randolph Hearst, Lessing's employer. According to Gaynor and Lessing, Hearst agreed privately to endorse Gaynor, then publically denied having done so when Gaynor ran on the Tammany Hall ticket. A letter from Lessing to Gaynor, confirming Hearst's support, appeared on the front page of the *New York Times*, but apparently Hearst did not think the matter warranted the dismissal of his faithful employee (even though Gaynor went on to win by a large majority). The *Times* also revealed that Gaynor had arranged for Lessing to receive some lucrative city commissionerships worth over $11,000 between 1906 and 1909. Nothing ever came of the implicit suggestion by the *Times* that Lessing was in Gaynor's employ, but the

incident does document the fact that Lessing was becoming well off and solidly established. His new affluence is most clearly evident in his famous collection of walking sticks—some 1,400 items gathered from around the globe—which was appraised at $250,000 and donated to the Smithsonian in 1929.

Riding the popularity of his periodical publications, Lessing had a second collection, *With the Best Intention*, published in 1914. Retaining the humorous elements but eliminating much of the pathos, Lessing again uses the ghetto for his setting and introduces Lapidowitz, the schnorrer, who was to become his only significant character. Lessing defines schnorrer almost immediately in the first episode: "A schnorrer, if you have never met one, is a member of the Jewish community who lives by his wits, never works if he can help it, knows every line of the Torah and Talmud that can possibly be used as an appeal for charity, eats, drinks, wears, and smokes anything that is given to him, and is usually quite amiable."

Lapidowitz reaches Ellis Island with seventy-six dollars in his pocket, and from his first days in America, when he accidentally finds and spends a friend's lost money, the schnorrer bumbles his way through the streets of the Jewish East Side. Lessing closely approximates the structure of a novel in this book, for though no dominant plot connects the segments, the events occur chronologically, and the character of Lapidowitz serves to unify the collection. Further, Lessing calls each story a chapter, rather than implying that the segments are unrelated, as he does in *Children of Men*.

This Dickensian character proved to be so popular that in 1915 a second book of stories about Lapidowitz was published, *Lapidowitz the Schnorrer*, *"With the Best Intention,"* which has now become a rare collector's edition. The stories in this work, most of which were published previously in periodicals, are very much akin to those of the 1914 collection; in fact, several stories appear in both books. The element of pathos is likewise absent in the second Lapidowitz collection, the emphasis residing clearly in the hopeless exploits of the schnorrer in constant schemes to marry or get rich quick. He serves as a ladle by which Lessing dishes out generous portions of the activities of the Jewish community. None of the moral or emotional intensity which marks the earlier *Children of Men* is present.

After 1919 Lessing had no more fiction published. Except for a catalogue (privately printed) of his cane collection, his writing until his death in

Arizona in 1940 consisted entirely of journalistic accounts in a column entitled "Vagabondia," based on his worldwide travels and syndicated by the Hearst chain.

Bibliography:
David M. Fine, "Lessing Bibliography," *American Literary Realism*, 6 (Summer 1973): 183-185.

Meyer Levin
(8 October 1905-9 July 1981)

Mashey M. Bernstein

See also the Levin entries in *DLB 9, American Novelists, 1910-1945*, and *DLB Yearbook: 1981*.

BOOKS: *Reporter* (New York: Day, 1929);
Frankie and Johnnie: A Love Story (New York: Day, 1930); revised as *The Young Lovers* (New York: New American Library, 1952);
Yehudah (New York: Cape & Smith, 1931; London & Toronto: Cape, 1931);
The Golden Mountain (New York: Cape & Ballou, 1932); republished as *Classic Hassidic Tales* (New York: Citadel, 1966);
The New Bridge (New York: Covici Friede, 1933; London: Gollancz, 1933);
The Old Bunch (New York: Viking, 1937);
Citizens (New York: Viking, 1940);
My Father's House (New York: Viking, 1947);
In Search: An Autobiography (New York: Horizon, 1950; Paris: Authors' Press, 1950; London: Constellation, 1951);
Compulsion (New York: Simon & Schuster, 1956; London: Muller, 1957);
The Story of the Synagogue, by Levin and Toby K. Kurzband (New York: Behrman House, 1957);
Eva (New York: Simon & Schuster, 1959; London: Muller, 1959);
The Story of the Jewish Way of Life, by Levin and Kurzband (New York: Behrman House, 1959);
God and the Story of Judaism, by Levin and Dorothy Kripke (New York: Behrman House, 1962);
The Fanatic (New York: Simon & Schuster, 1964);
The Stronghold (New York: Simon & Schuster, 1965; London: Allen, 1965);
The Story of Israel (New York: Putnam's, 1967);
Gore and Igor: An Extravaganza (New York: Simon & Schuster, 1968; London: Allen, 1968);

The Haggadah. Retold, music by Harry Coopersmith (New York: Behrman House, 1968); republished as *An Israel Haggadah for Passover* (New York: Abrams, 1970);
The Settlers (New York: Simon & Schuster, 1972);
The Obsession (New York: Simon & Schuster, 1973);
The Spell of Time (New York: Praeger, 1974);
The Harvest (New York: Simon & Schuster, 1978);
The Architect (New York: Simon & Schuster, 1981).

PLAYS: *The Good Old Days*, Paris, 1951;
Compulsion, New York; Ambassador Theatre, 24 October 1957;
Anne Frank, Israel, The Israel Soldiers Theatre, 1966; Walton, Mass., Brandeis University, 1972.

SCREENPLAYS: *My Father's House*, World View Films / Levin, 1947;
The Illegals, MAB, 1948;
Mountain of Moses, 1968;
The Falashas, 1970;
The Unafraid, 1978.

OTHER: *The Rise of American Jewish Literature*, edited by Levin and Charles Angoff (New York: Simon & Schuster, 1970).

Although a writer on the American-Jewish scene for over fifty years, Meyer Levin never received the kind of critical or popular acclaim bestowed on many of his contemporaries. Despite this fact, Levin was a consistent writer who produced a wide variety of works touching on almost every aspect of Jewish and American-Jewish life in the twentieth century. He was also one of the first writers to deal with the Holocaust and the creation of the state of Israel. In neither instance did he write as

Meyer Levin, shortly before his death in 1981
(photo by Layle Silbert)

writers. He eschewed the concept of the schlemiel, the pathetic underdog of the ghetto, or the idea of the Jew as some kind of universal existential man. Instead, he created a Jew that paralleled the type of Jew that the state of Israel was in the process of creating when he visited there in 1925. He found in Israel a Jew, free from the shackles of the past, able to escape negativity, even shame, and affirming his Jewishness in positive and inspiring ways. In his autobiography *In Search* (1950), Levin states as his credo that he can accept the messianic ideal so long as he can embody it "in the people" instead of an individual Messiah. For Levin, "the example of Jewish history in the past few years can give courage to all humanity." This is a thesis that permeated his entire oeuvre.

The child of East European parents Joseph and Goldie Batiste Levin, Levin was born and raised in Chicago and began his career as a reporter for the *Chicago Daily News* in 1923, while still a student at the University of Chicago. He graduated in 1924. A trip through Europe and Palestine in 1925 helped forge many of the ideas and concepts that were to stay with him all his life. In Europe, he met the artist Marek Szwarc (and his daughter Tereska, who would later become Levin's second wife), and in his circle Levin began to change his ideas about his religion. Hitherto, he had felt that religion would be a negative factor in his chosen career, but now he began to realize that it had much to offer him. He began to explore his Jewish roots and to look for a way by which to fuse its lessons with his art meaningfully.

This newfound feeling was cemented further by his visit to Palestine, where he covered the opening of the Hebrew University and worked for the Jewish Telegraphic Agency. He returned to the United States but decided to try and settle in Palestine. In 1929, he joined Kibbutz Yagar near Haifa. About this time, however, his literary career was beginning to blossom, and after a year he returned to the United States. Eventually, he made his home in Israel, with frequent visits to America. In many ways, this personal history finds a reflection in his literary concerns and interests.

His first novel, *Reporter* (1929), was based on his experiences as a journalist in Chicago but was withdrawn shortly after publication under threat of a libel suit by a newspaperwoman who believed Levin had used her as a model for one of the characters. Levin's second venture was entitled *Frankie and Johnnie* (1930). This unsuccessful novel of love in the big city was reviewed by Theodore

an outsider or as a tourist, but as one who had fully absorbed the history and experiences of both seminal events.

Nonetheless, his novels failed to capture the imagination of the public, and with the exception of his novel *Compulsion*, he never enjoyed a major success. A reason for the public's lack of interest may have been that stylistically Levin never escaped his days as a newspaper reporter and his prose style had a certain blandness and Dreiseresque flooding of detail. Overall, he wrote in a realistic quasi-documentary style with a highly moralistic frame of reference. Thus, his characters, especially his Jewish characters, were presented in affirmative and optimistic tones, and they lacked the more universal implications that Saul Bellow and Bernard Malamud were able to elicit from their Jewish backgrounds.

Levin deliberately avoided portraying the kind of Jew that had been created by the Yiddish writer and the more popular of American-Jewish

Purdy in the *Saturday Review of Literature* as a "bleak and uncomfortably fleshy tale, unleavened by pity or tenderness"; it "succeeds rather in disgusting the reader than in moving him to pity." Leaving the environs of Chicago, Levin drew on his own intimate knowledge and understanding of kibbutz life for his next novel *Yehuda* (1931), which deals with the struggle a violinist faces when he feels torn between an artistic career and working for his kibbutz. This novel was one of the first to deal with this relatively new way of life. It received generally high praise from the critics, including Lionel Trilling in the *Nation*, who praised Levin's ironic realism.

With his 1932 collection retelling the legendary tales of the Baal-Shem-Tov, *The Golden Mountain*, Levin gave expression to another of his primary interests, the mystical elements of Hasidism, which heightened his already growing sense of positive identification with Jews as a people. If physically Levin constantly journeyed between America and Palestine, spiritually he also moved back and forth from the gritty realism of Chicago to the magical aspirations of the Hasidic movement.

For his next novel, the dour *New Bridge* (1933), Levin returned to life in the big city, in this instance a tenement building in New York. This story takes place over a twenty-four-hour period and deals with the eviction of a family from the building. In resisting the eviction a boy is killed. Once again, Levin received praise, especially for the first part of the book in which he describes the tenants and the action leading up to the killing. Critics were less pleased with the second part, in which police and marshals are captured and tried by the tenants in an attempt to fix responsibility for the killing.

One of the critics of *The New Bridge* noted that its style reminded him of a play, and indeed during this period Levin had opened a marionette theater in Chicago. He later taught puppetry at the New School for Social Research in New York. Levin's interest in drama and film were to play an increasingly important part in his life in later years.

After reporting from the Loyalist side in the Spanish Civil War, Levin produced a work which must be considered among his most significant, the novel *The Old Bunch* (1937). Levin returned to the Chicago slums of his childhood in a broad and comprehensive novel that has its roots in Dos Passos and the proletarian novels of the era. *The Old Bunch* depicts the lives of a dozen Jewish boys and girls from 1921 until the Century of Progress World's Fair in 1934. Each of these youths, different from one another in emotional makeup, ends up in a different career but is never able to escape those

aspects that always have defined his limitations, his Jewishness, and also his Americanness. While receiving high praise, the novel was not without its detractors who felt that it was cumbersome and without dramatic conflict. As Philip Rahv commented in the *Nation*, "Though written with complete sincerity and in a language whose color and association keep pace with the movement of events, the novel's comprehensiveness and fidelity of social observation do not wholly make up for its lack of tension."

Levin's next novel, *Citizens* (1940), is a fictionalized version of the slaying of ten steel mill strikers in Chicago on Memorial Day, 1937, when the police prevented the striking workers from establishing a picket line in front of the plant. Levin brought his powers as a reporter to the fore, utilizing them to the utmost, though this technique was not without drawbacks. In his review of *Citizens* James T. Farrell sums up the strengths and weaknesses of Levin as a novelist, criticism which Levin never really escaped throughout his career: "In his general narrative, Mr. Levin writes in a manner similar to Sinclair Lewis, except that he lacks Lewis' pungency when Lewis is at his best. Mr. Levin sees details with a reportial eye: he seems to have that dictator's view of characters and moments which is characteristic of the reporter. His style is that of a competent journalist. At times, however, one feels as if one were reading the warmed-over headlines of yesterday's 'extra' rather than the vivid recreation of characters and events which one expects to find in the pages of an admittedly realistic novel."

The decade of the 1940s with its crucial significance for Jews in the events of the Holocaust and the creation of the state of Israel was to have a tremendous impact on Levin as a writer, and his major work since that time never escaped its implications. Levin joined the Office of War Information and worked on films in the United States and England and also served with the Psychological War Division in France. He accompanied American forces in their liberation of Europe and the concentration camps, visiting Buchenwald, Dachau, and Theresienstadt. After the war, he covered the plight of the Jewish illegals who attempted to enter Palestine in the face of British opposition and witnessed Israel's War of Independence. From these experiences, he wrote the novel *My Father's House* (1947), a story that covers both the Holocaust and the efforts of Jews to enter Palestine. That same year he turned the novel into a feature-length documentary. He also wrote and produced another documentary, *The Illegals* (1948); his autobiography

In Search recounts all of these events in detail and tries to put them into focus for himself and for Jews and non-Jews alike.

The decade of the 1950s produced two major events in Levin's career that mark the nadir and apex of his life's work: the trial over his dramatic version of *The Diary of Anne Frank* and the success of his novel *Compulsion*. Levin's wife Tereska discovered a French edition of the diary and showed it to Levin who arranged to have it published in America. His review of it in the *New York Times Book Review* played a large part in its gaining attention and acclaim. Levin had plans to turn the book into a play and wrote a draft which was accepted by the Broadway producer Cheryl Crawford. Crawford showed Levin's version to the playwright Lillian Hellman who felt that the play was "unactable." She suggested that the husband-and-wife Hollywood writing team Frances Goodrich and Albert Hackett could produce a better version. Crawford followed her advice, and Goodrich and Hackett wrote the play which became a great success.

Levin, however, was bitter at his mistreatment and sued Goodrich, Hackett, Otto Frank, and Kermit Bloomgarden. After years of litigation, he won a Pyrrhic victory. He was awarded fifteen thousand dollars in damages, and he agreed to give up all rights, avoid further controversy, and not have his version produced. This last agreement caused Levin considerable anguish, because he felt that the Goodrich-Hackett version had appropriated much of his material but was not faithful to the Jewish ideas and feelings in Anne Frank's diary. Levin never got over his sense of having been wronged and never reconciled himself to this defeat. (In more recent years, his version has been produced in Israel and in the United States.) The events were described and the characters involved thinly disguised in his novel *The Fanatic* (1964) and more openly in his autobiography *The Obsession* (1973).

In 1956, however, Levin achieved his greatest popular and critical success with his documentary novel, *Compulsion*. The work retold the Leopold and Loeb abduction and murder of Bobby Franks in 1924 and recreated events of the subsequent trial which Levin had covered as a young reporter. Levin divided the book into two main sections: the first part probes deeply into the psychological aspects of the crime, and the second part is devoted to the trial. Even though reviewers took note of its sexual and scatalogical content as well as its graphic language, the acclaim was universal. The *New York Herald Tribune* compared it to "an American Tragedy" while the *New York Times* called it a "masterly

achievement in literary craftmanship."

The novel was dramatized by Levin with great success in 1957, though he once again was embroiled in a lawsuit with his producer, whose version was the one produced. In 1959 *Compulsion* became an equally acclaimed feature film.

Eva (1959), Levin's next novel, met with mixed responses. In its use of a young girl living through the horrors of World War II and the concentration camps, the similarity to Anne Frank's story was obvious. Because Levin used a first-person narrative, the stylistic deficiencies in his work became all too apparent. The *New York Herald Tribune* called *Eva* a "thin ersatz" of the actual material contained in the Nuremberg Trials and other documentary works appearing at that time. Others were less kind, calling it "propaganda rather than literature" and "drab." The *Saturday Review* summed up the problem succinctly: "The survival of individuals masks the multitudes who perish. Survival is a happy ending but I am not sure that the final response to it is a satisfactory one. Tragedy so massive is better expressed by an Anne Frank than an Eva, finally a happy mother in Israel." (A further comparison of it with William Styron's *Sophie's Choice* [1980], which shares several similar plot lines, reveals the serious lack of imaginative power in Levin's novel.)

Levin returned to the Holocaust again in *The Stronghold* (1965), which places characters, among them Kraus, an Eichmann-like Nazi; his hostage, a Jewish ex-premier named Vered; and several Nazis and traditional Germans, into a serious discussion about attitudes toward Jews. In Levin's hands, in the words of one reviewer, it became a "passionately moral book."

His last works were concerned with Israel, where he had finally settled in 1958. He had bought a small lighthouselike building at Beit Yanndi, north of the seaside resort town of Netanya, and felt he had finally come home. Maybe this sense of contentment explains the genesis of *Gore and Igor* (1968), his only comic novel. Subtitled *An Extravaganza*, the book details the story of two very different characters, Gore, a Californian, and Igor, a Russian, who end up in Israel fighting in the 1967 Six-Day War. Before this event, they roar through adventures and orgies and encounter an assortment of individuals.

Levin's novels on the early settlement in Israel, *The Settlers* (1972) and its sequel *The Harvest* (1978), met with generally poor reviews. In the first novel, Levin interweaves the adventures of a large Russian immigrant family, the Chaimovitches, with the events of the era which saw the triumph of the first

Dust jacket for Levin's first novel about early settlers in Israel. Its sequel, The Harvest, *was published in 1978.*

Dust jacket for Levin's last book, a novel based on the life of Frank Lloyd Wright

agricultural settlements, while the second continues the history up to Israel's independence. In his review of both novels in *Studies in American-Jewish Literature*, Irving Halperin noted, "it may be that [the novels] will retain some value as historical documents. But, despite Mr. Levin's energy and ambitiousness, their pretense at fiction is thin and uninteresting."

Levin's last novel, *The Architect* (1981), published posthumously, reveals a complete change in subject matter and style. Once again, Levin returns to Chicago in this novel which recounts the rise to fame of one Andrew Lane (a thinly disguised Frank Lloyd Wright) to the point at which personal scandal and tragedy mark an end to the early phase of his career. Lane may lack the rugged Teutonic individuality of Howard Roark, the architect hero of Ayn Rand's *The Fountainhead* and another figure based on Wright, but he is a figure far more simpatico.

The changes in style and attitude in Levin's last novel come as a complete surprise. Gone is the moralizing, the heavy-handed didacticism, and the turgid prose style that had marred so much of his work. In his style, there appears a lightness of touch, a flexibility and muscularity in the very structure of the sentence that sweeps readers along. Furthermore, the novel appears so free of anger and spite, so full of love and forgiveness, and so ripe in imagination that Levin seems to have found his own peace and joy through writing it. It marks a fitting summation to a life devoted to writing and creativity.

References:

Sol Liptzin, *The Jew in American Literature* (New York: Bloch, 1966), pp. 218-221;

Benno Weiser Varon, "The Haunting of Meyer Levin," *Midstream*, 22 (1976): 7-23.

Ludwig Lewisohn

(22 May 1882-31 December 1955)

Ralph Melnick
College of Charleston

See also the Lewisohn entries in *DLB 4, American Writers in Paris, 1920-1939*, and *DLB 9, American Novelists, 1910-1945*.

BOOKS: *The Broken Snare* (New York: Dodge, 1908);

A Night in Alexandria: A Dramatic Poem in One Act (New York: Moods, 1909);

German Style: An Introduction to the Study of German Prose (New York: Holt, 1910);

The Modern Drama: An Essay in Interpretation (New York: Huebsch, 1915; London: Secker, 1916);

The Spirit of Modern German Literature (New York: Huebsch, 1916);

The Poets of Modern France (New York: Huebsch, 1918);

The Drama and The Stage (New York: Harcourt, Brace, 1922);

Up Stream (New York: Boni & Liveright, 1922; London: Richards, 1923);

Don Juan (New York: Boni & Liveright, 1923);

The Creative Life (New York: Boni & Liveright, 1924);

Israel (New York: Boni & Liveright, 1925);

Modern German Poetry (Girard, Kans.: Haldeman-Julius, 1925);

The Case of Mr. Crump (Paris: Black Manikin Press, 1926; New York: Henderson, 1930; New York: Farrar, Straus, 1947; London: Bodley Head, 1948);

Holy Land; A Story (New York: Harper, 1926);

Roman Summer (New York & London: Harper, 1927);

Cities and Men (New York & London: Harper, 1927);

The Defeated (London: Butterworth, 1927); republished as *The Island Within* (New York & London: Harper, 1928);

Adam: A Dramatic History in a Prologue, Seven Scenes and an Epilogue (New York & London: Harper, 1929);

Mid-Channel: An American Chronicle (New York &

Ludwig Lewisohn (photo courtesy of Special Collections, College of Charleston Library)

London: Harper, 1929; London: Butterworth, 1929);

Stephen Escott (New York & London: Harper, 1930); republished as *The Memories of Stephen Escott* (London: Butterworth, 1930);

The Golden Vase (New York & London: Harper, 1931);

A Jew Speaks, edited by James Waterman Wise (New York & London: Harper, 1931);

The Last Days of Shylock (New York & London: Harper, 1931; London: Butterworth, 1931);

The Romantic: A Contemporary Legend (Paris: Black Manikin Press, 1931);

Expression in America (New York & London: Harper, 1932; London: Butterworth, 1932); republished as *The Story of American Literature* (New York & London: Harper, 1937);

This People (New York & London: Harper, 1933);

An Altar in the Fields (New York & London: Harper, 1934);

The Permanent Horizon: A New Search for Old Truths (New York & London: Harper, 1934);

Trumpet of Jubilee (New York & London: Harper, 1937);

The Answer; The Jew and the World: Past, Present and Future (New York: Liveright, 1939);

For Ever Wilt Thou Love (New York: Dial, 1939);

Haven, by Lewisohn and Edna Lewisohn (New York: Dial, 1940);

Renegade (New York: Dial, 1942);

Breathe Upon These (Indianapolis & New York: Bobbs-Merrill, 1944);

A Jewish Commonwealth in Palestine: Our Contribution to a Better World, by Lewisohn, Bernard A. Rosenblatt, and Albert K. Epstein (Washington, D.C.: Zionist Organization of America, 1944);

Anniversary (New York: Farrar, Straus, 1948);

The Man of Letters and American Culture (Brooklyn, N.Y.: College English Association, 1949);

The American Jew: Character and Destiny (New York: Farrar, Straus, 1950);

The Magic Word: Studies in the Nature of Poetry (New York: Farrar, Straus, 1950);

What Is This Jewish Heritage? (New York: B'nai B'rith Hillel Foundation, 1954; revised edition, New York: Schocken, 1964);

In a Summer Season (New York: Farrar, Straus, 1955).

OTHER: St. John de Crevecoeur, *Letters From an American Farmer*, introduction by Lewisohn (New York: Fox, Duffield, 1904);

George Sylvester Viereck, *Gedichte von George Sylvester Viereck; With an Appreciation by Ludwig Lewisohn* (New York: Progressive Printing Company, 1904);

Rudolf Hans Bartsch, *Elisabeth Koett*, translated by Lewisohn (New York: FitzGerald, 1910);

Ernst von Feuchtersleben, *Health and Suggestion: The Dietetics of the Mind*, translated and edited by Lewisohn (New York: Huebsch, 1910);

Hermann Sudermann, *The Indian Lily, and Other Stories*, translated by Lewisohn (New York: Huebsch, 1911);

Gerhart Johann Robert Hauptmann, *The Dramatic Works of Gerhart Hauptmann*, volumes 1-8 edited by Lewisohn (New York: Huebsch, 1912-1919);

David Pinski, *The Treasure*, translated by Lewisohn (New York: Huebsch, 1915);

Georg Hirschfeld, *The Mothers*, translated with an introduction by Lewisohn (Garden City: Doubleday, Page, 1916);

Max Halbe, *Youth*, translated with an introduction by Lewisohn (New York: Doubleday, Page, 1916);

A Modern Book of Criticism, edited with an introduction by Lewisohn (New York: Boni & Liveright, 1919);

Adolf Andreas Latzko, *The Judgment of Peace; a Novel*, translated by Lewisohn (New York: Boni & Liveright, 1919);

Bosworth Crocker (Mary Arnold Crocker Childs Lewisohn), *Humble Folk, One-Act Plays*, introduction by Lewisohn (Cincinnati: Stewart Kidd, 1923);

Jacob Wassermann, *Wedlock*, translated by Lewisohn (New York: Boni & Liveright, 1926);

Hanns Heinz Ewers, *The Sorcerer's Apprentice*, translated by Lewisohn (New York: Day, 1927);

Thelma Bowman (Spear) Lewisohn, *First Fruits*, foreword by Lewisohn (Paris: Black Manikin Press, 1927);

"The Pagan in the Heart: on the Attitude of the Citizen as an Influence for Peace or War," in *If I Could Preach Just Once* (New York & London: Harper, 1929), pp. 15-35;

Bernard Guttman, *Ambition*, translated by Lewisohn (New York & London: Harper, 1930);

Thomas Mann, *Death in Venice*, introduction by Lewisohn (New York: Knopf, 1930);

Otto Rank, *Art and the Artist*, introduction by Lewisohn (New York: Knopf, 1932);

Creative America, edited by Lewisohn (New York & London: Harper, 1933);

Rebirth: a Book of Modern Jewish Thought, edited by Lewisohn (New York & London: Harper, 1935);

Franz Werfel, *The Eternal Road: a Drama in Four Parts*, translated by Lewisohn (New York: Viking, 1936);

Franz Hoellering, *The Defenders*, translated by Lewisohn (Boston: Little, Brown, 1940);

Thelma Bowman (Spear) Lewisohn, *Many Mansions*, includes poems by Lewisohn (North Montpelier, Vt.: Driftwind Press, 1941);

Franz Werfel, *The Song of Bernadette*, translated by Lewisohn (New York: Viking, 1942);

Jewish Short Stories, edited by Lewisohn (New York: Behrman House, 1945);

Martin Buber, *For the Sake of Heaven*, translated by Lewisohn (Philadelphia: Jewish Publication Society of America, 1945);

Selma Stern, *The Spirit Returneth*, translated by Lewisohn (Philadelphia: Jewish Publication Society of America, 1946);

Rainer Maria Rilke, *Thirty-One Poems*, English versions by Lewisohn (New York: B. Ackerman, 1946);

Soma Morgenstern, *In My Father's Pastures*, translated by Lewisohn (Philadelphia: Jewish Publication Society of America, 1947);

Among the Nations, edited by Lewisohn (New York: Farrar, Straus, 1948);

Johann Wolfgang von Goethe, *Goethe, the Story of a Man; Being the Life of Johann Wolfgang Goethe as Told in His Own Words and the Words of His Contemporaries*, edited and translated by Lewisohn (New York: Farrar, Straus, 1949);

Max Brod, *Unambo*, translated by Lewisohn (New York: Farrar, Straus & Young, 1952);

Theodor Herzl, *Theodor Herzl: a Portrait for the Age*, edited with an introduction by Lewisohn (Cleveland: World, 1955);

Jacob Picard, *The Marked One, and Twelve Other Stories*, translated with an introduction by Lewisohn (Philadelphia: Jewish Publication Society of America, 1956).

SELECTED PERIODICAL PUBLICATIONS: "Books We Have Made," *Charleston [S.C.] News and Courier*, 5 July 1903-20 September 1903;

"German American Poetry," *Sewanee Review*, 9 (April 1904): 223-230;

"George Sylvester Viereck. An Appreciation," *Sewanee Review*, 9 (April 1904);

"A Plea for Passionate Poetry," *Current Literature*, 10 (September 1906): 290-292;

"The Garden of Passion," *Current Literature*, 7 (February 1907): 224;

"Dionysis," *Current Literature*, 8 (February 1909): 220;

"The Modern Novel," *Sewanee Review*, 14 (October 1909): 458-474;

"Symon's Romantic Movement," *Forum*, 6 (November 1909): 487-492;

"The Poet of Galilee," *Forum*, 9 (January 1910): 86;

"Germany in War Time," *Literary Digest*, 9 (16 October 1915): 856;

"Gertrude and I," *Internationalist*, 6 (April 1916): 122;

"A New England Fable," *Internationalist*, 11 (April 1917): 116-119;

"Foreshadowings of the New Novel," *Forum*, 12 (September 1918): 79-84;

"The Problem of Modern Poetry," *Bookman*, 5 (January 1919): 550-557;

"The Story Ashland Told at Dinner," *Smart Set*, 10 (February 1919): 14-21;

"The Jewish Art Theatre," *Nation*, 109 (13 December 1919): 747-748;

"Cult of Violence," *Nation*, 110 (24 January 1920): 118;

"Creation and Analysis," *Nation*, 110 (17 July 1920): 74-75;

"The Homeless Muse," *Nation*, 111 (1 December 1920): 622-623;

"William Ellery Leonard," *Nation*, 112 (12 January 1921): 44-45;

"Macbeth in the Void," *Nation*, 112 (2 March 1921): 349-350;

"Culture and Race," *Nation*, 112 (27 July 1921): 102;

"South Carolina: a Lingering Fragrance," *Nation*, 114 (12 July 1922): 36-37;

"Hauptmann on Broadway," *Nation*, 115 (11 October 1922): 392;

"The Negro Players," *Nation*, 116 (23 May 1923): 605;

"The Dance of Life," *Nation*, 117 (12 September 1923): 270;

"Un-Americanized Americans," *Independent*, 5 (29 March 1924): 173;

"The Death of Society," *Nation*, 119 (10 August 1924): 156;

"Blind Alley," *Menorah Journal*, 9 (December 1924): 495-498;

"Hunger and Holiness," *Menorah Journal*, 9 (February 1925): 62-66;

"The Art of Being a Jew," *Harper's Monthly Magazine*, 146 (May 1925): 725-729;

"Can an Artist Live in America?," *Nation*, 121 (14 October 1925): 423-424;

"The Fallacies of Assimilation," *Menorah Journal*, 10 (October 1925): 460-472;

"Martin Buber," *Menorah Journal*, 11 (February 1926): 65-70;

"The Jew and the State," *New Palestine*, 6 (1 March 1929): 159-160;

"The Jewish World Crisis," *Harper's Monthly Magazine*, 158 (November 1930): 701-709;

"Jewish Literature in Europe," *Opinion*, 5 (29 February 1932): 6-7;

"Germany's Lowest Depths," *Nation*, 112 (3 May 1933): 493-494;

"In a Pagan World," *Opinion*, 7 (January 1934): 13-15; 7 (February 1934): 9-12;

"The New Meaning of Revolution," *North American Review*, 42 (September 1934): 210-218;

"An American Comes Home," *Harper's Monthly Magazine*, 168 (October 1934): 513-520;

"Jews in Trouble," *Atlantic*, 57 (January 1936): 53-61;

"Clarifying Democracy," *Jewish Mirror*, 5 (August 1942): 5-11;

"Jewish Contributions to American Literature," *Jewish Mirror*, 5 (November 1942): 32-37;

"The Test," *Esquire*, 12 (May 1947): 23-32;

"The Sources of Being Jewish," *Congress Weekly*, 17 (13 December 1948): 6-7;

"Notes on Yiddish Poetry," *Jewish Frontier*, 10 (April 1949): 19-22;

"The Jewish Novel in America," *Congress Weekly*, 12 (5 December 1949): 5-7;

"The Future of American Zionism," *Commentary*, 5 (August 1950): 117ff.;

"To the Young Jewish Intellectuals," *Jewish Frontier*, 12 (April 1952): 5-8;

"Ghetto Boyhood," *Saturday Review*, 36 (3 September 1953): 14;

"Israel, American Jewry and the State Department," *Jewish Frontier*, 111 (October 1954): 7-10;

"The Stories of Jacob Picard," *Jewish Frontier*, 16 (June 1956): 16-18;

"Reflections on Crisis," *Judaism*, 2 (Summer 1956): 195-204;

"Thomas Mann," *Jewish Frontier*, 19 (March 1959): 4-11; 19 (April 1959): 18-24; 19 (June 1959): 14-19.

Ludwig Lewisohn was an imposing figure on the literary landscape of America and Europe during the first half of the twentieth century. A product of two continents and several ethnic communities, he sought to give new life to an American culture he believed moribund, to a Western society he saw as misguided by demogoguery, and to a Jewish community he found lost and without direction. At first seeking to assimilate within the dominant culture in America, he gradually came to realize the need to find a way to mix, in what were for him proper proportions, the elements of his diversified heritage.

The major themes of his life's work can be found even in his earliest writings—a concern for the development of a richer American literature and theater through exposure to the literary arts of Europe; the role of literature and the theater in the lives of the citizenry of all nations; the question of what he termed "Puritan" values and their role in the lives of the people on which they weighed heavily; the place of his Jewishness in his life and his own personal role in the future of the Jewish people. In love with the power of words, he wrote, edited, or translated over eighty-five books, hundreds of poems, and several thousand journal articles (many under pseudonyms) in an attempt to resolve what he felt were urgent questions in need of immediate answers.

Born into a culturally assimilated Berlin Jewish family, Lewisohn was brought by his parents, Jacques, a small businessman, and Minna (Eloesser), the highly educated daughter of a rabbi, to the rural hamlet of St. Matthews, South Carolina, in 1890. Moving to Charleston within two years of his arrival in the United States, he later distinguished himself as valedictorian of the Charleston High School (1897). After four years of study at the College of Charleston, during which time he became editor of its literary journal, he was graduated with honors at the age of nineteen with B.A. and M.A. degrees in English literature. Despite ten years of active participation in the Methodist Church, Lewisohn failed to secure a teaching position at the church-affiliated Porter Military Academy because of his Jewish origins, a position he needed desperately if he was to earn enough to attend graduate school the following year. Disappointed and bitter over what he perceived as prejudice against him as a Jew, he isolated himself and spent the year following his graduation writing poetry and several minor literary studies, while seeing his master's thesis, "A Study of Matthew Arnold," serialized in the *Sewanee Review* (1901).

Acceptance into the doctoral program in English literature at Columbia University and the financial assistance of family and local supporters brought the young literary scholar to New York in the fall of 1902. It was here that his world was broadened by exposure to the city's eclectic cultural life and by friendships with the poet William Ellery Leonard and the iconoclastic poet and journalist George Sylvester Viereck. It was here, too, that he more seriously pursued the problem of his life's direction, as doubts involving his Jewishness and its conflict with "Puritan" America, already present during his years in college, became ever more troubling. Constant warnings from two of his professors that a Jew would not be appointed to an English faculty at an American university or college finally convinced Lewisohn to leave Columbia with a master's degree before completing his dissertation, a reworking of the still highly regarded history of South Carolina literature, "Books We Have Made," that had been serialized in the Charleston newspaper the previous summer (1903). "Books We Have Made" was Lewisohn's valedictory to the world of Southern Christian gentility. While understanding the factors making for continued provincialism in the Deep South, there is a definite critical stance assumed by him toward this land he no longer felt a part of—thus, the ironic "We" of the title. His initial negative reaction to New York,

made more severe by the separation from his parents, lessened as he found his place within the Yankee world.

After the disappointment of failed literary pursuits and his dismissal from Doubleday, Page (where he worked briefly as an editor) because of labor agitation, Lewisohn returned to Charleston in the winter of 1904. In the spring of 1906 he was followed to Charleston by Mary Arnold Crocker (pseudonym, Bosworth Crocker), a minor playwright twenty years his senior and a divorcée with children. Lewisohn, who had met her in 1904, later claimed that in 1906 she had forced him into a marriage made unbreakable by society's Puritan restraints. He taught extension courses for the College of Charleston (which awarded him an honorary D.Litt. degree in 1914) while working on one-act plays and short stories in an attempt to end his financial dependence upon his parents. But literature offered little opportunity in Charleston for him, and in the fall of 1907, he returned to New York with Mary. With his baggage he carried his just-completed novel, hoping that its sale would give him the financial backing to pursue the poetry he then thought his clearest statement. Entitled *The Broken Snare* (published with the help of Theodore Dreiser in 1908), the novel was a work ostensibly concerned with a young woman's growing acceptance of her inner thoughts, artistic dreams, and sexual desires, but had far deeper personal meaning for him. It was, for Lewisohn, the point of departure from the rigid world of his youth into a new life of freedom and creativity, a life in tune with his inner nature—a major step in his metamorphosis from provincial American to cosmopolitan figure.

Harsh criticism from those same Charlestonians who had once raised funds to send him to Columbia but who now saw this work as scandalous made his return to New York, on hindsight, less of a strain than the separation from his parents, particularly his mother, had been in the past. The three years that followed were marked by hardship, hunger, and despair—until in 1910 an appointment was offered to him in the German department at the University of Wisconsin through the urging of his old friend William Ellery Leonard, a member of the school's English faculty. During this three-year period Lewisohn's reputation as a writer and literary figure had begun to grow. *The Broken Snare* had been favorably received outside of Charleston, with a particularly positive and encouraging review by W. M. Payne in the *Dial* (1 November 1908). In Payne's view, the book was the daring work of a first-time novelist, beautifully written by one who,

Letter from Lewisohn to Lancelot Minor Harris, who was his mentor at the College of Charleston. The letter was written a few months before publication of Lewisohn's first novel, The Broken Snare *(Special Collections, College of Charleston Library).*

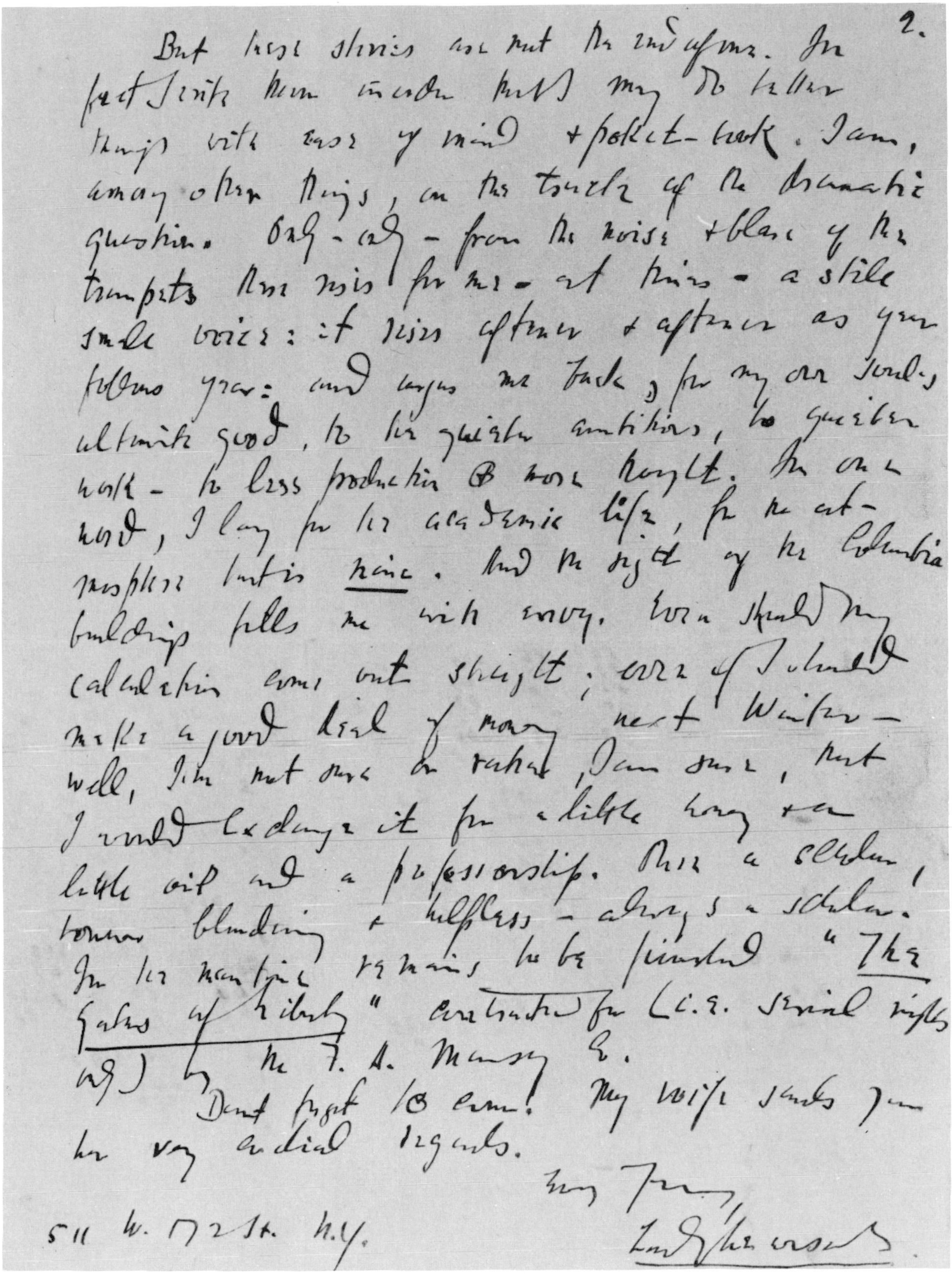

2.

But these stories are not the end of me. In fact I write them in order that I may do better things with ease of mind + pocket-book. I am, among other things, on the track of the dramatic question. Only—only—from the noise + blare of the trumpets there rises for me—at times—a still small voice: it rises oftener + oftener as years follow years: and urges me back, for my own soul's ultimate good, to the quieter ambitions, to quieter work—to less production & more thought. In one word, I long for the academic life, for the atmosphere that is mine. And the sight of the Columbia buildings fills me with envy. Even should my calculations come out straight; even if I should make a good deal of money next Winter—well, I'm not sure or rather, I am sure, that I would exchange it for a little honor + a little ease and a professorship. Once a scholar, however blundering + helpless—always a scholar! In the meantime remains to be finished "The Gates of Liberty" contracted for U.S. serial rights only by the F. A. Munsey Co.

Don't forget to come! My wife sends you her very cordial regards.

Ever Yours,

Ludwig Lewisohn

511 W. 172 St. N.Y.

Page two of Lewisohn's letter to Harris

in baring his soul, had brought a new awareness of the cultural shackles surrounding the lives of all Americans. A year later, Lewisohn's one-act dramatic poem *A Night in Alexandria* (1909), inspired by the need for money, brought him further critical acclaim. His now rather frequent journal appearances (*Cavalier, All-Story, Town Topics, Sewanee Review, Current Literature, Forum*) and his book *German Style: An Introduction to the Study of German Prose* (1910) added to his growing stature as a scholar, most notably as interpreter and translator of German literature to an English readership.

After a year in Wisconsin, a particularly difficult period emotionally and financially, Lewisohn moved to the German department at Ohio State University, where he remained until 1917. The strain of life with Mary and her children continued, complicated by his mother's illness and death and his father's subsequent mental breakdown—all of which took every penny he could earn as teacher and writer. It was, however, a fruitful period as he became respected by faculty and students for his abilities in the classroom (he was throughout his life a riveting speaker) and as his literary output began to increase dramatically. As editor and translator of the first eight volumes of *The Dramatic Works of Gerhart Hauptmann* (1912-1919), he began to propagate his own notion of literary naturalism, more fully developed three years later in his study *The Modern Drama* (1915), a work in praise of Ibsen, Strindberg, the French realists, O'Casey, and, of course, Hauptmann, whom Lewisohn considered the fullest expression of this movement. This treatment of literary naturalism was extended in a work on *The Spirit of Modern German Literature* (1916), a comprehensive account of the literary arts of the land of his birth. This concentration on German literature was more than a scholar's interest. Rejected by those who preserved English literature as the private domain of Anglo-Saxon blood, he fell back on the literature of his fatherland and found in it a richer contemporary body of work unknown to, and far more enlightened than, the world of English literary scholarship.

While in Ohio, Lewisohn began once again to reexamine the role of his Jewishness in his life, finding new meaning in it, in large part as a reaction to the rejection of others and to his continuing sense of alienation. As a child he had had limited exposure to his parents' heritage. His father, cutting himself off from the Old World and its ways, had totally rejected Jewish traditions, declaring himself a secularist, a modernist, and an American of democratic persuasion—even if society continued

to deny him an opportunity to give expression to this self-image he had created. Lewisohn's mother, as the daughter of a rabbi, had continued to practice, against her husband's wishes, a few of the traditions she had known as a child before coming to Berlin. Lewisohn himself had followed his mother to a distant corner of their home each Friday evening to light candles, but as the years passed and the pressure of schoolyard peers increased, it became ever more difficult for him to divide his life between the Methodist he was to the outside world (a role his mother had chosen for him as a means of Americanization) and his inner existence as a Jew. By the time he had entered college, the rejection of his mother's Judaism had been internalized, though some vestige remained buried in his consciousness. But as the social rejection of his college peers continued unabated, he began to use his alien roots as a foil. Throughout his college publications (whether poetry, short story, or literary essay) there is a sense of the ever present, alienated Jew, looking from outside the wall of Christian culture, longingly, but cognizant of its impenetrable nature and of its role in denying him access to the means of expression for the desires he believed to be natural and moral. *The Broken Snare*, beyond its affirmation of man's fundamental nature, is a carefully disguised Jewish polemic against this Puritan ethos. The passage from Psalm 124 quoted at the opening of the book—"Our soul is escaped as a bird out of the snare of the fowlers. The snare is broken, and we are escaped"—is preceded in the full text, not quoted by Lewisohn, with the following: "Let Israel now sing; 'If it had not been the Lord who was for us, When men rose against us, Then would they have swallowed us up alive. . . . Blessed be the Lord, Who hath not given us as prey to their teeth.' "

The short stories written before and after *The Broken Snare* have, like the antagonistic and catalytic Held of this novel, a character clearly modeled after Lewisohn, who acts as the agent of resolution for whatever conflict exists—and always as the aid to Christians in distress, physical or emotional. This theme is repeated as late as 1927 in *Roman Summer*, in which a Jewish woman offers a Gentile the means of personal renewal, and again in 1934, with *An Altar in the Fields*.

The death of Lewisohn's mother precipitated his final conflict over the role of his Jewishness. Wishing earlier to identify with the dominant culture, he had moved closer to his father by rejecting the ways of his mother. Yet his mother was the closer parent, and thus, he was never able to complete the transformation of his own identity. The momentary feeling of freedom following her death in 1912 enabled him to reject as totally as he could the Jewishness he had always found so burdensome, despite its usefulness as a weapon against a rejecting and repressive environment. This liberation soon turned to confusion, and not until 1915 had Lewisohn finally begun successfully to work through this identity crisis, coming to terms with the secular life he wished to live outside the Jewish world—the world of European literature—and with the Jewishness he now realized was so integral a part of who he was. In that year he lectured to the fledgling Menorah Society at Ohio State and saw the publication of his translation of David Pinski's Yiddish work *The Treasure*, thereby expressing his increasing commitment to Jewish themes, as well as a continuation of socialist leanings, first evidenced in his college debates. This commitment to finding the role of his Jewishness in his life was strengthened by his father's death in a mental hospital in 1920, for which he blamed Puritan America's refusal to allow his father the opportunity to fulfill his dreams, while encouraging him to abandon his Jewish identity.

Lewisohn's academic career came to an abrupt end in 1917 following America's entrance into the European conflict, which made his political neutrality untenable. As a proponent of German culture, he struggled against the hysteria of the times which he believed would negate the very important human contribution made by Germany in modern philosophy, literature, and the arts. Lewisohn was more concerned with the breakdown of humane civilization than with German culture as such. He had become an internationalist and would give no quarter to the chauvinism of World War I America. In the spring of 1917, he was requested by Ohio State to take a sabbatical leave, at half pay and with the understanding that he not return at its conclusion. He went to New York somewhat relieved to be rid of the strictures of teaching duties and of a Midwestern environment, overly patriotic and intolerant of dissent. He had been working on a study of German and French poetry but changed the focus of the book under the direction of the publisher because of intense anti-German sentiment. *The Poets of Modern France* (1918) discusses thirty symbolist poets, accompanied by selections from their writings—a work far different from the initial comparative study, part of which was salvaged years later in *Modern German Poetry* (1925).

Translations from the German and periodical articles (appearing in *Internationalist, Forum, Bookman, Smart Set, Nation*, and other journals), a posi-

tion as Latin instructor at a YMCA-related preparatory school, and a six-month renewal of his sabbatical at one-third pay, kept food on the table until 1919, when Lewisohn was invited by Oswald Garrison Villard to become drama critic and fiction editor for the prestigious *Nation* (he had been book reviewer of German material for over a year at this point), a position he held for five years, ending his tenure as associate editor in 1924. A promoter of the avant-garde stage, of the Yiddish and black theaters, and of the works of European dramatists being performed in small off-Broadway theaters, he built a reputation as a serious critic. Old friendships deepened and new ones were formed as he counted among his closest associates Theodore Dreiser, Sinclair Lewis, Horace Liveright, Edgar Lee Masters, H. L. Mencken (with whom he had an on-again, off-again relationship), Upton Sinclair, Carl Van Doren and his brother Mark. His dramatic criticism was collected in 1922 as *The Drama and The Stage*, testimony to his acknowledged position as a significant critic.

In the same year Lewisohn published the work for which he is perhaps best known, his impressionistic autobiographical work *Up Stream*. He had worked on it for several years, but his father's death gave him the final impetus he needed to complete the work. In a lifetime of controversial works, this was the most disputed of all, for it was accusatory, indeed inflammatory, and it tore at the very heart of American culture. Its reception by the press was anything but neutral. Mencken gave a glowing review of it in the *Nation*, but Brander Matthews (Lewisohn's former teacher at Columbia) in the *New York Times* echoed the sentiments of many when he held Lewisohn at fault for not being able to find a place in society. Matthews went so far as to condemn Lewisohn for being a member "of a militant group of un-Americanized aliens, loudly proclaiming that they and they alone are Americans." In so doing, he unwittingly confirmed Lewisohn's contention that he had been rejected for reasons Lewisohn characterized as "racial." Matthews, acknowledging that "racial prejudices . . . may have made his path somewhat thornier," affirmed the justice of this condition, for "the literature of a people is a record of the life of those who speak its language; and no alien by birth can expound the spirit of this literature as the natives of that speech want to have it expounded." This was precisely what Lewisohn had complained about and what the Jewish novelist and short-story writer Anzia Yezierska objected to in her response to Matthews in the *New York Times* of 19 April 1922: "It is the glory of America that it is not composed of a single race, one single strain like the other nations of the world. . . . To us newer Americans, *Up Stream* is not merely a book. It is a vision, revelation. It is our struggles, our hopes, our aspirations and our failures made articulate. It is the cry of young America to old America not to confine literature, education and thought to the formula of a small group. *Up Stream* is a dynamic protest against the sanctification of a priestcraft in education, a revolt against the existence of an Anglo-Saxon intellectual aristocracy in a country that is the gathering together of peoples from every corner of the earth."

Yezierska gave the last word to Lewisohn himself by quoting from *Up Stream*: "I have written of America for the simple reason that I am an American, and I have spoken strongly for the simple reason that the measure of one's love and need is also the measure of one's disappointment and indignation. . . . Among the masses of our countrymen I see no stirring, no desire to penetrate beyond fixed names to living things, no awakening from the spectral delusions among which they pursue their aimless business and their sapless pleasures. But the critical spirit which is also the creative spirit has risen among us, and it has arisen, naturally and inevitably, in the form of a protest and rebellion. . . . Life among us is ugly and mean and, above all things, false in its assumptions and measures. Somehow we must break these shackles and flee and emerge into some beyond of sanity, of a closer contact with reality, of nature and of truth."

Lewisohn's marriage, in trouble almost from its beginning nearly two decades earlier, had been proof enough of the unnatural constraints of a "Puritan" society. By breaking with it, he could free himself of the masks he had worn, of all the pretense he had been forced to perpetuate. Mary, and the search for acceptance over the years, had been parts of an attempt to be what he knew he was not. Each author "writes a confessional," he noted in *Up Stream*—"each is a lyricist at bottom." As with so much of his writing, a novel he had been at work on, *Don Juan* (1923), became the means by which he worked through the end of his relationship with his wife. Here he explored the conflict between marriage and personal freedom; here he decried the demands of an inhumane legal system opposing the needs of the individual—needs he felt more earnestly with the deepening of his feelings toward a woman twenty years his junior, Thelma Spear. An aspiring opera singer, she sought the patronage of a recognized critic. Lewisohn, desperate for a new life, believed he had found in this younger woman a

chance for a new beginning. Proclaiming the artist's right to freedom in *The Creative Life* (1924), Lewisohn and Spear departed for Europe.

By 1920 Lewisohn had become a committed Zionist, and it was Chaim Weizmann's invitation to undertake a secret fact-finding mission in Eastern Europe and Palestine that made the voyage abroad possible. The tour of major Jewish population centers completed, Lewisohn returned to Paris, only to find himself stranded there; his and Spear's passports had been revoked because they had falsified information on their visa applications. Their pose as husband and wife—despite his plaint that spiritually they were wed—was caught by U.S. State Department officials forewarned by an avenging Mary Lewisohn, who would refuse to relinquish her grip for another fifteen years.

The decade he was to spend in Europe (partially recounted in a follow-up to *Up Stream*, the 1929 autobiographical *Mid-Channel*) saw an amazing literary outpouring dealing with both his Jewishness and his concern for a broader cultural transformation. His tour and his thoughts on Jewish life were summarized several months after his arrival in Paris in a book entitled *Israel* (1925), a call to his fellow Jews to reject the temptations of assimilation and to renew themselves through a return to their people's traditions. The notion of a worldwide redemption and the emphasis upon pacifism, both rooted in the biblical prophets, gave indication that Lewisohn saw himself as the Jews' standard-bearer in a darkening age. The pacifist theme would be repeated four years later in a stirring essay, "The Pagan in the Heart: on the Attitude of the Citizen as an Influence for Peace or War," though the growing Nazi tide of the 1930s would eventually sweep away these ideals, seen by Lewisohn as untenable in the face of Nazism's destructive potential.

This struggle against assimilation and the concomitant pursuit of personal and communal Jewish integrity were to dominate much of Lewisohn's efforts in the years ahead. In book after book, article after article, he juxtaposed the Christian and the Jew, the ethos of one against that of the other, portraying the ways of his own people as the more natural, sane, healthy approach to life. In 1928 he implored his fellow Jews to seek *The Island Within* themselves, as he recounted the epic of a family's transition from traditional Jewish life in mid-nineteenth-century Poland to affluence in early twentieth-century New York, all told against the backdrop of centuries of Jewish history, heightened by the transition of the assimilated grandson back to a strong identification with his people. Not unlike Lewisohn himself, the protagonist Arthur Levy left behind his successful psychiatric practice in New York and his Christian wife to undertake a Jewish mission to Eastern Europe, as much for the sake of his people as for himself.

Lewisohn moved farther back into history to portray the persecution of the Jews in his imaginative recreation of *The Last Days of Shylock* (1931), resuming Shakespeare's story at the point of its conclusion but with flashbacks to childhood scenes of poignancy and foreboding. The historical again served as the means of portraying contemporary problems in *This People* (1933), a series of vignettes ranging from the Purim story as told by Mordecai to the self-destructive life of a Jew-turned-Bolshevik whose denial of his Jewishness leads to his death. Particularly moving is "The Saint," the tale of an elderly Jew who, lost in his liberal secularism, fails to find the peace which the return to Judaism has given his son. Parallels with Lewisohn's life are clearly present in "The Saint"—his father's eventual madness and his own escape from it through a turning toward the ways of his mother and away from the ideas of his youth (more forcefully expressed a year later in *The Permanent Horizon: A New Search for Old Truths*).

The problem of marriage, ever on his mind, became for Lewisohn another chance to explore the implications of his Jewishness. In the tale of *Stephen Escott* (1930), he speaks of the healthy relationship enjoyed by a Jewish couple, contrasting it with the Gentile marriages that fail because of a denial of what he saw as the natural basis of all such unions—sexual pleasure and spiritual compatibility. Lewisohn reworked this theme in *An Altar in the Fields* (1934), this time, however, combining earlier memories of Charleston names and events with the often repeated use of the Jew as the light to the Gentiles. In this novel the floundering marriage of a prosperous American Christian couple on holiday in Europe is aided by a Jewish psychiatrist who leads them back to a natural life via a trip to the African desert.

Despite this absorption in the Jewish problems of his life, the role he had earlier chosen for himself, that of literary figure and scholar, remained one of extreme importance, if only because it offered a way into the larger world and the means of extending his critique of Western civilization beyond a Jewish audience. The Paris of the 1920s and 1930s was an exciting center of literary activity, and Lewisohn sought his place there in the decade of his residence. The friendships he had in America carried over to Europe, where new personal ties were established. Lewisohn's attraction to psychological models led to his short-lived analysis under Freud (he feared that Freud would cure him of the neuroses that made him an effective writer), though he eventually sided with his close friend Otto Rank in the latter's dispute with the master. In 1932, Lewisohn wrote the introduction to Rank's *Art and the Artist*, a work in which Lewisohn saw himself fulfilling the self-sacrificing destiny of the artist. As a continuing lover of German culture, he soon met Thomas Mann, with whom he formed a lifelong friendship of mutual respect and artistic appreciation that was strengthened by Mann's open opposition to the Nazi regime. Familiar with the "charmed circle" of Gertrude Stein, he preferred the literati that surrounded James Joyce. In fact, according to Sylvia Beach, proprietress of the bookshop and lending library Shakespeare and Company, it was Lewisohn who wrote the first draft of the legal brief against those who had pirated *Ulysses*. Completing Lewisohn's own circle was Sisley Huddlestone, editor and fellow pacifist, Cass Canfield of Harper and Brothers, and a host of others in the theater, most notably Regis Michaud and Paul Robeson.

But of all the relationships Lewisohn developed over these years, perhaps the most important was with Edward Titus, owner of the Black Manikin Book Shop and the publishing house that grew out of it. Aided financially by his wife, Helena Rubenstein, Titus brought out, as his first book-length publication, Lewisohn's controversial autobiographical novel *The Case of Mr. Crump* (1926), a frankly told account of his marital bondage to Mary. Mary Lewisohn succeeded in having it banned in America for reasons of libel and sexual explicitness (though a pirated edition was published in the United States in 1930), but *The Case of Mr. Crump* was recognized as a literary triumph, called by Freud "an incomparable masterpiece" and praised by Mann as a work standing "in the forefront of modern epic narrative," the story "of the inferno of a marriage." The novel was an opportunity for Lewisohn to further exorcise the demons of childhood and of the adult life he now saw as a series of lies to himself and the world. In time, it would be translated into many languages and published again and again, most recently in England in 1980, with sales of well over a million copies since its first publication.

A work of equal magnitude and the first full treatment of American literature from a Freudian perspective was Lewisohn's *Expression in America* (1932), an interpretation of American thought from the colonial period to the present. He had been at work on this study in his thoughts ever since his college days, and when money became scarce in Paris, he contracted with Harper to put his thoughts on paper. For three years he labored on this massive undertaking (659 pages), once again venting his spleen on "Puritan" values, using Freud to demonstrate the injustice and unhealthy nature of American life. Walt Whitman and those who followed his lead had attempted to give the people a new life— and Lewisohn sang their praise. But so many others had done so little to liberate their fellow citizens—these he condemned. Reviewers called it "a beautiful book" and a "challenge to those who . . . believe in the good life"; Joseph Wood Krutch noted how "profoundly interesting" Lewisohn's "intelligible thesis" was: "I know of no other book on American literature more genuinely stimulating." The following year Lewisohn produced a companion anthology, *Creative America* (1933), in which he tried to demonstrate more clearly, through the evidence he selected, the thesis of *Expression in America*. In the *Nation* Carl Van Doren praised the efforts of his old colleague for a "work of art . . . provocative of debate, . . . the most exciting anthology of the whole of American literature that has ever been made."

Lewisohn's continuing marital problems, no longer a function of "Puritan" persecution as he believed it had been with his first wife, had become critical by the time of his return to America with Thelma Spear in 1934. Her career as an opera singer, despite Lewisohn's efforts and financial backing, had never flourished. As time passed, she became increasingly bitter and blamed him for her failure. He was aware of the slow disintegration of their relationship, and as early as 1927 he wrote about a man whose departure from America in search of the means to rekindle his imagination in the *Roman Summer* of his middle years ends in failure because the woman he had hoped would give him new life could not give of herself. But self-doubt dogged him in the years that followed— could he, too, have been at fault? In 1931, he wrote again, in *The Golden Vase*, of a middle-aged American, a successful writer who leaves for Europe (this time Nice, a frequent resting place for the Lewisohns), where he finds a woman whose love inspires him; but he pulls back and ends the relationship, despite the woman's desire to continue it. Lewisohn had matured and had come to the realization that the reticence he now experienced was the result of wounds suffered during his years

with Mary, wounds so deep that they had brought an end to whatever relationships he had had in the years that followed their stormy marriage.

He had always wished for a son, and the birth of his only child (James Elias) in 1933 was an occasion of immense satisfaction for him. Spear vacillated between love and disdain for the "bastard," as she often referred to her son, blaming him (as she did Lewisohn) for her failure as a singer. The return to America in 1934, following years of struggle with the U.S. State Department that ended through the influence of prominent Jewish leaders (Louis Marshall and Rabbi Stephen Wise, an old associate of Franklin Roosevelt), temporarily calmed the mounting domestic crisis. Continued failure as a singer, extended absences by Lewisohn as he plied his trade as a lecturer around the country, and the pressures of motherhood led to a final break after fifteen years.

In 1939, while on a lecture tour in Upstate New York, Lewisohn met Edna Manley, a journalist who had spent many hours of her confinement for tuberculosis reading his works. Their relationship flourished immediately, and marriage followed a year later, Mary having finally agreed to a divorce in 1939. The marriage to Edna Manley dissolved in 1943, though the three years she and Lewisohn had together had been full ones, marked by legal battles for the custody of his son (told in great detail in their coauthored account of 1940, *Haven*), an attempt by Lewisohn at Hollywood screenwriting (which produced the 1948 novel *Anniversary*, the story of Edna's search for her self and her break from her wealthy father's hold on her life), Edna's literary apprenticeship under Lewisohn, and their life in Tucson as part of a small colony of writers and artists.

In the years between Lewisohn's return in 1934 and the break-up of his third marriage in 1943, he had become a spokesman for American Jewry, attacking Nazi Germany and demanding a Jewish refuge in Palestine. Articles, books, and lectures (the volume often occasioned by financial need) repeated these concerns with growing intensity as persecution changed to extermination. Even before his return from Europe, his correspondence warned of a growing sickness in German society; by 1933, he could no longer remain silent, and in a searing *Nation* article he told of "Germany's Lowest Depths," only to see Germany sink even further. Conditions had reached an unspeakable state by 1944 when Lewisohn, outraged by the British closing of Palestine to escapees from Hitler's inferno, recounted in heartrending detail the sinking of the refugee ship *Struma* in his novel *Breathe Upon These* (1944).

His relationship with the Zionists, dating to the early 1920s, had cooled on occasion. Wishing to remain above reproach in the eyes of the world, the Zionist leadership cut their ties with him when he left Thelma Spear for Edna Manley, and there ensued extensive newspaper coverage of his affairs that added a greater degree of notoriety to his reputation than the Zionists thought their situation could permit. Lectures were cancelled, and articles became more difficult to place. But the need for a strong, passionate voice as the 1940s wore on and his new life with Louise Wolk of Chicago brought Lewisohn back into favor, particularly through the efforts of his old friends Stephen Wise and Saul Spiro. By 1944, Lewisohn was the editor of the ZOA's journal, *New Palestine*, giving him four stormy years of access to the Jewish public.

Brandeis University's first faculty in 1948 was composed of both young scholars of great promise and older, established masters whose Jewish backgrounds had barred them from the academies of America. Lewisohn, at the age of sixty-six, found himself teaching Shakespeare for the first time in his life at a university. Given the title of professor of comparative literature and later of university librarian, he brought other distinguished faculty to the campus and became a source of financial support as his contacts and presence were used to build a Jewish university. Yet Brandeis's lack of what he considered an adequate Jewish atmosphere and program with Jewish content brought him into continuous contention with the administration. During the Brandeis years, his nationwide lecture tours continued as did his writing on Jewish themes, particularly those related to the struggle against assimilation and to his contention that a Jewish rebirth in America was possible only if the level of Jewish education could be raised significantly within the next generation. To these activities he now added the translation of refugee Jewish writers into English, a way of assisting their transition and of exposing America to a world destroyed by madmen.

Shortly before his death in 1955, Lewisohn finished what was to be both a summary of the course of his seventy-three years and a final word to be passed on to the generations that would follow. In *In a Summer Season* (1955), with the fading light of winter's evening upon him, Lewisohn reflected: "All I've ever heard . . . from my college days on,

strikes me now as just so many words, however big and brash. And they didn't even come out with what they meant at bottom. There still remains the me, the I, the innermost—the creature who wants: what, what, after the needs of the body are taken care of? I wouldn't have dared to say that even to myself two years ago. We're so bedeviled by the shouters and the boosters. What I want are two things: faith and love. Ah, love is the turbid thing—the strangest in all its commonness, its supposed universality. All seek love. How few find it! Do they even seek it? Do they know how to seek it? Did I seek it, did I seek love, when I 'fell in love'? . . . No, I've never loved, if love has any real meaning. Do I even know how to love? We love beauty or what seems beauty to us; we can't, most of us, do without it. We shouldn't, I suspect. But it's so little on which to build life. . . . Goodness is other, deeper, darker. The stresses of life reveal it; upon it and upon it alone the pain and disappointment of life can lean. How is it to be sought? Where is it to be found? . . . Faith, some kind of faith, a sufficient faith—that ultimate point from which a rational life can proceed to be lived—is it not almost, Heaven help me, more easily found than love is to be found among the confusions of our lives? . . . Who am I? A very humble person who must try to keep hold of the insight that has been granted him, who must try not to lose it again amid the clamor of the world. . . ."

References:

Stanley Chyet, "Lewisohn, a Zionist," in *Studies in Jewish Thought* (Tel Aviv: Sifriat Poalim, 1947), 103-136;

Chyet, "Ludwig Lewisohn in Charleston," *Publications of the American Jewish Historical Society*, 54 (March 1965): 296-322;

Chyet, "Ludwig Lewisohn: The Years of Becoming," *American Jewish Archives*, 11 (March 1959): 125-147;

Adolph Gillis, *Ludwig Lewisohn: The Artist and His Message* (New York: Fox, Duffield, 1933);

Seymour Lainoff, *Ludwig Lewisohn* (Boston: Twayne, 1982);

Ralph Melnick, "Ludwig Lewisohn: The Early Charleston Years," in *Studies in the American Jewish Experience* (Cincinnati: American Jewish Archives, 1984);

Melnick, "Oedipus in Charleston: Ludwig Lewisohn's Search for the Muse," in *Studies in Jewish American Literature*, 3 (1983);

Saul Spiro, *The Jew as Man of Letters: Being Some Notes on Ludwig Lewisohn* (Burlington, Vt.: Vermont Zionist Youth, Masada, 1935).

Papers:

Lewisohn's correspondence, journals, diaries, and scrapbooks are located in dozens of repositories throughout the United States. The two largest collections are at the American Jewish Archives, Hebrew Union College (Cincinnati), and the Special Collections Department of Goldfarb Library, Brandeis University (Waltham, Mass.).

Norman Mailer
(31 January 1923-   )

Andrew Gordon
University of Florida

See also the Mailer entries in *DLB 2, American Novelists Since World War II; DLB 16, The Beats: Literary Bohemians in Postwar America; DLB: Documentary Series 3; DLB Yearbook: 1980*; and *DLB Yearbook: 1983*.

SELECTED BOOKS: *The Naked and the Dead* (New York: Rinehart, 1948; London: Wingate, 1949);

Barbary Shore (New York: Rinehart, 1951; London: Cape, 1952);

The Deer Park (New York: Putnam's, 1955; London: Wingate, 1957);

The White Negro: Superficial Reflections on the Hipster (San Francisco: City Lights Books, 1957);

Advertisements for Myself (New York: Putnam's, 1959; London: Deutsch, 1961);

Deaths for the Ladies and Other Disasters (New York: Putnam's, 1962; London: Deutsch, 1962);

The Presidential Papers (New York: Putnam's, 1963; London: Deutsch, 1964);

An American Dream (New York: Dial, 1965; London: Deutsch, 1965);

Cannibals and Christians (New York: Dial, 1966; London: Deutsch, 1967);

The Bull Fight: A Photographic Narrative With Text by Norman Mailer (New York: Macmillan, 1967);

The Deer Park: A Play (New York: Dial, 1967; London: Weidenfeld & Nicolson, 1970);

Why Are We in Vietnam? (New York: Putnam's, 1967; London: Weidenfeld & Nicolson, 1969);

The Short Fiction of Norman Mailer (New York: Dell, 1967);

The Idol and the Octopus: Political Writings on the Kennedy and Johnson Administrations (New York: Dell, 1968);

The Armies of the Night (New York: New American Library, 1968; London: Weidenfeld & Nicolson, 1968);

Miami and the Siege of Chicago (New York: New American Library, 1968; London: Weidenfeld & Nicolson, 1968);

Of a Fire on the Moon (Boston: Little, Brown, 1970; London: Weidenfeld & Nicolson, 1970);

Maidstone: A Mystery (New York: New American Library, 1971);

King of the Hill: On the Fight of the Century (New York: New American Library, 1971);

The Prisoner of Sex (Boston: Little, Brown, 1971; London: Weidenfeld & Nicolson, 1971);

The Long Patrol (New York: World, 1971);

Existential Errands (Boston: Little, Brown, 1972);

St. George and the Godfather (New York: New American Library, 1972);

Marilyn (New York: Grosset & Dunlap, 1973; London: Hodder & Stoughton, 1973);

The Faith of Graffiti (New York: Praeger, 1974); republished as *Watching My Name Go By* (London: Matthews, Miller, Dunbar, 1974);

The Fight (Boston: Little, Brown, 1975; London: Hart-Davis, 1976);

Genius and Lust: A Journey Through the Major Writings of Henry Miller (New York: Grove, 1976);

Some Honorable Men: Political Conventions 1960-1972 (Boston: Little, Brown, 1976);

A Transit to Narcissus (New York: Howard Fertig, 1978);

The Executioner's Song (Boston: Little, Brown, 1979; London: Hutchinson, 1979);

Of Women and Their Elegance (New York: Simon & Schuster, 1980; Sevenoaks, U.K.: Hodder & Stoughton, 1980);

Norman Mailer (photo by Patrick Ward)

Pieces and Pontifications (Boston: Little, Brown, 1982; London: New English Library, 1983);
Ancient Evenings (Boston: Little, Brown, 1983; London: Macmillan, 1983).

SCREENPLAYS: *Wild 90*, Supreme Mix, 1968;
Beyond the Law, Supreme Mix/Evergreen Films, 1968;
Maidstone, Supreme Mix, 1971.

Norman Mailer has labored for most of his literary career to repudiate what he himself describes as "the one personality he found absolutely insupportable—the nice Jewish boy from Brooklyn. Something in his adenoids gave it away—he had the softness of a man early accustomed to mother-love." Mailer would probably agree with the complaint of Philip Roth's Portnoy: "Because to be *bad*, Mother, that is the real struggle: to be bad—and to enjoy it! That is what makes men of us boys, Mother." If the central question of Saul Bellow's fiction is Joseph's in *Dangling Man* (1944)—"How should a good man live?"—then the central ques-

tion of Mailer's fiction might be posed as "How should a bad man live?" Mailer has struggled to become an American male and an American writer worth noticing by deliberately making himself *bad*, the official Bad Boy of contemporary letters, staking out as his territory the extremes of experience often excluded from American-Jewish fiction, including murder, rape, orgy, suicide, and psychosis. His persistent themes have been sex, violence, and power, and the interconnections among all three in American life. But behind his radicalism is a conservative, moral, proselytizing (one might even say rabbinical) streak. What gives his work continuity despite its many radical changes in form and style is a continuing quest for a hero fit for our times: a man powerful enough and egotistical enough to resist the drift of history and help to shape the future. From the fictional Sergeant Croft in *The Naked and the Dead* (1948) to Gary Gilmore in *The Executioner's Song* (1979), to Menenhetet II in *Ancient Evenings* (1983), the central figures in Mailer's work struggle heroically but fail.

Mailer's upbringing was stable and fairly conventional. His father, Isaac Barnett (Barney) Mailer, of Russian-Jewish background, served in the British army and immigrated to America via South Africa and London after World War I. His mother, Fanny Schneider Mailer, had family in the hotel business in the Atlantic resort town of Long Branch, New Jersey. Mailer, their first child, was born in 1923. He has a sister, Barbara. The family moved in 1927 to the Eastern Parkway section of Brooklyn, which Mailer calls "the most secure Jewish environment in America." The family remained in Brooklyn, where his father worked as an accountant until his death in 1972, and where his mother still lives. Mailer is fond of his Brooklyn roots and maintains an apartment in Brooklyn Heights overlooking the harbor.

Mailer has never written about his childhood. For that matter, he has never written a novel in which the majority of the characters are Jews, and his heroes tend to be either WASPs or only part Jewish. Perhaps this is because he prefers to think of himself as an American rather than a Jewish-American writer, or perhaps because, as he admits, "My knowledge of Jewish culture is exceptionally spotty."

Mailer was a bright, confident child who got excellent report cards in school and was interested in playing the clarinet and building model airplanes. He also went to Hebrew school. He enjoyed reading romances such as Rafael Sabatini's *Captain Blood*. Mailer started scribbling stories at the age of seven, his earliest being a science-fiction novel patterned on the "Buck Rogers" comic strip, but his first published work, at Boys' High School in Brooklyn, was an article on building model planes. His high grades allowed him to choose between the Massachusetts Institute of Technology and Harvard at age sixteen; he picked Harvard because M.I.T. wanted him to attend another year of school.

The precocious Mailer entered Harvard to study aeronautical engineering. However, he writes, "Before I was seventeen I had formed the desire to be a major writer; . . . all through December 1939 and January 1940 I was discovering modern American literature." His early models were neither Jewish nor Jewish-American writers but 1930s novelists John Dos Passos, James T. Farrell, and John Steinbeck. Farrell's proletarian novel, *Studs Lonigan*, made Mailer aware for the first time that his life and those of the people around him were fit subjects for fiction. Shortly after his initial discoveries, he acquired a passion for Thomas Wolfe, William Faulkner, and Ernest Hemingway.

Jews were at a social disadvantage at Harvard

in 1939. Although Mailer was, according to a classmate, "blatantly and abrasively Jewish," he did not practice the religion or join any campus Zionist organizations. He was eager to fit in and soon won acceptance because of his literary talent, becoming an associate editor of the literary magazine, the *Harvard Advocate*, in his sophomore year and being elected to the elite Signet society. Years later Mailer said that "the peculiar juxtaposition of a Brooklyn culture and a Harvard culture have had the most external importance I could name in making me wish to write."

His first story, "The Greatest Thing in the World," about the adventures of a hobo in a pool hall, was published in the *Harvard Advocate* his sophomore year. At the suggestion of Robert Gorham Davis, his Harvard writing instructor, he sent it to *Story* magazine's annual college fiction contest and won first prize. Although Mailer included it in *Advertisements for Myself* (1959), he finds the story embarrassingly crude and derivative, "like the early work of a young man who is going to make a fortune writing first-rate action, western, gangster, and suspense stories." A still derivative but far more seasoned tale, "A Calculus At Heaven," appeared in Edwin Seaver's *Cross Section: A Collection of New American Writing* in 1944 and is also included in *Advertisements for Myself*. This early war story, written before Mailer served overseas in World War II, anticipates the form and themes of *The Naked and the Dead*. Before entering the U.S. Army, he also completed other stories and two novels: "No Percentage" (unpublished) and *A Transit to Narcissus*, which was published in 1978 in a facsimile edition of the typescript.

Mailer confesses that right after Pearl Harbor "I was worrying darkly whether it would be more likely that a great war novel would be written about Europe or the Pacific. . . ." He graduated with honors and a B.S. in engineering from Harvard in 1943 and married Beatrice Silverman (the first of his six wives) in 1944. He was drafted into the army, serving in the Pacific with the 112th Cavalry until April 1946, first as a clerk and then as a rifleman with a reconnaissance platoon in the Philippines. If Mailer had imitated the WASPs at Harvard, he defended himself against the anti-Semitism of his fellow soldiers by absorbing a Texas accent. Thus he added to his repertoire of American roles.

In the fifteen months following his discharge he completed *The Naked and the Dead*, departing for Europe in September 1947. The novel's huge critical and popular success overtook him in 1948, when he was living with his wife in Paris and studying on the GI Bill at the Sorbonne. The novel topped the best-seller lists for months and was purchased by the movies.

Today, although it seems rather old-fashioned in form and style when compared to other novels of the 1940s such as Saul Bellow's *Dangling Man* (1944), *The Naked and the Dead* remains one of the classic novels of World War II. It clearly derives from the harshly realistic novels of the 1930s and stands as a summation and perhaps dead end of that tradition, its importance lying in its epic scope and in the profundity and complexity of its themes. Mailer did not attempt a novel of precisely this epic form again until thirty years later, in *The Executioner's Song*.

The Naked and the Dead is a sweaty, bleak, mercilessly realistic view of men at war, littered with decaying corpses and filled with the overpowering scent of jungle rot. Death is omnipresent, and the men's violent struggle to preserve their lives and their manhood consumes them. Their unsatisfactory confrontation with the civilian forces that have determined their characters (revealed in compressed "Time Machine" flashbacks) seems only a preparation for the carnage of the battlefield. Mailer criticizes not the war or the army but the overwhelming institutions of modern America that serve to crush the individual.

The action takes place on a Pacific island the Americans are trying to recapture from the Japanese. For purposes of comparison and contrast, scenes in the officers' camp, commanded by the autocratic General Cummings, are juxtaposed with scenes in a reconnaissance platoon led by the cruel, hard-driving Texan Sergeant Croft. The link between the two is Lieutenant Hearn, a Harvard graduate and alienated liberal. Mailer, who divides his attention among all the characters, is interested in the fate of each man.

A division of sympathies also occurs in his treatment of the two Jewish soldiers, Roth and Goldstein. Mailer maintains the same objectivity toward them as he does toward the rest of the mixed platoon, which includes a Texan, a Southerner, an Irish-American, an Italian-American, and a Polish-American. Roth is an upwardly mobile, assimilated Jew. A college graduate, he resembles Hearn: because he feels superior and distant from the men, he is universally disliked. The woeful, self-pitying Roth makes a poor soldier. Lacking any defense against the abuse of the platoon, he is goaded to the breaking point. (Mailer always tries to reveal character by pushing his characters to their limits and beyond.) Unable to jump a chasm in the

mountain, Roth finally knows himself and loses his fear of Croft and the anti-Semitic bully Gallagher. He realizes he could force the patrol to turn back from its senseless mission, but he lacks the courage to refuse and have to face the men afterward. Roth jumps, only to fall to his death.

In contrast to Roth, Goldstein has the courage to endure. Goldstein was raised in a candy store in the New York ghetto. Poorly educated but nourished by his religious faith, he has the survival ability of a peasant. Significantly, his best friend in the platoon is Ridges, a religious fundamentalist and illiterate son of a sharecropper. The two carry their burden, the dying soldier Wilson, for days on a stretcher through the jungle, persisting even after Wilson dies, only to see his body wash away as they try to ford the rapids of a river. In bitter frustration, Goldstein wonders if all the centuries of Jewish suffering, carrying the burden, are also simply lost, "all statistics in the cruel wastes of history." Nevertheless, Goldstein has formed a bond of friendship with Ridges through their shared burden, and theirs is really the only unselfish male friendship in the novel.

Mailer admires the heroism of ordinary individuals who carry their burdens to the limit, despite the inevitability of failure. His radical criticism of American society seems to espouse a return to traditional values, even if his belief in those values is tempered by an existential pessimism about the vicissitudes of nature and fate.

With the success of *The Naked and the Dead*, Mailer returned from Europe in July 1948 and was active that fall in Henry Wallace's unsuccessful presidential campaign. He spent part of 1949 in Hollywood writing a screenplay for Metro-Goldwyn-Mayer, who rejected it. His first child, Susan, was born. He toyed with the idea of a novel about the labor movement, but returned to New York to finish a work he had begun in Paris, *Barbary Shore*.

Mailer writes that after *The Naked and the Dead* "my life seemed to have been mined and melted into the long reaches of the book. And so I was prominent and empty, and I had to begin life again." *Barbary Shore* (1951) is a product of that period, a novel of education or initiation. If Mailer's first novel was long and fairly mechanical in form, impersonal in its omniscient narration, panoramic and crowded with characters, *Barbary Shore* in contrast is a short, first-person narrative, concentrating on a handful of characters in a Brooklyn boardinghouse. It is an intensely personal, even claustrophobic, work, reflecting the novelist's agony at having to begin all over again, having to grow up in Brooklyn a second time. Thus it seems less like a second novel and more like the kind of flawed, semiautobiographical first novel many young writers produce.

Barbary Shore is an intriguing failure, an ambitious but unsuccessful attempt to mix political allegory with existential closet drama and family romance. It hovers between realism and a grotesque surrealism. Nonetheless, today it seems to have been ahead of its time, an anguished shout of political prophecy from the depths of the McCarthy era. Like George Orwell's *1984*, it is set in an imaginary near-future dystopia intended as a warning to the present.

The narrator of *Barbary Shore*, Mikey Lovett, is an amnesiac who lost his identity, perhaps in the war. He must start life over again in the postwar world. An aspiring novelist, he rents a room for a summer in a boardinghouse where he becomes involved in the intrigues of the inhabitants. No one is what he or she appears to be; gradually, Lovett realizes he has moved into a nest of spies, double agents, and ex-Communists.

But the political concerns vie with the sexual ones, as the characters indulge in a frenzied round-robin of affairs. Mailer's view of American society as perverse and corrupt and his attempt to explore the unconscious motivations of that society were leading him away from the literary realism of his first novel and into the feverish distortions of a dream vision, akin to the novels of Nathanael West, but in *Barbary Shore* the two forms clash. Consequently, the novel seems overdefensive and overwrought, and critics and readers found it puzzling or repellent. Mailer was stung by the failure, but the novel was nevertheless a useful transition work for him.

In *Barbary Shore*, although none of the characters is identified as Jewish, the Brooklyn setting evokes the world of Mailer's childhood and adds a note of ghetto claustrophobia to the novel. In addition, Mailer is clearly writing as a disillusioned left-wing Jewish intellectual. Hovering over the book are the historical figures of Trotsky and Stalin: Trotsky, the martyred Jewish idealist, and Stalin, the brutal anti-Semite who, in ordering Trotsky's assassination, betrayed the revolution. In the absence of any viable politics or religion, Mailer's hero must find a substitute faith in order to go on living.

After the failure of *Barbary Shore*, Mailer again fashioned a new life for himself, divorcing Beatrice Silverman, moving to Greenwich Village, and marrying the painter Adele Morales, by whom he had his second and third children. With Daniel Wolf and Edwin Fancher he helped to found and began to write columns for the progressive newspaper the *Village Voice*.

Mailer conceived an admittedly "Napoleonic" plan for an eight-part epic work, "the prologue to be the day of a small, frustrated man, a minor artist manqué. The eight novels were to be eight stages of his dream later that night, and the books would revolve around the adventures of a mythical hero, Sergius O'Shaugnessy." This dream epic, part of Mailer's continuing quest for a hero fit for our times, consumed his energies as a writer for the remainder of the 1950s. The only completed segments of this project, however, are *The Deer Park* and two short stories, "The Man Who Studied Yoga" (intended as the prologue) and "The Time of Her Time."

"The Man Who Studied Yoga" (1952) and "The Time of Her Time" (1959), both included in *Advertisements for Myself*, are Mailer's two finest stories. "The Man Who Studied Yoga" anticipates the concerns of his next three novels: self-betrayal into the deadening trap of American life, middle-class security and freedom from dread purchased at the price of one's soul. Sam Slovoda, protagonist of "The Man Who Studied Yoga," is a failed radical and failed artist subsiding into a middle-class coma, an assimilated Jew whose analyst and wife have him effectively hemmed in. Perhaps Mailer wrote the story partly to exorcise his bitterness over the failures of his first marriage and his second novel. In any case, Sam the Jew becomes a poignant archetype of mass man alienated and powerless in mass society. Bereft of faith in both politics and religion, Sam yearns for a substitute faith in art, but he is no artist.

When Rinehart, publisher of Mailer's first two novels, rejected *The Deer Park*, Mailer was forced to send it all over town until G. P. Putnam's accepted it. In the meantime, he decided to revise the novel to create a more confident voice for its narrator, Sergius O'Shaugnessy. The rewrite process, described in *Advertisements for Myself*, was a forced march into himself, fueled by liquor, marijuana, Benzedrine, Miltown, Seconal, and finally, mescaline.

The Deer Park (1955) is a Hollywood novel, reminiscent of Nathanael West's *The Day of the Locust*. It could almost be a rewrite of *Barbary Shore* in a more realistic vein. There is the same hectic mix of politics and sex and the same corrupt, repressive climate of the 1950s. There are even the same types of characters: a young first-person narrator (Sergius), a wounded war veteran and aspiring novelist; an older man (Charles Eitel), a defiant leftist who serves as mentor to the hero; and a psychopathic young man (Marion Faye), a kind of "bad brother" to the narrator and his rival for the affections of Eitel and Eitel's woman, Elena. There is the same mythic pattern concerning the quest of the orphan hero for his identity and the same family-romance plot, a complex web of incestuous relationships.

The main difference is that *The Deer Park* deals more realistically with the human cost of politics and sex and introduces a new theme about the nobility of art, which becomes Mailer's "substitute faith." Eitel and Sergius are both artists, one a movie director and the other a would-be writer. Each is pressured by the authorities and tempted with offers of power if he submits to their demands. Sergius passes the test, but Eitel, after initially refusing to cooperate with congressional investigators, caves in and names names to their committee so he can get his Hollywood job back.

The Deer Park demonstrates the interlocking power relationships in America of sex, money, politics, and the dream factory of Hollywood, which keeps the public pacified with illusions. Desert D'Or, a resort for the movie crowd, is a sterile place of false fronts, a labyrinth where people forever chase the mirages of love or money.

Mailer sees Hollywood as dominated by Jews, but as in *The Naked and the Dead*, he portrays two very different kinds of Jews. Herman Teppis is the caricatured vulgar Jewish movie tycoon with a cigar, out to crush the noble but frail Jewish artist Eitel. They represent the conflict between movies as a business and movies as art. The villainous Teppis is created with a great deal of comic relish. Mailer views him alternately as a whoremaster marketing his stars or a ringmaster cracking the whip over his stable of performing animals.

The problem with the novel is that Desert D'Or is an inferno of endlessly repeated actions. Only Sergius escapes, but Sergius is an unconvincing character in spite of Mailer's rewrite, a passive stick-figure narrator like Lovett. The artistic alternative he finds is not dramatized. The interest in the novel instead is in the sad love affair between Eitel and Elena and in Marion Faye, a self-torturing pimp who is the secret hero of the book. Faye is a prototype of the hipster or "White Negro" who dominates Mailer's later fiction.

The Deer Park was better received by both critics and readers than *Barbary Shore*, but it was not the

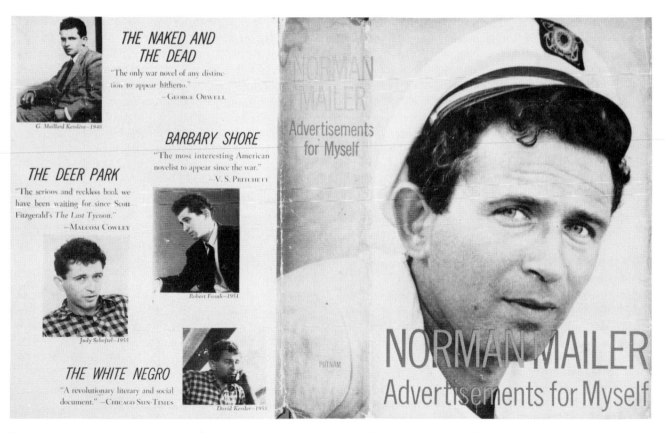

Dust jacket for Mailer's collection of writings from the first eighteen years of his career. In the autobiographical "advertisements" written to join selections together, Mailer candidly describes the pressures that success, money, liquor, and drugs have exerted on his work.

enormous success Mailer anticipated. Once again he reassessed the direction of his career. The result was *Advertisements for Myself*, a selection of pieces from his first eighteen years as a published writer tied together by brilliant introductory essays or "Advertisements," in which Mailer candidly analyzes his strengths and weaknesses as a writer. He conspicuously omits *The Naked and the Dead*, no longer wanting to be known only as the author of that novel.

The controversial *Advertisements for Myself* was a turning point in his career. It is the most candid confession of the pressures of success, money, liquor, and the literary marketplace on the serious American writer since F. Scott Fitzgerald's "The Crack-Up" (1936). To all the forces which drove Fitzgerald over the edge, Mailer adds the peculiar torment of a post-World War II American writer: the sense of being irrelevant or impotent, one more entertainer competing with all the other distractions in the circus of contemporary American life. Mailer was furious at his inability to effect change in the bland, repressive 1950s, whose cultural and political atmosphere he saw as increasingly "cancerous." But one also senses in the book the personal frustration of an outsider, a Jew, clamoring for attention from a society that refused to take him seriously.

The writing in the autobiographical passages of *Advertisements for Myself* was Mailer's best yet, establishing a new voice crackling with energy. He was throwing his hat in the ring in an open bid to be the first Jewish president of American letters. *Advertisements for Myself* did establish Mailer's claim to be a writer worth listening to, if not as a novelist then as a spokesman for himself. From that point on, he vacillated between the rather oblique rewards of the novel and other pseudofictional forms in which he placed himself at the center as the American hero for our times he had been seeking.

In *Advertisements*, Mailer includes his famous essay about a new archetype, the "White Negro" or "philosophical psychopath," a mythical hero concocted out of the psychology of Wilhelm Reich and the influence of the Beat Generation. This rebel hero is a white man who has absorbed the survival instincts of Black-American culture, a man supposedly in touch with his deepest self, who accepts each moment as it comes and lives for extreme experience, proving his manhood by immersing himself in the underworld of drugs, crime, violence, and in the quest for the perfect orgasm.

This existential hero, a rebel for the atomic age, is Mailer's instrument in his next few novels for exploring and unlocking the repressed powers of the instinctual and the irrational. He wanted to shake America back to its senses. Mailer abandoned the tradition of literary realism which had constrained him in his earlier fiction. Having performed variations on the war novel, political novel, and Hollywood novel, Mailer now began to write far bolder, more unconventional works. He forged a rhetoric that at its best is rich, playful, and vigorous (at its worst it is clotted, pretentious, and lumbering) to convey simultaneously levels of both conscious and unconscious meaning. His characters were no longer realistic, but deliberate superstereotypes, grotesques who belong in a universe of super-meaning and superrealism. He centered each work on one strong central hero who embodies the ceaseless war between the id and the superego, between the White Negro and the nice-Jewish-boy side of Mailer.

"The Time of Her Time" represents a breakthrough in Mailer's fiction and anticipates the form, style, and themes of *An American Dream*. The hero, a revitalized Sergius O'Shaugnessy, is a hipster, the antitype of the weak Jew Sam Slovoda. Mailer pits Sergius against Denise Gondelman, a "proud, aggressive, vulgar, tense, stiff and arrogant Jewess," in a sexual struggle for power. It is intended to shock the reader with the story's sexual explicitness.

Some critics see the story as Mailer's attempt to work out his Jewish self-hatred by having the first-person, Aryan narrator rape the sexually repressed Jew. Clearly one of Mailer's literary strategies has been identification with the aggressor. In both fiction and in public, he enjoys adopting the role of the antitype of the Jew: the hard-bitten Texas rifleman, the tough-talking, heavy-drinking Irishman, or the mafioso.

The 1960s were a turbulent but productive decade for Mailer. In 1960, he stabbed his wife Adele with a penknife (she recovered) and was briefly admitted to Bellevue Hospital for psychiatric observation. The incident later contributed to his novel *An American Dream*, in which a celebrated writer murders his wife. He ran unsuccessfully for mayor of New York twice, in 1960 and 1969, introducing some intriguing ideas to solve the city's problems but proving a poor politician. He had two more wives (Lady Jeanne Campbell and actress Beverly Bentley) and fathered three more children. Mailer branched out into new fields, reporting on presidential conventions and heavyweight title matches, writing a play version of *The Deer Park* which was staged off-Broadway, and directing and starring in three sporadically interesting but uneven, improvised films (*Wild 90, Beyond the Law*, and *Maidstone*). He also became a celebrity to nonreaders with his provocative statements and unpredictable behavior on television talk shows. He was attempting to become a Renaissance man, hoping that one activity would feed into another.

He put together two more collections along the lines of *Advertisements for Myself* (*The Presidential Papers*, 1963, and *Cannibals and Christians*, 1966), expounding at length on his theories about American "totalitarianism," the evils of technocracy and the plastic society, cancer, sex, excrement, the combat between God and the Devil, and the need for an existential hero to reunite the two halves of the divided American psyche. These ideas became the bases of his two novels of the decade, *An American Dream* (1965) and *Why Are We in Vietnam?* (1967). He also briefly tried to make connections between his idiosyncratic, American existentialism and Jewish mysticism, writing a series of essays for *Commentary* on the existential theologian Martin Buber.

Finally, in the 1960s, Mailer developed a hybrid form, "history as a novel," in *The Armies of the Night* (1968) and *Miami and the Siege of Chicago* (1968). This method of journalism reported on real events and real people, using the entire range of techniques for ordering experience and creating subjective meaning available to fiction. These techniques also allowed Mailer to thrust himself center stage as the hero of his own novels, a logical progression from the self-scrutiny of his critical collections.

An American Dream, because of its style, its narrative energy, and its levels of allegorical meaning, may be Mailer's best work, apart from his nonfiction novels. Written under deadline pressure for serialization in *Esquire* in 1964 and revised for publication in 1965, it reads like a single, nonstop action. Critics have either denounced it as fatuous, self-indulgent, overwritten, and morally repugnant or praised it as a powerful dream-vision of American life. In its extreme violence and hallucinatory power, it is in the tradition of Nathanael West.

This novel about a man who murders his wife and gets away with it depends upon the morality Mailer had evolved in "The White Negro," which posits a necessity sometimes to fight evil with evil, to commit violence in order to prevent the death of the soul. Mailer believes that individual, presumably "authentic" acts of violence are preferable to the collective violence of the modern bureaucratic superstate.

An American Dream acts out the explosion to the surface of the hero's (and some of Mailer's) repressed desires. In this psychological monodrama, Stephen Rojack is a kind of war correspondent reporting on the civil war inside himself. Like all Mailer heroes, he is compelled to push his obsessions to the limit and beyond, to test himself and gain masochistic pleasure from his own anxiety. Mailer is back on the exhausting long patrol of *The Naked and the Dead*, except that here it is clearly a forced march and guerrilla raid into the unconscious.

As usual, Mailer is concerned with the interplay between the various forms of American Power, including sex, politics, and money, which he conceives of in increasingly fabulous, magical terms, so that the opening page of *An American Dream* invokes Fitzgerald's fantasy of "a diamond as big as the Ritz." The Irish-Catholic Fitzgerald and the Jewish Mailer both possess the ambivalence of outsiders toward WASP American success and wealth, a combination of awed fascination and revulsion. Mailer's part-Jewish hero journeys through the levels of American society, from the underground of slum tenements to a penthouse suite in the Waldorf. This is America as dream and nightmare, seen by a Jewish outsider.

As American reality pushed on in the 1960s to new heights of violence and absurdity, so Mailer's fiction kept pace, pushing to comparable extremes in *Why Are We in Vietnam?* Taking his cue from William Burroughs's *Naked Lunch*, Mailer wrote a novel of corrosive obscenity. His hero and first-person narrator, D. J., is a lovable, incorrigibly foulmouthed Texas teenager, a modern-day Huckleberry Finn who sees through the corruption and hypocrisy of adult society, "sees through shit" as he puts it. Like *Huckleberry Finn*, *Why Are We in Vietnam?* is a tall tale and a savage comedy indicting an entire civilization.

D. J. conducts a nonstop monologue, like a mad-genius disk jockey broadcasting our dream desires. Along the way, he recounts the story of his hunting trip to Alaska with his father, Texas corporate tycoon Rusty Jethroe, and his teenage buddy, mortician's son Tex Hyde. The cowardly technological violence of the hunt, complete with excess firepower and helicopters, becomes analogous to the American experience in Vietnam.

Mailer's choice of a hero from Texas relates to then-President Lyndon Baines Johnson, a Texan Mailer had reviled in an antiwar speech at Berkeley, California, in 1965. Mailer identified Johnson as "a member of a minority group," not in the sense of being a Negro or a Jew, but as a man "alienated from the self by a double sense of identity." By this definition, said Mailer, nearly all Americans are members of a minority group, and Johnson expresses "the near insanity of most of us, and his need for action is America's need for action; not brave action, but action; any kind of action. . . . A future death of the spirit lies close and heavy upon American life, a cancerous emptiness at the center which calls for a circus." Vietnam is that bloody circus. Faced with irresolvable ambivalence and confusion of identity, at the novel's end D. J. and Tex Hyde (Jekyll and Hyde) are eagerly off to join the army: "Vietnam, hot damn."

The critic Leslie Fiedler has speculated that the rise of the American-Jewish novelist in post-World War II America is due to the fact that the Jew is the specialist in alienation, and more Americans than ever were feeling alienated. Mailer sees that alienation as a division in self or split in identity. Perhaps he was projecting the split that he sensed in his own identity as Jew and as a potential "all-American" writer and hero.

Although the theories behind *Why Are We in Vietnam?* may be intriguing, it does not succeed as fiction. Mailer inflates a short-story idea, with a minimum of conflict and grotesque caricatures instead of characters, into a novel by depending almost entirely on style. Everything is subordinated to the word—in particular, to the supposedly magical restorative power of the four-letter word. The redeeming feature of *Vietnam* is its humor, which was notably lacking in the deadly serious *An American Dream*. It paves the way toward Mailer's finest comic work, *The Armies of the Night*.

The Armies of the Night is one of the most influential works of the New Journalism of the 1960s, a movement in which reporters abandoned the pretense of objectivity toward their subjects and gave subjective responses or even participated in the events they reported. *The Armies of the Night* is an autobiographical work written in the third person about a hero named Norman Mailer. It recounts the events surrounding Mailer's arrest and imprisonment stemming from his participation in an anti-Vietnam War march on the Pentagon in 1967.

Mailer as comic hero of *The Armies of the Night* resembles in part his own antihero, the Jewish schlemiel Sam Slovoda in "The Man Who Studied Yoga." The comedy in both works depends upon the disparity between the hero's grandiose visions and the petty realities of his life. And in both works the narrator contemplates the hero's foibles with detached affection and ironic amusement.

But Mailer as hero of *The Armies of the Night* has another side he calls "the Beast." This alter ego is the antithesis of Sam, who is humane, pacifistic, and Jewish. Instead, he more closely resembles the Big Bad Wolf, Sergius in "The Time of Her Time." As the critic Richard Levine argues, "Sergius, the Cossack in Mailer, fearlessly enters the fray, while Sam, the Jew, watches from the sidelines in terror."

Mailer tends to see the Jewish side of himself as unmanly, a weak momma's boy. In *The Armies of the Night* he notes that this Jewish Mailer is too modest for his taste, "and he hated this because modesty was an old family relative, he had been born to a modest family, had been a modest boy, a modest young man, and he hated that, he loved the pride and the arrogance and the egocentricity he had gathered over the years. . . ." One senses in *The Armies of the Night* how much Mailer has attempted to remake his image over the years, to suppress what he views as his loathsomely weak side—Sam Slovoda, the Jewish intellectual—and defend against it through aggressive action and shameless exhibitionism, qualities he and many other Americans mistakenly equate with manhood. The modest, gentle Jewish man who is also part of him he sees as "a fatal taint." As he writes, "The trouble with being gentle is that one has no defense against shame."

The comedy in *The Armies of the Night* helps to balance the aggressiveness of Mailer's attack on himself, on liberal academics, and on the middle class. Mailer comes across as a heroic schlemiel, urinating on the floor in a darkened men's room, making a broken-field run in a three-piece suit to get himself arrested, exchanging insults with a Nazi in a police van ("Dirty Jew." "Kraut pig."), and being released from prison through the skill of a clever Jewish lawyer who impresses the WASP judge. In contrast to Mailer as Jewish schlemiel is the heroic dignity of poet Robert Lowell, who represents for Mailer the conscience of WASP America.

The march on the Pentagon was an inconclusive, ambiguous event, not a turning point in national history. If it is recalled today, it is largely because Norman Mailer was there and chose to write about it. He does succeed, nevertheless, in capturing and making comprehensible for us the drift of American history in the 1960s and the behavior of an individual caught up in a crucial event of a mass movement.

Later Mailer applied similar novelistic techniques to his reports on the 1968 presidential conventions in *Miami and the Siege of Chicago* (1968) and on man's landing on the moon in *Of a Fire on the Moon* (1970). However, these works are not as compelling as *The Armies of the Night* because Mailer was more of a reporter than an active participant in these events; readers are deprived of the focus on the adventures of a comic hero to unify the action and hold interest.

Mailer's twenty-year-long experiment with form—from omniscience, to first-person, to essays and reportage, to self-interviews—culminated in *The Armies of the Night*, in whose third-person narration and formal tone he found a congenial solution to the problem of presenting himself in print without seeming too aggressive or too egotistical. He harnessed his aggression and ambivalence in a form and style that yielded maximum dividends. The problem was that, having found the most successful form with which to express his warring tendencies, he began to repeat himself and to fall, like Hemingway, into self-parody. After *The Armies of the Night* the form wore thin; the voice became overly familiar; the one major character (Norman Mailer) was overexposed; and the constant forcing of reality into warring opposites (good versus evil, God versus Devil) became boring and predictable. In the 1970s, Mailer produced a prodigious amount—the moon-landing book, a biography of Marilyn Monroe, more accounts of boxing matches and political conventions, two more collections of assorted pieces, an attack on the Women's Movement (*The Prisoner of Sex*, 1971), and an homage to Henry Miller—but it seemed as if he were marking time. Temporarily he lost his major asset as a writer, the ability to shock and startle us.

His private life was as busy as ever: two more wives (Carol Stevens and Norris Church) and two more children, for a current total of six marriages and eight offspring. In 1974, in the wake of Watergate, he announced the organization of a citizen's group called the Fifth Estate to investigate the FBI and the CIA. Nothing has been heard of this plan since. The same year, he signed a reportedly million-dollar contract to write an epic novel for Little, Brown. Mailer needed the money to keep up with taxes and large alimony and child support payments. The novel, *Ancient Evenings*, was eventually published in 1983. By then, Mailer's contract with Little, Brown had been renegotiated to four million dollars: *Ancient Evenings* was going to be part of a trilogy. The epic he had been promising and demanding of himself for so long was on its way.

In 1979, Mailer again displayed his astonishing versatility as a writer, combining his talents as reporter and storyteller in *The Executioner's Song*, a "True Life Novel" recounting the last year in the life of Gary Gilmore, the Utah murderer who in 1977 became the first prisoner executed in the United States in a decade. The work won the Pulitzer Prize.

In this massive novel, Mailer seems to have come full circle, returning to the omniscient point of view, the relatively plain style and objective narration, and the panoramic sweep of *The Naked and the Dead*. Selecting from thousands of pages of interviews with dozens of people, Mailer pieced together his own imaginative re-creation and synthesis of events, fashioning a moving, painstakingly thorough account of the life and death of a charismatic criminal and the extraordinary effect he had on those around him.

If the cold-blooded killer Gilmore seems at first a surprising hero for a work by an American-Jewish author, he turns out in the end to be of possibly Jewish descent. Circumstantial evidence suggests he may have been the child of the illegitimate son of Harry Houdini, the Jewish magician. The narrative frequently compares Gilmore to Houdini; both were escape artists who made a living risking their lives. When one of the characters shakes hands with Gilmore as the convict faces the firing squad, "It was as if he was saying good-bye to a man who was going to step into a cannon and be fired to the moon, or dropped into an iron chamber at the bottom of the sea, a veritable Houdini."

Mailer's counterpart in the work is Lawrence Schiller, the promoter who buys the rights to Gilmore's story. Schiller is an outsider, a Sammy Glick-style hustler who nevertheless suffers moral qualms about his part in the media circus surrounding the execution: "I don't know any longer whether what I'm doing is morally right."

Negative criticism of the book centered on this same moral issue: was Mailer exploiting real people and tragic events and glorifying a vicious criminal? But Mailer's work had been criticized on moral grounds in the past. He thrives on moral controversy, and it is unlikely to deter him from future investigations of the full range of human behavior.

Mailer found himself once again embroiled in real-life controversy in 1982. The book on Gilmore led him into a correspondence with a convict at Utah State Prison, Jack Henry Abbott. Mailer promoted the publication of Abbott's eloquent prison letters in a volume entitled *In the Belly of the Beast* and helped him gain release on parole. Abbott, however, soon stabbed to death a young waiter in New York, and Mailer was called to testify on Abbott's behalf. Mailer was severely criticized by the media, since he appeared once again to be defending or romanticizing violence by placing a writer above the law.

His next work of fiction was *Of Women and Their Elegance* (1980), an expensive book containing photos of beautiful women and the text of a novel, a first-person story narrated by Marilyn Monroe. The work continues Mailer's obsession with the actress, to whom he had already devoted "a biography in novel form." Both books are filled with lurid speculation and projection of motives onto her which tell far more about the author than they do about Monroe. This work will add little to his reputation as a writer.

In 1982, Mailer's *Pieces and Pontifications*, a collection of interviews and essays from the 1970s, was published. This kind of volume—Mailer has produced one every few years since *Advertisements for Myself*—serves the author as a means of organizing his output and taking stock of his ideas before he moves on to new projects.

Finally, in 1983, after ten years of intermittent labor on the project, Mailer's long-promised epic, the Egyptian novel *Ancient Evenings*, was published. It is the first volume of a proposed trilogy intended to range from ancient Egypt into our future. Mailer claims the three novels will total nearly a million words and says, "I've got a terribly tricky way of tying them up."

Ancient Evenings is the most ambitious and daringly innovative of Mailer's fictions. He takes

Mailer at New York's Books & Company, giving a prepublication reading from Ancient Evenings *(photo by Layle Silbert)*

large risks in terms of form, style, and subject matter (although the gambles do not always pay off). The reviews have been mixed: many critics found Mailer's obsession with scatology and sodomy repetitious, even ludicrous and embarrassing. But granted Mailer's excesses in this regard, the novel is still a significant and worthwhile experiment.

Ancient Evenings is best evaluated not as a work of realism or even as historical fiction but as fantasy. Mailer has veered toward fantasy before: *Barbary Shore* is set in an imaginary near future, *An American Dream* operates by dream logic, and *Why Are We in Vietnam?* is filled with mysticism. But setting a novel entirely in ancient Egypt allows Mailer to work out on a grand scale his theories about the interconnections of sex, violence, and power. In this historical fantasia, he is completely freed from the limitations of the contemporary scene and the restrictions of novelistic realism. Instead he is able to create a world of the imagination: a sweeping panorama of kings, gods, and devils, barbaric violence, and epic fornications. *Ancient Evenings* is a tale of mysticism and magic, introduced with an epigraph from Yeats and concerned with extrasensory perception, life after death, and reincarnation.

The introduction of a narrator who is a ghost (or rather the "Ka" or spiritual double of the dead Menenhetet II, or Meni) and who has telepathic powers allows Mailer to experiment with point of view, combining some of the advantages of first-person and omniscient narration. Mailer has used "ghost" narrators before, in "The Man Who Studied Yoga" (1952) and "Advertisements for Myself on the Way Out" (1959), but not until *Ancient Evenings* does he exploit such a narrator's potential in a long fiction.

Through fantasy, Mailer is also able to create a mythical hero who lives many lives. The bulk of the narrative (it is constructed of tales within tales and shuttles between the past and the land of the dead) concerns the lives of Menenhetet I, Meni's great-grandfather, who has supposedly been reincarnated four times. In the end, the souls of Meni and of his great-grandfather mate; the two heroes become one, and our new hero struggles to be reborn.

If the florid prose style Mailer concocts to convey his fantastic tale at times becomes overblown or silly, it is also capable of effects of lyric beauty or horror, as in the descriptions of the great battle of Kadesh. Finally, his purple prose is necessary to transport us to a world as alien as some distant planet.

Another primary critical objection to *Ancient Evenings* is that, in writing about ancient Egypt,

Dust jacket for Mailer's most recent novel, the first volume of a projected trilogy which, by the author's estimate, will total nearly a million words

tell us—precisely because they came before the Judeo-Christian era—about power, wealth, sex and death, and right in there is waste, excrement. . . . It's no secret that Freud gave us a firm set of connections between anality and power . . . and what I learned about Egypt seemed a kind of confirmation." In other words, in Mailer's estimation he is not so much rebelling against the Judeo-Christian ethic as he is trying to discover what preceded it.

The body of Mailer's fiction thus far, for all its unevenness, shows a wide scope and flexibility, a willingness to experiment and to tackle controversial, major themes which place him in the top rank of American-Jewish novelists. The irresolvable contradictions in Mailer's personality, between the "nice Jewish boy from Brooklyn" and the all-American wild man, paradoxically make him remarkably open to a range of experiences and themes alien to most American-Jewish fiction.

Interviews:

Robert Begiebing, "Twelfth Round," *Harvard Magazine* (March-April 1983): 40-50;

George Plimpton, Interview with Norman Mailer, *People* (30 May 1983): 53-59.

Bibliography:

Laura Adams, ed., *Norman Mailer: A Comprehensive Bibliography* (Metuchen, N.J.: Scarecrow, 1974).

Biography:

Hilary Mills, *Norman Mailer: A Biography* (New York: Empire Books, 1982).

References:

Laura Adams, *Existential Battles: The Growth of Norman Mailer* (Athens: Ohio University Press, 1976);

Adams, ed., *Will the Real Norman Mailer Please Stand Up?* (Port Washington, N.Y.: Kennikat, 1974);

Jennifer Bailey, *Norman Mailer: Quick-Change Artist* (New York: Harper & Row, 1979);

Robert J. Begiebing, *Acts of Regeneration: Allegory and Archetype in the Works of Norman Mailer* (Columbia: University of Missouri Press, 1980);

Leo Braudy, ed., *Norman Mailer: A Collection of Critical Essays* (Englewood Cliffs, N.J.: Prentice-Hall, 1972);

Philip M. Bufithis, *Norman Mailer* (New York: Ungar, 1978);

Robert Ehrlich, *Norman Mailer: The Radical as Hipster* (Metuchen, N.J.: Scarecrow, 1978);

Mailer has slighted his own Jewish heritage. In particular, Leslie Fiedler claims that "the return to Egypt becomes for Mailer a deliberate inversion of the myth of the exodus—in which he is able to project once more his lifelong fantasy of becoming the 'Golden Goy,' as his surrogate, Menenhetet, rises . . . to sit at the right hand of a king who is also a god and makes it into the bed of his wife." Moreover, notes Fiedler, in Mailer's novel Moses is "demoted to the status of a second-rate magician." Finally, Fiedler claims that Mailer's obsession with the act of homosexual rape is a way to transgress "all the laws of Israel."

Mailer defends himself in interviews by explaining that he is trying to write about the world *before* the Judeo-Christian era, about a time in which the Jews were still "a race of tribes and barbarians," not yet taken seriously. He worked hard to eliminate all Judeo-Christian ideas from his novel. Mailer's point is that "the Egyptians have much to

Leslie Fiedler, "Going for the Long Ball," *Psychology Today* (June 1983): 16-17;

Joe Flaherty, *Managing Mailer* (New York: Coward-McCann, 1970);

Richard Foster, *Norman Mailer* (Minneapolis: University of Minnesota Press, 1968);

Andrew Gordon, *An American Dreamer: A Psychoanalytic Study of the Fiction of Norman Mailer* (Cranbury, N.J.: Associated University Presses, 1980);

Stanley T. Gutman, *Mankind in Barbary: The Individual and Society in the Novels of Norman Mailer* (Hanover, N.H.: University Press of New England, 1976);

Donald L. Kaufmann, *Norman Mailer: The Countdown (The First Twenty Years)* (Carbondale: Southern Illinois University Press, 1969);

Barry Leeds, *The Structured Vision of Norman Mailer*

(New York: New York University Press, 1969);

Robert F. Lucid, ed., *Norman Mailer: The Man and His Work* (Boston: Little, Brown, 1971);

Peter Manso, ed., *Running Against the Machine: The Mailer-Breslin Campaign* (Garden City: Doubleday, 1969);

Robert Merrill, *Norman Mailer* (Boston: Twayne, 1978);

Jonathan Middlebrook, *Mailer and the Times of His Time* (San Francisco: Bay Books, 1976);

Richard Poirier, *Norman Mailer* (New York: Viking, 1972);

Jean Radford, *Norman Mailer: A Critical Study* (New York: Harper & Row, 1975);

Robert Solotaroff, *Down Mailer's Way* (Urbana: University of Illinois Press, 1974);

W. S. Weatherby, *Squaring Off: Mailer vs. Baldwin* (New York: Mason/Charter, 1977).

Bernard Malamud
(26 April 1914-   )

Leslie Field
Purdue University

See also the Malamud entries in *DLB 2, American Novelists Since World War II*, and *DLB Yearbook: 1980*.

BOOKS: *The Natural* (New York: Harcourt, Brace, 1952; London: Eyre & Spottiswoode, 1963);

The Assistant (New York: Farrar, Straus & Cudahy, 1957; London: Eyre & Spottiswoode, 1959);

The Magic Barrel (New York: Farrar, Straus & Cudahy, 1958; London: Eyre & Spottiswoode, 1960);

A New Life (New York: Farrar, Straus & Cudahy, 1961; London: Eyre & Spottiswoode, 1962);

Idiots First (New York: Farrar, Straus, 1963; London: Eyre & Spottiswoode, 1964);

The Fixer (New York: Farrar, Straus & Giroux, 1966; London: Eyre & Spottiswoode, 1967);

A Malamud Reader, edited by Philip Rahv (New York: Farrar, Straus & Giroux, 1967);

Pictures of Fidelman: An Exhibition (New York: Farrar, Straus & Giroux, 1969; London: Eyre & Spottiswoode, 1970);

The Tenants (New York: Farrar, Straus & Giroux,

1971; London: Eyre Methuen, 1972);

Rembrandt's Hat (New York: Farrar, Straus & Giroux, 1973; London: Eyre Methuen, 1973);

Dubin's Lives (New York: Farrar, Straus & Giroux, 1979; London: Chatto & Windus, 1979);

God's Grace (New York: Farrar, Straus & Giroux, 1982; London: Chatto & Windus, 1982);

The Stories of Bernard Malamud (New York: Farrar, Straus & Giroux, 1983; London: Chatto & Windus, 1984).

Bernard Malamud writes Jewish-American fiction. He has been a leader in this field for years and has received international acclaim for his novels and short stories. His first short story, "Benefit Performance," appeared in *Threshold* in 1943. Forty years later, of his more than forty stories he selected twenty-five which he considered his best for publication in *The Stories of Bernard Malamud* (1983).

Malamud has also had six novels and one novella published. One novel, *The Fixer* (1966), and one short story, "Angel Levine," have been made

Bernard Malamud (photo by Layle Silbert)

into movies. His first novel, *The Natural* (1952), is scheduled for the movies in 1984, with Robert Redford starring as outfielder Roy Hobbs.

In May of 1983 Malamud was the recipient of one of the most prestigious honors that can be given to American writers: the Gold Medal for Fiction from the American Academy and Institute of Arts and Letters. Bennington College, in its *Quadrille* "Faculty Notes," pointed out that Malamud was "cited for his variations on themes from scripture," which he treated with "dignity, humor, honor."

The *Quadrille* further reported that when Malamud accepted his award he recalled Virginia Woolf's personal and writing trials: "Her life reminds me of many fine writers working in every wind and weather, some rich, some poor, all laboring in good and bad times—perhaps like ours today—to create their best forms, conscious of their privilege to live their lives in art. I have had that privilege for a while, and would gladly embrace it again if I could do the work better than before."

Malamud was born in Brooklyn, New York, in 1914, to Max and Bertha Fidelman Malamud. His parents, Russian-Jewish immigrants, ran a Mom-and-Pop grocery store in Brooklyn; this milieu later provided Malamud with the Depression-America context for *The Assistant* (1957). The ambience of Malamud's early life in Brooklyn is fictionalized in many of his stories and novels. From 1928 to 1932 he was a student at Brooklyn's Erasmus Hall High School. There his earliest stories were published in the literary magazine, the *Erasmian*. In 1936 Malamud received his B.A. from the City College of New York; he earned his M.A. from Columbia University in 1942. His M.A. thesis dealt with Thomas Hardy's *The Dynasts*. Critics have noted the strong resemblance between Hardy's and Malamud's brooding protagonists. Malamud planned to teach English in the New York public schools; however, during the pre-World War II period jobs were still scarce. So he took a job in Washington, D.C., with the Bureau of Census.

But he soon returned to New York, taught English in the evenings at Erasmus Hall High School, and wrote during the day. Then on 6 November 1945, he married Ann De Chiara, an Italian-American. He has often said that through his wife he gained an appreciation of the rich Italian culture in the United States and Italy. He and his wife have been frequent visitors to Italy, where his wife still has family, and it follows that many of the locales of his stories are Italian.

In his early married years Malamud continued to work at teaching and nonteaching jobs. His last New York teaching position at this time was in 1948-1949, evenings, at Harlem High School. Simultaneously, his short stories appeared in a variety of magazines; they reflected his experiences with and interest in the minority peoples of New York: Italians, blacks, Jews, and others.

In 1949 Malamud accepted an English instructorship at Oregon State University at Corvallis. Eventually he was promoted to associate professor, and he stayed at Oregon State until 1961. The university and its environs became the subject of his satiric academic novel, *A New Life* (1961). While living in the West and teaching a full load of composition at this agricultural and technical arts university, he found time to continue writing his fiction. Before he left the East, in 1947, his son Paul was born. Then in 1952, while he was at Oregon State, his daughter Janna was born. In 1956 the Malamud family interrupted their stay at Corvallis to live in Rome and travel in Europe. A *Partisan Review* fellowship helped defray the European expenses. Malamud's Italian sojourn is fictionalized in stories such as "The Lady of the Lake," "Naked Nude," and others which became a significant part of his first three collections of stories, especially *Pictures of Fidelman* (1969).

In 1961 Malamud accepted a position at Bennington College in Vermont in the Division of Language and Literature. He is still a member of the Bennington faculty and usually teaches one course there per year and divides his time between residence in rural Bennington and an apartment in New York City. His latest writings draw heavily upon the Vermont locale for setting and atmosphere, most notably in *Dubin's Lives* (1979). Periodically he interrupts his Bennington-New York life to travel and lecture. In 1963 he visited England and Italy. In 1965 he traveled through the U.S.S.R., France, and Spain. From 1966 to 1968 he was a visiting lecturer at Harvard University. In 1968 he toured Israel. In 1983 he was in Italy once again, at the Bellagio Study and Conference Center, which is a retreat for writers and scholars endowed by the Rockefeller Foundation.

In a recent interview with Karen Heller for *USA Today*, Malamud talked about his latest collection of short stories: "These are my best stories," he said. "I am a universal writer. I think I'm generally recognized as that. . . . There is some sense of me in all of [my fiction]. . . . It's my given experience. I'm merely addressing a vital but necessarily limited experience. . . . I am an inventive writer. . . . If you stay locked in one place you don't grow. . . . I like to work from city to city, from garden to garden, writing about what I know."

The plots of Malamud's novels are deceptively simple, and in some ways Malamud's short stories are simple also. For example, the straightforward opening sentences of his earliest stories are stylistically instructive: "Kessler, formerly an egg candler, lived alone on social security." "Manischevitz, a tailor, in his fifty-first year suffered many reverses and indignities." "Henry Levin, an ambitious, handsome thirty, who walked the floors of Macy's book department wearing a white flower in his lapel, having recently come into a small inheritance, quit, and went abroad seeking romance." "Not long ago there lived in uptown New York, in a small, almost meager room, though crowded with books, Leo Finkle, a rabbinical student in the Yeshiva University."

Malamud's first novel, *The Natural*, is a sports story. Roy Hobbs, the protagonist, is a baseball player who wants to be the best. He does achieve success, but he abandons the people who mean most to him as he furthers his own career. In *The Natural* Malamud sees baseball history as "the distillation of American life." In interviews he admitted that he used real events to avoid contrivance and to reveal baseball as the ritual for expressing American life. Other elements, Arthurian legend and Jungian mythic psychology, which are used to interpret the ritual, make baseball into a symbol, according to Earl R. Wasserman in "*The Natural*: World Ceres," of "man's psychological and moral situation."

However, Wasserman points out, even this early work foreshadows what was to become a typical Malamud hero or antihero. Malamud's baseball hero became an "amalgam of the heroic myth and its democratic offspring, the Horatio Alger story." Roy Hobbs can be seen as a *failed* hero because he cannot act within the prescribed mythology.

After *The Natural*, Malamud continued to write short stories. In 1958, after his second novel, *The Assistant*, had appeared, he received several national awards, including the Rosenthal Foundation Award of the National Institute of Arts and Letters and the Daroff Memorial Fiction Award of the Jewish Book Council of America. Because of *The Assistant*'s depiction of ethnicity, Malamud became classified as a Jewish-American writer—that class of American writers which includes Saul Bellow, Henry Roth, Philip Roth, and Edward Lewis Wallant—as distinguished from the Yiddish-American schmaltz industry housing writers of ethnic sentimentality.

The Assistant, set in Brooklyn, has as its main characters the Jewish proprietor of a run-down grocery store, Morris Bober, and the young man who will become his assistant, Frank Alpine, an Italian-American. In this novel much is made of Bober's bad luck as contrasted with the good fortune of others. The tangled love affair between Morris's daughter, Helen, and Frank provides a strong motif. But the most important part of the tale focuses on the father-son relationship between Morris and Frank and the difficult question of the meaning of Jewishness.

In *The Assistant* Malamud constructs two cultures, one based on Jewish tradition and the other on the American heritage. And he depicts a collision between Old World wisdom and New World practicality with its ethos of success. But critics recognized that the characters in this novel relate to both worlds ironically, in many ways presenting a continuation of Malamud's twisted heroes.

In 1958, Malamud's first collection of short stories, *The Magic Barrel*, was published to wide acclaim. Although some of Malamud's finest short stories appear in *The Magic Barrel*, it may be more instructive to examine the collection of six stories called *Pictures of Fidelman*, which appeared as a unit

Dust jacket for Malamud's first story collection, winner of a 1959 National Book Award

in 1969 but which had been published over a period of twelve years. A close reading of the stories reveals complexity of theme and motif to counteract simplicity of plot. "The Last Mohican" was part of *The Magic Barrel*. Others were included in Malamud's second collection, *Idiots First* (1963); two of the final three stories were published in magazines. And then all six were brought together in somewhat revised form as *Pictures of Fidelman: An Exhibition*.

In this book, Malamud resurrects his antihero—Arthur Fidelman—conceived years earlier in "The Last Mohican" as a young Jewish-American art critic in Rome. Fidelman continues his adolescence as a would-be artist in Rome and Milan in "Still-Life" and "Naked Nude," achieves schlemieldom's young manhood—still as artist—in other Italian cities (in "A Pimp's Revenge" and "Pictures of the Artist") and, finally, emerges as an adult artist-schlemiel in Venice. His emergence

takes place in the last story, "Glass Blower of Venice," in which, ostensibly, the schlemiel discovers life and the true meaning of love, gives up art per se, and goes back to America to become a *mensch*, or human being.

So ends the saga of Arthur Fidelman—or is it only the beginning of an understanding not only of this book but of much of the rest of Malamud's work?

Had Malamud simply created the Yiddish figure of the schlemiel, he might have ended with farce or slapstick. However, in this story sequence, as in the novels, Malamud seems intent on unfolding his themes bit by bit as he reveals character. Fidelman's habitual pattern is that of apprenticeship or education. And the subgenre he belongs to falls into the category which has been distinguished by German criticism as the Bildungsroman, or, because the book traces the growth of a hero as creative man, the Künstlerroman. In 1961, as readers were getting accustomed to Malamud the short-story writer, the baseball-story writer, the Jewish-American novelist, he put his stamp on another subgenre, the academic novel, with the publication of *A New Life*.

In *A New Life* the hero is S. Levin, who comes from New York City to be an instructor of English at an agricultural and technical college in the Pacific Northwest. Levin wants to "awaken" his students, but his new life awakens him too. Much of the novel is a satire of academic life.

After *A New Life*, the short stories continued, and new ones were collected in *Idiots First*. Then in 1966 *The Fixer* was published. In *The Fixer*, set in early twentieth-century czarist Russia, Yakov Bok moves out of the ghetto and passes himself off as a non-Jew. He is accused of the ritual murder of a Christian boy and imprisoned. In prison he discovers much about himself and the Jewish heritage which he had previously rejected.

This novel departs drastically from the subjects of Malamud's earlier stories and novels. Some dismissed *The Fixer* as merely another historical novel in the Dreyfus or Sacco-Vanzetti mold, except that in this instance the victim was modeled on Mendel Beiliss, who had been accused of using blood of a young Christian to bake Passover matzoth. Others, usually perceptive Malamud critics, moved back and forth in the body of Malamud's work—from his early short stories through his recent novels—to show significant patterns which, if they do not negate the periodic classifications of Malamud's work, at least put them into new perspectives and certainly emphasize a sophisticated and consistent schematization.

From Roy Hobbs of *The Natural* and Frank Alpine of *The Assistant*, through Seymour Levin of *A New Life*, Yakov Bok of *The Fixer*, and especially Arthur Fidelman, who comes to rest in *Pictures of Fidelman*, the Malamud schlemiel is used to realize a variety of themes and motifs. The pattern continues in Harry Lesser of *The Tenants* (1971), a novel about two writers—Lesser, a Jew, and Willie Spearmint, a militant black—who are the sole occupants of a New York City tenement scheduled soon for demolition; in William Dubin, the biographer caught up in a mid-life crisis in *Dubin's Lives* (1979); and in Calvin Cohn, sole survivor of "the thermonuclear war between the Djanks and the Druzhkies," in the novella *God's Grace* (1982).

The schlemiel also appears in the recent stories collected in *Rembrandt's Hat* (1973). In "The Silver Crown," for example, a young biology teacher purchases a silver crown from a wonder rabbi for $986, ostensibly to cure his father of cancer. The father dies. In "Man in the Drawer" Howard Harvitz, a writer, leaves America to forget his troubles, and in all the great expanse of Russia, he is the one, miraculously, to stumble on a Jewish taxi driver / author who pushes a forbidden manuscript on him, one which, if he agrees to smuggle it out of the country, can land the American in trouble much more serious than that he had originally tried to escape. And in the story which gives the collection its name is a final scene showing Rubin, the schlemiel, in the men's room "regarding himself in the mirror in his white cap, the one that seemed to resemble Rembrandt's hat. He wore it like a crown of failure and hope."

Of course the schlemiel is merely one theme or motif that many critics have noted in Malamud's fiction from *The Natural* to *God's Grace*. Whether the schlemiel epitomizes the born loser, the hard-luck guy, the poignant misfit, or collectively world Jewry, he has a long and honorable history. He can be traced back to the nineteenth-century Yiddish writers who created types like Tevye the milkman and extended forward to the New-World Herzogs and Fidelmans. The schlemiel is a composite of history, legend, myth, and folklore. And underlying all is the comic element. More often than not the comic figure of the schlemiel seems to be a victim, but because he and his creators redefine his world, in the end he achieves the moral victory often denied to others.

When Malamud has been asked for his reaction to the many recent commentaries on the use of the schlemiel in his fiction, he has replied "with

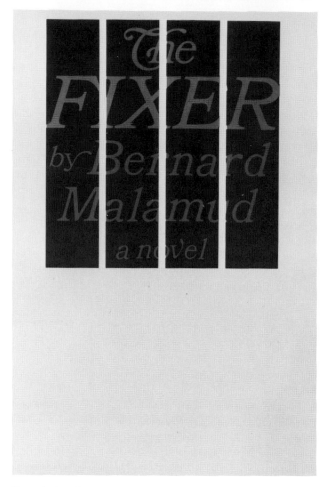

Dust jacket for Malamud's fourth novel, winner of both a Pulitzer Prize and a National Book Award

many apologies" that he does not "much care for the Schlemiel treatment of fictional characters." Of course he has a point if the schlemiel is used as a reductive approach. But just as there must be a built-in tension between the president and the press, so there must often be tension between an author and the community of critics.

In *The Fixer*, winner of a National Book Award and a Pulitzer Prize, all the themes which Malamud had introduced in his earlier works are refined and brilliantly reworked into their most powerful, controlled, and effective statement. In an interview Malamud reaffirmed his concern with several of these interrelated themes. Some of the most significant are a search for a new life in the manner of the Bildungsroman; the prison motif; the necessity for moral involvement, or freedom versus responsibility; the value of suffering; the meaning of Jewishness; the ritualistic and mythic elements in life; the search for a father or a son displacing a "father," or the scapegoat and orphan motifs; and consuming concern with Humanity (*Menshlechkeit*), Love, Mercy (*Rachmones*). Although it may be difficult to separate these themes sharply because they are so closely interwoven, through an examination of these elements which permeate the works before and after *The Fixer* the continuity and development of Malamud's essential concerns as a writer can be seen.

The theme of a new life involves the protagonist's leaving his home in search of change, a second chance, new opportunities. Sometimes the change brings good, sometimes not. On the surface, the change may involve only different surroundings. But the change should—to be beneficial—involve growth in the person from boyhood to manhood, that is, a giving up of the selfish concerns of youth for involvement in the problems of mankind, an acceptance of life's responsibilities.

In *The Assistant*, Frank Alpine's conversion to Judaism leads to such a change. But for Roy Hobbs, the failed hero of *The Natural*, the change in his physical surroundings does not include this necessary interior growth, and thus he is a failure. S. Levin, in the novel *A New Life*, goes west to a new career in new surroundings and freedom. What he finds, eventually, is a third new life when he gives up the Greek dream of freedom for the Jewish acceptance of responsibility and moral entanglement. When Henry Levin, in "The Lady of the Lake" (collected in *The Magic Barrel*), changes his name to Henry Freeman to escape his Jewishness, this denial of his past leads to the loss of his beloved, a concentration-camp survivor who says she has suffered too much for her heritage to betray it. Because Levin-Freeman refuses to accept his Jewishness, his change brings him no good.

In his search for increased opportunities outside of the prison-life confines of the *shtetl*, Yakov Bok shaves off his beard and changes his name. This change brings disaster. Ironically, however, inside the actual prison Yakov learns that the purpose of freedom is to create it for others. His change brings moral growth. By refusing to confess and betray Russian Jewry, he accepts responsibility for the Jewish community and becomes actively involved in the fate of his people.

In *Dubin's Lives*, Malamud's most recent novel, William Dubin is in constant movement from old life to new. As a biographer he moves from "ice-cold" H. D. Thoreau to his current project, "red-hot" D. H. Lawrence. As a man he also moves in a sense from cold to hot, from age to youth, that is, from Kitty, his wife of many years, to barefoot Fanny, who is young and voluptuous. In the end Dubin ambiguously seems to have reconciled himself to both youth and age, then and now.

In Malamud's fictional world, there is always a prison. It can lie in the physical environment—a grocery store, a tenement, an artist's garret, a bordello, a *shtetl*, or a real prison cell. But it can also lie in being imprisoned by one's own self and within one's self, being confined by one's ineptitudes and thus becoming a victim of one's own self.

Some critics have said that Malamud's central metaphor of Jewishness is the prison, a perfect symbol for the human and most particularly the Jewish condition. Metaphorically, the prison becomes an acceptance of life's limitations and responsibilities, and thus, ironically, in imprisonment there can be freedom.

In "Jewishness as Metaphor" Robert Alter says that the prison "is Malamud's way of suggesting that to be fully a man is to accept the most painful limitations; those who escape them . . . achieve only an illusory self-negating kind of freedom, for they become less than responsible humans." And Malamud himself has said in a 1975 interview that the prison is "a metaphor for the dilemma of all men throughout history. Necessity is the primary prison, though the bars are not visible to all. Then there are the man-made prisons of social injustice, apathy, ignorance. . . . Our most extraordinary invention is human freedom."

Malamud's work argues the necessity for moral involvement over the seductions of freedom (disengagement) and examines the value of suffering. The reader becomes immersed in this area in much that is elusive and overlapping, and not in the least in Malamud's often-cited enigmatic statement that "all men are Jews." A few years back Malamud recalled that he had said "all men are Jews except they don't know it." To be sure, he did not expect people to take his words literally. But he does believe that it is "an understandable statement and a metaphoric way of indicating how history, sooner or later, treats all men." It is doubtful that Malamud has said his last word on this matter. However, at this time his definition of Jewishness includes such universal human virtues as moral obligation to one's fellow man and the community, acceptance of responsibility, involvement in the suffering of others, and learning from one's own suffering. Thus an expanded definition or a metaphoric elaboration emerges.

In Malamud this metaphor seems to find its most comprehensive application in the gallery of Jewish characters—Bober, Bok, Levin, Fidelman,

Lesser, Dubin, and Cohn. Bok as paradigm becomes the father-hero if the focus is on his last vision. Here he symbolically kills the czar, the Little Father of Russia, and it may be assumed, as in ritual, thus displaces and replaces the father. He reminds the czar that because, as leader of his people, he has failed to rule with justice and mercy, he has failed in his charge. According to Bok's view of Spinoza, if the State "acts in ways . . . abhorrent to human nature it's the lesser evil to destroy it." And, "better him the Czar than us." The reader should remember that "us."

Yakov Bok learns to accept his Jewishness, too. "We're all in history . . . but some more than others, Jews more than some." As Bok concludes, "One thing I've learned . . . there's no such thing as an unpolitical man, especially a Jew." Truly, as Malamud writes, "he has stepped into history."

As for the value of suffering, Bok says while in prison, contemplating death because he thinks he can endure no more, "What have I earned if a single Jew dies because I did . . . if I must suffer, let it be for something." Here, of course, he is echoing Morris Bober as he defines his role of suffering Jew to Frank Alpine in *The Assistant*. When his lawyer says to him, "You suffer for us all," Bok answers, "It's without honor." Nevertheless, by this time he has accepted his fate. How far he has come in seventy pages. Earlier, "His fate nauseated him. Escaping from the Pale he had at once been entrapped in prison. From birth a black horse had followed him, a Jewish nightmare. What was being a Jew but an everlasting curse? He was sick of their history, destiny, blood guilt." In the last pages, however, *they* becomes *we*. Earlier he had said that "he suffers for no one but himself." At the end he acknowledges that he has suffered for all Jews. He notes that he has learned from and been changed by his experiences: "I'm not the same man I once was." Before the trial Bok decides to fast "for God's world." The guard says, "I thought you didn't believe in God." Bok answers, "I don't."

Despite the complexities and nuances, it does seem that the Bobers, Boks, Lessers, and many other Malamud characters are ultimately revealed as people who become involved in one way or another, but always positively, and always with the Jewish milieu.

A considerable body of Malamud criticism has been devoted to discovering and analyzing his use of myth, ritual, and symbolism: vegetation rituals, seasonal patterns, fertility myths, Grail quests, the myth of Fisher King, the figures of the orphaned hero and the scapegoat, Christian symbols, and the symbolism of names. Much of this complex analysis is dependent upon a close examination of the texts; unfortunately, popular commentary on Malamud's fiction often ignores the intricate symbolism and the patterns of meaning which Malamud so painstakingly weaves into his work.

Working with Yakov Bok's name and the idea of the scapegoat, some of the complexities and nuances become apparent. In old Hebraic use a scapegoat is literally a live goat; the meaning is extended to a person or group bearing the guilt for a larger group. The name Bok means goat, and his patronymic Shepsovich means son of a sheep. The charge of ritual murder against Bok is really an indictment against the entire Jewish nation, Bok simply being the "accidental" victim standing for all Jewry.

Seasonal patterns of myth are also apparent in *The Fixer* and are quite important in *The Natural, The Assistant, A New Life*, and *Dubin's Lives*. Certain events occur appropriately at specific seasons, thus leading the reader to tie the present to the sweep of history and to ancient myths and rituals.

Perhaps one of the most important of the mythic elements in Malamud's work involves the search for a father—either real or spiritual, within or outside of oneself. Although the theme is found frequently in Greek literature and in the folklore of all peoples, historically the search for a father is central to Jewish writings. Beginning with the Jewish patriarchs—Abraham, Isaac, Jacob—the motif finds further expression in the story of Moses and the Exodus and runs through the great history of biblical kings where there occurs between the ambivalent Davids and Solomons hostility and acceptance, hate and love. Overarching all is the tension between the acceptance and the rejection of the Father of us all—the One God. In this sense Malamud is a very Judaic writer, who tends, ironically, to undercut the Christian themes that appear in his work. Most of his heroes or antiheroes or schlemiels are still young and are either orphans or have vague, ineffectual fathers somewhere in their backgrounds.

In almost all cases Malamud depicts men who are free spirits, who insist upon freedom—but at the same time are destroying themselves because of that freedom. They have no purpose, no goal. And there is no one to guide them; there is no authority. Even though Frank Alpine, S. Levin, Yakov Bok, and William Dubin do not realize it, they are looking for that authority or guide which is represented by a real or substitute Father and/or God. Frank Alpine accepts and then becomes Morris Bober. S. Levin accepts responsibility as a father. Yakov Bok accepts Raizl's child as his own. Harry Lesser accepts Willie Spearmint as brother-son. Even William Dubin, a much older protagonist, seems to accept the responsibility of marriage. It may be that one of the most important elements in Malamud's handling of this theme is that the Yakov Boks accept themselves, their families, their communities; they step out of a nebulous history in limbo into the Judaic tradition of Abraham, Isaac, Jacob—and the covenant with God. Whether or not they would approve this formal Judaic tradition, they have indeed become *menshen*.

This change brings up the Humanity or *Menshlechkeit* theme in Malamud—Love, Mercy (*Rachmones*). It is more than a coincidence that *The Tenants* ends with a struggle to the death by the two writers—Harry Lesser, a Jew, and Willie Spearmint, a black man. The final thoughts in the novel are given to the Jew: as both men die, Lesser is convinced that "each . . . feels the anguish of the other." Then Malamud writes "THE END." After this formal ending the chorus of the Jewish landlord: "Mercy, the both of you, for Christ's sake . . . *Hab Rachmones*, I beg you . . . Mercy Mercy Mercy. . . ." *Mercy* is then repeated more than one hundred times.

It is necessary to recall, too, the final scenes in *The Fixer*: Yakov Bok, as he rides in the carriage from prison to the Russian Hall of Judgment, imagines his confrontation with the czar—the so-called father of Russia. "*Rachmones*, we say in Hebrew—mercy, one oughtn't to forget it," Yakov says to the czar. Because the czar has no *Rachmones*, he is destroying the Jewish people; therefore, Bok, who in his imagination destroyed the czar, is leaving the way open for the reappearance of the true father of the Jews and all people—the God of Mercy, the God who has *Rachmones*. Traditionally, the Jewish God is considered the God of law, of judgment, and the Christian deity, or Jesus, the God of love, of mercy. Of course this dichotomy is oversimplification. Nonetheless, it does seem that in this area Malamud's strongest synthesis of the Judaic and Christian appears.

In 1958—when Malamud was achieving recognition, he said in an interview that "The purpose of the writer . . . is to keep civilization from destroying itself." "My premise," he said, "is that we will not destroy each other. My premise is that we will live on. We will seek a better life. We may not become better, but at least we will seek betterment." "My premise," he continued, "is for humanism—and against nihilism. And that is what I try to put into my writings." In the following year—1959—in his address accepting a National Book Award for *The Magic Barrel*, Malamud once again emphasized the important role of humanism in his writing.

In April 1968, Malamud, now famous, was in Israel on a brief lecture tour. When asked about his role as a Jewish-American writer, he said: "What has made the Jewish writers conspicuous in American literature is their sensitivity to the value of man." "Personally," he concluded, "I handle the Jew as a symbol of the tragic experience of man existentially. I try to see the Jew as universal man. Every man is a Jew though he may not know it. The Jewish drama is a . . . symbol of the fight for existence in the highest possible human terms. Jewish history is God's gift of drama."

In 1973, Malamud may have inadvertently uttered a prophetic warning to mankind when he reiterated these sentiments, adding that to call every man a Jew is a way of "indicating how history, sooner or later, treats all men."

Despite Malamud's own words and evidence culled from his works, it may be possible that Malamud should be placed not centrally within the Jewish tradition, but marginally. To be sure, even a cursory examination of Malamud's work reveals that Jewishness and the Jewish milieu are central to it. An exhaustive list of Jews can be catalogued in Malamud's short stories. These Jews and the Jews of the novels are not simply incidental Jews; they are Jews involved in things Jewish.

But if the Jew and Jewishness are central to Malamud, the gnawing question—one which has concerned critics for some time—still persists: What kind of Jew and Jewishness? Obviously, Malamud's fiction is interwoven with bits and pieces of Judaism. But what of the essence of Judaism, whatever that may mean? Does Bober's explanation to Frank Alpine constitute that which is central to Jewishness? Does Yakov Bok's closing statement in *The Fixer*? Or what of stories such as "The Lady of the Lake," in which the conflict arises from the protagonist's denial of his Jewishness and his fair lady's ultimate rejection of him because she has a concentration-camp number on her arm and must therefore preserve her special Jewish identity? Ostensibly, she would have married him had he not attempted to pass for a non-Jew. And, finally, what kind of Jewishness is represented in the concluding lines of "Angel Levine" in *The Magic Barrel*: " 'A wonderful thing, Fanny,' Manischevitz said. 'Believe me, there are Jews everywhere.' "

It is not easy to define the Jewishness of Malamud's fiction. But it has been observed that in this area Malamud is timid. That is, he backs off. When Morris Bober explains his Jewishness and suffering to Frank Alpine, the explanations are the tip of the iceberg. Below the surface are anti-Semitism, pogroms, the Holocaust. Morris, almost asphyxiated by gas in his upstairs flat, has a horrible dream—a Jewish nightmare. He sees the outsiders, the non-Jews, closing in on him, his family, his home, his store, his life. It is as much the classic rape and defilement as when Morris's daughter Helen is actually raped by Frank and she yells "Dog—uncircumcised dog!" Morris is constantly being revealed, undressed. From top to bottom. Sweater, shirt, trousers, drawers. Finally, the shoes. First one shoe. And then the reader waits. The other never drops.

And such is the case with Malamud's other characters, too. The second shoe never seems to drop. Some think it does with Yakov Bok. But this is far from certain. And so Malamud straightens out the record. It was the Beiliss case. But it could have been Sacco and Vanzetti. "It could have been." A Malamud refrain. *Could have been* is marginality. *Is* is Jewishness.

Of course Malamud is a Jewish-American writer within the loose tradition of that special breed of Jewish writer. He is a brother to the many intellectual and literary Jews who years ago left the *shtetl* and traditional Judaism to reach out into the world. They rejected the confines of their past as they accepted "enlightenment." In so doing they as people and the characters they created took on all the qualities of marginality as these writers ignored, skirted, homogenized, or rejected important concerns of the Jewish people.

Nevertheless, by many tests Malamud is a great American writer. A reading of his stories and novels reveals that he is able to capture Jewish themes and commonplaces in his fiction. On one hand, he seems to have grasped and powerfully rendered the idiom of the Old World Jew in a New World context much as Faulkner was able to do with the Snopeses, the Sartorises, and the South against the macrocosm of the United States and the world. On the other hand, one can say of Malamud what has often been said of Hawthorne. Both have been concerned with man and some of the deepest forces that have moved him, whether they be religion, myth, folklore, or ritual. And just as Hawthorne was never interested in merely portraying his characters in a Puritan society in order to dissect Puritanism, so Malamud has never been overly concerned with

Dust jacket for Malamud's 1983 collection for which he chose the twenty-five short stories he considers his best

depicting American Jews in order to discuss Judaism. Both, apparently, are acutely conscious of the significant influence of religion on man—either the home-grown or the imported variety. But that is just the point. Neither one is interested in wrestling with the force itself, as Melville was. Malamud is saying, in effect, as Hawthorne did before him: Powerful forces are at work to mold man. (But my fiction is not meant to constitute an encyclopedia of forces.) Now what does man do and how does he act when confronted with these forces—whether they be American, European, or other? In short, Malamud, like all great writers before him, is circumscribed by predilections and limitations. But also like other great writers he is concerned with man, the human animal, evolving *his* world within a world he never made. And how man chooses his own world and what happens to man in the process of that choice constitute the significant world of Bernard Malamud's fiction.

References:

Richard Astro and Jackson Benson, eds., *The Fiction of Bernard Malamud* (Corvallis: Oregon State University Press, 1977);

Sandy Cohen, *Bernard Malamud and the Trial by Love* (Amsterdam: Rodopi, 1974);

Robert Ducharme, *Art and Ideas in the Novels of Bernard Malamud* (The Hague & Paris: Mouton, 1974);

Leslie A. Field and Joyce W. Field, eds., *Bernard Malamud and the Critics* (New York: New York University Press, 1970);

Field and Field, eds., *Bernard Malamud: A Collection of Critical Essays* (Englewood Cliffs, N.J.: Prentice-Hall, 1975);

Sheldon J. Hershinow, *Bernard Malamud* (New York: Ungar, 1980);

Bates Hoffer, ed., *Malamud's Barrel of Magic*, special issue of *Linguistics in Literature*, 2 (Fall 1977);

Rita Kosofsky, *Bernard Malamud: An Annotated Checklist* (Kent, Ohio: Kent State University Press, 1970);

Glenn Meeter, *Bernard Malamud and Philip Roth: A Critical Essay* (Grand Rapids, Mich.: Eerdmans, 1968);

Sidney Richman, *Bernard Malamud* (New York: Twayne, 1966);

Daniel Walden, ed., *Bernard Malamud: Reinterpretations*, special issue of *Studies in American Jewish Literature*, 4 (Spring 1978).

Papers:

The Library of Congress has manuscripts, typescripts, and proofs of *The Natural, The Assistant, A New Life, The Fixer, Pictures of Fidelman,* and parts of *The Magic Barrel, Idiots First,* and various short stories.

Wallace Markfield
(12 August 1926-   )

Frank Campenni
University of Wisconsin-Milwaukee

See also the Markfield entry in *DLB 2, American Novelists Since World War II*.

BOOKS: *To An Early Grave* (New York: Simon & Schuster, 1964; London: Cape, 1965);

Teitelbaum's Window (New York: Knopf, 1970; London: Cape, 1971);

You Could Live If They Let You (New York: Knopf, 1974);

Multiple Orgasms (Bloomfield Hills, Mich. & Columbia, S.C.: Bruccoli Clark, 1977).

PERIODICAL PUBLICATIONS:
Fiction:
"Notes On the Working Day," *Partisan Review*, 13 (September-October 1946): 460-463;

"Ph.D.," *Partisan Review*, 14 (September-October 1947): 466-471;

"The Patron," *Partisan Review*, 21 (January-February 1954): 80-86;

"The Country of the Crazy Horse," *Commentary*, 25 (March 1958): 237-242;

"The Big Giver," *Midstream*, 4 (Summer 1958): 35-46;

Wallace Markfield (photo by James P. Armstrong)

"A Season of Change," *Midstream*, 4 (Autumn 1958): 25-48;

"The Decline of Sholem Waldman," *Reconstructionist*, 17 October 1958;

"Eulogy for an American Boy," *Commentary*, 33 (June 1962): 513-518;

"Under the Marquee," *New York Herald Tribune*, 13 February 1966.

Nonfiction:

"By the Light of the Silvery Screen," *Commentary*, 31 (March 1961): 251-254;

"Yiddishization of American Humor," *Esquire*, 64 (October 1965): 114-115;

"Dark Geography of W. C. Fields," *New York Times Magazine*, 24 April 1966, pp. 32-33ff.;

"Play It Again, Sam, and Again," *Saturday Evening Post*, 240 (22 April 1967): 72-76ff;

"Oh, Mass Man! Oh, Lumpen Lug! Why Do You Watch TV?," *Saturday Evening Post*, 241 (30 November 1968): 28-29;

"Kong and I," *New York Times Magazine*, 12 December 1976, pp. 36-37ff.

Although he has received scant critical and scholarly attention, Wallace Markfield deserves recognition as a very talented chronicler of the urban world of second-generation Jews in America. Like the early Bernard Malamud, he concentrates on the working-class and lower-middle-class milieu of the 1930s through the 1950s. Like Philip Roth, his viewpoint is largely satirical, though more affectionately so, as he traces the transition from the culture of the candy store and the movies to the culture of the universities and the literary quarterlies. He is keen-witted and sometimes wickedly funny, in the manner of black humor, and his work is as saturated with the details of popular culture and recent political history as the fiction of Irvin Faust. These comparisons with others in the crowded field of competent Jewish writers suggest two probable reasons for the lack of critical recognition of a writer who merits attention. He lacks a clearly staked-out territory in the densely populated landscape of Jewish fiction. Also, he recalls vividly a vanished time of feverish striving, complete with comic accent and naive hungers, which his natural audience of contemporary Jews does not recall or may prefer to forget.

Markfield was born in Brooklyn on 12 August 1926, where he later attended *cheder*, Abraham Lincoln High School (as did Daniel Fuchs, Joseph Heller, and Herbert Wilner), and Brooklyn College. After receiving his B.A. in 1947, he did graduate work in history at New York University but took no degree. Although his fiction reflects a preoccupation with history, his disenchantment with academia was reflected in an early short story, "Ph.D." The pervasive influence of the movies upon Markfield and his childhood friends is readily seen in the film reviews he wrote for the *New Leader* while still a student in the late 1940s, in a one-year stint as film critic for that periodical from 1954-1955, in such stories as "Under The Marquee," and in frequent references to movies in his novels and articles. Aside from the modest income from three novels and about one hundred articles, reviews, and stories, Markfield supported himself and his family for about a dozen years as a publicist for Jewish agencies, and lately he has returned to part-time public-relations work. He has also taught as resident writer at San Francisco State College, Queens College, Columbia University, and other schools; while he enjoys teaching, he has satirized academic sterility and pomposity in "The Graves of Academe." He received a Guggenheim fellowship in 1965 and an award in 1966 from the National Council on the Arts. Markfield has been married to Anna May Goodman since 1949, and they have one child, a daughter. Although all of his novels involve family relationships, Markfield has not made use of his immediate family in his work. He has reached back instead to his days as the son of Max (a clothing cutter, social historian, and trade unionist) and Sophie Monete Markfield. From first to last, however, it is not the particular details of Markfield's personal experiences, drawn upon as they are, which characterize and flavor his work, but rather the density of American-Jewish idiom, custom, and angle of vision. His fictional world is as wholly Jewish in its secular, American way as is that of Sholem Aleichem or Isaac Bashevis Singer.

For a time, Markfield seemed about to embark as precociously upon a literary career as had so many second-generation Jews a decade earlier, from Howard Fast to Alfred Kazin. He sold a story to the *Partisan Review* at the age of nineteen and then another when he was twenty. These introspective stories, such as "Ph.D." (1947), showed talent but were derivative, somber, and self-pitying tales of young men searching for their true roles in life or seeking to bury their loneliness: "Gentlemen of the examining board, I have learned that the Jew chokes his fear only by the sheer quantity of books he has read." "The Patron" (1954) marked an advance toward Markfield's later métier of comedy; a family invites an arrogant young writer to live with them in the hope that he will marry their daughter. When the "patrons" discover that his stories avidly describe his love bouts with their daughter, the mother tears up his obscene posters and pornographic playing cards and then "addressed herself to the gutting of the typewriter, so that as they left the room, its keys stood up like broken fingers." The highpoint of Markfield's apprenticeship was in 1958, when nearly half of his short-story output had been published and he began to concentrate on the hard-luck incompetents and buffoons who would people his novels. In "A Season of Change," accountant Monroe Krim ("Where others had passed their C.P.A. exams with ease, he had needed two tries") fights off his bullying employer and nagging mother in order to escape to Europe and, presumably, from his dull life. "The Decline of Sholem Waldman" is a poignant tale of an unlovable professional mourner who quarrels with everyone in the strange land of America and waits, unrepentant, for death. The best of these tales of hapless Jews is "The Country of the Crazy Horse," which traces the home-visit of an errant, uneasy son. The symbolic opening scene describes a frightened horse which, long ago, had impaled itself on an iron fence near the narrator's home. The tale moves swiftly to the narrator's encounter with a deranged lady on the subway muttering about aggravation, to his memo-

ries of candy stores and magical egg creams, to his failed, bitterly sarcastic parents. Through all of these details, the narrator struggles with the bitter grip of the spent past and the guilt engendered by his lonely parents:

> A cold wave of penance moves through the room. I feel suddenly like promising all kinds of things: long visits, phone calls to relations, a greater interest in the family, a donation to the Synagogue. My father leans back against the chair. How bad he looks, I realize, how narrow and gray his face, how thin his hair and flabby his jaws, how cruelly shaven his cheeks.
>
> "It's time, it's time," I announce, like a nervous innkeeper.

While writing stories about Jews, enjoying the literary life of Greenwich Village, writing reviews and articles about films, and reading Joyce, Eliot, and Bellow, Markfield was storing material and experiences for a novel. Prodded by a friend, he finally began that novel in 1960 and completed *To An Early Grave* in 1963, when he was thirty-seven years old. Critics, such as Stanley Edgar Hyman, praised the novel when it appeared the following year, and there were glowing tributes on the book jacket from Joseph Heller, Brian Moore, and Harold Rosenberg. Others made reference to the apparent influence of James Joyce, but only critic Melvin Friedman specifically underscored the link between the four-man carriage trip to Paddy Dignam's funeral in *Ulysses* and the four-man Volkswagen journey to Leslie Braverman's funeral that essentially constitutes the story of *To An Early Grave*. Markfield considers that parallel accidental or unconscious without disclaiming it, stressing instead his debt to Italo Svevo's 1923 novel *Confessions of Zeno* as the inspiration for his book (Joyce actively promoted Svevo's work). Certainly, the parallels with Svevo are stronger: in Markfield and Svevo's novels the funeral odyssey goes astray (Markfield's protagonists go to the wrong synagogue, Svevo's to the wrong cemetery); the dead man, in each case, is a philanderer with marital troubles; the protagonist of each novel, as friend and rival to the deceased, sexually pursues the widow, who has held him in thrall for years. Finally, both protagonists are owed money by the dead man and both are comically portrayed as schlemiels or *schlimazls*.

From the moment that Monroe Rieff learns that literary journalist Leslie Braverman has died at forty-one until the day's end when he can finally, like Tommy Wilhelm in Saul Bellow's *Seize the Day*, weep for himself at the early grave of his hopes, the tone of the novel is curiously lighthearted and darkly comic at once. The novel has been viewed as a satire on the Jewish literary establishment of New York, especially some recognizable figures connected with *Commentary* (which had published the funeral eulogy from the work-in-progress). Despite the icy relations thereafter between Markfield and *Commentary*, neither the four men in the Volkswagen nor the deceased Braverman resemble members of any literary establishment anywhere, except in broad caricature. Rieff, like his creator, is a fund-raiser; fifty-eight-year-old Felix Ottensteen grinds out articles for a Yiddish daily; Barnet Weiner, lecher and aging mama's boy, had once earned a place in *New Critics: 1944*, but "he had published nothing in years"; Holly Levine, owner of the Volkswagen, is viewed pecking out clichés in a hilarious parody of book-reviewing (which he alternates with compulsive peeking at a *Playboy* centerfold). Levine calls the roll of "The Fathers" like a litany, "Trilling . . . Leavis . . . Ransom . . . Tate . . . Kazin . . . Chase," yet his own best boast that he has had a piece "anthologized twice . . . !" establishes his

meager level of achievement. But all of them (save Ottensteen) spring to life in trivia contests, for in naming characters from radio serials, comic strips, and B movies they return to their true love, popular culture. These permanent children tease and insult each other, sing boyhood songs, stop for snacks, hint at sexual exploits, get lost, and crash the car; Levine has a preposterous street fight with a Jewish cabbie. In short, they struggle with desperate gaiety to relive their boyhood memories while on their way to commemorate their lives' ends.

To An Early Grave is conventionally written and tightly structured despite its offbeat plot of attending—or missing—a funeral. But separate chapters—especially the pompous but slangy eulogy, Reiff's impressment as an assistant cemetery pretzel seller, and Holly Levine's fumbling among clichés for a critical review—take on memorable, almost classic status. Markfield's remarkable ear for dialogue and dialect, his gallery of peculiar Jewish cab drivers, peddlers, and semibereaved widows, as well as the poignant parting of the quartet of friends, add up to a triumphant entry into the novel form. Markfield's early subjects are all reflected here: death, loneliness, boyhood memories and

Dust jacket for Markfield's first novel, viewed by some as a satire aimed at New York's Jewish literary establishment

Dust jacket for Markfield's second novel, set in Brooklyn during the Depression

friendships, the lure of lowbrow culture, the pain and pleasure of Jewishness, the clash between thought and feeling.

His second novel, *Teitelbaum's Window* (1970), was more ambitious and in many ways a better novel, though not as well received. Essentially, it is a Bildungsroman—many American-Jewish novels have either traced the growing consciousness of a bright child or the clash of feelings within the family—the life of Simon Sloan in the 1930s, ending with his entrance into the army at eighteen. But the novel is also a brilliant documentary of Brooklyn's Brighton Beach Jews of the working class and the hard-pressed merchants of grocery and candy stores, the street characters, complaining *yentas*, and lecherous dentists, and what Alfred Kazin termed "a warehouse of Brooklyn Jewish folklore." Here, again, we come to the heart of Markfield's problem of not receiving adequate recognition. Some reviewers complained that "we have known them all" and accused Markfield of "telling a hundred-and-twice told tale," while others, such as Kazin, sarcastically described the "Brighton Beach Jews in the 1930's" as "a very hilarious thing to be."

Markfield's composite portrait of a people and an era is a fond evocation of the sense of family and community, one throbbing with life and undefeatable spirit. The dramatic exception is a stunning scene of a window-jumper who changes his mind and then falls. Somehow, the episode seems quintessentially Jewish, as garment-worker Mertz endlessly explains his life's travails, stoop-sitting housewives exchange comments with and about him, and the teeming tenement life absorbs and overpowers the comi-tragedy of Mertz's inept fall. Young Simon, meanwhile, races through this crowded milieu, seeking adventure in streets and in movie fantasies, dodging the movie-usher father who unaccountably hates him and the doting, self-pitying mother who calls herself "Malvena the Orphan." He comes to a sexually aroused adolescence and to political awareness (managing to remain steadfastly anti-Stalinist in that environment), then becomes a fledgling writer caught among pretentious asses, as Markfield's dislike of self-important highbrows is again underscored. But the world of work is even worse, peopled with tricky bosses, crazy workers, charlatan employment counselors.

This second novel, though covering familiar ground, is far more varied in form than *To An Early Grave*. The title, for example, refers to the window of Teitelbaum's grocery, and the book's first sentence quotes one of the grocer's crudely lettered signs, unimaginable in a non-Jewish neighborhood: "President Roosevelt had a hundred days but you got only till this Monday to enjoy such savings on our Farm Girl pot cheese." The long opening sentences of subsequent chapters summarize the events of passing years, referring both to local doings and world events, including the growing rumors of new-style pogroms abroad. Otherwise, much of the novel is told through Simon's diary, letters, list of "things to do," snatches of song, and minutes of meetings. The result is a composite of Dos Passos's techniques in *U.S.A.*, which integrates separate newsreel, camera eye, narrative, and biographical divisions. The Jewish flavor and Markfield's dark humor are evident in this curse by a blowsy mother upon a wayward, insolent daughter: "Don't get killed and live a long time. Only while you live I would love you to walk like President Roosevelt, to see good the way Helen Keller sees good, to eat what John D. Rockefeller eats, and to be good-looking like Primo Carnera."

Markfield's third and most recently completed novel, *You Could Live If They Let You* (1974), attempted to strike out in new directions, both in form and in material. Markfield says he began it as a monologue by "a Jerry-Lewis comedian," with events taking place during a forty-eight-hour telethon. The form was too confining, and Markfield adopted a narrator, Chandler Von Horton (could the name be any more Anglo-Saxon?), who is writing a biography of the stand-up comedian, Jules Farber. Despite the comments of reviewers, Farber is not a fictionalized Lenny Bruce, even though Markfield had recently reviewed Albert Goldman's biography of Bruce in the *New York Times*. Farber is, instead, a composite of Jewish "insult" comics with others who comment irreverently upon contemporary matters (his name is probably derived from Manny Farber, a movie critic and friend admired by Markfield). Farber's story is told through Van Horton's notes and dreams, tapes from Farber onstage and in frenzied conversation, remembrances by Farber's sister, Lilian Federman, and through parodies of Jewish newsletters and scholarly books (where Farber is not a stand-up comic but a "vertical monologist" and an "irony-monger"). Farber, a master parodist, frequently ridicules his own past, and he also attacks the Jews in his audience, who worship him, but he is equally unsparing of middle-American culture.

Each of Markfield's novels has less plot than its predecessor. Farber keels over dead from an unexplained heart attack about one-third of the way through this short novel, and there is virtually no story line, sequence, or cumulation here, since Farber is the victim neither of his culture nor of a drive toward self-destruction, but merely a bad heart. In lieu of story or character development, Markfield places growing emphasis on wit, dialogue, a sense of place, and a gallery of Dickensian characters. For all of Farber's stings, *You Could Live If They Let You* celebrates Jewish values and resiliency. Markfield convinces us that Farber is brilliant, mordant, and funny, and that he could only have been raised in New York and as a Jew. Van Horton, who is Farber's Nick Carraway, is genuinely envious of the richness of Farber's "aggravating" past and gradually becomes indistinguishable from the "other Jews" at Farber's funeral. In 1965, Markfield had written an *Esquire* article entitled "Yiddishization of American Humor," a title and text forecasting a subtheme of this novelistic tribute to the wisdom of stand-up comics and their roots in the tough Jewish past. Van Horton is an interesting switch on the familiar Jewish-novel conflict of assimilation versus *Yiddishkeit* in the Jewish novel, for there is little threat to Jewish identity in a country that is cheerfully becoming Jewish.

Markfield planned two other novels with Jewish characters and themes. One of them was to contain about twelve chapters, each taking place in a movie theater, with events reflecting what was up on the screen. The short story, "Under The Marquee," published in 1966, might have served as a first chapter, but the project never developed. The other work, *Multiple Orgasms*, was published as a fragment by Bruccoli Clark in 1977, although Markfield abandoned it after 178 manuscript pages. Events in this aborted novel were being told to a caseworker by Laura Pauline Goodfriend, a Manhasset, Long Island, housewife of forty-three, who is explaining how she came to be arrested for shoplifting a cashmere sweater from Bloomingdale's. There are, as usual, funny lines and odd characters (particularly the female arresting officer), while Laura Pauline, hearing time's wings, fantasizes about having "sex while carrying on a lengthy conversation with Lionel Trilling or Jacques Barzun about the merits of Edmund Wilson." But Markfield wisely recognized that "I'd grown tired, after three novels, of chronicling the Jewish experience in

America" and told himself to "tell no more Jewish jokes which they neither get nor care to get, drink no more egg creams, enter no more candy stores, stay away from talk of *shtetls*, stop salting and peppering your speech with all that Yiddish. . . ."

For the past few years, Markfield, a slow writer, has been at work on a political thriller, tentatively called "Radical Surgery." That working title suggests a critical change in his literary career. Thus far, there is only one Jewish character, and he speaks no Yiddish. According to Markfield, the work is intended to be "a serious, solidly plotted novel with a traditional beginning, middle and end."

References:
Matthew J. Bruccoli, "Wallace Markfield," in *Con-*

versations with Writers 1 (Detroit: Bruccoli Clark / Gale, 1977), pp. 216-236;

Melvin J. Friedman, "The Enigma of Unpopularity and Critical Neglect: The Case for Wallace Markfield," in Louis Filler, ed., *Seasoned Authors For A New Season: The Search For Standards in Popular Writing* (Bowling Green, Ohio: Bowling Green University Popular Press, 1980), pp. 33-42;

Friedman, "Jewish Mothers and Sons: The Expense of *Chutzpah*," in Irving Malin, ed., *Contemporary American-Jewish Literature* (Bloomington: Indiana University Press, 1973), pp. 156-174;

Review of Contemporary Fiction, Wallace Markfield and Douglas Woolf issue (Spring 1982): 4-59.

Jay Neugeboren
(30 May 1938-   )

Cordelia Candelaria
University of Colorado

BOOKS: *Big Man* (Boston: Houghton Mifflin, 1966);

Listen Ruben Fontanez (Boston: Houghton Mifflin, 1968; London: Gollancz, 1968);

Corky's Brother (New York: Farrar, Straus & Giroux, 1969; London: Gollancz, 1970);

Parentheses: An Autobiographical Journey (New York: Dutton, 1970);

Sam's Legacy (New York: Holt, Rinehart & Winston, 1974);

An Orphan's Tale (New York: Holt, Rinehart & Winston, 1976);

The Stolen Jew (New York: Holt, Rinehart & Winston, 1981).

OTHER: Martha Foley, *The Story of Story Magazine*, edited with an introduction and afterword by Neugeboren (London & New York: Norton, 1980).

SELECTED PERIODICAL PUBLICATIONS:
Fiction:
"My Son, the Freedom Rider," *Colorado Quarterly*, 13 (Summer 1964): 71-76;

"The Application," *Transatlantic Review 17* (Autumn 1964): 52-58;

"Something is Rotten in the Borough of Brooklyn," *Ararat*, 8 (Autumn 1967): 27-35;

"Connorsville, Virginia," *Transatlantic Review 31* (Winter 1969): 11-23;

"The Place Kicking Specialist," *Transatlantic Review 50* (Fall/Winter 1974): 111-126;

"His Violin," *Atlantic*, 242 (November 1978): 48-50;

"Star of David," *TriQuarterly 45*, 44 (Spring 1979): 5-15;

"The St. Dominick's Game," *Atlantic Monthly*, 244 (December 1979): 54-58;

"Visiting Hour," *Shenandoah*, 31 (March 1980): 23-29;

"Poppa's Books," *Atlantic*, 246 (May 1980): 59-63;

"Bonus Baby," *John O'Hara Journal*, 3 (Fall/Winter 1980): 10-21;

"Noah's Song," *Present Tense*, 7 (Winter 1980).
Nonfiction:
"A Modest Protest with Feline Feeling," *Fellowship*, 28 (May 1962): 27-28;

"Hoadley's Test Case in Indiana," *New Republic*, 149 (21 September 1963): 14;

Jay Neugeboren (photo by Layle Silbert)

"They Didn't Have to Tell the Truth," *NEA Journal*, 53 (November 1964): 21-22;

"Writing a First Novel," *Writer* (January 1967): 17;

"Humphrey and the Now Generation," *New Republic*, 156 (18 March 1967): 32-35;

"Disobedience Now!," *Commonweal*, 86 (16 June 1967): 367-369;

"Dave Stallworth: I'm One Lucky Man," *Sport* (January 1970);

"Your Suburban Alternative," *Esquire*, 74 (September 1970): 113;

"Mall Mania," *Mother Jones*, 4 (May 1979): 21-31;

"The Diamond Jubilee," *Present Tense*, 8 (Winter 1981): 15-18.

Several American-Jewish writers have used America's preoccupation with sports as the basis for their fiction; Bernard Malamud's *The Natural* and Philip Roth's *The Great American Novel* come immediately to mind. Jay Neugeboren first gained a modest readership through his sports fiction, and his accomplishments in this area are original, often elegant evocations of the subtleties of a modern phenomenon most encounter only superficially in the public arena. Neugeboren's novel about basketball, *Big Man* (1966), exemplifies the author's acute sensitivity to both the individual athlete's and the game's manifold complexities. Similarly, his treatment of baseball in several works transmutes the sport's legendary history, raw vitality, and essentially aesthetic form into a remarkable literary motif at once realistic and romantic. Despite his success in dealing with the literary possibilities of sports, the direction Neugeboren's writing has taken since his fourth book, *Parentheses: An Autobiographical Journey* (1970), is toward the fictive interpretation of traditional Jewishness as it is expressed in contemporary, secular society. That direction accounts for the author's strongest works to date—*An Orphan's Tale* (1976) and *The Stolen Jew* (1981)—though he is also adept at merging his concerns for the meaning of sports and of Jewishness in stylistically startling, inventive ways. His style, which in the early books showed greater promise than achievement, began to assert its peculiar grace and power in *Sam's Legacy* (1974), and with *The Stolen Jew* it has developed into a distinctive mastery of technique, language, and form.

Born and raised in Brooklyn, Neugeboren lived in a neighborhood about equally divided between Catholics and Jews, and he attended racially integrated schools. His parents (father, David Neugeboren, a printing jobber; mother, Anne Nassofer Neugeboren, a registered nurse) harbored many of the attitudes now associated with an immigrant mentality. Thus Jacob Mordecai, Neugeboren's name at birth, became Jay Michael because, as Neugeboren wrote in his autobiography, *Parentheses*, his father "wanted his sons to be 'Americans' "; "after [only] a few months" in yeshiva Neugeboren was transferred to a Brooklyn public school for the same reason. Although he completed a "novel" at the age of nine, "sports, at least until the age of fourteen, were [his] whole life." Indeed, when he graduated from public school his yearbook entry under "Career Ambition" was "professional baseball player, commercial artist." If unaware during his childhood of his future as a writer, Neugeboren was nonetheless absorbing all his early experiences with the vivid intensity of an artist, for they later found their way into his fictional works, where they often appear exactly as they are presented in *Parentheses*. At other times, his early Brooklyn experiences account for the immediacy and verisimilitude of his fictional cityscapes and their haunting inhabitants, as in the short stories in *Corky's Brother* (1969) and the novel *Listen Ruben Fontanez* (1968).

Working his way through Brooklyn's Erasmus

Hall High School in sundry jobs from elevator operator and busboy to postal worker and yeoman on a merchant marine ship allowed Neugeboren, as he put it in *Parentheses*, "the means to an end . . . a college education"; "to lower-middle-class Jewish families such as mine, living still with the irrational and profound fear that anything you owned could be snatched away in a moment . . . nonmaterial possessions were the most valuable ones." Accordingly, when he entered Columbia in 1955 his singular dedication to "the major literature, art, music, and history of Western Civilization" derived as much from the family values that had directly shaped him as from the 1950s conservatism that dominated the political opinion in the United States. Although he was destined to join the earliest dissidents of the 1960s, as an undergraduate English major Neugeboren along with his peers, "collected no data on Columbia's involvement in the military-industrial complex . . . instead we savored gossip, legends concerning teachers, former students (many, in those years, about [Allen] Ginsberg and [Jack] Kerouac)."

When he first enrolled at Columbia, Neugeboren indicated his career interests to be advertising, television, and architectural engineering—some remove from his earlier ambition of baseball player-commercial artist, but still not decisively literary. Nevertheless, between his sophomore and his junior years he completed his first novel (discounting his forty-page effort as a fourth grader) and elicited the praise of one of his teachers, Charles Van Doren, who sent it to several publishers. Though the book was rejected, Neugeboren continued writing and completed his second novel by the end of his senior year. Again his work received the warm interest of a Columbia literary eminent, Richard Chase, who also wrote a letter for Neugeboren, bringing the manuscript to his own publisher's attention. Again his work was rejected, but Neugeboren made the important discovery that "the only thing that mattered" was "to write novels."

Consequently, to support himself while he wrote and "to get farther away from Brooklyn," after receiving a B.A. from Columbia in 1959, he entered graduate study on a fellowship to Indiana University, but within a year he left graduate school to become an executive trainee for General Motors in Indianapolis. In this way he got "a job that would . . . [be] separate in all ways from my writing, a means to an end only, something that would give me the time, money, and freedom of mind to write." At General Motors he was exposed to "the organization man's" life and its various forms of automated dehumanization; he also had his first encounter with overt bigotry in the antiblack attitudes of his coworkers and in the lack of upward mobility for minorities in the company. These experiences sparked his latent revolutionary politics into expression, albeit in private form at this time.

Besides providing him with an Indiana University M.A. (1963) and provoking him to read a broad array of radical political writings, both contemporary and from the past, his Hoosier experience also led to what he termed a new "way of seeing things . . . [one that] came more and more from the black man's point of view." This transformation of outlook had important implications for his writings in that it led to the development of his ability to imagine and sustain unlikely narrative voices plausibly, and it also led to the awakening of the myriad voices he had unconsciously internalized as a child. A quick review of some of his most effectively realized characters makes the point: the title protagonist and narrator of *Big Man* is black; the narrator of *Listen Ruben Fontanez* is an elderly Jewish man, while the title character is Puerto Rican; the main character of *Sam's Legacy* is a hip Jewish bachelor, while another key character, Tidewater, who narrates a long story within the novel, is an elderly black man; and the central character in *An Orphan's Tale* is a thirteen-year-old Jewish boy. In addition, Neugeboren frequently interpolates into his primary narratives sequences presented or narrated by other, sometimes minor, characters.

These results of his Indiana General Motors period were accompanied, however, by continued rejections from publishers. Before receiving his first formal acceptance notice in 1962 (from *Fellowship*, a peace publication, for a piece he described as "a satirical protest against bomb shelters written in the form of a letter from John F. Kennedy's cat"), Neugeboren had completed four novels and was nearing completion of a fifth. He had become an accomplished letter writer for leftist causes, and his views were disseminated in newspapers, in mimeographed form at rallies, and through correspondence with other 1960s antiestablishmentarians. He had also discovered his abilities in another genre, the short story. In sum, he had found his true vocation, intermittently subsidized by teaching salaries and graduate-school stipends, but he had not found a publisher for any of his books.

By 1965, at the age of twenty-seven, he had written seven novels and over a dozen short stories; he had gotten married to Betsey Bendorf, and one of his "political successes in Indiana," an essay he had written on the 1960s, had been published by the

New Republic. More importantly one of his short stories, "The Application," had appeared in the *TransAtlantic Review* in 1964, after having received over thirty rejections. During this time Neugeboren also vowed, in appropriately tentative terms, "to *begin* to think about giving up the idea of being a novelist" if he did not have a book published by the time he was thirty. But his luck changed in 1965. Martha Foley, editor of the annual *Best American Short Stories* anthology, selected "The Application" for inclusion in her 1965 anthology. Impressed with the story, an editor at Houghton Mifflin solicited a book-length manuscript from Neugeboren, and he submitted his just-completed eighth novel, *Big Man*, which was published in 1966. His career as a professional writer began in earnest. Within a decade he had published five additional books with four major publishers and had placed over fifteen pieces of short fiction, three of which received Best Fiction awards. His novels, too, received serious critical notice. Ian Watt, for example, wrote that "Neugeboren understands, and makes us understand, things we could hardly surmise from the works of most of his contemporaries: that even if we are all a part of . . . the increasing tempo of historical degradation, we are not defined merely by disillusion and defeat. . . . I cannot doubt that Neugeboren will go his own way, and far."

Neugeboren has indeed realized Watt's prophecy by continuing to write fiction characterized by formal ingenuity and thematic depth. Three important threads weave a distinctive narrative pattern in Neugeboren's corpus; two are thematic, and the third is stylistic. Though identifiable and distinct constituents of most of his early writings, these threads intertwine seamlessly in his maturest work.

First, the central theme of his work concerns the nature of individual identity and the relationship of the subjective self to objective experience or, stated differently, the relationship of private consciousness to public manifestations of reality. Subsumed within this theme is the author's interest in probing the role of the imagination in shaping one's self-identity; typically this interest appears in the brothers metaphor, through which that, or a siblinglike, relationship suggests the mirroring (or doubling) effect of the subjective/objective aspects of identity.

Neugeboren's concern with the nature of identity appears in his first published novel, *Big Man*, in his portrayal of Mack Davis, the book's title character, a former college-basketball celebrity. Confined to the sidelines and sandlots because of

his involvement in a gambling scandal, Davis is a "pariah" who bears "the mark of Cain on [his] forehead." His story was Neugeboren's attempt to answer the question "what . . . would you do with your life if you couldn't do the thing you loved?" Through Davis's realistic, first-person narration we view his struggle to develop a meaningful identity outside the arena of fame, success, and the game which has fashioned his life. The novel also offers a tentative sketch of the brothers motif which assumes greater significance in the later works. Here, Mack's younger brother represents Mack's conscience or better self, and he also serves as emblem of the physical bond between Mack and others in Mack's life not associated with basketball, the community that Mack forgot while he was a star.

In Neugeboren's collection of stories, *Corky's Brother*, the focus on identity is developed primarily through the character profiles which constitute the basis of each short story. The book contains a wide range of character types comprising a variety of ages, ethnicities, occupations, and settings. The

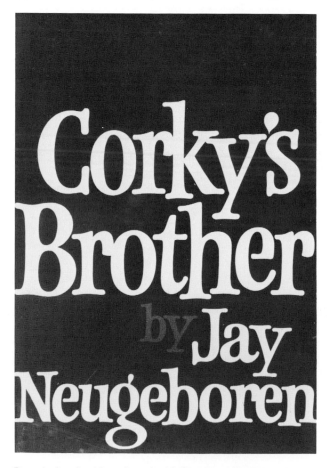

Dust jacket for Neugeboren's 1969 story collection. The title novella deals with the relationship of two siblings, an often repeated theme in Neugeboren's work.

collection's title novella explicitly deals with the sibling relationship that holds such an important place in the author's mind. Neugeboren's relationship with his own younger brother, Robert, appears to have provided the psychological donnée for this motif, but its rich symbolic possibilities have been heightened through careful literary craftsmanship. Another story in the collection—"The Pass"—deserves noting because its subject, a deranged boy in a mental hospital, again hints at this biographical link, for Robert also experienced institutionalization before emerging, Neugeboren recalls in *Parentheses*, "whole . . . back again for better or worse in the 'real' world." In addition, Neugeboren returns to the siblings motif and his own relationship to Robert in his latest novel, *The Stolen Jew*.

The second major thematic thread in Neugeboren's work relates to the inherent possibilities *and* limitations associated with ancestral roots, both familial and cultural. For Neugeboren (like Faulkner, unlike Hemingway), it is axiomatic that the past is defined by the interplay of one's ancestral heritage with one's repertoire of memories. The interest then resides in the rendering of the effect of that past both on present experiences and on individual perceptions of that experience. A significant metaphor here is cross-generational contact—that is, the encounter/confrontation of youth with age quite outside the commonplace dichotomy of innocence versus knowledge. Thus, Neugeboren's young characters usually share with his aged characters virtues and flaws, hope and despair, insight and blindness.

This thread is dominant in *Listen Ruben Fontanez*, presented through the first-person narration of sixty-four-year-old Harry Meyers, recently widowed and retired from public-school teaching. Through Meyers's persistent reveries about the past—his youth, his Jewishness, his wife, his experiences as a teacher—his character takes form for the reader. His friendship with Puerto Rican teenager Fontanez, which involves him in the quotidian excitement and violence of contemporary New York City, helps complete the portrait. In addition, the Meyers/Fontanez relationship in this novel (like the Ben Rosen/Mack Davis connection in *Big Man* and Tidewater/Sam Berman in *Sam's Legacy*), symbolizing at one level the inescapable intersection of the past with the present, points toward the culmination of Neugeboren's cross-generational metaphor in *The Stolen Jew*.

Sam's Legacy continues Neugeboren's interest in the tension between the possibilities and the limitations of ancestral roots where, he wrote in a 1981 essay in *Present Tense*, the "ideas of roots and continuity [are] not abstractions." To a large extent this third published novel smooths the ragged edges apparent in the treatment of the theme in *Listen Ruben Fontanez*, in which Neugeboren's craftsmanship failed to exploit the full possibilities of the genre. In *Sam's Legacy* Ben Berman's (Sam's father) observance of certain traditional Jewish practices combined with old Tidewater's meticulous chronicle, "My Life and Death in the Negro American Baseball League—A Slave Narrative," provide the indifferent Sam, a sports fan/gambler, with palpable evidence of the living quality of the past. When Tidewater gives his "Slave Narrative" to Sam, the act binds the two as closely, albeit on different terms, as Tidewater and Ben are bound in their fraternallike relationship. Besides marking Neugeboren's continued improvement in the evocation of theme and the use of metaphor, *Sam's Legacy* also shows technical development and experimentation. The skillful use of interior monologues and of the Tidewater manuscript to call attention to the intrinsic nature of the storytelling text underscores Neugeboren's perception of reality as a complex interplay between subjective consciousness (including memory and imagination) and the objective experiences the individual shares with others.

The third stylistic thread that dominates Neugeboren's canon may be described as post-Modernist fictionmaking in which the narrative mode raises questions about the validity of the storytelling text. Such fictions present the narrative consciousness as stemming from multiple viewpoints, and the reader is forced to assume an active, creative role in decoding the text—or, in the new vocabulary, the writer's "construct." Neugeboren experiments in this self-reflexive form of construction but in a way that allows him to explore both traditional literary themes and traditional Jewish beliefs. Hence, though post-Modernist, his technique operates within a framework of orthodoxy that is amenable to ethical interpretations usually considered out-of-step with the "new" fiction. This is quite fitting, for Neugeboren admires fiction that conveys "a love of storytelling" as well as "a sense of the price at which things such as beauty and art and knowledge and happiness [are], when they [do] come to one in this life, bought."

An Orphan's Tale exemplifies the third thread through the author's fine control of style. In the words of Barbara Bannon, reviewer for *Publishers Weekly*, it tells a compelling story in which "the elements of comic relief . . . present in ethnic dislocation are deftly interwoven with the cultural and ritual minutiae of Jewish observance." The story focuses on thirteen-year-old Danny Ginsburg, resident of the Maimonides Home for Jewish Boys in Brooklyn. When the book opens the home houses only fourteen boys and, early in the story, Danny runs away in a scheme intended to prevent the home's imminent closing. To help him save the home, Danny seeks out one of its former residents, Charlie Sapistein, known to the boy solely from his photographs on the walls of the orphanage. When Danny finds Charlie and is temporarily "adopted" by him, the boy continually tests the real Charlie against the person he had created in his mind while at the home. Through its plot, then, the novel introduces Neugeboren's concern for the role of the imagination in shaping individual identity, a theme which allows him to experiment with multiple narratives—third-person omniscient, Danny's first-person diary accounts, and the fictive narrators of Danny's stories. The multiple viewpoints, the use of Yiddish and Hebrew phrases, and the fact that, at the end, Danny's literal reality is bound up with the way his ingenious imagination confronts his complex Jewish heritage—all force the reader to a new comprehension of the view that fiction, *in its quintessential fictiveness*, is fact distorted into truth.

Neugeboren's immersion in explicitly Jewish topics in *An Orphan's Tale* follows a progression traceable to his early novels where Jewishness constituted random fragments of an overall New York City mosaic. Those works usually included Jewish figures and motifs as foils for their non-Jewish characters and subjects. Here, however, Danny Ginsburg, endowed with a precocity beyond his years, reflects upon an abundance of Jewish lore, both biblical and sociohistorical, trying to find his orphan's place as "an endangered species" within such a tragically glorious culture. Accordingly, the novel voices a wide range of concerns regarding fundamental Jewish issues, focusing in particular on the schism between Uncle Sol, the *macher*, and Dr. Fogel, the scholar. Dr. Fogel "said that Zionism represented the greatest heresy of all time . . . [for] 'ZIONISM IS AN ATTEMPT TO ESTABLISH A JEWISH KINGDOM ON EARTH WHICH WAS AND ALWAYS WILL BE THE PRIVILEGE OF THE MESSIAH ALONE.' " Uncle Sol, on the other hand, offers a pro-Zionist opinion that has appeal primarily because of his congenial and compassion-

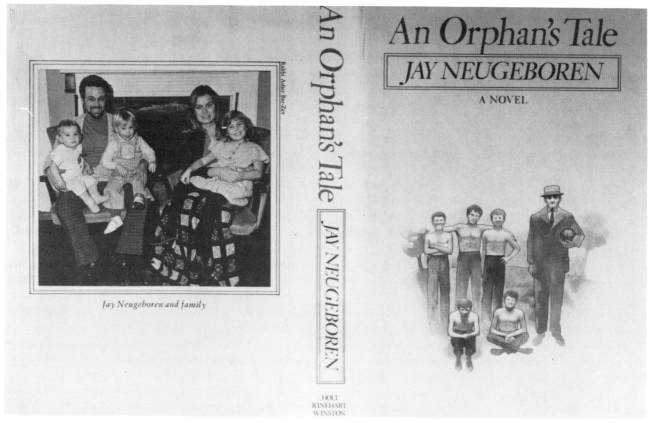

Dust jacket for Neugeboren's third novel, in which the author investigates the role of the imagination in shaping personal identity and addresses a wide range of explicitly Jewish topics

ate nature. Danny weighs the merits of these opinions and decides to grope toward answers on his own.

The Stolen Jew, Neugeboren's latest novel, indirectly offers Danny some answers and also, characteristically, poses a greater array of intriguing questions, all derived from the three distinct threads identified earlier as important in Neugeboren's writing. What role does the imagination play in the development of individual identity? Do childhood experiences define adulthood, or through the process of recollection does the mature personality distort the past to fit the needs of the present? Can a Jew's moral vision be anything but tragic if it is to be historically grounded? For tragedy to be "Jewish" must it be informed by humor, by a comic element? What formal features and structures, literary figures and symbols are most effective in seeking answers to these questions?

Not long before he finished *The Stolen Jew*, in 1978 Neugeboren described the novel-in-progress as "intensely Jewish." It is that, and it is also a splendid culmination of the author's stylistic skills and storytelling powers. Through an amalgam of stories within stories, it records the experiences of Nathan Malkin, a wealthy sixty-four-year-old Brooklyn businessman voluntarily retired and transplanted to Israel after his only son's death. The writer of a novel titled *The Stolen Jew*, a critically acclaimed best-seller, Nathan is embarrassed when reminded of his single literary triumph because he—who his brother Nachman thought would "be greater than Tolstoy"—never followed that accomplishment with another. Receiving word of Nachman's death, Nathan returns to New York; reunites with members of his family; lodges at the house in Brooklyn where he and his brother grew up and which Nachman's son, Michael, a psychiatrist, has bought for its "sentimental value"; and then accompanies Michael on a trip to Russia on behalf of that country's Jewish "refuseniks." Ever the hero, Michael schemes an elaborate escape for Alexander Cherniak, an imprisoned dissident writer, but the unsuccessful plot results in Michael's detainment in Russia and Nathan's solitary return to the United States.

Even the barest outline of the novel suggests its relation to Neugeboren's previous work. By having Nathan's *Stolen Jew* exist as a fiction within Neugeboren's book of the same title, the self-reflexive nature of fictionmaking underscores itself. This is further emphasized by Nathan's decision to revise and disguise parts of the original manuscript in order to fool Soviet authorities about the nature of his work. Thus a fictional character

takes on the task of making more fictive his original fiction which, of course, exists only in Neugeboren's fiction. Like *An Orphan's Tale*, with its shifts in narrative viewpoints which include Danny's attempts at writing stories, and like *Sam's Legacy*, with its use of Tidewater's embedded "Slave Narrative," *The Stolen Jew* focuses on both the act and the effect of fictionmaking to reveal the centrality of the imagination in one's perception of reality. The interplay between the imagination and external reality determines the particular form individual identity will take.

Also paralleling Neugeboren's other writings is the brothers motif in *The Stolen Jew*, which contains the author's most explicit and, simultaneously, his finest treatment of the subject. Though the Nathan/Nachman pair is the novel's primary instance of the motif, there are other important sibling pairs adding emphasis. The biographical significance of the theme and, especially, its treatment in this novel relate to Neugeboren's attempt to understand his own relationship with his younger brother. For instance, in the introduction to one of his short stories, Neugeboren has written that his twenty-third year "was a hard year for me. . . . My brother Robert, with whom I was very close, had a mental breakdown. . . . and I felt, for most of that year, that I would never escape. I would wind up in a hospital with my brother. I would never write again. I would never be published." Nathan expresses similar sentiments about his younger brother Nachman in *The Stolen Jew*, in which Nachman is described through flashbacks and dialogue as the adorable, favored son who eventually suffered complete derangement. Though Nachman does not appear in the book as a living character, he is such a vivid presence in the protagonist's mind that Nathan even has extensive conversations with him as if he were, in fact, alive. Besides contributing to the novel's delightful humor (an appealing feature of all Neugeboren's work), Nathan's conversations with his dead brother serve the ironic purpose of propelling him to move out of his private, subjective world toward a reconnection with others in the world of shared experience.

The brothers motif also has a manifold aesthetic function in *The Stolen Jew*, one that coheres the three primary threads apparent in all Neugeboren's novels. It reminds the reader, as one passage suggests, of "all the great Biblical stories that [tell] of brothers: Cain and Abel, Isaac and Ishmael, Jacob and Esau, Joseph and his brothers," thus providing a historical framework for the novel that is simultaneously Jewish and universal. Through this framework Neugeboren can tell a wide assortment of stories about the struggle for "a kind of freedom, personal and collective, that Jews had rarely, in history, known." Likewise, he can employ the motif as a mirroring device through which such opposites as good and evil, love and hate, sanity and insanity, past and present, life and death are, like brothers, inextricably linked. Neugeboren captures the total effect of these yoked polarities in *The Stolen Jew* through an allusion to a Jewish-Russian "fable in which the hero is to come on his white horse to a road that forks in two and [he] must . . . decide [which to choose] and no matter which road he [chooses] he is to die." Finally, the mirroring effect of the brothers motif thematically underscores the fictionmaking process of both the craft of fiction and the individual's involvement in the process of constructing reality. Ultimately, however, the novel's repeated references to writers such as Willa Cather, Tolstoy, Chekhov, contemporary "refuseniks" in the Soviet Union, and to other American-Jewish writers; its stories within stories; its blurring of Neugeboren's "real" characters with those created by his protagonist; its use of metafictional self-criticism—all these combine to reify one of Nathan's/Neugeboren's boyhood beliefs that "*God created the world because He loved stories*."

Neugeboren is one of those writers who, despite consistently favorable critical notice, remains largely unknown to a national readership. All five of his novels have been praised in a variety of forums and by established literati from Ian Watt to James Michener; yet all his books have had disappointing sales. About his first book, *Big Man*, Rex Lardner wrote, "this is a moving novel. . . . The author's great triumph is his poignant characterization of Davis [the protagonist]." His later work has drawn similar favor and many comments about his "unmistakable talent." *The Stolen Jew* has been described by Barbara Bannon in *Publishers Weekly* as "a major work . . . complex in theme, layered with multiple ironies, subtle, witty, intelligent." Though the same reviewer found the novel "often overwrought and heavy with tortured emotions. . . , [the] book-within-a-book is haunting and powerful, throbbing with life. . . . The book is provocative, unsettling, and in places, beautifully written. It should be read." Recipient of the Kenneth B. Smilen/*Present Tense* Award for Best Novel of 1981, *The Stolen Jew* appeared in paperback edition in 1983, Neugeboren's first novel to enjoy a second edition.

Thus, it seems that the same persistence that eventually turned the difficulties of his early years as a writer into the success of consistent publication will no doubt see this remarkable writer through this period of relative popular neglect. He continues to write, currently working on "David Voloshin," a novel he describes as "long" and "ambitious." He is also writing short fiction and collaborating on "a couple of screenplays." He teaches writing and literature at the University of Massachusetts, Amherst, where he has been writer-in-residence since 1971.

References:

Cordelia Candelaria, "A Decade of Ethnic Fiction by Jay Neugeboren," *MELUS*, 5 (Winter 1978): 71-82;

Charles Moran, "Parentheses," *Massachusetts Review*, 11 (Summer 1970): 613-616;

Michael Willis, "From Kerouac to Koch," *Columbia College Today* (Winter/Spring 1971).

Hugh Nissenson
(10 March 1933-)

Liela H. Goldman
University of Michigan-Dearborn

BOOKS: *A Pile of Stones: Short Stories* (New York: Scribners, 1965);

Notes From the Frontier (New York: Dial, 1968);

In the Reign of Peace (New York: Farrar, Straus & Giroux, 1972; London: Secker & Warburg, 1972);

My Own Ground (New York: Farrar, Straus & Giroux, 1976; London: Secker & Warburg, 1976).

To read the works of Hugh Nissenson is to confront such issues as the meaning of existence, the brutality of life, the nature of evil, God's relationship to man, man's need and search for redemption, and being Jewish in a hostile world.

Hugh Nissenson made his debut as an American-Jewish writer with the publication, in 1965, of his collection of, as one critic notes, "superbly crafted" short stories entitled *A Pile of Stones*, winner of the Edward Lewis Wallant Memorial Award. These stories, some of which appeared previously in journals such as *Commentary* ("The Groom of Zlota Street" and "The Law"), *Harper's* ("The Blessing" and "The Well"), *Esquire* ("A Pile of Stones"), and *American Judaism* ("The American"), encapsulate Nissenson's progress as a writer, while the tripartite division of *A Pile of Stones* — "Then: Poland," "Now: Israel," and "Then and Now: America" — adumbrates Nissenson's ideational and artistic development.

Like other American-Jewish writers, specifically Bernard Malamud, Nissenson uses Jewishness as the metaphor for what he has to say about the universe. The elaboration of this metaphor is uniquely his, yet he uses a specifically Jewish approach, one that is employed most successfully by Saul Bellow in his novels. The epigraph to *A Pile of Stones*, "Let me go, for the day breaketh," is taken from Genesis, from the biblical narrative which concludes the nightlong struggle of Jacob and his antagonist, the angel. This tale fascinates Nissenson because it epitomizes the Jewish experience—the constant life-and-death struggle, the renascence of Israel, the persistent conflict with evil incarnate, the spirit of Esau—and, by extension, that of mankind.

Hugh Nissenson (photo by Layle Silbert)

Critics are, in a sense, confused as to where to place Nissenson. He has been termed a "genuinely religious writer." Cynthia Ozick calls his stories *"Midrashim*, revelatory commentaries," and in a 1977 interview with Diane Cole he refers to himself as a "classic religious personality." Yet unlike Isaac Bashevis Singer, who feels redemption lies in the return to tradition, to the ancestral heritage of our forefathers, Nissenson claims to be a "militant atheist" and does not "believe in God." He is, however, obsessed with mythology—Jewish, Sumerian, Hindu, Greek, Christian, and American—and incorporates it into his writings. Although religious and Jewish metaphors permeate his work, he should not be mistaken as espousing Orthodox Jewish epistemology. Nissenson sees the Bible as a rich compilation of Jewish myth.

Hugh Nissenson was born in Brooklyn in 1933. His father, Charles Nissenson, lived in Warsaw until his immigration to the United States as a youth in 1910. He settled, as did many other Jews, on New York City's Lower East Side. He first worked in a sweatshop sweater factory and then as a traveling salesman, becoming one of the great American drummers fictionalized in Theodore Dreiser's *Sister Carrie*. This experience totally Americanized Charles Nissenson. He dropped his Yiddish and became fully articulate in the American idiom. His tales to his son of Jewish life both in Warsaw and on the East Side in the early 1900s serve as the background for some of Nissenson's stories and his novel *My Own Ground* (1976), while the American experience is captured in other stories as well as in his most recent novel, "The Tree of Life," which has been accepted for publication by Harper and Row. Nissenson's mother, Harriette Dolch, also of Polish parents, from the city of Lvov, was born in Brooklyn, New York.

Although Nissenson says his father is a "deeply religious man," unlike many of his contemporary second-generation American Jews, Nissenson did not receive religious training as a boy. By his account, he did receive a "religious sensibility" from his father, who related to him stories of the Bible and instilled in him "a sense that there is a God who has a special relationship with His people." His mother was the secularist in the family.

Growing up in the 1930s and 1940s, the central experiences for Nissenson—those which transformed his youthful belief and molded his ideas to the maturity of his present thought—were the tragedy of the Holocaust and the creation of the State of Israel. Evil, Satan, God and Israel, combined with the cycle of death and rebirth, became Nissenson's literary motifs and the inspiration for his artistry.

Nissenson attended the Fieldston School in New York and later went to Swarthmore College, from which he graduated Phi Beta Kappa in 1955. In 1961, he was a Wallace Stegner literary fellow at Stanford University.

In his interview with Diane Cole, Nissenson reveals that during his college years in the 1950s, he "passed through a series of intensely profound mystical experiences." He attempts to recapture and articulate the sense of these experiences in his short stories. He singles out the story "The Pris-

oner" in his collection *A Pile of Stones* as addressing itself to this task. In his estimation, he wrote his first "mature" short story, "The Blessing," at the age of twenty-five.

In the 1960s his stories began to appear in *Commentary, Esquire,* and *Harper's*. By this time, Nissenson was beginning to doubt his faith in God. In 1961, he went to Israel to cover the Eichmann trial for *Commentary*. Having previously read one of Martin Buber's works, wherein Buber comments about the "dark aspect of God," Nissenson decided to visit him in Israel. For a period of time, Buber was a major influence in Nissenson's thinking. He borrowed from Buber the idea that God can be demonic as well as benevolent. He has since, as he states, "repudiated" Buber. Presently, Nissenson views the cosmos as a "universe of blind chance."

Nissenson returned to Israel in 1965 and again during the Six-Day War in 1967, spending time with friends on the northern border settlement of Kibbutz Mayan Baruch in order to do research for his second book, *Notes From the Frontier* (1968). He has returned to the country several times since then, professing his love for Israel and his love for the Jews.

He and his wife, Marilyn Claster Nissenson, reside in New York City, on the Upper West Side, with their two daughters, Kate and Kore. He has taught at Manhattanville College and lectured on contemporary fiction, modern Jewish literature, and the Bible. He does not, however, hold a permanent teaching position, preferring the freedom of free-lance writing of fiction, articles, and television scripts.

A Pile of Stones commences Nissenson's spiritual autobiography and marks the beginning of his odyssey into the realm of Jewish mysticism. Though the themes of these stories present the classical tensions of Jewish literature—the impecunious saint and the prosperous sinner, death of the innocent and belief in a benevolent and merciful God, anti-Semitism and the chosenness of the Jewish people—Nissenson's unifying concern, as Lawrence Berkove suggests, is the problem of belief. He uses a theological and mystical framework (the number of stories in this compilation, seven, is carefully chosen for its religious and mystic significance) to set forth the values of traditional Judaism in an attempt to penetrate the mystery of God's relationship with Israel.

One of the basic tenets of Jewish epistemology is the belief in free will or freedom of choice. It is this freedom that makes man independent and allows him to control his destiny. Whether the Jew is in Poland, Israel, or America, his choices will define his experience. At times, the choice is simple, involving quotidian exigencies; at other times the choice is august, involving a life-and-death struggle. Three stories in *A Pile of Stones* illustrate the value of choice effectively.

The first, "The Groom of Zlota Street," set in Warsaw "in the first decade of the century" during Russian domination of Poland and its concomitant oppression of the Jews, forcefully depicts the primary position that choice plays in the life of an individual. It supersedes all other considerations, even that of physical sustenance. Yechiel, a cousin of the narrator, David, comes to live with David's family in the shop on Mila Street after his parents die. However, because the shop hardly provides for David and his parents, Yechiel must earn his own living selling carriage whips. Yechiel, defying modernity, plies his trade in the garb of the Orthodox Jew of the times—beard, gabardine, and skullcap. Whenever he leaves the shop he is tormented by the Russian sentries who take great pleasure in pulling his beard and beating him. David's mother blames herself for Yechiel's troubles and for those of the family, and David attempts to console her by saying "there's nothing else we can do." Yechiel knows that this is not so, that what sustains him is not the food that he eats, which only nourishes his body. More important to him is his soul, to be able to choose his fate. Regardless of how lowly he may appear, this choice makes him one with the Godhead, a partner with his Creator. This is the lesson he teaches David when he takes David to visit the groom on Zlota Street, who has offered to buy one whip every time Yechiel allows him to pull his beard. The family needs the money. It is before the Sabbath and Yechiel has only a ruble in his pocket. Yet he chooses not to allow the groom to pull his beard. He explains to David that he comes to the groom because the groom gives him a choice: "There's always a choice to be made. . . . Remember that. . . . God provides." The choice may be difficult, the consequence painful. Nevertheless, the courageous exercising of one's will sanctifies man while affirming a belief in God.

This kind of difficult choice is viewed in another light in the story set in the United States and called "The American." The tale reflects upon the inhuman choices that at times have to be made, choices that many may disapprove but which seem to have divine sanction. Moscowitz, in immigrating to the U.S., had to leave his sick daughter in Hamburg, Germany, because the captain of the boat would not allow her on board for fear of infecting

the others. His remorse at having left his daughter is assuaged by his success in the United States. Moscowitz's choice is painful. It displays a disbelief in the beneficence of God—he felt he could not stay in Hamburg with his daughter, hoping that God will provide for them—while affirming man's strength. Moscowitz's decision was godlike, and he had the courage and fortitude to live with his choice. He prospers in America, becomes a supporter of the temple where he attends services, and lives to an old age. This story questions God's relationship to man in context of the brutality and seeming injustice of life.

When this brutality becomes demonic, then freedom of choice as a basic Jewish value is used to negate a belief in God. Nissenson's second story, "The Prisoner," reveals the effect of absolute evil on a firm believer. A Jew is held in prison for political reasons; he has written a book criticizing the czarist regime. The prisoner, once a great sage, was witness to a pogrom. From his hiding place, he saw murder, looting, and the brutal rape of a fourteen-year-old girl by a gang of drunken peasants who afterward cut open her stomach with a sickle and stuffed it with feathers. The one-time sage chooses to renounce his service to God in favor of serving the Party and becomes a Communist, but the choice he makes does not free him from the burden of his life. His mystical dream of the obliteration of differences among men is disturbed by the recurring vision of the fourteen-year-old girl. This image forces the prisoner to acknowledge the Deity, but now it is a malevolent Deity, one that causes him to suffer and is responsible for the suffering of mankind. Although this story is set in the first decade of the twentieth century, in 1906, the rape and brutal murder of the girl may be seen as a metaphor for the heinous crimes committed against the Jewish people during the Holocaust. The reaction of the prisoner reflects Nissenson's own movement away from belief, and, of course, the reaction of countless survivors.

God's role in the suffering of the innocent is questioned once again in the third story, "The Blessing," set in modern Israel. An eight-year-old boy has died of cancer. His secularist father is resentful and refuses to attend his son's funeral. Esther, a relative, who is a survivor of Belsen, comes to the house to assist in the preparations. Upon hearing of the death of her nephew, she had uttered the traditional Jewish response to such news, "Blessed be the true Judge"—an acknowledgment of man's inability to understand the ways of the Lord and the meaning of death. Esther explains to the father that she too was resentful, wanted to curse God, and denounce her belief. "Still," she says, "one must live." Nissenson is stating, through Esther, that belief in God is necessary for man. It orders his universe; it gives him reason for continued existence; it offers him a measure of peace within himself. Those who rebel against God are left with a void.

Nissenson is one of the few American-Jewish writers who expresses an attitude toward Israel which is not merely positive but exuberant as well. He says: "I am frankly enamored, in love, with Israel, as one would love a woman. I mean the country of Israel and also what that represents." Nissenson sees in Israel the coming of age of the Jewish people—the "abjure[ment] of the idea of Messianic salvation" in favor of personal redemption via the creation of a "viable civilization."

Divided into two sections, *Notes From the Frontier* is a nonfiction record of two of Nissenson's trips to Israel: "Summer 1965" reports on life prior to the Six-Day War, the apprehensiveness, preparedness, and strength of the people attempting to lead normal lives despite the imminence of danger; "June 1967" describes the war itself, Nissenson's difficulty getting into the border kibbutz of Mayan Baruch, the liberation of Jerusalem, and his trip through the Golan.

Notes From the Frontier gives the reader an intimate glimpse into collective farming life and the individual needs of kibbutz members. Nissenson views the kibbutz mostly as an observer and recorder. The difficulty with the work is point of view. The characters appear to be dramatis personae of a play about a kibbutz, and their monologues attempt to reconcile socialist idealism with traditional bourgeois background.

Shlomo Wolfe and his wife, Aliza, Nissenson's friends with whom he stays at the kibbutz, jointly express the author's denial of God. For Aliza, Auschwitz negated the concept of religious intervention or divine sanction or guardianship; Shlomo relates piety with pacifism, which he feels has no place in a modern world. Religious ritual is meaningless to him, but he has not found adequate substitutes for basic religious ideas. Consequently, he and his wife secularize religious concepts—the Sabbath, the Bar Mitzvah, Redemption, Israel, the Bible—and have no heritage for their children.

The one religious Jew in this work, the *saba*, or grandfather who has joined the kibbutz to be with his daughter and grandchildren, is the least convincing character presented. He embodies the ancient concept of Judaism, and his piety contrasts markedly with the militant atheism and secularism of Shlomo Wolfe. The *saba* provides the axis around which the religious-secular debate can revolve. Ultimately, Nissenson's stance is equivocal; he is not sure that it is "possible to create a humane civilization without God."

In the progression of Nissenson's spiritual autobiography, the works that follow *A Pile of Stones* focus upon this question raised in *Notes From the Frontier*. Nissenson, having lost his own belief in God, must come to terms with this problem, and the second collection of short stories, *In the Reign of Peace* (1972), continues the dialectic of belief. As Cynthia Ozick in her review of this work in the *New York Times Book Review* suggests, although this volume appeared seven years after *A Pile of Stones*, it is a continuation of the first in "style and movement." Traditional Jewish values are also at the core of this work, but the unifying concern here is the problem of redemption, as indicated by the epigraph, "The Son of David will come when one generation of man is either totally guilty or totally innocent."

In Nissenson's fiction, redemption comes in a variety of guises. It can be the traditional messianism of Chaim in the short story "In the Reign of Peace," the communism of the prisoner in the story named for him in *A Pile of Stones*, the socialism and nationalism of the Israelis in *Notes From the Frontier* and *In the Reign of Peace*, or the Sabbatianism of Rabbi Isaacs in Nissenson's 1976 novel, *My Own Ground*. The short stories in Nissenson's second collection depict the period of turmoil that precedes "the reign of peace." Of the eight stories, all but two take place in Israel. All deal with the problem of good and evil and indirectly question the role of God in the affairs of man.

The most poignant rendering of the need for redemption is in the title story. The setting is a northern Israeli kibbutz. The secular-religious agon continues in the dialogue between the narrator, a secularist kibbutz member, and Chaim, a religious Jew from Morocco who lives in the nearby village of Kiryat Shemona but works on the kibbutz. Chaim finds it preposterous that Jews should work on the Sabbath, that they should eat nonkosher meat, and that they should not believe in God. The most paradoxical, however, to Chaim, is the idea that Jews can function without a belief in the Messiah. The narrator explains that he does believe in redemption, but a redemption of the socialist kind as found on the kibbutz, wherein all men share the benefits of the community. For him, redemption is the kibbutz. For Chaim, this is insufficient. Redemption to him is more than an egalitarian belief.

It is not only equality, but peace and justice as well. Chaim illustrates the traditional concept of redemption by showing the narrator the plight of a mouse caught in a hole in the concrete. Stuck halfway through the hole, the mouse is being eaten alive by ants. When the narrator admits that things of this nature are commonplace, Chaim tells him, "But not in the reign of peace. . . . When the Messiah comes."

This need for peace to end violence and suffering is the subject of three other stories in this collection. "The Throne of Good" deals with the relationship of good and evil. Set during the tumultuous period prior to Israel's statehood, right after World War II during the British mandate in Palestine, the tale reflects upon the problem of the end justifying the means—whether doing evil, defying British law, committing acts of terror for the eventual attainment of good, statehood, and security for Jews in their own land is warranted. A youthful survivor of the Holocaust, who had been detained in Cyprus but smuggled into Palestine, has enlisted for an unspecified terrorist activity. He quotes the Baal-Shem-Tov, founder of the Hasidic movement, to support his actions: "Evil is only the throne of good." The skeptical narrator, however, questions whether "any good can come of it."

Nissenson had provided an answer in *Notes From the Frontier*. In relating the story of the capture

Self-caricature by Neugeboren (collection of Burt Britton)

of Lod during the War of Independence, Nat, a kibbutz member says: "Once we had denied God and decided to acquire power to redeem ourselves, we were destined to become like everyone else. Murderers." The idea voiced is that Israel and the Jews are different from all other people. As God's chosen people, their Law sets them morally above others. This theme is repeated in the story "The Crazy Old Man" from *In the Reign of Peace*. The old man believes that Israel's survival depends on the new generation's establishment of a new world order, whereby "swords will be turned into ploughshares." Nissenson interweaves Christian thought with Jewish morality in this ambiguous tale of messianism, God's relationship to Israel, Israel's rebirth, and the problem of good and evil.

Another expression of the pacifist-militant, religious-secular dialectic and the effect the denial of God has upon the individual is presented in the story "Forcing the End," a modern retelling of an incident in the life of the first-century sage Yochanan Ben Zakkai. In Nissenson's narrative, Rabbi Jacobi, a religious scholar and an outspoken pacifist, wants to go to Yavneh to establish a school, but the authorities, who consider him a controversial figure, refuse to grant him permission to leave Jerusalem. He has himself smuggled out, as Ben Zakkai did, in a coffin in a mock funeral procession, but he is killed in Yavneh by a terrorist group which disapproves of pacifism and peace with the Arabs. Each group feels that its way is the only method to bring about the "reign of peace." Yet the murder of Rabbi Jacobi indicates the loss of a moral standard and leads back to the questions: "Is it possible to create a humane civilization without God?" Or, is evil really "only the throne of good?"

Of the four other stories in the collection, two more are set in Israel: "Going Up," which presents a novel interpretation of a saying in the 121st Psalm ("Behold, the guardian of Israel neither sleeps nor slumbers"), and "Lamentations," which examines death and rebirth and the nexus that binds the present to the past. Two tales are set in the United States: "Charity" and "Grace." Like *A Pile of Stones*, *In the Reign of Peace* contains one tale with a non-Jewish background, as if in preparation for Nissenson's work in progress "The Tree of Life."

Nissenson's most recently published novel, *My Own Ground*, is a troublesome work. Its tone is harsh, and it deals with the seamy side of Jewish life. Its world of pimps, prostitutes, and brothels is difficult to reconcile with Nissenson's earlier writings. Focusing on the impoverished Jewish community of New York's Lower East Side in the early part of the

—115—

29 March, 1812.   Easter Sunday. What follows almost verbatim
is the sermon delivered by the Rev. at dawn from atop the log in
Central Park, Mansfield:
      "' & if Christ be not risen, then is our preaching vain &
your faith is also vain.' 1 Cor. 15:14.
      "The Apostle Paul hits the nail on the head. Did Christ
rise from the dead today or not? I say, 'Yes. He did!' John
is the witness who convinces me. Listen how he describes
himself & Peter in Chap. 20, Verses 4 - 7;   *John*
      "'So they ran both together; and the other disciple did
outrun Peter and came first to the sepulchre. & he stooping
down & looking in, saw the linen clothes lying, yet went he not
in. Then cometh Simon Peter, following him, & went into the
sepulchre, & seeth the linen clothes lie. & the napkin, that
was about his head, not lying with the linen clothes but wrapped
together in a place by itself.'
      "Being younger than Peter, John outruns him; he stoops at
the entrance to the tomb, sees them linen clothes, but don't go
in. How come? Think! Because he's thunder-struck at the sight
 -- burial clothes in a heap on the floor! Meanwhile, Peter
pushes past. He spots not only the clothes, but that napkin,
'wrapped together in a place by itself.'
      "What's so important about that? Think again! Think
again! Jesus kept Himself neat. That's common sense. Picture
it. After rising from the dead, He wraps up the napkin. How
like Him!
      "That's why John then tells us in Verse 8,
      "'Then went in also that other disciple, which came first
to the sepulchre, & he saw, & believed'
      "Sure he did. So do I. 'I believe in God the Father
Almighty, Maker of Heaven & Earth; & in Jesus Christ, His only
Son Our Lord; who was conceived by the Holy Spirit, born of the
Virgin Mary, suffered under Pontius Pilate, was crucified, dead,
& buried; the 3rd. day He rose from the dead; He ascended to
Heaven & sitteth at the rt. hand of God the Father Almighty;
from thence He shall come to judge the quick & the dead. I
believe in the Holy Spirit; the Holy Catholic Church, the
Communion of Saints, the forgiveness of sins, the resurrection
of the body & the life everlasting. ~~Amen.~~' The wrapped up
napkin clinches it for me."

31 March.   Bought this morn. of Jones, at his store,
               Mans., 3 sheets of Royal size drawing
               paper @ .03. - - - - - -   .09.
               Bought of the above, 4 oz. India ink. - -   .04.
               Bought of the above, 4 oz. white lead. -   .02.

Swapped him my glasses for a stronger pair.

Corrected typescript page from Nissenson's forthcoming novel "The Tree of Life" twentieth century, the work is narrated by Jacob Brody, who relates his memoirs of the summer of 1912 and the tragedy of Hannah Isaacs.

In terms of his spiritual autobiography, Nissenson illustrates in this work that a viable civilization needs the admixture of spiritual and physical elements. The chaste and destitute Hannah's progression from the pious puritan, who lived by her father's exaggerated interpretation of the Law, to the whore of Babylon, as she sinks into a life of sexual perversity, only succeeds in confusing her so that she finally destroys herself.

Viewed in terms of Nissenson's other works, *My Own Ground* is a fusion of classical and biblical mythologies focusing on the dark side of humanity: the descent into Hades, the nightlong struggle with an adversary. It also bears a striking similarity to Isaac Bashevis Singer's *Satan in Goray*. While Singer's work, written prior to World War II, is set against the background of the Chmelnicki massacre and foreshadows the Holocaust, Nissenson's narrative is burdened by the heinous events that decimated European Jewry, destroyed humanity, and shook man's faith in God's sovereignty. The Holocaust is never mentioned—the events in the work predate the Holocaust by some twenty years—but the darkened vision that is presented, the plunge into depravity as forcing the advent of messianism, is an allegorical representation of the Holocaust. In biblical fashion similar to Solomon's Song of Songs, Nissenson employs a woman to represent Israel, and her fate—her seduction, debasement, and suicide—becomes the fate of the Jewish people. The work does not end on a note of death, however. It concludes with the promise of birth and a dream scene. The struggle of Jacob and the adversary in this novel, unlike the biblical narrative, is lost. Israel is defeated but not vanquished.

My Own Ground is somber, reflecting the author's metaphysical progression. It deals with the themes that have preoccupied Nissenson heretofore: good and evil, God's role in the universe, man's relationship to man, death and rebirth, redemption. The conclusion implied in this work is expressed in the moral which ends *Satan in Goray*: "LET NONE ATTEMPT TO FORCE THE LORD: TO END OUR PAIN WITHIN THE WORLD: THE MESSIAH WILL COME IN GOD'S OWN TIME. . . ."

Nissenson, as yet, has not achieved the renown he deserves. Critical attention has been slight. Yet his works are incisive, sensitive, and powerful, especially *A Pile of Stones*, which makes a major statement. Nissenson's problem is how to transcend his own barrier. Yet the mystery of death and rebirth, which Nissenson recognizes enveloping Israel's existence, is an enigma which must be confronted.

References:

Lawrence I. Berkove, "American *Midrashim*: Hugh Nissenson's Stories," *Critique*, 20, no. 1 (1978): 75-82;

Diane Cole, "A Conversation With Hugh Nissenson," *National Jewish Monthly*, 92 (September 1977): 8-16;

Arthur Kurzweil, "An Atheist and His Demonic God: An Interview with Hugh Nissenson," *Response*, 11 (Winter 1978-79): 17-23;

Cynthia Ozick, Review of *In the Reign of Peace*, *New York Times Book Review*, 19 March 1972, pp. 4, 22;

Alvin Rosenfeld, "Israel and the Idea of Redemption in the Fiction of Hugh Nissenson," *Midstream*, 26 (April 1980): 54-56.

Tillie Olsen

(14 January 1913?-   )

Marleen Barr
Virginia Polytechnic Institute and State University

See also the Olsen entry in *DLB Yearbook: 1980*.

BOOKS: *Tell Me a Riddle* (Philadelphia: Lippincott, 1961; London: Faber, 1964);
Yonnondio: From The Thirties (New York: Delacorte, 1974; London: Faber, 1974);
Silences (New York: Delacorte/Seymour Lawrence, 1978; London: Faber, 1978).

OTHER: "A Biographical Interpretation," in *Life in the Iron Mills*, by Rebecca Harding Davis (Old Westbury, N.Y.: Feminist Press, 1972).

SELECTED PERIODICAL PUBLICATIONS: "I Want You Women Up North to Know," *Partisan*, 1 (March 1934): 4;
"There is a Lesson," *Partisan*, 1 (April-May 1934): 4;
"Thousand-Dollar Vagrant," *New Republic*, 80 (August 1934): 67-69;
"The Strike," *Partisan Review*, 1 (September-October 1934): 3-9;
"Requa," *Iowa Review*, 1 (Summer 1970): 54-74.

Tillie Olsen (photo by Leonda Fiske)

Tillie Olsen, feminist and working-class writer, grew up in Wyoming and Nebraska, areas which have not often been the childhood homes of America's Jewish authors. This might explain why, despite the fact that some of her urban working-class characters are Jewish, Olsen's work does not center around the Jewish experience. Feminism and humanism—not Judaism—are at the heart of her writing. While American-Jewish writers often explore the relationship of assimilation and identity to American-Jewish life, Olsen deals with these two concerns in terms of the lives of women and the poor. Hence, like Norman Mailer, Saul Bellow, and Bernard Malamud, Olsen does not restrict herself to that which is exclusively Jewish. Because Henry Roth's depiction of ghetto life in *Call It Sleep* (1934) is analogous to her descriptions of urban poverty, he is the Jewish writer whose fiction is closest to her own.

In addition to her attention to working-class people, Olsen explores the literary tragedy of silenced writers, creative spirits killed by such potent poisons as class and gender. She reminds readers that, because they had to work and serve as their household's "essential angel," some of Shakespeare's sisters failed to write. As she explains in her most recent book, *Silences* (1978), Olsen's own responsibilities came close to thwarting her artistic pursuits: "As for myself, who did not publish a book until I was fifty, who raised children without household help . . . who worked outside the house on everyday jobs as well . . . who could not kill the essential angel (there was no one else to do her work) . . . [I was] as distant from the world of literature most of my life as literature is distant (in content too) from my world." There is a mirroring, reciprocal relationship between the facts of Olsen's life and the major concerns of her work. Her fiction bridges the distance between her own world and the world of literature. Her personal remarks describe instances when words die, the tragedy of a writer who is often silenced:

> The habits of a lifetime when everything else had to come before writing are not easily broken, even when circumstances now often make it possible for writing to be first; habits of years—response to others, distractibility, responsibility for daily matters—stay with you, mark you, become you. The cost of "discontinuity" . . . is such a weight of things unsaid, an accumulation of material so great, that everything starts up something else in me; what should take weeks takes me sometimes months to write; what should take months, takes years.
>
> I speak of myself to bring here the sense of those others to whom this is in the process of happening (unnecessarily happening, for it need not, must not continue to be) and to remind us of those (I so nearly was one) who never come to writing at all.

So close herself to being unable to write, Olsen speaks for those who do not have the wherewithal to produce art and for those whose art has not received the attention it deserves. This woman who has articulated the suffering of humanity; participated in the public, political sphere; reclaimed women's "lost" texts; and examined the relationship between creativity, sex, and class, has successfully combated silence. Although Olsen's output is small, her work is important because it gives a voice to people who are routinely not heard. Her characters speak with the authentic cadences of ordinary people. Here, for example, is the voice of Whitey in "Hey Sailor, What Ship?": "Wha's it so quiet for? Hey, hit the tune box. . . . Wha time's it anyway? Gotta. . . ."

Olsen, who was born in 1913, was the second of Samuel and Ida Lerner's seven children. The Lerners were Jewish immigrants who had fled Russia after the 1905 rebellion. While she was growing up, she lived in an environment where economic pressure was juxtaposed with political commitment: Samuel Lerner, who labored as a farmer, packinghouse worker, painter, and paper hanger, also became state secretary of the Nebraska Socialist party. Like her father, Olsen of necessity held many jobs, but these did not stop her from being politically active. After being forced to leave high school be-

fore graduating, she worked as a trimmer in a slaughterhouse, a power-press operator, a hash slinger, a mayonnaise-jar capper in a food processing plant, and a checker in a warehouse. Olsen carried on the family tradition of trying to better people's lives by joining the Young Communist League. She was arrested in Kansas City for trying to organize packinghouse workers. While in jail, where she did not have adequate medical care, she became ill with pleurisy which almost developed into tuberculosis. By 1933, Olsen had moved from the Midwest to California, which became her permanent home. She continued her political activities as a participant in the San Francisco Warehouse Strike of 1934. She worked at union headquarters and, once again, spent time in jail. In 1936 she married Jack Olsen, a printer and union man. She had three daughters and worked to support them by holding such jobs as waitress, shaker in a laundry, secretary, transcriber in a dairy-equipment company, and Kelly Girl.

When she won a Stanford University creative-writing fellowship for eight months in 1956-1957, just a year after enrolling in a San Francisco State University creative-writing course, Olsen was given the economic freedom which enabled her to create Whitey and other characters. Instead of having to work outside her home, Olsen wrote "I Stand Here Ironing," "Baptism" (published as "O Yes" in *Tell Me a Riddle*, 1961), and "Hey Sailor, What Ship?"; she also began "Tell Me a Riddle." In 1957, when she had to return to regular employment, Olsen was again silenced. This period of silence was broken in 1959 when a Ford Foundation grant enabled her to complete "Tell Me a Riddle" and to have it published in the collection which bears its name. "Tell Me a Riddle" won the O. Henry Award for the best short story of 1961.

David and Eva, the protagonists of "Tell Me a Riddle," are a Jewish immigrant couple who have struggled to survive—and struggled with each other—throughout their forty-seven-year marriage. Although both of them worked hard, the story stresses that Eva's lot is worse than that of her husband. While David at least found pleasure in the company of friends at his lodge, Eva did not have access to the company of the authors she enjoyed: "She thought . . . of that young wife, who in the deep night hours while she nursed the current baby, and perhaps held another in her lap, would try to stay awake for the only time there was to read. She would feel again the weather on the outside of his cheek when, coming late from a meeting, he would find her so, and stimulated and ardent, sniffing her skin, coax: 'put the book away, don't read, don't read.' " Because she fulfills the needs of others, she has no time to read, no time to fulfill herself.

Eva, who was imprisoned in Russia when she was young, has not found freedom in America. As Selma Burkom and Margaret Williams explain, "Eva's position is no better in America; at least in the coherent culture of the shtetl, women *did* have a respected place. . . . In America, Eva goes without the support of a community which shares her values; nor is she allowed to fulfill her individual needs." For this woman who is tied to a house which never stays clean, to children who drain her energy, to a husband whose needs must be satisfied, life in America is no panacea. As he berates her and sarcastically calls her names according to the particular situation at hand, David's language reflects the fact that Eva is not free to be herself. He calls her "Mrs. Enlightened," "Mrs. Cultured," and "Mrs. Unpleasant" without realizing that Eva might be unpleasant because she has been deprived of literary culture and enlightenment.

Eva, who could not find refuge in books, is also denied a literal place of refuge. She wishes to keep her home; David desires to retire to his union's Haven, a cooperative for the aged. Eva does not have the power to enforce her wish, and, after she learns that she has cancer, David takes her on a cross-country trip. Like a yo-yo, she moves from the house of one of her children to that of another while David holds the controlling string. Eva creates her own prison to escape from her children, grandchildren, and husband: she crawls into a closet and reflects upon her penal servitude in Russia.

It is clear that for Eva marriage has also been a form of penal servitude. Even during her last days, her needs are sacrificed to satisfy others. David enjoys traveling; her children and grandchildren enjoy visiting with her; Eva yearns to return home to a dwelling which she may no longer own: "your children cannot show enough how glad they are to see you, and you want to go home. . . . We cannot be with the children at home." She will never go home again.

In addition to being denied access to her home and to her books, in the end Eva is also denied the truth about the severity of her illness. Her still vigorous husband sees her die in a hospital bed. He is free to go to his Haven. The story implies that women can find no haven, in life—and even in death: "Religion that stifled and said: in Paradise woman, you will be the footstool of your husband, and in life . . . ground under, despised trembling in cellars." Even in paradise, Eva might find herself in a prison or in a closet.

"I Stand Here Ironing," the first story in *Tell Me a Riddle*, begins with the voice of a mother: "I stand here ironing, and what you asked me moves tormented back and forth with the iron." This sentence typifies Olsen's fiction: a mother/worker, an ordinary person, is given an opportunity to speak, is invited to tell her story. This particular mother, like many mothers, is concerned that she did not raise her daughter properly. And, like many mothers, the necessity of earning a living prevented her from spending sufficient time with her child, Emily: "Her father left me before she was a year old. I had to work her first six years when there was work, or I sent her home and to his relatives. There were years when she had care she hated." Lack of money kept Emily's "child cry"—"That time of motherhood . . . when the ear is not one's own but must always be racked and listened for the child cry, the child call"—from reaching the attentive ear of her mother. Emily's cries, then, were silenced.

The story focuses upon the waste of artistic, as well as maternal, creativity. Emily, who is not pretty, not popular, and not studious, does excel in one area: audiences respond to her enthusiastically when she performs as a clown. Yet, because there is not enough money, her talent becomes "eddied inside, clogged and clotted": "You ought to do something about her with a gift like that—but without money, or knowing how, what does one do?"

The mother wishes her daughter to know that, even though a lack of money has hampered Emily's personal and creative development, "there is still enough left to live by." Emily is an individual, "more than this dress on the ironing board, helpless before the iron"; she is more than a member of a certain economic class who can be helplessly molded and shaped by her social position. After all, like Emily, Olsen received neither her mother's full attention nor the funds to pursue her talent. Emily, like Olsen, can escape from being completely controlled by her disadvantages.

"Hey Sailor, What Ship?," the story which follows "I Stand Here Ironing" in *Tell Me a Riddle*, also discusses the waste of human potential. Whitey, the protagonist, is a sailor who has never developed close familial relationships. The family of his friend Lennie, whose life he once saved, provides "the only house in the world he can come into and be around people without having to pay." Yet, because Whitey is different, because a sailor's language is not appropriately spoken in a respectable home, he pays

Page from Olsen's notebook for Tell Me a Riddle. *The original page is approximately 3" x 5".*

the price of exclusion. Jeannie, the daughter of this family who also appears in "Tell Me a Riddle," articulates her concern: "I've got some friends coming over. . . . Whitey, please, they're not used to your kind of language." Whitey, then, is another of Olsen's characters who is silenced because of his social position. The sailor who carries a card which reads "When in Managua it's Marie's for Hospitality" does not find hospitality in his friend's home.

Hence, he will have to pay for all the hospitality he receives. Money cannot buy him a place in Lennie's family; money cannot buy him permanent rights to feel a child's warmth: "this helpless warmth against him, this feel of a child—lost country to him and unattainable." Although he has the money to buy women and to buy gifts for Lennie's family, he does not have access to the love of a woman and to the gift of familial love. He is aware that his relationships are empty: "Shove it, Lennie. So you're a chunk of my life. So?" When he leaves Lennie's house and looks down at similar houses in San Francisco, he knows that he will be forever barred from the relationships which are lived out in those buildings: "he can see the city below him, wave after wave, and there at the crest, the tiny house he has left, its eyes unshaded." The story questions the value of a life without a family, the value of spending all of one's time making a living on the crest of real waves. Even though Lennie's family has less money than Whitey, they, at least, have each other. Like Emily, for them "there is still enough left to live by."

"O Yes," the third story in *Tell Me a Riddle*, also focuses upon a terminated relationship. It tells why the friendship between Carol, a white girl, and Parialee, a black girl, is destroyed by economic and social pressures. Young Carol enters the black world and hears the words which give the story its title: "*Any day now I'll reach that land of freedom, Yes, O Yes.*" When Carol questions the intensity of these words, her mother thinks, "emotion . . . a characteristic of the religion of all oppressed peoples." The girls' friendship is strained as society encourages them to assume the roles of the oppressed and the oppressor. Blacks and whites inhabit separate worlds, environments whose differences are illustrated by the fact that Carol faints while she is in the black church.

The girls are exposed to different social expectations. Parialee is immersed in the black experience, "collecting things." "Like her own crowd. Like jivetalk and rhythmandblues. Like teachers who treat her like a dummy and white kids who treat her like dirt." Carol learns "how they sort," the appropriate mode of dress and behavior for a proper white girl. The economic and social reasons for the rift between them cannot be separated. While Carol enjoys herself after school, Parialee must return home to compensate for the absence of her working mother: "Carol is off to a club or skating or library or someone's house, and Parry can stay for kickball only on rare afternoons when she does not have to hurry home where Lucy, Bubbie, and the cousins wait to be cared for, now that Alva [her mother] works the four to twelve thirty shift." It is clear, then, that the girls' friendship is wrenched apart because "Parry's colored and Carrie's white." Here, again, Olsen describes how economic need and the demands of a large family stifle an individual's personal development.

The story ends with a note of hope, however. Upon discovering the existence of evil, instead of complacently accepting this knowledge Carol questions her mother: "Oh why is it like it is and why do I have to care?" Like the mother in "I Stand Here Ironing," Carol's mother communicates values to her daughter. The girl learns that she may one day again be friends with Parialee, "As Alva and I are." O yes, despite the difference of race and class, there is a chance that the girls will resume their friendship. Individuals *can* circumvent social rules and economic differences.

After the publication of *Tell Me a Riddle*, Olsen received fellowships from the Radcliffe Institute (1962-1964) and the National Endowment for the Arts (1968). Between 1969 and 1972 she taught at three universities: Amherst, the University of Massachusetts (Boston), and Stanford. While she was writer-in-residence at M.I.T. (1973), she received a grant from the MacDowell Colony. Olsen then returned to the University of Massachusetts (1973-1974) as Distinguished Visiting Professor.

The MacDowell Colony's support allowed her to publish *Yonnondio* (1974), whose first chapter, "The Iron Throat," appeared in *Partisan Review* in 1934. "A Note About This Book" explains that the novel has "ceased to be solely the work of that long ago young writer and, in arduous partnership, became the older one's as well." Hence *Yonnondio*, which derives its title and epigraph from Walt Whitman's "Yonnondio"—a lament for the aborigines whose "wailing word is borne through the air for a moment, / Then blank and gone and still, and utterly lost"—is a once-silenced text which has been reclaimed.

Yonnondio, which keeps the word of the unknown among America's working class from becoming utterly lost, resembles the work of another nearly silenced writer: Rebecca Harding Davis, whose writing was reclaimed by Olsen. Davis, the author of *Life in the Iron Mills*, a text which also speaks for the working class, has been Olsen's model since she was a teenager. She explains her identification with Davis in *Silences*: "myself so nearly remaining mute. . . . ; herself . . . so close to remaining mute." Olsen suggested that the Feminist Press republish *Life in the Iron Mills*, and she wrote the introduction to the press's 1972 edition. (The Feminist Press also republished Agnes Smedley's *Daughter of Earth* and Charlotte Perkins Gilman's *The Yellow Wallpaper* at Olsen's suggestion.) Both *Life in the Iron Mills* and *Yonnondio* are, in Olsen's words, "fiction which incorporates social and economic problems directly, *and in terms of their effects upon human beings*," books which say, "Literature can be made out of the lives of despised people." Hence, *Yonnondio*, like *Tell Me a Riddle*, directly addresses the problems of these "despised people": large families, temporary residences, lack of educational opportunities, lack of resources to nurture creativity.

In *Yonnondio*, the descriptions of the working person's lot are more graphic than those found in *Tell Me a Riddle*. This is what happens to meatpacking industry workers who are in the path of emissions from a broken steam pipe: "Peg and Andra and Phelomena and Cleola directly underneath fall and writhe in their crinkling skins, their sudden juices. Lena, pregnant, faints. . . . Ella, already at the work of calming, of rescue, thinks through her own pain: steamed boiled broiled cooked *scalded*." These "ordinary" victims with romantic-sounding names are not at the center of this novel whose focus is quite difficult to pinpoint. The text is at once a call for political action, the story of the Holbrook family's futile life, the story of young Mazie Holbrook's development, and a statement about the suffering of the working class.

These elements coalesce when *Yonnondio* is viewed as more than a working-class novel; it is a feminist working-class novel. The scalded workers are all women; Mazie is the only young Holbrook who emerges as a distinct individual; and, despite all the problems of Jim Holbrook, it is his wife Anna who receives most of the reader's sympathy. When *Yonnondio* depicts the lives of the working class, it stresses that certain members of this class must cope with the worst conditions: poor women, those who are silenced even on the rare occasions when men of their class are allowed to speak. The novel directly states that women do the most unpleasant jobs, that women work where men will not: "Breathing with open mouth, the young girls and women in casings,

where men will not work. Year-round breathing with open mouth, learning to pant shallow to endure the excrement reek of offal, the smothering stench from the blood house below." However, instead of concentrating upon the horrible experiences of women factory workers, the novel describes the problems of one woman whose life revolves around the domestic sphere. Mazie's conversation with her mother implies that women unfairly assume the burden of domestic responsibility:

> "Why is it always me that has to help? How come Will [her brother] gets to play?"
> "Will's a boy."
> "Why couldn't *I* get borned a boy?"

This conversation occurs at the end of the novel, after Mazie has grown up watching her mother's biological and social victimization. Anna cannot make enough money; she cannot stop making too many babies.

In addition to speaking about man's inhumanity to working men, *Yonnondio* also refuses to be silent about working men's inhumanity to their wives. Jim Holbrook uses his family—and especially his wife—as scapegoats upon which to vent his emotions: "For several weeks Jim Holbrook had been in an evil mood. The whole household walked in terror. He had nothing but heavy blows for the children, and he struck Anna too often to remember." Anna has no such outlet. Nor can she relieve her frustrations verbally. Jim complains about the quality of her work: "Any time I want sewage to eat I can get it on the job"; Anna complains to no one.

He does not welcome her words: "Goddam woman—what's the matter with her anyhow? Don't even have a wife that's a wife anymore—just let her say one word to me and I'll bash her head in." And, when she does voice an objection, her words are unheard, silenced.

Anna becomes dangerously ill as a result of miscarriage. In addition to her poverty, Jim is a major cause of Anna's suffering. He holds one terrible job at a time. She holds three simultaneously: wife of an insensitive husband, mother to children whose lives will ultimately be as hopeless as her own, and part-time laundress. Like Eva in "Tell Me a Riddle," Anna is defeated because she satisfies others at her own expense: "She fed and clothed the children, scrubbed, gave herself to Jim, clenching her fists against a pain she had no strength to feel." What Jim describes as "a woman's goddam life" is much worse than his own.

Hopelessness pervades the novel. Jim makes no progress even though he strives to give his family a better life. When readers first encounter him, he is employed as a miner; at the novel's end, although he has held many jobs, he again works in a hole in the earth. Anna suffers from satisfying the demands of her large family, and, when she satisfies her husband's demands, her family grows larger. Because they will not receive an adequate "edjication," the Holbrook children will eventually relive their parents' problems. This might explain why, with the exception of Mazie, the children are not given individual characteristics. Since it is virtually impossible for them to escape filling a predetermined social niche, they are robbed of their individuality. Regardless of how many times their family moves, or how many jobs their father holds, a better life is beyond their reach.

Five-year-old Will Holbrook already understands the implications of this statement: "Five years. I'm wearin your [Mazie's] old coat, a girl's coat. For why?" Although Will may spend his life questioning his poverty, he may never find the answer of how to escape its generational cycle. Young Will, who must wear a girl's coat, is the son of a man who cannot afford to buy the proper attire for his job. Regardless of their labor, the Holbrooks are excluded from the good life, despised.

Mazie thinks about this exclusion while she and members of her family traverse the lawns of the rich in search of dandelions for their table: "A vague shame, a weedy sense of not belonging, of something being wrong about them, stirred uneasy through Mazie." The Holbrook family has grown haphazardly, and it must take root where it can: "when the seed strikes stone; the soil will not sustain; the spring is false; the time is drought or blight or infestation; the frost comes premature," Olsen writes in *Silences*.

It is not surprising that Olsen was thinking about writers—especially women writers—when she wrote those words. In addition to creating memorable female characters like Anna and Eva, Olsen is an important feminist educator. Her courses, which have titles such as "Literature of the Working Class and the Human Struggle for Freedom" and "Women in Fact and Fiction," have introduced male and female students to long-forgotten works by women. After it was published in the *Women's Studies Newsletter*, the reading list she developed was used widely in women's studies courses. And her articles, "Silences: When Writers Don't Write" (*Harper's*, October 1965), and "Women Who Are Writers In Our Century: One Out of Twelve" (*College English*, October 1972), have been included in many women's studies courses throughout the United States. These two essays are republished in *Silences* (1978), a collection of Olsen's work which "is concerned with the relationship of circumstances—including class color sex; the times, climate into which one is born—to the creation of literature." Appropriately, *Silences*, the work of an influential college professor who never had a formal college education, "is not an orthodoxly written work of academic scholarship." Like her fiction, Olsen's nonfiction "came slow, hard won."

Since "Silences" begins by mentioning the silences of great men—"Thomas Hardy, Melville, Rimbaud, Gerard Manly Hopkins"—it illustrates that the articulation of feminist discourse is slow and hard won. In the essay women are only one of the four categories of "mute inglorious Miltons": "those whose waking hours are all struggle for existence; the barely educated; the illiterate; women." It insists upon including men: "we are in a time of more and more hidden and foreground silences, women *and* men." When ideas in "Silences" were first made public as Olsen's oral presentation at the Radcliffe Institute (1962), the members of the Institute's weekly colloquium heard her say that both class and gender are responsible for eradicating creativity. The essay, which does not focus solely upon women, names and defines the circumstances which retard the work of women writers. The following explanation is offered by Olsen, a member of the working class and a mother: "But women are traditionally trained to place others' needs first, to feel these needs as their own . . . their sphere, their satisfaction to be in making it possible for others to use their abilities. . . . motherhood means being instantly interruptable, responsive, responsible. It is distraction, not meditation, that becomes habitual; interruption, not continuity. . . ." The reason why "Silences" is a feminist essay is analogous to the reason why *Yonnondio* is a feminist novel. *Yonnondio*, a working-class text, includes the viewpoint of women; "Silences" a text whose subtitle includes the generic term *writers*, includes a discussion of writers who are women. Neither text silences the consideration of that which is specifically feminine.

Although the silences of women are discussed separately in Olsen's essay about human silences, the piece seems finally to reject categories. She mentions Rebecca Harding Davis together with luminaries. And, a discussion of her personal silences appears with a consideration of those of famous male writers. When "Silences" gives a voice to women, it refuses to silence men.

Not so for "One Out of Twelve: Writers Who Are Women In Our Century." Published seven years after "Silences," it is the more vehemently feminist of the two pieces. Its subject is "the lives and work of writers, women, in our century. . . ." It literally lists the social and critical attitudes which devalue the work of women writers. Olsen, a teacher of teachers, encourages female professors to correct a curriculum which fosters such devaluation: "Teach women's lives through the lives of the women who wrote the books, as well as through the books themselves; and through autobiography, biography, journals, letters." Her personal remarks, which are included so that others will learn from her experience, are quite congruent with the essay's didactic tone: "I speak of myself to bring here the sense of those others to whom this [discontinuity] is in the process of happening . . . and to remind us of those . . . who never come to writing at all." Strong words conclude her personal remarks: "We who write are survivors."

"Survivors" brings class to mind as does Olsen's discussion of Virginia Woolf's "angel in the house." Olsen defines another angel who is not a part of privileged women writers' lives: *the essential angel*" who "must assume the physical responsibilities for daily living, for the maintenance of life." Olsen's essay reminds readers that not all women writers have servants; it speaks for the lower-class woman writer, as her fiction speaks for the woman worker.

The two opening essays of *Silences*, like all of Olsen's written work, state that no one should be barred from experiencing "the whole of *human life*." Women—all people who do not belong to the privileged class—should not be confined to a sphere where their full, human creative potential is denied. Olsen's feminism is an integral part of her humanism.

Olsen, in the words of Van O'Connor, "is a writer of tremendous skill and power. Her productivity has been small, but she would not have to write a great deal more than she has to earn a place among the eminent writers of short stories." She had to overcome many obstacles to be a writer; she would call herself a "survivor." Olsen has done more than merely survive, though. She is an "ordinary" person who became a feminist hero.

While discussing Rebecca Harding Davis in *Silences*, Olsen states, "What Virginia Woolf wrote of Elizabeth Barrett Browning characterizes Rebecca as well: 'a true daughter of her age: passionate interest in social questions, conflict as artist and woman, longing for knowledge and freedom.'" Olsen might well have added that these words also describe her own life and work.

References:

Sandy Boucher, "Tillie Olsen: The Weight of Things Unsaid," *Ms.*, 3 (September 1974): 26-30;

Selma Burkom and Margaret Williams, "De-Riddling Tillie Olsen's Writings," *San Jose Studies*, 2 (1976): 65-83;

William Van O'Connor, "The Short Stories of Tillie Olsen," *Studies In Short Fiction*, 1 (1963): 21-25.

James Oppenheim
(24 May 1882-4 August 1932)

Charles Hackenberry
Pennsylvania State University

SELECTED BOOKS: *Doctor Rast* (New York: Sturgis & Walton, 1909; London: Melrose, 1910);

Monday Morning and Other Poems (New York: Sturgis & Walton, 1909);

Wild Oats (New York: Huebsch, 1910);

The Pioneers: A Poetic Drama in Two Acts (New York: Huebsch, 1910);

The Nine-tenths (New York & London: Harper, 1911);

Pay Envelopes: Tales of the Mill, the Mine, and the City Street (New York: Huebsch, 1911);

The Olympian: A Story of the City (New York & London: Harper, 1912);

Idle Wives (New York: Century, 1914; London: Nash, 1914);

Songs for the New Age (New York: Century, 1914; London: Richards, 1915);

The Beloved (New York: Huebsch, 1915);

War and Laughter (New York: Century, 1916);
The Book of Self (New York: Knopf, 1917);
Night: A Poetic Drama in One Act (New York: Arens, 1918);
The Solitary (New York: Huebsch, 1919);
The Mystic Warrior (New York: Knopf, 1921);
The Golden Bird (New York: Knopf, 1923);
Your Hidden Powers (New York: Knopf, 1923);
The Sea (New York: Knopf, 1924);
Lyrics to the Olympian Deities, as Jamus Jay (New York: Mayflower, 1925);
A Psycho-analysis of the Jews (Girard, Kans.: Haldeman-Julius, 1926).

OTHER: Randolph Silman Bourne, *Untimely Papers*, edited with a foreword by Oppenheim (New York: Huebsch, 1919).

James Oppenheim's literary works are no longer widely studied, though some of his fiction occasionally appears in anthologies such as Daniel Walden's *On Being Jewish* (1974), which includes a portion of Oppenheim's *Doctor Rast* in the section entitled "The Immigrant Experience." Oppenheim himself described his stories as "bad prose with a streak of poetry in them," but with the possible exception of "The Slave," even his poetry, of which several volumes were published during his lifetime, is largely unread today, as are all of his self-help books, strongly influenced by Jungian theories and written for a popular audience. Although Robert E. Spiller calls him "an important member of the [Imagist] movement," Oppenheim will probably be longest remembered as the ambitious and controversial editor of the short-lived and ill-fated *Seven Arts*, a periodical which became one of the most important and influential voices of the World War I period.

Born in St. Paul, Minnesota, Oppenheim was the eldest son of Matilda and Joseph Oppenheim, modestly successful and financially secure American Jews. He and his parents moved to New York City while he was still in his infancy, and growing up in the center of publishing and the book trade strongly influenced the course of his life. His father's death in 1888 proved to be the traumatic event of his early years. He attended public schools and came under the influence of Dr. Felix Adler, who guided him toward a system of rigorous moral scrutiny. Adler's strong, upright character may be reflected in the central figure of *Doctor Rast*, Oppenheim's first published novel. Oppenheim took classes at Columbia University, but left without a degree for employment as secretary, clerk, social

Portrait of Oppenheim by Gertrude S. Gertrude used as the frontispiece for his 1924 poetry collection, The Sea

worker, and teacher. In 1905 he married Lucy Seckel and accepted the position of superintendent at the Hebrew Technical School for Girls, a post he resigned in 1907 when his increasing radicalism brought him into conflict with the school's governing body.

Turning to literature, he wrote short stories and novels aimed at the popular audience. These works are heavily laced with a saccharine sentimentality that is unredeemed by Oppenheim's continuing interest in themes of social justice, transcendental idealism, and the plight of the poor—the last of which, at least, he had ample opportunity to observe firsthand during his earlier tenure as the head of the Hudson Settlement on the Lower East Side, from 1903 to 1905.

Pay Envelopes (1911) is a collection of a dozen stories of dreary working-class life, half of which are set in New York and half in Pittsburgh. Peter and Annie of "The Great Fear" gain a measure of personal strength from their marriage; they muster the courage to continue on in a life of grinding poverty amid the troubles that beset them. In a story named for her, Meg is responsible for having her husband sent to jail. His incarceration teaches him to value his wife and the other blessings bestowed on him, for he begs her to resume their wedded life after he is released. Most of the stories in this collection show Oppenheim's concern with the effects of hardship on the human spirit and the ability of the individual to overcome whatever trials circumstances hold in store. As in much of Oppenheim's fiction, the plots are worked out in domestic environments. Idealized women, suffering children, and the preparation of innumerable dinners are often repeated features.

The Olympian (1912) is the coming-of-age story of Kirby Trask. The central character of the novel, through trial and disaster, rises to a position of power and respectability by means of his virtue and diligence while managing to retain his values, a fate not shared by others in the work. In one sense, *The Olympian* is the transposition of the Horatio Alger myth to an industrial setting.

Doctor Rast, first published in 1909, combines idealistic themes in a form which is variously considered as either a collection of interlocking short stories or as a highly episodic novel with storylike chapters. In "The Battle" Morris and Nell discover that service to the community by "modern men of God," a category which includes magazine writers and doctors, is more important than either success in the eyes of the world or financial gain. "Everyday," a paean to the rewards and spiritual quality of family life, is set in the loving home of an organ-grinder and his wife as they celebrate their golden wedding anniversary. "The Family" shows Dr. Rast in the act of saving a would-be suicide; Annette Mishkin tries to shoot herself because she feels that her husband no longer loves her, and since both she and her spouse no longer believe in God, the rabbi is powerless to supply a reason for living. Dr. Rast, apparently remembering his Donne, explains that everyone is needed—grocers, butchers, teachers, and even doctors. What the world wants of her is her love. Six months later Annette gives birth to a son. From such materials as these Oppenheim fashioned his fiction: sentimental, often insipid, yet rooted in the soil of common life.

The cast of characters, with the exception of Dr. Rast and his wife, changes from scene to scene, but each subnarrative deals with Jews caught in the snares of poverty and working toward assimilation into a broader spectrum of American culture while attempting to preserve traditional values. "Groping Children," for example, focuses on a family of Russian-born immigrants whose grown children study law and medicine while the younger children and mother labor in the home to provide means for

the education that will, they hope, move the family into comfortable, fully American society. Dr. Rast provides the moral as he speaks to the erring elder daughter: the self-sacrificing parents are the earth's true nobility. Dr. Rast, himself a Jew, cites the example of Jesus as healer and benefactor of the multitudes.

Transmutation of the Jesus image recurs in Oppenheim's poetry, as in the following portion of "Hebrews" from *The Golden Bird* (1923):

> Amongst the swarms fixed like the
> rooted stars, my folk is a streaming Comet,
> The Wanderer of Eternity,
>   the eternal Wandering Jew.
> . . . .
>   Ho! we have turned against the mightiest
>   of our young men
>   And in that denial we have taken on
>   the Christ,
>   And the two thieves beside the Christ,
>   And the Magdalen at the feet of
>   the Christ,
>   And the Judas with thirty silver pieces
>   selling the Christ,
>   And our twenty centuries in Europe
>   have the shape of a Cross
>   On which we have hung in disaster
>   and glory.

Here, as in much of Oppenheim's poetry, the influence of Whitman is evident in the piling of detail upon detail, in the parallel structure from line to line, and in the sweeping cadence of the verse. Louis Untermeyer has commented on Oppenheim's second volume of poetry, *Songs for the New Age* (1914): "The speech, echoing the Whitmanic sonority, develops a music that is strangely Biblical and yet alive." To *The Book of Self* (1917) Untermeyer is less kind: "Most of it reads like *Leaves of Grass* translated by Freud."

Although *Songs for the New Age* is made up of sections entitled "We Dead," "We Living," and "We Unborn," the reader who expects poems narrated from these perspectives will be disappointed. The first poem of the book, "Let Nothing Bind You," sounds a revolutionary note that pervades the work:

> Let nothing bind you:
> If it is Duty, away with it.
> If it is Law, disobey it.
> If it is Opinion, go against it.

This tone of freedom and openness is much more of a unifying device than the superficial structure that is implied by the sectional arrangement. A wide variety of topics is found here: sin, civilization, the millennium, and sex. One part of "We Living" is devoted to the physical aspects of love; another loosely organized part of this section is called "Jottings"—and is as various as the title suggests.

Oppenheim himself came to realize the influence that his psychoanalytic studies were having upon his poetry, for in his introduction to *The Book of Self* he notes: "This little book owes its best to that science [psychology], especially as it is developed by Dr. Carl Jung in Zurich and Dr. Beatrice M. Hinkle in New York. To the latter is due even a certain sort of phrasing." Here, as in *Songs for the New Age*, the poet favored a sectional arrangement for the work. Following the example of Whitman, Oppenheim further partitioned the verse in the first two sections, "Self" and "The Song of Life," by using Roman numerals. In "Self" the influence of the language of psychoanalysis is strongest:

> Man, the Creator!
> But why be man-the-anything?
> Man's a dubious venture:
> A split-off Question from Understanding:
> He and Nature he knows as "I" and "It."
> This sundering: what has he gained by it?

"The Song of Life" turns the journey of self-discovery into a more or less continuous narrative of psychological, if not epic, proportion:

> But the body felt strangely light in his arms,
> And, curious, he looked, and behold!
> There lay, not a woman, but a child in
> his arms.
> And curiously he looked closer,
> And he thought he knew the dead,
> bleeding child.
> And then he saw that the child was himself
> Even as he was in the earlier days.

The final third of *The Book of Self* contains the poetic drama *Creation*—which is aptly subtitled *A Symbolic Drama of the Life of Man*. This work is even more of a closet drama than Oppenheim's *Night*, which saw production by the Provincetown Players during November of 1917 and publication the following year in the Flying Stag Plays for the Little Theatre series.

The Sea, published in 1924, is probably Oppenheim's most important book of poetry, for it gathers together the best of his poems from pre-

ceding years. The volume is marred, however, by the inclusion of transitional verses which attempt to fuse the selections into a cohesive whole.

The zenith of Oppenheim's literary career was his editorship of *Seven Arts*. Begun in November of 1916, the journal published the works of such writers as Amy Lowell, Sherwood Anderson, Kenneth MacGowan, Stephen Vincent Benét, Walter Lippmann, Theodore Dreiser, Max Eastman, S. N. Behrman, Eugene O'Neill, John Dos Passos, and H. L. Mencken. The *Seven Arts* advisory board included Kahlil Gibran, Louis Untermeyer, Van Wyck Brooks, and Robert Frost—most of whom, in addition to associate editor Waldo Frank, contributed regularly to the journal.

The introductory issue included a manifesto, probably written by Oppenheim, which set forth the literary and political position of the venture: "We have no tradition to continue; we have no school of style to build up. What we ask of the writer is simply self-expression without regard to current magazine standards. We should prefer that portion of his work which is done through a joyous necessity of the writer himself."

Immediately following this statement, the editorial praises Romain Rolland's "America and the Arts" which appeared in the same number; it lauds Rolland's idealism and applauds the French writer's espousal of Whitman.

The editor's politics, personality, and taste flavor the journal from the first issue to the last. In one of the regular features of the magazine, "The Seven Arts Chronicle," Oppenheim turned the occasion of Thoreau's birthday into an opportunity for contemporary political comment: "Thoreau is a perpetual reminder, the most vivid reminder our history affords us, that it is the toughness, the intransigence of the spiritual unit which alone gives edge to democracy. As our epoch of expansion draws to a close and we are obliged more and more to test the mettle of our social consciousness, we shall be brought back to this truth, apprehended in so many ways by our fathers in the forest. The days will come when easy solutions no longer have any charm for us and we shall have attained the strength to fashion ourselves in the face of the multitudinous modern world."

The journal became increasingly militant in its pacifism, taking a firm stance against the World War. This position, probably more than anything else, brought on the downfall of this often brilliant literary enterprise, for the periodical's financial backers became more and more patriotic as the war in Europe continued and American involvement increased. No attempt has yet been made to collect Oppenheim's periodical pieces.

Dejected and ill after the magazine ceased publication, Oppenheim deepened his self-directed psychoanalytical studies. Because he had found some relief from his personal problems through his reading, he dabbled in psychoanalysis for a time, but the influence was detrimental to his creative efforts, especially his poetry. Having divorced his first wife in 1914 he married Linda Gray and tried to support himself by writing volumes of popularized psychiatric self-help, some of which were published by Harper and others by Knopf, who had brought out his literary works; he also produced at least ten titles for the Haldeman-Julius Company's Little Blue Book series on various topics: marriage, sex, writing, and "nervous troubles." His final years were plagued by illness, a declining income, and

virtual anonymity. At fifty he died of tuberculosis in New York.

Although James Oppenheim hardly ranks among the great men and women of American-Jewish letters, his smoldering verse occasionally flares into brilliance. His fiction, while not of permanent literary value, epically portrays the heroic struggles of the foreign-born and the poor to achieve a place of dignity in American culture, to make the American Dream a reality. His editorship of an important literary periodical, if not his more creative endeavors, was a sound accomplishment.

Reference:

Robert Phelps and Peter Deane, *The Literary Life: A Scrapbook Almanac of the Anglo-American Literary Scene from 1900 to 1950* (New York: Farrar, Straus & Giroux, 1968).

Samuel Ornitz
(15 November 1890-11 March 1957)

Gabriel Miller
Rutgers University

BOOKS: *The Sock*, as Don Orno (Brooklyn, N.Y.: Three Pamphleteers, 1918);

Haunch, Paunch and Jowl, anonymous (New York: Boni & Liveright, 1923; London: Wishart, 1929);

Round the World with Jocko the Great (New York: Macaulay, 1925);

A Yankee Passional (New York: Boni & Liveright, 1927);

Bride of the Sabbath (New York: Rinehart, 1951).

SCREENPLAYS: *The Case of Lena Smith*, story, Paramount, 1929;

Chinatown Nights, story, Paramount, 1929;

Sins of the Children, adaptation, Cosmopolitan Productions-Metro, 1930;

Hell's Highway, story by Ornitz, Robert Tasker, and Rowland Brown, RKO, 1932;

Secrets of the French Police, screenplay by Ornitz and Tasker, RKO, 1932;

Men of America, screenplay by Ornitz and Jack Jungmeyer, RKO, 1932;

One Man's Journey, screenplay by Ornitz and Lester Cohen, RKO, 1933;

One Exciting Adventure, dialogue, Universal, 1934;

The Man Who Reclaimed His Head, adaptation by Ornitz and Jean Bart, Universal, 1935;

Three Kids and a Queen, screenplay by Ornitz and Barry Trivers, Universal, 1935;

Fatal Lady, Wanger-Paramount, 1936;

Follow Your Heart, screenplay by Ornitz, Lester Cole, and Nathanael West, Republic, 1936;

A Doctor's Diary, story by Ornitz and Joseph Anthony, Paramount, 1937;

The Hit Parade, screenplay by Ornitz and Bradford Ropes, Republic, 1937;

It Could Happen to You, adaptation by Ornitz and West, Republic, 1937;

Portia on Trial, Republic, 1937;

Two Wise Maids, Republic, 1937;

King of the Newsboys, story by Ornitz and Horace McCoy, Republic, 1938;

Army Girl, screenplay by Ornitz and Trivers, Republic, 1938;

Little Orphan Annie, screenplay by Ornitz and Budd Schulberg, Paramount, 1938;

The Miracle on Main Street, story by Ornitz and Boris Ingster, Columbia, 1939;

Samuel Ornitz (Culver Pictures)

Three Faces West, story and screenplay by Ornitz, F. Hugh Herbert, and Joseph Moncure March, Republic, 1940;

They Live in Fear, screenplay by Ornitz and Michael Simmons, Columbia, 1944;

Little Devils, Monogram, 1944;

Circumstantial Evidence, adaptation, 20th Century-Fox, 1945.

PERIODICAL PUBLICATIONS: "What the 'Gun-Fighter' Thinks About It," anonymous, *Review* (August 1912);

"In New Kentucky," *New Masses* (3 April 1934);

"Lester Coven Jumps Both Ways," *Clipper* (November 1941);

"A Jew Confronts the Un-American Committee," *Jewish Life* (December 1947).

Samuel Ornitz would not have claimed to be a dedicated or professional man of letters, because he had too many other concerns which he considered sometimes more important than his writing. As a result, his output as a novelist was sporadic and relatively small. Yet his novels remain arresting on several levels, and his literary career, all but forgotten, deserves attention and evaluation.

Samuel Badisch Ornitz was born in New York City in 1890, the son of Polish immigrants. Though he would write dramatically and realistically about the poverty and squalor of the Lower East Side, his own childhood there was not a deprived one, and he lived in comparative comfort in the midst of extreme poverty. He attended the Henry Street School and went to *cheder* until he was bar mitzvahed. From an early age, Ornitz showed an inclination to be a writer. As a child he enjoyed sitting in the park or on the stoops of apartment buildings and listening to the older men talk; from their memories and tales came some of the material he would incorporate into *Haunch, Paunch and Jowl*. Early interested in social causes, he was a soapbox orator by the age of twelve. He spent two years at

City College of New York and took some law courses at New York University, but he never formally graduated from college.

After leaving college, Ornitz held various odd jobs, which were later reflected in his fiction: he ran copy for news syndicates at the criminal courts, drove a hansom cab, was a leader of boys' clubs and a manager of summer camps. For five years he represented the Protestant members of the New York Prison Association at the Tombs Prison. Later he became assistant superintendent of the Society for the Prevention of Cruelty to Children in Brooklyn, serving as that body's Jewish expert.

Ornitz's work for the Prison Association resulted in his first publication, an article presented anonymously in the *Review* (August 1912), a monthly periodical published by the National Prisoners' Aid Association. The anonymity was probably an editorial decision, meant to give the illusion that the essay, "What the 'Gun-Fighter' Thinks About It," was actually written by a gang member. The piece employs street dialect and displays a naturalistic bent in its evaluation of the effect of the environment on character and the basically animalistic nature of man: "Every kid belongs to a gang, because every kid has got it in him to like the idea, and loves a fight." Ornitz then differentiates various ethnic gangs, particularly Italian and Jewish gangs: "The Yiddish gangster is another proposition. He's full of business."

An early play, *Deficit* (1919), also displays Ornitz's social concerns, for it deals with a religious Jewish woman's resort to prostitution in order to help pay for food for her family. She is eventually arrested by a vice-squad detective in front of her husband; the one-act play concludes as the husband turns on the gas, killing himself and the children. Like many of Ornitz's early pieces, this play was never published, though it was performed.

Ornitz's first novel, *Haunch, Paunch and Jowl*, caused a literary furor when it was published anonymously in 1923. Horace Liveright, his publisher, felt the book would sell better if the public thought it the actual memoir of a judge who had died five years earlier. Press releases claimed that Ornitz had prepared the manuscript because of his acquaintance with "all the facts and the characters involved."

The impetus for writing the book was, in part, economic. Ornitz had married Sadie Lesser in 1914, and they had two sons. After a failed venture in the woolen business with one of his brothers, he was operating a small newsstand and bookstore in the Bronx. In a desperate bid to supplement the meager income this afforded, he worked eighteen hours a day for three months to turn out his first novel. The second impetus was, characteristically, social concern; he told an interviewer: "I kept thinking the East Side leaders were a rotten example. The boys and girls I knew, brought up between two cultures, had caught with racial idealism the spirit of the New World. Then they grew older and saw the successful of their people playing a mean and sordid game."

The novel is a kind of Bildungsroman, focusing on a rogue hero named Meyer Hirsch, a boy of Orthodox Jewish upbringing, whose rebellion against his heritage leads to a picaresque tour of the larger world. At first drawn to the gang life of the streets, he soon learns that the real business of his society consists of fighting and extortion. Hirsch knows how to live by his wits, and, activated by this lesson, he rises swiftly, from runner for local courts and aide to dishonest lawyers, to successful lawyer, to politician. He becomes adept at bribery, conspiracy, and the uses of violence, and eventually his society rewards him with an appointment to the Superior Criminal Court. Certainly one of the vilest characters in American-Jewish literature, Hirsch delights in his ability to manipulate individuals, politics, and the system to his own advantage, and he openly scorns people who believe in a spiritual life or devotion to the public good.

His portrait is further detailed in juxtaposition to the story of his uncle Philip, who, after observing the ways of the Lower East Side, decides to become powerful and make money: "I am not a worm. I am as smart as the German Jews any time, and I found out the secret of their success. Simple. The quick turnover profits from cheap immigrant labor. Their pious dollars, their charitable, respectable dollars are sweated from your carcasses. But I'll go them one better. I'll beat them at their own game. I'm not as elegant as they are. I'm not veiling myself with hypocrisy. I'm going to make money direct from the cheapest greenhorn labor I can find." In stressing this man's consuming resentment of the German Jews, Ornitz ruthlessly exposes the bitterness of the infighting among various segments of the Jewish community. Philip vows to become an "ancestor," to break into the German Jews' social world, and, by the novel's end, he has succeeded in doing so.

As is common in Jewish success novels of the period, there is a muted regret about abandoning the spiritual values of an earlier generation. Hirsch never succeeds in winning the love of Esther, a girl who eventually devotes her life to serving the poor, and this loss is a recurring source of regret to him. Also, the novel ends with a reminder of the Old World when Hirsch is called to a dinner of *gedamfte brust* and *patate lahtkes* (potted breast and potato pancakes), but such echoes of a forsaken past provide only an undertone of sadness. Hirsch admits none of the regrets or longings of his literary forebear Abraham Cahan's David Levinsky but remains unrepentant to the end. *Haunch, Paunch and Jowl* is thus perhaps the most corrosive novel of the first generation of American-Jewish writers.

Like most of Ornitz's work, *Haunch, Paunch and Jowl* is stylistically awkward. Ornitz seemed impatient with matters of form and structure, but his lack of discipline cannot obscure the evidence of real artistic temperament and insight. The novel provides moments of poetry, and it clearly displays Ornitz's sensitive ear for dialogue and dialect. The narrative moves quickly, pulsating with the exuberance of the street life it depicts. Running through it are many stories in addition to those of Hirsch and his uncle; these introduce the world of theater and songwriting and also a more tragic aspect of East Side life—those who died because of their criminal ways and unhealthy living conditions.

The book attracted much attention. Contemporary newspaper accounts chronicle sermons by rabbis who damned it as "lecherous and degrading." One such denunciation, by Rabbi Dr. Samuel Schulman, drew a response from Ornitz in the *Jewish Tribune*: "most gratifying to me was the spontaneous testimony of non-Jewish men and women, who spoke, expressing surprise that the Jews, themselves, were reading race consciousness into the book, while, they, the non-Jews, read it as a book of general or universal significance, in which they found sympathy, beauty, truth and understanding. One speaker, sounding the true keynote, resented the fact that 'Haunch, Paunch and Jowl' was regarded in any way other than a book of Americans by an American. . . . Their answer explains why Dr. Schulman now finds himself on the defensive; he has written the hurt and harm into my book." On the other hand, many Jews and Jewish organizations praised the novel. It was serialized in two working-class papers, the *Morning Freiheit* in America and, years later, in the *Rote Fahne* in Germany. It was also later dramatized and staged by the working-class theater the Artef. *Haunch, Paunch and Jowl* was Ornitz's only commercial success, selling in excess of one hundred thousand copies.

Ornitz's next book was for children, *Round the World with Jocko the Great* (1925). It, too, is concerned with social justice, recounting the adventures of a monkey named Jocko who is kidnapped from the jungle to be sold to the circus.

In 1927, Boni & Liveright published Ornitz's second novel, *A Yankee Passional*, a novel quite different from *Haunch, Paunch and Jowl* yet related in its concern with reform and its conviction of the necessity for moral behavior. Ornitz here deals with the ministry of Dan Matthews, a New England mystic from the Maine woods, who dreams of a consolidated world religion. Coming to New York, he embraces Catholicism and is thrown in with Irish politicians, priests, social reformers, bishops, and gunmen. He spends much of his time trying to reform the Church and Tammany Hall, and then sets up a home for wayward boys, for which action he is harassed by the Church and other groups suspicious of his motives. In the end he is killed by a mob while on a retreat in Maine.

Like *Haunch, Paunch and Jowl*, this novel is picaresque in form, but its canvas is a broader one. While much of it is devoted to a portrait of New York City in the 1890s, Matthews also travels about the country, collecting experiences for his ministry. Again, in this very long and ambitious work, Ornitz occasionally loses control of his material. Too many characters and incidents are introduced; some characterizations are too broad, others lack differentiating detail. But there are scenes of extraordinary power, particularly the description of the lives of Pittsburgh steelworkers in the novel's most effectively controlled literary sequence. And, as in the earlier novel, Ornitz vividly evokes the street life of the Lower East Side.

A Yankee Passional is a scathing attack on Catholicism; yet it is not the work of a cynic, but a very tender novel, full of indignation directed by its author's keen mind and sensitive imagination. It is Ornitz's most richly textured work; it stands as his finest novel, a testament to what he could have done had he decided to devote his life to literature.

It was, however, to be Ornitz's last novel for many years. In 1928, at the encouragement of Herman Mankiewicz, he came to Hollywood to write for Paramount Studios. His first project was a film (now lost) made with Josef von Sternberg, called *The Case of Lena Smith*; its story was derived from a case Ornitz had handled while with the Prison Association.

Ornitz disliked Hollywood and left it several times before settling there permanently. Prompted to more direct involvement in social causes by the onset of the Depression and the rise of fascism in Europe, Ornitz abandoned writing fiction. He would observe later, "To write novels seemed as

John Dos Passos, Theodore Dreiser, and Samuel Ornitz in 1931, when they served on a committee investigating conditions among coal miners in Harlan, Kentucky (Wide World Photos)

puerile as they were profitless." He devoted most of his time to studying fascism and speaking against it, and he helped to organize the Hollywood Anti-Nazi League. Meanwhile he continued to write films in order to support himself and his family. His career as a screenwriter was not distinguished, as he cared little about it and devoted little mental energy to its advancement. At times he tried to interest producers in socially topical films, but these attempts generally failed. Among his films were *Follow Your Heart* (1936), *The Hit Parade* (1937), *Three Faces West*, (1940), and *Circumstantial Evidence* (1945).

Most of his time and his interest, however, went into fighting for social causes. He worked to free the Scottsboro Boys, and in 1931 he went with Theodore Dreiser, John Dos Passos, and others to help starving coal miners and to investigate labor conditions in Kentucky. From this experience came a short play, *In New Kentucky*, which portrays the miners' growing awareness of their degrading working conditions, their resolve to strike, and a concluding confrontation with some hired gunmen, in which some miners are killed. This work, published in *New Masses* in 1934, demonstrates Ornitz's skill in assimilating local speech patterns and reproducing them in dialogue, and in evoking a realistic social setting. In addition, he borrows some Brechtian devices, such as his use of sets—the backdrop for one scene is a list of food prices.

During the late 1930s and early 1940s, Ornitz devoted himself mostly to speaking out against war and fascism and against the threat of anti-Semitism. He traveled around the world to speak and learn and contributed his support to the cause of the Loyalists during the Spanish Civil War.

After World War II he soon became embroiled in another struggle—against the forces of repression in the film industry. Despite the fact that he had not really been working in films for three years, when the House Un-American Activities Committee's investigations into Communist infiltration in the film industry began, Ornitz felt compelled to stand up and join those writers, producers, and directors who decided to challenge Congress's right to ask questions about individuals' political affiliations. Ornitz became one of the group later known as the Hollywood Ten, which stood on the First Amendment and challenged the right of the committee to exist. He later wrote about his decision: "I felt I had to make a conscientious stand on the right to silence. After all, this right was the very soul of what I was writing. During the Nazi extermination, this right meant survival for Jewish babies whom Christians were sheltering more with their silence than with their care; even nuns in orphan asylums avowed this right to silence and thus saved Jewish children. The first Christians worshiped in secret in catacombs. The right to silence saved them from the Roman Security Police who wanted to arrest them on the charge of atheism because they denied Rome's numerous gods in acknowledging only One."

Called before HUAC, Ornitz refused to say whether he was a member of the Communist party or a member of the Screenwriters' Guild, explaining that it involved "a serious question of conscience for me." He was not allowed to read his prepared statement, which accused John E. Rankin, a leading member of the committee, of being an "outstanding anti-Semite" and one who "revels in this fact." He would have gone on to say: "It may be redundant to repeat that anti-Semitism and anti-Communism were the number one poison weapon used by Hitler—but still terribly relevant, lest we forget." Denied the opportunity thus to speak his piece and convicted for his refusal to cooperate, Ornitz was sentenced to a year in prison at Springfield, Missouri.

It was in prison that he completed writing the work that he had been researching so passionately during the 1940s. It was to be a study of prejudice and the schizophrenia in the national psyche that Ornitz considered "the number one health problem in our country . . . the very thing that makes me say early in the book that Walt Whitman's dream of a 'nation of nations' is in reality a nation of ghettos." He particularly focused on anti-Semitism and the Jews' problems with assimilation. In an explanatory note for the book's dust jacket, he wrote: "Now I will tell you for whom I wrote this book—for the several million Americans who are bewildered by their peculiar isolation who must want to know how they got that way and their own contribution to it. I want them to understand why they are isolated in uniqueness as a result of trying to be more Ameri-

can than the Americans—in other words, how their fathers and mothers did it to them in the hope of solving the Jewish Questions for them. And there are millions of non-Jews who are bewildered by it and want an answer to the mystery. I think it will help them be better Christians to read and study this book. I think I can help them see when I get all through, why Christianity has failed to come off." This novel, which Ornitz had titled "Face of Heaven," was published as *Bride of the Sabbath* in 1951.

It is divided into two parts. The first is the story of the ghetto, and again Ornitz weaves a rich tapestry of detail and character. The protagonist is Saul Cramer, raised in an Orthodox manner amid the poverty of the Lower East Side. Like Meyer Hirsch, Saul has an uncle (Mendel), a journalist and socialist who attacks all kinds of hypocrisy. Book two deals with Saul's (now Sal's) conversion to Catholicism and his search for a religion to include all religions. It also deals with the three women who play important parts in Saul's development: Pauline Kaplan, a childhood friend hateful of her people and consumed by a need to escape the ghetto; Becky Rosenberg, a Marxist and union organizer; and Nancy Fitzgerald, a devout Catholic whom Saul marries and who later leaves him to become a nun.

Again, the work is uneven; the second part lacks the power and authenticity of the first. Cramer is a more convincing figure when placed against the dramatic background of the ghetto, whereas later he seems to dwindle to a mere mouthpiece for the author's ideas. Ornitz editorializes too much and interrupts the narrative too often with historical asides and philosophical discussions. Yet the novel remains an important record, perhaps the most profound fictional record produced, of the struggles, both physical and psychological, of first- and second-generation Jews in adapting to America.

Bride of the Sabbath did not sell well, and so Ornitz put aside work on a sequel. After his release from prison in 1951, he was also working on a novel about homosexuality in prisons, a condition that had much disturbed him during his nine months' incarceration. Neither work was completed, for Ornitz died of cerebral hemorrhage in 1957, at the age of sixty-six.

Samuel Ornitz's three novels display a degree of intelligence and talent that might have made him an important writer. Yet the record of his life shows that Ornitz always considered life more important than art. If his novels lack the finesse and discipline of great literature, it is because Ornitz always felt the need to move on to another course or another project. His output was small, but his work stands as the lasting contribution of a man who never stopped believing in human progress and in man's innate capability to set things right.

Papers:
The State Historical Society of Wisconsin at Madison has Ornitz's papers, including manuscripts, letters, plays, and some screen work.

Cynthia Ozick
(17 April 1928-)

Diane Cole

See also the Ozick entry in *DLB Yearbook: 1982*.

BOOKS: *Trust* (New York: New American Library, 1966; London: MacGibbon & Kee, 1967);
The Pagan Rabbi and Other Stories (New York: Knopf, 1971; London: Secker & Warburg, 1972);
Bloodshed and Three Novellas (New York: Knopf, 1976; London: Secker & Warburg, 1976);
Levitation: Five Fictions (New York: Knopf, 1982; London: Secker & Warburg, 1982);
Art and Ardor: Essays (New York: Knopf, 1983);
The Cannibal Galaxy (New York: Knopf, 1983; London: Secker & Warburg, 1983).

TRANSLATIONS: *A Treasury of Yiddish Poetry*, edited by Irving Howe and Eliezer Greenberg (New York: Holt, Rinehart & Winston, 1969)—includes translations by Ozick of the poetry of David Einhorn, H. Leivick, and Chaim Grade;
Translation of A. Tabachnik, "Tradition and Revolt in Yiddish Poetry," in *Voices from the Yiddish: Essays, Memoirs, Diaries*, edited by Howe and Greenberg (New York: Shocken, 1975).

SELECTED PERIODICAL PUBLICATIONS: "The Sense of Europe," *Prairie Schooner*, 30 (June 1956): 126-138;
"Visitation," *Prairie Schooner*, 36 (Fall 1962): 271;
"Bridled," *Chelsea Review*, 15 (June 1964): 64;
"Red-Shift," *Chelsea Review*, 15 (June 1965): 65;
"An Opinion: On the Ovarian Mentality," *Mademoiselle*, 66 (March 1968): 20, 25;
"America: Toward Yavneh," *Judaism*, 19 (Summer 1970): 264-282;
"In the Synagogue," *Jewish Spectator*, 35 (December 1970): 9;

Cynthia Ozick (photo by Layle Silbert)

"Forster As Homosexual," *Commentary*, 52 (December 1971): 81-85;
"Reconsideration: Truman Capote," *New Republic*, 168 (27 January 1972): 31-34;
"In the Reign of Peace" (review of short stories by Hugh Nissenson), *New York Times Book Review*, 19 March 1972, p. 4;
"Literary Blacks and Jews" (review of Bernard

Malamud's *The Tenants*), *Midstream*, 18 (June/July 1972): 10-24;

"If You Can Read This, You Are Too Far Out," *Esquire*, 79 (January 1973): 74, 78;

"In the Days of Simon Stern" (review of the novel by Arthur A. Cohen), *New York Times Book Review*, 3 June 1973, p. 6;

"Mrs. Virginia Woolf," *Commentary*, 56 (August 1973): 33-44;

"All the World Wants the Jews Dead," *Esquire*, 82 (November 1974): 103-107, 207-210;

"The Riddle of the Ordinary," *Moment*, 1 (July/August 1975): 55-59;

"Hadrian and Hebrew," *Moment*, 1 (September 1975): 77-79;

"Justice (Again) to Edith Wharton," *Commentary*, 62 (October 1976): 48-57;

"How to Profit More from the Teachings of Clara Schacht than from All the Wisdom of Aristotle, Montaigne, Emerson, Seneca, Cicero, Et Al.," *Esquire*, 87 (May 1977): 92-93, 134-138;

"Shots," *Quest/77*, 1 (July/August 1977): 68-74;

"Letter to a Palestinian Military Spokesman," *New York Times*, 16 March 1978, A26;

"My Grandmother's Pennies," *McCall's*, 106 (December 1978): 30-34;

"Judaism and Harold Bloom," *Commentary*, 67 (January 1979): 43-51;

"Notes Toward Finding the Right Question (A Vindication of the Rights of Jewish Women)," *Lilith*, 6 (1979): 19-29;

"The Shawl," *New Yorker*, 56 (26 May 1980): 33-34;

"Carter and the Jews: an American Political Dilemma," *New Leader*, 63 (30 June 1980): 2-23;

"The Mystic Explorer," *New York Times Book Review*, 21 September 1980, pp. 1, 32-35;

"Rosa," *New Yorker*, 59 (21 March 1983): 38-71.

The author of two novels and dozens of essays, Cynthia Ozick is best known for her three collections of short fiction, *The Pagan Rabbi and Other Stories* (1971), *Bloodshed and Three Novellas* (1976), and *Levitation: Five Fictions* (1982). Despite the relatively small body of her work, she belongs to the front rank of American writers today.

Few contemporary authors have demonstrated her range, knowledge, or passion. Her novel *Trust* (1966) is an epic work, a vast psychological novel. By contrast, the novellas and short stories bring to mind writers as diverse as Thomas Mann, Isaac Babel, and Chekhov. Although these tales almost all concern American Jews, Ozick uses only incidentally such traditional subjects of American-Jewish fiction as the immigrant experience and contemporary family life. In turning to the oldest religious sources for her inspiration, Ozick has opened a path that other American-Jewish writers may follow.

Cynthia Ozick was born in New York City on 17 April 1928. Her parents were William and Shiphra Regelson Ozick; her father was the proprietor of the Park View Pharmacy in the Bronx. She was educated at New York University, from which she graduated Phi Beta Kappa in 1949, and at Ohio State University, from which she received a master's degree in 1950. In those years, she steeped herself in fiction, particularly the work of Henry James. She was, she says, "besotted with the religion of Literature."

After college Ozick served a lengthy apprenticeship, devoting seven years to a long philosophical novel which she finally abandoned. Only two excerpts from that book have seen print—"The Butterfly and the Traffic Light," which appears in *The Pagan Rabbi and Other Stories*, and "The Sense of Europe," a Jamesian tale published in *Prairie Schooner* in 1956. Between 1952 and 1953 she also labored as an advertising copywriter at Filene's Department Store in Boston. In 1952 she married Bernard Hallote; they have one daughter.

In this period she also wrote poetry—formal work, often on religious subjects that are reflected in such titles as "The Wonder Teacher" and "In the Synagogue." Although Ozick's verse appeared in many literary journals, few readers are aware of this aspect of her career. She composed her "last true poem" at the age of thirty-six, she says. (Her translations of Yiddish poetry can be read in *A Treasury of Yiddish Poetry* [1969], edited by Irving Howe and Eliezer Greenberg.)

It was during her apprentice years, too, that Ozick began her intensive reading of the literature, history, and philosophy of Judaism. Fluent in Yiddish from girlhood on, she had studied Hebrew in college. She did not develop her own course of study, however, until the age of twenty-five, when she discovered the work of the German-Jewish philosopher Leo Baeck. Along with Martin Buber, Franz Rosenzweig, and Hermann Cohen, Baeck was one of the major figures of the German-Jewish Renaissance that ended with World War II.

Trust, Ozick's first published book, forcefully announces the author's themes and obsessions. She worked on it for seven years, between the ages of twenty-nine and thirty-six, and it appeared in 1966 to generally appreciative reviews. "In writing *Trust*," Ozick says, "I began as an American novelist and ended as a Jewish novelist. I Judaized myself as I wrote it." Again and again, in the novel and in the stories that follow, characters are torn between the opposing claims of two religions. One is always pagan, whether it be the worship of nature or the idolatrous pursuit of art, whereas the other—Judaism—is sacred. It is characteristic that Ozick titled her unpublished volume of poetry "Greeks and Jews"—or, one might say, Pagans and Jews.

In Ozick's work, the struggle between Pan and Moses, between the pagan and the holy, is the figure in the carpet that becomes ever clearer. What is at stake is the possession of man's soul. But though in the end she stands with the rabbis to condemn all pagan rites and magic as abominations, Ozick worries that a part of her sides with the devil.

Ozick weaves her tales with technical brilliance. In *Trust*, however, she is still in the process of sharpening her narrative and dramatic gifts. It is her lyric impulse that she here shows to best effect. Sentence for sentence, *Trust* is nearly perfect. Paragraphs are crafted as carefully as poems. The rhythms are sure and smooth, the imagery rich and suggestive. Yet for all its intelligence, playfulness, and polish, the novel as a whole never comes fully alive.

The plot is intricate. The first-person narrator remains nameless throughout the book's some 600 pages. An American innocent who has just received her college diploma, she has traveled in Europe—the Europe of the Nazi death camps. Her mother, Allegra Vand, is wealthy, selfish, ambitious, and intellectually pretentious. William, Allegra's first husband and current lawyer, manages her vast estate—her "trust." He knows Allegra's secrets and is tainted by them; he has mastered the art of using and abusing the family's trust, both legally and morally. But neither William nor Allegra's second husband, Enoch Vand, is the narrator's true father. Her decision to go in search of that father—a mysterious figure named Gustave Nicholas Tilbeck—sets *Trust* in motion.

Here Ozick runs into a curious difficulty. Though the conditions of their lives change, Allegra, William, Tilbeck, and the narrator herself are static. Their past yields an interesting story, but they play essentially the same parts, no matter what the time or place.

Only Enoch undergoes a transformation. Though less space is devoted to him than to others, it becomes increasingly clear that he is the novel's central figure. The book's only Jewish character, he infuses *Trust* with his sensibility. He is fond of paradoxes, which Ozick quotes at length. (At one point she gives us several pages of his aphorisms at once.) Here is an example of Enoch at his best, as he tells Allegra not about trust but truth: "if you see the truth too soon you naturally accommodate yourself to what you see; and by the act of accommodating yourself you change whatever the circumstance was when you originally saw it; and by changing the circumstance you alter the ground from which the truth springs, and then it can no longer grow out that same truth which you foresaw: it has become something different. So you see it is impossible to see the truth too soon, for when its moment of commitment arrives, it has changed its nature and it is already too late. The truth is always seen too late. That is why hell is always with us."

Perhaps Enoch is capable of change precisely because he can envision both a heaven and a hell. He has seen hell as a minor administrative official assigned to bear witness to the aftermath of the German death camps, and it has stayed with him.

Ozick describes Enoch alternately as a magician and as one aspiring to the messianic, as a prophet and as an atheist. He is a creature of history, ever adaptable to circumstances. Finally, he is an embodiment of the mythical Jew: "He had something in him of the refugee, which was absurd, because he had been born in Chicago. But he was both visionary and resourceful, one of those 'interior' refugees of the kind which America throws off from time to time, adventurers . . . who turn up all over the world practicing the cult of a single idea." His single idea is this: "I want to prove that the world is of a piece, top and bottom. I want to demonstrate how creation is an unredeemed monstrosity." The world is not only unredeemed, it is unredeemable. Yet part of Enoch also believes that "man finds the world unwell in order to heal it."

In order to prove his point—and in order to survive—Enoch must change his skin many times, starting as a socialist youth leader in the 1930s and aspiring finally to a comfortable ambassadorship in a conservative administration. At novel's end, he loses the ambassadorship. Rather than breaking him, though, this last blow seems to free him. Once ambition is lost, Ozick seems to be saying, virtue may be found and the soul, perhaps, redeemed. "Let God be the kind of God who would allow the sort of world in which it is possible to lead a virtuous life," Enoch had once pledged, "and I would repay him by dedicating my days . . . to constant praise of his holy name." On the novel's final page, we learn that Enoch has begun his study of the Hebrew Bible and the Talmud.

If Enoch casts his lot with Moses and the Jewish God, the narrator's father, Gustave Nicholas

Tilbeck, is described in turn as a pagan, a "male muse," a magical Pied Piper, an aimless drifter, a bum, a blackmailer, an elusive spirit who cannot be defined or owned because he cares to own nothing except himself. Tilbeck is, in short, in league with the god Pan—the antithesis of Moses and thus of Enoch. "Pan Versus Moses" is the title of Enoch's projected essay. "It's Moses making the Children of Israel destroy all the grotto shrines and greenwood places and things," Allegra explains. "It's about how Moses hates nature."

Nature is where Tilbeck and Pan reside. While most of *Trust* takes place indoors or within the intellectual landscapes of the narrator's mind, the final chapters move outdoors—to Duneacres, Allegra's ruined island estate and Tilbeck's current home. There the narrator will meet her natural father. The scene has the makings of a forest idyll out of Shakespeare, but a squatter family called the Purses are more reminiscent of Dickens, and the convention is turned around further when William's son brings his fiancée to the island for a romantic tryst. As she watches Tilbeck seduce the fiancée, the narrator believes herself to have "witnessed the very style of my own creation." She has discovered everything about her past that she need know.

She has discovered everything, yet she remains curiously unchanged. Without identifying herself as a writer, she has an author's meditative sensibility. She absorbs everything, orders it, and sets it down for us to read. She also has the precocious intellectual's negative self-image. Always the outsider, she proclaims herself to be unattractive, ineffectual, and socially inept. She asserts herself through her use of language—in caustic dialogue, clever questions, and innumerable puns which she refuses to resist.

If Allegra, Enoch, Tilbeck, and the others try their best to ignore her, the narrator compensates by ignoring nothing. No descriptive detail, no philosophical argument escapes notice. It is as if Ozick and her narrator had decided to cram everything—all knowledge—between the covers of one book. Like many nineteenth-century novels, *Trust* takes Gentile high society as its milieu, but Ozick adds psychology, philosophy, religion, history, and literature itself—a heady brew.

Perhaps because its range is so wide, at times the book seems to lose its focus. It is as if Ozick had perfected her canvas section by section, but had not taken enough steps back from it to view it as a whole. In *Trust*, all too often intellectual concerns are declaimed in monologues or debated in lengthy con-

Self-caricature by Ozick   (collection of Burt Britton)

versations that have not been fully dramatized or integrated into the novel as a whole. As beautiful as the prose is, certain descriptive paragraphs have the feel of set pieces, too evocative to omit yet slowing the narrative pace. The novel boasts little in the way of bravura action, and most readers will have guessed the secret of the narrator's birth long before it is revealed. For all the plot's twists and turns, suspense is oddly lacking. In its form—though not in its themes—*Trust* is unlike anything Cynthia Ozick has had published since. A work of great moral seriousness, it is brilliant, ambitious, and flawed—one of those "loose and baggy monsters" that Ozick's master, Henry James, both admired and deplored.

The Pagan Rabbi and Other Stories appeared in 1971 to high critical praise. "In this new book of seven stories," Johanna Kaplan wrote in the *New York Times Book Review*, "all that was best in the novel—that relentless, passionate, discovering and uncovering intelligence—is present and instantly recognizable, but there is now a difference in the prose. It is sharpened, clarified, controlled, and above all beautifully, unceasingly welcoming."

With *The Pagan Rabbi and Other Stories*, Ozick finds her narrative voice. She now puts her gift for linguistic invention along with her intellectual brilliance at the service of the drama. The themes that appeared in *Trust* are now polished and refined. Enoch Vand's unwritten essay "Pan Versus Moses" sounds suspiciously like the seed for the collection's title story, "The Pagan Rabbi." The writer who in that story turns to religion to decode the world is the same writer who created Enoch Vand and Gustave Nicholas Tilbeck. There is this difference: the author has learned economy. Instead of attempting to demonstrate all of Enoch Vand's paradoxes and theorems at once, Ozick now explicates them one by one, in stories that are concisely wrought, rich in imaginative detail, and powerfully suggestive.

Of the seven stories that make up the collection, four are excellent: "The Pagan Rabbi," "Envy; or Yiddish in America," "The Dock-Witch," and "Virility." The other three—"The Suitcase," "The Doctor's Wife," and "The Butterfly and the Traffic Light"—are more conventional exercises in the short-story form. "The Doctor's Wife" is a quiet, evocative tribute to Chekhov, while "The Butterfly and the Traffic Light" reminds us of Henry James and of Ozick's earlier manner in *Trust*. "The Suitcase" returns to a subject introduced by Enoch Vand in *Trust* and one which Ozick will explore both more fully and more successfully in her story "Bloodshed"—the moral burden of the Holocaust and its meaning in history. In "The Suitcase," Ozick quotes a passage from Thomas Mann which she seems to have taken as an emblem for herself: "It is better to ruin a work and make it useless for the world than not to go to the limit at every point." In those first four stories, Ozick goes to the limit and succeeds.

"The Pagan Rabbi" draws the reader in with its opening sentence: "When I heard that Isaac Kornfeld, a man of piety and brains, had hanged himself in the public park, I put a token in the subway stile and journeyed out to see the tree." Rabbi Kornfeld, it is learned from notes and essays he has left behind, has strayed from the holy path and allowed himself to be seduced by nature. In a brilliant flight into the supernatural, Ozick describes his ravishment by the dryad who inhabits the tree from which he ultimately hangs himself. The follower of Moses has fallen prey to the charms of Pan.

The rabbi's soul is at war with his earthly longings for natural beauty. The soul "denies every spirit . . . and all gods diversiform, it spites even Lord Pan, it is an enemy." It declares that "The sound of the Law is more beautiful than the crickets. The smell of the Law is more radiant than the moss. The taste of the Law exceeds clear water." But while the soul cares "only to be bound to the Law," the flesh is pagan and lusts after nature.

Ozick has taken her epigraph from a passage in the Ethics of the Fathers: "Rabbi Jacob said: 'He who is walking along and studying, but then breaks

off to remark, "How lovely is that tree!" or "How beautiful is that fallow field!"—Scripture regards such a one as having hurt his own being.' "

Even so, the story's narrator—along with Ozick—can find some sympathy for the rabbi's plight. Ruth R. Wisse has pointed out that "one of the most pervasive subjects of the modern Yiddish and Hebrew literary tradition is the rediscovery of those natural human instincts which would free the dust-choked ghetto Jew from the stifling repressions of *halakhah* and religious inhibitions. In the works of Mendele, Sholem Aleichem, Peretz, Bialik, Feierberg, and Tchernikhowsky, the physical world of sun, storm, trees, and rivers provides a model of freedom counterposed to the self-denial of *shtetl* culture." "The Pagan Rabbi," then, both introduces a new note to American fiction and expands the traditional themes of Yiddish and Hebrew literature.

The story also strikes a chord familiar to readers of the well-known story by Isaac Babel, "The Awakening." There, too, the central figure is the studious urban Jew who knows nothing of nature. Part of Ozick may very well fear the old man's admonition to Babel's young narrator: "And you dare to write! A man who's not part of nature like an animal or a rock will never write two worth-while lines in his whole life." It is, perhaps, this conflict within Ozick herself that gives "The Pagan Rabbi" its power, high drama, and passion.

"The Dock-Witch," like "The Pagan Rabbi," dramatizes complex intellectual conceits through the use of fantasy and the supernatural. The story presents a secular version of Rabbi Kornfeld. George, who narrates "The Dock-Witch," is a lawyer, a man whom the life of the office has assimilated and consumed. Whereas Rabbi Kornfeld has abandoned the holy to follow Pan, George has lived his life uncommitted to any scheme of values except, perhaps, the routine of the ordinary. He exists on the edge of possibility—until Undine, a water sprite, comes into his life. His obsession with her becomes his salvation and his doom.

Like the dryad in "The Pagan Rabbi" or like Tilbeck in *Trust*, she inspires those who encounter her to seek fulfillment in nature or to follow the calling of art. But George the lawyer knows nothing of art, even after Undine abandons him. He is left to wander the world like a lost soul, bereft of everything.

In "Envy; or Yiddish in America" and "Virility" Ozick stays more rooted in the realistic world, but her imagination is no less fierce. Instead of rabbis who run after dryads or lawyers who fall victim to sea nymphs, these tales present writers who worship fame and the dream of immortality.

In "Envy," the Yiddish poet Edelshtein, now living in New York, engages in an unsuccessful search for English translators. He directs his bitterness and envy at his colleague Ostrover, a famous Yiddish storywriter whose themes and plots are reminiscent of Isaac Bashevis Singer. Ozick's novella details the particularities of the immigrant experience in America. America means success, ambition, new life in a new world—and the old world of the Yiddish language is dead. Or is it? In a moment of revelation, Edelshtein wonders if "the ghetto was the real world, and the outside world only a ghetto. . . . Talmud explains that when the Jews went into Exile, God went into Exile also. Babi Yar is maybe the real world, and Kiev with its German toys, New York with all its terrible intelligence, all fictions, fantasies. Unreality." Edelshtein's lusting after Western civilization and the dream of success in America may be only another lusting after idols.

In "Virility," the Russian immigrant Elia Gatoff transforms himself into the poet Edmund Gate. His rise to fame is meteoric, his fall into oblivion just as spectacular when it is discovered that his poems, acclaimed for their masculine strength, were in fact composed by an elderly woman, Edmund's impoverished aunt.

Ozick calls "Virility" not a story but a tract, and on one level it is the dramatization of a paragraph Ozick wrote in her feminist essay "The Demise of the Dancing Dog": "I have never—repeat, *never*—read a review of a novel or, especially, of a collection of poetry by a woman which did not include somewhere in its columns a gratuitous allusion to the writer's sex and its supposed effects. The Ovarian Theory of Literature is the property of all society, not merely of freshmen and poor Ph.D. lackeys: you will find it in all the best periodicals, even the most highbrow."

Like "Envy," "Virility" attacks the cult of ambition. The worship of fame, after all, is as idolatrous as the worship of nature. Ozick has already established that the muse of poetry is a pagan god. "Virility" affirms that the muse is neither male nor female. The poet who truly hears its call possesses no gender, but is only an Artist.

Like "The Dock-Witch" and "The Pagan Rabbi," "Virility" and "Envy" are virtuoso performances. Ozick successfully integrates within her texts poems, essays, lectures, tales within tales, jokes, and various lists. She takes her characters seriously, but at the same time her stories are satiric

gems. The philosophical or intellectual premises upon which she bases her stories are acted out by specific people whose conflicts and obsessions—however peculiar—are made to engage her reader's interest.

From page to page, Ozick will shift from an elevated Biblical inflection to the stilted Yiddish of the Russian immigrant to a slangy American vernacular; from sharply focused realism to fantastical flights into the supernatural. Magical transformations abound—of women into sea nymphs, trees into dryads, virile young poets into elderly androgynes. Ozick is always in control, yet the stories surprise us with their invention and their spontaneity. Her surfaces are bright and shiny, but there is nothing hollow about the complex passions and intellectual concerns that lie within. For *The Pagan Rabbi and Other Stories* Ozick won the B'nai Brith Jewish Heritage Award (1971), the Edward Lewis Wallant Memorial Award (1972), and the Jewish Book Council Award for Fiction (1972).

Bloodshed and Three Novellas, Ozick's next collection of fiction and winner of her second Jewish Book Council Award, can be praised for the same qualities found in *The Pagan Rabbi and Other Stories*. Witty and erudite, the four tales—"A Mercenary," "Bloodshed," "An Education," and "Usurpation (Other People's Stories)"—fuse passion with knowledge. They also serve to illuminate further, each tale from a different angle, the struggle between the pagan and the holy. The figure in the carpet is there to see, but it takes so many shapes and disguises that it retains its power to surprise and delight and to provoke us to thought.

When *Bloodshed and Three Novellas* appeared, the majority of critics applauded Ozick's virtuosity and imaginative range, but others voiced some puzzlement as to the author's intentions. Ozick had sought to answer her readers' questions in advance in the volume's preface—an essay occasioned by *New York Times* book reviewer Anatole Broyard's comments on the novella "Usurpation (Other People's Stories)," a first-prize winner in the O. Henry short story awards for 1975. "I must admit that I don't enjoy being tantalized," Broyard wrote of "Usurpation" in his review of the 1975 volume of O. Henry Award winners. "I want a story to *give* me something, not to tease me with possibilities. Technique as mystification, as a device for creating suspense, seems to me to be a sterile intellectual game."

Ozick's response was itself one of puzzlement: "I was astounded," she admits in her preface to *Bloodshed*. "I agreed with all his premises.

Literature-as-game was exactly what I have been devotedly arguing against inside my mind for half a decade." Why, then, she wonders, is so intelligent a critic as Broyard mystified? In seeking her answer, she looks to a far broader philosophical issue than simply the relationship between writers and their readers.

" 'Usurpation,' " Ozick writes in her preface, "is a story written against story-writing; against the Muse-goddesses; against Apollo. It is against magic and mystification, against sham and 'miracle,' and, going deeper into the dark, against idolatry. It is an invention directed against inventing—the point being that the story-making faculty itself can be a corridor to the corruptions and abominations of idol-worship, of the adoration of magical event."

Ozick worries "whether Jews ought to be story-tellers." The story warns that in condemning idolatry, the Second Commandment also condemns the writer of tales. It also allows Ozick—who dreads magic yet "lusts after stories more and more and more"—to wonder, "Why do we become what we most desire to contend with?"

In "Usurpation," magical transformations abound. The tale contains more metamorphoses than a Greek legend or a story out of Ovid. Like "Envy" and "Virility," it is another story about ambitious writers and their pagan muse. It also contains several brilliant mirror effects—stories within stories within stories. "Usurpation" may be the most complex of Ozick's tales, but it also yields the richest rewards.

The narrator—herself a writer, and a persona which should not be confused with an autobiographical portrait of Cynthia Ozick—hears a well-known author read a short story recognizable as Bernard Malamud's "The Silver Crown." The story moves her; she feels it "belongs" to her. But it has been usurped—written by somebody else. She comes into possession, instead, of the manuscript of a story belonging to an aspiring writer referred to as "the goat." The story's plot concerns ambition, envy, and idolatry, and it contains a vision of the Hebrew poet Tchernikhovsky. Eventually, the narrator finds her way to the goat's aunt, who with Saul, the aunt's husband, had cooked up the "real-life" scheme on which "The Silver Crown" was based. Saul's rabbinic paradoxes are reminiscent of Enoch Vand's aphorisms. Is Saul a charlatan or a prophet? As she ponders this, the narrator is forced to choose between the "Creator or the creature. God or god. The Name of Names or Apollo."

She chooses Apollo, as all artists must. The vision that accompanies this choice—a pagan vision

with overtones of Ezekiel—reminds her painfully that "when we enter Paradise there will be a cage for storywriters, who will be taught . . . All that is not Law is levity."

The art of telling stories is a pagan art, Ozick must conclude, and therefore an abomination. Yet because the fiction of Cynthia Ozick deals in paradox and thrives on ambiguity, few entertainments have succeeded so well and so cleverly in delivering so dark and biblical a prophecy.

Unlike "Usurpation," "A Mercenary" contains little plot. Rather, it draws contrasting portraits of two men who should be more alike than they are: Polish-born Stanley Lushinski, the "paid mouthpiece" for a developing black African nation which he visited once, for fourteen months, before his twentieth birthday; and his colleague Morris Ngambe, a native of the country which they both serve.

Lushinski lives in a state of perpetual metamorphosis. Although his personal history is elusive, Nazi persecution always plays a part in whatever story he invents to tell about himself. He is the master of many languages who has no mother tongue—a Jew whose mistress is descended from German royalty, a resident of New York who has lived on three continents but belongs to none of them, a traveler who retains several passports, each with a different identity. Like a chameleon, he periodically transforms himself for the purpose of survival. Along with Enoch Vand in *Trust*, he is the contemporary embodiment of a mythical figure—the resourceful, adaptable Jew.

By contrast, Morris is a man with both a heritage and a country. In a show of virtuosity, Ozick invents a language, a religion, a mythology, a poetic literature, a store of Yiddish-sounding folk sayings and curses to go with Morris's homeland. To Morris, Africa is the continent of light and of nature, whereas "in Europe you fled, it was flight, you ran like prey into shadows: Europe the Dark Continent"—the continent of persecution.

Educated in England and confused by America, Morris considers "how inventiveness and adaptability marked his father and all his father's brothers." But Morris is destined to question those same qualities in himself and in Lushinski. He wonders, "If you jump into someone else's skin . . . doesn't it begin to fit you?" Dressed in a Western suit and tie, he feels himself to be "self-duped, an impersonator."

But who is the "real" impersonator? To the African prime minister, Lushinski is "a true advocate." To Morris, Lushinski remains a Jew, no matter how vehemently he denies it. To himself, Lushinski is "the century's one free man." History, Ozick seems to be saying, has cast these two men in different roles. Each one must carve out for himself the identity that fits the particular historical moment. As the moment changes, so will each man's identity; so will the men themselves.

At one point in "A Mercenary," Lushinski declares that "every survivor is free. Everything that can happen to a human being has already happened inside the survivor. The future can invent nothing worse. What he owns now is recklessness without fear."

That same recklessness without fear belongs to the Holocaust survivors who inhabit the collection's title story, "Bloodshed." Bleilip, a skeptical American Jew, visits a community built by survivors. The Hasidic Jews who live, work, and study sacred texts there are as foreign to him as he is to them. He observes them as clinically as a sociologist would a pagan tribe. Still, as he listens to the rebbe's messianic sermon, Bleilip yearns for "a certain piece of truth, not too big to swallow."

He gets more than he bargains for. When the rebbe orders him to empty his pockets, Bleilip removes two guns. One is authentic; the other is a toy. Only the toy need be feared, the rebbe declares—only the symbol, the idea, "the incapable." In the end, the rebbe suggests, Bleilip remains as "bloody as anyone" who, like the believers at the ancient Temple on Yom Kippur, would sacrifice a goat to expiate the congregation's sins; as guilty as anyone who "would slaughter an animal, not for sustenance, but for an idea. . . . For animals we in our day substitute men." Thus, Bleilip must carry within him both the fact of his Jewishness and the moral burden of the Holocaust. He cannot escape his destiny or his morality. "Bloodshed" is a dark, difficult, evocative story which yields many meanings.

Unlike the other tales that make up *Bloodshed*, "An Education" does not carry an overtly Jewish theme. It does concern worship, however—the worship of people who allow themselves to be perceived as idols. Una, the story's protagonist, falls under the spell of a young, attractive, and seductively conniving couple called the Chimeses. (They had changed their name from its original, Chaim—the Hebrew word for life—but they are anything but life-giving.) Una idealizes them, follows them, makes herself their slave. She worships them as selflessly as any pagan idolator. Her education commences only when she can begin to smash her idols and free herself from their magic.

The title story of Ozick's next book, *Levitation: Five Fictions* (1982), is the most provocative in the collection. At the heart of this virtuosic fantasy lies a sharp and biting portrait of New York's "literary" Upper West Side. Feingold, who is Jewish, and his wife Lucy, a minister's daughter who has converted to Judaism, are self-admitted "secondary-level" novelists who feed on gossip and self-pity. Consumed by the same envy that plagued the mediocre poet Edelshtein in "Envy; or Yiddish in America," Feingold and Lucy try to validate their undistinguished literary careers by throwing a party. But even in this they fail: none of the invited luminaries deigns to appear.

Instead, the "friend from the Seminary" who had administered Lucy's conversion brings an unnamed "refugee," whom Ozick describes as possessing "a nose like a saint's. The face of Jesus." This prophetlike survivor of the Holocaust describes the horrors he has witnessed in a hypnotic whisper which casts a spell upon the party. Literally, a spell: His listeners soon begin to levitate, to ascend "like an ark on waters." But only the Jews are able to rise into the air, "kidnapped . . . by a messenger from the land of the dead."

The Jews rise, the others remain below. Nor does Lucy, the convert, choose to complete her conversion by ascending also. Tiring of the refugee's endless tales of death, she is drawn instead to a different vision—of Christian and pagan rites: "Lucy sees how she has abandoned nature, how she has lost true religion on account of the God of the Jews." She chooses nature, the gods, the earth, even as the holy messenger of God hovers above her. Only the Jews, the Chosen People, will ascend; the pagan nature-worshippers will always remain below. The separate worlds of the holy and the pagan remain separate. But "Levitation" also suggests a more disturbing interpretation: a mere conversion, the story seems to say, cannot convert the pagan to the holy, cannot ever gulf the abyss of Jewish history, the Holocaust.

Refugees and artists appear in two more stories in *Levitation*. "Shots" presents a photographer who deals in graven images, in what the narrator-artist confesses is necrophilia: "I have fallen in love with corpses. Dead faces draw me." In a sense, this photographer is herself dead, drawn more to the inanimate images of her art than to the possibilities of life. Perhaps reflecting that deadness, the narrative lacks the vigor and energy that characterize Ozick's best work.

In the least satisfying story in the collection,

"From a Refugee's Notebook," Ozick takes a lesson from the postmodernists and draws under one heading two seemingly unrelated fragments "found . . . behind a mirror in a vacant room-for-rent on West 106th Street, New York City." In the first fragment, titled "Freud's Room," the narrator speculates that "Sigmund Freud wished to become a God," creating out of his own imagination the religion of psychoanalysis.

This first fragment reads more like an essay than a work of fiction. The second fragment, "The Sewing Harems," is a peculiar satire. Here it is not Freud but Ozick who takes upon herself the role of creator, inventing a fictional world called Acirema (America spelled backwards). There, a sect emerges of women who stitch closed the passage leading to the womb. The complex sociology of the group and its forbidden offspring—at first cherished, later cast off as pariahs—reminds one at first of the complex politics of any social movement. Is this, as Peter Prescott suggested in *Newsweek*, a "sendup of the women's movement?" Or are the pagan rituals of the sewing harems a far darker warning to any group that would set its own code of laws in opposition to God's?

In the last two of *Levitation*'s five fictions, "Puttermesser: Her Work History, Her Ancestry, Her Afterlife" and "Puttermesser and Xanthippe," Ozick displays her talents at their brightest. With wit, brio, and brilliance, she relates the saga of Ruth Puttermesser, a serious yet dreamy spinster who labors as a civil servant for the city of New York. She may be an unlikely heroine, but Ozick invests her with so rich an inner life that Puttermesser's fantasies cannot help but spill over into the mundane existence of her daily life.

In "Puttermesser: Her Work History, Her Ancestry, Her Afterlife," Puttermesser dreams of a *gan eydn* where she can sit beneath the shade of a tree, gorge on fudge, and read all the books on the shelves of the public library. She may live alone in a decaying apartment in the Bronx, but as she studies Hebrew, she invents for herself a roguish holy ancestor who will teach her the holy tongue. She may have been cast out of her first job at a white-shoe law firm because she was both Jewish and female—even though she felt no particular allegiance to either her religion or her sex—but in her dreams she seeks to claim a connection with her Jewish past.

But Puttermesser's dreams, like her career, are doomed to fail. Even Puttermesser's "biographer" seems to tire of her, for suddenly, abruptly the story ends: "Hey! Puttermesser's biographer!

What will you do with her now?," Ozick asks out loud. As the title promised, Ozick has presented Puttermesser's work history, her ancestry, her afterlife. But what next?

"Puttermesser and Xanthippe," one of Ozick's finest and most inventive tales, provides the answer. Puttermesser is older, but still a spinster, still a civil servant for the city of New York. She lives in Manhattan now—her apartment in the Bronx has been vandalized and destroyed—and she is about to lose her job.

Puttermesser also still studies Hebrew, and one night she inadvertently calls to life a golem—the famed automaton of Jewish legend. As Ozick goes through the history of the genus golem, it becomes clear that what sets Puttermesser's creation apart is that this is the first female golem. Puttermesser, the rationalist, calls her Xanthippe, after the shrewish wife of Socrates, but Xanthippe more accurately identifies Puttermesser as the mother who created her—the mother, and also a god-usurper who takes God's role upon herself to breathe life into inanimate matter.

At first the size of a child, Xanthippe grows quickly, and the mother and daughter soon become locked in a seemingly humorous struggle which can only end tragically when one destroys the other. First, however, Xanthippe will help Puttermesser the civil servant realize her fantasy of triumph in becoming mayor of New York and thus boss of all the city's civil servants. More like a messiah than a mayor, Puttermesser magically redeems the city from dirt, vandalism, crime, and corruption.

But the messiah is a false messiah, and the god-usurper Puttermesser will pay heavily for her creation. Her golem-daughter becomes greedy, insatiable, a corrupt example which other citizens quickly follow. Garbage, crime, inefficiency plague the city once more. The mother must kill the daughter even as she brought her to life. In the end, Puttermesser the godlike creator has wrought only destruction. She is left to mourn: "O lost New York! . . . O lost Xanthippe!"

A god-usurper and a struggle between a mother and her daughter also animate Ozick's second novel, *The Cannibal Galaxy* (1983). Under 200 pages in length, this tightly constructed novel is more firmly grounded in the realistic world than any of Ozick's works since *Trust*. The writing resonates with passion and care. As with *Trust* she has filled her canvas with a multitude of details, but unlike *Trust* the painting works both at close range and as a whole.

At the book's center stands Joseph Brill, a mediocre school principal who seeks to usurp the role of a god by decreeing which of his students shall succeed and which shall not. Having survived the Holocaust by hiding first in a convent cellar and then in a barn's hayloft, the Parisian-born Brill eventually escapes to America and founds a Jewish day school in an unnamed Midwestern city. There, everything is of the middle: the middle-aged, middle-brow refugee finds himself "beleaguered by middling parents and their middling offspring."

Unlike the refugee in "Levitation," Brill does not ascend to the heights. In fact, he has long since abandoned his study of astronomy and with it any heavenly aspirations. He attempts to coax great achievements from his pupils with his private motto, *Ad astra*, "to the stars," but he himself suffers from a stunted vision of the universe.

When he meets the linguist Hester Lilt, the brilliant mother of his least promising pupil, Principal Brill seeks in vain to enlarge his vision. "You stopped too soon," Hester reproves him: he has cut short his own quest for the stars by remaining a bachelor and childless, by choosing to educate other men's children, by letting his telescope lie unused. He has also stopped too soon as a teacher. On the basis of a poor aptitude test, he has doomed Hester's child, Beulah, to failure. To chide the principal, Hester invites him to a public lecture in which she cites the following Talmudic midrash:

> "There ran the little fox," she said, "on the Temple Mount, in the place where the Holy of Holies used to be, barren and desolate, returned to the wild, in the generation of the Destruction. And Rabbi Akiva was walking by with three colleagues, Rabbi Gamliel, Rabbi Elazar, and Rabbi Joshua, and all four saw the little fox dash out. Three of the four wept, but Akiva laughed. Akiva asked, 'Why do you weep?' The three said, 'Because the fox goes in and out, and the place of the Temple is now the fox's place.' Then the three asked Akiva, 'Why do you laugh?' Akiva said, 'Because of the prophecy of Uriah and because of the prophecy of Zechariah. Uriah said, "Zion shall be ploughed as a field, and Jerusalem shall become heaps." Zechariah said, "Yet again shall the streets of Jerusalem be filled with boys and girls playing." So you see,' said Rabbi Akiva, 'now that Uriah's prophecy has been fulfilled, it is certain that Zechariah's prophecy will also be fulfilled.' . . . [Therefore,] To stop at Uriah without the expectation of Zechariah is to stop too soon. And when the pedagogue stops too soon, he

misreads every sign . . . and takes aggressiveness for intelligence, and thoughtfulness for stupidity, and diffidence for dimness, and arrogance for popularity, and dreamers for blockheads, and brazenness for the mark of a lively personality. And all the while the aggressive and the brazen one is only a fox!—a false and crafty creature running in and out of a desolation and a delusion. The laughter of Akiva outfoxes the fox."

The phrase "the cannibal galaxy" derives from astronomy: "the cannibal galaxies, those megalosaurian colonies of primordial gases that devour smaller brother-galaxies." Does Brill devour his pupils for his vanity, as Hester suggests? Yet in using her daughter's plight as the text for a lecture, Hester is, according to Brill, herself guilty of cannibalization. Brill accuses her: "Without Beulah to show the way you wouldn't have a subject matter! A thesis! Without Beulah where would you get your ideas about pedagogy? About silence? About emptiness? You'd be a barren pot! . . . You need her to be nothing, so you can be something. She's Genesis Chapter One, Verse Two—*tohu vavohu*, unformed and void, darkness over the deep, so you can spin out your Creation from her! . . . You call *me* despot? Look how you use, you eat, you cannibalize your own child!"

In time, Beulah, whose eyes once seemed dull, as dull and unformed as a golem's, will indeed outfox the fox. Her sudden and magical transformation from blockhead to celebrated artistic genius is one of Ozick's most realistic metamorphoses, but it is also among her most inspired. Beulah's eyes will shine more brightly than anyone's, and as they peer at Brill from a television screen, they will haunt him with his failure: Principal Brill, who aspired to the stars, mistook an undiscovered planet for a speck of dirt on his telescope's lens. But Beulah's piercing gaze will also mock Hester. Interviewed as a celebrity artist, Beulah cracks sardonic jokes at her mother's expense. Does the daughter cannibalize the mother, too?

The Cannibal Galaxy is a masterful and disturbing work. As tautly constructed as one of Ozick's stories, this slim volume is a far cry from Ozick's epic-length first novel, *Trust*. Yet here, too, Ozick at times falls prey to the vice of overwriting, particularly in the novel's opening chapters. These chapters subtly foreshadow Brill's future, and they describe, often brilliantly, Brill's childhood, adolescence, and life in hiding during World War II. But they remain more description than dramatization,

Advertisement from the New York Times Book Review *for Ozick's most recent novel* and it is not until Brill meets and confronts Hester Lilt that the novel takes flight. From that point on, *The Cannibal Galaxy* can be counted one of Ozick's most stunning achievements.

Ozick has also proven herself a masterful literary critic and essayist in her collection of essays aptly titled *Art and Ardor* (1983). Ozick can be counted among those few contemporary fiction writers who approach criticism as an art in itself, not as an occasion to simply improvise. Like her fiction, Ozick's essays frequently explore the dimensions of the holy. Here, as in her fiction, she distinguishes between ideas that derive their power from unreasoned magic and those that carry the weight of justice and morality. Perhaps because Ozick argues her beliefs as ardently in her essays as she does in her fiction, critics of Ozick the critic have at times accused her of being a polemicist.

Only a fraction of Ozick's essays have been collected, and these address a wide range of literary, feminist, political, and religious subjects. In her literary essays, in particular, she often plays a role similar to that of the narrator in her novella "Usur-

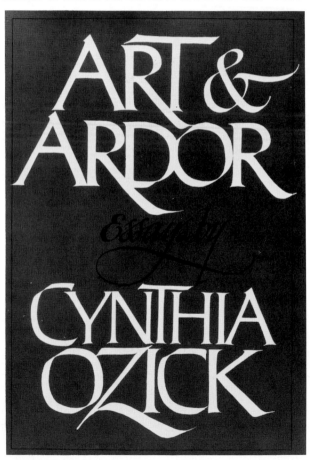

Dust jacket for Ozick's first collection of critical pieces, published in 1983

pation": confronted with a worthy work which is somehow flawed, she seems to imagine how the book would appear if her own sensibility had been brought to bear upon it—a sensibility that separates the holy from the pagan. Thus both Truman Capote and Harold Bloom are shown to be pagan idolators. But few writers could enter more fully or generously into the art of Isaac Bashevis Singer than Ozick does in her appreciation of that writer's collected stories.

In both her fiction and her essays, Ozick continues to pursue themes that have haunted her throughout her career. She addresses herself to the questions: What is holy? What is pagan? What separates the two? What is the burden of Jewish history? She continues to find new ways to refine what has become for her a central metaphor—the biblical story of Terach, the maker of idols, and his son Abraham, who smashed his father's idols and banished them from the household. In fact, as she dramatizes the rise and ultimate fall of idol-worshippers and god-usurpers such as Puttermesser and Principal Brill, she herself plays the role of Abraham, exposing the evils of paganism.

At times, Ozick says, she feels cramped by a language she uses as skillfully as anyone today. "English," she wrote in her preface to *Bloodshed and Three Novellas*, "is a Christian language. When I write English, I live in Christendom." She seeks a way, then, to translate Jewish ideas—and Jewish ideas are holy ideas, Ozick would say—into the Christian language, English.

The Jewish past, the burden of the Holocaust, the Bible, all Jewish thought and literature, the religion itself and the men and women who practice it—these are the subjects of Cynthia Ozick's fiction. They are her primary sources, but not her only sources, for her imagination ranges freely through all of literature and history. Her vision is both religious and obsessive. Though she maintains a Jewish viewpoint, Ozick worries that she may secretly follow Terach—that her true allegiance lies with the idolatrous religion Art. Again and again, her stories dramatize the opposing claims of art, nature, and God. Her characters go in search of what is holy, and are waylaid by temptations that the rabbis must label pagan. This spirited conflict between the sacred and the profane yields an art that is complex, elusive, and richly suggestive.

References:

Anatole Broyard, Review of *Art and Ardor*, *New York Times*, 27 April 1983, C23;

Diane Cole, "I Want to Do Jewish Dreaming," *Pres-*

ent Tense (Summer 1982): 54-57;

Leslie Epstein, Review of *Levitation: Five Fictions,* *New York Times Book Review,* 14 February 1982, pp. 11, 25;

Johanna Kaplan, "The Pagan Rabbi," *New York Times Book Review,* 13 June 1971, pp. 7, 14;

David Lehman, "Chatting with the Zeitgeist," *Newsweek,* 101 (30 May 1983): 91-92;

Elenore Lester, "Author Cynthia Ozick Advocates Jewish Ideas in Fiction," *Jewish Week* (8 April 1983): 14, 24;

Julian Moynahan, "Bloodshed," *New York Times Book Review,* 11 April 1976, p. 8;

Eve Ottenberg, "The Rich Visions of Cynthia Ozick," *New York Times Magazine,* 10 April 1983, pp. 46-47, 62-66;

Katha Pollitt, Review of *Art and Ardor, New York Times Book Review,* 22 May 1983, pp. 7, 35;

Peter S. Prescott, *Quick-Change Artist, Newsweek,* 99 (15 February 1982): 85;

Earl Rovitt, *The Bloodletting, Nation,* 234 (20 February 1982): 207;

David L. Stevenson, "Daughter's Reprieve," *New York Times Book Review,* 17 July 1966, p. 29;

Ruth R. Wisse, "American Jewish Writing, Act II," *Commentary,* 61 (June 1976): 40-45.

Grace Paley
(11 December 1922-)

Adam J. Sorkin
Pennsylvania State University

BOOKS: *The Little Disturbances of Man* (Garden City: Doubleday, 1959; London: Weidenfeld & Nicolson, 1960);

Enormous Changes at the Last Minute (New York: Farrar, Straus & Giroux, 1974; London: Deutsch, 1975).

OTHER: "Some Notes on Teaching: Probably Spoken," in Jonathan Baumbach, ed., *Writers as Teachers/Teachers as Writers* (New York: Holt, Rinehart & Winston, 1970), pp. 202-206.

PERIODICAL PUBLICATIONS: "A Symposium on Fiction," by Paley, Donald Barthelme, William Gass, and Walker Percy, *Shenandoah,* 27 (Winter 1976): 3-31;

"Dreamers in a Dead Language," *American Review,* no. 26 (November 1977): 391-411;

"Somewhere Else," *New Yorker,* 54 (23 October 1978): 34-37;

"Friends," *New Yorker,* 55 (18 June 1979): 32-38;

"Love," *New Yorker,* 55 (8 October 1979): 37;

"The Seneca Stories: Tales from the Women's Peace Encampment," *Ms.* (December 1983): 54-62, 108.

Grace Paley's short stories are vivid examples of twentieth-century American local color and regional sensibility. Populated by many a hue and caste of New York citizen and narrated in a supple, percussive urban demotic, Paley's sketches and tales good-naturedly celebrate the toughness and endurance, the humor and resiliency of the human spirit. In both of her books, the author delves with comedy and sympathy into the anguish, perplexity, and mixed joy and frustration of what the title of her first collection of stories terms "the little disturbances of man."

Paley's fictions are sometimes quite brief. Her plots are often gestures, anecdotes, or monologues, mere snatches of the loneliness of the petty triumphs and the pale ordinariness of the losses and tragedies of neighborhood life. But more than from plot, the momentum and liveliness of Paley's stories derive from their telling, the bright oral tonality and often wildly funny colloquial twists and deadpan ironic turns that underlie the terse comic narrative energy of her works and her sharply etched, sometimes razor-tongued characters. Often seen as a writer's writer whose compressed, circuitous, tangential, and consequential stories are greatly admired by her peers for their concision and seemingly casual, spontaneous artistry, Paley achieves in her best works a complex sense of life's richness, cheerfully accepting human limitations while honoring our capacity to care, to grow, to act deliberately. Few contemporary writers are at once so tough-minded and open-eyed yet so optimistic—or

Grace Paley (photo by Layle Silbert)

perhaps generous—in assessing mankind. Few possess so much street savvy yet retain so much hope and wonder. It is as much for these qualities as for the writer's antic humor and her remarkable ear for the rhythms and inflections of city speech that her stories are memorable.

Grace Paley is thoroughly a product of New York City. She was born and grew up in the Bronx, was educated at city schools and colleges, and now lives in Manhattan and commutes to the suburbs to teach. Her father, Isaac Goodside, "M.D., artist, and storyteller" (according to the author's dedication in her second collection of stories), retired from his practice at sixty to concentrate on painting and was an important influence on his young daughter who as a child, like her Shirley Abramowitz of "The Loudest Voice," was a talkative youngster "absolutely entranced" by the conversation and oral tales of her family. Both Dr. Goodside and his wife, the former Mary Ridnyik, were, Paley notes, "very political people" who had been exiled early in life, Paley's father to Siberia when he was a young man, her mother to Germany. Their political concerns

seem to have been inherited by their daughter, a radical activist who described herself in the mid-1970s as a "somewhat combative pacifist and cooperative anarchist."

As a writer, Paley began as a poet and in the early 1940s studied with W. H. Auden at the New School for Social Research in New York. But she had little interest in formal academic study and, although she also attended Hunter College in 1938 and 1939 after her graduation from Evander Childs High School and later took courses at New York University, she has no college degree. In 1942, at the age of nineteen, she married motion picture cameraman Jess Paley, the father of her two children; they were divorced over twenty years later. By then, after having been a typist and housewife most of the time since dropping out of college, Grace Paley had begun to undertake what might be called almost a second dual career: she had commenced her political involvement with community action and civil defense protests starting in the early 1950s, and she had turned to the writing of short fiction in the middle of the same decade. After many form letter rejections, most of Paley's earlier works were published in book form by Doubleday in 1959 as *The Little Disturbances of Man*, a collection of eleven stories only three of which had previously appeared in magazines.

The collection, while not widely reviewed, was admiringly received: the *New York Times Book Review* welcomed Paley's "well-defined and artfully guileless form of narrative progression" and her wry, "serio-comic" manner of "salvag[ing] laughter from lamentation," and the *Herald Tribune* reviewer hailed her a "sure and individual . . . impressive and extremely articulate writer." Philip Roth wrote that Paley "has deep feelings, a wild imagination, and a style whose toughness and bumpiness arise . . . out of . . . the daring and heart of a genuine writer of prose." The volume developed a loyal following, and in 1968, less than ten years after publication—in a largely unprecedented event for commercial American publishing, especially for a book of short stories—*The Little Disturbances of Man* was republished in hardcover by a different publisher, Viking. Ivan Gold greeted the return to print of Paley's "subtle, fanciful, energetic, wild, and undeniably unique" prose by emphasizing the "rare identity of her mode of expression and her deepest concerns" about "the levels of feeling and turmoil" beneath ordinary human lives.

In the book, the writer's masterly use of diction, her ear for dialect, and her gift for colorful turns of phrase in a variety of idioms infuse her world of often lonely, loveless people with vibrant life. In particular the volume's many voices animate a cityscape of impressive variety. Paley's characters range widely. There are the precocious Josephine, brash and innocent nymphet of "A Woman, Young and Old," with her competitive mother and her placid, wise grandmother, feminist by experience; the almost philosophically passive air-conditioner installer, blandly ironic Charles C. Charley of "An Irrevocable Diameter"; and the cranky, wise-cracking Eddie Teitelbaum, stubborn, defeated idealist of "In Time Which Made a Monkey of Us All," who inadvertently makes a gas chamber of his father's pet shop and suffers, almost by choice, a mental breakdown. Paley's women include Dotty Wasserman, the assertive seeker of marriage who with her boyfriend's help wins a trip to Israel in "The Contest" but loses him, and Rosie Lieber, in love with life and with love itself, a female schlemiel who, "fat and fifty," pathetic and outrageous, belatedly gets her man, once "the Valentino of Second Avenue," in "Goodbye and Good Luck." Equally self-reliant, but very different, are Anna of "The Pale Pink Roast," recently remarried but going to bed with her previous husband "for love," and the author's gently self-mocking alter ego, Faith, with her former and current husbands, Livid and Pallid, in "The Used-Boy Raisers."

Paley's women in this volume—which the author intended to be subtitled, with emphasis on the former, "Stories of Women and Men at Love,"—possess tremendous, indomitable vitality. In part they have to, for as a small boy says in a story from the author's second book, "Mostly nobody has fathers" on the playgrounds of her fiction's city. The writer's own attitude is self-conscious: "I think of myself as a woman who has been a writer and who has been in a tradition which is largely male," Paley noted in 1975. Well before the rise of contemporary feminist consciousness, Paley's work treated from within and unprogrammatically the experience of women's lives. Often linked by the sympathy of motherhood and a communicativeness among themselves—"Women . . . have been the pleasure and consolation of my entire life," asserts Josephine's grandmother—the females of Paley's works sometimes feel men are, again in Grandma's words, "first grouchy, then gone," or, like Anna, they cannot forget that cannibals see man as "the great pig, the pale pink roast." But whether grieving or a trifle devouring, they nonetheless are never bitter and know that, emotionally and irrationally, they need men. Frequently fatalistic, Paley's women are also kind, and in reality are often glad to let men

go their way "having established tenancy" (or thinking that they have), staunchly sending them off "easy and impervious," insouciant and perhaps ultimately irrelevant, like Anna's Peter "cartwheel[ing] eastward into the source of night."

Three excellent stories in *The Little Disturbances of Man*, which like all of Paley's work concerns itself not only with love but also with "time past and upon us," are set in the immigrant past of America's Jews, and more than half of the others take place in the apartments and lives of the second and third generations. Paley is skillful at evoking the tones, the speech, the sometimes grim, sometimes buoyant laughter of the ghetto milieu. Her works retrieve for the contemporary reader the departed narrowness and glamour of Aunt Rose's world of sweatshops and the Yiddish theater, the post-Holocaust gloom of Eddie Teitelbaum's father, the dour assimilationism of Yankee ingenuity in Eddie's hopes, and the enthusiastic, ironic Americanization of irrepressible Shirley Abramowitz, bringing this world alive—in Shirley's words—"still as full of breathing as me." Similarly moving is the tense contrast between the older generations, with their background of Old-World famine, immigrant hardships, and—as one story most sardonically puts it—the deaths from "Jewishness in the epidemics of '40, '41," and the younger generations who, even when unhappy or bitter, perhaps having had "to grow up in the shadow of another person's sorrow," are never as deeply touched by "the cruel history of Europe."

Compelling also—a hallmark of the Paley manner in both her books—are repeated moments of effortlessly achieved folk wit and aphorism, or sardonic one-liners, of sparkling description. "From Coney Island to the cemetery. . . . It's the same subway; it's the same fare," observes genial Mr. Abramowitz, who shares with Shirley the philosophy that "In the grave it will be quiet." Aunt Rose, mocking her younger sister's pity of her unmarried state, admits, "my heart is a regular college of feelings and there is such information between my corset and me that her whole married life is a kindergarten." In a later story, "Wants," a Paley woman describes her ex-husband's "habit . . . of making a narrow remark which, like a plumber's snake, would work its way through the ear down the throat, halfway to my heart." Paley's acerbic, pushy, slightly boozy Irishwoman, Mrs. Raftery, who like many of the author's characters appears in both collections, speaks of her husband's mistress as "a skinny crosstown lady, . . . [who] wears a giant Ukrainian cross in and out of the tub, to keep from going down the drain, I guess," and taunts her son, "tell me, young man, how you'll feel married to a girl that every wild boy on the block has been leaning his thumbs on her titties like she was a Carvel dairy counter, tell me that?" But just as effective, if less quotable, are the moments of understated irony, the tension between parents and children, the combat for self-definition of lovers, wives, and husbands, and the instances of oblique insight into the many ways that—as Paley's Ginny, deserted wife who becomes mistress of Mrs. Raftery's loyal, kindly son John, observes—"All that is really necessary for survival of the fittest, it seems, is an interest in life, good, bad, or peculiar."

Grace Paley's career in letters flourished with the publication of *The Little Disturbances of Man*, and in the early 1960s the author taught at Columbia University and Syracuse University, the latter her only teaching outside the New York metropolitan area except for summer writers' workshops in such places as Vermont, North Dakota, and California. Currently Paley commutes from her Greenwich Village apartment, where she resides with her second husband, Robert Nichols, poet, playwright, and landscape architect, to teach at Sarah Lawrence College in nearby Bronxville. She is well known as a sympathetic and effective creative-writing teacher.

Paley's concern and respect for her students in the classroom and the deep feeling for mankind that the reader finds in her stories reflect a sensibility for which the artistic, the political, and the moral are one. To Paley, it is "a bad habit" to say "A Work of Art" instead of a "Work of Truth." For "art . . . makes justice in the world" and "to tell . . . stories as simply as possible" is, in a sense, "to save a few lives." Paley's life over the last twenty years bears witness to a determined commitment to justice and peace. If her production of stories has slackened (the seventeen stories of her second collection took fifteen years), it is because of the importance she places on activism and nonviolent protest. She was an early and resolute agitator against the inhumane conditions of one of New York City's worst prisons, the Women's House of Detention, in which she herself served six days for, as she put it, "sitting down in the middle of Fifth Avenue for about three minutes among people, lilacs, and daisies in order to confront tanks, missiles, and people" in the "symbolic action" of attempting to block the annual Armed Forces Day parade in 1966. In 1961, Paley was one of the founders of the Greenwich Village Peace Center, and throughout the 1960s the author donated much of her time to antiwar activities, to handing out political leaflets, pamphleteering, par-

ticipating in rallies and protests, and counseling young men and their parents about draft resistance. Her 1966 arrest was neither her first nor her last. An active member of both the local and national committees of Resist, she became prominent in the peace movement despite a self-effacing posture. In 1969 Paley flew to Hanoi to arrange for the return of three prisoners of war as part of an invited four-person U.S. delegation that also included Rennie Davis, member of the Chicago Seven and coordinator of the National Mobilization Committee to End the War in Vietnam. In 1973, she attended the World Peace Conference in Moscow and joined with the Reverend Paul Mayer, cochairman of the American delegation, in presenting a provocative statement on human rights also signed by linguist Noam Chomsky, poet-priest-activist Daniel Berrigan, David Dellinger of the Chicago Seven, and two other left-wing and pacifist spokesmen. The document bluntly condemned Soviet repression of free thought and speech and suppression of dissident intellectuals, but it also criticized the dissidents' "naive views of the political situation in the United States," the beliefs of Andrei Sakharov and especially of Aleksandr Solzhenitsyn that the United States is "a very benign place."

Passages from an uncompleted novel were published in little magazines in the late 1960s, but it was not until 1974 that Paley's next book, *Enormous Changes at the Last Minute*, appeared. Paley has noted in an interview that aiming at a novel was "the wrongest thing I ever did. . . . I did it because people said I should." This second collection of short fiction is darker in mood, quieter in style, more experimentally open in method, at once more truncated and hyperbolic, more economical in technique and powerfully symbolic in scope. "I think the language in my writing now may be simple, but the stories are not so simple," Paley observed upon the book's publication. The volume is also more self-conscious in its social and political themes. These represent the author's concern with and highly synoptic specification of "the facts of money and blood," the "economic arrangements" according to which "people are rich or poor, make a living or don't have to, are useful to systems, or superfluous" and "the way people live as families or outside families or in the creation of family"— elements Paley contends that even "the slightest story ought to contain." The world of the volume is often that of the three-page story "Living," a bleak tale about death, survival, loss, and friendship in which the bleeding Faith tells her dying friend, "We've had nothing but crummy days and crummy

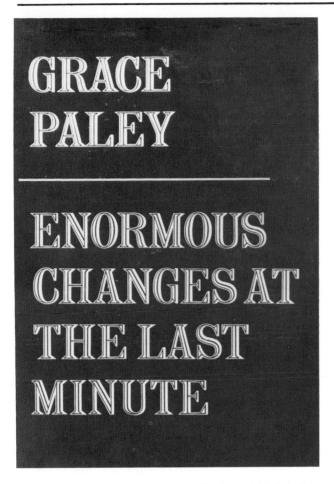

Dust jacket for Paley's second story collection. "I think the language in my writing now may be simple," Paley observed when the book was published, "but the stories are not so simple."

guys and no money and broke all the time and cockroaches and nothing to do on Sunday but take the kids to Central Park and row on that lousy lake." In this second book, characterizations, while precise, are generally less immediately appealing; passion, joy, and grief are more greatly understated; and the exploration of the theme of time—"I don't understand how time passes," confesses the narrator of "Wants," who could be speaking for almost any Paley character—offers no warmly nostalgic detailed evocations of the ever more distant ethnic past, set in and, as it were, voiced by memory's "inheritance."

In a sense, as the collection makes clear in its broader range and in its more muted portrait of Paley's New York, all women and men are immigrants in time's neighborhood. Lonely, rejected, mortal, they share with Mrs. Raftery "a long hopeless homesickness" for the "young days" of the past when—like "The kids! the kids! . . . optimistic,

humorous, and brave," whom the hippie songwriter and cabdriver Dennis eulogizes in the title story—they intended enormous, positive, last-minute changes. The feel of the volume is clear in Paley's "Distance," a fascinating retelling from the self-justifying perspective of Mrs. Raftery, "the lady who appreciated youth," of the story of her son's relationship with Ginny, which the reader heard from Virginia's more matter-of-fact, self-mocking, but also more triumphant tongue in "An Interest in Life" in the earlier book. Despite her claims of victory and rightness in life, Mrs. Raftery pathetically asks near the end, "What the devil is it all about, the noisiness and the speediness, when it's no distance at all?" In the closing story, "The Long-Distance Runner," one of the collection's most surrealistic and ambitious, Paley's persona, Faith, who is Mrs. Raftery's and Ginny's neighbor, jogs in her silk shorts across the short blocks and the long lifetime back to "where her childhood happened" and stays for three weeks with the black family who now lives in what used to be her family's apartment. After Faith returns home to find her children well and her sometime boyfriend Jack on the scene, Paley summarizes: "A woman inside the steamy energy of middle age runs and runs. . . . She learns as though she was still a child what in the world is coming next." Faith's optimism is also her creator's. "You have a rotten rosy temperament," insists the grim Jack in "The Immigrant Story," an accusation—if it is one—that could apply to the "hospitable remarks" of the author as well. Thus change—"change is a fact of God," Rose Lieber suggests in the opening of the first story of the author's first book—is accepted and respected, intended enormously for the good by the living while nonetheless welcomed in the mixed state of the world.

Many of the stories in Paley's second volume, as well as two brief, linked sketches in *The Little Disturbances of Man*, center upon Faith, and in a sense the collection can be seen as containing a novel. Paley admitted to an interviewer, "Maybe there really is a novel in that book. . . ." However, she added perceptively, "I couldn't have done it any other way." In any event, very important to *Enormous Changes at the Last Minute* are two stories in which characters—in one Faith, in the other a woman very much like Faith—visit parents in their old-age homes (in both, as in the title story, the old men, a note tells us, are Paley's father, "no matter what story he has to live in"). In "Faith in the Afternoon" the protagonist, daughter of a Jewish immigrant but fully "an American . . . raised up like everyone else to the true assumption of happiness," visits her parents in the Children of Judea. Recently deserted by her husband, ashamed at her family's solicitude, prodded by the persecuting, paranoid Mrs. Hegel-Shtein, Faith weeps over dismaying news of the once hopeful friends of her youth and in parting with her father insists she cannot again visit until she is happy; her "capacity for survival" and "her susceptibility to abuse" hang in delicate balance. In "A Conversation with My Father," an important fictional statement about Paley's art, the narrator-writer (whom we identify with the author) tries to improvise at her eighty-six-year-old father's request a "simple story" in the style of Maupassant or Chekhov, governed—the writer says—"by plot, the absolute line between two points which I've always despised. Not for literary reasons, but because it takes all hope away." But she only winds up angering the old man; he believes in finality—"Tragedy! Plain tragedy! Historical tragedy! No hope. The end."—and decries her "jokes" and her insistence that such a woman as the story tells about could change, both in fiction and in life. And central to the volume is its longest work, "Faith in a Tree," a story about change in which a symposium of urban voices, largely those of many "a co-worker in the mother trade," ascends to Faith in a hardy urban sycamore. After her furious son chalks on the sidewalk the slogan of a passing antiwar parade hounded out of the neighborhood park by the local cop, the first-person narrator-protagonist concludes, "And I think that is exactly when events turned me around, changing my hairdo, my job uptown, my style of living and telling."

It was precisely for these overt political notes that, aside from some unevenness in the collection, *Enormous Changes at the Last Minute* met sporadic condemnation. The book was widely reviewed in the United States and Great Britain and was warmly praised. For instance, while "the fuzzy failures" of occasionally unrealized sketches or ill-conceived parables of urban dynamics was admitted by Vivian Gornick in the *Village Voice*, her notice insisted that "Paley when she is good is so good that she is worth 99 'even' writers. . . ." Lis Harris, in the *New York Times Book Review*, also found occasional stories marred by shrillness or by pat or precious endings, perhaps the result of Paley's attention to politics, but she stressed, "I can't think of another writer who captures the itch of the city, or the complexities of love between parents and children, or the cutting edge of sexual combat as well as Grace Paley does"; and Gabriele Annan, in the *London Times Literary Supplement*, found Paley "a conscious and deliberate artist" whose characters' voices "always sound au-

thentic" and "are often funny and sometimes witty in a dry, wry, punchy, even brutal way." But the reviewers in *Commentary* and *Saturday Review* expressed abhorrence at, respectively, the author's "reductive," "narrow-minded attitudes . . . borrowed wholesale from the communitarian/utopian ethos of the radical Left" and her "sociological shorthand" which proves "that progressive politics . . . is a downright heavy burden on the art of fiction." More levelheaded, if unswervingly enthusiastic, was Jonathan Baumbach in *Partisan Review* who suggested that the differences in atmosphere between Paley's two books were conscious and artistic, not the ether of spoiled politics. To Baumbach, *Enormous Changes at the Last Minute* "is not, as advertised by some reviewers, inferior to *The Little Disturbances of Man*. It is a different book by the same author . . . a further exploration . . . made up of a number of seeming fragments, an indication not of haste . . . but of a distillation of materials. . . ."

Paley's slow pace of writing stories and her indefatigable political agitation have continued since the publication of this volume. Since the mid-1970s, only a handful of Paley stories have appeared in print in the *New Yorker* and elsewhere. In 1978, on Labor Day, in a simultaneous demonstration with another group of War Resisters League members in Red Square near the Kremlin, Paley and ten others unfurled a banner on the White House lawn condemning both U.S. and U.S.S.R. nuclear weapons and nuclear power. For this, "the Washington Eleven" were given $100 fines, 180-day suspended jail sentences, and two-to-three-year terms of probation during which time they were forbidden to participate in any protest in Washington. At her sentencing, Paley commented, "We were trying to speak beyond the range of our own voices, and we succeeded. We stepped on the lawn to be *heard*. . . ."

The notion of voice, of speaking out loud, is important not only as an adjunct to Paley's political principles but also as the basis of the characteristic effects of her fiction and as a principal theme of her writing. At the heart of her narrative technique lies the assertion of the storywriter in "A Conversation with My Father" that "everyone, real or invented, deserves the open destiny of life." The achievement of a sense of this openness is one of the foremost appeals of a Paley story and reflects the author's firm belief in change and potentiality. Philip Roth has pointed out about the careful contrivance and sophistication behind Paley's seemingly improvisatory manner: "for a writer like Grace Paley . . . creating the illusion of intimacy and spontaneity is not just a matter of letting your hair down and being yourself, but of inventing a whole new idea of what 'being yourself' sounds like and looks like. . . ." Identity is, as it were, created in utterance.

As a demonstration of the ongoing human spirit, art likewise speaks of ourselves and our lives beyond the range of the individual voice. Verbal art, like Mrs. Darwin's framed photograph of baby Faith "fixed . . . with glass to assail eternity," delivers humanity from impermanence, from the closed sequence of mute mortality in time (the storywriter's father's "tragedy," "the end of a person"), indeed from the grave's silence that Shirley and her father cite. Thus in "Debts," the author-narrator decides she possibly does "owe" a debt of transforming for family and friends the "inheritance" of "knowing" to the "remember[ing]" of "telling." The artist's "responsibility," the writer asserts to her aged father in opposing his tragic perspective, is to her neighbor and main character in her story, her "knowledge" and "invention." Moreover, art also delivers humanity from isolation and ignorance. In speaking out, listening, and telling stories together, people reconfirm human "community," reaffirm "mutual aid and concern." In short, the verbal is the essence of the human. To Paley, talk is vitality, fellowship, and hope, and in it are an inherent politics, art, and morality. Behind these conceptions stands the distant influence of the European tradition of Yiddish stories in which the Deity spoke (and could be talked back to) and the word was supreme. The politics and morality of the spoken word are most clear in Paley's story "Faith in the Afternoon," where Faith and her parents remember an episode when Mr. Darwin is arrested for distributing leaflets along the Coney Island boardwalk and Mrs. Darwin tells the policeman, "Shut up, you Cossack!" Faith's father explains, "You see . . . to a Jew the word 'shut up' is a terrible expression, a dirty word, like a sin, because in the beginning, if I remember correctly, was the word!"

Grace Paley pays great homage to this conception of the word in both her life and her art. The ultimate seriousness of her writing is camouflaged in her two books by the humor, the apparently conversational openness and simplicity, the finely wrought casualness of her manner. In the conven-

tions of her work, it has been said, she "combines what has been called the 'tradition of new fiction' in America with the abiding concerns of the old." In recognition of her artistry, Paley received a Guggenheim fellowship in 1961, a National Endowment for the Arts grant in 1966, and an award for short-story writing from the American Institute of Arts and Letters in 1970. In 1980 she was elected a member of the Institute. The importance of her work has also been acknowledged by her peers. Baumbach wrote that "Paley is a major writer working in what passes in our time as a minor form." Fellow practitioner of the art of the postmodern short story, Donald Barthelme, noted, "Grace Paley is a wonderful writer and troublemaker. We are fortunate to have her in our country."

Interviews:

Leonard Michaels, "Conversation with Grace Paley," *Threepenny Review*, 1 (Fall 1980): 4-6;

Joan Lidoff, "Clearing Her Throat: An Interview with Grace Paley," *Shenandoah*, 32 (1981): 3-26.

References:

Jonathan Baumbach, "Life Size," *Partisan Review*, 42, no. 2 (1975): 303-306;

Nancy Blake, "Grace Paley's Quiet Laughter," *Revue Française d'Etudes Américaines*, 4 (November 1977): 55-58;

Marianne DeKoven, "Mrs. Hegel-Shtein's Tears," *Partisan Review*, 48, no. 2 (1981): 217-223;

Blanche Gelfant, "Grace Paley: Fragments for a Portrait in Collage," *New England Review*, 3 (Winter 1980): 276-293;

Anne Z. Mickelson, *Reaching Out: Sensitivity and Order in Recent American Fiction by Women* (Metuchen, N.J.: Scarecrow Press, 1979), pp. 206-207, 221-234;

Harriet Shapiro, "Grace Paley: 'Art Is on the Side of the Underdog,' " *Ms.*, 2 (May 1974): 43-45;

Adam J. Sorkin, " 'What Are We, Animals?': Grace Paley's World of Talk and Laughter," *From Marginality to Mainstream: A Mosaic of Jewish Writers, Studies in American Jewish Literature*, 2 (1982): 144-157.

Chaim Potok

(17 February 1929-   )

S. Lillian Kremer

BOOKS: *The Chosen* (New York: Simon & Schuster, 1967; London: Heinemann, 1967);

The Promise (New York: Knopf, 1969; London: Heinemann, 1970);

My Name Is Asher Lev (New York: Knopf, 1972; London: Heinemann, 1972);

In the Beginning (New York: Knopf, 1975; London: Heinemann, 1976);

Wanderings: Chaim Potok's History of the Jews (New York: Knopf, 1978; London: Hutchinson, 1979);

The Book of Lights (New York: Knopf, 1981; London: Heinemann, 1982).

PERIODICAL PUBLICATIONS: "Provisional Absolutes," *Commentary*, 39 (May 1965): 76-78;

"Martin Buber and the Jews," *Commentary*, 41 (March 1966): 43-49;

"Interaction in the Adopted Land," *Saturday Review*, 51 (7 December 1968): 37-40;

"Reply to a Semi-Sympathetic Critic," *Studies in American Jewish Literature*, 2 (Spring 1976): 30-35;

"A Tale of Two Soldiers," *Ladies' Home Journal*, 98 (December 1981): 16-19;

Review of *The Dean's December*, by Saul Bellow, *Philadelphia Magazine*, 73 (March 1982): 71-75;

"Teaching the Holocaust," *Philadelphia Magazine*, 73 (April 1982): 130-144;

"The Gifts of Andrea," *Seventeen*, 41 (October 1982): 152;

"The Bible's Inspired Art," *New York Times Magazine*, 3 October 1982, pp. 58-69.

Chaim Potok, rabbi and critical scholar of Judaic texts, has demonstrated in his literary career that the American novel is indeed a viable genre for writing about Jewish theology, liturgy, history, and scholarship. He has brought to American fiction a feeling for biblical exegesis, Talmudic study, and the mystical writings of the Cabala and the Zohar. Born in New York on 17 February 1929, to Polish-Jewish immigrants Mollie Friedman and Benjamin Max Potok, the novelist's formative years were spent in a traditional Jewish home, and he was edu-cated in Jewish parochial schools. In early adolescence, Potok read Evelyn Waugh's *Brideshead Revisited*, which has given major direction to his creative activity. Potok recognized in Waugh's work the capacity of the novel to successfully transport readers into cultural environments foreign from their own, and he determined that fiction would be his vehicle to weave Jewish civilization into American literature. With that end in mind, he undertook a rigorous religious and secular education at Yeshiva University, where he earned the B.A. summa cum laude in 1950; at the Jewish Theological Seminary, where he received the M.H.L. and rabbinic ordination in 1954; and at the University of Pennsylvania, where he earned a Ph.D. in philosophy in 1965. Potok's interest in Jewish studies and the influence of Evelyn Waugh are evident in his efforts to show man in relation to God and to examine the importance of religion in a secular age and society. Potok's characters, like Waugh's, display a strong sense of continuity with national history and are often presented against a backdrop of the demands of family and religion. Furthermore, the interplay, as in *Brideshead Revisited*, of two sensitive, intelligent young men of parallel yet divergent interests has become Potok's major character construct.

Unlike his fellow American-Jewish novelists, to whom scholarship in Judaica has been of peripheral interest, Potok stands in the European tradition of Sholem Aleichem, Isaac Leib Peretz, and Chaim Nachman Bialick, pursuing a Judaic professional role in conjunction with that of the creative artist. Following service as a U.S. Army chaplain in Korea (1956-1957), Potok married Adena Sarah Mosevitzky and began a distinguished teaching and publication career in Jewish studies. He taught at the University of Judaism in Los Angeles (1957-1959), served as scholar in residence at Har Zion Temple in Philadelphia (1959-1963), and taught at the Jewish Theological Seminary Teachers' Institute (1963-1964). His career in publishing has included positions as managing editor of *Conservative Judaism* (1964-1965) and editor for the Jewish Publication Society (1965-1974). In his role as special projects editor for the Jewish Publication Society (since 1974), he has collaborated with other

232

Chaim Potok (photo by Layle Silbert)

scholars and rabbis to prepare the new authorized translation of the work that is at the heart of Judaism, the Hebrew Bible. Their labors have resulted in three volumes, *The Torah* (1962), *The Prophets* (1978), and *The Writings* (1982). Potok acted as committee secretary for the final volume, coordinating the translation and occasionally, he says, acting "as arbiter of English style" in an effort to bring the work "into line with modern scholarship and language." *Wanderings: Chaim Potok's History of the Jews* (1978) is a compendium of scholarship about Jewish civilization and its relation to the myriad cultures with which Judaism has come into contact. As in the novels, Potok's structural scheme in this work is cultural confrontation, exploring Jewish encounters with Egypt, Greece, Rome, Christianity, Islam, and modern secularism. Potok's scholarly and critical articles have appeared in *Commentary, Saturday Review of Literature*, the *New York Times, Conservative Judaism*, the *Reconstructionist*, and *American Judaism*.

The novel serves as Potok's primary vehicle for the examination of the modern Jewish experi-ence. The genesis and substance of every Potok novel is Jewish religious, historic, and cultural experience in a non-Judaic world. His philosophic and ethical views are derived from Judaic sources. The novelist's affirmative vision, veneration of life, positive assessment of human nature, and pervasive striving for meaning in the midst of chaos, for good in the face of evil, derive from Judaism. He joins other American-Jewish novelists in advocating the Jewish view of a sanctified world and an enduring and noble humanity, revealing a vital philosophy to counter twentieth-century alienation and despair.

Potok's characters are conversant with Jewish theology, liturgy, and rabbinic commentaries, and it is through these intellectual resources and their life experiences that they strive to comprehend the human condition. They are frequently presented in the context of synagogue, yeshiva, and observant Jewish home, engaged in activities historically associated with Judaism: prayer, study, and communal service. They do not share the assimilationist goals of the Jews about whom Saul Bellow and Philip Roth write. They do not dream, as does Bellow's Tommy Wilhelm, of becoming a Hollywood star; they do not desire, as does Bellow's Moses Herzog, to break down the social bastions of Luddeyville, Massachusetts; they do not aspire, as does Bellow's Humboldt Fleisher, to be valued members of Princeton University's English department. Nor do Potok's characters hope, as do Roth's Zuckerman and Lonoff, to be accepted as American writers; or like Bernard Malamud's Freeman, to pass as Christian. In the instances when Potok's characters enter the secular public world, they maintain orthodox private lives.

The central subject of every Potok novel is, the author notes in a recent interview, "the interplay of the Jewish tradition with the secular twentieth-century." He writes of Jews "who are at the very heart of their Judaism and at the same time . . . encountering elements that are at the very heart of the umbrella civilization." In *The Chosen* (1967) and *The Promise* (1969) two sets of core-to-core confrontations evolve: one within the context of Orthodox Judaism between traditionalists and Hasidim, and the second between religious orthodoxy and Western secular humanism. In *My Name Is Asher Lev* (1972) the confrontation is with Western art; in *In the Beginning* (1975), with scientific biblical criticism and modern Western anti-Semitism; and in *The Book of Lights* (1981), with the Orient and the destructive implications of atomic physics. Each of the novels considers whether American Jewry has succumbed to secularism or has used its freedom to reeducate itself—as Potok writes in *Wanderings*—"to rebuild its core from the treasures of our past, fuse it with the best in secularism, and create a new philosophy, a new literature, a new world of Jewish art, a new community, and take seriously the word 'emancipation.'"

The Chosen, Potok's first novel, examines contemporary American-Jewish identity. The Crown Heights-Williamsburg section of Brooklyn, an area heavily populated by Jews, is the setting for a drama of religious commitment. The antagonists are Hasidim, known for their mystical interpretation of Judaic sources and intense devotion to their spiritual leaders, and Orthodox Jews, who emphasize a rational, intellectual approach to Judaic law and theology. Paradoxically, the supportive relationship which is developed between the Hasidic and Orthodox boys begins in conflict. Potok employs a quintessentially American device, a baseball rivalry, as objective correlative of the dichotomies. The Hasidic zealots are led by Danny Saunders, son of a charismatic leader. The traditional Orthodox team is led by Reuven Malter, son

of a modern scholar who applies textual explication to Talmud studies. An injury sustained by Reuven at Danny's hands is the catalyst which brings the boys together and exposes each to the father and antithetical religious attitudes of the other. The novel chronicles the attempts of the fathers and sons to understand and sustain religious life and tradition in a predominantly secular age and society and emphasizes the fathers' efforts to rear sons who will be strongly committed to Judaism and Jewish causes. The elder Malter, patterned after the novelist's beloved father-in-law, Max Isaac Mosevitzky, is the idealized Jewish teacher, a dedicated scholar and humanitarian. Just as he fuses the best in Judaic scholarship with the best in secular culture, his son combines intellectual excellence in sacred and secular studies, complementing Talmudic studies with forays into symbolic logic, mathematics, and secular philosophy. In marked contrast to the Malters' relationship is the strained silence between Reb Saunders and Danny, who is meant to succeed him as Hasidic spiritual leader. Counterpointing the intellectual exploration Malter encourages is Reb Saunders's circumscribed grooming of Danny for his dynastic role. Recognizing, as did the early Hasidim, the danger of relegating the soul to the dominance of the mind, Saunders uses silence to teach Danny the value of heart and soul. When they are not engaged in Talmudic study, Saunders builds a wall of silence between them in an effort to strengthen Danny's soul through suffering and thereby help ready his son to assume the burdens of his followers. The father fails. Although Danny remains an observant Jew, he rejects the traditional role of spiritual guide and becomes instead its secular counterpart, a clinical psychologist.

That Potok stands alone among American-Jewish novelists in the realm of Judaic studies becomes evident in the comparison of his schoolroom scenes with those of other writers. Potok transforms scholarship to drama. Whether Talmudic debate is presented to an entire congregation or in private tutorial sessions or in the context of classroom discussion and dialogue, Potok's delineation of Hebrew higher education is superb. After a plethora of early educational scenes limited to ineffectual instructors and recalcitrant young boys, the standard fare of American-Jewish fiction, it is refreshing to encounter Potok's able treatment of serious scholarship, progressing beyond rudiments of Hebrew to Talmudic tractate and textual emendation. A case in point is Reuven's class. His teacher is soft of voice, gentle, an exciting, knowledgeable instructor who teaches Talmud, "concentrating for days on a few lines and moving on only when he is satisfied that . . . his students understood everything thoroughly." No other work in recent American-Jewish fiction captures the joy and intensity of Talmudic learning as does the scene of Reuven preparing a tractate for discussion. Potok brings the research process to life. In addition to the time-honored yeshiva method of memorization of text and accompanying rabbinic commentaries, Reuven examines cross-references for parallel texts and checks the Palestinian Talmud discussions against those of the Babylonian Talmud to reconstruct a correct text. He triumphs when he rejects mere dialectics and offers instead an explanation based on a controversial modern method of critical analysis to a professor known for hostility to the approach. Potok's descriptive and dramatic portrayal of scholarly endeavor brings new depth and breadth to American-Jewish fiction.

In addition to using religious and scholarly interests to authenticate the Jewish milieu, Potok gracefully parallels his youths' inner quests for Jewish identity with historic events: the demonic Nazi mission to destroy Jewry and the search for physical and spiritual salvation in a Jewish national homeland. Although the Holocaust remains a muted topic in this first novel, it is presented as a hovering pestilence in the larger context of America at war. Potok links the Holocaust and the creation of the State of Israel, a theme to which he will return in later works. Out of the ashes, Malter insists, new life must emerge. The only meaning to be derived from the destruction of one-third of world Jewry is the rebirth of a nation, the Zionist goal of the establishment of a Jewish state in its ancient territory. Beyond its thematic import, Zionism is integrated into the novel's dramatic conflict between the Malters and Saunders. Predictably, Reb Saunders supports a postmessianic Israel and bitterly denounces secular Zionism, while the Malters support the Zionist goals. The yeshiva students talk of little but Israel during the early days of independence when the infant state was under attack by five Arab nations. Zionist youth groups become increasingly active, in one instance loading supplies for delivery to the Haganah, as had Chaim Potok. The final third of the novel is narrated in the context of the Zionist struggle, and the experiences of the characters are intimately bound with the history of Israel. Unlike the assimilated suburbanites of Roth and the intellectual assimilationists of Bellow, Potok's characters reflect the concern of American Jewry for the survival of Israel. The novel concludes emblematically with chapter eighteen. In Hebrew the number

eighteen is transcribed *chai*, which also spells the word *life*. In this manner Potok symbolically suggests a renaissance for the Jewish people in the State of Israel and a new beginning for Danny in psychology and Reuven in rabbinic studies.

Potok's second novel, *The Promise*, is a sequel to *The Chosen*. The novelist continues to trace the careers of the two friends and the influence of their fathers in their lives. Reuven is preparing for rabbinical ordination at an Orthodox seminary while Danny is adjusting to secular life in pursuit of a psychology degree at Columbia University. Shorn of beard, earlocks, and Hasidic garb, Danny nevertheless remains a Hasid in spirit. Paralleling his separation from his traditional Hasidic role in *The Chosen* is his departure from orthodox psychiatric practice in *The Promise*. While Reuven continues to work in Judaic studies, he is faced with the dilemma of opposing his traditional instructor's insistence that he remain true to classic Talmudic scholarship and refrain from using modern textual criticism. The fathers play significant roles in the sequel. Reb Saunders's dominating presence is somewhat diminished, but David Malter's parental and scholarly influence is extended. The influence of the fathers is dramatized through Danny's adaptation of Reb Saunders's technique for creative suffering through silence to clinical psychology and Reuven's adoption of Malter's critical method to elucidate the Talmud. The fathers defined themselves within the Jewish context, and, despite the incursion of secular interests, the sons find their elemental and existential purpose in Judaism. Every struggle is undertaken within the sphere of a dynamic Judaism, and each character defines himself, understands himself, and celebrates himself as a twentieth-century Jew.

As in the first novel, the dramatic conflict and thematic emphasis is in the arena of Judaic scholarship. Religious dichotomy dramatized in *The Chosen* between Hasidic and traditional Orthodox Judaism is extended in *The Promise* to explore the relationship and distinctions between Orthodox and Conservative Judaism. Using a structural scheme reminiscent of medieval morality drama, the novelist casts his rabbinical student at the center of discord between rivals. Reuven is at odds with a key member of his ordination committee, a fundamentalist who fears and resents Reuven's preference for his father's critical method of analyzing and emendating texts. The teacher views such critical emendation as sacrilege and enlists Reuven's assistance to help him understand the method so he may attack it in the Orthodox scholarly press. In addition, Reuven is drawn into further conflict with his fundamentalist teachers when he challenges the rabbinic court's excommunication decree to study the works of and befriend a radical scholar, Abraham Gordon.

In addition to characters and themes, the sequel is further linked to its predecessor by the structural device of a game to engage principal characters and introduce conflict and theme. Unfortunately, the device which served Potok so vibrantly in the first novel pales by comparison in the second in which it is less carefully integrated. In *The Promise* a carnival pitch game is employed to introduce another father and son duet, the Gordons. Michael Gordon, an emotionally disturbed youngster who is to become Danny Saunders's patient, correlates a carnival barker's misrepresentation of his score with the unjust vilification his father has suffered in the Orthodox press and rabbinic court which has excommunicated him for heretical publications. The child relates the dishonest pitchman to the authors of vitriolic attacks against his father, critics who argue that the apostate Gordon is lethal to Judaism, a threat to scripture and religion. On a metaphoric level the game is emblematic of the core-to-core conflict within contemporary Judaism, a conflict between those who read scripture as divine revelation and those who insist on human attribution.

In addition to using theological dispute to represent the diversity of twentieth-century Judaism, Potok contrasts Hasidic and Conservative factions by juxtaposing their social and religious customs in the betrothal and marriage of Danny Saunders and Rachel Gordon. Accused by critics such as Judah Stampfer of having presented an unduly bleak portrayal of Hasidic life in *The Chosen*, Potok now turns his attention to Hasidic joy and enthusiasm, to the tumultuous song and dance of the betrothal and wedding feasts in *The Promise*.

Pre-Potok American-Jewish fiction often failed to delineate either the rich diversity within Orthodox Judaism or the scope and variety of other Jewish denominations. The theological underpinning and the cultural and social manifestations of American Judaism had, until Potok's novels, gone largely unexplored. Where others have been brief and superficial, Potok has been substantial and substantive. In so doing, he has made an important contribution to American literature.

The third novel, *My Name Is Asher Lev* (1972), is once more structured around cultural confrontation, counterpointing ardent Hasidic religionists and their son, whose devotion is to art. As Danny

Saunders had abandoned the role of Hasidic spiritual leader for that of secular healer, so Asher Lev rejects his designated role of Hasidic emissary for a place in the Western artistic tradition. The ensuing conflict between parents and sons takes the form of the traditional novel of initiation charting the coming of age of an artist working in a society inherently hostile to his endeavor. In this work Potok abandons his customary third-person narrative and achieves the immediacy and vividness of the first-person narrative without paying the heavy price of limitation of knowledge. The book is the mature artist's retrospective portrait of his childhood, a reexamination of his attitudes and the external forces which shaped his vision and judgment. The occasion for the narrative is the artist's response to Hasidic detractors to whom he has become "the notorious and legendary Lev of the Brooklyn Crucifixion." Although Lev is an observant Jew, he is judged guilty of betraying his religious heritage and encroaching upon a tradition sacred to Christianity. Variously depicted as "a traitor, an apostate, a self-hater, an inflicter of shame" upon his family, his friends, and his people, Lev's autobiographical reflections defend his actions.

The Levs are Ladover Hasidim, a sect patterned on the Lubavitcher Movement, who have escaped European persecution and settled in the Crown Heights section of Brooklyn to rebuild their community. Among Asher's ancestors are the Rebbe of Berdichev, a celebrated Hasidic leader, and a grandfather recognized as a genius, "a dweller in the study halls and synagogues, and academies," who uprooted his family and journeyed to a distant Russian town to join the Ladover Hasidim and eventually became their leader's Russian emissary. The artist's father, Aryeh Lev, continued his father's work and expanded it from national to international dimension as history warranted. In European cities, where Jews had suffered enormous losses, Aryeh created centers of Hasidic learning. Similarly, Asher's mother, Rivkeh, carries on her murdered brother's mission to serve Jews in the name of the Rebbe. Beyond disappointment in their son's failure to work in behalf of Jewish causes, the Levs despair of his dedication to Western art, considering it blasphemous at worst and mere indulgence of personal vanity at best. Asher persistently defies his father's demand that he sacrifice art to religion, and a deep rift develops between them.

Consumed with self-doubt and guilt, the aspiring artist suffers nightmares in which his mythic ancestor accuses him of failing to continue the family tradition of service. The ancestor's nocturnal visits recur intermittently and in a manner reflecting Asher's transgressions, ranging from a mild admonition for "playing, drawing, wasting time" to a formidable rebuke for his refusal to join the family in Vienna on a Hasidic mission. In that dream the mythic ancestor, dressed in dark caftan and fur-trimmed hat, thunders through the Russian forest to confront the errant child. As father and son become increasingly polarized, Asher dreams of the venerable old man "moving in huge strides across the face of the earth" to berate him for being unequal to the courageous Russian Jews who risk death pursuing Judaic education in the clandestine religious schools and frozen barracks of Siberian prison camps. Community disapproval of Asher's art is foreshadowed when a classmate discovers Asher's absentminded portrait of the threatening Rebbe in his Bible. Asher is bewildered and frightened when he recognizes the nature and degree of his antagonism toward the spiritual leader. Censure of Asher's drawing, until now limited to his family, becomes brutally vociferous and public. Paradoxically, it is only the Rebbe who understands Asher's talent. Others associate the artist's talent with the demonic. Since the spiritual guide regards Asher's ability as a divine gift, he forbids the father to uproot the son and engages a mentor to work with the young artist.

Under the mentor's tutelage, Asher undergoes a program of expansion and discovery which transports him from the religious community to the secular, to the subjects and modes of Western art. Whereas to Asher progress toward self-realization as an artist demands that he learn to paint in the Western tradition of nudes and crucifixions, to his father that activity is an abomination, for in his eyes it is an abandonment of Torah and Talmud. Where the artist son sees the cross as an aesthetic mold stripped of Christological import, the father sees a river of Jewish blood replenished throughout a two-thousand-year history of Christian anti-Semitism.

The artist's torment, resulting from conflict between critical and public acclaim offset by family and Hasidic denunciation, is expressed in his "Brooklyn Crucifixion." Lev has portrayed his suffering mother tied to the Venetian blinds of her parlor window in a posture of perpetual agonized waiting, waiting for the warring husband and son to return home in peace. Thus Asher records his struggle to be an artist and the tragic division he has imposed on the family. In the painter's mind,

"Brooklyn Crucifixion" expresses not religious martyrdom, but the artist's psychological plight. Despite the assertions of his antagonists, Lev maintains that in secular art the cross is emptied of vicarious atonement and serves only as an aesthetic reference. He uses the form because, as Potok remarked in a 1978 interview, he finds no comparable "aesthetic mold in his own religious tradition into which he could pour a painting of ultimate anguish and torment." Potok explains that "For Asher Lev the cross is the aesthetic motif for solitary protracted torment." To the victims and descendants of victims of Christian anti-Semitism, the Lev painting is but another painful reminder of a two-thousand-year burden of deicide libel. Informed by the Rebbe that he must leave the community to which he has brought such pain, Asher paints his Russian ancestor and experiences an epiphany, becoming fully aware of the divine and demonic possibilities of the creative impulse. Lev is now ready for a new beginning, ready to join forces with the ancestor and express the world's anguish, ready to use his artistic talents to give shape and form to human pain. Thus Asher Lev shares with James Joyce's young artist the knowledge that his vocation as an artist demands a period of exile of him. It is worth noting here that Potok, like Joyce, treats the artist's isolation and alienation from family, school, religious community, culminating in exile, as a progressive step that will become more positive with the artist's maturity, one that will lead to reconciliation of the spiritual and aesthetic natures.

The autobiographical fourth novel, *In the Beginning*, fuses Potok's traditional interests in Jewish education and twentieth-century history, a history that has violently touched his family. The novelist's parents, described in *Wanderings* as "the bearded young man who hated Poles and Russians and the lovely young woman who was nearly raped by cossacks," migrated to America "from the apocalypse that was eastern Europe after the Bolshevik Revolution and the First World War." Benjamin Max Potok, who "saw himself mirrored in the eye of most American gentiles as Jewish Caliban," is the model for Max Lurie, the novel's militant Jew who learned while serving as a Polish soldier that Gentile Poles wanted him, not as an equal, but as a scapegoat, ever ripe for persecution, an ever ready object on which to vent one's lust for mayhem. A postwar pogrom, which was the elder Potok's reward for service to his country, is the fate of the Lurie brothers and the occasion of the murder of the protagonist's uncle.

In this novel, as is typically the case in Potok's fictional universe, the young Jewish boy from whose

1) His right hand, resting upon the cold sill of the window, tingled vaguely — the hand with which he had respectfully shaken the hands of the man who had helped to build & the man who had given the order to drop the (first) atomic bomb. He felt cold & weary with a strange & looming dread. What was it? He did not know precisely. It was perhaps his growing inability to bear his slowly heightening sense of the disconnectedness of things. Nothing seemed truly a part of anything. Even between himself & Karen the lines were tenuous & fragile. He felt the world as separate bits & pieces floating & whirling. All seemed to him discrete entities. Particles, bits of cold dead light. His aunt & uncle, Keter & Malkuson, the old man in the synagogue, his classmates, the dean of students, Arthur — whom did he really know? And who really knew him? Choose. Choose what? Why choose? Events began & did not end. There seemed no firm structure to anything. He himself floated & drifted & blew about. He did not even know on what or whom to focus the rages he sometimes felt. Ahead was always some elusive enticing truth. Always ahead. But here & now all seemed random & terrifying, shot through with gaping holes & cluttered with severed lines. Why so sad, Gershon? Why so sad?

He stood there gazing at the snow & wondering what he would do with his life. He shivered in the cold air that radiated inward from the window. After a while he dressed &

perspective the tale is told has a broader view of international history than has generally been true of characters in American fiction. Reflective of Potok's own experience, David Lurie is a studious, thoughtful child, whose status as a child of immigrants makes him more sensitive to European influences on American life and policy than are our Tom Sawyer, Huck Finn, Nick Adams, and Holden Caulfield. There is familiar Potokian material and manner in this work: an articulate friendship between two sensitive, intelligent boys and positive mentor-student and father-son relationships. But there are also significant departures and much exploration of new issues. *In the Beginning* examines hostile forces which impinge on the Jewish consciousness. Whereas contact with secular society was limited in the Hasidic and Orthodox enclaves of the early fiction's Williamsburg locale, this novel is set in a multiethnic Bronx neighborhood like that in which Potok was reared. The result is encounter between Jew and Gentile. Because his purpose is to show the violent Gentile impact on his young protagonist, more often than not the setting is on bustling sidewalks, in school yards, commercial districts, and the zoo, with short counterpoint scenes staged in the traditional Potokian environments of home, library, synagogue, and classroom. The gentle, nostalgic tone of Potok's first novels gave way in the third to a strident tone as he recorded Stalinist Era persecution of Russian Jewry. *In the Beginning* alternately employs bitter and melancholy tones to reflect Jewish despair in the wake of Depression and Holocaust era anti-Semitism. The corresponding pathologies of Christian and Nazi anti-Semitic evils emerge from what Potok has called "the dark underbelly of Western civilization," as he renders the encounter of Jew and anti-Semite.

Just as Reuven Malter had endured scholarly battles paralleling his father's conflicts with the Orthodox educational establishment, so David Lurie is the object of Polish-American anti-Semitic outbursts which correspond, in a diminutive form, to the abuse his father suffered. David's childhood nemesis is Eddie Kulanski, who hates Jews with a "kind of mindless demonic rage." The youthful perpetrator of hooliganism and harassment repeating the lessons of his father and father's fathers is the product of an evolutionary process: "his hatred bore the breeding of a thousand years." Potok presents European anti-Semitism as a continuum which reaches its nadir in the Holocaust. The father's Polish encounters with anti-Semitism are reflected in David's American childhood. European anti-Semitic escalations from encroachment of

civil rights to denial of human rights and then to mass murder are paralleled as the young Kulanski's torment of the Jew begins with boorish harassment and progresses to repeated attempts to push David and his tricycle into oncoming traffic. Characteristic of Potok's historicity is his treatment of anti-Semitism in the ambush of the unsuspecting David at the Bronx Zoo. "For Christ's sake," is the rallying cry employed by Eddie Kulanski and his cousin as they unwittingly echo the Crusaders and their emulators who went about the sacred business of rampage, plunder, rape, and murder against European Jewry throughout twenty centuries of Christianity.

A measure of Potok's maturing craftsmanship in the fourth novel is his use of a stream of consciousness to integrate public event and private drama. When David hears a graphic account of the 1929 Hebron Massacre, he is overwhelmed by visions of an innocent Jewish community of scholars "shot, stabbed, and chopped to pieces, . . . their eyes pierced and their hands cut off, . . . burned to death inside their homes and inside the Hadassah Hospital." Potok uses the irony of the massacre, the irony of Jews leaving European persecution only to be slaughtered in Israel as the catalyst for a stream of consciousness revenge vision in which the impotent child revels in his father's militant response to the cossacks who had "Jewish blood on their sabers . . . Jewish flesh on their whips." In this sequence Potok skillfully fuses anti-Semitic references; David's recollection of a photograph of an armed secret Jewish self-defense league, talk of the Lemberg Pogrom in which his uncle lost his life, and an attack on his father in the presence of fellow soldiers by a bandit confident that wounding a Jewish soldier would provoke no retribution from his Polish countrymen. These memories merge with David's own anti-Semitic encounters, experiences which are paralleled by those of Potok's youth.

The natural integration of liturgy, theology, and imagery patterns in this novel reflects the author's maturing talent. His introduction of the Holocaust in the context of a Yom Kippur memorial prayer is exemplary. As David chants the ancient lament for the martyred Torah sages of the Roman era, he also mourns the death of a Nazi victim. As World War II news is released, David enters an imaginary realm reflecting contemporary horrors. He retreats into the dark rectangle of a window shade containing his visions of Nazi demonstrations with flags, banners, and twenty thousand brown-shirted men shouting and saluting. The acceleration of wartime atrocities is suggested by a vision in which Potok deftly combines nightmarish imagery with mythic legend. This fantasy is composed of the Golem of Prague, a legendary Jewish protector, burning a German building. In the recesses of David's imagination he and the golem perform together heroically, breaking up demonstrations, shouting down the Nazi rage, and furtively entering strategy sessions the better to spy out Nazi secrets. Finally, the impotent real boy becomes the dream hero, the savior of God's word. He battles smoke and flame to rescue endangered Torah scrolls from a burning synagogue. Potok thus registers the frustrations and grief of American Jews at the tragedy befalling European Jewry. These fantasy sequences render the impotence of the Jews, alone and armed with little more than ancient myth in the face of overwhelming odds to halt Germany's genocidal endeavor. Finally, Potok effectively links the Holocaust with earlier historic manifestations of anti-Semitism through the integration of the golem legend with the traditional Passover liturgy. During the Passover seder service celebrating the historic deliverance of the Israelites from Egyptian bondage, David prays for another Moses, a historic deliverer to replace his weary, ineffectual imaginary warrior. These references to the mythology and history of the Jews are splendidly woven into the dramatic context of the novel when David and his cousin struggle against roaming gangs of thugs who attack yeshiva boys and old men.

Consistent with his Dos Passos-style use of journalistic headline juxtaposed with private experience to render contemporary Jewish history in the earlier novels, Potok again evokes the impact of the Holocaust through reference to newspaper photographs of Bergen-Belsen. Like the novelist's own family, the fictional Luries suffered enormous losses: more than 150 family members perished. Potok's dramatization of the Lurie response parallels the experience of his own family. Potok, who was David's age at war's end, learned the truth of the camps as his protagonist did, from "newspaper photographs, memorial assemblies, the disbelief in the faces of friends, the shock as news came of death and more death." Potok's "father's rage" and "mother's soft endless weeping," both described in *Wanderings*, are the models for Max Lurie's anger and Ruth's grief. Although Potok has not yet confronted the subject of the Holocaust frontally, its ever increasing presence in the novels attests to the novelist's conviction in *Wanderings* that "the Jew sees all his contemporary history through the ocean of blood that is the Holocaust."

Of the American-Jewish novelists who have treated the Holocaust in their fiction, Potok alone has related it to the revitalization of Judaism: two major aspects of this phenomenon, American Judaic scholarship and support for Israel as a Jewish nation, have been among Potok's recurring themes. *In the Beginning* presents both, exemplified in the son's dedication to biblical scholarship and the father's active support of Israel. David's motivation to pursue a career in biblical criticism employing techniques held suspect by fundamentalists is the same that Potok attributes to his friends who entered the field "to change the attitude of the discipline toward Jews." Like the scholar-novelist himself, whose work in biblical studies and translation is well known, the protagonist loves Torah and determines to use the tools of its detractors to prove them wrong, to demonstrate that the Hebrew Bible is, indeed, a light to the nations. The second component of the Potok equation for a revitalized Jewry, a vibrant Israel, is Max Lurie's cause. Like Potok's father, who supported the Revisionist party and Vladimir Jabotinsky in efforts to gain home rule for Jews and Israeli independence from British dominion, Max is a fervent supporter of Jabotinsky and the Irgunists in their struggle to assert Jewish rights. Potok, more than other American-Jewish writers, has created characters who reflect American-Jewish support for Israel.

Attention to Potok's interest in post-Holocaust revival of Judaism clarifies the novel's biblical analogies. From its title, which is a translation of *Berashit*, the Hebrew word which begins Genesis, to the novel's structural parallel with the subject of Genesis, Potok draws thematic and allusive connections regarding the relationship of the Jewish people with surrounding Gentile societies. Similarly, Potok's portrayal of Judaism emerging from the Holocaust to rebirth in America and Israel parallels the conclusion of Genesis when Joseph recapitulates the lesson of his career, teaching that God brings good out of evil; that He will deliver the Jewish people out of Egypt and bring them to the land He promised the patriarchs. Significantly, it is during the worst period of Jewish suffering of the Holocaust that the nineteen-year-old David recalls his bar mitzvah Torah portion and its accompanying Prophetic reading. The passages deal with the entry of the Jews into Egypt and the promise of the restoration of the fortunes of Israel, of the rebuilding and habitation of ruined cities. Thus *In the Beginning* reiterates the convictions expressed in *The Chosen* and is a fictive reflector of the novelist's commitment to contribute to a new Jewish civilization, one which rebuilds its core from the treasures of the past and fuses that with the best of the surrounding world.

In *The Book of Lights* (1981), Potok portrays Judaism as giving two powerful beacons to the world, the creative light of Judaism, represented in this instance by the mystical brilliance of the Zohar (*The Book of Radiance*), and the destructive light, the atomic bomb, designed in part by distinguished Jewish physicists. Although the characters are now older, this novel is also the story of a friendship, the relationship of two young rabbis, Gershon Loran and Arthur Leiden, from the period of their seminary studies through their search for meaning in the Judaic tradition while living in a secular society. The narrative is presented from the point of view of Gershon Loran, who started rabbinic study in the traditional Talmudic fashion and was drawn to Cabala, Jewish mysticism, by a brilliant teacher, Jacob Keter, modeled on the famous scholar Gershom Scholem. Arthur Leiden travels the road to the rabbinate indirectly by way of penance for his father's sin. The familiar Potokian pattern of counterpointing two sensitive, intelligent young men from different religious or educational backgrounds is intact.

The influence of Waugh's *Brideshead Revisited* on Potok's method of character interaction and thematic concern is nowhere more evident than in *The Book of Lights*. Here, as in all his fiction, Potok affirms the validity of religious commitment, even in a secular society. And in this work too, he emulates Waugh's pattern of placing young men of divergent backgrounds in each other's paths. However, unlike Waugh's distinctive foils, both of Potok's men are believers. Gershon Loran, orphaned as a child when his parents were killed in Jerusalem, has been reared in an economically depressed Brooklyn neighborhood by an impoverished aunt and uncle who were themselves mourning a son killed in World War II. Loran's life is bleak until at age sixteen he experiences a vision of radiance after witnessing the birth of pups on an apartment house rooftop. This epiphany leaves him with a feeling of being "all caught up in the life of heaven and earth, in the mystery of creation, in the pain and inexhaustible glory of the single moment." Loran's subsequent study of Cabala is emblematic of his desire to recapture the awesome awareness he experienced at the moment of his rooftop epiphany. Arthur Leiden, on the other hand, seeks the religious life in expiation for his father's role in atomic research. Leiden, himself a Harvard graduate in physics, expresses moral anguish in every seemingly glib utterance. In Leiden's

dialogue a new tone and diction enter Potok's fiction. Juxtaposed with moral introspection and exclamation are satiric barbs, invective, vulgar colloquialism which register Leiden's fury at his atomic heritage—a heritage which fills his memory with visions of incinerated birds in his Los Alamos backyard and incinerated people in Hiroshima. Through Leiden's plight Potok grapples with the terrible truths of our time, the reality of a promising technological age which delivered devastation.

Like Waugh's Sebastian Flyte and Charles Ryder, Arthur Leiden and Gershon Loran are students together, in this instance, in the rarefied atmosphere of Riverside Hebrew Institute, a thinly veiled portrayal of Potok's old school, the Jewish Theological Seminary. While the Leidens are not members of a social aristocracy comparable to Waugh's upper-class Britons, they are members of an American aristocracy of talent, respected members of the intellectual and scientific elite; Mrs. Leiden is a professor of art history and her husband is a prominent physicist. Among their friends are Einstein, Teller, Fermi, Szilard. Einstein is "Uncle Albert" to Arthur. It is because of Leiden that President Truman and Albert Einstein appear at the seminary graduation, Truman to accept an honorary degree and Einstein to award Loran a memorial scholarship in honor of the Leidens' son killed in World War II. As Charles Ryder was drawn to Sebastian Flyte's family history, so too, on a less intimate scale, does Loran become involved with the Leidens.

As Evelyn Waugh's young men leave idyllic Oxford to make their way in the world, so do Potok's characters leave the haven of academia to gain knowledge of the world. And like their creator, the characters leave the seminary to fulfill ordination requirements by serving as army chaplains in Korea. Again mirroring Potok's experience, Loran finds great beauty in the "pagan" world of Japan. Echoing the rabbi-novelist, these young rabbis react strongly to Hiroshima, expressing feelings of guilt for the human destruction wrought by the bomb. While Potok's anguish is understandable, his complete assignment of blame to the Jewish project physicists is inexplicable. He appears to ignore the fact that the bomb was an American project, for he leaves unimplicated in his righteous indignation the non-Jews who collaborated on the project, and most enigmatic is his failure to indict the politicians and military advisors whose decision it was to drop the bomb.

On pilgrimage in Hiroshima the young rabbis mourn the dead, reciting the ancient Jewish prayer, the Kaddish, which extols God's wonders. At the center of destruction they pray in the language and liturgy of a people who sanctify life and the creative spirit of God.

For Loran, the spiritual trauma of the Hiroshima experience is deepened by Arthur Leiden's death in an airplane crash. Although it is clear that Leiden would have viewed his own death as symbolic expiation for the lives lost as a result of his father's scientific sins, Loran is tormented by the capriciousness of the penitent's death and is unable to pray. The only solace Loran finds is in Cabala. His tour of duty over, Loran seeks the Talmud teacher who had disapproved of his mystical interest at the expense of legal studies. This teacher directs Loran to a new beginning, convincing him that prayer is not the only commandment and that the study of texts also fulfills God's law. The Talmud teacher thus legitimizes Loran's mystical and scholarly directions by reiterating Potok's recurrent thesis: "the scientific study of sacred texts is a sacred act." In his bleakest moment, Loran returns to the rooftop site of his first epiphany, descends to the deepest recesses of self, and emerges to the voice of his departed friend urging him to reject the notion of nothingness and instead to search for meaning. Now, as at Hiroshima, the answer lies in the Jewish reverence for life expressed in the inspiring words of the Kaddish, the sacred public affirmation of God which marks Loran's return to prayer. He prays ardently for the broken people of his generation and for future generations to mend the world and share in God's work through peaceful endeavor. Appropriately, the novel concludes in the Jewish New Year season, the season of spiritual introspection, repentance, hope, moral rehabilitation, mercy, and forgiveness. Shortly after the solemn New Year devotions, Loran takes up the last stage of the spiritual quest and journeys to Jerusalem to study the mystical texts with his Cabala mentor.

This novel is the most ambitious in the Potok canon, representing significant technical experiment. In his quest for the meaning of human experience in God's creation, Potok has moved outward spatially, thematically, and technically from his traditional Orthodox environments of New York to the Orient, from the Talmudic intellectual core of traditional Judaism to the mystical sphere of Cabala. Although he employs the time-honored literary device of the spiritual quest, he does so in an area previously unexplored in his fiction. In the earlier fiction Potok successfully delineated the dynamics of studying a page of Talmud. In this novel, he undertakes the aesthetic challenge of delineation of the dynamics of a page of Cabala, of creating visions and the interplay of people in the visions. The quest carries the seeker from newfound religious awareness on a Brooklyn rooftop through the traditional routes of religious study and discipline in seminary and clerical office to introduction to the countercultures of East and West. Paradoxically, it is in a civilization he describes as "pagan" that Loran most fully comprehends the grandeur of God's creation, that he knows beauty. The truth learned in the Orient leads the quester to Jerusalem at the culmination of his journey. It is appropriate to this novel and consistent with Potok's earlier work that the American Jew's search for spiritual meaning culminate in Jerusalem, the heart of Judaism. This novel shares with the earlier fictions the resolve of the protagonist to commit his life to Judaic studies. With *The Book of Lights* Potok has again demonstrated that he stands in the forefront of American-Jewish fiction for his capacity to bring to fiction material that had hitherto been uncharted, namely Jewish theology, philosophy, law, scholarship, and mysticism.

Critical response to Potok's writing has ranged from denunciation to acclaim. Potok's detractors frequently center their criticism on the novelist's style, charging him with composing banal speech and employing a pompous tone. Others have complained about the predictability and lack of complexity in his characters. In "The Hasid as American Hero," Curt Leviant judges the dialogue between the young men of *The Chosen* "more like a mature man's bookish presumption of what their talk should sound like than authentic speech itself" and objects to Potok's rendition of Hasidim void of humor and zest for life. In his review of *The Chosen*, "The Tension of Piety," Judah Stampfer also rejects Potok's description of a joyless, rigid Hasidic lifestyle, seeing in it "only the most superficial resemblance of its outer behavior," but Stampfer lauds Potok's rendition of yeshiva life and regards that aspect as the novel's strongest asset. Most often Potok is extolled for examining serious social, philosophical, and theological problems and praised for his concern with ideas and issues.

Criticism of the subsequent fiction has thus far followed lines similar to those which characterized the reception of *The Chosen*. In his analysis of *The Promise*, James Murray faults Potok as being "concerned far more with matter than with form," for "reluctance to dramatize," and praises the novelist's use of "historical background, analysis, commentary, explication, . . . an intelligent discussion of . . .

religiosity in twentieth century America." Others, such as Hugh Nissenson, believe *The Promise* is "a brilliantly and intricately conceived thematic elaboration of the quote from Pascal with which Potok prefaces the book" and concludes that whereas "*The Chosen* established Chaim Potok's reputation as a significant writer, *The Promise* reaffirms it." Writing about *My Name Is Asher Lev*, Guy Davenport assesses Potok's writing as "deceptively plain" and asserts that the novelist needs neither ostentatious style nor rhetorical flourish for his subject. Davenport praises the work as "a tragedy of terrifying dimensions" which shows Potok's "sure sense of how to diagram tragic misunderstanding . . . in a contest of faith and love." R. J. Milch joins those critics who perceive maturation in Potok's craftsmanship when he argues that Potok's treatment of Judaism in *My Name Is Asher Lev* is superior to the earlier volumes because its Jewish concerns are no longer restricted by authorial voice but now "define themselves in the course of the ongoing revelation provided by action and character." Comparing Potok to other American-Jewish writers, Milch concludes that Potok is "the real thing." In "Rectangles of Frozen Memory," Leonard Cheever commends *In the Beginning* as a "great novel," one of richness and complexity, and celebrates Potok's framing metaphors for their dramatic intensity and illumination of the protagonist's thoughts. In a review of *The Book of Lights* for *Commentary*, Ruth Wisse takes Potok to task, charging that "the historicity of the novel is selective," that Potok has superimposed "current attitudes and cultural trends on events of three decades ago." Further, Wisse attacks Potok for Judaizing the atomic bomb and indulging in a "drama of Jewish self-accusation and expiation." Wisse laments Potok's departure from his original authentic representation of Jewish life, "validating traditional Judaism" and taking "his cues from the culture at large." Prior to the charge leveled by Ruth Wisse, most knowledgeable critics assessed Potok's treatment of Jewish life and thought as among the finest in American literature. Sheldon Grebstein's assessment that Potok has rendered Orthodox Judaism authentically is the characteristic judgment. Explaining the reasons for Potok's popularity in an article for *Studies in American Jewish Literature*, Grebstein identifies the elements which assure Potok a significant place in American-Jewish fiction. Among these are "moral fervor, strong emotions experienced by sensitive characters, the portrayal of ancient and deeply felt traditions, the depiction of intimate family life, and an essentially affirmative view of human nature."

Interviews:

C. Forbes, "Judaism Under the Secular Umbrella," *Christianity Today*, 22 (8 September 1978): 14-21;

S. Lillian Kremer, "Interview with Chaim Potok," *Studies in American Jewish Literature*, 4, forthcoming (1984).

References:

Sam Bluefarb, "The Head, the Heart, and the Conflict of Generations in Chaim Potok's *The Chosen*," *College Language Association Journal*, 14 (June 1971): 402-409;

Leonard Cheever, "Rectangles of Frozen Memory: Potok's *In the Beginning*," *Publications of the Arkansas Philological Association*, 4 (n.d.): 8-12;

Michael T. Gilmore, "A Fading Promise," *Midstream*, 16 (January 1970): 76-80;

Sheldon Grebstein, "Phenomenon of the Really Jewish Best-Seller: Potok's *The Chosen*," *Studies in American Jewish Literature*, 1 (1975): 23-31;

Curt Leviant, "The Hasid as American Hero," *Midstream*, 13 (November 1967): 76-80;

Daphne Merkin, "Why Potok Is Popular," *Commentary*, 61 (February 1976): 73-75;

Dorothy Rabinowitz, "Sequels," *Commentary*, 50 (May 1970): 104-108;

Ellen Schiff, "To Be Young, Gifted and Oppressed: The Plight of the Ethnic Artist," MELUS, 6 (1979): 73-80;

Judah Stampfer, "The Tension of Piety," *Judaism*, 16 (Fall 1967): 494-498;

Studies in American Jewish Literature, special Chaim Potok issue, 4 (1984);

Sam Sutherland, "Asher Lev's Visions of His Mythic Ancestor," *Re: Artes Liberales*, 3 (1977): 51-54;

Ruth R. Wisse, "Jewish Dreams," *Commentary*, 73 (March 1982): 45-48.

Charles Reznikoff

(31 August 1894-22 January 1976)

Sanford Pinsker
Franklin and Marshall College

SELECTED BOOKS: *Rhythms* (Brooklyn, N.Y.: Privately printed, 1918);

Poems (New York: Samuel Roth, 1920);

Uriel Acosta: A Play and a Fourth Group of Verse (New York: Cooper Press, 1921);

Chatterton, the Black Death, and Meriwether Lewis: Three Plays (New York: Sunwise Turn, 1922);

Coral, and Captive Israel: Two Plays (New York: Sunwise Turn, 1923);

Nine Plays (New York: Privately printed, 1927);

Five Groups of Verse (New York: Privately printed, 1927);

By the Waters of Manhattan [novel] (New York: Boni, 1930);

Jerusalem the Golden (New York: Objectivist Press, 1934);

Testimony (New York: Objectivist Press, 1934);

In Memoriam: 1933 (New York: Objectivist Press, 1934);

Early History of a Sewing Machine Operator, by Reznikoff and Nathan Reznikoff (New York: Privately printed, 1936);

Separate Way (New York: Objectivist Press, 1936);

Going To and Fro and Walking Up and Down (New York: Privately printed, 1941);

The Lionhearted (Philadelphia: Jewish Publication Society of America, 1944);

The Jews of Charleston, by Reznikoff with the collaboration of Uriah Z. Engleman (Philadelphia: Jewish Publication Society of America, 1950);

Inscriptions: 1944-1956 (New York: Privately printed, 1959);

By the Waters of Manhattan: Selected Verse (New York: New Directions, 1962);

Family Chronicle, by Reznikoff, Nathan Reznikoff, and Sarah Reznikoff (New York: Privately printed, 1963);

Testimony: The United States 1885-1890: Recitative (New York: New Directions, 1965);

Testimony: The United States (1891-1900): Recitative (New York: Privately printed, 1968);

By the Well of Living and Seeing and The Fifth Book of the Maccabees (New York: Privately printed, 1969);

By the Well of Living and Seeing: New & Selected Poems,

Charles Reznikoff (photo by Layle Silbert)

1918-1973 (Los Angeles: Black Sparrow Press, 1974);

Holocaust (Los Angeles: Black Sparrow Press, 1975);

Poems 1918-1936: Volume I of the Complete Poems of Charles Reznikoff, edited by Seamus Cooney (Santa Barbara: Black Sparrow Press, 1976);

Poems 1937-1975: Volume II of the Complete Poems of Charles Reznikoff, edited by Cooney (Santa Barbara: Black Sparrow Press, 1977);

The Manner "Music" (Santa Barbara: Black Sparrow Press, 1977).

OTHER: *Louis Marshall: Champion of Liberty, Selected Papers and Addresses*, edited by Reznikoff (Philadelphia: Jewish Publication Society of America, 1957).

TRANSLATIONS: Emil Cohn, *Stories and Fantasies from the Jewish Past* (Philadelphia: Jewish Publication Society of America, 1951);

Israel Joseph Benjamin, *Three Years in America, 1859-1862* (Philadelphia: Jewish Publication Society of America, 1956).

Charles Reznikoff's poetry has not only influenced the direction and shape of American-Jewish poetry but it has, in effect, created the possibility of such a poetry. In a recent interview Kenneth Koch asked Allen Ginsberg the following question: "Could you tell me briefly which 20th-century poets have influenced your work?" It is, of course, a standard query, one that poets like to dodge. Ginsberg's reply, however, is instructive: "Most recently, enormously, Charles Reznikoff, for his particular focus on sidewalks, parks and subways of New York." It is Reznikoff's work—rather than, say, Karl Shapiro's—that has provided a shaping force to the urban Jewish imagination, that brought Jewish concerns and Modernist technique into a juxtaposition. Indeed, it is hard to think of another American-Jewish writer in any genre whose work so spans the nightmare of our century or whose vision divides so neatly between tightly wrought Imagist poems about the urban landscape and longer meditations on Jewish history. The sheer range of Reznikoff's canon is impressive: some fifteen books of poetry, a handful of plays, several novels, translations, editions, anthologies, Charles Reznikoff was the complete Jewish man of Jewish letters.

Charles Reznikoff was born in Brooklyn, New York, on 31 August 1894, the son of Nathan Reznikoff, a businessman, and Sarah Yetta Wolvosky Reznikoff. He attended Boys' High School in Brooklyn, graduating in 1909. He spent the following year at the University of Missouri and completed his study for an LL.B. at New York University in 1915. Reznikoff was admitted to the Bar of the State of New York in 1916, although he never seriously practiced law. Instead, he worked in Hollywood as a writer, put in time in the family business (manufacturing hats), contributed to encyclopedias, and did stints as a legal writer. During these years—and indeed for long stretches of his life—Reznikoff tried his hand at marginally profitable employments so that he could give his major effort to writing poetry. That he labored in obscurity is something of an understatement. That he lived long enough to receive a full measure of the kudos he deserves is also true. But the neglect that becomes both the lot and the mythos of the Modernist poet mattered less to him than his poems. And it is his poems—rather than the bare facts of his life—that have endured.

Reading Reznikoff's work from the earliest poems in *Rhythms* (privately printed in 1918) to the final ones in *Poems 1937-1975: Volume II of the Complete Poems* (1977) is to notice the influences that mattered and the developments he made and, at the same time, to be struck, again and again, by the concerns that abided throughout his extraordinarily long creative life. Here is a section from *Rhythms* that Reznikoff himself set into print when he was twenty-four:

> On Brooklyn Bridge I saw a man drop dead.
> It meant no more than if he were a sparrow.
> Above us rose Manhattan;
> Below, the river spread to meet sea
>   and sky. . . .
> The shopgirls leave their work
> quietly.
> Machines are still, tables and chairs
> darken.
> The silent rounds of mice and roaches
>   begin . . .
> I walked through the lonely march
> Among the white birches.
> Above the birches rose
> Three crows,
> Croaking, croaking.
> The trumpets blare war
> And the streets are filled with echoes.

The title of Alfred Kazin's memoir of growing up in Brooklyn—*A Walker in the City*—comes to mind as a phrase that could be aptly applied as well to Charles Reznikoff. Indeed, Reznikoff was fabled as a "walker," as one who knew the streets of New York with an intimacy few could match. And as with Kazin, there was a part of Reznikoff that yearned for a "world more attractive," a part of himself that was never quite at home in the city he spent most of his life trying to understand.

Reznikoff was, above all, a poet, and there are no snug harbors for such an ambition. And too, Reznikoff found his "career" as a lawyer interrupted by World War I and then by work as a drummer for his parents. It was Reznikoff's task to sell their hats to jobbers and large department stores. In the late 1920s he worked on *Corpus Juris*, an encyclopedia of law; in the 1930s he worked at Paramount Pictures in Hollywood. Much of this biographical data is given a fictional form in *The Manner "Music"* (1977), a novel which splits Reznikoff's psyche into an unnamed narrator who is a salesman and Jude Dalsimer, a composer who sacrifices everything on the altar of experimentation only to end in abject poverty and loneliness, burning his manuscripts and embracing madness. Reznikoff's salesman-narrator is, no doubt, a corrective to the mounting doubts he must have had about "Objectivist" poetry. At one level the novel offered Reznikoff a chance to see his own situation writ large, but from an altered perspective. As the narrator puts it after Dalsimer's untimely death: "Jude had undoubtedly gotten nowhere with his music, unless the insane asylum or the grave is a place to get to. I read Wordsworth's poem 'The Leechgatherer' after Jude had praised it and the words 'we poets whose lives begin in gladness whereof in the end comes to misery and madness' stuck in my mind. The quotation may not be accurate but it's near enough. . . . If Jude had wanted to write his music and had not done his best to do so, he might have lived longer and more pleasantly but, as he might have explained, it is as if one enlists in the army or perhaps is drafted: he must fight and may fall but may not desert."

Reznikoff, of course, survived not only the Depression of the 1930s but also the anxious decades which followed—earning his living as a free-lance writer, translator, and editor, whatever private depressions may have haunted him. In his Introduction to *The Manner "Music,"* Robert Creeley rehearses the oft told story that Reznikoff's novel was written in response to a late 1940s letter by William Carlos Williams urging him to keep writing at any cost, and to try his hand at a novel. Creeley elaborates the situation this way: "Stories are changed in the telling, of course, so this one is not a simple rehearsal of a part of a man's life. There are, in fact, many stories here, 'the manner, *music*,' an interweaving of a complex of 'things' happening, being recalled and told." Nonetheless, there must have been times when Reznikoff wondered, like Jude Dalsimer, if the commitment to poetry was worth it. But Reznikoff's story has a happier ending than does that of his character in *The Manner "Music."* When New Directions published *By the Waters of Manhattan: Selected Verse* in 1962, Reznikoff's poetry attracted the attention it so richly deserved. Then came, in something like rapid order, the Jewish Book Council of America Award for poetry in 1963 and, in 1971, the Morton Dauwen Zabel Award for Poetry by the National Institute of Arts and Letters.

On 27 May 1930, Reznikoff married Marie Syrkin, a woman who shared his deep concern about Jewishness and supported his commitment to poetry. Later she became a distinguished professor at Brandeis University. Meanwhile, Reznikoff's *Jerusalem the Golden* was published by the Objectivist Press in 1934 after sixteen years of self-publishing. Whatever the noble history of self-publishing may be (Whitman was only one in a long string of American "advertisers for themselves" that stretches both before and after him), poets yearn for more stable arrangements. The Objectivist Press consisted of Louis Zukofsky, George Oppen, and Reznikoff. It grew out of the "Objectivist" issue of *Poetry* magazine (February 1931) and Zukofsky's *An "Objectivists" Anthology* which had been published in France in 1932. As an offshoot of Ezra Pound's famous directives about Imagism —"The image is itself the speech"; "Go in fear of abstractions"; "The natural object is always the adequate symbol"— "Objectivism" (which always retained the quotation marks surrounding its name) was less a school than a temperament, less a defined program than a mode of seeing. For Reznikoff, the *seeing* was centrally important; the theatrics of reforming the literary world—so dear to Pound's heart—were not.

Nonetheless, Zukofsky, Oppen, and Reznikoff formed a cooperative to publish "their own work and that of other writers whose work they think ought to be read." Writers do this all the time—out of necessity or community or a sense of shared mission—but it is hard to think of another group that managed to weather nearly fifty years of labor in a common enterprise. No doubt their very looseness about definition was a saving grace; even the Jewishness of the members may have had something to do with it. In any event, Reznikoff provided this cryptic description of his understanding of "Objectivist" verse in 1970: " 'Objectivist,' images clear but the meaning not stated but suggested by the objective details and the music of the verse; words pithy and plain; without the artifice of regular meters; themes, chiefly Jewish, American, urban." The others, of course, may not have agreed, but one thing is clear—in describing "Objectivist" verse, Reznikoff was describing—and defending—his own poetry.

In Reznikoff's own words: "With respect to the treatment of subject matter in verse and the use of the term 'objectivist' and 'objectivism,' let me . . . refer to the rules with respect to testimony in a court of law. Evidence to be admissible in a trial cannot state conclusions of fact: it must state the facts themselves. . . . The conclusions of fact are for the jury and let us add, in our case, for the reader."

Reznikoff's *In Memoriam: 1933* (published by the Objectivist Press the following year) is replete with the historical consciousness we associate with Jewish poetry. There are dramatic monologues set in Samaria of 722 B.C.E., in Spain of 1492, in Poland of 1700, and in Russia of 1905.

Reznikoff's poetic genius captured the essentials of Jewish experience in its broad, historical sweep as well as in its gritty American particulars. For him, Jewishness meant both. He could describe clouds as "piled in rows like merchandise" or the last moments of his mother's illness:

> In her last sickness, my mother took
> my hand in
> hers tightly: for the first time I knew
> how calloused a hand it was, and how soft
> was mine.

During the 1960s—and particularly in the poems of *By the Well of Living and Seeing*, which was published in one volume with *The Fifth Book of the Maccabees* in 1969—Reznikoff's work increasingly reflected the changes that occur as immigrant groups replace one another. At the same time, however, Reznikoff also understood the high costs of

Jewish assimilation in an America that sometimes cajoled, sometimes shoved its newer arrivals into the melting pot. As in these lines from "By the Well of Living and Seeing," he could be especially sharp to those Jews who placed a five-foot shelf of the Harvard classics between themselves and Jewishness:

> You understand the myths of the Aztecs
> and read with sympathy
> the legends of the Christian saints
> and say proudly:
> though you were born a Jew
> there is nothing Jewish about you.
> But the ancient Greeks would still have
> thought you a barbarian
> and even the Christian saints might not have
> liked you;
> and the Nazis
> would have pried from your witty mouth
> your golden teeth.

Poems 1937-1975: Volume II of the Complete Poems includes a section entitled "Last Poems" that includes some previously unpublished pieces. They are extraordinary, especially when one remembers that Reznikoff was eighty-one years old when he died, and by every indicator, a vigorous, imaginatively productive eighty-one. He was working on volume two of his *Complete Poems* (volume one was in press at his death) and, of course, he continued work on new poems. "Walking in New York" is an example not only of the power that still remained in "Last Poems" but also of Reznikoff's lifelong affection for the city and for an "Objectivist" way of rendering it. The humanity and passionate social concern of Reznikoff's verse never lost touch with the poor, the unnoticed, the downtrodden. Reznikoff could not *not* see the world around him and remain silent. In that sense he was an *activist*, but as the word modified *poet* rather than as a noun unto itself. Reznikoff once explained that he chose not to practice law because "I wanted to use whatever mental energy I had for my writing." The same priority no doubt applied to politics as it is usually conceived.

George Oppen's poem "In Memoriam: Charles Reznikoff" puts these matters of commitment and congenial material, of sacrifice and talent, "objectivistically":

Front cover for the volume that was in press when Reznikoff died

> . . . this is
> heroic this is
> the poem
> to write
> in the great
> world small.

Reznikoff did write "small" in "the great world" because he was a truly great poet. Future generations of readers will count themselves fortunate that his work has been collected into attractive, scholarly, and accessible editions. There is much to learn from both his life and his art.

References:

Michael Heller, "Charles Reznikoff," *New York Times Book Review*, 16 May 1976, p. 47;

David Lehman, "Holocaust," *Poetry* (April 1976): 37-39;

Sanford Pinsker, "On Charles Reznikoff," *Jewish Spectator*, 43 (Spring 1978): 57-60;

John R. Reed, "A Review of *Poems 1918-1936: Volume I of the Complete Poems of Charles Reznikoff*," *Ontario Review*, 6 (Fall-Winter 1976-1977): 85-86.

Norma Rosen
(11 August 1925-   )

Ruth Rosenberg
University of New Orleans

BOOKS: *Joy to Levine!* (New York: Knopf, 1962; London: Joseph, 1962);

Green: A Novella and Eight Short Stories (New York: Harcourt, Brace & World, 1967);

Touching Evil (New York: Harcourt, Brace & World, 1969);

A Family Passover, by Rosen, Anne Rosen, and Jonathan Rosen, photographs by Laurence Salzmann (Philadelphia: Jewish Publication Society of America, 1980);

At the Center (Boston: Houghton Mifflin, 1982).

SELECTED PERIODICAL PUBLICATIONS: "Apples," *Commentary*, 27 (January 1959): 43-53;

"The Open Window," *Mademoiselle*, 48 (April 1959): 169-178;

"What Must I Say to You?," *New Yorker*, 39 (26 October 1963): 48-53;

"Sister Gertrude," *Redbook*, 122 (November 1963): 60-61;

"A Thousand Tears," *Redbook*, 123 (June 1964): 42-43;

"Sheltering A Life," *Redbook*, 125 (October 1965): 88-89;

"Walking Distance," *Commentary*, 52 (November 1971): 63-68;

"Mount Holyoke Forever Will Be," *New York Times Magazine*, 9 April 1972, pp. 37ff.;

"A Forum: Women on Women," *American Scholar*, 41 (Autumn 1972): 599-627;

"Living in Two Cultures," *Response* (Winter 1972-1973): 105-111;

"Making Connections," *Hadassah Magazine*, 54 (June 1973): 12-13;

"Who's Afraid of Erica Jong?," *New York Times Magazine*, 28 July 1974, pp. 8-9;

"The Holocaust and the American-Jewish Novelist," *Midstream*, 20 (October 1974): 54-62;

"Between Guilt and Gratification: Abortion Doctors Reveal Their Feelings," *New York Times Magazine*, 17 April 1977, pp. 70-71;

"What is Hanukkah but the Symbol of Few Against Many?," *New York Times*, 9 December 1982, C2;

"In the 'Empty Nest,' a Newly Created, Lonely, 'Only Child,'" *New York Times*, 23 December 1982, C2.

What Isaac Babel did for Russian Jews, what Franz Rosenzweig did for German Jews; Norma Rosen has, in four critically acclaimed books, attempted to do for American Jews. Her three novels and her collection of short stories record encounters with a heritage that became soul-shaking conversion experiences. Her disaffiliated characters confront the tradition they disavowed and find their perceptions totally altered. These secularized, assimilated characters are brought through complicated plots and ironic turns of events to the point where a sudden glimpse of the ethical ideals of

Norma Rosen (photo by Layle Silbert)

Judaism make the American quest for self-fulfillment unthinkable.

Norma Gangel Rosen was born in Borough Park, Brooklyn. As she put it in a 1982 essay for the *New York Times*, "I grew up an only child but hardly knew it. For years I lived my after-school days and part of my evenings at my grandparents' house. It was full of children—my aunts and uncles. I knew they weren't my brothers and sisters, but I felt as if they were. My mother was the first-born and my grandmother had gone on bearing a long time, so that my youngest aunt was only a few years older than I."

When Rose Miller and Louis Gangel, a businessman, moved to Manhattan, their daughter entered Julia Richman High School and was forced to accept her status of truly being an only child. It was then that she became a writer: "I read read read in my room, kept diaries, wrote stories."

The sympathy all her later stories show with those who were dislocated from their own culture stems partially from her feeling that she had had no

formal Jewish education as a child. Her parents did not want to burden her with the history of anti-Semitism. Neither were they particularly observant, as she explained in her 1972 article "Living in Two Cultures":

> Some years, my father went to reform services on the extra-special, extra-"high" days. But not my mother, who could not stand even this skimpy slice of official Jewish life. I think now that she was an early women's liberationist, at least in Jewish matters. Even then I know that she bitterly resented the treatment of women in her mother's orthodox synagogue—on the one hand, the denial of women's spiritual life, on the other, the physical wearing down of women under the burdens of Jewish home-making.
>
> No religion, no philosophy, no language, no literature, no custom. My parents were giving me all this....

Their intentions were, she continues, to free her from the indignities their parents had endured, to allow her to grow up as an American. However, from the Borough Park neighborhood itself, which is the setting of many of her short stories, she had "inherited, literarily speaking, a trust fund. Without even trying, one had certain speech rhythms in one's head—colloquialisms that were inherently funny, relationships always good for a cutting down by wit, and a large, energy-radiating store of culture-abrasions," she wrote in "The Holocaust and the American-Jewish Novelist," a 1974 piece published in *Midstream*.

She had also been "lucky enough to grow up with the sound of my grandparents' Yiddish in my ears for the first twelve years of my life." The Yiddish idioms and the exuberant comedy of Rosen's first novel derive from those memories.

Rosen attended Mount Holyoke College, where she studied modern dance with José Limon and Martha Graham and did choreography for the New Dance Group. Three decades later her tribute to her alma mater, "Mount Holyoke Forever Will Be," was published in the *New York Times Magazine*. She graduated cum laude and a member of Phi Beta Kappa in 1946. For the next three years, she taught English and dance at a private girls' academy, the Riverdale School, and had several interviews, reviews of recitals, and articles published in *Dance Magazine*.

Rosen did her graduate work at Columbia University, which in 1953 awarded her a master's degree for a thesis on the novels of Graham Greene. What interested her was his use of dogma, as she explained in her 1974 article in *Midstream*: "When Graham Greene in *The Heart of the Matter* has Scobie, a Catholic, commit adultery and then suicide, the special dimension of pain comes from the acknowledgement that it is, precisely, a Catholic who commits these acts." Since she, herself, had been raised without a theology, it was particularly the sense of sin which comes from having transgressed a rigorous code that most interested her.

Rosen began studying book designing at New York University. From 1954 to 1959 she worked at Harper and Row. Like the protagonists of her first two novels, she did copy editing, studied typography, and prepared manuscripts for the printer. This profession gave her a whole new set of terms that served her well in her first novel *Joy to Levine!* (1962), which she began writing in the evenings and on weekends. In it Arnold Levine works for a declining firm that publishes business-school texts: he "took pleasure in specifying, with a flourish: 'Printer: 10 on 12 Boldoni Bold X 16 picas. One-em rule all around.'"

When Rosen found her first novel taking form, she quit her job to devote herself full-time to composing it. In the summer of 1959 she worked on it at the MacDowell Colony, and she received a Eugene F. Saxton Grant in 1960 to finish the book.

On 23 August 1960, she married Robert S. Rosen, a professor in the department of modern languages at Baruch College. Their daughter, Anne Beth, was born 5 August 1961, and their son, Jonathan Aaron, was born 25 February 1963. Rosen's husband had had an extensive Jewish education in Vienna, which inspired her to begin studying Jewish philosophy and history. When the family moved to Brookline, Massachusetts—a move described in the story "Walking Distance" published in *Commentary* in 1971—she attended weekly *shiurim*, or study groups, held by Rabbi Joseph Soloveitchik.

The sophisticated techniques with which Rosen has reworked the theme of rediscovering the ethical concepts embodied in Jewish thought were further developed by her own teaching and her continual participation in writers' workshops. She perfected her craft at the New School for Social Research, at the Bread Loaf Writers Conference, and at the University of Colorado. From 1966 to 1969, she taught creative writing at the New School, where she became known as an inspiring teacher. In 1970, she was appointed visiting professor of creative writing at the University of Pennsylvania. From 1971 to 1973, she was a fellow in creative writing at

the Radcliffe Institute. From 1975 to 1976, she taught at Herbert H. Lehman College. She was awarded a New York State Creative Artists Public Service Grant in 1975. Since 1977, she has been teaching at the College of New Rochelle.

The publication of her first book in 1962 was greeted with critical accolades. The reviewer for the *London Times Literary Supplement* wrote: "Joy, indeed to Levine, and joy to the reader of this dry, wry, tender, and blessedly funny book." Whitney Balliett, in the *New Yorker*, said: "Mrs. Rosen has two priceless gifts: she can write, and she knows how to laugh in the face of life. *Joy to Levine!* is an auspicious beginning." Paul Pickrel, in *Harper's*, described the novel as "a marvelously gentle book, beautifully poised between pathos and comedy . . . an altogether winning piece of work."

What is most refreshing about this first novel is that it is an anti-Bildungsroman. Its protagonist is an inept, accident-prone young man working for a moribund firm whose declining business exactly suits his own propensity for failure. At the office Arnold meets, and tentatively woos, an overweight stenographer, who, he assumes, is not Jewish. The shy courtship is conducted in the library, where Arnold lets Theresa teach him the Rutborough method of shorthand. All of his needless agonizing about the problems of intermarriage is dispelled when he meets his future father-in-law. Mr. Bialo's Italian-sounding name is the creation of an immigration authority. His views on life are compatible with Arnold's modesty. He says: "If a person makes a living, if he has what to eat, and his family has what to eat—enough! Nobody should want it too good." With this congenial family, Arnold finally feels at home, having made good his escape from his own pushy father who was continually pressuring him to succeed, to accomplish, to be more aggressive.

Acclaimed both for its wit and for its compassion, the book proved to be a popular as well as a critical success and was published in paperback by Curtis. What seemed so new in competitive America was actually an ancient genre. The author had refurbished the Yiddish wisdom tale which preferred goodness to material prosperity and morality to physical beauty.

Rosen's *Green: A Novella and Eight Short Stories* was published in 1967. James Frakes, in the *New York Times*, thought the three stories about young mothers and Jamaican nurses were "quiet tales" of "almost perfect form." He particularly praised "What Must I Say to You?": "To watch the nurse's plaintive Christianity meshing with and eventually transcending the combat over Judaism between husband and wife is an experience to which no reader can fairly deny the epithet 'beautiful.' " This moving story was included in Julia Wolf Mazow's *The Woman Who Lost Her Names: Selected Writings by American Jewish Women* (1980). Its autobiographical basis was confirmed by Rosen's 1982 *New York Times* essay, "What is Hanukkah but the Symbol of Few Against Many?," in which she mentions the "devout woman" who "helped care for our children" who asked, on every Christian holiday, what greeting she could properly give in return: "What must I say to you?"

The exuberantly comic story from *Green* "The Open Window" was televised by the Canadian Broadcasting System. It was also reprinted as one of the *40 Best Stories From Mademoiselle*, and the title novella "Green" was described by the *Times* reviewer as a "study of the corrosion of 'green' ideals by human demands" in which "no scene is arbitrary, no insight redundant." He found it "right in terms of narrative movement, modulation of tone, and character revelation."

Like *Joy to Levine!* Rosen's second novel, *Touching Evil*, published in 1969, has a protagonist who is a book designer. The novel is about two women who watch the televised Eichmann trial together daily and find their lives totally changed by that shared experience. They are so profoundly affected by the horrors of Belsen and Auschwitz that they can no longer think of leading normal lives. After the evils of Buchenwald have been admitted into one's consciousness, nothing can, ever again, be what it was before.

Judy Rousuck in the *Cleveland Press* called *Touching Evil* "a modern classic," a book "infused with the mystical, the terrible, and the evil from which it takes its title." Ruth Bauerle in the *Cleveland Plain Dealer* applauded the novel's complexity of form, the merging of points of view through diaries, letters, commentary, and manuscripts so as to convey "a universalized terror." She also noted that: "The subject is Dostoevskian: what do sensitive people do when their hard (but ordinary) task of trying to be genuine, loving human beings is broken in upon by a great evil?" Rosen's important article "The Holocaust and the American-Jewish Novelist" describes her conception of this novel and of its critical reception.

Rosen's most recent novel, *At the Center*, was published in 1982. It has as its protagonist Hannah Selig, a character involved in the "special dimension of pain" that had fascinated Rosen in the works of Graham Greene. Hannah's observant parents had escaped from the death camps only to be murdered

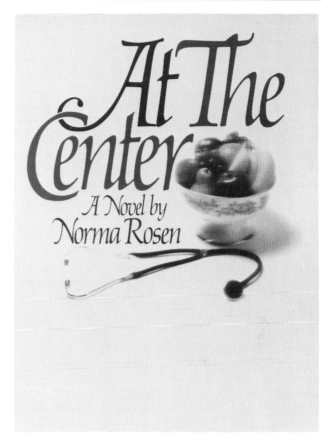

Dust jacket for Rosen's 1982 novel about Hannah Selig, who rediscovers her commitment to Hasidism through her work at an abortion clinic

in their Williamsburg kitchen. Hannah at first assumes that she is being terribly punished for her refusal to marry, for her wish to study at a university, for her desire to leave the community. She begins a "war with God" by transgressing every prohibition. Every intricate rabbinical elaboration of a law affords her more opportunities for violating ordinances. It is after she has tested all the strictures that she arrives at a cabalistic insight. Summed up in the Hebrew phrase *lo samnu* is the vision of her parents' congregation that the work of creation is unfinished. Human beings must assume the obligation of completing that work, of uplifting the divine sparks, of redeeming the earth from evil. By participating in the suffering of others at The Center, an abortion clinic founded by the idealistic Dr. Bianky as a memorial to his sister who died from an illegal abortion, Hannah is enabled to return with renewed commitment to the Hasidism she had sought to escape. In the relationship of the two Jewish doctors Charles and Paul, who are Dr. Bianky's partners, intricate ethical problems arise.

These, Hannah Selig attempts to mediate. Her interventions inspire Paul to discover what it truly means to be Jewish. Then she flees, to allow him to become the good and giving man he wishes to be.

Robert Miner wrote in the *New York Times Book Review* that the novel "earns its troubling power from Mrs. Rosen's steady exploration of this human dilemma, which in 1982 seems as critical as ever." He finds her writing to be "startling and elegant, sweeping the dark landscape with beautiful lights . . . with an energizing, passionate wit." He applauds the "moral strength" of the novel for bravely confronting "the hard questions" which still exist about this issue.

Norma Rosen's fiction is so technically accomplished that she can transform the stuff of ordinary lives into art. It is this recognition of the everyday existence that we require from literature in order to confirm ourselves. Rosen's narratives tell of integrity, kindness, but entangle them with ambivalences, ensnarl them in ironies, as good impulses are complicated in actuality. The characters remain, ultimately, mysteries to themselves, yet moved, in spite of everything, to do the humanly

decent thing. Although stubbornly resisting, they are impelled toward a vision of what might be, of what man could become. Deprived of the heritage they needed, a glimpse, no more, is offered them. The touch of that tradition becomes a conversion experience.

The return of Paul, the Jewish doctor in *At the Center*, to a Jewish vision is paradigmatic for Rosen's protagonists. Paul had so longed for a meaningful background that he bought himself an heirloom watch at a pawnshop to symbolize an inheritance. After he studied the notebooks Hannah left behind her when she fled, he began to perceive the traditions which were his to claim.

This was the way, as Rosen writes in "The Holocaust and the American-Jewish Novelist," "that the encounter with devout Polish Jews acted upon the Russian writer Isaac Babel, who wished to be assimilated into the Red Cavalry, the Cossacks; and upon the young German intellectual, Franz Rosenzweig, who saw them praying on Yom Kippur, just before he was to effect his conversion to Christianity. Both men, through these encounters, became Jews."

Isaac Rosenfeld
(10 March 1918-15 July 1956)

Bonnie Lyons
University of Texas at San Antonio

BOOKS: *Passage from Home* (New York: Dial, 1946);
An Age of Enormity: Life and Writing in the Forties and Fifties, edited by Theodore Solotaroff (Cleveland: World, 1962);
Alpha and Omega (New York: Viking, 1966; London: MacGibbon & Kee, 1967).

An extraordinary, gifted, vital man, Isaac Rosenfeld has been warmly remembered and vividly characterized in the memoirs of his friends, including Saul Bellow and Alfred Kazin. The memory of the man is, unfortunately, stronger than the impact of his work. Rosenfeld's literary legacy is small: one novel published in his lifetime, one collection of short stories, and one volume of reviews and essays, the latter two posthumously by friends and admirers. Although his fiction is uneven in quality, several stories, including one of his earliest

("The Hand That Fed Me") and his latest ("King Solomon"), are of lasting quality. And despite the limitation of scope and length of many of his reviews, Rosenfeld's nonfiction is noteworthy for his humanist stance vis à vis literature, the brilliance of his analysis, and the compactness and directness of his style.

Isaac Rosenfeld was the only child of a lower-middle-class Jewish family in Chicago. The central event of his childhood was the death of his mother when he was twenty-two months old. Following his father's remarriage and the birth of a half sister in 1929, he became more or less estranged from the home atmosphere, and a gap between him and his father and stepmother developed. Both the early loss of his mother and the subsequent increasing alienation from his father and stepmother resonate throughout Rosenfeld's life and fiction,

Isaac Rosenfeld

especially *Passage from Home* (1946).

Yiddish was Rosenfeld's first language, and he attended Sholom Aleichem schools (Yiddish language afternoon schools) for several years. A superbly accomplished Yiddishist, Rosenfeld in his mature years translated Sholom Aleichem stories, wrote fables and stories in Yiddish (his Yiddish prose style has been praised as almost as fine as Isaac Bashevis Singer's), and is remembered by friends for a hilarious Yiddish translation of "The Love Song of J. Alfred Prufrock." Rosenfeld was also one of the earliest writers to enrich his English with translated Yiddish idioms. Throughout his career Yiddish and *Yiddishkeit*, the culture of Yiddish-speaking Eastern European Jews, were major interests.

In a brilliant essay "Sholom Aleichem," Rosenfeld discusses the intimate connections between language and culture, between Yiddish and *Yiddishkeit*. The fact that Yiddish "was never allowed to develop an affinity for the natural world" and was "poor in subject names" correlates with Yiddish culture's refusal to accept exile, to cease longing for Jerusalem, the true home. Likewise, the liberal sprinkling into Yiddish of Hebrew, "the language

historically of the true home and faithful tradition, lends poignancy to the half-tones of exile, and an incongruity that mirrors in its humor the whole incongruity of Jewish dispersal."

As a boy he was somewhat sickly and a "butterball," according to his friends. He was also precociously brilliant in a particularly verbal way. In a fictionalized memoir, "The World of the Ceiling," he reminisced: "I was a serious young man, interested only in philosophy and politics, with a way of wrinkling my face in thought which I had copied from a portrait of Hegel. . . . I had no girl friends, no frivolities; I had a *Weltanschauung*." In a memoir written shortly after Rosenfeld's death, Saul Bellow, a close friend from childhood years, reminisced about Rosenfeld holding forth on Schopenhauer with perfect authority and seriousness—as a thirteen-year-old wearing short pants. The ferocious intellectuality was matched by traits characteristic of many first- and second-generation Jews in America: what Irving Howe has called a "heritage of discomfort before the uses and pleasures of the body" and a lack of at-homeness in nature. Rejecting the usual American ideals summed up in the word *baseball*, this culture looked instead to European and Jewish ideals of intellect, sensibility, and political awareness. As a teenager, Rosenfeld was active in the Trotskyist Spartacus Youth League and the Young People's Socialist League during its Trotskyist phase, when it was known as "YPSL Fourth" after the Fourth International.

Highly ambivalent about his own body, Rosenfeld, like one of his cultural heroes, Kafka, occasionally seemed to think that intellectuality precluded good health. This disdain for good health was more than a personal quirk; according to Bellow, Rosenfeld's poor yellowish color during their college years was the "preferred intellectual complexion." On the other hand, the search for physical well-being and healthy physicality is a major theme in Rosenfeld's fiction and became a dominant drive in his life during the 1940s.

Attending the University of Chicago after graduating from Tuley High School, Rosenfeld was a prize pupil of Eliseo Vivas and Rudolph Carnap and was interested in both symbolic logic and Dewey's pragmatism and naturalism. In those years the University of Chicago offered a heady intellectual and political experience. Rosenfeld characterized those years in "Life in Chicago": "Politics was everywhere, in a measure, one ate it and drank it; and sleep gave no escape, for it furnished terror to our dreams: Hitler, Mussolini, the Moscow Trials, the Spanish Civil War, . . . Stalinism, the short gaps of NRA, WPA and the New Deal, and the approach of inevitable war."

During his college years, Rosenfeld left home and lived in a series of boardinghouse rooms. Associating the neat, clean atmosphere of his father's home with pinched, repressive petit-bourgeois values like correctness, propriety, and soul-destroying habit, Rosenfeld began his lifelong pattern of living in various kinds of disorder. What started as a gesture of bohemian freedom in these early years gradually deepened into a paradoxically rigid commitment, an enforced asceticism of physical squalor.

Besides pursuing his interests in philosophy and politics during his college years, he also wrote fiction and poetry. In 1937 he received the John Billings Fisk Prize for a group of five related lyrical poems. The derivative tone (full of echoes of *The Waste Land*) and a forced quality mark these poems as juvenilia; however, two subjects that haunt Rosenfeld's work first appear: his interest in Jews and Judaism ("the stories of my race") and the possibility or impossibility of love and community ("the thought of the shared life").

After graduating with an M.A. in 1941, Rosenfeld married Vasiliki Sarantakis, a fellow University of Chicago student, and moved to New York City to work on a Ph.D. in logic at NYU. During his first year in New York, while suffering from one of his perennial bouts of pleurisy, he reread *Moby-Dick* and suddenly "no longer believed in logical positivism." He gave up his studies in logic and began to write. This dramatic conversion from the Theory of Signs is an example of one of Rosenfeld's lifelong patterns. Forever looking for "the Way," the truest life pattern, he was immensely affected by a series of figures whom he considered great, among them Tolstoy and Gandhi. In each man and in each literary work central to his imagination, he sought a unifying intellectual world view. Like an alchemist seeking the philosopher's stone, he searched for a model, or an all-embracing synthesis, with unremitting, feverish dedication.

Despite his often wildly fluctuating enthusiasms, Rosenfeld throughout his career remained interested in Jews, Judaism, and Jewish life in both America and Europe. The most positive scene in his fiction occurs in the novel *Passage from Home* when the protagonist Bernard accompanies his grandfather to the house of a Hasidic rebbe and experiences a transcendent moment of joy in sharing the wisdom and ecstatic dancing of Reb Feldman and his followers. In a seminal review of Abraham Cahan's *The Rise of David Levinsky*, Rosen-

feld sees Levinsky as Diaspora Man, the "essential type of the Jewish Dispersion," wed to dissatisfaction, bound to "endless yearning after yearning." Rosenfeld notes that despite the seeming disparities, Jewish and American culture and character share a "similar play on striving and fulfillment," and this congruity made for Jews' "virtually flawless Americanization."

Despite his basic love of things Jewish and the ghetto sensibility in particular, some of his essays on Jewish culture were controversial and met with alarmed or negative response. In particular, an essay analyzing Jewish dietary laws announces that the kosher laws could easily become "an insidious ruin of life" because of the disguised antisexual meaning: the food taboos, according to Rosenfeld, symbolize "forbidden exogamy" and worse, the separation of milk and meat mean the separation of male and female. Thus the dietary laws are a covert prohibition against sexual intercourse. Rosenfeld's response to the Holocaust was personal and profound. For him the destruction of six million Jews was a radical break in history and undermined and nullified all previous conceptions of man or morality. For him the necessary new categories were "terror beyond evil and joy beyond good."

Between 1941 and 1945, Rosenfeld became a regular contributor of poetry, fiction, and criticism to the *New Republic* and joined the staff as an editor for a brief period. By the end of the war he was also a regular contributor to *Partisan Review, Commentary,* the *New Leader*, and the *Nation*. The early years in New York were ebullient with excitement and literary triumph. He achieved early success in fiction with his "The Hand that Fed Me," which appeared in *Partisan Review*'s winter 1944 issue. Like Bellow's *Dangling Man*, which was published the same year, this is the story of an American underground man, a clearly Dostoevskian character. The next year Rosenfeld won *Partisan Review*'s Novelette Award for "The Colony," a chapter from a novel set in India that he never completed.

The 1940s were Rosenfeld's most productive decade, and few careers seemed more promising in the early years. Most of his stories, reviews, and essays were written during these years, and his only novel, *Passage from Home*, a tale of a sensitive adolescent boy's search for meaning and love, appeared in 1946. In this loosely autobiographical Bildungsroman, the fifteen-year-old Bernard, "as sensitive as a burn," feels alienated from his bourgeois father and stepmother and leaves home to live with his aunt and a Gentile drifter. Instead of finding freedom and a more expansive and vital life, he finds emotional dishonesty and confusion. When he returns home, he and his father evade facing the crucial questions about themselves, and Bernard concludes despairingly, "I might as well never have left, or never come back." Neither the middle-class family nor the shabby bohemian life offers him the values he seeks, and because of the inconclusiveness of both his search and homecoming, "Now there would only be life as it came and the excuses one made to himself for accepting it."

The theme of alienation dominates Rosenfeld's fiction. In the best stories, such as "Alpha and Omega," the ideas are seamlessly embedded in the fictional elements; the characters and plot support the themes. In the less successful fiction, however, the themes are inadequately dramatized, and the characters seem mere vehicles to announce the themes. Despite his deep desire to be a major novelist, Rosenfeld's gifts as a critic were the shortcomings of his fiction; the same talent for explanation and analysis that gives strength to his essays makes his weaker stories lifeless and discursive.

Rosenfeld's focus on character was central to his life, his fiction, and his criticism. In his journals one finds parallel messages to himself as man and writer. To the writer he insisted that he was eager to write about himself, his family, his friends, about "people, flesh and blood, reality," and that he had had "enough psychological abstractness." To himself as a man he declared: "I want to find myself, Me! Not a reaction formation, an oral sadistic neurosis, a fixation, but myself!" Unfortunately, unlike his friend Bellow, Rosenfeld was unable to combine his gifts for analysis and philosophy with fiction; his mind was not long detained by surface phenomena. The "thinginess" of the world eluded him, and by natural bent and under the influence of Kafka, he often wrote bloodless allegories which proclaimed rather than developed his themes.

Although *An Age of Enormity* (1962) does not contain all of Rosenfeld's essays or reviews, it clearly indicates his strengths and limitations as a critic. Rosenfeld wrote for the generally educated, not the specialist. Believing in the human uses of literature, he rejected the idea of literature as a specialist's subject, judged writers by their feeling for and knowledge of life, and wrote criticism marked by

Dust jacket for Rosenfeld's posthumously published collection of essays and reviews

lucidity and directness. In the 1980s, when the most influential critics insist that literature means anything or nothing and that criticism is an art form not in any way subsidiary to literature, Rosenfeld's criticism seems modest, straightforward, and refreshingly sane. Surprisingly, given his theoretical bent, there is no overall system, no abstruse jargon. Rather, he takes the position of an intelligent individual equipped with no tool other than human intellect and emotion.

Many of his book reviews are ephemeral, because the books themselves lacked weight, causing an ironic disparity between his subtle perception and the object of his analysis. Besides the ephemeral nature of some of his subjects and the brevity dictated by the journals he wrote for, there are other limitations to his criticism. He addresses himself only to fiction and to fiction only of a realistic or naturalistic approach; nowhere does he grapple with the great modernists. His general strategy is to analyze the fiction writer's handling of character as the dramatic and moral center of the work. The failure of much contemporary English and American fiction, according to Rosenfeld, emerged from the same source: the failure to deal adequately with emotion. In American fiction this was compensated for and demonstrated by cheap hard-boiledness (John O'Hara) or forced apocalyptic fervor (Kenneth Patchen), while English writers (Henry Green) fled timidly from both emotion and sex.

Rosenfeld's early successes as a fiction writer and critic proved deceptive. By the late 1940s he was severely blocked. Believing that his writer's block was symptomatic of deeper, more personal problems, he turned to the theories of Wilhelm Reich as a solution and world view. Reich's combination of Freudian and Marxist insight seemed to offer a vision that adequately explained and linked the internal, especially sexual, forces and social and political structures. Reich fulfilled Rosenfeld's demand for political consciousness, for acknowledgment of the vast social and economic forces impinging on man, without neglecting the deepest personal sexual needs. As a total and messianic world view, Reichianism promised redemption in the power of the unblocked libido.

Although ambivalent and vacillating in his response to Reich's theories, Rosenfeld did build a bargain-basement orgone box in his bedroom and for several years questioned friends about their sexual lives, categorizing people according to Reich's theories of character types.

Unfortunately Reichianism did not unblock Rosenfeld. His second novel, "The Enemy," a Kafkaesque allegory, was rejected by several publishers and never published; the rejection undermined his already diminished confidence. He worked fitfully for several years on "The Empire," a novel based in part on his ideas about Gandhi.

His marriage broke up, and after ten years in the City, he left New York in 1951. Because New York represented the hub of intellectual and artistic life as well as the scene of his youthful aspirations and success, this departure was symbolic. After 1951 his work slackened and few reviews appeared. Rosenfeld taught for two years at the University of Minnesota and then returned to the University of Chicago. He died of a heart attack in a shabby furnished room on Walton Street on Chicago's Near North Side. Bellow and others believe that Rosenfeld finally experienced a psychic breakthrough at the very end of his life; "King Solomon," one of his best stories, was written during the last months. But the overall pattern of the last years is one of depression and withdrawal.

References:

Saul Bellow, Foreword to *An Age of Enormity* (Cleveland: World, 1962);

Alfred Kazin, *New York Jew* (New York: Knopf, 1978), pp. 47-52;

Bonnie Lyons, "Isaac Rosenfeld's Fiction: A Reappraisal," *Studies in American Jewish Literature*, 1 (Spring 1975): 3-9;

Mark Shechner, "From Isaac Rosenfeld's Journals," *Partisan Review*, 47, no. 1 (1980): 9-28;

Shechner, "Isaac Rosenfeld's World," *Partisan Review*, 43, no. 3 (1976): 524-543;

Shechner, "The Journals of Isaac Rosenfeld," *Salmagundi*, 47 (Spring 1980): 30-47;

Shechner, "Yiddish Fables," *Prooftexts*, 2 (1982): 131-145;

Theodore Solotaroff, Introduction to *An Age of Enormity* (Cleveland: World, 1962).

Henry Roth
(8 February 1906?-   )

Bonnie Lyons
University of Texas at San Antonio

BOOKS: *Call It Sleep* (New York: Ballou, 1934; London: Joseph, 1963);
Nature's First Green (New York: Targ Editions, 1979).

PERIODICAL PUBLICATIONS: "Impressions of a Plumber," *Lavender* (May 1925): 5-9;
"If We Had Bacon," *Signatures: Work in Progress*, 1 (1936): 139-158;
"Broker," *New Yorker*, 15 (18 November 1939): 45-48;
"Somebody Always Grabs the Purple," *New Yorker*, 16 (23 March 1940): 37-38;
"Equipment for Pennies," *Magazine for Ducks and Geese* (Fall 1954): 15-16;
"Petey and Yotsee and Mario," *New Yorker*, 32 (14 July 1956): 70-74;
"At Times in Flight: Story," *Commentary*, 28 (July 1959): 51-54;
"The Dun Dakotas: Story," *Commentary*, 30 (August 1960): 107-109;
"The Surveyor," *New Yorker*, 42 (6 August 1966): 22-30;
"Segments," *Studies in American Jewish Literature*, 5 (Spring 1979): 58-62.

Henry Roth

Henry Roth's literary reputation rests entirely and securely upon *Call It Sleep* (1934). The single novel is so emotionally moving and so artistically elegant that it has made Roth an important literary figure, even though he has never completed another novel.

There is considerable interest in Roth's biography both because of the desire to know how such an artful novel could be a writer's first and last and because the novel has biographical links with the author's own youth. Henry Roth was born in Tysmenitsa, near Lemberg, Galicia (then an Austrian Crownland), to Herman and Leah Roth. Eighteen months later his mother brought him to New York. Roth's life is clearly reflected in the opening section of the novel: Roth's father like Albert Schearl had come to America before his wife and child and earned money for their passage to New York. As in the novel, before the mother and child arrived, the parents were emotionally estranged, for Henry Roth's birth date and paternity were in question, as is that of David Schearl, the novel's protagonist.

The parental strife affected all the family relationships: Leah Roth drew her son ever closer to her, while Herman favored their daughter Rose, who was born in America two years after Henry's birth. In addition to the emotional strain of this Oedipal situation, the Roths suffered the more general immigrant problem of adaptation to the New World. For Eastern European Jews like Roth's parents, the move to New York meant a move in time as well as place: they left a secure, if stagnant, pastoral

257

village for the chaos and anonymity of a modern city. Unlike Albert Schearl in the novel, Herman Roth was a diminutive man in physical stature, but in his son's eyes, he exuded the ever-impending rage and barely suppressed violence of the fictional figure. Just as Roth increased his father's physical dimensions in *Call It Sleep* to emphasize the child's fear of his parent's unpredictability and power, he depicted his mother in an artful and not simply biographical way. In the novel, Genya, the mother, is aloof, contemplative, almost regal, while her sister Bertha is talkative, vulgar, and extroverted. Leah Roth possessed both sets of traits and was the source of both fictional characters.

With his immediate family polarized—father and daughter on one side, mother and son on the other—it is not surprising that much of Henry Roth's security derived from the community in which he grew up rather than from his family. The Roths, like the Schearls, settled down in the Brownsville section of Brooklyn at first, but two years later in 1910, Roth's family moved to the Lower East Side of Manhattan.

Despite poverty, overcrowding, and poor sanitary conditions, the Lower East Side was an emotionally satisfying place to live because the residents maintained their internal vitality and aspiration. Moreover, the Lower East Side offered the young Henry Roth a sense of belonging, of community; it provided him the emotional haven and protection he never felt in his home. When his family left the area in 1914, the departure caused him deep anxiety.

Torn from a homogeneous and tightly knit community, the eight-year-old Roth found himself in a much more mixed and threatening environment in Harlem. The abrupt move was also crucial to him because his sense of Jewishness and of Jewish identity was severely shaken. At the time his family left the Lower East Side, Roth had not yet reached the stage of translation in religious school: he could pronounce the Hebrew words but not understand their meaning. Translation might have opened up the deeper religious aspects of Judaism and riveted him to his religion. But Roth felt trapped in an alien, threatening environment and wanted to adapt to this Gentile Irish neighborhood as quickly as possible. One of the conditions for adapting was moving away from Judaism.

The parents' faith had never been deeply felt. Partly in reaction to the fanatical orthodoxy of her own father, Leah Roth was somewhat ironic in her faith. Herman Roth observed some of the prominent Jewish holidays but was not devout. Nominally observant, Roth's parents did not reinforce religion at home enough to help their son withstand the anti-Jewish external pressures he felt impinging on him from outside.

The move from the Lower East Side to Harlem, with its dual loss of sense of community and Jewish identification, apparently caused serious changes in Roth's personality and development: he became a poor student, grew fat, and withdrew into himself. One source of pleasure for him during these tense Harlem years was reading, particularly fairy tales. The influence of fairy tales on Roth's work is apparent in two ways. First the gripping narrative line of the fairy tale is apparent in the narrative strength of *Call It Sleep*. Second, fairy tales often embody archetypal patterns of initiation, as does the novel, particularly in the climactic chapter.

After graduating from DeWitt Clinton High School in Manhattan in 1924, Roth enrolled in City College of New York. His goal at the time was to become a biology teacher or zoologist. Two events occurred during his freshman year which were to deflect him from his original aim and to shape his entire future: his first publication appeared and he met Eda Lou Walton.

Told by his freshman English teacher to write an expository essay on an experiment or construction, Roth chose to write a piece about how to install plumbing pipes. Although the assignment was to write an expository theme, Roth's essay turned into an impressionistic piece. Roth's teacher was so impressed by the essay that he recommended that it be published in the *Lavender*, City College's student magazine. "Impressions of a Plumber" is hardly a major piece, but it shows the writer's budding interest in character and reveals several of Roth's lifelong interests and special touches: a firm sense of structure, a clever use of dialogue, and a good ear for dialect and speech patterns.

Roth's freshman year brought him into contact with Eda Lou Walton, a New York University professor and poet. This contact proved crucial to both his personal life and his literary career. Roth met Walton through a high-school friend who was then attending NYU and had Walton for a freshman English instructor. Walton formed a club for aspiring writers to which she invited contemporary poets to read their work; Roth met her at one of these meetings. Interested in and knowledgeable about the contemporary modernist literary scene, Walton encouraged aspiring young writers.

When Roth began living with Walton in 1928, he was already emotionally estranged from his family. The fact that he was living with a non-Jewish woman twelve years his senior perhaps deepened but did not cause any breach with his family. Roth had already dissociated himself from family and Judaism. While Roth and Walton moved in an active intellectual circle which included the anthropologist Ruth Benedict and poet Hart Crane, Roth felt basically isolated as a man and as an artist. The world of his childhood and that of his present life were too disparate and unconnected for him to feel at ease in his present milieu.

In the summer of 1930 Walton was invited to Peterborough, New Hampshire, the art colony; Roth accompanied her and stayed at a nearby inn where he began to write *Call It Sleep*. The only real writing he had done before the novel was "Impressions of a Plumber," and the leap from that slight, boyish essay to the full-blown achievement of *Call It Sleep* is one of the most extraordinary facts of Roth's literary career.

As with "Impressions of a Plumber," Roth began writing the novel in the first person as a straight autobiography and slavishly kept to the facts for about seventy-five pages. But just as the more literary and impressionistic aspects of the essay emerged despite the assignment, here the impulse toward fiction and significant form became insistent. His fabricating side eventually conquered his original autobiographical impulses, and he spent the next two weeks outlining furiously. Writing in pencil in little blue examination booklets which were readily available in Walton's apartment, he not only outlined the events of the novel but also consciously decided to focus the novel more sharply by transforming real-life figures into literary characters: that is when he split his mother into Genya and Bertha and increased his father's magnitude. The fact that the ending of the novel with its deep sense of artistic inevitability was not part of the original plan shows how far Roth moved from what promised to be a loose chronicle to an unusually well-constructed novel.

Although the first major steps were rapid, the novel developed slowly over the next three and a half years. Roth learned how to write a novel by writing one. As he became more self-conscious as an artist, more aware of formal problems, he continued to revise and rearrange his material. Financially and emotionally supported by Walton, he spent these years working in a strikingly hermitic way—showing his work to no one. Part of the time he worked in her apartment, part of the time he worked in a studio for which she paid, and he spent one memorable and productive period in Norridgewock, Maine, in 1932. By late 1933 he had his first presentable draft; in early 1934, he sent *Call It Sleep* to several publishers, including Harcourt, Brace, which turned it down on the grounds that the material would not have much market in Depression-locked America.

Call It Sleep is a profound psychological study of David Schearl, who is at once a sensitive child and a mystic in search of divine illumination. Redemption, the underlying theme of the novel, is developed through an intricate pattern of symbols. Although the novel is superficially constructed in an episodic manner, certain symbols, specifically cellar, picture, coal, and rail, provide a firm unifying structure, as well as the names of the four books of

Dust jacket for Roth's only novel, an autobiographical work based on memories and impressions of his childhood

the novel. In the first book, David associates the cellar with filth, bodily corruption, shameful sexuality, guilt, and death. The picture represents the past, including Genya's previous sexual relationship with a non-Jew in Poland and Albert's highly charged relationship with his own father. While the symbol of the cellar involves uniformly negative connotations and the picture's meanings are ambiguous, the symbol of the coal combines conflicting or opposing meanings. Because it is black and dirty, coal has inevitable connections with uncleanliness for David. He confuses this ordinary coal with the coal or burning ember which purified Isaiah and is unable to reconcile the blackness of coal he knows with purity. In the brilliant last section of the novel, David, who believes that God's purifying coal is in the car-tracks, rushes madly through the streets and plunges a milk ladle into the tracks. Knocked unconscious, he experiences a vision which enables him to transcend the horrors of the cellar, the oppression of the picture, and the conflict of the coal.

The central theme, the search for redemption or mystical transfiguration, is universal, and the delicacy and artistry with which Roth develops his material grow ever more apparent the more the novel is studied. The intricate symbolic structure, complex interweaving of motifs, wide variety of narrative techniques, and archetypal initiation patterns combine with realistic detail, rounded characters, accurate dialect, and compelling plot to produce a novel with the compression and intensity of poetry.

The emotional atmosphere surrounding Roth during the years he was writing the novel and underlying the circumstances of its publication were complex and sometimes most ironic. The circumstances of the publication of *Call It Sleep* by the Robert O. Ballou publishing company are a case in point. David Mandel, who later married Walton, was her lover during part of the time Roth was living with her. On the one hand, Mandel's liaison with Walton was disturbing to Roth; on the other hand, Mandel was instrumental in having Roth's novel published: Mandel was a partner in Ballou, and Walton pressured him to publish *Call It Sleep*.

Similarly, Roth's financial dependence on Walton was both essential to the production of *Call It Sleep* and emotionally taxing to its author. The novel was written during the Depression years; coming from a poor family himself, Roth would not have been able to spend the years completely absorbed in writing his novel without her assistance. On the other hand, this financial cushioning was psychologically damaging. It filled him with intense

guilt feelings about the poverty around him and kept him from feeling self-sufficient.

One way Roth's guilt expressed itself was that in 1933 he joined the Communist party. Although Walton herself became politically active several years later, she opposed what she thought was his premature politicalization and thought it would ruin him as a writer. Roth himself now believes that his joining the Party was both sentimental and forced. His membership in the Communist party temporarily assuaged his guilt about living comfortably in the midst of poverty and filled the tremendous gap left in his life when his family moved from the Lower East Side nineteen years earlier. Like so many other Jews who had lost their religious faith, he saw communism as an opportunity to identify with a larger whole outside himself.

When *Call It Sleep* appeared in December 1934 the critical reception was, in general, extremely favorable, especially for a first novel. Considering the times, the novel sold well, going through a first printing of fifteen hundred copies and a second of twenty-five hundred. The chief adverse criticism the novel received was for its frank language and sexual descriptions. The liberal press gave *Call It Sleep* remarkably adulatory reviews, but particularly noteworthy is the wide variety of things the critics found to praise, including its realism, vision, use of language, characterization, and plot.

The novel received quite a different reception in the Communist press. In an unsigned one-paragraph review in the *New Masses*, it was attacked for being too long, too impressionistic, too introspective and febrile, and for the vile spelling in rendering dialects and for overemphasizing the sex phobias of a six-year-old Proust. This dismissal of the novel did not go unanswered by other left-wing sympathizers. There was a considerable pro-Roth outcry following the *New Masses* review; each of the advocates of the novel felt called upon to defend it in political terms. The sine qua non of every review was Roth's or the novel's political acceptability. Even Walton apparently saw *Call It Sleep* in sociological or proletarian terms. In an essay published in 1936 (by which time she was politically active), she asserted that Roth, like James T. Farrell and Edward Dahlberg, was attacking capitalism in his novel. The original negative review in the *New Masses*, the subsequent defense, and Walton's analysis all suggest the seemingly inevitable politicalization in the 1930s.

Even though Roth himself believed that the proletarian revolution was the necessary step for establishing a just society, he never accepted the prevailing Communist slogan that art was a class weapon. But while he did not succumb to the slogans of the period, the prevailing political atmosphere made itself felt in his work in a more subtle way: the fact that Roth chose to focus his second novel on a Midwestern American worker who becomes a Communist after being injured in an industrial accident reflects the political preoccupations of the times. Through the Party Roth had met a man he planned to use as a model for the protagonist of this second novel; the man was an illiterate, tough, second-generation German-American who prided himself on his physical self-reliance and brawled his way through life until he lost his right hand in an industrial accident and learned to turn to others.

Roth began this second novel in 1935. He carefully gathered material about his character's life, wrote approximately one hundred pages, and submitted them to Scribners, which had bought the rights to his second novel from Robert O. Ballou, when the latter folded. Maxwell Perkins was extremely impressed with the material submitted, and everything seemed to be going well for Roth. But as soon as Perkins accepted the section, Roth found that he did not want to write any more. In 1936, a twenty-page opening section of this second novel was published in *Signatures: Work in Progress* under the title "If We Had Bacon." But Roth never completed the novel and, except for "If We Had Bacon," destroyed all he had written several years later.

A highly complex combination of situations contributed to his failure to complete this second novel—a failure Roth believes was crucial to him psychologically. Roth probably should have finished the novel before showing it to anyone. This had been his procedure with *Call It Sleep*, on which he worked for three and a half years, showing it only to Walton, to whom the novel is dedicated. Giving the fragment to Perkins and publishing "If We Had Bacon," while seemingly signs of literary success and progress, ironically signaled disaster.

Other aspects of Roth's life in the mid-1930s probably contributed even more to his failure to complete the second novel. *Call It Sleep* is an autobiographical novel in which Roth used memories and impressions of his own childhood. But while the partial autobiographical veracity probably gives the novel a special convincingness and sense of reality, it is also the basis of an artistic problem, how to go on to write another, presumably less subjective novel.

This quite common "second novel" problem was compounded for Roth by the fact that, in his own analysis, he belonged to that category of writer who has to write about the stages of his own development. By not writing about his own adolescent years and, instead, trying to write about a Midwestern worker who becomes a Communist, he abandoned his own natural bent, apparently under the influence of the current Weltanschauung.

Still other facets of Roth's personality and life contributed to his literary problems after *Call It Sleep*. During the years in which he wrote *Call It Sleep* Roth felt that he was in a kind of general mystical state and had a sense of unifying force or power in the universe. This mystical power is, no doubt, the underlying source of the extreme potency of the novel. As Roth wrote *Call It Sleep* he was a possessed artist; while the works of such writers are probably the deepest and most movingly written, the cost to the artists is extreme.

Because in *Call It Sleep* Roth looked inward and back in time toward his childhood, he was unable to live in his own emotionally self-sustaining world. After *Call It Sleep* he was more dependent on his environment and found himself unable to finish his second novel. Even Eda Lou Walton's financial support worked against Roth psychologically; there was no pressing financial need for him to finish the second novel.

Deciding that he had made a mistake in focusing his second novel on a Midwestern Communist, Roth abandoned this project and began to write another novel which was to deal with his own adolescence. This work was to be more ambitious and have greater scope than *Call It Sleep*; in it Roth intended to deal with the Jewish intellectual embracing many more elements of the social world. But in the wake of his inability to finish the second novel, Roth found himself floundering emotionally and artistically. He no longer felt sure of himself, no longer felt he had a point of view.

Roth's failure with the second novel proved crucial; he was unable to mold the subsequent novel about his own adolescence to his own satisfaction. He felt increasingly inadequate in both his personal life and his career. During the summer of 1938 Roth went to Yaddo, the artists' colony at Saratoga Springs, New York. While there he met Muriel Parker, a young composer. After Roth's return to New York City, he and Eda Lou Walton separated permanently.

The following year Roth and Muriel Parker married and settled in New York, supported largely by WPA work and relief. During the next two years Roth tried halfheartedly to write short stories for a living. "Broker" appeared in the *New Yorker* in 1939 and "Somebody Always Grabs the Purple" a year later. Both of these stories are related to actual incidents in Roth's life. "Broker," which is about a Negro truck driver with a seemingly accursed truck, developed out of an incident Roth witnessed. The second story has a young protagonist, who, like Roth himself as a child, has a passion for fairy tales. Despite this proof that he was still able to write and have his work published, Roth recognized that the creative force working in *Call It Sleep* was much weaker in the stories. Without the former inspiration, writing seemed to him simply a task. Giving up the attempt to support himself by writing, and even more importantly, giving up the idea of himself as a writer, he found the possibility of pursuing any semiliterary job distasteful.

Instead, he obtained a steady job as a substitute teacher at Theodore Roosevelt High School in the Bronx, where he taught until 1940. By that time the world was involved in World War II; additional skilled craftsmen were needed to keep up with the increased volume of war materials, and Roth decided to apply his interest in mathematics and become a precision metal grinder.

Although he was pleased by the slow, demanding exactness required for precision grinding, Roth's feeling of intense dissatisfaction with himself for having failed as a writer transferred to the scene of his failure, and he developed a distaste for New York. In 1945 he and his family moved to Cambridge, Massachusetts, and Roth worked in Boston for one and a half years at the same kind of job he had done in New York. But while he was a member of the working class economically, his background and personality kept him an alien in the lower-class environment. By 1945 the Roths had two small sons, Jeremy (or Jeb) and Hugh, ages three and one respectively. The older boy developed a stammer, and a doctor suggested a change of environment. A move to the country seemed like a good idea for his sons; in addition, Roth wanted to get away from the literary world in which he felt that he had completely failed. Thus the move represented a further retreat, a complete escape. Looking around for a place to settle, he discovered that Maine real estate was extremely cheap. Moreover, memories of the happy and productive months he had spent in Maine in 1932 while writing *Call It Sleep* made it seem a desirable place to settle. With the move Roth was convinced that his whole literary career was over. Feeling that his literary past no longer had any bearing on him, he destroyed the fragmentary second and third novels.

Roth sent his family to Montville, Maine, on Memorial Day 1946, the farm having been purchased the previous winter; he joined them on Labor Day. Roth's 110-acre farm, which he bought for $1200, was something like a ribbon in shape; a couple of hundred yards wide and extremely long. During the next few years Roth was busy trying to make a living and rear his sons. For a year he taught in a one-room schoolhouse where he tried to educate children of eight different grades. Later he worked as a psychiatrist aide at the Augusta State Hospital. He was promoted to a supervisory position but soon asked to be relieved of this position because he felt that the increase in pay was not commensurate with the increase in responsibility and because he found himself in sympathy with his underpaid and overworked subordinates. After leaving the hospital in 1953 because he saw no real future for himself there, he decided to try to raise waterfowl. With the help of his sons, he began to raise ducks and geese and slaughtered for other farmers.

For Roth the best part of these years was the closeness to his sons that developed during their work together. The family closeness was especially important to him, because he had cut himself off from his past in New York and because he felt no real intimacy with his neighbors. Still nagged by a desire to write, he once again tried to write about his Harlem years. "Petey and Yotsee and Mario," published in the *New Yorker*, was written during this period from 1953 to 1955, but in general, he felt dissatisfied with his output.

In "Petey and Yotsee and Mario" the narrator recalls how in his youth he was saved from drowning by three Gentile neighborhood boys. Subsequently the narrator's mother gives the boys a cake as a gesture of thanks, despite her son's fear that they will spurn the Jewish-style baking. The three boys in the story are similar to the three boys in *Call It Sleep* who force David Schearl to push a child's toy sword into the trolley tracks. There is a striking difference however; in the novel, the three boys are anti-Semitic, while in the story they are not. The difference reflects a profound shift in Roth's ideas about himself and his own past. At the time he wrote the novel in the early 1930s, he thought he was honestly portraying his childhood. By the time he wrote "Petey and Yotsee and Mario" Roth believed that David Schearl was based on an idealization of himself as a superior and consequently persecuted child.

In 1956, when Roth turned fifty, he experienced a profound depression: this chronological milestone underlined his failure in his own eyes. Ironically, the year also marked the beginning of the rebirth of *Call It Sleep*. Although the novel had not been totally forgotten over the years, 1956 was clearly an important year in its resurrection. That year the *American Scholar* invited various outstanding scholars and critics to suggest the book of the last twenty-five years that they considered most undeservedly neglected. Selected by both Alfred Kazin and Leslie Fiedler, *Call It Sleep* was the only book mentioned more than once. And after going virtually unmentioned in literary histories for over twenty years, in the same year, 1956, the novel was acclaimed the most distinguished proletarian novel by Walter B. Rideout in *The Radical Novel in the United States*.

While critics continued to praise the novel highly, the next major event in its strange saga was a serendipitous meeting two years later of the novelist Charles Angoff and Roth's sister Rose. Angoff passed along the information about Roth's whereabouts to Harold U. Ribalow, critic and anthologist of American Jewish literature, who began corresponding with Roth and visited him in Maine in the summer of 1959. Ribalow's efforts on behalf of *Call It Sleep* resulted in its republication in hardback in 1960 by Cooper Square Publishers.

Roth's extraordinary rediscovery by the literary world resulted in an interest in the author as well as his work. Of special interest was the question of what happened after *Call It Sleep*. In two short parables which appeared in *Commentary* in 1959 and 1960 ("At Times in Flight" and "The Dun Dakotas") Roth addressed himself to this question. In "At Times in Flight" Roth deals with the summer of 1938, which he spent at Yaddo. The Roth character sees a horse that while warming up for a race seems "at times in flight" destroyed when the race becomes "real." So, too, one might interpret, was Roth's art destroyed by the reality of life. In the second parable Roth considers the problem of his artistic collapse in less personal terms, in relation to the atmosphere of the 1930s. This parable closes on a note of muted hope: an Indian chief who for twenty-five years had stopped an expedition party trying to cross a "waste land" now "motioned them the way of their journey." This hopeful tone, suggesting a reawakening in the author after years at an impasse, parallels chronologically the rebirth of the novel in 1960.

Although the Cooper Square edition is handsome the novel did not receive much notice from the general reading public or from critics until republication in paperback in 1964, thirty years after its original publication. With this publication as an Avon Books paperback, the novel achieved astonishing popular and critical success. On 25 October 1964, *The New York Times Book Review* printed a front-page review of the novel by Irving Howe—the first time a paperback reprint had ever been given such coverage. The following year Roth received a grant from the National Institute of Arts and Letters.

While Roth greeted his success with no small amount of apprehension, he recognized that the money resulting from it brought freedom and time to write, and the critical acclaim and popularity prodded him to do so. Later in 1965, while traveling in Seville, Spain, with his wife, Roth felt a strong urge to write about the Spanish Inquisition. His interest in the Spanish persecution of the Jews centuries ago came as a surprise to Roth himself. Since childhood he had not identified himself with Judaism. In fact, in 1963 he had commented in a *Midstream* symposium that he rejected his Orthodox upbringing and recommended total assimilation.

Although Roth never completed the work he was contemplating about the Inquisition, the *New Yorker* published his story "The Surveyor," in which the central characters are an American couple very much like Roth and his wife, who try to discover the long-forgotten location of the *quemadero* (where heretics were burned during the Inquisition) and to place a wreath on the spot. Thematically the story explores the Roth-like character's ambiguous, contradictory attitudes toward religious faith and disbelief. Subsequently Roth came to believe that his interest in the Inquisition was in fact his attempt to find his way back to something related to Judaism.

Roth found the outlet he was seeking a year later when the Six-Day War broke out in the Middle East. He found himself identifying intensely with the Israelis. Roth no longer believes in assimilation, although he still does not have any great attachment to Diaspora Judaism; his primary Jewish identification is with Israel.

After 1965 the Roths traveled extensively in Mexico, Europe, and Israel. They left their Maine farm permanently in 1968. In the summer of that year, Roth was named the eleventh D. H. Lawrence Fellow at the University of New Mexico and spent the summer at the secluded Lawrence ranch near Taos. Delighted with the Southwest, the Roths stayed on in Albuquerque, where they now live. Roth has given several interviews over the years, and written several short pieces including the memoir *Nature's First Green* (1979); he continues to work on a long journal.

Interviews:

David Bronsen, "A Conversation with Henry Roth," *Partisan Review*, 36, no. 2 (1969): 265-280;

Bonnie Lyons, "An Interview with Henry Roth," *Shenandoah*, 25 (Fall 1973): 48-71;

John S. Friedman, "On Being Blocked & Other Literary Matters: An Interview," *Commentary*, 64 (August 1977): 27-38.

Bibliography:

Debra B. Young, "Henry Roth: A Bibliographical Survey," *Studies in American Jewish Literature*, special Roth issue, 5 (Spring 1979): 62-71.

References:

James Ferguson, "Symbolic Patterns in *Call It Sleep*," *Twentieth Century Literature*, 14 (January 1969): 211-220;

Leslie A. Fiedler, "Henry Roth's Neglected Masterpiece," *Commentary*, 30 (August 1960): 102-107;

William Freedman, "Henry Roth and the Redemptive Imagination," in *The Thirties: Fiction, Poetry, Drama*, edited by Warren French (De

Land, Fla.: Everett/Edwards, 1967), pp. 107-114;

A. Sidney Knowles, Jr., "The Fiction of Henry Roth," *Modern Fiction Studies*, 11 (Winter 1965-1966): 393-404;

Kenneth Ledbetter, "Henry Roth's *Call It Sleep*: The Revival of a Proletarian Novel," *Twentieth Century Literature*, 12 (October 1966): 123-130;

Bonnie Lyons, *Henry Roth: The Man and His Work* (New York: Cooper Square, 1977);

Sanford Pinsker, "The Re-Awakening of Henry Roth's *Call It Sleep*," *Jewish Social Studies*, 28 (July 1966): 148-158;

Mary Edrich Redding, "Call It Myth: Henry Roth and *The Golden Bough*," *Centennial Review*, 18 (Spring 1974): 180-195;

Tom Samet, "Henry Roth's Bull Story: Guilt and Betrayal in *Call It Sleep*," *Studies in the Novel*, 7 (Winter 1975): 569-583;

Studies in American Jewish Literature, special Roth issue, 5 (Spring 1979).

Papers:

Henry Roth's letters and unpublished papers are in the Mugar Memorial Library, Boston University. Drafts of portions of *Call It Sleep* are in the Berg Collection, New York Public Library.

Philip Roth
(19 March 1933-   )

Sanford Pinsker
Franklin and Marshall College

See also the Roth entries in *DLB 2, American Novelists Since World War II*, and *DLB Yearbook: 1982*.

BOOKS: *Goodbye, Columbus and Five Short Stories* (Boston: Houghton Mifflin, 1959; London: Deutsch, 1959);

Letting Go (New York: Random House, 1962; London: Deutsch, 1962);

When She Was Good (New York: Random House, 1967; London: Cape, 1967);

Portnoy's Complaint (New York: Random House, 1969; London: Cape, 1970);

Our Gang (New York: Random House, 1971; London: Cape, 1971);

The Breast (New York: Holt, Rinehart & Winston, 1972; London: Cape, 1973);

The Great American Novel (New York: Holt, Rinehart & Winston, 1973; London: Cape, 1973);

My Life as a Man (New York: Holt, Rinehart & Winston, 1974; London: Cape, 1974);

Reading Myself and Others (New York: Farrar, Straus & Giroux, 1975; London: Cape, 1975);

The Professor of Desire (New York: Farrar, Straus & Giroux, 1977; London: Cape, 1977);

The Ghost Writer (New York: Farrar, Straus & Giroux, 1979; London: Cape, 1979);

A Philip Roth Reader (New York: Farrar, Straus & Giroux, 1981; London: Cape, 1981);

Philip Roth (photo by Nancy Crampton)

Zuckerman Unbound (New York: Farrar, Straus & Giroux, 1981; London: Cape, 1981);

The Anatomy Lesson (New York: Farrar, Straus & Giroux, 1983; London: Cape, 1983).

TELEPLAY: *The Ghost Writer, American Playhouse*, PBS, 17 January 1984.

One of the dominant voices of American-Jewish literature during the past two decades, Philip Roth has had an ambivalent, even troubled, response to the Jewishness of his congenial material. He was born in Newark, New Jersey, and shares that birthplace with such luminaries of contemporary letters as Allen Ginsberg, Leslie Fiedler, and Imamu Amiri Baraka (LeRoi Jones). At best, only traces of Newark still cling to the others: Allen Ginsberg bangs his prayer wheel, squeezes his harmonium, and gives every impression of being a bodhisattva; LeRoi Jones has metamorphosed into a true son of Africa; and Leslie Fiedler headed west, literally to Montana and figuratively to that place in his imagination where black men and American Indians are really "Jewish" under the skin. Only Philip Roth has

remained faithful, in his fashion, to what it meant to grow up Jewish in lower-middle-class Newark, the son of Beth Finkel and Herman Roth, a salesman for the Metropolitan Life Insurance Company.

Philip Roth's first story—"The Day It Snowed"—was published in the Fall 1954 issue of the *Chicago Review*. He was twenty-one years old. The bone-chilling despairs one associates with Chicago were less apparent than the heady promises of a big city and the prestigious University of Chicago. But in 1954 Chicago must have looked like Roth's kind of town. He graduated from Newark's Weequahic High School (a version of its football cheer, probably slightly embellished, is included in *Portnoy's Complaint*) and in 1950 took his freshman year at Newark College of Rutgers University. He transferred to Bucknell University the following year and graduated three years later with a B.A. *magna cum laude* and a member of Phi Beta Kappa.

In 1955, the year Roth earned his University of Chicago M.A., his story "The Contest for Aaron Gold" was published in *Epoch* and anthologized. Having a story included in Martha Foley's *Best American Short Stories* does not make a career, but it did establish a launching pad from which larger successes would spring. With *Goodbye, Columbus* (1959), success arrived—along with a notoriety that has followed Roth ever since.

Goodbye Columbus and Five Short Stories was published during the year that Roth married Margaret Martinson, at a moment wedged between the innocence that had characterized the 1950s and the permissiveness that was to dominate the next decade. Roth would, of course, write about both sensibilities, almost as if he were unsure where his strongest allegiance lay. He could be, in Philip Rahv's division of American literature, the Jamesian "paleface" as well as the anarchist "Indian"; frequently, he struck his critics as embracing both simultaneously. For better or worse, Roth became a remarkably accurate barometer for the radical shifts occurring in American social attitudes. To be sure, the benefit of hindsight turns such judgments into commonplaces; in 1959 *Goodbye, Columbus* looked very odd indeed.

On one hand, Roth's first collection of short fiction reminded one of F. Scott Fitzgerald's *This Side of Paradise* in an American-Jewish idiom; on the other, it was satire à la Evelyn Waugh, but without the saving graces of his urbane civility. Most of all, *Goodbye, Columbus* made it clear that Roth was a force to be reckoned with. The work not only won its twenty-six-year-old author a National Book Award and the Jewish Book Council of America's Daroff

Award but also, and more important, it changed the ground rules by which one wrote about American-Jewish life. If an older generation of writers had insisted, in Bernard Malamud's phrase, that "All men are Jews!," Roth's vision was the converse—in his fiction, all Jews were men.

To be sure, Roth was hardly the first American-Jewish writer to cross verbal swords with the "official" Jewish community. Artists, regardless of ethnic affiliation, rarely cultivate good public relations. As early as 1917 charges of "self-hatred" and "Jewish anti-Semitism" had been leveled against Abraham Cahan, the author of a respected and yet often unflattering portraiture of a successful immigrant businessman called *The Rise of David Levinsky*. Secular writing, whether in the newly acquired English of Cahan or the Yiddish of an East European satirist like Mendele, was usually followed by the slings and arrows of outraged rabbis. Angry defenses were, in short, nothing new. But Roth's book brought the antagonisms to a rapid boil. Granted, no social critic has an easy task. The "glad tidings" he or she brings us about ourselves are never welcome, and, quite understandably, offended readers go to great lengths to prove that such writers are morbidly misanthropic, clearly immoral, merely insane—or, as in Roth's case, all of the above.

At this early stage in Roth's career, Irving Howe enjoyed playing the self-proclaimed role of "defender of the [aesthetic] faith." After all, enough self-protectiveness was enough. Those who dismissed Roth as a self-hating Jew cried out for instruction. And in a review of *Goodbye, Columbus* which appeared in the 15 June 1959 issue of *New Republic*, Howe used the occasion to talk about Roth's aesthetics (Roth's stories lack "imaginative transformation," drive "openly to moral conclusions") and to take a few swipes of his own at the meretriciousness of suburban Jewry. In effect, by calling Roth a "self-hating Jew," the need for self-examination disappears. Howe strongly suggests it shouldn't. Later (in a scathing essay entitled "Philip Roth Reconsidered" in the December 1972 issue of *Commentary*) Howe would accuse Roth of being a vulgarian, of reducing his characters to objects of easy derision. But in 1959, Howe felt duty-bound to talk about this new, exciting voice in American-Jewish fiction.

"Goodbye, Columbus" is a love story of sorts, played out against a backdrop of what it means to be both Jewish and nouveau riche. Brenda Patimkin is fated to forever be the ur-JAP, a Jewish-American Princess, the archetype for Jewish Bitch Goddesses

to follow. Neil Klugman is cast as the young man presumably grown sadder and wiser from his encounter with Brenda and her materialistic family. The problem, of course, is that Neil is at least Brenda's match where being "spoiled" is concerned. The story begins at poolside. Warnings about the ashy taste "success" is likely to have had been sounded before—in *The Rise of David Levinsky* and later in a spate of proletarian novels—but Roth's devastating eye for realistic detail and his sharp ear for contemporary speech rhythms had a power all their own. It hurt to look into this particular mirror held up to American-Jewish nature. Moreover, it was meant to.

Brenda is a product of Short Hills, New Jersey, an Edenic suburban world where sweat is the result of grueling tennis matches rather than of hard work. Sport abounds—from the swimming pool to the driving range to the basketball court—along with the more literal fruits of the leisure class: cherries, plums, watermelons. Roth uses food as an index that keeps the Klugmans forever separated from the more affluent Patimkins. At dinner, Neil's Aunt Gladys wonders if he is "going to pick the peas out is all?," while at the Patimkins' "fruit grew in their refrigerator and sporting goods dropped from their trees." For an author who claimed, in 1961, that "Small matters aside—food preferences, a certain syntax, certain jokes—it is difficult for me to distinguish a Jewish style of life in our country," it is these "small matters" that dominate the texture of "Goodbye, Columbus." Here people really *are* what they eat.

Of the other stories in the collection, three have been the objects of special praise: "Conversion of the Jews," "Defender of the Faith," and "Eli, the Fanatic." In each, Roth explores what it means to be a man (a subject that will haunt his subsequent fiction) as that preoccupation rubs against the forces of the superego (nearly always defined as "the Jewish Community"). Taken as a whole, the fictions in *Goodbye, Columbus* established patterns that have persisted throughout the Roth canon. It also set in motion a system of critical responses that have persisted just as tenaciously. Neutral criticism, whether of the sort that collects images or discovers structures, hardly exists where Roth's work is concerned. His readers tend to have strong attachment to one end or the other of the evaluative yardstick, which is to say, people either love his fiction or they hate it. Gray areas are rare indeed.

Roth's career has also had a nasty habit of not developing in ways his admirers or, for that matter, his detractors, had envisioned. Just when he seemed

Richard Benjamin and Ali MacGraw in the 1969 film version of Roth's Goodbye, Columbus

destined to write tightly constructed, Jamesian fictions such as *Letting Go* (1962), the freewheeling *Portnoy's Complaint* (1969) was published; just when a constituency grew comfortable with the fabulist experimentations of *The Breast* (1972), the modernist *My Life as a Man* (1974) appeared. The effects were unsettling; reviewers, critics, and readers alike were not shy about issuing directives to Roth about where his fiction ought to go. Roth's most recent fictions have settled on the trials and tribulations of an alter ego named Nathan Zuckerman. In *The Ghost Writer* (1979) Roth's protagonist is a very young, very vulnerable writer who discovers that life and art have a strange, interpenetrating relationship. One of his stories (suspiciously like those that appeared in *Goodbye, Columbus*) has deeply upset his family: artistic truth is all well and good, they tell him, but some things should remain private. After all, what will non-Jews think when they read such a distasteful story? The task of making Zuckerman see the light falls to Judge Leopold Wapter, a man who takes a special delight in arranging a series of questions designed to domesticate the satirist in Zuckerman and to turn Zuckerman, the would-be artist, into the Jewish commu-

nity's public relations man. One suspects that Philip Roth has had to face similar questions, in and out of print, long before. In *Zuckerman Unbound* (1981) the price of fame exacts even higher tolls, and nastier mail.

Not surprisingly, Roth responded in kind. If Auden is right about "mad Ireland" hurting William Butler Yeats into poetry, it is equally true that nagging criticism could sting Roth into self-serving/self-justifying criticism. He launched the counterattack early, with an article entitled "Writing American Fiction" (*Commentary*, March 1961) and then added some scathing remarks to a *Commentary* symposium on "Jewishness and the Younger Intellectuals" in the same issue. In fact, Roth has been a tireless booster of Philip Roth—with articles, with interviews, with a wide assortment of occasional pieces. In 1975 many of these were collected between the covers of a book. It was entitled *Reading Myself and Others*, and the title said it all: In talking about others (be they Saul Bellow or Bernard Malamud, Franz Kafka or Richard Nixon), Philip Roth always had his eye firmly on the main chance. This, of course, is hardly a new phenomenon. Writers have an itch to knock off the competition, and the literary essay is an excellent way to settle old scores or to chart some new territory where one's peers might be afraid to tread.

The short story had been a perfect form for the flip postures of *Goodbye, Columbus*. With *Letting Go* reviewers invoked no less a craftsman than Henry James as Roth tried his hand at that difficult, nearly un-American form called the "novel of manners." The result was an unrelievedly grim saga of how the lives of Gabe Wallach (largely a self-portrait of Roth), a sad-sack, graduate student named Paul Herz, and Elizabeth (Libby) DeWitt were inextricably intertwined. Part of the blame for this novel that strained for significances on one hand and dazzled with small brilliances on the other must rest on Chicago, a locale Roth writes about with a pinch-faced grimness. Part of the problem is built into its context as an "academic" novel, especially for a writer like Roth who finds it hard to effect a compromise between satirical aloofness and passionate self-righteousness. But these are small matters, not necessarily fatal to a novel with as much sense of disarming detail and localized vision as *Letting Go* has. The important flaws lie deeper, at a level where plot gives way to disconnected threads and moral implications exhaust themselves through sheer weariness.

The action of *Letting Go* begins in the predictable shabbiness that is both the nostalgic memory and the grim truth of graduate-student life. That is, apartments furnished in early Salvation Army, cars on the edge of collapse, threadbare coats, and embattled spirits. Gabe Wallach, however, is spared whatever ravages genteel poverty might exact from the human spirit; instead, he is beleaguered by long-distance calls from his father and bombarded by checks he seldom bothers to cash. Like a character in a James novel, leisure is his vaguely unhappy lot, the cross he bears with dilettantish grace.

By contrast, Paul Herz is a graduate student etched in more familiar terms. In Gabe's description, Paul was "forever running . . . and forever barely making it": "Once, shopping for some bread and milk, I saw him nearly break several of the major bones in his body at the entrance of a downtown grocery store. The electric eye swung the door out at him just as he had turned, arms laden with packages, to watch a cop stick a ticket under the single wiper of his battered, green, double-parked Dodge." To Gabe, Paul Herz seems to find a perverse pleasure in "saying to the world: Woe is me." All the small, daily sufferings that the flesh can endure increase his spiritual standing in the hypersensitive academic community. Such a fellow *must*

be more "sensitive," better than the fat souls that surround him. Besides, Paul is a would-be writer, presumably suffering for the art he presumably will make.

The Paul-Libby-Gabe triangle tests Roth's growing interest in the spidery nets human hearts spin. Money functions as the binding cement. In a realistic novel readers expect a sense of how much a loaf of bread costs and how characters earn their ready cash. *Letting Go* is filled with moments when price tags intrude on idealistic dreams, when bank accounts (or the lack of them) signify all. This is particularly true when Paul marries Libby (over his family's strenuous objections) and Gabe watches as poverty grinds away at their dreams. In such a world even an eight-dollar hairdo at the Carita Salon looms as a foreboding detail. Libby insists on having such a coiffure before facing Paul's family, while Paul can only wonder "Eight dollars!," amazed that the undergraduate Libby could be so bourgeois after all. Hadn't he taught her about the Good, the True, and the Beautiful? Where does beauty-parlor extravagance fit into *that*? "I can't afford stuff like that, Libby. We're going to have to live a frugal life. A sensible life."

Power, particularly when human relationships are concerned, is what *Letting Go* is all about. Paul simultaneously abandons the illusions of getting his Ph.D. and/or becoming a writer, opting, instead, for a less competitive job teaching high school. For Libby, the old hysterias no longer matter; happiness is feeling "Jewish," complete with aching wrists from grating potatoes and a daughter named Rachel. Even Gabe's father is no longer the lonely man on the other end of a long-distance telephone call. He has found Fay Silberman and the possibility of "fun" in his old age.

Only Gabe is left to drift as uncommitted at the end of the novel as he was at the beginning. If Libby is a pale copy of the Jamesian heroine, Gabe bears more than little resemblance to those American innocents such as Christopher Newman who hide out abroad. As Gabe's letter to Libby, at the conclusion of the novel, puts it: "It is only kind of you Libby, to feel that I would want to know that I am off the hook. But I'm not, I can't be, I don't want to be—not until I make some sense of the larger hook I'm on."

If it is truth that Roth has a habit of biting Jewish hands that have fed him, it is also true that he can occasionally snap at Midwestern WASPs. In a brief flirtation with the New Journalism entitled "Iowa: A Very Far Country Indeed" (*Esquire*, December 1963), Roth bid a satiric farewell to that state where he labored for two years as a member of the Iowa Writers Workshop (1960-1962). The exercise apparently warmed him up because four years later Roth struck at the Midwest again. This time it was called *When She Was Good* (1967) and, this time, critics—both Jewish and non-Jewish alike—had the pinched feeling of shoes being forced on the wrong feet.

When She Was Good, the saga of a Midwestern Madame Bovary named Lucy Nelson, was a conscious effort to prove that Roth could write about non-Jews in a non-Jewish setting. Reviewers were quick to point out that, like Lucy, when Roth was good (his ear for native American speech was once again singled out for especial praise) he was very, very good, but when he was bad, he was horrible. Liberty Center, the setting of *When She Was Good*, is the heartland as Easterners imagine and fear it to be. Roth's ambition seems less a matter of rendering the Midwest than an attempt to show the American Nightmare lurking just on the other side of the American Dream. Granted, portraying the American female as a castrating bitch is hardly an innovative idea; such monsters have a cherished, even traditional, place in the American novelist's psyche. But Roth alters the usual ground rules by arming her with narrative perspective and a filtering consciousness. With the exception of the opening chapters, *When She Was Good* is Lucy's saga, told with what, at first glance, looks like narrative sympathy. However, what her strident voice first insists upon is more than countered by the soft whispers of Roth we hear underneath. Here is a representative sample, when she discovers that she is pregnant and that a marriage to the ineffectual dreamer Roy Bassett would mire her forever in the ordinary: "I don't want to marry him. I don't want to lie to you. I hate liars and I don't lie, and that's the truth! Please, hundreds and hundreds of girls do what I did. And they do it with all different people! . . . But I'm not bad! . . . I'm good." *When She Was Good* is a darkling tale, one that pays off debts for the unhappy years Roth spent in Iowa and at the same time established him as the author with the wherewithal to transpose Madame Bovary onto American literary soil.

Portnoy's Complaint (1969) changed everything—including charges of misogyny against Roth. Now he was, if anything, even worse: an ungrateful son and a mother baiter. Parts of *Portnoy's Complaint* had already appeared in *New American Review* (of which Roth's Chicago friend Theodore Solotaroff was the editor), in *Partisan Review*, and in *Esquire*. Publicity about it was everywhere—on television talk shows, in newspapers, and, of course,

among indignant congregations of synagogues. Unlike, say, Saul Bellow's *Herzog*, this was a novel that American Jews both owned and read. Many were shocked rather than delighted at what they found between its covers. The word the reviewers had missed was *schmutz*, a term of contempt that its English translation—*dirt*—only approximates. The anti-Roth crusade that the rabbis began with *Goodbye, Columbus* turned into a full-scale suburban war.

The Roth-haters got some measure of consolation when Marya Mannes called Portnoy "the most disagreeable bastard who ever lived"—this in the pages of *Saturday Review* (22 February 1969) and Jacqueline Susann fired off her oft-repeated quip about Roth being a good writer, although not the sort of person you'd like to shake hands with; but, by and large, measured, academic cadences were more typical. Here, for example, is a representative sampling from Lois G. Gordon's "*Portnoy's Complaint*: Coming of Age in Jersey City" (in *Literature & Psychology*, no. 19, 1969): "The theme of the book—and a significant and universal one—is . . . this dichotomy and tension between the public and private man, between consciousness and unconscious motivation, between the adult ideal one strives for and the childhood fantasy one cannot relinquish, between abstract morality with its noble dictates and the unconscious, parental, superego precipitates that are the source of morality."

Portnoy's Complaint is simultaneously a confessional act and an attempt to exorcize lingering guilts. His is a complaint in the legalistic sense of an indictment handed down against those cultural forces that have wounded him; it is a complaint in the old-fashioned sense of an illness (one that Dr. Spielvogel, his analyst, comically describes as "a distortion in which strongly-felt ethical and altruistic impulses are perpetually warring with extreme sexual longing, often of a perverse nature"); and, finally, it is a complaint in the more ordinary, existential sense of the word. Even Portnoy has trouble distinguishing the truth behind his compulsive needs to complain, to confess, to project guilt, to accuse, to rationalize, to wallow in self-pity: "Could I really have detested this childhood and resented these poor parents of mine to the same degree then as I seem to now, looking backward upon what I was from the vantage point of what I am—and am not? Is this the truth I'm delivering up, or is it just plain *kvetching*? Or is *kvetching* for people like me—a *form* of truth?" Roth insists that the book only became possible when he "got hold of guilt . . . as a comic idea." Then he could find the voice of the troubled analysand—"the voice that could speak in behalf of both the 'Jewboy' (with all that word signifies to Jew and Gentile alike about aggression, appetite, and marginality) and the 'nice Jewish boy' (and what that epithet implies about repression, respectability, and social acceptance)"—and, thus, raise "obscenity to the level of a subject." Those sentiments (republished in *Reading Myself and Others* from earlier interviews) were not Roth's last words on the subject. Roth's 1981 book *Zuckerman Unbound* is about the heavy toll that being famous takes, especially if you happen to be the author of a scandalous best-seller like *Carnovsky* (that is, *Portnoy's Complaint*). And Roth is still busy at the business of separating the Artist from his Art, of explaining, of defending, of looking quizzically into the faces of people who think of him not as a quiet, retiring, hard-working writer, but as an "enemy of the [Jewish] world."

Portnoy's Complaint is a darkly comic family romance in an American-Jewish idiom. Sophie Portnoy is more Borsht-Belt fantasy than actual person, the easy villain in Alexander's self-constructed Rorschach. As the capital-S Superego, she was so embedded in little Alexander's consciousness that "for the first year of school I seem to have believed that each of my teachers was my mother in disguise." Sophie is, of course, the Jewish-Mother joke incarnate, full of sardonic, but ultimately castrating wit. It is Sophie who looms over the terrified Alex "with a long bread knife in her hands" and Sophie who locks him out of the apartment when he is bad. In her dual roles of "nurturer" and "devourer," she is the figure of the Mother outlined in anthropological studies such as Robert Graves's *The White Goddess*. But most of all, she is "thorough": "For mistakes she checked my sums; for holes, my socks; for dirt, my neck, every seam and crease of my body. She even dredges the furthest recesses of my ears by pouring cold peroxide into my head."

By contrast, Portnoy's father provides a poignant model of all his darling son seeks to avoid. As Jack Portnoy's comic version of the Cartesian formula would have it: I am a Jewish father; *ergo* I'm constipated. As long-suffering as Sophie is constantly tormenting, Portnoy's father is the grumbling stoic, a man resigned to his inevitable fate as a chewer of Ex-Lax. He *provides* (everybody, he insists, needs an "umbrella [an insurance policy] for a rainy day"), but can find no "relief" for himself.

And yet, for all Portnoy's insistence that his parentage is the alpha and omega of his malady, socioeconomic factors as well as purely psychological ones play a significant role. Portnoy belongs to that culture of sons for which immigrant Jewish

parents worked. As Portnoy puts it as he considers his father: "where he had been imprisoned, I would fly: that was his dream. Mine was its corollary: in my liberation would be his—from ignorance, from exploitation, from anonymity." Portnoy is, in effect, a scorecard of both the assets and the liabilities of such a program. Groomed to succeed, he does. But what Norman Podhoretz calls the "small-print costs" of America's "brutal contract" (the terms are from *Making It*, his account of how he came to be *Commentary*'s editor) are also there. The curious intertwining love and hatred Alex feels are no doubt matched by similar, albeit silent, emotions on the other end of the generational spectrum. As Naomi, the tough-minded Israeli Marxist, puts it: "You seem to take a special pleasure, some pride, in making yourself the butt of your own peculiar sense of humor." *Portnoy's Complaint* is an extended exercise in special pleading, one that can also plead guilty to Naomi's charges. Nonetheless, the novel itself is a minor classic. It does for growing up Jewish what *The Catcher in the Rye* does for the "hard time" served in prep schools. Both do their respective subjects in, exhaust the possibilities, and give their imitators a bad name in advance.

The avalanche of human folly is as much a curse as it is a blessing to the writer of contemporary fiction, particularly if he has the satirical bent of Philip Roth. As early as March 1961, Roth put it this way: "the writer in the middle of the twentieth century has his hands full in trying to understand, describe, and then make *credible* much of American reality. It stupefies, it sickens, it infuriates, and finally it is even a kind of embarrassment to one's own meager imagination. The actuality is continually outdoing our talents, and the culture tosses up figures almost daily that are the envy of any novelist. Who, for example, could have invented Charles Van Doren? Roy Cohn and David Schine? Sherman Adams and Bernard Goldfine? Dwight David Eisenhower?" Although Roth was elected to the National Institute of Arts and Letters in 1970, in the years following *Portnoy's Complaint* it became increasingly difficult for Roth to find a congenial home for his sizable talents. The grotesquery of contemporary America chipped away at what a literary imagination might conceive, always threatening to outdo in life what one has patterned into art.

The late 1960s took a particularly fearful toll. Roth's next books were pitched on that shaky ground called the playful gimmick. For a writer without his reputation, the results, no doubt, would have been fatal. For Roth, however, even the slimmest straw can lead to a darkly comic drowning. A decade earlier, J. D. Salinger discovered that short stories such as "Franny" and "Zooey" could be marketed as a thin, wide-margined book. Roth used the same tactic in *Our Gang* (1971) and *The Breast* (1972).

Our Gang was written in the white heat of indignation and outrage. Much of the novel is hopelessly dated even now, but in the context of 1971—with the war in Vietnam still raging and American citizens still deeply divided about its moral justification—critics tended to respond to the righteousness of Roth's position rather than the artfulness of his book. *Our Gang* takes President Richard Nixon's 3 April 1971 statement about abortion ("Unrestricted abortion policies, or abortion on demand, I cannot square with my personal belief in the sanctity of human life—including the life of the yet unborn. For, surely, the unborn have rights also") as a starting point, and then fantasizes wildly about a news conference in which a "troubled citizen" asks Trick E. Dixon the following:

> "What if Lieutenant Calley gave her an abortion without her demanding one, or even asking for one—or even wanting one?"
> "As an outright form of population control, you mean?" [the President replies].
> "Well, I was thinking more along the lines of an outright form of murder."

Roth's satire turns John Kennedy into John Charisma, San Clemente into San Dementia. The result is a series of loosely connected sketches rather than a cohesive novel. President Dixon, for example, bursts into speeches such as the following: "As always, I want to make everything as perfectly clear to you as I can. That is why you hear me say over and over again, in my speeches and press conferences and interviews, that I want to make one thing very clear, or two things, or three things, or as many things as I have on my agenda to make very clear."

To shore up his dwindling constituency, President Dixon appeals to the unborn for support. After all, isn't he on record as a defender of their rights? Nonetheless, things worsen, and Dixon (dressed in a football uniform) holds a "skull session" in his blast-proof underground locker room. One strategy involves a "secret operation for the surgical removal of the sweat glands from his upper lip"; another requires the courage Dixon wrote about in *Six Hundred Crises*: "if I have to go on TV and say I am a homosexual, then I will do it. I had the courage to call Alger Hiss a Communist. I had the courage to call Khrushchev a bully. I assure you,

I have the courage to call myself a queer!"

Ultimately, Dixon consults his "enemies list" to find a suitable fall guy and settles on Curt Flood (ex-baseball player, instigator of a lawsuit against organized baseball and recent defector to Copenhagen). In a mad world he is a "sensible" choice.

Roth's next novel—*The Breast*—confirmed a wide range of suspicions: that Roth was a black humorist; that he was a male sexist pig; that he was America's most interesting, most daring, and most experimental fabulist. *The Breast* is a static novel, one even more severely limited by its controlling gimmick than *Our Gang* was. But this time the premise is literary rather than political, and the result is a version of comic allegory rather than satirical invective. In this novel Roth can give his spiritual kinship with Franz Kafka full comic rein. The result is a contemporary version of Gregor Samsa's strange metamorphosis—Alan David Kepesh turns into a female breast rather than a beetle—and one that translates the angst of Kafka's age into the self-conscious, stridently flip postures of Roth's. The result is something of an academic in-joke, as Kepesh, a professor of comparative literature, becomes the unwitting victim of too much teaching, too intensely done. As Kepesh hypothesizes, what has happened to him "might be my way of *being* a Kafka, being a Gogol, being a Swift. They would *envision* these marvelous transformations—they had the language and those obsessive fictional brains. I didn't. So I had to live the thing." To Kepesh's list of impressive "theys," we must now, presumably, add the name of Philip Roth. Roger Sale, writing in *Hudson Review* (Winter 1972-73) spoke for large segments of the critical population when he insisted that *The Breast* was "stupefyingly bad; I read it through twice, surely more than Roth himself has done, just trying to fathom what could have made him write it. . . . It will, and should, be read, if at all, standing up in a bookstore."

As if this weren't a low enough point in Roth's career, Warner Brothers released a film version of *Portnoy's Complaint*—surely one of the most disappointing adaptations of any novel—in 1972. Unlike the Paramount version of *Goodbye, Columbus* (released in 1969), this one failed, even in an age of "liberation."

In a memorable moment from William Dean Howells's *A Hazard of New Fortunes* (1889), a gingerly would-be writer wonders if he can put a character "into literature just as she was, with all her slang and brag"; he decides that he cannot and resigns himself to the view that "the great American novel, if true, must be incredible." Whatever faults Roth might have as a writer, timidity is not one of them. *The Great American Novel* (1973) is full of "slang and brag." Half an attempt to give the whole notion of the G.A.N. the comic burial it deserves, half an attempt to write that "big book" his critics kept demanding, the results could only be disappointing. It was yet another installment in the shell game Roth played with his critics and critics played with Roth. From his side, there was the bravado, the big promise, the shameless chutzpah of his title; from theirs, the feeling that, this time, Roth had gone *too* far.

Ironically enough, the same Philip Roth who had been chastised for passing off jeux d'esprit like *The Breast* as hardbacked books was now hectored for his overly large ambition.

The Great American Novel turns the baseball diamond into stage center. Never before—even in a self-consciously mythic novel such as Bernard Malamud's *The Natural* or Robert Coover's *The Universal Baseball Association*—has the game taken so many wacky, allusive curves: "Who is Moby Dick [asks an eighty-seven-year-old ex-sports reporter named Word Smith] if not the terrifying Ty Cobb of his species? Who is Captain Ahab if not the unappeasable Dodger manager Durocher, or the steadfast Giant John McGraw? Who are Flask, Starbuck, and Stubb, Ahab's trio of first mates, if not the Tinker, Evans, and Chance of the Pequod's crew?" It is Smitty who tells the tragicomic tale of the Rupert Mundys. Once a noble ball club (in the days when superstars Luke Gofannon, Base Ball, and Smoky Woden made the Mundys a household word), they have degenerated into the sad sacks of organized baseball. When their owners, who have a quick eye for the fast buck, realize that Mundy Park can be turned into a wartime embarkation camp, they jump at the chance to combine patriotism with big profits. Homeless, the Rupert Mundys must play their entire schedule on the road, and as the perpetual visitors, they find themselves paraded through the opposition's streets in garbage trucks.

The treatment is as cruel as it is appropriate to inveterate schlemiels. They are, after all, a ragged lot: the Mundys boast a one-legged catcher, a one-armed pitcher, an outfielder with a penchant for running into walls, and a group Smitty describes ruefully as "the has-beens, should-have-beens, would-have-beens, never-weres and never-will-bes." There is even a fourteen-year-old who desperately wants that essential of big-league ballplayers—a nickname all his own: " 'How about

Hank?' he asked his new teammates his very first day in the scarlet and white, 'don't I look like a Hank to you guys?' He was so green they had to sit him down and explain that Hank was a nickname for Henry. 'Is that your name, boy—Henry?' Nope. It's worse. . . . 'Hey, how about Dutch? Dutch Damur. It rhymes!' 'Dutch is for Dutchmen, knucklehead.' 'Chief?' 'For Indians.' 'Whitey?' 'For blondes.' " In the end he is called Nickname Damur.

Only a team like the Mundys could sport a player like Specs Skinir, who sustains a whole raft of comic injuries while sitting out the season on the bench: "Look, look how I chipped my tooth on the water fountain in Independence. My glasses got steamed up on account of the heat, and I went in too close for a drink, and I chipped my tooth on the spout. . . . Look, Cholly, look at my shins, they're all black and blue—tripped over Big Jawn's foot just going down to the clubhouse in Terra Inc. to take a leak. Imagine—just taking a leak is dangerous in these damn things. . . . Nine innings just on the bench and at the end of the game I'm a wreck!"

In *The Great American Novel*, Roth includes nearly every gag about baseball that has been thought and said. Small wonder the novel topples over two-thirds of the way through under the sheer pressure of its parodic weight.

My Life as a Man (1974) is yet another trip to the Roth confessional, where, this time, the protagonist—Peter Tarnopol, with *his* fictional alter ego, Nathan Zuckerman—shores up the ruins of his life against the "big book" he cannot quite imagine. He has been had by Literature. When in the 1950s the noble subject of discussion was "responsibility," and literary criticism was full of solemn pronouncements about "the human tragedy," poor Tarnopol listened, read Thomas Mann and others, and dreamed of writing such fictions himself.

My Life as a Man is Tarnopol's turn at last. Unfortunately, life has not cooperated by staying either as firm or as neat as Tarnopol had been led to believe it would. Nonetheless, "all I can do with my story is tell it. And tell it. And tell it. And that's the truth." If his sprawling autobiographical narrative keeps grating against the decorum of high art, what he calls "Useful Fictions"—two short stories about the adolescence and subsequent marriage of Nathan Zuckerman—set the stage for Tarnopol's brooding. In effect, Roth adds yet another refracting mirror to the technique he pioneered in *Portnoy's Complaint*. The gripes of Roth (this time, more adult and considerably more agonizing) are collapsed into a fictional persona who, in turn, collapses them still further into the objects of his interior fictions. The result is those literary Chinese boxes we identify as the reflexive mode: "A reader of Conrad's *Lord Jim* [Zuckerman/Tarnopol declares of himself in outrage and hurt] and Mauriac's *Therese* and Kafka's 'Letter to His Father,' of Hawthorne and Strindberg and Sophocles—of Freud—and still I did not know that humiliation could do such a job on a man. . . . For I cannot fully believe in the hopelessness of my predicament, and yet the line that concludes *The Trial* is as familiar to me as my own face: 'it was as if the shame of it must outlive him!' Only I am not a character in a book, certainly not that book. I am real. And my humiliation is equally *real*."

Roth's best characters talk. Alexander Portnoy complains; David Kepesh, in *The Professor of Desire* (1977), lectures. Later Kepesh will become *The Breast* of Roth's earlier novel (here is a case in which the sequel moves backward rather than forward in chronology), but now he has all the savage energy associated with Roth's portraits of artists as unhappy young men. In this sense, the young David Kepesh is caught between temptation and restraint, between the impulses of exhibitionism and the aftermaths of shame. He claims that "At twenty I must stop impersonating others and Become Myself, or at least begin to impersonate the self I ought to be." Like Peter Tarnopol, Kepesh desires to transmogrify himself into a serious person, a priest of the critical imagination. In short, he reads voraciously. And like other Roth protagonists, he desires. The result is a sybarite willing to sacrifice everything on the altar of desire. At the same time, however, he is also an incurable academic, the sort of professor who draws his lectures from a curious interpenetration of the great modernist works (Chekhov, Flaubert, Kafka) and his own chaotic life. In this sense, he is exactly the sort of professor who will be metamorphosed into a breast.

At the same time, however, the dedication of *The Professor of Desire* to Claire (Bloom) suggests some important changes in Roth's own situation. From roughly 1975 onward he has been living with the distinguished actress Claire Bloom (Margaret Martinson Roth had been killed in an auto accident in 1968), and they have become, for better or worse, an "item" in the public eye. Warmth, even human love—as opposed to temper tantrums and spoiled Jewish Princess theatrics—now loom as a possibility. From *The Professor of Desire* onward, fathers-and-sons (with the attendant problems of approval, of blessing, of love) become more important than momma jokes and the saga of one's childhood. The

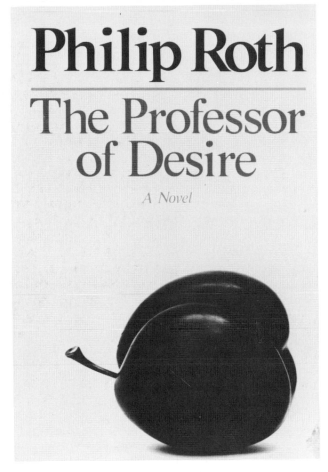

Dust jacket for Roth's 1977 novel, which he dedicated to actress Claire Bloom

ending of *The Professor of Desire*, in which Kepesh and his father are reunited at the family hotel, is as lyrical and as moving as anything the supremely talented Roth has written thus far.

In *The Ghost Writer* (1979), Roth returned—in the guise of Nathan Zuckerman (from *My Life as a Man*)—to his earliest days as a fiction writer and the controversies born along with *Goodbye, Columbus*. It is an exercise in both having-it-out and making peace, of charting the territory of the imagination that the genuine artist must explore with honesty, and of asking, once again, what one's responsibilities to the American-Jewish community actually are. Here, for example, is the barb that Roth has been carrying around in his craw for some twenty years; the speaker is Zuckerman's father, a man in a highly agitated state because of an unpleasant story Nathan has just written: "from a lifetime of experience I happen to know what ordinary people will think when they read something like this story. And you don't. You can't. You have been sheltered all your life. . . . But I can tell you. They don't think about how it's a great work of art. They don't know about art. Maybe I don't know about art myself. Maybe none of our family does, not the way that you do. But that's my point. People don't read art—they read about *people*. And they judge them as such. And how do you think they will judge the people in your story, what conclusions do you think they will reach? Have you thought about that?"

Hungry for approval, nonetheless, Zuckerman makes a pilgrimage to the Massachusetts home of E. I. Lonoff, a fictional character who seems for all the world a composite of Bernard Malamud and Isaac Bashevis Singer. *The Ghost Writer* is Zuckerman's recollections of that emotional visit, some twenty years after the fact. It is a triumph of the sustained, fictional voice—surely Roth's best performance since *Portnoy's Complaint*. And yet, John Leonard, writing in the *New York Review of Books* (25 October 1979) puts his finger on problems that surface again, with a vengeance, in the second novel of Roth's trilogy, *Zuckerman Unbound* (1981): "The trouble with reviewing *The Ghost Writer* a few weeks late is that Roth had already explained it for us. He is forever explaining. Like David Susskind, he can't shut up. *The Ghost Writer*, he told readers of *The New York Times*, 'is about the surprises that the vocation of writing brings,' just as *My Life as a Man* 'is about the surprises that manhood brings' and *The Professor of Desire* is 'about the surprises that desire brings.'. . . This isn't Nabokov's ice-blue disdain for the academic ninny-hammers who went snorting after his truffles. Roth, instead, worries himself, as though a sick tooth needed tonguing. He is looking over his shoulder because somebody—probably Irving Howe—might be gaining on him."

If anything, *Zuckerman Unbound* is an even worse tooth-tonguing—this time about the surprises that followed (actually "haunted" would be a better word) poor Zuckerman after the publication of *Carnovsky*, a novel that bears more than a few resemblances to *Portnoy's Complaint*. *Zuckerman Unbound* is about the trials of being rich and famous. This is hardly a universal theme, and those who are poor and relatively obscure are certain to be resentful. What, after all, did Roth/Zuckerman expect?

The third novel of the Zuckerman trilogy and Roth's most recent book finds Nathan Zuckerman at what seems the end of his twenty-year career as a writer. The list of problems with which *The Anatomy Lesson* (1983) begins summarizes Zuckerman's plight: suffering from excruciating, incapacitating back pains, he is in the care of a "harem of Florence Nightingales" and in the grip of alcohol, writer's block, and a growing sense of regret: "He'd never had so many women at one time, or so many doctors, or drunk so much vodka, or done so little work, or known despair of such wild proportions." Although Roth is certainly not the first contemporary writer to turn his fear of never producing again into the subject of his fiction, he is perhaps the first American-Jewish author to have confronted the problem so directly. Zuckerman has run out of things to write about, and there is nothing left to conquer: "A first-generation American father possessed by the Jewish demons; a second generation son possessed by their exorcism; that was his whole story"—a story already told which reached its peak when Zuckerman's *Carnovsky* made the best-seller list.

The Anatomy Lesson also provides Roth the opportunity to take to task Irving Howe—thinly disguised as the critic Milton Appel—for his scathing comments in "Philip Roth Reconsidered." Howe's 1972 essay is cited verbatim, as Zuckerman, whose collapse takes place in 1973, unleashes his rage against Appel: "in that bloodthirsty essay you have the . . . gall to call my moral stance 'superior'! You call my sin 'distortion,' then distort my book to show how distorted it is! You pervert my intentions, then call me perverse! You lay hold of my comedy with your ten-ton gravity and turn it into a travesty! My coarse, vindictive fantasies, your honorable, idealistic humanistic concerns! I'm a sellout to the pop porno culture, you're the Defender of the Faith! Western Civilization! The Great Tradition! The Serious Viewpoint! As though seriousness can't be as stupid as anything else!"

Philip Roth did not begin his career as either a compulsive explainer or a paranoid defender of his work. Well-meaning critics and well-intentioned rabbis have been hectoring him since those halcyon days when Neil Klugman held Brenda Patimkin's glasses. It would be hard to think of a love/hate affair in contemporary American literature that has been its equal. Meanwhile, Philip Roth is fifty years old and at the top of his form; though *The Anatomy Lesson* may be the final Zuckerman book, it is not likely to be Roth's swan song. He has a distinctive voice, and, for better or worse, it is impossible to talk about American-Jewish literature during the last two decades without coming to grips with books such as *Goodbye, Columbus*; *Portnoy's Complaint*; *My Life as a Man*; and *The Ghost Writer*. If they aren't the sacred modernist texts that Roth's protagonists can

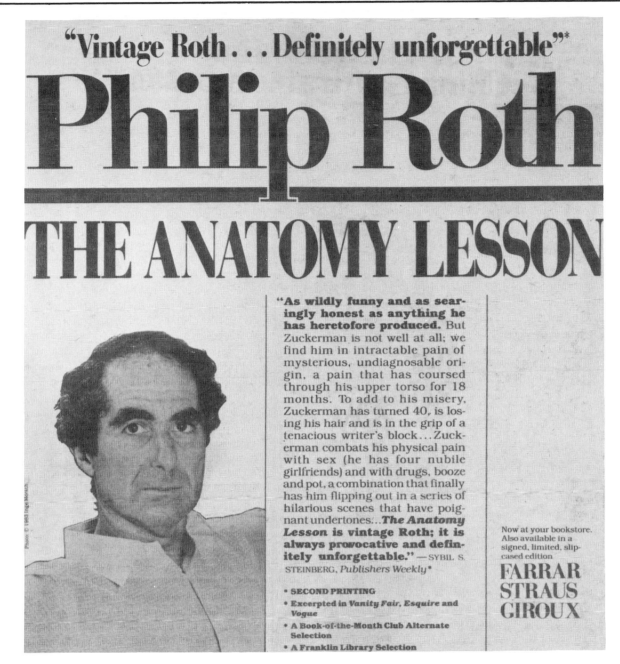

"Vintage Roth... Definitely unforgettable"*

Philip Roth
THE ANATOMY LESSON

"**As wildly funny and as searingly honest as anything he has heretofore produced.** But Zuckerman is not well at all; we find him in intractable pain of mysterious, undiagnosable origin, a pain that has coursed through his upper torso for 18 months. To add to his misery, Zuckerman has turned 40, is losing his hair and is in the grip of a tenacious writer's block...Zuckerman combats his physical pain with sex (he has four nubile girlfriends) and with drugs, booze and pot, a combination that finally has him flipping out in a series of hilarious scenes that have poignant undertones...**The Anatomy Lesson is vintage Roth; it is always provocative and definitely unforgettable.**" —SYBIL S. STEINBERG, *Publishers Weekly**

* SECOND PRINTING
* Excerpted in *Vanity Fair*, *Esquire* and *Vogue*
* A Book-of-the-Month Club Alternate Selection
* A Franklin Library Selection

Now at your bookstore. Also available in a signed, limited, slip-cased edition

FARRAR STRAUS GIROUX

Advertisement in the New York Times Book Review *for Roth's most recent novel*

never quite shake free from, they are, in a word, *essential* ones. In reading his works, we read ourselves. That alone explains something of the animosity his fiction generates, and it also suggests something of its continuing value.

Bibliography:
Bernard F. Rogers, Jr., *Philip Roth: A Bibliography* (Metuchen, N.J.: Scarecrow Press, 1974).

References:
John McDaniel, *The Fiction of Philip Roth* (Haddonfield, N.J.: Haddonfield House, 1974);

Sanford Pinsker, *The Comedy That "Hoits": An Essay on the Fiction of Philip Roth* (Columbia, Mo.: University of Missouri Press, 1975);

Bernard F. Rogers, Jr., *Philip Roth* (Boston: Twayne Publishers, 1978).

Susan Fromberg Schaeffer

(25 March 1941-   )

Susan Kress
Skidmore College

BOOKS: *The Witch and the Weather Report* (New York: Seven Woods Press, 1972);
Falling (New York: Macmillan, 1973);
Anya (New York: Macmillan, 1974; London: Cassell, 1975);
Granite Lady (New York: Macmillan, 1974);
The Rhymes and Runes of the Toad (New York: Macmillan, 1975);
Alphabet for the Lost Years (San Francisco: Gallimaufry, 1976);
Time in Its Flight (Garden City: Doubleday, 1978);
The Bible of the Beasts of the Little Field (New York: Dutton, 1980);
The Queen of Egypt (New York: Dutton, 1980);
Love (New York: Dutton, 1980);
The Madness of a Seduced Woman (New York: Dutton, 1983).

SELECTED PERIODICAL PUBLICATIONS: "The Unwritten Chapters in *The Real Life of Sebastian Knight*," *Modern Fiction Studies*, 13 (Winter 1967-1968): 427-442;
"The Editing Blinks of Vladimir Nabokov's *The Eye*," *University of Windsor Review*, 8, no. 1 (1972): 5-30;
"*Bend Sinister* and the Novelist as Anthropomorphic Deity," *Centennial Review*, 17 (Spring 1973): 115-151;
" 'It is Time That Separates Us': Margaret Atwood's *Surfacing*," *Centennial Review*, 18 (Fall 1974): 319-337.

Susan Fromberg Schaeffer (photo by Layle Silbert)

Susan Fromberg Schaeffer is a full-time teacher/scholar and a full-time writer. To date, in addition to her scholarly articles and reviews, she has completed five novels, five books of poetry, and a volume of short stories. Her works have been reviewed in poetry magazines, the *New York Times Book Review*, and in several other publications, including *Time*, the *New Yorker*, and *Saturday Review*, but Schaeffer is still awaiting an extended critical evaluation which will attempt to assess the importance of her total achievement.

Schaeffer's imaginative range is impressive. She has worked successfully in both poetry and fiction and has tried major experiments within each genre. She is attracted to realism and fantasy; her material is sometimes based on historical or biographical fact, sometimes pure invention. She ranges in historical time and geographical space from nineteenth-century New England (*Time in Its Flight*) to Poland at the time of World War II (*Anya*). Always interested in the relationships between parents and children, particularly between mothers and daughters, Schaeffer sometimes pursues this theme across several generations of a family. She often creates Jewish characters, but Jewish issues are rarely a central concern. She does regard herself as an American-Jewish writer, but, as she points out to Harold Ribalow in an interview in *The Tie That Binds: Conversations with Jewish Writers,* "Partly the reason I wouldn't call myself a Jewish writer is because I'm not trying deliberately to write on Jewish themes." Thus she tells more about assimilation than separation. Acknowledging the tradition established by James, Faulkner, Woolf, and Nabokov, the great modern innovators, Schaeffer experiments with time—with the relationship between time and fictional form, and with the relationship between time and consciousness.

Susan Fromberg Schaeffer was born on 25 March 1941 to Irving Fromberg and Edith Levine Fromberg in Brooklyn, New York. Irving Fromberg earned a law degree, but then worked in the wholesale clothing industry; Edith Fromberg taught Spanish at Andrew Jackson High School in Queens. Schaeffer was the firstborn of three children and the only daughter. She was fascinated early by the fairy tales of Oscar Wilde and the brothers Grimm, and learned to read because she wanted to read about Bluebeard for herself. *Anne of Green Gables* was an influence in fifth and sixth grades, and she began the Brontës' novels early, continuing to reread them with deepening levels of appreciation. Schaeffer remembers writing all through her childhood and through college until the middle of her sophomore year. She attended PS 206 in Brooklyn and, later, Southside High School in Rockville Center, New York.

Schaeffer started her college career at Simmons College, Boston. She was interested in medicine but because of the sexist bias of the times found it politic to tell her parents that she wanted to be a nurse. She disliked Simmons intensely and asked her philosophy professor to suggest a college that would be very different from Simmons. On his recommendation, she transferred to the University of Chicago and found herself liberated by the atmosphere of a university where academic excellence was paramount. She earned her B.A. in 1961, and then went to Boston for a year, working in the medical order department of Little, Brown and Company, the publishers. She returned to Chicago, completed her M.A. with honors in 1963, and went on to complete her Ph.D. with honors in 1966; her dissertation, the first on Vladimir Nabokov, is entitled "Folding the Patterned Carpet: Theme and Form in the Novels of Vladimir Nabokov."

A fully committed teacher, Schaeffer began her teaching career at Wright Junior College, Chicago, in 1964, and then went to Illinois Institute of Technology, Chicago, where she remained from 1965 to 1967. After she had completed her dissertation, she began writing poetry again. In 1967 Schaeffer moved to Brooklyn College of the City University of New York, where she is presently a full professor. She married Neil Jerome Schaeffer, now an associate professor in the English Department at Brooklyn College, on 11 October 1970, and they have two children, Benjamin Adam, born 6 November 1973, and May Anna, born 10 April 1977. Schaeffer has continued to teach full-time, valuing the contact with students and the ways in which, as she said to an interviewer, teaching helps her to "organize [her] entire life."

In June 1972, Schaeffer wrote her first published prose work, "The Toad Who Wanted to Be King" (later collected with one other prose tale in *The Rhymes and Runes of the Toad*, 1975). This was followed soon after by *Falling* (1973), which was chosen as one of *Time* magazine's ten best novels of the year and received enthusiastic reviews in *Time* (18 June 1973) and in the *New York Times Book Review* (20 May 1973), where Wayne C. Booth praised Schaeffer's comic treatment, defined the novel as "serious fiction," and claimed that "Except maybe for Cynthia Ozick, Susan Fromberg Schaeffer is the finest new talent we've seen in a long while." Close examination of *Falling* confirms the novel as the source book for all Schaeffer's later long fiction. Elizabeth Kamen, the Jewish protagonist of *Falling*, attempts suicide and must make the slow journey back to psychological health; the novel tells the story of her sessions with Dr. Greene, a psychoanalyst, her reminiscences of childhood and of various family members, her teaching experiences, her relationships with a series of men, her search for "a Jewish husband," and, finally, her marriage. But to describe the novel this way is not to do justice to the experimental nature of its form; in this novel, time is fractured and the narrative stream is discontinuous as the protagonist attempts to recover her personal history and establish her consciousness through dream and memory.

The protagonist's memories focus on pain and violence, and she recalls with special vividness childhood injuries and illnesses and the ferocious battles between parents and children. Only toward the end of the novel does she realize the reciprocal nature of this violence: "Now at thirty-one, she was seeing the parent at the throat of the child, the child at the throat of the parent. She could see both pictures; time was double-exposed." (In her interview with Harold Ribalow, Schaeffer and Ribalow agree that the obsessive relationships between parents and children are especially characteristic of Jewish families.) The novel ends with a marriage; out of thematic disunity and formal discontinuity come symbolic unity and continuity. Marriage represents a reconciliation between past and present, parent and child, and puts the protagonist in touch with her personal history—especially the Jewish immigrant grandparents whose story of settlement in the new country is briefly narrated in the opening section of the book. One of the minor characters in *Falling*, Armand, spent time in a concentration camp. Not much attention is paid to this character; indeed, Elizabeth Kamen spends a good deal of time avoiding him and his stories of disaster and war.

Anya (1974), Schaeffer's second novel, which earned great praise from critics and won both the Friends of Literature Award and the Edward Lewis Wallant Award, confronts the Holocaust experience directly. Schaeffer said that before she wrote *Anya* she was not particularly conscious of her Jewish identity; afterward, she had strong views about the Holocaust and the precarious position of Jews in modern times. She began to think about writing *Anya* after the shock of discovering that a friend whom she thought she knew well had, in fact, lived through the experience of a concentration camp. Schaeffer became obsessed by what had happened to the Jews, what it meant, and began the long process of research. Books did not tell her what she needed to know about the Holocaust, and so she interviewed survivors.

Anya is the story of a young woman born into a comfortable life in Vilno, Poland, and later devastated by the events of World War II. In the opening section of the novel, the narrator, Anya herself, details the street where she lives, her apartment, its rooms, the minutiae of housekeeping. Richly, carefully, the texture of orderly, everyday life in prewar Poland is conveyed. Easy in their assimilation, Anya and her family are not particularly conscious of being Jews, but such knowledge is forced upon them as the war disrupts and destroys their lives. Anya, sent to the camps, describes the humiliations and degradations, and the pain of separation from her daughter. Eventually, she escapes, lives through the war, is reunited with her daughter, and starts a new life in America. In the final section of the book, a much older Anya reflects on her life, her memories, the difficulties of her relationship with her daughter.

As in *Falling*, Schaeffer's achievement is to show how consciousness can be rendered in fictional terms; unlike many writers of Holocaust fiction, she is not interested only in sensational details but in the full range of Anya's awareness and perceptions as well. She spoke of the task she set for herself to Ribalow: "What I wanted to do and what people I talked to wanted to do were poles apart. I wanted to write a book which began with a normal life which was interrupted by history when history collided with it. But people who have survived the war want to start to talk about their experiences when they really became dreadful, beginning with the ghetto." William Novak, in his favorable review of *Anya* in the *New York Times Book Review* (20 October 1974), seems to have understood Schaeffer's expressed intentions: "But though Anya suffers, this is not a book about suffering, nor about the horrors of the holocaust; its substance is, rather, fictionalized memory which seeks to dwell on human goodness more than on depravity and evil."

Schaeffer sees *Time in Its Flight* (1978), a main selection of the Book-of-the-Month Club, as her most ambitious novel to date and as her favorite fictional work, although the critical reception was cool. The particular impetus for writing the book was Schaeffer's coming across a daguerreotype of a young child lying in bed, photographed through an open window. She later discovered that the boy was not asleep but dead and that such daguerreotypes were extremely common in the nineteenth century. She became fascinated by the sensibility which was drawn to take such pictures and as a result invented the Steele family: Edna, her husband John the doctor, their children and grandchildren. The daily lives of the family—marriages, births, deaths—are explored in meticulous detail, and the family's history is built up through the consciousness of several of the characters, but mostly that of Edna. Indeed, the novel is a kind of encyclopedia of information about the sensibilities of characters rooted in nineteenth-century New England; the narrative includes sustained reflections on time, religion, medicine, law, photography, etiquette—even jokes. Once again, the form is experimental; as Schaeffer has said she tries to counterpoint the conventional family-saga form with a meditation on immortality. The result is, however, uneven; there seems to be too much undigested theoretical material; too much is explained rather than enacted. As Lynne Sharon Schwartz pointed out (*Saturday Review*, 24 June 1978), "When [the novel's] themes are embodied in action or event, the results are admirable, but they are too often pursued in an expository, didactic manner." The form, ambitious though it certainly is, seems to inhibit rather than release creativity.

In *Love* (1980), Schaeffer finds a form perfectly adapted to her needs. As in *Falling* and *Anya*,

Dust jacket for Schaeffer's fourth novel, the story of Russian Jew Esheal Luria, who comes to America, enters pharmacy school, marries, and has a family

more sophisticated at rendering consciousness—even pure consciousness—as she demonstrates in the experimental ending of the novel. Even Lore Dickstein in her somewhat cautious review (*New York Times Book Review*, 11 January 1981), conceded that Schaeffer wrote "a stunning finale to an otherwise unimaginative novel." One notes in this novel, too, far more compassion for the characters. The compassion that Elizabeth Kamen of *Falling* must work for, the perspective she must earn, is here achieved.

Schaeffer has said that all her novels are fundamentally about mortality and that she is concerned with the possibilities of presenting in fiction both the limits of personality in time and the duration of personality in the memories of others. Agnes Dempster, the protagonist of Schaeffer's latest novel, *The Madness of a Seduced Woman* (1983), is haunted by the personalities of her grandmother, her mother, and her sister Majella, who was killed in an accident with boiling water shortly before Agnes was born; as Agnes declares of herself, she was "a ghost, a child constructed out of the ebbing and flowing shadows of the lives that had gone before [her]." In 1896, the sixteen-year-old Agnes, feeling unloved by a mother who doted on Majella, leaves her home in North Chittendon, Vermont, and prepares to fend for herself in Montpelier. Nurtured by a steady diet of romantic fiction, she is fully prepared for a passionate obsession with Frank, a stonecutter with the talent of an artist. Their relationship changes after Agnes has an abortion, and Frank turns from her to Jane, who has been a shadowy, background figure in the story. Agnes takes a gun, intending to shoot herself, but shoots Jane instead and wounds herself while attempting suicide.

The shooting is the novel's focal point, and the narrative attempts to explore the meaning of that act and the significance of medical and legal interpretations of Agnes's crime. As in Schaeffer's other novels, the narrative strategy is complicated, for, while Agnes, at the end of her long life, tells most of the story, her narrative includes other characters' versions of events; the narrative also moves outside her point of view at the beginning and end of the novel and after she describes the shooting. Such a strategy implies the complexities of interpreting individual acts and events and demonstrates Schaeffer's continuing interest in the ways in which the individual consciousness takes impressions of the interactions between its own and others' versions of experience.

The Madness of a Seduced Woman is a densely

Schaeffer tells the story of a Jewish family; indeed, this book covers some of the same narrative ground explored in *Falling*—but in a quite different way. Schaeffer has said that she was haunted for many years by the fact that her maternal grandfather was shot, and in *Love* she undertakes to tell the story of Esheal Luria, a man who dies in the same way. Esheal, abandoned by his mother at her remarriage, sojourns with the *zenshina*, a mysterious woman out of Russian folktale. Finally, he moves to America, enters pharmacy school, marries, and produces children. The fictional mode shifts from fantasy to realism as the locale changes from Russia to America. The combination works beautifully, especially as, once again, Schaeffer's interest is in the fluidity of consciousness as it holds the memories of people, places, and sensations. *Love* may use some of the same material as *Falling*, but the narrative viewpoints shift and expand, depicting events from many different angles. Schaeffer has become much textured book, exploring the nature of Agnes's madness; the dangers—especially for women—of splitting mind from body, self from nature, and the importance of integration; the degree to which characters are controlled by fate or shape their own lives; and the intricate relationship between past and present, the dead and the living. Most of all, as in some of her other works, Schaeffer probes the violence of love and obsession in family life and in relationships between men and women, but in this work she also suggests the possibility of love and friendship between women.

Once again, Schaeffer sets herself an ambitious task in this novel, though, as in *Time in Its Flight,* there is sometimes an uneasy balance between the demands of character and the demands of the ideas Schaeffer holds up for scrutiny. Critical response to this novel has been positive with particular appreciation for the way in which Schaeffer has been able to portray the passionate nature of Agnes Dempster. Julie Greenstein (*Ms.*, July 1983) called the novel "beautifully constructed and intelligently written," and while Rosellen Brown (*New York Times Book Review*, 22 May 1983) found the book's ideas somewhat limited, she praised Schaeffer's "poet's talent for creating images and making

them reverberate through repetition."

Although *Time in Its Flight* and *The Madness of a Seduced Woman* are not concerned with Jewish characters and themes, some of Schaeffer's other works offer glimpses into Jewish life; the short stories "His Daughter's House" and "Antiques" (collected with other short fiction in *The Queen of Egypt*, 1980) and the poem "Yahrzeit" are especially vivid vignettes. Schaeffer says she is not an observant Jew and never has been, but she regards her sensibility as profoundly Jewish. Her primary concerns are not Jewish themes and Jewish identity; even in *Anya* her main object is to demonstrate the ways in which consciousness processes the events and meanings of a lifetime. Nevertheless, her Jewish identity is important to Susan Fromberg Schaeffer; in her own words, she regards her Jewishness as "like the wallpaper in every room [she has] ever been in."

Reference:

Harold U. Ribalow, "A Conversation with Susan Fromberg Schaeffer," in his *The Tie That Binds: Conversations with Jewish Writers* (San Diego & New York: Barnes, 1980), pp. 77-92.

Budd Schulberg
(27 March 1914-   )

Josephine Zadovsky Knopp
Harcum Junior College

See also the Schulberg entries in *DLB 6, American Novelists Since World War II, Second Series, DLB 26, American Screenwriters*, and *DLB Yearbook: 1981*.

BOOKS: *What Makes Sammy Run?* (New York: Random House, 1941; London: Jarrolds, 1941);
The Harder They Fall (New York: Random House, 1947; London: Bodley Head, 1948);
The Disenchanted (New York: Random House, 1950; London: Bodley Head, 1951);
Some Faces in the Crowd (New York: Random House, 1953; London: Bodley Head, 1954);
Waterfront (New York: Random House, 1955; London: Bodley Head, 1956);
A Face in the Crowd: A Play for the Screen (New York: Random House, 1957);

Across the Everglades: A Play for the Screen (New York: Random House, 1958);
The Disenchanted: A Drama in Three Acts, by Schulberg and Harvey Breit (New York: Random House, 1959);
What Makes Sammy Run?: A New Musical, by Schulberg and Stuart Schulberg (New York: Random House, 1964);
Sanctuary V (New York & Cleveland: New American Library/World, 1969; London: Allen, 1971);
Loser and Still Champion: Muhammad Ali (Garden City: Doubleday, 1972; London: New English Library, 1972);
The Four Seasons of Success (Garden City: Doubleday, 1972; London: Robson, 1974); revised as *Writers in America: The Four Seasons of Success*

Budd Schulberg

(New York: Stein & Day, 1982);

Swan Watch, by Schulberg and Geraldine Brooks (New York: Delacorte, 1975);

Everything That Moves (Garden City: Doubleday, 1980);

On the Waterfront: A Screenplay (Carbondale & Edwardsville: Southern Illinois University Press, 1980);

Moving Pictures: Memories of a Hollywood Prince (New York: Stein & Day, 1981; London: Souvenir Press, 1982).

PLAYS: *The Disenchanted*, by Schulberg and Harvey Breit, New York, Coronet Theatre, 3 December 1958;

What Makes Sammy Run?, book by Schulberg and Stuart Schulberg, New York, Fifty-fourth Street Theatre, 27 February 1964.

SCREENPLAYS: *Little Orphan Annie*, screenplay by Schulberg and Samuel Ornitz, Paramount, 1938;

Winter Carnival, screenplay by Schulberg, Maurice Rapf, and Lester Cole, United Artists, 1939;

On the Waterfront, Columbia, 1954;

A Face in the Crowd, Warner Bros., 1957;

Wind Across the Everglades, Warner Bros., 1958.

OTHER: *From the Ashes: Voices of Watts*, edited by Schulberg (New York: New American Library, 1967);

William Spratling, *File on Spratling*, edited by Schulberg (Boston & Toronto: Little, Brown, 1967).

SELECTED PERIODICAL PUBLICATIONS: "The Real Viennese Schmaltz," *Esquire*, 16 (September 1941): 68, 102-103;

"A Second Father," *Playboy*, 4 (February 1957): 16-18ff.;

"The Barracudas," *Playboy*, 4 (December 1957): 23-24ff.

Budd Wilson Schulberg's first novel, *What Makes Sammy Run?*, was published in 1941. Its principal character, Sammy Glick, is, in Schulberg's words, "about as unpalatable a character as ever came down the pike"—a Hollywood type who rises from newspaper office boy to motion picture mogul. The narrative is hard-hitting, biting and cynical, a chronicle of a kind of life Schulberg knew firsthand.

Schulberg was born 27 March 1914, in New York City to B. P. and Adeline Jaffe Schulberg. When he was five years old his family moved to Hollywood, where his father, one of the industry's most important producers, was head of production at Paramount Famous-Lasky studios. Schulberg describes his life from about 1920 to 1937 as "Hollywood": "The studio backlot was my playground and hundreds of nights I went off to sleep with the drone of interminable story conferences as my lullaby music." Between 1931 and 1936 Schulberg attended and graduated from Deerfield Academy and Dartmouth College. The move east was a significant one for Schulberg: "I looked around in some wonderment at this green world of the Connecticut Valley. Until that time I must have believed that Western Civilization had its center at the corners of Vine Street and Hollywood Boulevard."

Between 1936 and 1939, Schulberg was an apprentice screenwriter, during which time he also had a series of short stories published, several of which became bases of his later novels. In 1939, Schulberg left Hollywood and moved to Norwich, Vermont, just across the state line from Dartmouth College. It was here that he completed his first novel, *What Makes Sammy Run?*

Schulberg spent three and one-half years (1942-1946) in the U.S. Navy, working for the Office of Strategic Service in Washington and Europe, gathering photographic evidence for the Nuremberg trials. Much of this material he used as the basis for several short stories. One of these, "Nazi Pin-Up Girl" concerns Leni Riefenstahl, the director of the classic documentary *Triumph of the Will*. The other, "100,000 Years at Hard Labor," was described by the *New York Post* as revealing how the U.S. Army "scientifically and humanely is reducing and remitting long sentences of 90,000 soldiers convicted in World War II court martials." In spite of his war record, Schulberg, in 1951, voluntarily testified before the congressional Un-American Activities Committee that he had been a Communist briefly during the 1930s but broke with the party "when communists sought to dictate how he should write *What Makes Sammy Run?*"

What Makes Sammy Run? was an immediate success. Robert C. Ruark of the *New York World-Telegram* described the novel as a "biting but nonvicious appraisal of Hollywood" and lauded the fact "that it dealt honestly with fundamental issues." Commenting on his novel in the Modern Library edition (1952), Schulberg wrote that he "committed this character to public attention because I found significance in him. I tried to suggest Sammy's as a

way of life that was paying dividends in the first half of the twentieth century."

The work is brilliantly effective because it is completely of its time, with snappy, brittle dialogue and repartee. For Schulberg, Hollywood of the 1930s was a microcosm of America with its success drive, motivated by the belief that only winning counts. In a very real sense, Sammy Glick is a victim of the American Dream, caught up in the vicissitudes of success and failure. Sammy's drive for money and prestige tells, in a very real sense, something about the first generation of Americans who came from impoverished immigrant families, determined to "make it"—fast and aggressively—and willing to sacrifice everything in order to do so. Schulberg has referred to Sammy as a victim of the American cultural condition, a "frantic marathoner" who finds the country's moral atmosphere "so suitable and the underfooting so conducive to his kind of climbing." Because Sammy is a victim, caught up in the panoply of the modern predicament—love, money, guilt—he becomes a sympathetic villain/hero who must be betrayed but about whom we must say, as one critic put it, "Oh, the utter waste!"

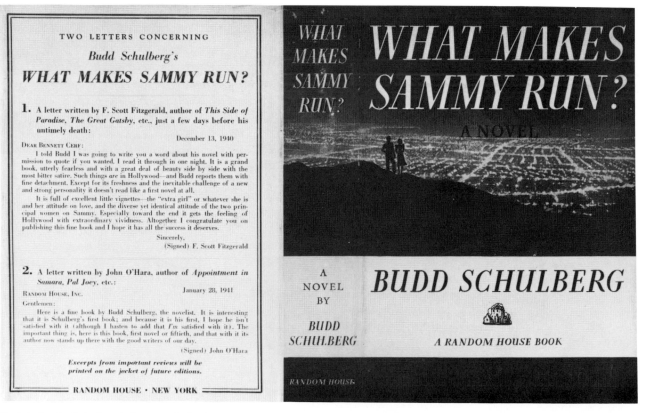

Dust jacket for Schulberg's first novel. In the introduction to the 1952 Modern Library edition, Schulberg described his protagonist Sammy Glick as a "frantic marathoner" victimized by the American dream of success.

To deny the charge that *What Makes Sammy Run?* was an anti-Semitic work, Schulberg claimed that he was only writing about the world he knew. Citing Dorothy Parker, who in her review of the novel said, "Those who hail us Jews as brothers must allow us to have our villains, the same, alas, as any other race," Schulberg felt that the attacks on Sammy as anti-Semitic and himself as a self-hating Jew were strikingly parallel to those attacks on Richard Wright's *Native Son*, also published in the same year: "I believe that for any single reader of *Native Son* who came away with a feeling of revulsion for the Negro race, ten closed the book with a deepened understanding of the conditions, the processes that turn a Bigger Thomas from a strong, ambitious, socially useful human being into a hunted animal that kills and hides. . . . I planned and hoped that my book would have a similar effect." Schulberg admitted that "the fear the bigots might be able to turn his book against his own people and the democratic ideal" was unavoidable. But this could only be done, said the author, "by wrenching characters out of their cultural sockets and paragraphs out of their continuity."

This theme of American cultural dislocation is continued in Schulberg's second novel, *The Harder They Fall*, published in 1947. The work, written in the same terse style and vivid detail as *What Makes Sammy Run?* and based on the life of Primo Carnera, is the story of an exploited prizefighter through whom Schulberg exposes the prizefighting business. The language is cruel and idiomatic, revealing the author's disgust for the corrupted—the fighters, the promoters, the hangers-on, and the public. These fighters are victims who, in their last days become, more often than not, the battered and punch drunk veterans of a racket that passes for a sport. Once again Schulberg's notion is to present an ugly but poignant reflection of American culture. The "Sammy drive" is all too apparent, to be found, says the author, "in every field of endeavor and among every social group." And it will survive, he continues, "as long as money and prestige and power are ends in themselves."

The Disenchanted, published in 1950, concerns the last days and sentimental reminiscences of a once-famous writer trying to make a comeback by collaborating on a Hollywood script. Manley Halliday, the diabetic and alcoholic protagonist of the work, is generally thought to be a portrait of F. Scott Fitzgerald, whom Schulberg knew in Hollywood and with whom he collaborated on the script for *Winter Carnival* (1939), set against the background of the Dartmouth festival, as is *The Disenchanted*.

Schulberg insists, however, that the work was drawn from his experiences as a "junior writer" assigned to "collaborate with a number of older and well-established novelists and playwrights." His purpose in the novel was once again to reveal a seamy side of Americana—great writers who are forced by their culture to sell themselves for money. "The theme of success has always fascinated me," Schulberg has said. "Each of my novels has been concerned with it: I believe Hollywood is rather an ideal microcosm in which to study it; and for this reason I hope to write more novels about the dream factories and their heterogeneous personnel."

Despite Schulberg's denial that this work was a portrait of Fitzgerald, the critics thought otherwise. *Time* magazine described *The Disenchanted* as a "piece of spiritual biography." The *New York Herald Tribune* reviewer wrote that "there is something of a decade here, and much of a man and one lively and subtle mind probing the behavior of another," and according to the *New Yorker*, "the trouble with the book is that approval which starts from creative sympathy and understanding." But Schulberg did pity Fitzgerald. In an earlier article commemorating Fitzgerald Schulberg said, "He was not meant,

Schulberg (right) and his brother Stuart, with whom he collaborated on the 1964 stage version of What Makes Sammy Run?

temperamentally, to be a cynic, in the same way that beggars who must wander through the cold night were not born to freeze." Eight years after publication of the novel, Schulberg and Harvey Breit adapted *The Disenchanted* for the stage. The play opened on 3 December 1958 at New York's Coronet Theatre, where it had a 189-performance run.

The themes of rapid success and the psychic losses of public winners that run through Schulberg's first three novels also appear in many of the stories collected in *Some Faces in the Crowd*, published in 1953. Several stories, some of which were written in the late 1930s, deal with the familiar Schulberg subjects of Hollywood and boxing, and as Frank Campenni has suggested, "compromise with self, betrayed by or of others, doubt, guilt, isolation and fear haunt and shame his restless characters."

Waterfront (1955), Schulberg's fourth novel, is an adaptation of his screenplay for the 1954 *On the Waterfront*. Schulberg based the screenplay about one man's struggle against union corruption on Malcolm Johnson's Pulitzer Prize-winning series of articles entitled "Crime on the Waterfront," published in the *New York Post* in November and December 1948. Every major Hollywood studio turned the film down (it was finally produced independently by Sam Spiegel), and problems plagued production: lawsuits were brought against Spiegel and Schulberg; union boss Joe Ryan threatened a labor boycott of the production crew; and director Elia Kazan required the services of a bodyguard to protect him during shooting. The film, starring Marlon Brando and Eva Marie Saint, was nevertheless one of the most critically acclaimed and commercially successful of 1954: it earned more than six million dollars at the box office and won eight Academy awards, including that for best screenplay. Schulberg's novel duplicates the film's sympathetic yet brutally realistic treatment of the dockworkers around the New York harbor, void of illusion and romance. James Kelly in his appraisal in *Saturday Review* puts it most aptly when he says, "In Schulberg's land, the heels are at work, the realities are squalid, and the prognosis is dreary."

After a fourteen-year absence from the novel, Schulberg's *Sanctuary V*, a melodramatic study of a failed revolution and the ruinous effects of sudden power, was published in 1969. Justo Suarez, the provisional president of a Latin American country, has fled from the corrupted revolutionary leader, Angel Bello, to take sanctuary in a corrupt embassy among corrupt and perverted refugees and jailors. Critics did not receive *Sanctuary V* as warmly as they had its predecessors.

In the 1970s Schulberg produced three nonfiction works, *Loser and Still Champion: Muhammad Ali* (1972), *The Four Seasons of Success* (1972), and *Swan Watch* (1975). His most recent work of fiction, *Everything That Moves* (1980), is, in Schulberg's phrase, a "documentary novel" patterned after the career of Teamster president Jimmy Hoffa. Schulberg's memoirs, *Moving Pictures: Memories of a Hollywood Prince*, were published in 1981.

About his own writing Schulberg says he has been influenced by Mark Twain, Frank Norris, John Steinbeck, and the so-called social novelists. "I believe in art, but I don't believe in art for art's sake. . . . I believe in art for people's sake. I believe the novelist should be an artist turned sociologist. I think he should see his characters in social perspective. I think that is one of his obligations." This does not mean that Schulberg is not aware of the novelist's obligation to entertain. For him, the novel "should run a double track."

In the final analysis, however, Schulberg is "proud that *What Makes Sammy Run?*, *On the Waterfront* and *The Harder They Fall* caught the public attention and perhaps, even in a small way, made it more aware of social sores, the corruption that springs from the original Adam Smith ideal of individuality. The humanist writer of novels may be slightly out of style, but there are miles and decades of many more books before he sleeps." Schulberg, referred to as a "writer with a sensitive and gentle compassion," has been described as a socialist-realist, an apt title.

Delmore Schwartz

(8 December 1913-11 July 1966)

Mark I. Goldman
University of Rhode Island

BOOKS: *In Dreams Begin Responsibilities* (Norfolk, Conn.: New Directions, 1938);

Shenandoah (Norfolk, Conn.: New Directions, 1941);

Genesis: Book One (New York: New Directions, 1943);

The World Is a Wedding (Norfolk, Conn.: New Directions, 1948; London: Lehmann, 1949);

Vaudeville For a Princess and Other Poems (New York: New Directions, 1950);

American Poetry at Mid-Century, by Schwartz, John Crowe Ransom, and John Hall Wheelock (Washington, D.C.: Library of Congress, 1958);

Summer Knowledge: New and Selected Poems 1938-1958 (Garden City: Doubleday, 1959);

Successful Love and Other Stories (New York: Corinth Books, 1961);

Selected Essays of Delmore Schwartz, edited by Donald A. Dike and David H. Zucker (Chicago & London: University of Chicago Press, 1970);

In Dreams Begin Responsibilities And Other Stories, edited by James Atlas (New York: New Directions, 1978);

Last and Lost Poems of Delmore Schwartz, edited by Robert Phillips (New York: Vanguard, 1979).

OTHER: Arthur Rimbaud, *A Season in Hell*, translated by Schwartz (Norfolk, Conn.: New Directions, 1939; revised edition, 1940);

Syracuse Poems, 1964, edited with a foreword by Schwartz (Syracuse, N.Y.: Department of English, Syracuse University, 1965).

Delmore Schwartz in the 1940s

The renewal of interest in Delmore Schwartz may be due to a fascination with his life, with the now familiar history of the *poète maudit* in the modern world, but for the serious reader the real concern is always with the work, with Schwartz's poetry, stories, and critical essays. His reputation as a poet has remained constant enough to guarantee a place in the anthologies for some of his best-known poems, such as "The Ballad of the Children of the Czar," "In the Naked Bed, in Plato's Cave," and "The Heavy Bear Who Goes With Me," but atten-

tion to Schwartz's work since his death has also resulted in republication of *Summer Knowledge* in 1967, the appearance of a collection of the critical essays in 1970, and a new edition of the stories in 1978. With much of the major writing now in print, then, critical recognition or reevaluation is both appropriate and desirable.

It is important to consider Schwartz's work in the context of two traditions: that of American-Jewish writing and that of literary modernism, the powerful phenomenon of the period between the two world wars. These two traditions or movements converge in Schwartz's mind and art, as his work reveals a search for identity in the face of alienation, both as an American-Jewish writer, one of the "sons," and as a modern poet. Schwartz's poetry, stories, and criticism all seem to focus on the theme of alienation or separation, and a concomitant striving for oneness or identity.

Delmore David Schwartz was born in Brooklyn, New York, the son of immigrant parents, Harry and Rose Nathanson Schwartz, who had left Eastern Europe while still very young to settle in the golden land. When he was fourteen, Schwartz moved with his family to the Washington Heights section of Manhattan, graduating from George Washington High School in 1931. He spent his freshman year at the University of Wisconsin but transferred the following year to New York University, where he majored in philosophy and studied under Sidney Hook, James Burnham, and Philip Wheelwright. Schwartz was a brilliant student of philosophy and went on, after receiving his B.A. in 1935, for graduate study at Harvard. Though again fortunate in having such famous teachers as Alfred North Whitehead, Harry Wolfson, and David Prall, he did not feel at home in Brahmin Boston and suddenly left Cambridge, after failing to get a fellowship, in March 1937. He was, in any case, eager to pursue a literary career in New York, as well as the woman, Gertrude Buckman, he hoped to marry when he had his first successful book published. In June 1938 he married Buckman, and in December his first book, *In Dreams Begin Responsibilities*, did appear to critical acclaim. At the age of twenty-four Schwartz was suddenly famous.

The volume demonstrated Schwartz's ambitious literary scope, containing his famous title story; the long narrative poem "Coriolanus and His Mother"; two groups of lyric poems; and a play, *Dr. Bergen's Belief*, which has never been republished. The title story, which many believe to be his masterpiece, appeared in the Autumn 1937 issue of the *Partisan Review* and was included in Schwartz's first collection of stories, *The World Is a Wedding* (1948). It is an extraordinary work, a stroke of imaginative light in the midst of a darkened theater where the narrator goes to watch a film about the courtship of his own parents. Schwartz's parents had a stormy marriage, which found young Delmore in the middle of many confrontations and separations until his father left in 1923 and moved to Chicago. The dream sequence in the theater must be understood, then, against the background of Schwartz's own experience as a child, trapped himself between forces that would affect his early life and determine his eventual struggle for freedom against the past.

At first the young man enjoys the turn-of-the-century summer in Brooklyn but then suddenly breaks down and weeps, for his parents and for himself, while an old lady tries to reassure him that "it is only a movie, young man, only a movie." The narrator calms down for a time, but when his father proposes, he suddenly stands up and shouts: "Don't do it, it is not too late to change your minds, both of you. Nothing good will come of it, only remorse, hatred, scandal, and two children whose characters are monstrous." Warned by the usher, he sits down but finally cannot contain himself and begins to shout again, until the usher leads him out into the lobby and the cold light of dawn as he wakes from his dream to snow and the morning of his twenty-first birthday.

Schwartz called the second work in his book a narrative poem, but it is also an attempt at verse drama, with prose interludes between the five acts. In retelling the Coriolanus story, he follows Shakespeare but gives it a modern twist by using a surrogate narrator and a series of ghostly commentators, including Aristotle, Marx, Freud, and Beethoven, who discuss the conflict between self or freedom and fate and determinism. As a Kafkaesque dream play, "Coriolanus and His Mother" is an ironic version of classical drama, suggesting the same forces at work, but now in Marxist and especially Freudian terms, as the title implies. Conrad Aiken, reviewing a number of poets, singled out Dylan Thomas and Delmore Schwartz as "the two most completely satisfactory poets of the moment" and Schwartz's "Coriolanus and His Mother" as "altogether the finest and profoundest long poem, narrative poem, which has come into English literature for a very long time. It is beautifully designed, rich in detail—magnificent." Schwartz's use of commentators in his verse play and autobiographical works, such as *Shenandoah* (1941) and *Genesis: Book One* (1943), is an attempt to show the protagonist in tragicomic terms. Consciousness, or knowledge, which the ghostly commentators in "Coriolanus and His Mother" possess, is no help in death, as it is of little use to Schwartz's autobiographical heroes, lost in a past they can understand but no longer control.

Part three of *In Dreams Begin Responsibilities* contains two groups of poems, "The Repetitive Heart" and "Twenty-Four Poems," under the general heading "Poems of Experiment and Imitation." These groups appear, in reverse order, in *Summer Knowledge: New and Selected Poems 1938-1958* (1959), preceded by the title "The Dreams Which Begin in Responsibilities." Schwartz's finest poems are in this collection, justifying the high praise by Allen Tate, Mark Van Doren, Wallace Stevens, and John Crowe Ransom when the volume appeared. For Van Doren, the distinction of Schwartz's poetry is "that it restores a rich, wide world of reference which latterly has been lacking in the art. . . . Considered in itself, it is what very little poetry has been for a long time: it is interesting. . . . I do not assume that it will lose its interest any more than that it will lose its goodness. For by calling it interesting I have meant to call it good—as good as any poetry has been for a long while, say at least a literary generation." Though influenced by Yeats, Eliot, and Auden, Schwartz brought to the poems his own imaginative power and a sensibility striving for lyric grace in the flat, desolate voice of the 1930s. When these poems appeared in 1938, Robert Lowell and John Berryman, among those who would come under his influence, had not yet published anything.

Though Schwartz called the first group of poems imitations of the fugue form, he added that it would be more accurate to say "in a form suggested by the fugue, since the contrapuntal effect is of course impossible in language." The imitations seem more indebted to Mozart than Bach but are beautifully lyric or musical, in contrast to his more typically Audenesque voice found in the second group of poems. Only the famous "The Heavy Bear Who Goes With Me" could easily be included in the second section. Originally the poems were only numbered, but for republication Schwartz took the first line from each to provide the marvelous titles for which he is famous: "All of Us Always Turning Away for Solace," "Dogs are Shakespearean, Children Are Strangers," "A Dog Named Ego, the Snowflakes as Kisses." To illustrate his lyric fluency, one need only quote the first stanza from Poem two:

> Will you perhaps consent to be
> Now that a little while is still
> (Ruth of sweet wind) now that a little while
> My mind's continuing and unreleasing wind
> Touches this single of your flowers, this
>   one only,
> Will you perhaps consent to be
> My many-branched, small and dearest tree?

In Poem four, "Calmly we walk through this April's day," Schwartz manages to create his characteristic fusion of social consciousness and lyric beauty. The refrain, echoing Eliot, also sounds what will be a recurring note in Schwartz's poetry: time as the crucible or refining fire of our tragic lives. Poem nine is one of his finest pieces, "The Heavy Bear Who Goes With Me," a modern Kafkaesque lyric about the tragicomic conflict between body and spirit.

Among the second group of twenty-four poems are famous anthology pieces, such as "The Ballad of the Children of the Czar," "Far Rockaway," "In the Naked Bed, In Plato's Cave," as well as less famous but first-rate poems, such as "Socrates's Ghost Must Haunt Me Now" and "Tired and Unhappy, You Think of Houses," a remarkable lyric about the lonely poet as outsider, watching a bourgeois family inside their comfortable world, before turning away, like Matthew Arnold's Scholar Gypsy, toward the "underground," or isolated world of the imagination.

In 1940, Schwartz returned to Cambridge as a teacher of composition at Harvard. A revised edition of his translation of Rimbaud's *A Season in Hell*, which had been attacked for its careless attention to the original when it first appeared (1939), came out in 1940. During the 1940s, Schwartz moved from lyric poetry to verse plays, such as *Shenandoah* and the long autobiographical poem *Genesis: Book One*. Both works reflect his obsession with the symbolic nature of his own life. *Shenandoah* is about the naming of a child and is in prose and verse, the poetic passages delivered by the commentator Shenandoah Fish, who, at twenty-five, stands in the wings to watch himself as a baby being circumcised and fatally named. Painfully and ironically self-conscious about his own double-barreled, Gentile-Jewish name, Schwartz said that Shenandoah was a "rite of naturalization in America," as well as a defense against a joke "by telling the joke oneself."

Schwartz's obsession with character as the product of historical forces is clearly seen in *Genesis: Book One*, which was published as the first volume of an epic chronicle that was never finished. *Genesis* takes its hero, Hershey Green, only to his seventh year, so that the emphasis is naturally on the past or the lives of Hershey's grandparents in Eastern Europe and his immigrant parents pursuing their fate in the New World. Influenced by Thomas Hardy's *The Dynasts*, Schwartz uses a chorus of ghosts who visit Hershey in his room at night and comment on the narrative. Schwartz uses what he calls a "biblical prose" for his narrative and blank verse for the choric passages. Unlike the ghosts of "Coriolanus and His Mother," the spirits in *Genesis* are anonymous but suffer a similar fate, having attained knowledge without the ability to affect the living. While the poem is extremely long, at times portentous and overly concerned with the self, the verse can be very moving, and the narrative of the

Jewish migration to America, one of Schwartz's dominant themes, is vividly and dramatically present. Describing *Genesis* as a type of Bildungsroman, F. O. Matthiessen adds that Schwartz contributes "a peculiar freshness" to the genre, "a freshness that is owing to his most distinctive gift, irrespective of what medium he works in. He has a fine capacity for combining lyric immediacy with philosophical reflection, and can thus command both the particular and the general."

In March 1943, Schwartz and his wife agreed to separate, Gertrude going back to New York. In 1944 the divorce became final, and in January 1945 Schwartz was granted a sabbatical leave and moved to New York, settling in Greenwich Village like an exile returning home. He rejoined his old *Partisan Review* gang, the New York intellectuals of the 1940s, adding two new friends from Chicago, Saul Bellow and Isaac Rosenfeld. Returning to Cambridge the following year, he felt even more alienated; he applied for a position at Columbia, which he did not get, then suddenly left Cambridge without notifying Harvard to go back to his own city in the spring of 1947.

In New York, Schwartz turned to fiction, to the short stories which would embody the same themes he had explored in *Genesis*—Jewish immigration and his own plight as one of the sons, as an artist-intellectual drawn to but exiled from his own roots in this newfound land. *The World Is a Wedding*, Schwartz's first collection of fiction, appeared in 1948. The stories cover the entire spectrum of his thematic concerns, from the reprinted "In Dreams Begin Responsibilities" to the title story, which is about Paul Goodman's coterie, caught between egomania and the economic realities of the Depression; from his story *à clef* "New Year's Eve," which satirizes his *Partisan Review* friends, to a story about his wartime teaching at Harvard, "A Bitter Farce." Finally, there are the two fine stories about immigrant life in America, about the family, exile, and the artist: "America! America!" and "The Child is the Meaning of This Life." In his foreword to a later volume of Schwartz's stories, Irving Howe tries to see them from a new historical perspective: "The stories Schwartz wrote in the years between 'In Dreams Begin Responsibilities' and the publication in 1948 of his collection *The World Is a Wedding*, capture the quality of New York life in the 1930's and 1940's with a fine comic intensity—not, of course, the whole of New York life but that interesting point where intellectual children of immigrant Jews are finding their way into the larger world while casting uneasy, rueful glances over their backs. These were stories that helped one reach an emotional truce with the world of our fathers, for the very distance they established from their subject allowed some detachment and thereby, in turn, a little self-criticism and compassion."

Schwartz uses Shenandoah Fish once again as his protagonist in "America! America!" In this story he is a writer who has just returned from Paris to New York, a city from which he feels cut off. Out of touch with his friends, feeling the paralyzing effects of the Depression (it is 1936) on America, Shenandoah spends his mornings sitting at his mother's breakfast table listening to her long monologue on the past, and especially to her story of the Baumann family, a tale of Jewish immigrant life in middle-class America. Mr. Baumann is a successful insurance agent, the completely social man, an emissary carrying the wonders of America into the homes of his customers. At the heart of the story is Shenandoah's ambivalent response to his own people. As an intellectual and writer he sees that the separation from his past, from people like the Baumanns, has cruelly deprived him of his real subject and his true audience. But the story of rejection and acceptance is still more complex as it unfolds in Shenandoah's mind. His own sense of isolation from the tradition is a result of an earlier separation by the immigrant Jews from their European past. The story of the Baumanns, the blind embracing of the American dream of success, is itself a story of alienation from the European-Jewish past. And this loss of cultural identity is ironically compounded by the second-generation sons, by writers like Shenandoah Fish who in turn are drawn to the European culture which their parents have abandoned. At the end, a strong sense of belonging, of acceptance, merges with his former feelings of separation as Shenandoah reaffirms his unity with "these people." But affirmation soon gives way to doubt, as Shenandoah looks into the mirror, conscious of the modern sensibility that can fully understand what it cannot truly experience.

In June 1949 Schwartz married Elizabeth Pollet, a young writer he had met years before but who had been frightened away, she confessed, by his emotional outbursts. During the next summer, he was invited to teach at the Kenyon School of Letters, along with William Empson, Robert Lowell, Allen Tate, and Kenneth Burke.

In spite of personal and creative crises, Schwartz continued to write lucid, imaginative, highly intellectual criticism, as he had been doing steadily since the mid-1930s. Donald A. Dike and David H. Zucker, the editors of the posthumously published *Selected Essays* (1970), mention that a bibliography of Schwartz's critical writings would number at least 120 items. Like T. S. Eliot, Schwartz is primarily a poet-critic, though his essays are predominantly about modern poetry and criticism, with additional essays on fiction and its modern practitioners. As the editors put it, Schwartz's essays are "the inconsecutive record of an extraordinarily intelligent and sensitive mind, a mind nurtured on Joyce, Rilke, Eliot, the heroes of modernism. . . ."

Philip Rahv's review of the *Selected Essays* is a memoir and assessment of his friend and fellow editor of the *Partisan Review*, with Rahv lamenting the fact that the essays were not collected during Schwartz's lifetime and that he was undervalued as a critic because he was always seen (and saw himself) as a poet and short-story writer. Yet he was "an exceptionally able literary critic. Far too sophisticated intellectually and too much at home with conceptual matters to turn himself into an exponent of any given exclusive method, he also understood the pitfalls to which critical discourse is exposed when it oversteps its limits to indulge in philosophical or sociological divagations." Rahv points out that at the very time Schwartz wrote his early poems and stories, when he was only twenty-four, he had also written "three superb critical pieces." These are the essays on R. P. Blackmur's critical method, a long critique of Yvor Winter's *Primitivism and Decadence*, and a study of John Dos Passos.

The theme of alienation or separation is central to the essays on poets and poetry in the *Selected Essays*. In "The Isolation of Modern Poetry" (1941), Schwartz finds that the isolation of the poet is a function of the dislocation of modern society: "The fundamental isolation of the modern poet began not with the poet and his way of life; but rather with the whole way of life of modern society. It was not so much the poet as it was poetry, culture, sensibility, imagination, that were isolated." The so-called obscurity of modern poetry, then, results from the poet's isolation and concentration on the self as subject: "Since the only life available for the poet as a man of culture has been the cultivation of his own sensibility, that is the only subject available to him. . . ." In "The Vocation of the Poet in the Modern World" (1951), "Views of a Second Violinist" (1949), and "The Present State of Poetry" (1958), Schwartz continues his analysis of the relation between poetry and modern culture. The essays on major modern poets Yeats, Eliot, Pound, and Stevens are excellent examples of Schwartz's fine-tuned critical sensibility, and, in the case of Pound's *Cantos*, he reveals an admirable tolerance as he cuts

Portrait of Schwartz by Nela Walcott

through the linguistic jungle to the heart of the poetic matter.

While Schwartz avoids system and methodology in his own essays, he is an acute analyst of critical method in the work of others, as in the essays on T. S. Eliot, Yvor Winters, R. P. Blackmur, Edmund Wilson, and Lionel Trilling. The essay on Trilling, "The Duchess' Red Shoes" (1953), is a very witty response to the famous "Manners, Morals and the Novel" in Trilling's *The Liberal Imagination* (1950), while it is also a serious attack on Trilling's moral bias in emphasizing manners in the novel, a criterion that Schwartz finds too limited when applied to some of the great novels and to American fiction in general.

In the fall of 1950, Schwartz's *Vaudeville For a Princess* was published. The book is in three parts. The first, or Vaudeville, section has alternating verse and humorous prose commentaries on literature (including comic character studies of Othello, Hamlet, and Don Giovanni), existentialism, cars, and divorce. The second part consists of eight poems on the value of poetry; while the last section, "The Early Morning Light," is a sequence of forty sonnets. In spite of Schwartz's reputation by this time, the volume was dismissed, for the most part, as a minor achievement compared with his earlier work. There are, however, a few poems that recall his original powers, such as his tribute to great artists of the past, "The Masters of the Heart Touched the Unknown," and the much-anthologized "Starlight Like Intuition Pierced the Twelve," a series of monologues by Christ's disciples, disillusioned in their own lives after having witnessed "the unspeakable unnatural goodness of their master."

It is difficult to sum up Schwartz's life in the 1950s without echoing Saul Bellow's harrowing account in *Humboldt's Gift* (1975), the remarkable novel based in part on Schwartz's life. This was the period of Schwartz's move to the farm in New Jersey, his year at Princeton and Machiavellian efforts to obtain a professorship, his chronic insomnia and increasing dependence on alcohol and pills, and a growing sense of failure and loss of creative powers. In 1953 he was appointed poetry editor and film critic for the *New Republic*, which helped him financially and provided an outlet for his writing which, in recent years, had been devoted to frustrating attempts at fiction. After years of suffering from Schwartz's paranoid tyranny, Elizabeth Schwartz left him in the fall of 1955. What followed has also been dramatized in *Humboldt's Gift*: Schwartz, driven mad by jealousy, grew wilder and more destructive until he was finally confined, for a short period, at Bellevue Hospital and the Payne-Whitney Clinic.

Strangely, in the late 1950s, after years of struggling with fiction, his poetic gifts returned, and in 1959 *Summer Knowledge: New and Selected Poems 1938-1958* was published by Doubleday. In 1967, just after Schwartz's death, New Directions published a paperback edition of *Summer Knowledge: Selected Poems*. Almost all of *In Dreams Begin Responsibilities*, a short selection from *Genesis: Book One*, and three poems from *Vaudeville For a Princess* make up the first part of the book, while the later poems appear in part two under the "Summer Knowledge" heading. In the later poems, Schwartz turns from his earlier traditional patterns and preoccupation with the theme of urban exile and loneliness. Influenced by his reading of Whitman, he attempts to celebrate and affirm the natural world and the truth of those who are at one with life. In "The First Morning of the Second World," Schwartz returns, in free-flowing lines, to the lost world of childhood, and in "Summer Knowledge," to the innate truth of summer ripeness and fruition. These themes are repeated and most fully realized in the finest of the later poems, "Seurat's Sunday Afternoon Along the Seine." Finally, included among the later poems are three impressive verse epistles on literary figures—"Sterne," "Swift," and

"Baudelaire"—and a series of dramatic monologues on biblical characters—"Abraham," "Sarah," and "Jacob."

In 1960, Schwartz was awarded the Bollingen Prize for Poetry, and in 1961 a collection of his later fiction and his last book published in his lifetime appeared. The stories of *Successful Love and Other Stories* are curiously light in tone and seem to be trying to capture some image of innocence during the 1950s. In striking contrast to *The World Is a Wedding*, the stories in *Successful Love* are written in an alien manner about a suburban, *New Yorker* world, and the results are not very satisfactory. Only one story, "The Track Meet," is up to the earlier standard.

In spite of Schwartz's paranoid threats and abuse, his friends remained loyal and tried to help in 1962 by arranging for a professorship at Syracuse University, where he was to spend the next three years. Unfortunately, he was still very unstable and his teaching and behavior at Syracuse were highly erratic, though there were still times when he could summon up his old charm and brilliance, and he managed to surround himself with a small band of devoted students. In January 1966, apparently fearful about his chances for tenure, Schwartz suddenly left for New York and took a room at the Hotel Dixie in Times Square. Soon afterward, he moved to another hotel, the Columbia on West Forty-sixth Street. Here, on a hot July night, while trying to take out the garbage Schwartz suffered a heart attack in the elevator and died on the way to the hospital. For two days, his body lay unclaimed, since, in Saul Bellow's words, "there were no readers of modern poetry" at the morgue. Finally, family and friends took charge and N.Y.U. paid for the funeral, which was attended by almost 200 people. At the service, Dwight Macdonald, F. W. Dupee, and M. L. Rosenthal delivered eulogies, and telegrams were read from Meyer Schapiro and Robert Lowell.

Schwartz's death generated a revival of interest in his life and work, spearheaded by the memoirs of his *Partisan Review* friends, John Berryman's elegies in *The Dream Songs* (1969), Saul Bellow's best-selling novel *Humboldt's Gift*, and James Atlas's 1977 biography. Delmore Schwartz's achievement in poetry, fiction, and criticism clearly establishes him as a leading contributor to the modernist movement and as a significant figure in the history of American-Jewish literature.

References:
Conrad Aiken, "Schwartz, Delmore," in his *A Re-*

viewer's ABC: Collected Criticism, edited by Rufus A. Blanshard (New York: Greenwich/ Meridian, 1958), pp. 355-358;

James Atlas, *Delmore Schwartz, The Life Of An American Poet* (New York: Farrar, Straus & Giroux, 1977);

R. P. Blackmur, "Commentary by Ghosts," *Kenyon Review*, 5 (Summer 1934): 467-471;

Irving Howe, Foreword to Schwartz's *In Dreams Begin Responsibilities And Other Stories*, edited by James Atlas (New York: New Directions, 1978);

F. O. Matthiessen, "A New York Childhood," in his *The Responsibilities of the Critic* (New York: Ox-

ford University Press, 1952), pp. 112-115;

Richard McDougal, *Delmore Schwartz* (New York: Twayne, 1979);

Philip Rahv, "Delmore Schwartz: The Paradox of Precocity," in his *Essays On Literature And Politics, 1932-1972* (Boston: Houghton Mifflin, 1978), pp. 85-92;

Mark Van Doren, "Music of A Mind," *Kenyon Review*, 1 (Spring 1939): 208-211.

Papers:
Almost all of Schwartz's papers are in the American Literature Collection of the Beinecke Rare Book and Manuscript Library at Yale University.

Roberta Silman
(29 December 1934-   )

Evelyn Avery
Towson State University

SELECTED BOOKS: *Somebody Else's Child* (New York: Warne, 1976);

Blood Relations (Boston: Atlantic/Little, Brown, 1977);

Boundaries (Boston: Atlantic/Little, Brown, 1979; London: Sidgwick & Jackson, 1980).

PERIODICAL PUBLICATIONS: "Years Later," *Hadassah*, 58 (November 1976): 14, 15, 46-50;

"A View From The Mountain," *McCall's*, 104 (April 1977): 192-193, 237-250;

"Touchstone," *Atlantic Monthly*, 245 (February 1980): 62-67;

"A Labyrinth of Love," *McCall's*, 107 (February 1980): 94-95, 135-138;

"Loving A Married Man," *Mademoiselle* (March 1983): 111-124, 261-262;

"The Education of Esther Eileen," *Seventeen* (June 1983): 130-131, 142-143.

Roberta Silman, a second-generation Jewish-American, began writing in the 1960s and gained recognition with her highly praised short-story collection *Blood Relations* (1977) and her novel *Boundaries* (1979). Though she writes about Eastern European Jews, their assimilated offspring, and lonely, sensitive women, her work has universal appeal. In contrast to much contemporary feminist

fiction, Silman's subdued tone, broad themes, and compassionate characters represent a return to traditional literature.

Both her short stories and her novel contain biographical elements reflecting the author's American-Jewish background. Born in Brooklyn, New York, in 1934 to Herman Karpel, a Lithuanian-Jewish curtain manufacturer, and Phoebe Brand Karpel, an American Jew, Silman lived near Orthodox relatives in Borough Park, which became the setting for the story "The Grandparents." Although the family soon moved to a prosperous Long Island suburb, they frequently visited Brooklyn, enabling Silman to compare Orthodox and assimilated Jewish life. Years later she would write about the tensions between generations, between the immigrant and the native-born, and between religious and nonobservant Jews.

An excellent student and avid reader, Silman won a scholarship in 1952 to Cornell University, where she was elected to Phi Beta Kappa and earned a B.A. in English with honors. Upon graduation in 1956, she married fellow student Robert Silman, who later developed a successful engineering firm and who has consistently encouraged her talent. They live with their three children in Ardsley, New York.

In the 1950s as a science writer for *Saturday*

Roberta Silman (photo by Robert Silman)

Review, Silman gained valuable training and, she says, confidence in her ability to "write about anything." Convinced that imaginative writing and raising children were compatible, she determined to do both; her first child, Miriam, and her first story, "Wedding Day," were born in 1961. By the time Silman entered the Sarah Lawrence graduate writing program in 1972, she had produced several stories and impressed Grace Paley, who agreed to work with her. First appearing in the *Atlantic Monthly*, the *New Yorker*, and *McCall's*, the stories were later collected in *Blood Relations*. A year after Silman received her M.F.A. from Sarah Lawrence in 1975, her first book, *Somebody Else's Child*, was published; this fictional story about an adopted boy was selected by the Child Study Association as the best children's book of 1977. A dedicated writer, Silman is also active in P.E.N. Society of America and has offered writing workshops in Westchester County.

Blood Relations, published in 1977, is, according to Alfred Appel, Jr., a collection of sixteen "moving, humane, and tightly controlled stories." The traditional narratives focus on ordinary, de-

cent people confronting unavoidable losses. Graduations, weddings, births, and deaths announce the passage of time and underscore man's common fate. In "Giving Blood," "Lost," and "A Bad Baby," helpless mothers wrestle with the spectacle of their dying children. Even happy occasions can be bittersweet. In "Debut" a proud father applauds his son's musical achievement but cannot accept his sudden independence. Similarly, in the autobiographical "Wedding Day" the devoted father is ambivalent about losing his newlywed daughter. Such fears are generally unwarranted, particularly in the Jewish tales, which center on three generations of one family bound by blood, history, and love. Arranged nonchronologically, these stories cannot be fully appreciated until all three have been read and a composite emerges. For example, the opening story, "A Day in the Country," portrays the author's persona, Laura, a young mother and writer, debating with her crusty immigrant father, Herschel. Despite contrasting values and views, the two obviously love each other, proving Herschel's fears unfounded in "Wedding Day," which appears later in the collection. "In the German Bookstore" draws Herschel and Laura closer when he confides his European past to her, and also explains how his apprenticeship to a generous, intellectual German made it difficult for him later to condemn a whole nation.

"The Grandparents," perhaps the most Jewish story in tone, encompasses Eastern Europe, America, and Israel and provides a balanced portrayal of immigrant and American Jews. At the center are Avram Moshe and Henya Malke, Laura's paternal grandparents, sensitively but realistically drawn as they suffer and prosper, symbolizing the immigrant generation in America. Despite an ambivalent portrait of Avram, a brilliant rabbinic scholar but also a miserly man dedicated to the most traditional values, Silman comprehends the intense ties between the immigrant husband and wife and their children. Instead of condemning the grandparents' relationship, she describes an old photograph in which Avram, walking ahead of his wife, reaches behind for her hand, an old-fashioned statement of mutual need.

The need for tradition and continuity is not always satisfied in *Blood Relations*, but Silman affirms the quest, sympathizes with the characters, and allows them small victories. As Melvin Maddocks has noted, "at a time when the ego [dominates literature], Roberta Silman gives the reader history in all its connections: soil, blood, tribe, family." The volume earned honorable mention in the 1978

31

is an intravenous solution of sugar and water. He doesn't

seem to be in much pain, but sometimes makes a face when the

nurses have to turn him. My mother comes into the room every

half hour or so; ~~occasionally she lets~~ *gently* her hand graze~~s~~ his

~~then she kisses him and leaves.~~ *and occasionally she*

forehead. The nurses read or talk quietly to us. *bends over him*

+ kisses his

"I think he can hear," the day nurse tells me and my *parched*

lips.

sisters, so we talk to her about him and my mother and ~~our~~

families, comforted by the knowledge that perhaps the sound

of our voices gives him some solace.

For years _____ *(Hello, young man. I have*

~~they have been~~   Our husbands are more persistent. ~~When they come they~~

no sons, tell me your life.) they stand at the foot of the bed,

~~stand at the foot of the bed;~~ sometimes they wiggle his toes,

then say as loudly and clearly as they can,

"Herman, can you hear us?" ~~they speak as clearly as~~

love you, and we will miss you."

~~they can.~~ ~~"We want you to know that we love you."~~ Their

~~strong voices resound through the rooms of the quiet apartment.~~

~~(Hello, young man. I have no sons, tell me your life.)~~

Can you hear us   *ask over and over,*

"Herman, ~~are you listening~~?" they ~~say~~ again and again,

~~but all he can do in reply is lift his wispy eyebrows in reply,~~

~~and each time they try to speak to him my father's wispy eye-~~

~~brows lift,~~ *and his response is the merest ~~lift~~ of his now-*

~~wispy eyebrows.~~ ~~But all he can do is so do give~~

in reply is lift his now — ~~But the~~ *his* ~~only reply is the~~

~~merest lift of his now-wispy eyebrows.~~

~~and think back to those times when he wanted pills~~

It is his mother ~~and each time they ask to there is the merest lift my father's~~

familiar facial   *wispy eyebrows lift.*

reflex but I cannot   *and each time they call to him my father's wispy*

believe it is *only that.* *eyebrows give the merest lift. as if to ~~reassure them~~*

As I stand here *that it's not so bad ~~so all that he can hear~~ ~~us all~~*

and watch him *that whatever is happening ~~to him~~ ~~is not so bad~~ say. "I'm*

die *still here: listening, ~~and~~ it's not so bad that I can't*

to that."

Revised typescript page from Silman's short story "Heart-work" competitions for the Ernest Hemingway Foundation Award and the Janet Kafka Prize, and although some reviewers described the collection as uneven, most praised the author's taut prose, believable characters, and understanding of traditional values.

Even more positive reviews have been written about Silman's first novel, *Boundaries*, which actress Linda Lavin plans to produce as a film. A development of earlier themes, the novel examines minutely the emotions and behavior of Madeline (Mady) Glazer as her life is shattered by the sudden death of her beloved husband David, a talented, idealistic lawyer and a devoted husband and father. Thrust on her own, Mady is compelled to analyze all her relationships and to confront her Jewishness when she meets Hans Panneman, the son of a Nazi. Poetically, but realistically, the novel probes the memories, desires, and painful choices of an assimilated Jewish-American who must resolve her guilt toward her dead husband, disappointed children, and uncomprehending father who visualizes "storm troopers and spiked wires" when Hans speaks. Set against a background of the Vietnam War, Watergate, and social upheavals, Mady's struggle becomes representative of many in contemporary America, where blood relations are poisoned or undependable. But in the midst of disappointment hope flowers, and people tentatively reach out, inching toward each other as Mady and Hans do.

In *Boundaries* Silman draws upon her short stories' concerns and characters, but the novel is richer, more textured and complicated. Whereas some of the stories are related through one point of view, the novel varies viewpoints. Although the heroine's consciousness is central, the reader observes a sleeping Mady through Hans's eyes, his own guilt, and fear of losing Mady. Against their mutual nightmares are balanced common decency and needs and the author's conviction, evident in "In the German Bookstore," that even between a German and a Jew affection and respect are possible. In a *New York Times* review Nora Johnson acknowledges the novel as "a quiet, unpressured story [with] a slow tidal motion, incessant and inconclusive as life's events actually are."

Silman's fiction, thus far, reflects a preoccupation with characters under stress. Two forthcoming novels made possible by a 1979 Guggenheim Fellowship and a 1982 fellowship from the National Endowment for the Arts will examine further the reactions of people trapped in an increasingly violent world. "The Dream Dredger" traces the fortunes of a Viennese Jewish family from 1931 when they settle in a town on the Hudson River until their daughter meets a tragic fate in 1968. Another novel-in-progress departs from Silman's familiar New York setting and involves the effects of the Los Alamos bomb project on Jewish scientists and their families, a natural project for a former science editor.

As a Jewish woman writer Roberta Silman utilizes her background, but her fiction defies easy classification; her characters resist stereotyping. Though she focuses primarily on immigrant and middle-class Jews, their situations and responses will appeal to most perceptive readers. A traditional author, Silman avoids fashionable rhetoric, shocking subjects, and stylistic experimentation. Instead, she offers well-told stories and memorable characters whose struggles and occasional successes earn them applause.

Reference:

Easy Klein, "The Writer Who Came Out of the Attic," *New York Times*, 24 June 1979, XXII: 15.

Jo Sinclair
(Ruth Seid)

(1 July 1913-)

R. Barbara Gitenstein
Central Missouri State University

BOOKS: *Wasteland* (New York & London: Harper, 1946);
Sing at My Wake (New York: McGraw-Hill, 1951);
The Changelings (New York: McGraw-Hill, 1955);
Anna Teller (New York: McKay, 1960).

PLAYS: *Folk Song America*, Cleveland College, 1940;
The Long Moment, Cleveland Play House, 1951.

Jo Sinclair (pseudonym for Ruth Seid) is best known for her descriptions of wastelands of self-denial and self-destructiveness and of the torture they engender. Too often the reviews of Sinclair's novels are limited to criticism of her overly circumstantial accounts of characters' psychological backgrounds and to the discussion of her characters' problems with Jewish identification. However, Sinclair's interests are quite broad and her sympathy with characters from many backgrounds and suffering from many psychological afflictions is impressive. There is often a sociological perspective from which these sorrowing individuals are described, but it is their emotional responses to their lives that interest the author.

Sinclair was born to Jewish-Russian immigrants in Brooklyn, New York, but moved at age three with her parents, Nathan and Ida Kravetsky Seid, to Cleveland, where she still resides. Her careers have been many: she worked in a factory and on a WPA project; she served as assistant publicity director for the Cleveland American Red Cross; and she was an editor, secretary, and saleswoman. Since 1942, Sinclair has been a free-lance writer, producing two full-length plays, four radio plays, four novels, numerous anthologized short stories (published in *Of the People*, 1942; *America in Literature*, 1944; *This Way to Unity*, 1945; *Social Insight Through Short Stories*, 1946; *Cross Section*, 1947; *This Land, These People*, 1950; *A Treasury of American Jewish Stories*, 1961), and many short stories, essays, and poems for journals (*Accent, American Judaism, Chicago Jewish Forum, Cleveland College Skyline, Collier's American, Common Ground, Coronet, Crossroad,*

Jo Sinclair

Crisis, Epoch, Esquire, Harper's, Jewish Spectator, Ken, New Masses, Reader's Digest, Saturday Evening Post, and *Villager*).

Sinclair's greatest concerns in her novels are the psychological pains inflicted on the individual because of emotional wastelands suffered during childhood. Often her main characters are females, and often these females must also suffer the pain of the woman's place in the Western world of the twentieth century. Whether that individual be a sensitive tomboy and leader of a children's gang as in *The Changelings* (1955), the immature and sexually frustrated working mother of *Sing at My Wake* (1951), or the independent and proud European matriarch in *Anna Teller* (1960), Sinclair's female characters struggle against the passivity of American femininity and sexual repression. These women bear children whom they love, but rarely do they develop mature love for their spouses or their lovers. In Sinclair's world, in fact, the plight of women in the West is sexual denial and the redirection of sexual energies into child-love or into sensual gratification in the world of women, evident, for example, in the strong female friendship between Anna Teller and Margit Varga in Budapest or the lesbian affairs of Debby Braunowitz, sister of the protagonist in *Wasteland* (1946). The complexity of the individual human life bombarded by historical forces and familial histories is the foundation of Sinclair's work. Thus, the criticisms of overdetailed narrative, though well founded, often ignore the purpose for such detail. Each person must learn about his individual and group past in order to live in this world in contentment without excruciating pain.

Wasteland, Sinclair's most famous novel and the recipient of the ten-thousand-dollar Harper prize, tells of John Brown's (born Jake Braunowitz) self-destructive denial of his Jewish past. His hatred of his family and his roots stems from a revelation of the emptiness and crudity of his family during a seder service, as John is trying to recite the four questions. Not until the end of the novel, after months of psychoanalysis and soul-searching that help him understand and accept his family members, can Jake (no longer the Gentile John) recite the four questions at the seder. A photographer by profession, Jake must become honest about his pictures by photographing his family. In order to make honest pictures, he must learn of the value of his past, which he does through his sister Debby, a writer, who precedes Jake in psychoanalysis. She in some ways preempts Jake's role as son of the Braunowitz house: when Jake refuses to recite the questions at the seder, she recites them; she protects their mother from the anger and stinginess of their father. Jake's decision to accept his Jewishness is symbolized by the change of his name back to the original Jake Braunowitz and coincides with his enlistment in the army to fight in World War II, another indication of his maturation and acceptance of adult responsibility.

The critical reception of this most important of Sinclair's novels was tentative. The reviewers recognized the fullness, frankness, and intensity of the tale told, with Orville Prescott describing the book as "an intelligent, able, and psychologically convincing study." However, some critics, including Richard Plant in the *New Republic* and F. X. Connolly in *Commonweal*, felt that this fullness and frankness were carried too far, citing the vulgarity of the language or the case-history quality of the form as a consequence of Sinclair's use of Jake's therapy sessions to tell most of the story. Criticism of the excessive complexity of Sinclair's narratives has also appeared in reviews of *Sing at My Wake* and *Anna Teller*. But in all cases the fullness of Sinclair's vision stems from her attempt to present the entire context of the individual consciousness.

Though *Wasteland* is the best known of Sinclair's novels, the later novels seem more powerful and sensitive. Sinclair is much more successful when she presents female characters and when she attempts to show the integration of international, emotional, spiritual, religious features of the individual life. *The Changelings* presents the problems of a changing environment (the influx of blacks into a neighborhood of Eastern European immigrants) on the children of the community. The emotional trauma of change and the pain of hate are fully experienced by the young Judith Vincent.

The novels *Sing at My Wake* and *Anna Teller* are even more successful at portraying the pain of youth, the complexity of the parent-child relationship and the rarity of sexual fulfillment in a woman's life. Catherine Ganly of *Sing at My Wake* presents the unhappiness of a woman's existence in twentieth-century America. As a child her mercurial mother baffles her and as a young wife her husband's depression destroys her sexual satisfaction. Only in her affair with Paul Randolph, a sculptor, does Catherine realize herself as a woman. But this sexual awakening is, as Paul correctly puts it, conflation of sex and death. He likens their toast to Tristan and Isolde's drinking of the love potion and to the glorious singing at wakes in Ireland. Anna Hurvitz Teller is, on the other hand, the prototypical strong immigrant woman who overcomes this unhappiness of the twentieth-century American female by sheer determination. Perceived by outsiders, the Teller home is perfection; experienced by the participants, the home is a depressed one. In this novel, Sinclair associates Jewishness with pain and deformity and depression with sexual dissatisfaction.

Though Sinclair is often included in discussions of American-Jewish novelists, her interest in the painful psychology of the twentieth-century human transcends the boundaries such a category suggests. Her characters must confront their own pasts as well as learn to accept the values and pasts of others. The question of Jewishness is part of the background of Jake Braunowitz's self-hatred, but it is only part; his problems could just as easily have been those of any second-generation immigrant family or of any family whose children have moved into the middle class from the lower class. In *Anna Teller*, the Tellers' Jewishness is also quite peripheral. Emil feels unidentified with Jewish peoplehood, but joining a temple does not assuage his pain; acceptance of his mother as a strong, but human and loving woman does. In *Sing at My Wake*,

the only characters who are Jewish are Phil and Anne Barron, friends of the heroine, Catherine Ganly Huffman.

Jo Sinclair is an unfairly neglected author who should be appreciated for her attempts to portray the complexity and power of the past on the individual—a past which includes the family, the community, ethnic heritage, religion, the nation, and the world.

Isaac Bashevis Singer
(14 July 1904-   )

Barbara Frey Waxman
University of North Carolina at Wilmington

See also the Singer entry in *DLB 6, American Novelists Since World War II, Second Series*.

*SELECTED BOOKS: *The Family Moskat*, translated by A. H. Gross (New York: Knopf, 1950; London: Secker & Warburg, 1966);

Satan in Goray, translated by Jacob Sloan (New York: Noonday, 1955; London: Owen, 1958);

Gimpel the Fool and Other Stories, translated by Saul Bellow and others (New York: Noonday, 1957; London: Owen, 1958);

The Magician of Lublin, translated by Elaine Gottlieb and Joseph Singer (New York: Noonday, 1960; London: Secker & Warburg, 1961);

The Spinoza of Market Street, translated by Martha Glicklich, Cecil Hemley, and others (New York: Farrar, Straus & Cudahy, 1961; London: Secker & Warburg, 1962);

The Slave, translated by Isaac Bashevis Singer and Hemley (New York: Farrar, Straus & Cudahy, 1962; London: Secker & Warburg, 1963);

Short Friday and Other Stories, translated by Joseph Singer and others (New York: Farrar, Straus & Giroux, 1964; London: Secker & Warburg, 1967);

In My Father's Court, translated by Channah Kleinerman-Goldstein, Gottlieb, and Joseph Singer (New York: Farrar, Straus & Giroux, 1966; London: Secker & Warburg, 1967);

Zlateh the Goat and Other Stories, translated by Elizabeth Shub and Isaac Bashevis Singer

*This list includes only books published in English.

(New York: Harper & Row, 1966; London: Secker & Warburg, 1967);

Selected Short Stories of Isaac Bashevis Singer, edited by Irving Howe (New York: Modern Library, 1966);

Mazel and Shlimazel, Or the Milk of a Lioness, translated by Shub and Isaac Bashevis Singer (New York: Farrar, Straus & Giroux, 1967; London: Cape, 1979);

The Manor, translated by Joseph Singer and Gottlieb (New York: Farrar, Straus & Giroux, 1967; London: Secker & Warburg, 1969);

The Fearsome Inn, translated by Shub and Isaac Bashevis Singer (New York: Scribners, 1967; London: Collins, 1970);

When Shlemiel Went to Warsaw & Other Stories, translated by Isaac Bashevis Singer and Shub (New York: Farrar, Straus & Giroux, 1968; London: Longman Young Books, 1974);

The Séance and Other Stories, translated by Roger H. Klein, Hemley, and others (New York: Farrar, Straus & Giroux, 1968; London: Cape, 1970);

A Day of Pleasure: Stories of a Boy Growing Up in Warsaw, translated by Klemerman-Goldstein and others (New York: Farrar, Straus & Giroux, 1969; London: McRae, 1980);

The Estate, translated by Joseph Singer, Gottlieb, and Shub (New York: Farrar, Straus & Giroux, 1969; London: Cape, 1970);

Elijah the Slave, translated by Isaac Bashevis Singer and Shub (New York: Farrar, Straus & Giroux, 1970);

Joseph and Koza, Or the Sacrifice to the Vistula, trans-

Isaac Bashevis Singer (photo by Layle Silbert)

lated by Isaac Bashevis Singer and Shub (New York: Farrar, Straus & Giroux, 1970);

A Friend of Kafka and Other Stories, translated by Isaac Bashevis Singer, Shub, and others (New York: Farrar, Straus & Giroux, 1970; London: Cape, 1972);

An Isaac Bashevis Singer Reader (New York: Farrar, Straus & Giroux, 1971);

Alone In the Wild Forest, translated by Isaac Bashevis Singer and Shub (New York: Farrar, Straus & Giroux, 1971);

The Topsy-Turvy Emperor of China, translated by Isaac Bashevis Singer and Shub (New York, Evanston, San Francisco & London: Harper & Row, 1971);

Enemies, A Love Story, translated by Aliza Shevrin and Shub (New York: Farrar, Straus & Giroux, 1972; London: Cape, 1972);

The Wicked City, translated by Isaac Bashevis Singer and Shub (New York: Farrar, Straus & Giroux, 1972);

A Crown of Feathers and Other Stories, translated by Isaac Bashevis Singer, Laurie Colwin, and others (New York: Farrar, Straus & Giroux, 1973; London: Cape, 1974);

The Hasidim, illustrations by Ira Moskowitz (New York: Crown, 1973);

The Fools of Chelm and Their History, translated by Isaac Bashevis Singer and Shub (New York: Farrar, Straus & Giroux, 1973; London: Abelard-Schuman, 1974);

Why Noah Chose the Dove, translated by Shub (New York: Farrar, Straus & Giroux, 1974);

Passions and Other Stories, translated by Isaac Bashevis Singer and others (New York: Farrar, Straus & Giroux, 1975; London: Cape, 1976);

A Tale of Three Wishes (New York: Farrar, Straus & Giroux, 1975);

A Little Boy in Search of God: Mysticism in a Personal Light, illustrations by Moskowitz (Garden City: Doubleday, 1976);

Naftali the Storyteller and His Horse, Sus, and Other Stories, translated by Joseph Singer, Isaac Bashevis Singer, and others (New York: Farrar, Straus & Giroux, 1976; Oxford: Oxford University Press, 1977);

Yentl, by Singer and Leah Napolin (New York, Hollywood, London & Toronto: French, 1977);

A Young Man in Search of Love, translated by Joseph Singer (Garden City: Doubleday, 1978);

Shosha, translated by Joseph Singer and Isaac Bashevis Singer (New York: Farrar, Straus & Giroux, 1978; London: Cape, 1979);

Old Love, translated by Joseph Singer, Isaac Bashevis Singer, and others (New York: Farrar, Straus & Giroux, 1979; London: Cape, 1980);

Nobel Lecture (New York: Farrar, Straus & Giroux, 1979; London: Cape, 1979);

The Power of Light; Eight Stories for Hanukkah (New York: Farrar, Straus & Giroux, 1980; London: Robson, 1983);

Reaches of Heaven: A Story of the Baal Shem Tov (New York: Farrar, Straus & Giroux, 1980);

Lost in America (Garden City: Doubleday, 1981);

The Meaning of Freedom (West Point, N.Y.: U.S. Military Academy, 1981);

The Collected Stories of Isaac Bashevis Singer (New York: Farrar, Straus & Giroux, 1982; London: Cape, 1982);

The Golem (New York: Farrar, Straus & Giroux, 1982; London: Deutsch, 1983);

My Personal Conception of Religion (Lafayette, La.:

University of Southwestern Louisiana Press, 1982);

One Day of Happiness (New York: Red Ozier Press, 1982);

Isaac Bashevis Singer: Three Complete Novels (New York: Avenel Books, 1982)—includes *The Slave; Enemies, A Love Story;* and *Shosha;*

Love and Exile (Garden City: Doubleday, 1983)— includes *A Little Boy in Search of God, A Young Man in Search of Love,* and *Lost in America.*

In his novels and short stories, Isaac Bashevis Singer has created a world of ghosts, dybbuks, witches, and demons, a world of eccentric people strongly rooted in the *shtetls* of Poland and of disoriented émigrés haunted by memories of the *shtetls* as they walk the streets of Manhattan or Miami Beach. Singer has created a world that reaches beyond the perimeters of traditional Yiddish literature, of people yearning for erotic love and of people possessed by perverse or even demonic kinds of love. His fictional universe has fascinated readers from America to Japan and has carved for Singer a permanent niche both in Yiddish literature and in the literary history of the world—a niche strengthened by his winning two National Book awards and the 1978 Nobel Prize for Literature. Singer writes his works in Yiddish, often having them serialized in the Yiddish newspaper the *Jewish Daily Forward* before they are translated into English, often by him in collaboration with his editors. He not only writes fiction, but for the past forty-five years he has also written free-lance articles, reviews, and essays for the *Jewish Daily Forward*. More recently he has also contributed to such magazines as *Commentary, Esquire, Midstream,* and the *New Yorker*.

Singer was born in Leoncin, Poland, the son and grandson of rabbis who intended for him to become a religious scholar. He and his family moved to Warsaw when Singer was four, and he grew up there except for spending three years in his grandfather's village of Bilgoray when he was an adolescent. Experiences in Bilgoray later became the subjects of many of Singer's tales of *shtetl* life. Influenced by his older brother Israel Joshua, who later achieved prominence as a Yiddish novelist, Singer dramatically shifted his interests from sacred to secular writing. He followed his brother to America in 1935, leaving behind him a wife and a son. He settled in New York City and launched his career by associating with the *Jewish Daily Forward*. In 1937 Singer met a German-Jewish immigrant woman named Alma Hazmann, who became his wife three years later. He and Alma still live on New York City's Upper West Side. They also spend part of their time in their Surfside, Florida, condominium, and they travel several times a year to Israel, where his son by his first marriage, Israel Zamir (*zamir* is Hebrew for *singer*), lives with his wife and Singer's four grandchildren. Zamir, a journalist for *Al Hamishmar*, frequently translates his father's works into Hebrew for publication in Israel. Besides still actively writing, Singer frequently lectures at such different places as Bard College in New York, Virginia Commonwealth University in Richmond, Washington Hebrew Congregation in Washington, D.C., and Hebrew University in Jerusalem.

Although Singer has most frequently written about Jewish folklore and life in the Polish *shtetls*, in recent years he has begun to set some of his tales in America. These American tales will be our main concern here, but to understand them properly, it is important to note the atmosphere and major themes of Singer's fictional works and memoirs rooted in the Polish *shtetls* and the Warsaw Ghetto. These works range from his first serious novel, *Satan in Goray*, published in Poland in 1935 (and in English translation twenty years later), in which the protagonist, a cabalist, is possessed by Satan and by his own passion for the occult, while his village, Goray, is possessed by the "false messianism" rampant in seventeenth-century Poland, to *The Family Moskat* (1950), a realistic epic novel which, together with *The Manor* (1967) and *The Estate* (1969), forms a trilogy that Samuel H. Joseloff has described as "covering the Polish Jewish communities from the insurrections of 1863 until the Nazi conquest of 1939." These works, Singer's hundreds of short stories, and his memoirs of his boyhood, *In My Father's Court* (1966), enable us, says Joseloff, "to take . . . [a] journey into the past" of Jewish religious tradition, culture, and folklore. Other realistic novels, *The Magician of Lublin* (1960), set in nineteenth-century Poland, and *The Slave* (1962), set in seventeenth-century Poland, complete Singer's portrait of the Polish-Jewish past.

In many of these works, Singer's main characters struggle with intense, even pathological passions or obsessions which are frequently depicted as visitations by Satan or other demons and dybbuks, Singer's "spiritual stenography"—his own words—for his characters' psychological problems and often enigmatic behavior. Eroticism, "the weakness of the flesh," is also a prominent motif in these works; love and its transcendent power are treated with profound respect by Singer. In addition to the subject of passion, epistemological questions about truth and reality ("Is this life a dream?") also preoccupy Singer's characters, among them the protagonist-narrator of Singer's much admired short story "Gimpel the Fool" (collected in *Gimpel the Fool and Other Stories*, 1957). The "divine fool" Gimpel, though apparently easily deceived by his wife and fellow townsmen of Frampol, apprehends some profound and touching truths about love, reality, evil in human beings, and spiritual faith. Other collections of stories, such as *The Spinoza of Market Street* (1961) and *Short Friday and Other Stories* (1964), embrace this wide range of topics and feature Singer's rich Jewish folk characterizations. They display a rootedness in the *shtetl*, in Jewish folklore, in Jewish religious ritual, in Jewish history, in the past.

Given the intense attachment of his protagonists to the past and to their European-Jewish roots, it is no wonder, then, that when Singer shifts the locus in some of his more recent stories to America, his European immigrant characters are usually depicted as suffering the torments of dislocation and deracination. Some twenty-five short stories and three novels, *Enemies, A Love Story* (1972), "Shadows by the Hudson" (1957), and "A Ship to America" (1958) (only the first of which has been translated into English), take place in American settings, usually in New York City and its suburbs, Miami Beach, or the Catskill Mountains. Prominent in these American tales is the theme of disorientation, or "lostness." Leslie Fiedler has said that Singer's Yiddish-speaking emigrés to America usually view themselves as being in perpetual exile; for these protagonists, America is a limbo and they are lost "semi-ghosts." Perhaps Singer's preoccupation with the themes of lostness and rootlessness reflects his own disorientation when he arrived in America as a young man. In an interview with Richard Burgin, which appeared in two installments in the *New York Times Magazine* just after Singer won the Nobel Prize, Singer described his emotional state as that of a "greenhorn": "I felt that I had been torn out of my roots and that I would never grow any roots in this country." This concern with roots is apparent in most of Singer's American stories. In the Burgin interview, Singer claims that a writer must acknowledge his roots, or he fails as a writer: "No assimilationist can be a great writer."

Singer's nonassimilated lost souls are often actively in search of a God, while doubting His goodness. They are also frequently in quest of love, of union with a possessed, witchlike woman, a "metaphysical joining of male and female flesh," says Fiedler, "which goes beyond erotic mysticism of the *Zohar* into the realm of heresy." These American stories, like some of their European predecessors, are often preoccupied with forbidden passion, especially incest, and with the interrelationship between the sexual and the sacred. Are these stories of passion perhaps a tribute to his own passionate relationship with Alma, his wife of over four decades? Certainly there is a personal tone in these tales, since they are frequently narrated by a first-person narrator/protagonist, Singer's persona. The tone of this narrator is more often than not ironic, and the irony is occasionally aimed playfully against the narrator himself.

Most of all, Singer is concerned with being a spellbinding storyteller. In his Nobel Prize lecture, he declares that the masterful storyteller "must be an entertainer of the spirit . . . literally [must] intrigue the reader, uplift his spirit, give him the joy and escape that true art always grants." Although Singer is often criticized for being a skeptic or a pessimist, he claims he is, rather, a truth-seeker; in his Nobel lecture he says, "While the poet entertains he continues to search for eternal truths . . . he tries to solve the riddle of time and change, to find an answer to suffering, to reveal love in the very abyss of cruelty and injustice." Noting these words, it is no wonder that love's idealized, redemptive power is central among Singer's literary concerns.

Love, lostness, and a search for faith are all themes of *Enemies, A Love Story*. The protagonist Herman Broder is the epitome of the alienated and disoriented emigré, the "semi-ghost." He is, appropriately, a ghostwriter, producing sermons and essays for a spiritually underdeveloped rabbi. Yet not only is he a ghostwriter but he is also, as Fiedler suggests, literally a "ghost who writes," vanishing at the end of the novel without a trace. His ghostliness seems to have something to do with his being a Holocaust survivor who is haunted by his past. Broder's Holocaust experiences are the main reason for his alienation from American-Jewish society. Edward Alexander notes that Broder's "unease in American Jewish society" may be due to American Jewry's failure to save East European Jews during World War II. Broder's contact with American Jews who have never been touched by the Holocaust inspires him only "with revulsion and a metaphysical disgust at worldly existence." American-Jewish life repels him with its vulgarity and materialism and its incomprehension of the Holocaust survivor's experiences and mentality.

Tormented by recurrent dreams of Nazi horrors, Broder seeks escape through reckless hedonism in an affair with another Holocaust survivor, Masha. His Gentile wife, Yadwiga, cannot be the object of his love. But he knows his empty pursuit of pleasure with Masha must be abandoned as he struggles to form a commitment to God, Torah, and the Talmud. However, his commitment to Judaism is never really affirmed, largely because it cannot be sustained in the insubstantial American-Jewish cultural environment, which, the novel claims, has as its "aim to ape the Gentile." As Alexander aptly surmises, "nothing remains to him [Broder] but a spiritually inconclusive petering out." Ironically, only the Gentile Yadwiga realizes the importance of the Jewish people's preservation. Her giving birth to Broder's child—although Broder does not know it—will, Alexander points out—be "an affirmation that no member of the family of nations shall be removed from the world to satisfy the blood-lust of another member." Fiedler has characterized *Enemies, A Love Story*, especially because of its ending, as an "eminently astonishing, terrifying and satisfactory book."

Most critics agree that it is in the short-story form that Singer really excels. Remarking on Singer's "swift and dramatic" style, Irving Howe and Eliezer Greenberg say, "He is at his best in short forms, exciting bursts and flares of imagination." Singer himself acknowledges that for him the short story is more perfectible and controllable: "A short story is a lot easier to plan, and it can be more perfect, more accomplished, than a novel." Many critics, furthermore, consider his novels as traditional, while reading his short stories, as Alexander suggests, as "modernist excursions into diabolism, perversity, and apocalypse. . . ." Certainly some of these excursions are apparent in the stories which Singer sets in America. Stories selected from two of his collections, *Old Love* (1979) and *Passions and Other Stories* (1975), serve as examples.

As Singer explains in the author's note to *Old Love*, the title *Old Love* comes from a story collected in *Passions* but not republished here; love, Singer continues, is "the only hope of mankind"; the source of all love is "love of life." Three stories in the collection, "A Party in Miami Beach," "There Are No Coincidences," and "The Psychic Journey," explore love among the aging, but the love seems to be perverse, disturbing, entrapping or absurd, hardly reassuring if it is the "only hope of mankind." The stories may, however, suggest the sense of dislocation of European Jews in American society.

"A Party in Miami Beach" is one of Singer's many tales about a Holocaust survivor, only this survivor, Max Flederbush, has become a multimillionaire in America. His wealth no longer brings

Dust jacket for Singer's 1975 collection of twenty stories. In the author's note Singer describes his characters—"the Jews of Eastern Europe, specifically the Yiddish-speaking Jews who perished in Poland and those who emigrated to the U.S.A. The longer I live with them and write about them, the more I am baffled by the richness of their individuality and (since I am one of them) by my own whims and passions."

him solace after he loses his family in an automobile accident. Like Herman Broder, Max wavers between faith and doubt, saying, "Well, but that's how man is—he believes and he doubts." Such an attitude toward religion reflects Singer's own: "Since there is no evidence attesting to what God is, I doubt all the time. Doubt is part of all religion."

The first-person narrator of the story is a much lionized writer, a vegetarian, Singer's persona. Flederbush, an admirer of his, gives a cocktail party in his honor and then treats him to dinner at an elegant restaurant. In the midst of this luxury, however, Flederbush extols the virtues of the concentration camps: "in a certain sense, it's worse here than in the camps. There, at least, we all hoped." He

Singer in Israel, 1970s

contrasts the camp inmates' optimism to the hopelessness and purposelessness of the wealthy retired Miami Beach Jews, who sit around waiting to die.

Somehow Max Flederbush does not really live in Miami Beach. He dwells in the memories of his Holocaust experience, which he relates to the narrator: "three-quarters of a year behind a cellar wall . . . there were six of us men there and one woman." Flederbush says that the woman had sexual relations during this time with her husband and with him, "and she satisfied the others as best as she could," except for the two who turned to homosexuality. Despite his belief that "martyrdom and sex don't mix," Flederbush feels compelled to confess that the Jews of Poland "were people, not angels." While the love shared by the seven people may seem grotesque or even perverted, perhaps it saved their lives. It may have encouraged them to keep their hope, even while they experienced the "whole shame of being human." Flederbush, the narrator, and the narrator's friend who accompanies them to dinner, conclude that hope is what kept the Holocaust victims going; and hope will insure the

survival of the "crazy" Jews for the next ten thousand years. With its atmosphere of futility, however, Miami Beach and its Jewish populace will be underwater by then. The futility of the Miami Beach Jews is what repels Max Flederbush and alienates him from their society.

A similarly unbearable futility invests the atmosphere at a party set in a New York suburb in "There Are No Coincidences." At the party, one woman dominates the conversation with "sentimental claptrap" about her study of living conditions in Sing Sing Prison. The protagonist, another first-person narrator, is bored—this is not a cause to which he can relate. Nor can another guest, a woman who leaves the party when the protagonist does. The two wind up stranded together in this suburb on a miserably stormy night, unable to find a taxi to take them back to Manhattan. They are inexorably drawn together, first by their common reaction to the party—alienation—and then, in a primal sense, by needing one another: "Every degree of warmth was now of utmost value. Like two stray animals, we pressed hard against one another." A sympathetic night watchman provides them with shelter in the cellar of his building, where the two spend the night. They talk of the "guardian angels" in their lives who have saved them from crises, they discuss the difference between coincidences and miracles, and they question fate: "Why should fate continually play cat-and-mouse with a person? Why terrify and then make a last-minute rescue? It's simply that we explain every good coincidence as being a miracle and we blame all the adverse things on blind nature." Finally, they embrace and kiss passionately once. The narrator concludes that they were meant to be drawn together on this lonely night, that there "are no coincidences." Fate had meant them to act like two "idiots," stirred by a passion as electrical as the lightning bolts flashing all around them.

"There Are No Coincidences" thus begins with a mood of isolation in the narrator and ends with the narrator at least temporarily not alone; he is less lonely at the end than Max Flederbush, though like Flederbush, he is still not comfortably a part of any larger group. Moreover, there is no indication at the story's end that the momentary passion between the two is anything more than momentary. The implied question is, why does "fate" bother with such slight feelings at all?

In "The Psychic Journey" the theme of alienation is again pursued, but the male-female relationship that develops in this story appears to be more destructive and frightening than is loneliness. The first-person narrator Morris's encounter, first in New York and then in Israel, with a psychic named Margaret Fugazy develops into a perverse kind of love—on Margaret's part. She claims that meeting him has saved her from "deep crises" in her life, from suicide even. The two become guides for a group tour to Israel. Margaret acts possessive, paranoid, and hysterical when Morris decides to leave the tour in Tel Aviv. She curses him, and he superstitiously fears she is "trying to bring the powers of evil down upon" him. Her hysterical reaction may be understood if Margaret, not the male protagonist, is considered as the figure of alienation and dislocation in this story: "her black eyes exuded the melancholy of those who estrange themselves from their own environment and can never be at home in another." The two part as the Yom Kippur War starts exploding around them—a fit emblem of the explosive and destructive nature of their relationship, and also of Margaret's tormented, "witch-like" personality. "Love" has ultimately done Margaret and the narrator very little good. It has, on the contrary, for its duration created havoc in their lives and alienated them from one another.

Two selected stories from *Passions* similarly treat of passions gone awry and of lost souls. As Singer says, "People are victims of their passions and this makes for a perilous world; but it's equally perilous to be without them." Harry Bendiner, protagonist of the short story "Old Love," is, at age eighty-two, "perilously without" passion in his life. An affluent widower waiting to die in Miami Beach, he has nothing to look forward to until a wealthy younger woman, a widow named Ethel Brokeles, moves into a nearby apartment. They spend a day together and discover that they both have roots in the same Polish *shtetl*—a familiar element of Singer's American writings. They speak freely, even intimately, contemplate marriage, and embrace once. That is the end of their "old love." In the middle of the night Ethel jumps out of a window—to be with her dead husband—and Harry is left to meditate over "why a man is born and why he must die." Harry, like the protagonist of "The Psychic Journey," is left feeling emptier than he did before the meeting. And Ethel's loneliness and despair evidently could not be assuaged by the promise of passion in old age.

Singer at Stockholm's Concert Hall receiving the Nobel Prize from King Carl XVI Gustaf (The Jewish Daily Forward)

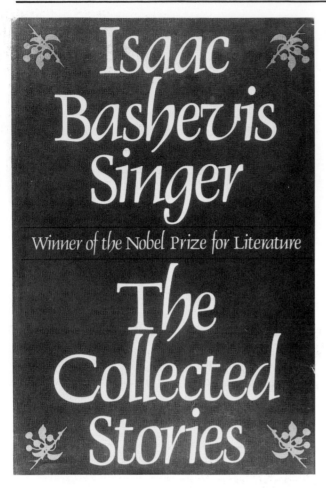

Dust jacket for Singer's 1982 collection of his favorite stories. In the author's note he writes, "It is difficult for me to comment on the choice of the forty-seven stories in this collection, selected from more than a hundred. Like some Oriental father with a harem full of women and children, I cherish them all."

noon together, including several alarming telephone calls from Elizabeth's family, Elizabeth's suffering some kind of fit, and a brief sexual interlude during which the narrator feels attracted to this sick, witchlike woman—another in Singer's long line of demonic females. The narrator seems to be the lover of Elizabeth's fantasies. We learn from the narrator that "every love is irrational" and that "no love of any kind is lost." Perhaps the love depicted in this story is redemptive, reflecting Singer's view of love in his Nobel lecture. Perhaps Elizabeth's love for the narrator has helped her briefly through some of her mental torment. Yet this does not seem the case for the narrator. Although the two never meet again, the narrator seems disturbed and haunted by this woman. She leaves behind in his apartment, and never reclaims, traces of her influence, tokens of their interaction: her umbrella and her grandfather's manuscript. Perhaps the only positive feature of this interaction is that a link has been forged between East European Jewry living in America and American-born Jewry. This link may ease the European Jew's sense of alienation.

This sampling from Singer's American oeuvre consistently reveals his preoccupation with the painful problems of readjustment to American culture experienced by European Jewish émigrés. Perhaps it is also Singer's own way of coping with his profoundly traumatic personal experience of entering American society in 1935. Singer's American tales emerge as a moving tribute to the human being's impulse to link in a meaningful way the precious, familiar, and timeless elements of his past to the dynamic, alien, and often threatening elements of his present and future.

Interviews:

Paul Rosenblatt and Gene Koppel, *A Certain Bridge: Isaac Bashevis Singer on Literature and Life* (Tucson: University of Arizona Press, 1971);

Richard Burgin, "Isaac Bashevis Singer Talks . . . About Everything" and "Isaac Bashevis Singer's Universe," *New York Times Magazine*, 26 November 1978, pp. 24-48, and 3 December 1978, pp. 39-52.

References:

Edward Alexander, *Isaac Bashevis Singer* (Boston: Twayne, 1980);

Irving Buchen, *Isaac Bashevis Singer and the Eternal Past* (New York: New York University Press, 1968);

Leslie Fiedler, "Isaac Bashevis Singer, or the

In "The Admirer" a mentally unstable young woman suffering from, among other things, a miserable marriage, has become a passionate admirer of the protagonist, who is another first-person narrator, a writer by trade and Singer's persona. She is one of the "eccentrics—odd, lost souls" who often visit the narrator. Like many of Singer's lost souls, Elizabeth Abigail de Sollar is trying to find herself and claims the narrator's works have helped her in her search. Like Harry and Ethel, Elizabeth and the narrator talk familiarly and discover they are probably related, her mother and the narrator having come from a Polish town, Klendev, where Elizabeth's grandfather had been the rabbi; both she and the narrator are evidently descended from the Klendev rabbi and from Rabbi Moses Isserles. A complex series of events occurs during their after-

American-ness of the American Jewish
Writer," *Studies in American Jewish Literature*, 1
(1981): 124-131;

Irving Howe, Introduction to *Selected Short Stories of
Isaac Bashevis Singer* (New York: Modern Library, 1966);

Samuel H. Joseloff, "Isaac Bashevis Singer," *Jewish
Spectator* (November 1971): 14-16;

Irving Malin, *Isaac Bashevis Singer* (New York:
Ungar, 1972);

Peter S. Prescott, "Singer the Magician," *Newsweek*,
92 (16 October 1978): 97-98.

Lionel Trilling
(4 July 1905-5 November 1975)

Stephen J. Whitfield
Brandeis University

BOOKS: *Matthew Arnold* (New York: Norton, 1939;
London: Allen & Unwin, 1939; revised edition, New York: Columbia University Press,
1949; London: Allen & Unwin, 1949);

E. M. Forster (Norfolk, Conn.: New Directions,
1943; London: Hogarth, 1944; revised edition, New York: New Directions, 1964; London: Hogarth, 1967);

The Middle of the Journey (New York: Viking, 1947;
London: Secker & Warburg, 1948);

The Liberal Imagination (New York: Viking, 1950;
London: Secker & Warburg, 1951);

The Opposing Self (New York: Viking, 1955; London: Secker & Warburg, 1955);

Freud and the Crisis of Our Culture (Boston: Beacon,
1955);

A Gathering of Fugitives (Boston: Beacon, 1956;
London: Secker & Warburg, 1957);

The Scholar's Caution and the Scholar's Courage (Ithaca,
N.Y.: Cornell University Libraries, 1962);

Beyond Culture (New York: Viking, 1965; London:
Secker & Warburg, 1966);

Sincerity and Authenticity (Cambridge, Mass.: Harvard University Press, 1972; London: Oxford
University Press, 1972);

Mind in the Modern World (New York: Viking, 1973);

The Works of Lionel Trilling, Uniform Edition, 12 volumes (New York & London: Harcourt Brace
Jovanovich, 1977-1980);

Of This Time, of That Place and Other Stories, selected
by Diana Trilling (New York & London: Harcourt Brace Jovanovich, 1979; Oxford: Oxford University Press, 1981);

The Last Decade: Essays and Reviews 1965-75, edited
by Diana Trilling (New York & London: Har-

Lionel Trilling

court Brace Jovanovich, 1979; Oxford: Oxford University Press, 1982);

Prefaces to the Experience of Literature (New York &
London: Harcourt Brace Jovanovich, 1979;
Oxford: Oxford University Press, 1981);

Speaking of Literature and Society, edited by Diana Trilling (New York & London: Harcourt Brace Jovanovich, 1980; Oxford: Oxford University Press, 1982).

OTHER: Henry James, *The Princess Casamassima*, 2 volumes, edited by Trilling (New York: Macmillan, 1948);

Mark Twain, *The Adventures of Huckleberry Finn*, introduction by Trilling (New York & Toronto: Rinehart, 1948);

The Portable Matthew Arnold, edited with an introduction by Trilling (New York: Viking, 1949); republished as *The Essential Matthew Arnold* (London: Chatto & Windus, 1969);

The Selected Letters of John Keats, edited with an introduction by Trilling (New York: Farrar, Straus & Young, 1951);

Leo Tolstoy, *Anna Karenina*, 2 volumes, introduction by Trilling (Cambridge, England: Limited Editions Club at University Press, 1951);

Gustave Flaubert, *Bouvard and Pécuchet*, introduction by Trilling (Norfolk, Conn.: New Directions, 1954);

Irvin Stock, *William Hale White (Mark Rutherford): A Critical Study*, foreword by Trilling (London: Allen & Unwin, 1956; New York: Columbia University Press, 1956);

Selected Short Stories of John O'Hara, introduction by Trilling (New York: Modern Library, 1956);

Jane Austen, *Emma*, introduction by Trilling (Boston: Houghton Mifflin, 1957);

Ernest Jones, *The Life and Works of Sigmund Freud*, edited and abridged by Trilling and Steven Marcus, with an introduction by Trilling (London: Hogarth, 1962);

Saul Bellow, *The Adventures of Augie March*, introduction by Trilling (New York: Modern Library, 1965);

Tess Slesinger, *The Unpossessed*, afterword by Trilling (New York: Avon, 1966);

The Experience of Literature: A Reader with Commentaries, edited by Trilling (New York, Chicago, San Francisco & Toronto: Holt, Rinehart & Winston, 1967);

Isaac Babel, *The Collected Stories*, edited and translated by Walter Morrison, introduction by Trilling (London: Methuen, 1967);

The Broken Mirror: A Collection of Writings from Contemporary Poland, edited by Pawel Mayewski, introduction by Trilling (New York: Random House, 1968);

Literary Criticism: An Introductory Reader, edited with an introduction by Trilling (New York,

Chicago, San Francisco, Atlanta, Dallas, Montreal, Toronto, London & Sydney: Holt, Rinehart & Winston, 1970);

Victorian Prose and Poetry, edited by Trilling and Harold Bloom (New York, London & Toronto: Oxford University Press, 1973).

Among American critics of the twentieth century, Lionel Trilling was especially illuminating, subtle, and wise. His consummate intelligence, which found its most congenial expression in the poise and discernment of his essays, earned an admiration that is likely to endure even if the influence of his particular judgments and opinions were to fade. He was also a minor novelist and writer of short stories.

Born in New York City and educated in the public schools there, Trilling was the son of Orthodox Jewish immigrant parents. His father, David Trilling, was a tailor and a furrier; and his mother, Fannie Cohen Trilling, had been born in England, a country whose culture was to exert a lifelong fascination for Trilling himself. Middle-class in its ideals and aspirations, his family spoke English at home and felt at ease in Gentile society, according to Diana Rubin Trilling, whom he married in 1929. (They were to have one son, James, born in 1948.)

Trilling placed no special emphasis on his Jewish origins, though he later acknowledged his ethnic background as "one of the shaping conditions of my temperament" and would have regarded any effort to disguise his Jewish identity as dishonorable. He resisted the tendency to be classified as a Jewish writer and disclaimed any intention to serve a communal or ethnic purpose. From 1923 until 1931 he was nevertheless a contributor and editorial assistant to the *Menorah Journal*, which under editor Elliot Cohen asserted the vitality and authenticity of Jewish life and culture in the United States. Its circle tended to be nonreligious and non-Zionist, and its writers hoped to foster ethnic pride and the sense of kinship. Trilling himself recalled that the pressure of anti-Semitism helped him and other associates of the *Menorah Journal* to "define ourselves and our society; we could discover who we were and who we wished to be." Such revelations made "society at last available to my imagination" and were important in the formation of his own identity.

As an avid reader since childhood, Trilling had intended to become a novelist, not a critic—a designation which, even when venerated for his interpretive powers, he considered odd. "I do not

Diana Rubin Trilling, 1960s (photo by Jim Theologos). She and Trilling were married in 1929.

say alien, I only say odd," he explained, because fiction appealed to him in its moral rather than its aesthetic dimensions. The twelve volumes of the uniform edition of his works (1977-1980) display little interest in the theory of criticism but much absorption in the complexity of social life that fiction has seemed peculiarly destined to disclose. In 1925 the *Menorah Journal* published Trilling's first short story, "Impediments," describing an encounter between two Jewish undergraduates. Its narrator suffers from a doppelgänger named Hettner, the threatening and unpleasant facet of the self. Their intellectual combat concludes with an insult and a premonition of death, but the defenses of the narrator have not been penetrated.

This slight tale was written when Trilling was a senior at Columbia, the university with which he was to be associated until his death half a century later. He graduated in 1925 and received his master's degree at Columbia the following year; and after teaching briefly at the University of Wisconsin and

at Hunter College, he served as an instructor from 1932 until 1938, when he was awarded his doctorate. Jews were then rare among the Columbia University faculty, and none had ever been permitted to remain in its English department. But the publication of Trilling's dissertation on Matthew Arnold attracted the attention of president Nicholas Murray Butler, who insured the bestowal of tenure upon the instructor whom the English department had intended to dismiss "as a Freudian, a Marxist, and a Jew." The intellectual promise which Butler perceived was to be fulfilled; Trilling became a full professor in 1948, the Woodberry Professor of Literature and Criticism in 1965, and University Professor in 1970. The honorary degrees he received from Harvard, Yale, Northwestern, Brandeis, and other universities in the United States and England were ornaments of a career that prefigured the extinction of academic discrimination against Jews in the humanities and other disciplines.

The elegance of Trilling's critical taste and the vigor of his judgments have overshadowed a pedagogic reputation that was by virtually all accounts brilliant. But he exercised a greater impact as a teacher of literature than as a creator of it; and of his short stories, only "Of This Time, of That Place" (1943) and "The Other Margaret" (1945) have ignited critical engagement. The former tale has an academic setting, recounting the relationship between a fastidious English instructor and poet (Joseph Howe) and two of his students—one (Tertan) an extravagant and intense devotee of philosophy and art who is not clinically sane, the other (Blackburn) a shallow, manipulative but successful opportunist. Part of the design of this concise and memorable story is, according to Trilling himself, the formulaic suggestion "that there are kinds of insanity that society does not accept and kinds of insanity that society does accept." "The Other Margaret," also published in the *Partisan Review*, is less striking and affecting. It is set within a New York family belonging to the urbane and cultivated upper crust, and its title refers to a black domestic with the same name as the progressively educated daughter in the family. The central incident is the maid's deliberate destruction of an objet d'art, an act of perversity which challenges liberal sentimentality and its evasion of the stern requisites of individual responsibility. Without betraying any explicit sympathy for conservative ideology, Trilling tested the limits of liberalism by suggesting to its adherents the pain and squalor of the interior life and the irreducible mysteries of mortal existence. Neither the meaning of tragedy nor the actuality of evil, he believed, could be accommodated to the liberal sensibility. Trilling therefore nominated himself a kind of faculty adviser to progressive Americans, instructing them through his fiction and criticism in the obdurate roughness of the emotional strife lurking beneath the surface of civility.

After World War II, Trilling produced only one other work of fiction, *The Middle of the Journey* (1947). His only novel is set sometime in the twilight years of the romance of American liberals with communism, but its locale is not Spain or even Harlan County but rural Connecticut. There John Laskell, an urban planner whose sudden illness has brought him close to death and whose girl friend has recently died, comes to recuperate at the home of Arthur and Nancy Croom, who have cared for him but who cannot share his effort to extract deeper wisdom from his ordeal. For the Crooms "death was politically reactionary"; it subverts their faith that progressive social forces and an ethic of rational self-control suffice to remedy injustice. Such assurance is further threatened by other characters: Duck Caldwell, an irresponsible local handyman who inadvertently murders his own daughter; and Gifford Maxim, a renegade from the underground Communist apparatus who is ablaze with apocalyptic right-wing passion. In the process of intensifying the awareness of mortality, Laskell, the embodiment of negative capability, comes to understand the inadequacy and even falsity of liberal optimism.

Although *The Middle of the Journey* has attracted admirers, it failed to generate—either in 1947 or later—much enthusiasm. Usually categorized as a political novel, it lacks the pungency of political dialogue and opinions and fails to trace the consequences either of engagement or of detachment. Trilling located himself in opposition to the Stalinism he attributed too widely to the cultivated middle class; and *The Middle of the Journey* has the virtue, in its characterization of Nancy Croom in particular, of defining the temper of the fellow traveler. But almost nothing of the agon of modern politics is registered in the novel. The tepid critical response to the book may be due as well to a treatment of mortality which is distinct from the primary tradition of American fiction. Death therein tends to be violent and sudden, random rather than meditated upon; it occurs not on the Magic Mountain but on Boot Hill. Yet Trilling's eccentricity of aim is not matched by vividness of execution; and it is not unfair to lament the flatness of a book produced by a critic who conceived of fiction as "an especially useful agent of the moral imagination, as the literary form which most directly reveals to us the complexity, the difficulty, and the interest of life in society, and best instructs us in our human variety and contradiction." The author's alter ego, the rather colorless Laskell, is simply not endowed with a voice of sufficient novelistic authority and resonance to affirm such variety and contradiction.

Like "Of This Time, of That Place" and "The Other Margaret," *The Middle of the Journey* incorporates no Jewish characters. In a novel composed out of the intellectual rendezvous with Stalinism, that is like writing a novel about white blues singers. In the 1930s and 1940s, radicalism exerted a special appeal for American Jews, whose immediate antecedents—Trilling's included—were formed in the poverty and bigotry of the doomed Romanov and Hapsburg Empires. Such memories, when combined with the continuing feeling of exclusion and estrangement from American institutions and with the ethical stringency and idealistic yearnings of the Judaic heritage, stimulated in Jewish intellectuals a radical commitment out of proportion to their numbers. Yet the absence of their distinctive disaffection and of their repudiation of "ideas in modulation" vitiates the power of *The Middle of the Journey* to communicate the vise of ideology.

Attuned to the nuances of cultural change, Trilling's writings might be designated as postsocialist. In the moral economy of his fiction, characters like Hettner, Tertan, the other Margaret, Duck Caldwell, and Maxim represent the frenzy and rage that advanced society had been unable to tame, the perversity and meanness that the liberal imagination could neither acknowledge nor assimilate. Haunted by Freud's *Civilization and Its Discontents* rather than by Marx's *Capital*, Trilling consecrated much of his critical writing to weighing the price that civilization exacts. He himself was willing enough to pay that price, but his own appearance hinted at the victory that gentility had won over the instinctual life. "There was immense and even cavernous subtlety to the man," as Alred Kazin portrayed him. "With the deep-sunk colored pouches under his eyes, the cigarette always in hand like an intellectual gesture, [and] an air that combined weariness, vanity, and immense caution," Trilling struck the younger critic as one who "quietly defended himself from the many things he had left behind." In his writing and in his person he conveyed the heroism of the struggle to produce articulate art and to fathom "the moral life in process of revising itself." Under the spell of the psychoanalytic system which he advocated so cogently, Trilling exemplified the triumph of the therapeutic over the allure of radicalism, which is why sociologist Philip Rieff considered him the preeminent "American Jew of culture."

Trilling invested all three terms with ambiguity and paradox. After the 1920s he showed no interest in the patrimony of Judaism and made no effort to quicken the interest of others. Though he never placed himself in an antagonistic relationship to Jewish rights or concerns, he defined himself as an independent intellectual and protested the subjugation of the individual will to any sort of collective purpose. Bereft of religious feelings, Trilling condemned in 1944 the "self-indulgent and self-admiring" nature of organized American Jewry and announced that he could not detect within it "a single voice with the note of authority—of philosophic, or poetic, or even the rhetorical, let alone of religious, authority." The rabbi of Temple Emanu-El nevertheless officiated at his funeral when Trilling died in New York City thirty-one years later.

Not a panoptic critic, he was undoubtedly most at home in British literature, especially of the nineteenth century. His only extensive studies of individual writers were devoted to Arnold and E. M. Forster, who exulted to an American visiting Cambridge: "Your countryman Trilling has made me famous!" The essays on Wordsworth's poetry, on Keats's letters, on *The Princess Casamassima* are among the exemplary performances in the canon of American criticism. But however thoughtful and radiant his analyses of particular texts could be, Trilling's larger importance remains his unrivaled gift for taking such texts as symptomatic. He made

them pivotal to the apprehension of the vicissitudes of culture. Having identified in the 1940s and 1950s the blindness of liberalism without ever doubting his own liberal credentials, Trilling vented in the 1960s his suspicions of modernism itself. He came to doubt what had once sustained him—the moral sovereignty of art, and he addressed the deepening crisis of humanistic learning within a culture that was becoming disconnected from its own past. Yet his readers could be fortified not only by the astuteness of his diagnosis but also by the freshness of Trilling's manner of expression. The mandarin prose, for all the risks it took with circumlocution and euphemism, was charged with grace, precision, resourcefulness, and energy. In his fiction as well as his criticism, as a teacher as well as a man of letters, Trilling remained vigilant in the defense of humanism—a term worn smooth by use which he made lustrous.

References:

Quentin Anderson, Stephen Donadio, and Steven Marcus, eds., *Art, Politics, and Will: Essays in Honor of Lionel Trilling* (New York: Basic, 1977);

Robert Boyers, *Lionel Trilling: Negative Capability and the Wisdom of Avoidance* (Columbia: University of Missouri Press, 1977);

William M. Chace, *Lionel Trilling: Criticism and Politics* (Stanford, Cal.: Stanford University Press, 1980);

Nathan A. Scott, Jr., *Three American Moralists: Mailer, Bellow, Trilling* (Notre Dame, Ind.: University of Notre Dame Press, 1973), pp. 153-225.

Edward Lewis Wallant
(19 October 1926-5 December 1962)

David R. Mesher

BOOKS: *The Human Season* (New York: Harcourt, Brace, 1960; London: Gollancz, 1965);
The Pawnbroker (New York: Harcourt, Brace & World, 1961; London: Gollancz, 1962);
The Tenants of Moonbloom (New York: Harcourt, Brace & World, 1963; London: Gollancz, 1964);
The Children at the Gate (New York: Harcourt, Brace & World, 1964; London: Gollancz, 1964).

OTHER: "I Held Back My Hand," in *New Voices 2: American Writing Today,* edited by Don M. Wolfe (New York: Hendricks House, 1955), pp. 192-201;
"The Man Who Made a Nice Appearance," in *New Voices 3: American Writing Today,* edited by Charles I. Glicksberg (New York: Hendricks House, 1958), pp. 336-353;
"When Ben Awakened," in *American Scene: New Voices,* edited by Wolfe (New York: Lyle Stuart, 1963), pp. 94-100.

PERIODICAL PUBLICATION: "The Artist's Eyesight," *Teacher's Notebook in English* (Fall 1963).

Edward Lewis Wallant (photo by Bob Anthony)

When Edward Lewis Wallant died of a stroke resulting from a cerebral aneurysm in 1962, at the age of thirty-six, he had been a published novelist for less than three years and a writer of serious fiction for little more than twice that. Yet Wallant had already gained recognition as one of the most important figures among postwar Jewish writers in the United States. His first published novel, *The Human Season* (1960), received the Daroff Memorial Fiction Award for the best novel of the year on a Jewish theme—an award since renamed for Wallant. His next work, *The Pawnbroker* (1961), a treatment of the Holocaust, firmly established Wallant as a major literary talent. Remarkably, Wallant's two posthumously published novels, *The Tenants of Moonbloom* (1963) and *The Children at the Gate* (1964), revealed their author's stark departure from the formula of his early successes, anticipating developments that have subsequently taken place in American-Jewish literature.

The accomplishment his work exhibits almost from the start may, in part, be attributed to his relative maturity as a novice writer: Wallant was nearly thirty when he began taking writing workshops that marked a shift of emphasis in his continuing interest in art and literature and soon led to the first publication of his stories. Wallant, the son of Sol Ellis and Ann Mendel Wallant, was born in 1926 in New Haven, Connecticut, where he grew up; during high school and later, he discovered his flair for writing and illustrating stories, but gradually concentrated on the latter talent. After sandwiching service in the U.S. Navy during World War II, as a gunner's mate in Europe, between two

310

semesters at the University of Connecticut, one each in 1944 and 1946, Wallant began studying draftsmanship at New York's Pratt Institute in 1947. The following year he married Joyce Fromkin. Upon graduating from Pratt Institute in 1950, he worked as a commercial artist in a series of four New York advertising agencies, eventually advancing to the position of an art director at McCann, Erickson. Wallant commuted to Madison Avenue from New Rochelle and, later, from Norwalk, Connecticut, where he and his wife raised a family of one son and two daughters.

Throughout his period as a commercial artist, Wallant retained the habit of voracious if unsystematic reading which he had acquired in his youth, and in 1951 he took an adult-education course in modern American literature at Hunter College. In his only published memoir, a brief but revealing piece entitled "The Artist's Eyesight" (1963) written shortly before his death, Wallant traces his developing tastes in fiction from Edgar Wallace, Howard Pease, and Edgar Rice Burroughs, through Twain, Defoe, and Dickens, to Sherwood Anderson, John Dos Passos, Thomas Wolfe, and, finally, Ernest Hemingway, all by age seventeen. Hemingway was later eclipsed by such writers as F. Scott Fitzgerald, Sinclair Lewis, Willa Cather, and the Russian writers of the nineteenth century, especially Dostoevski.

Wallant's love of reading was fostered by the conditions of his childhood. In "The Artist's Eyesight" he recalls how "books were part of my initiation into the magic of projection; with them I first learned to leave a sick-bed, escape a lonely house walled in by rain, transcend the solitude of a summer afternoon." The mood of this recollection accords well with the characterizations of Wallant's young protagonists: alone to the point of loneliness, isolated to the point of alienation, seeking imagined escapes. Such a character is Max Faibling, in Wallant's first published story, "I Held Back My Hand" (1955): the quintessential outsider with a passion for acting and writing plays, and creating "games of make believe in which he was the victim." Max is seen from the outside, through the eyes of a former friend, and the story is not so much Max's tragedy as that of the lasting effect Max's sad fate has on the narrator. Try as he might to overcome his sense of Max's strangeness, the narrator cannot extend to Max human sympathy at a crucial moment and is haunted by this failure into adulthood.

One of the major factors contributing to this concern for youthful alienation was the death of his father when Wallant was still a child. The insecurity

of a fatherless boy figures largely in both *The Children at the Gate* and *The Tenants of Moonbloom*, while its reverse, the depression endured by a father whose only son has died, is mirrored in both of the earlier published novels, *The Human Season* and *The Pawnbroker*. The situation is even more autobiographical in Wallant's first attempt at longer fiction, the unpublished "Tarzan's Cottage." This lengthy, unevenly written tale centers for the most part on Freddie Bussman and his father, Martin. The latter, like Wallant's own father, has contracted tuberculosis after being gassed in World War I and finally dies from the disease. The last scene of the novel, in which Freddie lets "himself be held back from his father" at Martin's deathbed, locates the emotional atrophy from which so many of Wallant's characters suffer in the blocked or failed relationship between father and son.

Wallant's mother never remarried, and he was brought up by her and two of his aunts. Though his family was not observant, Wallant seems to have received the minimal Jewish education usual in America: Sunday school and preparation for the ceremony of bar mitzvah, which, according to his widow, he did celebrate. As in other spheres, most of Wallant's knowledge of things Jewish was garnered secondhand as an adult, from his reading and from people around him. Wallant remembered listening to the stories of his Russian-born grandfather, material that no doubt found its way into the flashbacks of Jewish life in the Ukraine in *The Human Season*. According to Dan Wickenden, his editor at Harcourt, Brace, Wallant also had a close friend who had survived the death camps and may have related details relevant to scenes in *The Pawnbroker*. Indeed, it should be noted that the first two published novels are to a great extent constructed vicariously, from the experiences of others: *The Human Season* is dedicated to the memory of Mae Fromkin, Wallant's mother-in-law, whose husband was a plumber and the model for the characterization of the novel's bereaved protagonist, Joseph Berman; and, again according to Wickenden, Wallant spent time in the Harlem pawnshop of a relative, making observations of pertinence to *The Pawnbroker*. The importance to Wallant of these individuals—a storytelling grandfather, a father-in-law who lost his wife, a friend who survived the Holocaust, a pawnbroking relative—can be overrated, but Wallant's apparent need at this stage of his career, to focus his art on external points of reference, is more noteworthy. In his later writings, Wallant shifted focus more and more directly onto himself. The protagonists of the

The
Human
Season
a
novel
by
Edward
Lewis
Wallant

Dust jacket for Wallant's first published novel, which he dedicated to the memory of his mother-in-law Mae Fromkin. Her husband served as the model for Wallant's bereaved protagonist Joseph Berman.

final novels are both, like their author, fatherless sons; like Angelo DeMarco in *The Children at the Gate,* Wallant worked as a youth in a New Haven pharmacy across the street from a Catholic hospital, where he made deliveries; and while working on *The Tenants of Moonbloom,* Wallant moved briefly into a New York tenement, in October 1961, making notes about the conditions and residents in a bound ledger that is preserved with the rest of his papers.

Yet it would be wrong to overemphasize the autobiographical element in Wallant's fiction. Most of the images of him as isolated, introverted, or introspective relate to his childhood and youth; his mature life was by all accounts quite different. Wallant was characterized by a lively disposition and an affirmative outlook, which are glimpsed only rarely in his writing, notably at the end of his last novel, *The Tenants of Moonbloom.* Though his work as a commercial artist may not have offered the emotional

stimulation and aesthetic satisfaction he desired, Wallant was talented and successful. Eager for another artistic outlet, Wallant was excited about his new vocation as a writer long before his first works were published. After a full day of work, he attended writing workshops at the New School for Social Research in 1954 and 1955; there he studied under Don M. Wolfe and Charles I. Glicksberg, and his stories later appeared in anthologies of new writing which they edited. At home, Wallant composed fictions of loss and loneliness on the kitchen table, in the midst of his young and boisterous family.

Wallant's first attempt at a novel, the ungainly "Tarzan's Cottage," won him limited encouragement from Harcourt, Brace after having been flatly rejected by several other publishers. Within a year, Wallant submitted two manuscripts together to the publisher: another long, clumsy work entitled "The Odyssey of a Middleman," about the failure of a would-be artist; and a short novel which was quickly accepted and published in 1960 as *The Human Season.* The publication of *The Pawnbroker* the following year brought Wallant immediate critical recognition, a measure of popular success, and, among other honors, a Guggenheim Fellowship which allowed him to resign from his position at McCann, Erickson. Wallant spent the summer of 1962 traveling in Europe with his family and had planned to remain abroad longer after his wife's departure with the children for school in Norwalk, but he returned in the early fall as the Cuban missile crisis deepened. Most of his time in Europe was spent in Italy and Spain, and Wickenden remembers Wallant describing these countries in terms that might be applied to Wallant's writing, comedy and tragedy: "Italy was a comic-opera country, I was never scared there. Spain was a tragic country, and the whole time I was there I was scared." Though he claimed to have preferred the Spanish tragedy, in his fiction Wallant was turning increasingly to comedy. Before leaving for Europe, he had again submitted two manuscripts simultaneously, *The Children at the Gate* and *The Tenants of Moonbloom.* His editors at Harcourt, Brace requested extensive rewriting of the former and minor revisions in the latter. Wallant took both to work on while abroad.

When he returned in the fall of 1962, Wallant had completed work only on *The Tenants of Moonbloom.* Though it is essentially the earlier novel, with its first drafts finished before *The Tenants of Moonbloom* was begun, *The Children at the Gate* was received by Harcourt, Brace after Wallant's death in a version still requiring extensive editing. Wallant first noted symptoms of his illness in Europe, but examinations he underwent back in America failed to diagnose the disorder accurately. Indeed, Wallant's doctors may have complicated his condition by treating him for a suspected brain tumor. Nevertheless, Wallant continued to pursue an active schedule until the last week of his life, when rupture of the undetected aneurysm led to a stroke, coma, and death.

Despite the apparent paucity of his Jewish background—confirmed occasionally by errors in Jewish law or Hebrew or Yiddish—Wallant's first novel displays a higher degree of Jewish content and a greater depth of involvement in Jewish life than are to be found in work from the same period by more celebrated authors. Recent Jewish history, including life in the Pale of Settlement and the immigrant experience in America, provides the content of many of the main character's memories. Joseph Berman and his wife may replace traditional Jewish rituals with their own, but they never repudiate them; and the sense of such traditions and rituals is strong throughout the novel, culminating in Berman's final affirmation—"It *is* enough!"—a clear if subtle echo of the Hebrew *Dyanu* he has sung earlier when faced with anti-Semitism in America. Berman is also a modern Job, who discerns in the midst of his argument with God that no one is listening: the biblical comparison is not a cliché, but a parallel which Wallant skillfully develops into an underlying resonance, at times specifically referring to the biblical book. Not all the references to Job should be traced to the biblical source, however, for *The Human Season* is also Wallant's most consciously literary work. Berman's initials are the same as those of the title character in Archibald MacLeish's modernization of the Job drama, *J. B.* (1958), and there are other citations from MacLeish's work in the novel—including Wallant's title, from MacLeish's poem "Immortal Autumn." The novel's working title, "A Scattering on the Dark," derives from MacLeish's "Einstein" and is to be found within the novel in a description of the photograph of Berman's dead son; in one draft of the novel, Wallant used an epigraph from "Einstein."

Wallant also makes ample use of Berman's profession as a plumber to introduce an overwhelming sense of defilement, a resonant vocabulary of scatology, and a remarkable system of water imagery. More important than scatology of biblical and literary allusions, however, is the introduction of two central motifs in Wallant's art: the special relationship between father and son, and the au-

thor's construct of a "human season"—a period of weeks or months of extreme sensitivity and pain which irreversibly alters each of his main protagonists. Though Berman's wife has just died, it is his son's much earlier death in the war with which he must finally come to terms during the summer of the novel.

Like *The Human Season,* Wallant's second novel, *The Pawnbroker,* mixes an American narrative present—the life of Sol Nazerman, an immigrant Jewish pawnbroker in Harlem—with flashbacks from modern Jewish history: Nazerman's dreams and memories of the Holocaust. In locating such vivid, overpowering scenes of the destruction of European Jewry at the heart of his novel, Wallant confronts the most terrifying fact of modern existence and, in doing so, precedes by nearly a decade the great explosion of Holocaust novels written by American Jews in the late 1960s and 1970s. The criticism of *The Pawnbroker,* that its implicit comparison of the Nazis' Jewish victims with the blacks in Harlem tends to reduce the Holocaust to everyday dimensions, is partially valid and identifies the novel's central weakness; but such a view also misunderstands that the presentation of those very different horrors operates on two separate scales as a metaphor, and it ignores the significance of the novel as an early step in American-Jewish writing about the Holocaust.

The Pawnbroker is set on two very different stages: one, contemporary America, from the destitution of Harlem where Nazerman runs his pawnshop to the smug comfort of suburban Mount Vernon where he lives with his sister's family; and two, the Holocaust, recreated in Nazerman's thought and nightmares. This novel's "human season" is shorter—only a few weeks leading up to the anniversary of the Nazis' destruction of Nazerman's family. Nazerman has survived the death camp physically but not emotionally. Near the end, forcing himself not merely to survive but to bear witness to the atrocities, Nazerman dons "a pair of spectacles" which brings "the whole vast spectacle" of death "into horrid clarity." Wallant's wordplay emphasizes Nazerman's glasses as a symbol of vision, but later they become opaque shields, symbols of his indifference. In America, Nazerman sacrifices his own conscience for physical and material security in accepting the gangster's proposition which sets him up as a pawnbroker. As the novel begins, those lenses are moral blinders for his "glass-covered eyes."

The novel traces the pawnbroker's rebirth into human sensitivity from this depth of moral apathy.

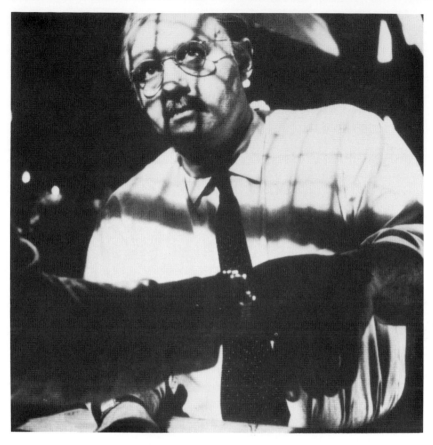

Rod Steiger in the 1965 film The Pawnbroker, *based on Wallant's second novel*

Many of the stages of that rebirth relate to incidents from the pawnbroker's memories, with important alterations: the barrel of a pistol stuck in Nazerman's mouth on the orders of his gangster "partner" recreates the scene in which Nazerman watches as his wife is forced to perform fellatio on a Nazi officer; and when Jesus Ortiz saves the life of Nazerman, his surrogate father, at the cost of his own, the novel has come full circle from the first italicized flashback, in which Sol is unable to save his own son David—indeed, is seemingly unwilling even to try. Yet Wallant achieves more than artistic symmetry in *The Pawnbroker*. Beginning with an imaginable horror—the despair and deprivation of Harlem—Wallant manages to suggest an incredible one—the Holocaust. Against such a background, Nazerman's emotional resurrection, limited as it seems to be, is a powerful expression of the author's ultimate faith in humanity.

The Pawnbroker has often been compared to Saul Bellow's *Mr. Sammler's Planet* (1970), another novel focusing on an isolated Jewish survivor of the Holocaust living in New York City and forced to confront atrocities in both his past and his present. Wallant's last two novels similarly anticipated developments in later novels by writers such as Bellow and Bernard Malamud, though this has received less critical comment. Between the writing of *The Pawnbroker* and *The Children at the Gate* Wallant began to focus more sharply on his own experiences, on fatherless sons in place of the sonless fathers, the spiritual descendants of Jesus Ortiz, not Sol Nazerman, who learn to avoid the latter's solemn pessimism. That shift of focus comprises other components as well. One is Wallant's discovery of humor as a narrative strategy. The laughter is perhaps a little forced in *The Children at the Gate,* where the final joke is the gruesome suicide by which Sammy Kahan teaches Angelo DeMarco to love life; but humor, not suffering, is the medium of instruction. In fact, the problems of this novel—Wallant's weakest—derive in large part from the forced, strident brand of comedy which Sammy affects. In a variation on the relationship between Sol Nazerman and Jesus Ortiz in *The Pawnbroker,* Sammy is a slightly older Jewish orderly at a hospital, where the young Catholic Angelo makes deliveries for a pharmacy; Sammy's suicide, like Jesus' death, is the ultimate lesson in humanity, following a series of incidents both at home and at the hospital which harden Angelo's cynicism. But Wallant's emphasis on the grotesque burdens the novel with a sense of bleakness which its questionable humor does little to dispel. Angelo laughs at Sammy's dying joke and learns to cry by the novel's end; but the reader experiences nothing like that range of emotions.

The humor is not only funnier but humane and genuine in *The Tenants of Moonbloom.* The concluding scene, in which Norman Moonbloom's laughter somehow seems to salve and almost explain his own pain and that of his fellow victims of life, represents a remarkable climax to Wallant's career. "Thick brown liquid" cascades on Norman from faulty plumbing in a description that is not all that removed from the imagery of Wallant's first novel, *The Human Season.* Norman is the consummate example of Wallant's fatherless sons. As manager of his brother's decaying apartment houses, the insulated Norman is slowly freed from his emotional swaddling of apathy and naiveté by close contact with the large cast of rather singular tenants. He begins as an ironic Cartesian: "his dream was an infinite series of reflections and all he could be sure of was that it existed and made him sure that *he* existed." Though Norman tries to avoid human contact with his tenants, after only the first round of collections "a tiny mark showed on the shell of his consciousness"—a shell cracked wide open by the end. In different apartments, Norman experiences the variety of love, hate, life, and death. He loses his virginity with a woman whose father is so blind to her flaws that he can look at the couple in flagrante delicto and only mutter to Norman that his daughter is pure as "driven snow." Norman learns to see through the artificiality of one couple's pornographic relationship, another couple's innocence that approaches unconsciousness, a nephew's playacting with his maiden aunts, the soft lighting in the flat of aged lovers, the passions of played-out musicians and a burned-out English teacher, the swinging life of a lonely woman; and he learns of the necessity for such pretenses in Sugarman the candy butcher's trinity of survival, "Courage, Love, and Illusion." Here, too, Wallant introduces the grotesque, but in *The Tenants of Moonbloom* he softens it with sympathy. And the insistent Christ imagery of *The Children at the Gate,* where Sammy walks on the water he is mopping and dies by mock crucifixion, has been exchanged for a more profitable and sub-

tle Grail: Norman, who writes "Astolat" in the dust of his office and wears a Red Cross pin, embarks on a crusade to repair his blighted realm, accompanied on his quest by the black janitor Gaylord Knight. And Norman's quest succeeds well beyond those of Wallant's other heroes when, at the end of the novel as a wall explodes in a shower of "vile and odorous viscosity," Norman shouts, "I'M BORN." Indeed he is—born into the endless possibilities of love and pain that are life.

In his earlier novels, Wallant explored the possibilities of victim literature, a dominant trend in American fiction following World War II, excellent examples of which are Bellow's *The Victim* (1947) and Malamud's *The Assistant* (1957). But in his later work, Wallant recognized the shortcomings of such a literature and turned from suffering to laughter as his central expression of the human condition. In so doing, Wallant foresaw a general reassessment that would subsequently include Bellow's *Herzog* (1964), in which the title character announces that he is "not going to be a victim. I hate the victim bit," and Malamud's *The Fixer* (1966), in which the title character comes to the conclusion that "what suffering has taught me is the uselessness of suffering." *The Tenants of Moonbloom* was one of the first novels to challenge the pervasive but limited metaphor of the Jew as victim and sufferer in American-Jewish literature and to enlarge upon it with humor.

Not all of Wallant's experiments and innovations proved as successful. The shift of focus in the middle of his career also diminished the Jewish content of his fiction. Though in both of the last novels main characters like Sammy Kahan and Norman Moonbloom are Jewish, their Jewishness is no longer an integral part of their characterizations, and Jewish history and traditions no longer contribute as significantly to the subject matter or themes. In a seemingly concomitant development, Wallant's Christ imagery escalates as the Jewish content declines. Use of the Christian myth is a common enough feature of American-Jewish fiction generally, as it is of all Western literatures. Wallant's employment of the myth is conspicuous in his first two novels, especially in *The Pawnbroker*, in which a character named Jesus imaginatively replaces the crucified figure with that of his own father, first, and then of Nazerman himself. And not only does the pawnbroker's last name have a Nazarene ring, but his first name and those of his family—Sol, David, Naomi, and Ruth—all derive from the biblical House of David, from which the messiah is to come. Subtly crafted, as in *The Pawnbroker,* such imagery enriches Wallant's art immensely; overdone, as in *The Children at the Gate,* the same allusions become as importunate as the strident humor of that novel. It seems hardly coincidental that *The Children at the Gate* is at once Wallant's worst published novel and his least Jewish.

　　None of this can detract from the very real accomplishments of all Wallant's work. All of the novels show a singular blending of American and Jewish themes and archetypes. The confidence man, for instance, that most American of frauds, reappears in various guises throughout all of the author's fiction, and the con artist's game becomes a metaphor for the author's art. Indeed, the artist and the con artist are often related in Wallant's work. And there is an important shift in Wallant's use of the confidence man in the early and later novels: he is the oily Kivarnik of *The Human Season* and Murillo the gangster in *The Pawnbroker*; but he assumes a more positive aspect in Sammy Kahan of *The Children at the Gate* and a beneficent one in *The Tenants of Moonbloom* as Sugarman and his disciple, Norman. That, after all, is the point of "illusion" in Sugarman's trinity of survival—to con yourself and others into well-being, an illusion Norman succeeds in creating. In Wallant's best works—*The Pawnbroker* and *The Tenants of Moonbloom*—the variety of humanity portrayed makes urban American society, as much as any single character, the central figure. Such achievements give Edward Lewis Wallant's fiction a stature and significance far beyond what might be expected of the four slim volumes to which it was limited.

References:

Jonathan Baumbach, "The Illusion of Indifference," in his *The Landscape of Nightmare: Studies in the Contemporary American Novel* (New York: New York University Press, 1965), pp. 138-151;

David Galloway, *Edward Lewis Wallant* (Boston: Twayne, 1979);

Robert W. Lewis, "The Hung-Up Heroes of Edward Lewis Wallant," *Renascence*, 24, no. 2 (1972): 70-84;

Thomas M. Lorch, "The Novels of Edward Lewis Wallant," *Chicago Review*, 19, no. 2 (1967): 78-91;

David R. Mesher, "Con Artist and Middleman: The Archetypes of Wallant's Published and Unpublished Fiction," *Yale University Library Gazette*, 56, nos. 1-2 (1981): 40-49.

Papers:

All of Wallant's unpublished writings and drafts of his published novels are housed in the American Literature Collection of the Beinecke Rare Book and Manuscript Library, Yale University.

Jerome Weidman
(4 April 1913-)

Edith Blicksilver
Georgia Institute of Technology

BOOKS: *I Can Get It For You Wholesale* (New York: Simon & Schuster, 1937; London: Heinemann, 1938);

What's In It for Me? (New York: Simon & Schuster, 1938; London & Toronto: Heinemann, 1939);

The Horse That Could Whistle "Dixie" and Other Stories (New York: Simon & Schuster, 1939; London & Toronto: Heinemann, 1941);

Letter of Credit (New York: Simon & Schuster, 1940);

I'll Never Go There Anymore (New York: Simon & Schuster, 1941; London & Toronto: Heinemann, 1942);

The Lights Around the Shore (New York: Simon & Schuster, 1943; London: Hale, 1948);

Too Early to Tell (New York: Reynal & Hitchcock, 1946);

The Captain's Tiger (New York: Reynal & Hitchcock, 1949);

The Price Is Right (New York: Harcourt, Brace, 1949; London: Hammond, 1950);

The Hand of the Hunter (New York: Harcourt, Brace, 1951; London: Cape, 1952);

The Third Angel (Garden City: Doubleday, 1953; London: Cape, 1954);

Give Me Your Love (New York: Eton, 1954);

Jerome Weidman (photo by Mary Morris Lawrence)

Your Daughter, Iris (Garden City: Doubleday, 1955; London: Cape, 1956);

A Dime A Throw (Garden City: Doubleday, 1957);

Fiorello!, book by Weidman and George Abbott, music and lyrics by Sheldon Harnick and Jerry Bock (New York: French, 1957);

The Enemy Camp (New York: Random House, 1958; London: Heinemann, 1959);

Before You Go (New York: Random House, 1960; London: Heinemann, 1961);

Tenderloin, book by Weidman and Abbott, music and lyrics by Harnick and Bock (New York: Random House, 1961);

My Father Sits in the Dark and Other Selected Stories (New York: Random House, 1961; London: Heinemann, 1963);

I Can Get It For You Wholesale, book by Weidman, music and lyrics by Harold Rome (New York: Random House, 1962);

The Sound of Bow Bells (New York: Random House, 1962; London: Heinemann, 1963);

Back Talk (New York: Random House, 1963);

Word of Mouth (New York: Random House, 1964; London: Bodley Head, 1965);

Where the Sun Never Sets and Other Stories (London: Heinemann, 1964);

The Death of Dickie Draper and Nine Other Stories (New York: Random House, 1965);

Other People's Money (New York: Random House, 1967; London: Bodley Head, 1967);

Ivory Tower, by Weidman and James Yaffe (New York: Dramatists Play Service, 1969);

The Mother Lover (New York: Dramatists Play Service, 1969);

Asterisk! A Comedy of Terrors (New York: Dramatists Play Service, 1969);

The Center of the Action (New York: Random House, 1969; London: Bodley Head, 1970);

Fourth Street East (New York: Random House, 1970; London: Bodley Head, 1970);

Last Respects (New York: Random House, 1972; London: Bodley Head, 1972);

Tiffany Street (New York: Random House, 1974; London: Bodley Head, 1974);

The Temple (New York: Simon & Schuster, 1975; London: Bodley Head, 1976);

A Family Fortune (New York: Simon & Schuster, 1978; London: Bodley Head, 1978);

Counselors-at-Law (Garden City: Doubleday, 1980; London: Bodley Head, 1981).

PLAYS: *Fiorello!*, book by Weidman and George Abbott, music and lyrics by Sheldon Harnick and Jerry Bock, New York, Broadhurst Theatre, 23 November 1959;

Tenderloin, book by Weidman and Abbott, music and lyrics by Harnick and Bock, New York, Forty-sixth Street Theatre, 17 October 1960;

I Can Get It for You Wholesale, book by Weidman, music by Harold Rome, New York, Shubert Theatre, 22 March 1962;

Cool Off!, book by Weidman, music by Howard Blackman, Philadephia, Forrest Theatre, 31 March 1964;

Pousse-Café, book by Weidman, music by Duke Ellington, New York, Forty-sixth Street Theatre, 18 March 1966;

Ivory Tower, by Weidman and James Yaffe, Ann Arbor, Michigan, 1968;

The Mother Lover, New York, Booth Theatre, 1 February 1969;

Asterisk! A Comedy of Terrors, New York, 1969.

SCREENPLAYS: *The Damned Don't Cry*, screenplay by Weidman and Harold Medford, Warner Bros., 1950;

The Eddie Cantor Story, screenplay by Weidman, Ted Sherdeman, and Sidney Skolsky, Warner Bros., 1953;

Slander, M-G-M, 1957.

TELEVISION: *The Reporter* [series], created by Weidman, CBS, 1964.

OTHER: *The W. Somerset Maugham Sampler*, edited by Weidman (Garden City: Garden City Publishing, 1943);

Traveler's Cheque, edited by Weidman (Garden City: Doubleday, 1954);

The First College Bowl Question Book, edited by Weidman and others (New York: Random House, 1961).

PERIODICAL PUBLICATIONS: "Some Important Fall Authors Speak for Themselves: Jerome Weidman," *New York Herald Tribune Book Review*, 11 October 1953, pp. 8, 22;

"How I Became a Connecticut Yankee," *Holiday* (September 1959): 34-47, 128, 131-133;

"Jerome Weidman: A Self-Portrait," *Esquire*, 58 (September 1962): 115.

"To be the child of immigrants from Eastern Europe," Delmore Schwartz has written, "is in itself a special kind of experience; and an important one to an author." Novelist, playwright, short-story writer, and essayist, Jerome Weidman bears witness to the moral and cultural influences of his childhood on New York's Lower East Side, where, Weidman recalled years later, there were "two cultures at war with each other"—the immigrant sensibility shared by almost everyone over the age of thirty and the sense of dislocation shared by their first-generation American children. He heard two languages throughout his childhood, one spoken with ease in the home, the other spoken by young Weidman in the streets and at school but spoken poorly by his parents. Drawing upon that duality and upon a heightened sensitivity to the nuances of dialect and character, he has created an impressive canon of fiction and drama that explores the complexities of emotional motives.

Born in 1913 to Joseph and Annie Falkovitz Weidman—his father an Austrian immigrant, his mother from Hungary—Weidman never spoke a word of English until he was five. A sense of shared traditions, secular and cultural identity-seeking, the generation gap, intermarriage, stereotypes fashioned by a hostile Gentile world, the ruthlessness of clawing one's way out of the urban ghetto, the material comforts obtained through success, and the price paid for their possession are the themes that have preoccupied first-generation American-Jewish writers. Weidman has fashioned stories that reflect this perception of the American experience,

blending the tonalities of New York with a Yiddish flavor and a rhythmic English dialogue.

The author's debt to his ethnic roots is extremely important: "My religion has influenced my work enormously," he admits. "All my characters are Jews even when I write them as Gentiles. This may seem contradictory, but . . . I cannot make a character come alive unless I step into his or her shoes and write as though I am writing about myself, and I cannot make this absolutely essential step except as a Jewish boy from East Fourth Street, regardless of what age I may be at the time I am writing a story. I have never written a line unless it dealt with some real experience I've had. I've changed the names, of course, but my biography is in my novels and stories."

In 1927 Weidman won a *New York Times* oratorical contest and spent the fifty-dollar prize on a typewriter. He studied at City College, 1931-1933, at New York University, 1933-1934, and worked as a newsboy, soda jerk, mail clerk, stenographer, and accountant. He was studying law at New York University when his first novel, *I Can Get It For You Wholesale* (1937), was published depicting the seamier aspects of the New York garment industry. The novel chronicles Harry Bogen's rise from fifteen-dollar-a-week clerk to successful manufacturer. Unable to find happiness with his devoted mother's cultural traditions or with the pretty neighborhood girl, he seeks diamonds and cars, and pursues the actress Martha Mills. "Anything money can't buy, I don't want" is his motto. Harry becomes a ruthless villain, and Weidman's swift-paced, savage indictment of unscrupulously ambitious men brought him success at the age of twenty-four. He abandoned his law career and devoted all his time to writing.

The critical response to *I Can Get It For You Wholesale* was overwhelmingly favorable. The *Philadelphia Record* compared Weidman's style with that of Faulkner's *Soldier's Pay*, and the *New York Times* paid tribute to the author's skill in creating believable characters: he "knows his subject about as well as Ernest Hemingway knew the Paris cafes, James M. Cain the postman who always rang twice, John O'Hara the life and death of Julian English." Marc Connelly admitted that he read the book "at one sitting," while Arthur Kober concluded that Weidman "doesn't write with his fingers—he pounds with his fists."

The *New York Herald Tribune* was impressed with the novel's ethical attributes: the book's "morality is vivid because it is so dramatically abused by its narrator, Harry Bogen, who is more pathetic than

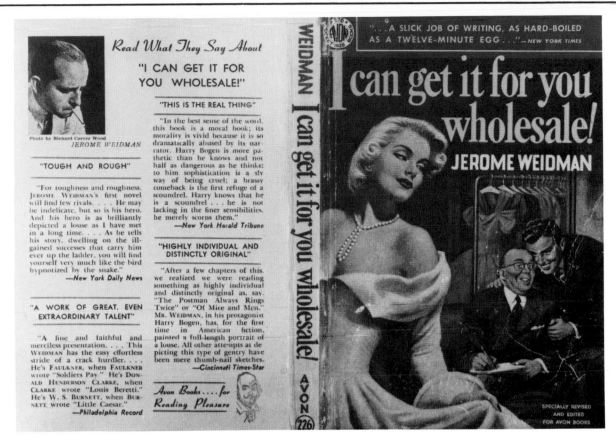

Cover for the first paperback printing of Weidman's first novel

he knows and not half as dangerous as he thinks. The story . . . is a crescendo of mockery." Ironically, this unscrupulous cloak-and-suiter's story depicts Jewish characters so repulsive to some that the publisher temporarily ceased printing the book in 1938.

But the novel was so popular that Weidman wrote a sequel, *What's In It for Me?* (1938)—which is exactly what Harry Bogen's egocentric life-style implied. In this novel once again Weidman shows the motives, reasoning process, and techniques of a clever scoundrel completely lacking in sensibilities, never able to perceive that he is an unsavory human being. Weidman delineates Bogen as a man unable to love, capable only of using people. The sequel concludes with this ruthless creature in lonely isolation.

In 1943 Weidman married Elizabeth Ann Payne Wright: "I cannot conceive of having written anything in the last forty-one years unless I had been married to her." They have two sons. During World War II, Weidman served with the U.S. Office of War Information, and he used his experiences in his satiric novel on propaganda techniques, *Too Early to Tell* (1946), and in several short stories.

The main concern of the novelist "is the labyrinth in which are concealed the secret chambers of the human heart," wrote Weidman in the introduction to his 1963 book of travel essays, *Back Talk*, admitting that he started writing short stories because he wanted to write novels, but he soon realized that the technique of the well-made novel differs radically from that of the short story. He began developing outlines headed by a one-sentence central idea, the point of the story he wanted to create. Beneath it he listed numerically the incidents observed or invented to illustrate his point, thrashing out problems of plot and structure. Regardless of what "brilliant turn of phrase" tempted him into "ornate digressions, and embroidered bypaths," he stuck to the outline, finding that the finished stories resembled closely those he had in mind.

In several scenes in Weidman's short narrative tale collections—*The Horse That Could Whistle "Dixie"* (1939), *The Captain's Tiger* (1949), *My Father Sits in the Dark* (1961), *The Death of Dickie Draper* (1965)—the reader is taken back to the author's origins. Many of the short stories utilize Eastern

European folk traditions and rituals associated with the cycle-of-life motif. Weidman has a sharp sense of the way in which the profound and the mundane exist parallel in our daily lives, and he is imaginative in his use both of traditional Jewish materials and of his modern renditions of them. Frequently, he writes about a strong-willed individual breaking free of environmental restrictions, and he is at his best in his shorter works when he evokes, often with a kind of tender tolerance as well as a biting fierceness, the reality encountered by the immigrant Jews and their Americanized children in the urban ghetto. The young son in the short story "My Father Sits in the Dark" wonders why this elderly man sits without the need for lights in the room, but realizes finally that the transplanted Austrian does not have to "see" the scenes of the past. He listens to his inner voices transporting him back to his boyhood Old World village. *Fourth Street East* (1970) is a touching autobiographical novel detailing events that befell a boy growing up in the early years of the twentieth century on New York's immigrant Lower East Side.

In many of Weidman's works characters are successful at first, but later defeated if they sacrifice their integrity to achieve financial rewards. Some of his protagonists are unable to see beyond an adolescent desire to gain power and wealth. They fail to understand, sometimes until it is too late, that there is no human resonance in that ambition and no outlet for the better qualities they possess. The contrast between the security of the home, fortified by parental love in spite of family quarrels, and the tensions of the world outside it, the economic and psychological dislocations caused by the Depression, are all sketched with painstaking accuracy.

Weidman is especially skilled in telling the Semitic dream of Eden, about Jews who fled from the European pogroms with thanksgiving and with faith, from a czarist variation of Egyptian bondage into a new Promised Land. These immigrants found waiting for them the sweatshops, the street fights, the corruption of Tammany Hall. He shows human beings in a particular time and place attempting to achieve their own brand of survival. Frequently his protagonists discover the source of their inner turmoil in the severe dislocations and inequalities of American society. It is to Weidman's credit that he is never quaint or condescending toward those who struggle nobly to change the system as long as they do not surrender their morality or their humanity.

The novel *The Lights Around the Shore* (1943) sketches the life-style of a charming woman, adrift in a sea of passion, danger, and global conflict. She fled her homeland in terror, but she is going back, knowing that the same dangers that threatened her still prevail. Weidman keeps the reader in suspense by not revealing the purpose of her return too early in the novel, implying that it is a secret, even to the man who worshiped her. She alone knows that at her journey's end awaits another man, the lover she desperately desires, who is a traitor, capable of sealing her doom. The work was praised as a fine psychological study moving with the pace and intrigue of a mystery story.

Based upon the author's wartime recollections and imaginative skills in combining fact with fiction, Weidman's *The Hand of the Hunter* (1951) characterizes a man unable to remain aloof from others during a tragedy at sea. Vincent Sloate is an American businessman on a journey abroad whose ship is icebound off the coast of Halifax. The novel details how frightened passengers, even a self-contained private person like Sloate, expose their inner lives when facing a natural crisis. The title is taken from the biblical injunction to "deliver thyself as a roe from the hand of the hunter and as a bird from the hand of the fowler," and the story reveals that this philosophy is impossible when the artificial barriers that divide human beings break down in times of stress. In *The Hand of the Hunter* Weidman suggests that "no man is an island," as he takes readers on a voyage that jolts complacency and, like all good adventure stories, enriches the mind by verifying that no one is safe and untouched by violence.

Weidman is a hardworking, disciplined writer, an expert storyteller, and a shrewd observer of modern life. His literary aspirations are evident in an article he wrote for the *New York Herald Tribune Book Review* in 1953: "In almost three decades of intensive reading, much of it devoted to the hope of picking up a few pointers for what Hemingway has called the serious trade of novel writing, only two men have ever taught me anything helpful. Conrad is one. James Gould Cozzens is the other. To be able to write as well as either of them seems to me to be as much as a man can ask."

He remembers teachers who encouraged immigrant children to appreciate the classics, recalling an amusing incident with obvious relish: "I was once asked by an interviewer for the most exciting reading experience in my life. I said *Vanity Fair*. He was derisive in the interview to a man who would say that. I still mean it." Not only was Weidman "fed Shakespeare, Dickens, Thackeray, Kipling, George Eliot," but he also appreciated the importance of his thorough knowledge of English literature. On his first trip abroad at the age of twenty-six, he remembers that he "stepped down from the boat train in London . . . and felt at home . . . in the world of David Copperfield and Pendennis." Among Weidman's other favorite books are *War and Peace, Emma, Huckleberry Finn*, and most works by James Gould Cozzens and W. Somerset Maugham. Weidman asserts that he has read his favorites more than once, actually "many times, and I still feel eager to read them again. . . . I get a dual pleasure from all of them: (a) they entertain me; (b) they make me feel that if I were dealing with that material that is exactly how I would have wanted to write it."

In 1953 Weidman wrote *The Third Angel*, which describes a town's guilty secret life behind a facade of prosperous respectability. The people lead lives filled with passion and greed, intrigue and deception, while one man threatens the stability of this Connecticut town through his powerful control over its economic and political leadership. In *The Third Angel* Weidman again shows his perception of human frailties.

The Enemy Camp (1958) depicts the tragic implications of anti-Semitism. The camp referred to in the title is the Gentile world, and Weidman's protagonist is George Hurst, who takes his uncle's advice that it is "more important to be a man than a Jew. Don't make a private ghetto for yourself and creep into it. . . ." Hurst is told to "do what your heart tells you, not your religion," which seems good advice to an adopted orphan boy growing up in poverty in the anti-Gentile society of New York's immigrant world, but Hurst never understands that advice—not even after he has left his childhood environment, become a successful accountant, married a Gentile and bought a Connecticut suburban home. One day the personal questions of a private investigator make Hurst face a painful moral dilemma that has threatened his marriage, his business, and community security. How Hurst handles the fears and ghosts of a past that he thought had been obliterated gives credit to Weidman's skills in sketching vigorous, three-dimensional personalities without resorting to maudlin maneuvers. Weidman's message is that nobody should be permitted to exploit others. Hurst's Jewishness ceases to be a problem when he realizes that no camp exists for a free spirit. *The Enemy Camp* was praised by the *New York Herald Tribune* as "a New York version of Maugham's *Of Human Bondage*."

According to London tradition, anyone born within the sound of bells of the church of St. Mary-le-Bow is a true Cockney, but Weidman's novel *The Sound of Bow Bells* (1962) is about neither London nor Cockneys. Instead, his protagonist, a successful slick-fiction writer, is a sort of New York Cockney who tries to rise above his Lower East Side origins. The time span covered in the story is a little more than a day, but using a flashback technique with graceful fluency, Weidman examines significant events in the thirty-six-year life of Sam Silver, whose ambitious mother, scheming wife, and two literary agents help propel him into the society of successful short-story writers and novelists.

As an author Silver faces internal frustrations in coming to terms with his Jewish origins; he discovers that one of his rejected stories is accepted when he changes the Jewish names. He becomes a superb technician, but by compromising his integrity, he realizes that he is not using his well-honed skills honestly. The final scene when he arranges for his son's bar mitzvah ceremony is eloquent testimony that he is no longer willing to deny his Old World origins for cheap success.

In *The Sound of Bow Bells*, Weidman's skills in sketching vivid vignettes are evident in his characterizations of an enterprising literary-manuscript typist and of an aging, pitiful major novelist. He avoids melodrama by underplaying emotional confrontations and focuses instead upon producing strong and vital portrayals. The novel also offers shrewd comments about the hazards and problems facing an ethnic writing about his own people.

Other People's Money (1967) details the activities of a ruthless character who seduces other men's wives and squanders their life savings. Weidman takes the reader through scenes of wealth and exploitation, sketching two men engaged in a savage competitive struggle with each other for success, power, and a woman's love. The novelist captures with mastery the personalities of sophisticated people who turn the quest for fame and fortune into the deadliest game human beings can play—destroying innocent lives.

One of Weidman's strongest plots, in which he relies upon confrontations, chicanery, suspense, and intrigue, informs *The Temple* (1975), telling about Dave Dehn's mission, an obsession so strong it profoundly changes the lives of all who come into conflict with him. Dehn's is a compulsion so powerful that it results in a loveless marriage, two suicides, and a murder. He has influenced presidents and controlled a financial empire but is ready to stake it all on his fanatic architectural ambitions and his religious zealotry. The reader is introduced to well-drawn characters: Bella Biaggi, the faithless, sensual woman whom Dehn married when he needed her land; Colin Babington, the tough, prejudiced lawyer who tries to sabotage the temple;

Renata Bazeloff, the shrewd, tireless reporter who probes deeply to discover the mysterious source of Dehn's wealth; and Lola Truscott, the beautiful widow who becomes the protagonist's staunchest ally. Weidman creates and sustains suspense as a master storyteller in this eventful novel that shows the tragic repercussions of one man's manipulative behavior and the ruined lives of people trapped in his dream.

The Center of the Action (1969), about Weidman's experiences in the publishing world, was inspired by Weidman's long affectionate association with Richard Simon of Simon and Schuster. "He was my big brother," the novelist recalled in his interview with *Publishers Weekly*. Simon, aware that the twenty-one-year-old author had never been anywhere except the Bronx and Manhattan, gave the novice an advance, making it possible for him to take a trip around the world which Weidman claimed "changed my life and gave me a whole new perspective." Although he used his own experiences when he wrote *The Center of the Action*, the story is fiction. "Whereas any good journalist can move in on a situation and report on it," the test of the novelist is what he lets his imagination add. "Without imagination, what the plate in your memory has recorded won't work," he said of novel-writing in *PW*. "Total recall won't make a good fictional scene. Your imagination has to push the scene around and get the essence of it." Convincing dialogue in a novel "is not reporting, it's selecting."

Weidman's travels in America, in England, and in the Mediterranean have given him material for more than a dozen novels, two hundred short stories, several plays and travel essays. His works have been translated into many languages, and in a 1962 *Esquire* article, Weidman admitted his pleasure in having his books appear in Hebrew, because the translations enabled his "mother and father, both in their eighties and both barely on speaking and not at all on reading terms with English, . . . finally . . . to find out what their oldest son has been up to these last thirty-one years."

Weidman's venture into writing plays brought him praise when the musical *Fiorello!* (1959) won a Pulitzer Prize, an Antoinette Perry (Tony) Award, and recognition from the New York Drama Critics' Circle in 1960. Weidman admits that these prizes gave him the greatest satisfaction in his career. During a 1962 interview for *Saturday Review* John Barkham asked Weidman if the theater was cutting too deeply into his time. Weidman laughingly responded that his theater work "consists mostly of conversation. It's a great relief to talk after sitting alone in a room all morning with a pad and pencil. I find I can't work continuously at one thing for more than three or four hours." At that time his mornings were devoted to "his serious writing" (his novels), afternoons to his stories or plays. His novels took two years from conception to publication, he told Barkham.

In response to how he learned to cope with adversity throughout seventy years, Weidman remembers an incident in the midst of the Second World War. During a London air raid which terrified him, he noticed that a British female officer assigned to accompany him continued her work "while the rest of us ducked into the shelter." Then Weidman "asked her what she thought about during a bad time like that. She thought for a moment, then said: 'One Must Be Able To Last It Out.' It still seems to me the best piece of off-the-rack philosophy I ever heard. I've tried to live by it. It's surprisingly useful," Weidman admits.

Not all his critics have been enthusiastic.

Dust jacket for Weidman's autobiographical novel about growing up on New York's Lower East Side during the 1920s

"Weidman is clever about people without being really wise about them," Lee Rogow wrote in *Saturday Review of Literature* in February 1949. "The emotional penetration and the understanding of the sources of human ethics are essentially superficial." But as Weidman put it recently, he has always been surprised by the critics' remarks: "I have tried to write stories because they were in my head, and it troubled me to have them there until I got them out on paper. . . . I have always been surprised by my reviews, I didn't try to do all the things the critics said I did, but I was very glad to hear that I'd done them. My first novel *I Can Get It For You Wholesale* has been called by serious critics a breakthrough achievement. I didn't realize this at the time it was published in 1937. I have just reread it in connection with a new 50th anniversary edition, and I've read some of the reviews. I think they were right."

Weidman's advice to aspiring authors is to "get an agent" who is also a good editor. "I have always felt that until it sees print I haven't really written it. Many works have never seen print. I would like to believe that they are good stories . . . but I have a stubborn inner feeling that they are probably not because if they were good somebody would have recognized their worth and printed them. This is depressing, but as long as your powers of invention continue to work, the depression is not too debilitating. There is always something else to write."

Weidman is still a foremost chronicler of the Lower East Side and the arduous trek uptown. His skill has been in developing the character of the ruthless, unscrupulous manipulator, the hustler; and, like Herman Wouk, he both entertains and instructs his readers. An adroit storyteller, an artist of the flashback, he draws his characters masterfully, and his satiric sense is deft and incisive.

As Weidman told the interviewer for *Publishers Weekly* in 1969, "If a man runs up to me and says, 'Hey! I just saw an Indian in a big feathered headdress walking down Seventh Avenue with a large pink stone tucked under his arm!'—I'm interested. I want to know what he's going to do with that stone. Because there may be a germ of a story there. . . ." Jerome Weidman's sharp eye for the minutiae of human life is his enduring strength as a novelist and the source of his finely drawn characters and intricate tales.

References:

John Barkham, Interview with Jerome Weidman, *Saturday Review*, 45 (28 July 1962): 38-39;

"Publishers Weekly Interviews Jerome Weidman," *Publishers Weekly*, 196 (28 July 1969): 13-15;

H. R. Warfel, "American Novelists of Today," *New York Herald Tribune Book Review*, 11 October 1953.

Papers:

Weidman's papers are on deposit at the Humanities Research Center, University of Texas at Austin.

Nathanael West
(17 October 1903-22 December 1940)

Daniel Walden
Pennsylvania State University

See also the West entries in *DLB 4, American Writers in Paris, 1920-1939*, and *DLB 9, American Novelists, 1910-1945*.

BOOKS: *The Dream Life of Balso Snell* (Paris & New York: Contact Editions, 1931);

Miss Lonelyhearts (New York: Liveright, 1933; London: Grey Walls, 1949);

A Cool Million: The Dismantling of Lemuel Pitkin (New York: Covici Friede, 1934; London: Spearman, 1954);

The Day of the Locust (New York: Random House, 1939; London: Grey Walls, 1951).

PLAY: *Good Hunting*, by West and Joseph Schrank, New York, Hudson Theatre, 21 November 1938.

SCREENPLAYS: *Ticket to Paradise*, by West and Jack Natteford, Republic, 1936;

The President's Mystery, by West and Lester Cole, Republic, 1936;

Follow Your Heart, by West, Cole, and Samuel Ornitz, Republic, 1936;

Rhythm in the Clouds, adaptation by West, Republic, 1937;

It Could Happen to You, by West and Ornitz, Republic, 1937;

Born to be Wild, Republic, 1938;

I Stole a Million, Universal, 1939;

Five Came Back, by West, Jerry Cady, and Dalton Trumbo, RKO, 1939;

Spirit of Culver, by West and Whitney Bolton, Universal, 1939;

Men Against the Sky, RKO, 1940;

Let's Make Music, RKO, 1940.

PERIODICAL PUBLICATIONS: "Euripedes—A Playwright," *Casements*, 1 (July 1923): 2-4;

"Miss Lonelyhearts and the Lamb," *Contact: An American Quarterly*, 1 (February 1932): 80-85;

"Two Chapters from *Miss Lonelyhearts*: Miss Lonelyhearts and the Dead Pan and Miss Lonelyhearts and the Clean Old Man," *Contact: An American Quarterly*, 1 (May 1932): 13-21, 22-27;

"Miss Lonelyhearts and the Dismal Swamp," *Contempo*, 2 (5 July 1932): 1-2;

"Miss Lonelyhearts on a Field Trip," *Contact: An American Quarterly*, 1 (October 1932): 50-57;

"Some Notes on Violence," *Contact: An American Quarterly*, 1 (October 1932): 132-133;

"Some Notes on Miss L," *Contempo*, 3 (15 May 1933): 1-2;

"The Dear Public," *Americana*, 1 (August 1933): 29;

"Business Deal," *Americana*, 1 (October 1933): 14-15;

"Bird and Bottle," *Pacific Weekly*, 5 (10 November 1936): 329-331.

Early in the twentieth century it was quite common for young Jewish men, especially those whose parents had come from Poland and Russia, to change their names. In an effort to make it easier to succeed in America, the "goldineh medina," that is, the golden land, and in the hope that one's identity as an American would be maximized, Isadore Baline became Irving Berlin and Hyman Altuck became Harold Arlen. Nathanael West, born Nathan Weinstein in New York City on 17 October 1903, changed his name and his identity for the same reasons, but his desire to shed the past and be assimilated into American ways coexisted with a desperate wish to hold himself above that new life. In Sholem Asch's novels, for example, the conflict in Jewish immigrants and their children between

Nathanael West, 1931

their respect for European culture and their dearly held passion for assimilation into American society are central concerns. Similarly, as Jay Martin has pointed out, all of West's novels are built "on the dramatic irony that the hero is drawn into the society which he scorns, while ever forced to remain alien from the ideal society, the impossible society, which he envisions." Although Nathanael West was not an American-Jewish writer in the sense that Saul

Bellow is (his characters and plots are not drawn from the essence of the Jewish experience), it is inconceivable for West to have written as he did had he not been Jewish, hated being Jewish, and suffered from the fact that he could not escape being Jewish.

In 1970, I. J. Kapstein, West's close friend from college days, commented that on the one hand West "had no Jewish heritage"; thus "it was likely less hostility than complete indifference to it that finally made it burdensome to him." On the other hand, Kapstein held, "What I do find is his getting even with a world that made him an outsider because he was a Jew, something he did not want to be anyway. He got even with Christianity: it professed to love all men (except Jews) and it kept him from belonging to fraternities and clubs and enjoying everywhere at any time the simple pleasure of belonging with the right people: hence the mockery of Christianity in *The Dream Life of Balso Snell* . . . and the exposé in *Miss Lonelyhearts* of Christianity as a stupid illusion having nothing to do with the reality of human nature and the hard truths of life."

In Kapstein's view West got even with American democracy as well, and with humanity itself, in "The Burning of Los Angeles" in *The Day of the Locust*: in fiction West "could discharge all the resentment he could not discharge in fact; in fiction he could rise above the world of fact and manipulate it to his will; as an artist in fiction he could prove to the world that had rejected him that it was wrong and that he deserved to be accepted by it. Indeed, having gone this far, I would say that this last was the driving force in the production of his work — that his writing was not an end in itself, but a means to an end: the achievement of acceptance, the dream life of Nathanael West come true." Kapstein's opinion, based on a close, lifelong acquaintance with West, is basic to understanding Nathanael West, Jewish writer manqué.

Nathanael West wrote four novels, one play, and a smattering of poems and essays. Of the four novels, *Miss Lonelyhearts* (1933) is widely considered a masterpiece; *The Dream Life of Balso Snell* (1931) is an exotic, imaginative, scatological novel; *A Cool Million: The Dismantling of Lemuel Pitkin* (1934) is a bizarre spoof of every Horatio Alger novel; and *The Day of the Locust* (1939) is a dark, satirical evisceration of the Hollywood dream and the people who create it. As Carter Carmer put it, West was probably the most experimental American novelist, with the exception of William Faulkner, who wrote his major works during the Great Depression. Perhaps the most neglected talent of the age, his genius

burned brightest, says Mark Schorer, when his passionate private vision found objectivization in an exacting search for technical perfection. His four novels are indictments of the emptiness of mass living. He knew, as he wrote in *The Day of the Locust*, that "Few things are sadder than the truly monstrous." Yet, prefiguring the black humorists of the 1960s, particularly Joseph Heller, and working in a characteristically Jewish way — laughing through his tears — he began with laughter and moved toward pathos and even horror.

Nathan Weinstein, the son of Max and Anna Wallenstein Weinstein, from Kovno, Lithuania, grew up in a home in which Americanization was all important. Refusing to speak Yiddish or Russian at home, the Weinsteins taught German to their children because they identified with the German-Jewish establishment in New York, learned English quickly, and took up residence in a house on 110th Street across from Central Park, part of what John Sanford, West's friend, called "The Gilded Ghetto." Here Max Weinstein rose in the world; as a successful contractor he showed his penchant for Americanisms by naming his buildings the Arizona, the Colorado, and the Colonnade. His patriotic zeal was also shown in his decision not to send his children to Hebrew school and in his present to Nathan, before Nathan was ten, of a set of Horatio Alger's books. The Weinsteins would not be part of what Emma Lazarus called "the wretched refuse of the teeming shore"; they would crowd the crucible, along with Germans, Frenchmen, Irishmen, Englishmen, Jews, and Russians, as in Israel Zangwill's *The Melting Pot* (1908), because "God is making the American."

A good American, Nathan learned early to love the outdoors, especially baseball, although he was never an athlete. He was called "Home-Run Weinstein" at Camp Paradox, a middle-class Jewish camp he attended during summers while he was in high school. He was also ironically called "Pep," a name that stuck with him, because he was awkward and spoke slowly. At P.S. 81 and P.S. 186 he was no more than an ordinary student. While attending DeWitt Clinton High School, however, largely because he was a frequent theater- and filmgoer and an omnivorous reader, he began to blossom. In 1920 when he left high school before graduation, already a rebel, he showed his scorn for the system his parents loved and admired by becoming an insider and caricaturing it in his adoption of its conventions. Although he lacked credits in Spanish, history, Latin, plane geometry, and physics, he manufactured a transcript from DeWitt Clinton

*Cartoon by West for the Camp Paradox newspaper, August 1920. At summer camp West was ironically known as Pep
because he was awkward and spoke slowly.*

with the aid of a friend, applied to, and was admitted to Tufts College, Medford, Massachusetts, in 1921. He understood that his family wanted above all else to be Americanized as quickly as possible. They provided him with no models for the absorption of values; success as a value he rejected. As he gradually evolved an individual philosophy, he first held to an ethics of scorn. An observer now, as he put it in his short story "The Adventurer," he stalked the tracks of college life. A snappy dresser who had plenty of money and wore his hair parted slightly off-center (according to photographs), he did everything well except go to classes. On 30 November 1921, he was asked to withdraw. Amazingly, although he had only some fifteen entrance credits and had been at Tufts for only two months, he used the transcript of another Nathan Weinstein (a few years older, who had gained a total of fifty-seven credits at Tufts before transferring to the medical school) to gain admittance to Brown University for spring 1922 with fifty-seven credits.

Over several years West had been evolving a new persona, shaping a legend. At Brown he told his roommate that his ancestors were of noble birth, that his name was Nathanael von Wallenstein Weinstein. Escaping the cocoon his family had imposed on him, he was creating his own romantic, heroic version of himself.

At Brown West enjoyed football, drinking, and hell-raising; food, alcohol, and women were his passions. As his roommate described him, he "accepted very much the rules of the game as it was then being played at Brown. . . . He got through college, as I did, on brains and hard work." He

"tooled around in our jointly-owned Stutz Bearcat (red, of course)" and wore "Brooks Bros norfolk jackets, Brooks buttondown shirts, and Locke and Collins and Fairbanks hats," the uniform of the Joe College dude of the day. West was also attracted to fraternity life. Unfortunately, he was not impeccably Nordic nor of distinguished ancestry and was refused acceptance to DKE, one of the most prestigious and extroverted fraternities at Brown. The irony is that he had only wanted to be asked to pledge, not to join, and when he was not invited he refused to accept his rejection by a fraternity he had already spurned.

At Brown West was a member of a group he called the Hanseatic League. Intended to recall the union of free German towns of the thirteenth century (including Kovno, the town his parents had come from), formed to protect and promote commerce, the League reflected West's enlightenment and modernism, the other side of the Joe College hedonist. But all the time, as a friend had it, West was ready to laugh at himself, at the dude and the modernist. He read widely and deeply in the Greek and Roman classics, religious literature, the French symbolists, Russian realists, and American and British modernists. He was preparing himself to be a writer. In his term paper on "Euripedes—A Playwright," which was published in the Brown literary magazine, *Casements*, in July 1923, with tongue in cheek he used his scholarship to accuse Euripedes of plagiarizing from others. Another seriocomic piece, written in June 1924 for his friend Quentin Reynolds, told the story of a flea named Saint Puce (French for flea) who was born under

Christ's armpit, fed on his body, and died at the moment of Christ's death. This story became the central metaphor for *The Dream Life of Balso Snell*, which West wrote from 1924 to 1930, off and on.

From October 1926 to January 1927, West visited Paris, frequenting the bohemian clubs and occasionally writing. Prior to his trip he had changed his name legally to Nathanael West, possibly inspired by the phrase "Go West, young man" or by the example of his Uncle Sam, who had been using the name West for some time. Whatever the source of West's new name, it is likely that he was seeking to find an identity that would remove him from his Jewish roots, and particularly from his parents' mantle. The funny thing, as Edmund Wilson remembered, is that in spite of his attempts to appear American, West exhibited a kind of Eastern European suffering and sense of the grotesque, a Russian-Jewish soul, a sad Jewish humor, and a Russian-Jewish imagination.

From 1927 through 1931 West, back in the States, worked as a night manager at the Kenmore Hall Hotel and later at the Suffolk Club Hotel. Friendly with S. J. Perelman (who later married West's sister Laura) and with Kapstein and Reynolds from college, he also made the acquaintance of Michael Gold, Maxwell Bodenheim, Edward Dahlberg, Nathan Asch, Dashiell Hammett, and Philip Wylie, all of whom were Greenwich Village habitués. At the *New Republic* he met Edmund Wilson and John Dos Passos. And on Sundays, at George Brownoff's Central Park West apartment, he discussed music, literary criticism, and such writers as Dostoevski, Chekhov, Ibsen, O'Neill, and Joyce with a group of young Jewish intellectuals.

By 1930 West had finished *The Dream Life of Balso Snell*, which was turned down by several publishers but finally accepted (only after William Carlos Williams recommended it) by Contact Editions, which David Moss and Martin Kamin had taken over from Robert McAlmon. West's first novel was published in 1931 in a printing of 500 copies. Without a public relations blitz, it sold badly and garnered only two reviews. West had to guarantee the sale of 150 copies, but as late as 1937 he still had a few copies left.

The Dream Life of Balso Snell is a satirical attack against literary games and against the perversion of art in a mass culture. Through scatological images, used to shock the pompous avant-garde and those whom H. L. Mencken labeled the "booboisie," the novel is directed to those pseudosophisticates West met in Paris in the 1920s who opted for escape to "Anywhere Out of This

World"—the title of Balso Snell's first song. Balso Snell is a kind of Babbitt who, finding absurd all the major historic events of Western civilization, concludes that "Art is a sublime excrement." Yet, even as he lampoons art as escapism, he criticizes the dream makers who divorce art from society.

In the beginning when Balso Snell enters the Trojan horse through its anus the shock is meant not only to affect the reader but also to symbolize man's deterioration into a subhuman species. For in satirizing the classical past, the Catholic religion, Joyce, Dostoevski, and Freud, West satirizes those who perverted them. To shock and shatter the complacency of the reader was important. To evoke disgust was part of his plan. How else to react to Balso who "had good cause to tremble, for the Phoenix Excrementi eat themselves, digest themselves, and give birth to themselves by evacuating their bowels?" Balso Snell is the grotesque product of a commercialized world.

Inside the horse Balso meets a Jewish guide, with "Tours" on the front of his cap—West's portrayal of a confidence man only too willing to publicize any culture for a profit. When Balso then suggests anti-Semitism the guide screams: "I am a Jew! and whenever anything Jewish is mentioned I find it necessary to say I am a Jew. I'm a Jew! A Jew!" When Balso attempts to placate the guide with the cliché that "Some of my best friends are Jews," the guide engages him in chitchat, meaningless drivel. In short, in describing the Jewish guide as a grotesque incongruity, an atomized person whose life is a sham, West ridicules affectation by creating incidents and images at once grotesque and comical. In getting revenge, for example, at the end of the third episode, Balso writes a play for the art theaters, patronized by art and book lovers, schoolteachers, sensitive young Jews who adore culture, librarians, homosexuals, newspapermen and advertising-copy people, and then insults their intelligence; and in case they didn't get the message he would have the ceiling of the theater open "and cover the occupants with tons of loose excrement. After the deluge, if they so desire, the patrons of my art can gather in the customary charming groups and discuss the play."

The Dream Life of Balso Snell is an experimental first novel but it is also a carefully written and structured novel, written and rewritten, as Jay Martin has pointed out, many times. Thematically, as William Bittner wrote, it strikes at "every weakness in the world's religions, and then swings into religious love." Norman Podhoretz, writing in the *New Yorker* in 1957, called it "a brilliantly insane surrealist fantasy that tries very hard to mock Western culture out of existence." Malcolm Cowley added ironically that "escape from the mass was becoming a mass movement." In Stanley Edgar Hyman's view, *The Dream Life of Balso Snell* is a vision of one vast dung heap. A brilliantly conceived comic novel, it is an obsessively scatological, anti-Catholic, and anti-Jewish novel as well. And if one seriously reads the opinion of John Raskolnikov Gilson, a character out of Dostoevski, that "I need women and because I can't buy or force them, I have to make poems for them," then the novel is misogynistic too.

West, unlike so many post-World War II Jewish writers, was unable, as Max Schulz has insightfully noted, to rest content suspended between heavenly aspirations and earthly limitations, belief and skepticism, order and disorder. It appears that all his novels represent a search for absolutes, for values. "If I could only discover the Real," Gilson cries, "a Real that I could know with my senses." Disillusioned, West too searched for something real, but in novel after novel he ended with a mocking denunciation of a false dream: in *The Dream Life of Balso Snell* it is the bardic dream; in *Miss Lonelyhearts* it is the Christ dream; in *A Cool Million* it is the Horatio Alger dream; and in *The Day of the Locust* it is the Hollywood dream. Ironically, for all his attempts to escape his Jewish heritage, it is West's shriek of laughter, Victor Comerchero noted, that "keeps breaking into a sob," a very Jewish phenomenon, that may be responsible for the less than complete success of all but *Miss Lonelyhearts*.

About the time of publication of *The Dream Life of Balso Snell*, William Carlos Williams invited West to be associate editor of *Contact: An American Quarterly*. In the journal's three issues parts of early drafts of West's second novel, *Miss Lonelyhearts*, appeared. The third and final issue, in October 1932, included his "Some Notes on Violence," which defended the way violence was portrayed in American writing on the grounds that "In America violence is idiomatic." Another chapter of *Miss Lonelyhearts* appeared in *Contempo* in 1932, and after *Miss Lonelyhearts* was published in 1933, the magazine offered "A Symposium on *Miss Lonelyhearts*" that included commentary by Josephine Herbst, Angel Flores, and William Carlos Williams, as well as West's "Some Notes on Miss L."

West got the idea for his novel in March 1929, when he and Perelman went to a New York Jewish restaurant where they met a female columnist for the *Brooklyn Eagle* who wrote under the pseudonym Susan Chester. Her description of the letters she received, which she thought West might see

humorously, struck West as utterly serious and a key to the social chaos of the day. In "Some Notes on Miss L," West described Miss Lonelyhearts as a "portrait of a priest of our time who has a religious experience." In the novel Miss Lonelyhearts, a lovelorn columnist with a "Christ complex," unable to tolerate his boss Shrike's cynical hedonism and antireligiousness, turns at last to love. "I'm a humanity lover," the columnist admits to Betty, his girl friend, whereas Shrike, almost as vicious as the bird whose name he carries, derisively suggests that "The church is our only hope, the First Church of Christ Dentist, where he is worshipped as Preventer of Decay. The Church whose symbol is the trinity new-style: Father, Son and Wirehaired Fox Terrier."

Reflecting on Freud's influence, in "Some Notes on Miss L" West wrote that "The great body of case histories can be used in the way that ancient writers used their myths. Freud is your Bullfinch; you cannot learn from him." That is, although West disdained the relationship of psychology to reality, he understood that psychology replaced the myths of religion with new myths. In that sense, going beyond satire and allegory, Miss Lonelyhearts's search for himself is destined to end in futility. A neurotic functioning as best he can as a columnist to whom people pour out their troubles, he suffers with them even as he wonders how to find sanity in an insane world. Unfortunately, according to West, "Man has a tropism for order" while "The Physical world has a tropism for disorder, entropy," and "Every order has within it the germs of destruction." Rendered impotent, unable to act, Miss Lonelyhearts withdraws, looking for harmony in his dreams, in the fantasy world. At first he had looked to sweet, simple Betty, but as he realizes: "Her world was not the world and could never include the readers of his column. Her sureness was based on the power to limit experience arbitrarily." Similarly, Shrike's cynicism, a mask to cover his inability to relate to others, is no solution. In a nutshell, Shrike is a false messiah, a kind of anti-Christ. On the other hand there is the husband of one of the letter writers, Fay Doyle. Peter, a cripple, cuckolded by his wife, willing to do all for love, is a touching example of selfless love, altruism, and at the same time he is Miss Lonelyhearts's murderer. At the end of the novel, Peter, having set out to kill Miss Lonelyhearts, sees Betty, struggles to put his gun away, and accidentally shoots Miss Lonelyhearts.

Love, of course, is no match for the cynicism and violence that colors *Miss Lonelyhearts*. In constructing a world in which the myths of love and compassion, so central to the Judeo-Christian tradition, are limned, West shows that such emotions are irrelevant, perhaps destructive, in the real world. Says Bruce Olsen, "The attack upon Christian compassion as a delusive myth is made to work by enforcing a quite contrary mythlike view—that the universe is composed of deterministic forces in which feeling has no relevance." In the novel, love can provide motivation and hope, but it cannot impose harmony; only if one can give up excessive individualism and greed can love work its magic. *Miss Lonelyhearts* uses an ironic perspective to illuminate a moral paradox; the reader sympathizes with the anguish of the narrator and yet laughs with him as well.

West was committed to American ways. He was also committed to the criticism of the American Dream of success. He understood, as he told a friend, "I'm not going to be able to change the course of anything, I just want to know." In the grip of the Great Depression he countered the myth perpetrated by Horatio Alger, that anyone with get-up-and-go who was honest and forthright could make it, by setting the myth in the midst of a huge nightmare, the American Dream. Undeniably, maturing during the 1920s he saw that there were differences between the reality and the myth. But as an outsider, despite his desire to be treated as an American, West felt the pain of those who suffered financially and emotionally. From that position he heaped scorn on the con artists and frauds of all kinds, who, vampirelike, grew fat and rich by feeding on the myth and its believers.

A Cool Million, originally titled "America, America," is a fable and a satire. Lemuel Pitkin, the protagonist, is a farm lad whose mother cannot pay the rent. Threatened by foreclosure of the mortgage by banker Nathan "Shagpole" Whipple, a cracker-barrel type who used to be president of the United States, Lemuel decides to seek his fortune. Inspired by Whipple's words "Don't be discouraged. This is the land of opportunity," Nathan leaves home with thirty dollars. Unhappily for him, every opportunity, which would have worked out well for Alger's heroes, is the key to a disaster. Robbed on the train, he is then arrested and, under the tutelage of a crazed prison warden, has his teeth pulled (for health reasons, it is said); and, successively, his right eye is removed, his leg is amputated, he is scalped, and finally killed—all, Alger fashion, in the name of "the right of every American boy to go out into the world and there receive fair play and a chance to make his fortune in industry and probity without being laughed at or conspired against by

sophisticated aliens." Beginning in comedy, says Jay Martin, West ends by showing that beneath the surface lies "the bitter salt tragedy of betrayed ideals." In reversing the Horatio Alger myth of success West comes up with a truth that satisfied him.

Pursuing humor and absurdity to their exaggerated conclusions in *A Cool Million*, West depicts the novel's heroine, Betty, at the House of All Nations to shoot down the myth of Aryan supremacy and uses the Sierra Mountain episodes, as Carter Carmer has demonstrated, to attack the violence propagated by the American myth of the Western bad man and the social irresponsibility incited by certain members of the intellectual class. Significantly, the Indian chief, Israel Satinpenny, is not only a severe critic of middle-class America, but he is also angry at the civilization that introduced syphilis, the radio, TB, the cinema, and "doubt, a soul-corroding doubt. He rotted this land in the name of progress."

In the end, as a social critic of the grotesque and the shoddy, West reminds the reader of the Jewish immigrant tradition. In a road show called the "Chamber of Horrors and Inanimate Hideosities," managed by pseudopoet Sylvanus Snodgrass, a dramatic skit titled "The Pageant of America or A Curse on Columbus," out of Abraham Cahan (and used later by Philip Roth), shows Quakers being branded, Indians brutalized, Negroes sold. The line between the grotesque and propaganda is very thin, West is saying. No wonder at the end, after Lemuel is killed—during a comedy scene—Whipple, the leader and dictator of a fascist party, celebrates Lemuel Pitkin's martyrdom (which he uses) by attributing his greatness to his faith in fair play and the rest of the Alger canon of virtues. Having purged the country of the alien diseases, the National Revolutionary Party shouts, in unison, "Hail Lemuel Pitkin! All hail, the American boy!" Victimized by myths, Pitkin, whose plight in ways reflects West's, looks for flesh-and-blood messiahs even as he tries to live his dreams and fantasies.

A Cool Million's evident strengths do not compensate for its weaknesses. In pointing out the violence latent in ordinary people, West reminds the reader of what had happened in history (and anticipates what would happen again very soon in Hitler-dominated Europe). Yet Lemuel Pitkin can be seen as a hero who is absurd or a schlemiel. If the novel does not work for the reader, then it is, to quote Stanley Edgar Hyman, a "formless, an inorganic stringing together of comic set-pieces"; on the other hand, as Alan Ross writes, "In its awareness of political technique, its devastating true analysis of

Drawing of West by David Schorr

sold badly. By February 1940 it had sold only 1,464 copies. From his four novels he made only $1,280.

The Day of the Locust, called by Malcolm Cowley the best novel ever written about Hollywood, is about Tod Hackett (note the first name is the German word for death and in English the last name can be a two-word command), a would-be painter who works as a set and costume designer and consorts with an assortment of Hollywood grotesques. In love with seventeen-year-old Faye Greener, whose father is a broken-down vaudevillian, Tod first finds to his chagrin that Faye prefers Earle Shoop, a cardboard cowboy, and then Miguel, Earle's Mexican friend. Also important are Abe Kusich, a dwarf, and Homer Simpson, a stereotypical Midwesterner who provides Faye with room and board and, in his innocence, expects nothing in return. Significantly, Homer reminds the reader of Wing Biddlebaum in Sherwood Anderson's *Winesburg, Ohio*, in that he reflects his anxieties and emotion through his hands. Homer's repressed emotions, however, break out at the end, when, driven almost to madness, he attacks a boy named Adore Loomis and incites a riot that ends with the burning of Los Angeles. The riot inspires Tod to complete his apocalyptic masterpiece, "The Burning of Los Angeles," that he has tried to work on throughout the book. Faye, the archetypal blonde femme fatale, "the dream dreamed by all of America," is an important figure in Tod's work. By most standards she looks inviting, but hers is in fact "an invitation to struggle, hard and sharp, closer to murder than to love." Faye is all things to all men, "completely artificial," yet so irresistible that, as Tod puts it, "Nothing less than rape would do." She is amoral, but to Homer she is "a fine, wholesome child." She is so wrapped up in herself that reality never intervenes. Like Homer, doomed to self-destruction, a perfect automaton, Faye has mechanical mannerisms and an artificial voice; her constant dream machine is a collage of movie heroines.

Paralleling the main characters are the movie-mad mobs who throng Hollywood and the premieres. "All their lives they had slaved at some kind of dull, heavy labor, behind desks and counters, in the fields and at tedious machines of all sorts, saving their pennies and dreaming of the leisure that would be theirs when they had enough." But once in California they discover that sunshine, fresh fruit, and the ocean are not enough. In West's Dream Dump the mass, incapable of responding normally to anything, becomes a violent mob: "A super 'Dr. Know-All Pierce-All' had made the necessary promise and they were marching behind

unrestricted capitalistic method, its foreshadowing of Americanism turned into a possible Fascism, *A Cool Million* is brilliantly successful." In any case it is a tour de force in its ability to portray the grotesqueries of the American way of life. But, in part because it was a hastily written novel, it did not get good reviews and did not sell well. What it did, however, was bring West to the attention of Samuel Goldwyn, who hired West to write screenplays in Hollywood.

In Hollywood from 1933 on, West fashioned quite a few screenplays, some of which were never produced. In 1935, he collected material for a new book on the underworld life of the film capital, a life in which he was peripherally involved, mainly as an interested, fascinated observer. While residing at an apartment hotel near Hollywood Boulevard he met stuntmen, bit players, comics, midgets, and the grips on the sets. He went to cockfights and boxing matches; he encountered Mexican-Americans, cops, and newspapermen. He worked as a studio writer for Republic, Columbia, RKO, and Universal. In 1938 he submitted *The Day of the Locust* to Random House, which published it in 1939 to good reviews—but, like its predecessors, West's novel his banner in a great united front of screwballs and screwboxes to purify the land. No longer bored, they sang and danced joyously in the red light of the flames."

Commenting on West's portrayal of Hollywood's artificiality and his gradual revelation of the primitivism and the savagery that lie beneath the surface, West's Hollywood acquaintance Allan Seager observed that *The Day of the Locust* "was not fantasy imagined, but fantasy seen." In Edmund Wilson's view, West "caught the emptiness of Hollywood; and he is, as far as I know, the first writer to make this emptiness horrible." The novel, F. Scott Fitzgerald wrote to S. J. Perelman, "puts Gogol's *The Lower Depth* in the class with *The Tale of Benjamin Bunny*."

Like Balzac, whom he admired, West had as his aim to expose the superior truth about the middle and the lower classes. He captured the horror of his age in which reality was perverted and values distorted. His sense of the pathetic is mirrored in the conclusion to *The Day of the Locust*: "It is hard to laugh at the need for beauty and romance, no matter how tasteless, even horrible, the results of that need are. But it is easy to sigh. Few things are sadder than the truly monstrous."

West understood, as he told Edmund Wilson, that "there is nothing to root for in my books, and no rooters." He saw that fundamental changes were difficult if not impossible to make. Disillusioned by the state of politics in the late 1930s, he turned to hunting as an escape and to screenwriting as a way to make enough money to buy the time for another book. In this mood he met and married Eileen McKenney, the model for her sister Ruth's book, *My Sister Eileen*. Eileen was gentle and gave him her love, both of which he responded to and needed. Although he had not produced a commercially successful book, he looked forward to more books, to a promising future in Hollywood. Suddenly life came to a close. On 22 December 1940, returning from a weekend hunting trip in Mexico, West and his new bride were killed in an automobile accident near El Centro, California. He was thirty-seven years old.

West pursued his quest of exposing America's myths relentlessly. Compelled to do what he had to do, he described the cancers that threatened American society, and in depicting these horrors, he made his readers shudder and laugh. Although his novels reflect the era in which he wrote, they are above all—in Jay Martin's words—"permanent and true explorations into the Siberia of the human spirit."

Bibliography:
William White, *Nathanael West: A Comprehensive Bibliography* (Kent, Ohio: Kent State University Press, 1975).

Biography:
Jay Martin, *Nathanael West: The Art of His Life* (New York: Farrar, Straus & Giroux, 1970).

References:
Roger Abrahams, "Nathanael West's *Miss Lonelyhearts*," in *Seven Contemporary Authors*, edited by Thomas Whitbread (Austin: University of Texas Press, 1966);

Robert M. Coates, "Messiah of the Lonelyhearts," *New Yorker*, 49 (15 April 1933): 59;

Victor Comerchero, *Nathanael West: The Ironic Prophet* (Syracuse: Syracuse University Press, 1964);

Malcolm Cowley, Introduction to *Miss Lonelyhearts* (New York: Avon, 1950), pp. ii-iv;

Leslie Fiedler, "Master of Dreams," *Partisan Review*, 34 (Summer 1967): 339-356;

David Galloway, "Nathanael West's Dream Dump," *Critique*, 6 (Winter 1963-64): 46-63;

Stanley Edgar Hyman, *Nathanael West* (Minneapolis: University of Minnesota Press, 1962);

James B. Light, *Nathanael West: An Interpretive Study* (Evanston: Northwestern University Press, 1961);

Bruce Olsen, "Nathanael West: The Use of Cynicism," in *Minor American Novelists*, edited by Charles A. Hoyt (Carbondale & Edwardsville: Southern Illinois University Press, 1970), pp. 81-94;

Miles D. Orvell, "The Messianic Sexuality of Miss Lonelyhearts," *Studies in Short Fiction*, 10 (Spring 1973): 159-167;

Randall Reid, *The Fiction of Nathanael West* (Chicago: University of Chicago Press, 1967);

Alan Ross, "The Dead Center: An Introduction to Nathanael West," *Horizon*, 18 (October 1948): 284-296; revised and republished in *The Complete Works of Nathanael West* (New York: Farrar, Straus & Cudahy, 1957), pp. vii-xxii;

Edmund Volpe, "The Waste Land of Nathanael West," *Renascence*, 13 (Winter 1961): 67-77, 112;

Walter Wells, "Shrieks of the Locusts," in *Tycoons and Locusts* (Carbondale & Edwardsville: Southern Illinois University Press, 1973), pp. 49-70.

Anzia Yezierska
(circa 1885-21 November 1970)

Charlotte Goodman
Skidmore College

BOOKS: *Hungry Hearts* (Boston & New York: Houghton Mifflin, 1920; London: Unwin, 1922);

Salome of the Tenements (New York: Boni & Liveright, 1923; London: Unwin, 1923);

Children of Loneliness (New York & London: Funk & Wagnalls, 1923);

Bread Givers (New York: Doubleday, Page, 1925; London: Heinemann, 1925);

Arrogant Beggar (New York: Doubleday, Page, 1927; London: Heinemann, 1927);

All I Could Never Be (New York: Brewer, Warren & Putnam, 1932);

Red Ribbon on a White Horse (New York: Scribners, 1950);

The Open Cage: An Anzia Yezierska Collection, edited by Alice Kessler Harris (New York: Persea Books, 1979).

Anzia Yezierska, novelist and short-story writer, belonged to that generation of Jewish immigrant authors who wrote about the Jewish migration from the pogrom-ridden Eastern European *shtetl* to the cities of America in the late nineteenth and early twentieth centuries. Like her contemporary Abraham Cahan, author of *The Rise of David Levinsky*, Yezierska focuses upon the struggles of her protagonists to become Americanized and to better themselves economically. She dramatizes as well the way in which traditional Jewish values— piety, dedication to religious studies, filial obedience, loyalty to one's own group—are eroded as her immigrant characters become increasingly assimilated. Yezierska's special contribution to American-Jewish literature, however, lies in her depiction of the Jewish immigrant experience from the point of view of the Jewish woman, whose struggles to achieve autonomy both within the family and in the larger American society she describes sympathetically and persuasively.

Born in a mud hut in Plinsk, on the Russian-Polish border, to Bernard and Pearl Yezierska, Anzia Yezierska immigrated to New York's Lower East Side with her family at the age of fifteen. By day she worked in a sweatshop and at other menial

Anzia Yezierska (Culver Pictures)

jobs, while at night she attended school to learn to read and write English. Three years after her arrival in America, she obtained a scholarship to study domestic science at Columbia University; however, her subsequent career as a teacher of domestic science was short-lived since she found herself to be temperamentally unsuited to the job of teaching. About 1910 she married an attorney, but after only a few months this marriage was annulled. Shortly thereafter she married Arnold Levitas, a teacher and author of textbooks, and gave birth to a daughter, Louise. However, finding domestic chores and maternal responsibilities to be oppressive, Yezierska left Levitas and soon after surrendered her daughter to his care. She devoted the remainder of her life to pursuing a career as a writer.

Yezierska describes again and again in her fiction the attempt of a spirited Jewish female protagonist from the ghetto to bridge the chasm between the chaotic though vital immigrant milieu and the orderly but ultimately repressed world of the uptown Jews and WASPs. Seeking to capture the essence of ghetto life and to approximate the rhythms of her native Yiddish tongue as well as the fractured English of her immigrant characters, she fashioned a series of Bildungsromane and short stories which delineate the metamorphosis of the immigrant girl from "greenhorn" to educated young lady and her subsequent liaison with either an urbane and assimilated Jewish young man or a scholarly WASP who serves as her mentor. Several of her short stories focus on the daily experiences of middle-aged and older women from the ghetto. Writing about her own literary efforts, Yezierska said, "I began to build a bridge of understanding between the American-born and myself. Since their life was shut out from such as me, I began to open my life and the lives of my people to them. . . . Writing about the Ghetto, I found America." To Yezierska, America was a miraculous country which afforded those immigrants possessing determination and intelligence the opportunity to "make a person" of themselves. By becoming educated, they would be able to escape the squalor and ugliness of the ghetto; in turn, they could infuse their warmth and vitality into the sterile, restrained Anglo-Saxon American culture. Frequently in her works, however, the protagonist, once she has become Americanized, finds herself suspended uncomfortably between the restrictive but colorful ghetto culture and the aseptic uptown world for which she had once yearned.

With the publication of her short story "Free Vacation House" in *Forum* in December of 1915, Yezierska's literary career was launched. Her story movingly describes the humiliating encounters of a Jewish mother from the Lower East Side tenements with benevolent but condescending charity workers. Though she and her children are able to escape temporarily from their dirty, overcrowded surroundings when they are sent to the country for a brief vacation, they are continuously reminded by their benefactors that they are recipients of charity and must behave accordingly.

In 1917 Yezierska made the acquaintance of John Dewey and obtained permission to audit his seminar in social and political thought at Columbia University. During the course of this year, a romantic relationship developed between the fifty-eight-year-old Dewey and Yezierska, who was then in her thirties. Included in *The Collected Poems of John Dewey* are several poems which he wrote to and about Yezierska in 1917 and 1918. Dewey was to serve as the prototype for the supportive though austere Anglo-Saxon male appearing again and again in her fiction in the role of mentor and sometimes lover of the young Jewish immigrant female protagonist. When Dewey's seminar concluded, he asked Yezierska to serve as translator for a group of graduate students who were conducting a study of the Polish community in Philadelphia. This experience is treated fictionally in Yezierska's novel *All I Could Never Be* (1932). Dewey and Yezierska parted in 1918, when he left for an extended trip abroad.

Recognition for her realistic fictional representation of immigrant life came to Yezierska when Edward J. O'Brien not only included her short story "The Fat of the Land" in *Best Short Stories of 1919* but also dedicated the volume to her. The story describes the feeling of alienation and loneliness that Hannah Breineh, an elderly Jewish woman from the ghetto, experiences after her affluent, well-meaning children install her in an elegant but sterile uptown apartment. Though she realizes how superior her new home is to her former shabby tenement dwelling, she misses the bustle and camaraderie of the ghetto.

The next year Yezierska published a volume of short stories about Jewish immigrant life, *Hungry Hearts* (1920). With the appearance of this book, she became a celebrity, for Hollywood producer Samuel Goldwyn purchased the film rights to the work and with much fanfare brought her out to Hollywood. Called "Queen of the Ghetto" and "The Immigrant Cinderella" by publicists of the day, Yezierska settled in California with the intention of pursuing her writing career there, but within the year she returned East because she discovered that when she was no longer living in the familiar milieu of New York's Lower East Side she could not write. After her return, she began her first novel, *Salome of the Tenements* (1923). This novel is based on the love affair and marriage of Yezierska's friend, the immigrant Socialist writer Rose Pastor, to Graham Stokes, scion of an upper-class WASP family. In the novel, Sonya Vrunsky, news reporter for the *Ghetto News*, falls in love with an American philanthropist named John Manning, a character who resembles philosopher John Dewey. Inspired by Sonya's impassioned concern for the poor, Manning decides to devote his life to social causes.

The short stories and sketches which subsequently appeared in Yezierska's *Children of Loneliness* (1923) and in the novels *Arrogant Beggar* (1927)

HUNGRY HEARTS

BY

ANZIA YEZIERSKA

BOSTON AND NEW YORK
HOUGHTON MIFFLIN COMPANY
The Riverside Press Cambridge
1920

Title page for Yezierska's first published book, a volume of short stories about Jewish immigrant life

and *All I Could Never Be* also deal with the immigrant experience, describing the female version of the American Dream and delineating as well the tensions between the values of the Old World and the New World. Though Yezierska's early works were on the whole favorably reviewed by the critics, those who had applauded the emotional power of her early fiction soon began to speak pejoratively of her unvarying style and subject matter. And while several of her short stories, including "Free Vacation House" and "The Fat of the Land," are memorable literary achievements, the novels, with their somewhat implausible plots and their frequently too predictable characters, are interesting at present primarily as fictional documents of the immigrant experience.

Yezierska's most fully realized fictional work is *Bread Givers* (1925), an autobiographical novel that was republished in 1975. Sara Smolinsky, the feisty first-person narrator of this novel, not only fights to escape from the oppressive tenement world but also

from the strictures imposed on Jewish women by the patriarchal pronouncements of the Orthodox Jewish religion, personified in the novel by Sara's father, Reb Smolinsky. Sara constantly challenges the authority of her domineering father, a religious scholar who studies his sacred books and drinks tea with his male cronies while his wife and four daughters struggle to bring in enough money from their menial jobs to sustain the impoverished household. Sara's three older sisters all fall prey to their father's schemes to marry them off to suitors chosen by him, men who he believes will help him to better his own economic situation. However, seeing the dreams of each of her older sisters betrayed, Sara is determined to avoid their fate by acquiring an education and becoming independent. "Woe to America where women are let free like men," Reb Smolinsky thunders. Undaunted by his imprecations, Sara resolves to free herself from the restraints imposed by poverty and lack of education, as well as from her father's dominion. She leaves her father's house and rents a room of her own with her meager wages, proclaiming, "I'm smart enough to look out for myself. It's a new life now. In America, women don't need men to boss them." In America, as Sara proves, women can also develop their intellectual capacities, something that only Jewish males were traditionally encouraged to do. *Bread Givers* is not only an indictment of patriarchal Jewish attitudes towards women; it is also a threnody for a culture whose vitality will be sapped by economic and social pressures. As Reb Smolinsky's holy books are moved to make room for boarders, and as he himself dons a grocer's apron in order to realize his own American dream of economic success, it becomes apparent that the Old World religious culture cannot survive intact amid the pressures of the secular New World. Yezierska's vivid portrayal of tenement life, of cultural conflicts, and most importantly, of the struggles of her young female protagonist to achieve autonomy, even if she must defy the traditions of her people to do so, makes this novel a memorable contribution to American-Jewish literature.

The Depression years brought economic hardship to Yezierska, as they did to many other writers. The royalties from her published books were negligible, and her modest savings disappeared with the stock-market crash. Like many other unemployed writers of this era, she was fortunate to find both a job and a community through the W.P.A. Writers' Project, though the work assigned to her—cataloguing the trees in Central Park—hardly made effective use of her creative

Drawing of Yezierska by Flavia Bacarella, 1982, created from a 1920 sketch and a 1952 photograph

talents. This period in her life, as well as the early years of her career, is vividly described in her autobiographical novel *Red Ribbon on a White Horse* (1950). The novel also recounts her brief sojourn in a small New Hampshire town after a ghetto acquaintance willed her some money and thus freed her for a time from the pressing necessity of earning a living. However, discovering once again, as she had during the year she lived in Hollywood, that she could not write when she was too far removed from the familiar ghetto world of her youth, she soon returned to New York City, where she lived until her death. Though she had no novels published after 1950, she continued to write short stories and book reviews. Her last published story, "Take up Your Bed and Walk," which describes the experience of an elderly Jewish woman, appeared in *Chicago Jewish Forum* in 1969, a year before her death, and has recently been republished in a volume of her collected fiction, *The Open Cage: An Anzia Yezierska Collection* (1979), edited by Alice Kessler Harris. With the publication of this collection and the republication of *Bread Givers*, Anzia Yezierska's fiction is now available to a new generation of readers.

References:

Alice Kessler Harris, Introduction to *Bread Givers* (New York: Braziller, 1975), pp. v-xviii;

Harris, Introduction to *The Open Cage: An Anzia Yezierska Collection* (New York: Persea Books, 1979), pp. v-xiii;

Louise Levitas Henriksen, Afterword to *The Open Cage: An Anzia Yezierska Collection*, pp. 253-262;

Babbette Inglehart, "Daughters of Loneliness: Anzia Yezierska and the Immigrant Woman Writer," *Studies in American Jewish Literature*, 1 (Winter 1975): 1-10;

Cecyle S. Neidle, *America's Immigrant Women* (New York: Hippocrene Books, 1976), pp. 264-267;

Carol B. Schoen, *Anzia Yezierska* (Boston: Twayne, 1982).

Books for Further Reading

Alter, Robert. *After the Tradition: Essays on Modern Jewish Writing.* New York: Dutton, 1969.

Alter. *Defenses of the Imagination: Jewish Writers and Modern Historical Crisis.* Philadelphia: Jewish Publication Society of America, 1977.

Baumbach, Jonathan. *The Landscape of Nightmare: Studies in the Contemporary American Novel.* New York: New York University Press, 1965.

Chapman, Abraham, ed. *Jewish-American Literature: An Anthology of Fiction, Poetry, Autobiography, and Criticism.* New York: New American Library, 1974.

Eisenberg, Azriel, ed. *The Golden Land: A Literary Portrait of American Jewry 1654 to the Present.* New York: Yoseloff, 1965.

Gittleman, Sol. *From Shtetl to Suburbia: The Family in Jewish Literary Imagination.* Boston: Beacon, 1978.

Gross, Theodore, ed. *The Literature of American Jews.* New York: Free Press, 1973.

Guttmann, Allen. *The Jewish Writer in America: Assimilation and the Crisis of Identity.* New York: Oxford University Press, 1971.

Hapgood, Hutchins. *The Spirit of the Ghetto,* ed. Moses Rischin. Cambridge, Mass.: Belknap, 1967.

Harap, Louis. *The Image of the Jew in American Literature From Early Republic to Mass Immigration.* Philadelphia: Jewish Publication Society of America, 1974.

Hassan, Ihab. *Radical Innocence: Studies in the Contemporary American Novel.* Princeton: Princeton University Press, 1961.

Howe, Irving, with the assistance of Kenneth Libo. *World of Our Fathers.* New York: Harcourt Brace Jovanovich, 1976.

Howe and Eliezer Greenberg, eds. *A Treasury of Yiddish Stories.* New York: Viking, 1954.

Klein, Marcus. *After Alienation: American Novels in Mid-Century.* Cleveland: World, 1964.

Liptzin, Sol. *The Jew in American Literature.* New York: Bloch, 1966.

Madison, Charles. *Yiddish Literature: Its Scope and Major Writers.* New York: Ungar, 1968.

Malin, Irving. *Jews and Americans.* Carbondale: Southern Illinois University Press, 1965.

Malin, ed. *Contemporary American-Jewish Literature: Critical Essays.* Bloomington: Indiana University Press, 1973.

Pinsker, Sanford. *The Schlemiel as Metaphor: Studies in the Yiddish and American Jewish Novel.* Carbondale: Southern Illinois University Press, 1971.

Rischin, Moses. *The Promised City: New York's Jews: 1870-1914*. Cambridge, Mass.: Harvard University Press, 1962.

Sanders, Ronald. *The Downtown Jews: Portraits of an Immigrant Generation*. New York: Harper & Row, 1969.

Schulz, Max. *Radical Sophistication: Studies in Contemporary Jewish-American Novelists*. Athens: Ohio University Press, 1969.

Solotaroff, Theodore. *The Red Hot Vacuum and Other Pieces on the Writing of the Sixties*. New York: Atheneum, 1970.

Tanner, Tony. *City of Words: American Fiction 1950-1970*. New York: Harper & Row, 1971.

Wisse, Ruth. *The Schlemiel as Modern Hero*. Chicago: University of Chicago Press, 1971.

Walden, Daniel, ed. *On Being Jewish: American Jewish Writers from Cahan to Bellow*. Greenwich, Conn.: Fawcett, 1974.

Contributors

Evelyn Avery .... *Towson State University*
Doris G. Bargen .... *Amherst, Massachusetts*
Marleen Barr .... *Virginia Polytechnic Institute and State University*
Mark Bernheim .... *Miami University*
Mashey M. Bernstein .... *Kansas City, Missouri*
Edith Blicksilver .... *Georgia Institute of Technology*
Julia B. Boken .... *State University of New York at Oneonta*
William J. Burling .... *Pennsylvania State University*
Frank Campenni .... *University of Wisconsin-Milwaukee*
Cordelia Candelaria .... *University of Colorado*
Jules Chametzky .... *University of Massachusetts*
Diane Cole .... *New York, New York*
Mildred Louise Culp .... *Seattle, Washington*
Cathy N. Davidson .... *Michigan State University*
Leslie Field .... *Purdue University*
R. Barbara Gitenstein .... *Central Missouri State University*
Liela H. Goldman .... *University of Michigan-Dearborn*
Mark I. Goldman .... *University of Rhode Island*
Charlotte Goodman .... *Skidmore College*
Andrew Gordon .... *University of Florida*
Charles Hackenberry .... *Pennsylvania State University*
Sheldon Hershinow .... *Kapiolani Community College, University of Hawaii*
Steven P. Horowitz .... *University of Iowa*
Josephine Zadovsky Knopp .... *Harcum Junior College*
S. Lillian Kremer .... *Manhattan, Kansas*
Susan Kress .... *Skidmore College*
Miriam J. Landsman .... *University of Iowa*
Bonnie Lyons .... *University of Texas at San Antonio*
Ralph Melnick .... *College of Charleston*
David R. Mesher .... *Portland, Oregon*
Gabriel Miller .... *Rutgers University*
Eva B. Mills .... *Winthrop College*
Keith M. Opdahl .... *DePauw University*
Sanford Pinsker .... *Franklin and Marshall College*
Ruth Rosenberg .... *University of New Orleans*
George J. Searles .... *Mohawk Valley Community College*
Peter Shaw .... *New York, New York*
Judith Rinde Sheridan .... *New York, New York*
Adam J. Sorkin .... *Pennsylvania State University*
Emily Toth .... *Pennsylvania State University*
Richard Tuerk .... *East Texas State University*
Daniel Walden .... *Pennsylvania State University*
Barbara Frey Waxman .... *University of North Carolina at Wilmington*
Stephen J. Whitfield .... *Brandeis University*

Cumulative Index

Dictionary of Literary Biography, Volumes 1-28
Dictionary of Literary Biography Yearbook, 1980-1983
Dictionary of Literary Biography Documentary Series, Volumes 1-4

Cumulative Index

DLB before number: *Dictionary of Literary Biography*, Volumes 1-28
Y before number: *Dictionary of Literary Biography Yearbook*, 1980-1983
DS before number: *Dictionary of Literary Biography Documentary Series*, Volumes 1-4

A

B

C

Cumulative Index

D

E

H

O

P

Q

R

S

W